Computer Vision

Models, Learning, and Inference

This modern treatment of computer vision focuses on learning and inference in probabilistic models as a unifying theme. It shows how to use training data to learn the relationships between the observed image data and the aspects of the world that we wish to estimate, such as the 3D structure or the object class, and how to exploit these relationships to make inferences about the world from new image data.

With minimal prerequisites, the book starts from the basics of probability and model fitting and works up to real examples that the reader can implement and modify to build useful vision systems. Primarily meant for advanced undergraduate and graduate students, the detailed methodological presentation will also be useful for practitioners of computer vision.

- Covers cutting-edge techniques, including graph cuts, machine learning, and multiple view geometry.
- A unified approach shows the common basis for solutions of important computer vision problems, such as camera calibration, face recognition, and object tracking.
- More than 70 algorithms are described in sufficient detail to implement.
- More than 350 full-color illustrations amplify the text.
- The treatment is self-contained, including all of the background mathematics.
- Additional resources at www.computervisionmodels.com.

Dr. Simon J. D. Prince is a faculty member in the Department of Computer Science at University College London. He has taught courses on machine vision, image processing, and advanced mathematical methods. He has a diverse background in biological and computing sciences and has published papers across the fields of computer vision, biometrics, psychology, physiology, medical imaging, computer graphics, and HCI.

Computer Vision

Models, Learning, and Inference

Simon J. D. Prince

University College London

CAMBRIDGE
UNIVERSITY PRESS

University Printing House, Cambridge CB2 8BS, United Kingdom

One Liberty Plaza, 20th Floor, New York, NY 10006, USA

477 Williamstown Road, Port Melbourne, VIC 3207, Australia

314-321, 3rd Floor, Plot 3, Splendor Forum, Jasola District Centre, New Delhi - 110025, India

79 Anson Road, #06-04/06, Singapore 079906

Cambridge University Press is part of the University of Cambridge.

It furthers the University's mission by disseminating knowledge in the pursuit of
education, learning and research at the highest international levels of excellence.

www.cambridge.org
Information on this title: www.cambridge.org/9781107011793

© Simon J. D. Prince 2012

First published 2012
3rd printing 2018

A catalogue record for this publication is available from the British Library

Library of Congress Cataloging in Publication data
Prince, Simon J. D. (Simon Jeremy Damion), 1972–
    Computer vision : models, learning, and inference / Simon J. D. Prince.
        p.   cm.
    Includes bibliographical references and index.
    ISBN 978-1-107-01179-3 (hardback)
    1. Computer vision.   I. Title.
    TA1634.P75   2012
    006.3´7–dc23   2012008187

ISBN 978-1-107-01179-3 Hardback

Additional resources for this publication at www.computervisionmodels.com

This book is dedicated to Richard Eagle, without whom it would never have been started, and to Lynfa Stroud, without whom it would never have been finished.

Contents

V Models for geometry

VI Models for vision

Acknowledgments

I am incredibly grateful to the following people who read parts of this book and gave me feedback: Yun Fu, David Fleet, Alan Jepson, Marc'Aurelio Ranzato, Gabriel Brostow, Oisin Mac Aodha, Xiwen Chen, Po-Hsiu Lin, Jose Tejero Alonso, Amir Sani, Oswald Aldrian, Sara Vicente, Jozef Doboš, Andrew Fitzgibbon, Michael Firman, Gemma Morgan, Daniyar Turmukhambetov, Daniel Alexander, Mihaela Lapusneanu, John Winn, Petri Hiltunen, Jania Aghajanian, Alireza Bossaghzadeh, Mikhail Sizintsev, Roger De Souza-Eremita, Jacques Cali, Roderick de Nijs, James Tompkin, Jonathan O'Keefe, Benedict Kuester, Tom Hart, Marc Kerstein, Alex Borés, Marius Cobzarenco, Luke Dodd, Ankur Agarwal, Ahmad Humayun, Andrew Glennerster, Steven Leigh, Matteo Munaro, Peter van Beek, Hu Feng, Martin Parsley, Jordi Salvador Marcos, Josephine Sullivan, Steve Thompson, Laura Panagiotaki, Damien Teney, Malcolm Reynolds, Francisco Estrada, Peter Hall, James Elder, Paria Mehrani, Vida Movahedi, Eduardo Corral Soto, Ron Tal, Bob Hou, Simon Arridge, Norberto Goussies, Steve Walker, Tracy Petrie, Kostantinos Derpanis, Bernard Buxton, Matthew Pediaditis, Fernando Flores-Mangas, Jan Kautz, Alastair Moore, Yotam Doron, Tahir Majeed, David Barber, Pedro Quelhas, Wenchao Zhang, Alan Angold, Andrew Davison, Alex Yakubovich, Fatemeh Jamali, David Lowe, Ricardo David, Jamie Shotton, Andrew Zisserman, Sanchit Singh, Vincent Lepetit, David Liu, Marc Pollefeys, Christos Panagiotou, Ying Li, Shoaib Ehsan, Olga Veksler, Modesto Castrillón Santana, Axel Pinz, Matteo Zanotto, Gwynfor Jones, Brian Jensen, Mischa Schirris, Jacek Zienkiewicz, Etienne Beauchesne, Erik Sudderth, Giovanni Saponaro, Moos Hueting, Phi Hung Nguyen, Tran Duc Hieu, Simon Julier, Oscar Plag, Thomas Hoyoux, Abhinav Singh, Dan Farmer, Samit Shah, Martijn van der Veen, Gabriel Brostow, Marco Brambilla, Sebastian Stabinger, Tamaki Toru, Stefan Stavref, Xiaoyang Tan, Hao Guan, William Smith, Shanmuganathan Raman, Mikhail Atroshenko, Xiaoyang Tan, Jonathan Weill, Shotaro Moriya and Alessandro Gentilini. This book is much better because of your selfless efforts!

I am also especially grateful to Sven Dickinson, who hosted me at the University of Toronto for nine months during the writing of this book; Stephen Boyd, who let me use his beautiful LATEX template; and Mikhail Sizintsev, for his help in summarizing the bewildering literature on dense stereo vision. I am extremely indebted to Gabriel Brostow, who read the entire draft and spent hours of his valuable time discussing it with me. Finally, I am grateful to Bernard Buxton, who taught me most of this material in the first place and has supported my career in computer vision and every stage.

Foreword

I was very pleased to be asked to write this foreword, having seen snapshots of the development of this book since its inception. I write this having just returned from BMVC 2011, where I found that others had seen draft copies, and where I heard comments like "What amazing figures!", "It's so comprehensive!", and "He's so Bayesian!".

But I don't want you to read this book just because it has amazing figures and provides new insights into vision algorithms of every kind, or even because it's "Bayesian" (although more on that later). I want you to read it because it makes clear the most important distinction in computer vision research: the difference between "model" and "algorithm." This is akin to the distinction that Marr made with his three-level computational theory, but Prince's two-level distinction is made beautifully clear by his use of the language of probability.

Why is this distinction so important? Well, let us look at one of the oldest and apparently easiest problems in vision: separating an image into "figure" and "ground." It is still common to hear students new to vision address this problem just as the early vision researchers did, by reciting an algorithm: first I'll use PCA to find the dominant color axis, then I'll generate a grayscale image, then I'll threshold that at some value, then I'll clean up the holes using morphological operators. Trying their recipe on some test images, the novice discovers that real images are rather more complicated, so new steps are added: I'll need some sort of adaptive threshold, I can get that by blurring the edge map and locally computing maxima.

However, as most readers will already know, such recipes are extremely brittle, meaning that the various "magic numbers" controlling each step all interact, making it impossible to find a set of parameters that works for all images (or even a useful subset). The root of this problem is that the objective of the algorithm has never been defined. What do we *mean* by figure and ground separation? Can we specify what we mean mathematically?

When vision researchers began to address these problems, the language of statistics and Markov random fields allowed a clean distinction between the objective and the algorithm to be drawn. We write down not the steps to solve the problem but the problem itself, for example, as a function to be minimized. In the language of this book, we write down formulae for all the probability distributions that define the problem and then perform operations on those distributions in order to provide answers. This book shows how this can be done for a huge variety of vision problems and how doing so provides more robust solutions that are much easier to reason about.

This is not to say that one can just write down the model and ask others to solve for its parameters because the space of possible models is so much vaster than the space of ones in which the solution is tractable. Thus, one always has at the back of one's mind a collection of models known to be soluble, and one always tries to find a model for one's problem, which is near some soluble problem. At that stage, one may well think in terms of strategies such as "I can probably generalize alpha expansion a bit to solve for the discrete parameters, and then I can use a Gauss-Newton method for the continuous ones, and that will probably be slow, but it will tell me if it's worth trying to invent a faster combined algorithm." Such strategies are common and can be helpful, provided one always retains an idea of the model underlying them.

However, even armed with the attitudes this book will engender, experienced researchers today can fall into the trap of failing to distinguish model and algorithm. They find themselves thinking thoughts like: "I'll fit a mixture of Gaussians to the color distribution. Then I'll model the mixture weights as an MRF and use graph cuts to update them. Then I'll go back to step 1 and repeat." The good news is that often such recipes can be turned back into models. Even if the only known way of fitting the model is to use the recipe you just thought of, the discipline of thinking of it as a model allows you to reason about it, to make use of alternative techniques, and ultimately to do better research. Reading this book is a sure way to improve your ability to make that jump.

So what is this language of probabilities that will allow us to become better researchers? Well, let me provide my "Engineer's view of Bayes' theorem." It is common to hear a distinction between "Bayesians" and "Frequentists," but I think many engineers have a much more fundamental problem with Bayes: Bayesians must lie. Their estimates, biased toward the prior mean, are deliberately different from the most probable reading of their sensor. Consider the example of an "I speak your height" machine whose sensor has a uniformly distributed ±1 cm error. You receive £1 every time you correctly predict someone's height to within 1 cm. Bayesian principles suggest that if your sensor reads 200 cm ±1 cm, you should report 199 cm; you will make more money than guessing the actual sensor reading, because more 199 cm people will appear than those of 200 cm. So I as an engineer believe in Bayes as a way of getting better answers, and thus very much welcome this book's pragmatic (but much more subtle than mine) embrace of Bayes. I wonder if it might even be considered a book on statistics with vision examples rather than a book on vision built on probability.

But it would be wrong to finish this foreword without mentioning the figures. They really are good, not because they're beautiful (they often are), but because they provide crucial insights into the workings of even the most basic of algorithms and ideas. The illustrations in Chapters 2–4 are fundamental to the understanding of modern Bayesian inference, and yet I doubt that there are more than a handful of researchers who have ever seen them all. Later figures express extremely complex ideas more clearly than I have ever seen, as well as representing fabulously "clean" implementations of fundamental algorithms, which really show us how the underlying models influence our capabilities.

Finally I believe it is worth directly comparing this book to the recent textbook by my colleague Richard Szeliski. That book too is marked by an enormously comprehensive view of computer vision, by excellent illustration, by insightful notation, and intellectual synthesis of large groups of existing ideas. But in a real sense the two books operate at opposite ends of the pedagogical spectrum: Szeliski is a comprehensive summary of the state of the art in computer vision, the frontier of our knowledge and abilities, while this book addresses the fundamentals of how we make progress in this challenging and exciting field. I look forward to many decades with both on my shelf, or indeed, I suspect, open on my desktop.

Andrew Fitzgibbon
Microsoft Research, Cambridge
September 2011

Preface

There are already many computer vision textbooks, and it is reasonable to question the need for another. Let me explain why I chose to write this volume.

Computer vision is an engineering discipline; we are primarily motivated by the real-world concern of building machines that see. Consequently, we tend to categorize our knowledge by the real-world problem that it addresses. For example, most existing vision textbooks contain chapters on object recognition and stereo vision. The sessions at our research conferences are organized in the same way. The role of this book is to question this orthodoxy: Is this really the way that we should organize our knowledge?

Consider the topic of object recognition. A wide variety of methods have been applied to this problem (e.g., subspace models, boosting methods, bag of words models, and constellation models). However, these approaches have little in common. Any attempt to describe the grand sweep of our knowledge devolves into an unstructured list of techniques. How can we make sense of it all for a new student? I will argue for a different way to organize our knowledge, but first let me tell you how I see computer vision problems.

We observe an image and from this we extract *measurements*. For example, we might use the RGB values directly or we might filter the image or perform some more sophisticated preprocessing. The *vision problem* or *goal* is to use the measurements to infer the *world state*. For example, in stereo vision we try to infer the depth of the scene. In object detection, we attempt to infer the presence or absence of a particular class of object.

To accomplish the goal, we build a *model*. The model describes a family of statistical relationships between the measurements and the world state. The particular member of that family is determined by a set of *parameters*. In *learning* we choose these parameters so they accurately reflect the relationship between the measurements and the world. In *inference* we take a new set of measurements and use the model to tell us about the world state. The methods for learning and inference are embodied in *algorithms*. I believe that computer vision should be understood in these terms: the goal, the measurements, the world state, the model, the parameters, and the learning and inference algorithms.

We could choose to organize our knowledge according to any of these quantities, but in my opinion what is most critical is the model itself – the statistical relationship between the world and the measurements. There are three reasons for this. First, the model type often transcends the application (the same model can be used for diverse vision tasks). Second, the models naturally organize themselves neatly into distinct families (e.g., regression, Markov random fields, camera models) that can be understood in relative isolation. Finally, discussing vision on the level of models allows us to draw connections between algorithms and applications that initially appear unrelated. Accordingly, this book is organized so that each main chapter considers a different family of models.

On a final note, I should say that I found most of the ideas in this book very hard to grasp when I was first exposed to them. My goal was to make this process easier for subsequent students following the same path; I hope that this book achieves this and inspires the reader to learn more about computer vision.

Chapter 1

Introduction

The goal of computer vision is to extract useful information from images. This has proved a surprisingly challenging task; it has occupied thousands of intelligent and creative minds over the last four decades, and despite this we are still far from being able to build a general-purpose "seeing machine."

Part of the problem is the complexity of visual data. Consider the image in Figure 1.1. There are hundreds of objects in the scene. Almost none of these are presented in a "typical" pose. Almost all of them are partially occluded. For a computer vision algorithm, it is not even easy to establish where one object ends and another begins. For example, there is almost no change in the image intensity at the boundary between the sky and the white building in the background. However, there is a pronounced change in intensity on the back window of the SUV in the foreground, although there is no object boundary or change in material here.

We might have grown despondent about our chances of developing useful computer vision algorithms if it were not for one thing: we have concrete proof that vision is possible because our own visual systems make light work of complex images such as Figure 1.1. If I ask you to count the trees in this image or to draw a sketch of the street layout, you can do this easily. You might even be able to pinpoint where this photo was taken on a world map by extracting subtle visual clues such as the ethnicity of the people, the types of cars and trees, and the weather.

So, computer vision is not impossible, but it is very challenging; perhaps this was not appreciated at first because what we perceive when we look at a scene is already highly processed. For example, consider observing a lump of coal in bright sunlight and then moving to a dim indoor environment and looking at a piece of white paper. The eye will receive far more photons per unit area from the coal than from the paper, but we nonetheless perceive the coal as black and the paper as white. The visual brain performs many tricks of this kind, and unfortunately when we build vision algorithms, we don't have the benefit of this preprocessing.

Nonetheless, there has been remarkable recent progress in our understanding of computer vision, and the last decade has seen the first large-scale deployments of consumer computer vision technology. For example, most digital cameras now have embedded algorithms for face detection, and at the time of writing the Microsoft Kinect (a peripheral that allows real-time tracking of the human body) holds the Guinness World Record

Figure 1.1 A visual scene containing many objects, almost all of which are partially occluded. The red circle indicates a part of the scene where there is almost no brightness change to indicate the boundary between the sky and the building. The green circle indicates a region in which there is a large intensity change but this is due to irrelevant lighting effects; there is no object boundary or change in the object material here.

for being the fastest-selling consumer electronics device ever. The principles behind both of these applications and many more are explained in this book.

There are a number of reasons for the rapid recent progress in computer vision. The most obvious is that the processing power, memory, and storage capacity of computers has vastly increased; before we disparage the progress of early computer vision pioneers, we should pause to reflect that they would have needed specialized hardware to hold even a single high-resolution image in memory. Another reason for the recent progress in this area has been the increased use of machine learning. The last 20 years have seen exciting developments in this parallel research field, and these are now deployed widely in vision applications. Not only has machine learning provided many useful tools, it has also helped us understand existing algorithms and their connections in a new light.

The future of computer vision is exciting. Our understanding grows by the day, and it is likely that artificial vision will become increasingly prevalent in the next decade. However, this is still a young discipline. Until recently, it would have been unthinkable to even try to work with complex scenes such as that in Figure 1.1. As Szeliski (2010) puts it, "It may be many years before computers can name and outline all of the objects in a photograph with the same skill as a two year old child." However, this book provides a snapshot of what we have achieved and the principles behind these achievements.

Organization of the book

The structure of this book is illustrated in Figure 1.2. It is divided into six parts.

The first part of the book contains background information on probability. All the models in this book are expressed in terms of probability, which is a useful language for describing computer vision applications. Readers with a rigorous background in engineering mathematics will know much of this material already but should skim these chapters to ensure they are familiar with the notation. Those readers who do not have this background should read these chapters carefully. The ideas are relatively simple, but they underpin everything else in the rest of the book. It may be frustrating to be forced to read fifty pages of mathematics before the first mention of computer vision, but please trust me when I tell you that this material will provide a solid foundation for everything that follows.

The second part of the book discusses machine learning for machine vision. These chapters teach the reader the core principles that underpin all of our methods to extract useful information from images. We build statistical models that relate the image data to the information that we wish to retrieve. After digesting this material, the reader should understand how to build a model to solve almost any vision problem, although that model may not yet be very practical.

The third part of the book introduces graphical models for computer vision. Graphical models provide a framework for simplifying the models that relate the image data to the properties we wish to estimate. When both of these quantities are high-dimensional, the statistical connections between them become impractically complex; we can still define models that relate them, but we may not have the training data or computational power to make them useful. Graphical models provide a principled way to assert sparseness in the statistical connections between the data and the world properties.

The fourth part of the book discusses image preprocessing. This is not necessary to understand most of the models in the book, but that is not to say that it is unimportant. The choice of preprocessing method is at least as critical as the choice of model in determining the final performance of a computer vision system. Although image processing is not the main topic of this book, this section provides a compact summary of the most important and practical techniques.

The fifth part of the book concerns geometric computer vision; it introduces the projective pinhole camera – a mathematical model that describes where a given point in the 3D world will be imaged in the pixel array of the camera. Associated with this model are a set of techniques for finding the position of the camera relative to a scene and for reconstructing 3D models of objects.

Finally, in the sixth part of the book, we present several families of vision models that build on the principles established earlier in the book. These models address some of the most central problems in computer vision including face recognition, tracking, and object recognition.

The book concludes with several appendices. There is a brief discussion of the notational conventions used in the book, and compact summaries of linear algebra and optimization techniques. Although this material is widely available elsewhere, it makes the book more self-contained and is discussed in the same terminology as it is used in the main text.

At the end of every chapter is a brief notes section. This provides details of the related research literature. It is heavily weighted toward the most useful and recent papers and

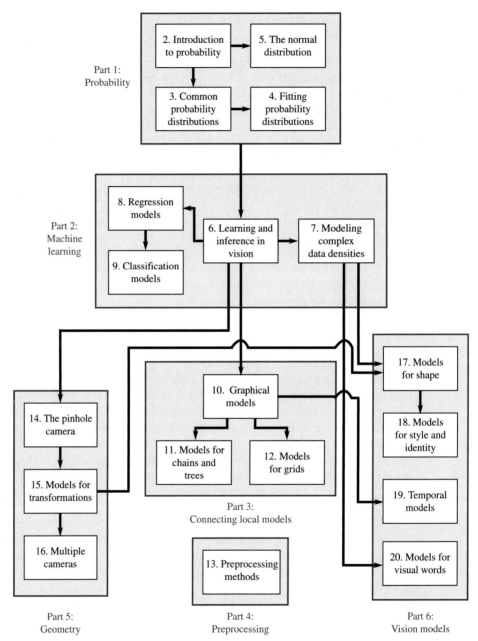

Figure 1.2 Chapter dependencies. The book is organized into six sections. The first section is a review of probability and is necessary for all subsequent chapters. The second part concerns machine learning and inference. It describes both generative and discriminative models. The third part concerns graphical models: visual representations of the probabilistic dependencies between variables in large models. The fourth part describes preprocessing methods. The fifth part concerns geometry and transformations. Finally, the sixth part presents several other important families of vision models.

does not reflect an accurate historical description of each area. There are also a number of exercises for the reader at the end of each chapter. In some cases, important but tedious derivations have been excised from the text and turned into problems to retain the flow of the main argument. Here, the solution will be posted on the main book Web site (http://www.computervisionmodels.com). A series of applications are also presented at the end of each chapter (apart from Chapters 1–5 and Chapter 10, which contain only theoretical material). Collectively, these represent a reasonable cross-section of the important vision papers of the last decade.

Finally, pseudocode for over 70 of the algorithms discussed is available and can be downloaded in a separate document from the associated Web site (http://www. computervisionmodels.com). Throughout the text, the symbol [⚙] denotes that there is pseudocode associated with this portion of the text. This pseudocode uses the same notation as the book and will make it easy to implement many of the models. I chose not to include this in the main text because it would have decreased the readability. However, I encourage all readers of this book to implement as many of the models as possible. Computer vision is a practical engineering discipline, and you can learn a lot by experimenting with real code.

Other books

I am aware that most people will not learn computer vision from this book alone, so here is some advice about other books that complement this volume. To learn more about machine learning and graphical models, I recommend '*Pattern Recognition and Machine Learning*' by Bishop (2006) as a good starting point. There are many books on preprocessing, but my favorite is '*Feature Extraction and Image Processing*' by Nixon and Aguado (2008). The best source for information about geometrical computer vision is, without a doubt, '*Multiple View Geometry in Computer Vision*' by Hartley and Zisserman (2004). Finally, for a much more comprehensive overview of the state of the art of computer vision and its historical development, consider '*Computer Vision: Algorithms and Applications*' by Szeliski (2010).

Part I
Probability

The first part of this book (Chapters 2–5) is devoted to a brief review of probability and probability distributions. Almost all models for computer vision can be interpreted in a probabilistic context, and in this book we will present all the material in this light. The probabilistic interpretation may initially seem confusing, but it has a great advantage: it provides a common notation that will be used throughout the book and will elucidate relationships between different models that would otherwise remain opaque.

So why is probability a suitable language to describe computer vision problems? In a camera, the three-dimensional world is projected onto the optical surface to form the image: a two-dimensional set of measurements. Our goal is to take these measurements and use them to establish the properties of the world that created them. However, there are two problems. First, the measurement process is noisy; what we observe is not the amount of light that fell on the sensor, but a noisy estimate of this quantity. We must describe the noise in these data, and for this we use probability. Second, the relationship between world and measurements is generally many to one: there may be many real-world configurations that are compatible with the same measurements. The chance that each of these possible worlds is present can also be described using probability.

The structure of Part I is as follows: in Chapter 2, we introduce the basic rules for manipulating probability distributions including the ideas of conditional and marginal probability and Bayes' rule. We also introduce more advanced ideas such as independence and expectation.

In Chapter 3, we discuss the properties of eight specific probability distributions. We divide these into two sets of four distributions each. The first set will be used to describe either the observed data or the state of the world. The second set of distributions model the parameters of the first set. In combination, they allow us to fit a probability model and provide information about how certain we are about the fit.

In Chapter 4, we discuss methods for fitting probability distributions to observed data. We also discuss how to assess the probability of new data points under the fitted model and how to take account of uncertainty in the fitted model when we do this. Finally, in Chapter 5, we investigate the properties of the multivariate normal distribution in detail. This distribution is ubiquitous in vision applications and has a number of useful properties that are frequently exploited in machine vision.

Readers who are very familiar with probability models and the Bayesian philosophy may wish to skip this part and move directly to Part II.

Chapter 2

Introduction to probability

In this chapter, we provide a compact review of probability theory. There are very few ideas, and each is relatively simple when considered separately. However, they combine to form a powerful language for describing uncertainty.

2.1   Random variables

A random variable x denotes a quantity that is uncertain. The variable may denote the result of an experiment (e.g., flipping a coin) or a real-world measurement of a fluctuating property (e.g., measuring the temperature). If we observe several instances $\{x_i\}_{i=1}^I$ then it might take a different value on each occasion. However, some values may occur more often than others. This information is captured by the probability distribution $Pr(x)$ of the random variable.

A random variable may be *discrete* or *continuous*. A discrete variable takes values from a predefined set. This set may be ordered (the outcomes 1–6 of rolling a die) or unordered (the outcomes "sunny," "raining," "snowing" upon observing the weather). It may be finite (there are 52 possible outcomes of drawing a card randomly from a standard pack) or infinite (the number of people on the next train is theoretically unbounded). The probability distribution of a discrete variable can be visualized as a histogram or a Hinton diagram (Figure 2.1). Each outcome has a positive probability associated with it, and the sum of the probabilities for all outcomes is always one.

Continuous random variables take values that are real numbers. These may be finite (the time taken to finish a 2-hour exam is constrained to be greater than 0 hours and less than 2 hours) or infinite (the amount of time until the next bus arrives is unbounded above). Infinite continuous variables may be defined on the whole real range or may be bounded above or below (the 1D velocity of a vehicle may take any value, but the speed is bounded below by 0). The probability distribution of a continuous variable can be visualized by plotting the *probability density function* (pdf). The probability density for an outcome represents the relative propensity of the random variable to take that value (see Figure 2.2). It may take any positive value. However, the integral of the pdf always sums to one.

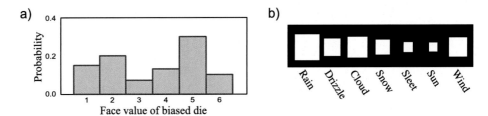

Figure 2.1 Two different representations for discrete probabilities a) A bar graph representing the probability that a biased six-sided die lands on each face. The height of the bar represents the probability, so the sum of all heights is one. b) A Hinton diagram illustrating the probability of observing different weather types in England. The area of the square represents the probability, so the sum of all areas is one.

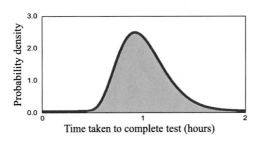

Figure 2.2 Continuous probability distribution (probability density function or pdf for short) for time taken to complete a test. Note that the probability density can exceed one, but the area under the curve must always have unit area.

2.2   Joint probability

Consider two random variables, x and y. If we observe multiple paired instances of x and y, then some combinations of the two outcomes occur more frequently than others. This information is encompassed in the *joint* probability distribution of x and y, which is written as $Pr(x, y)$. The comma in $Pr(x, y)$ can be read as the English word "and" so $Pr(x, y)$ is the probability of x *and* y. A joint probability distribution may relate variables that are all discrete or all continuous, or it may relate discrete variables to continuous ones (see Figure 2.3). Regardless, the total probability of all outcomes (summing over discrete variables and integrating over continuous ones) is always one.

In general, we will be interested in the joint probability distribution of more than two variables. We will write $Pr(x, y, z)$ to represent the joint probability distribution of scalar variables x, y, and z. We may also write $Pr(\mathbf{x})$ to represent the joint probability of all of the elements of the multidimensional variable $\mathbf{x} = [x_1, x_2, \dots, x_K]^T$. Finally, we will write $Pr(\mathbf{x}, \mathbf{y})$ to represent the joint distribution of all of the elements from multidimensional variables $\mathbf{x}$ and $\mathbf{y}$.

2.3   Marginalization

We can recover the probability distribution of any single variable from a joint distribution by summing (discrete case) or integrating (continuous case) over all the other variables (Figure 2.4). For example, if x and y are both continuous and we know $Pr(x, y)$, then

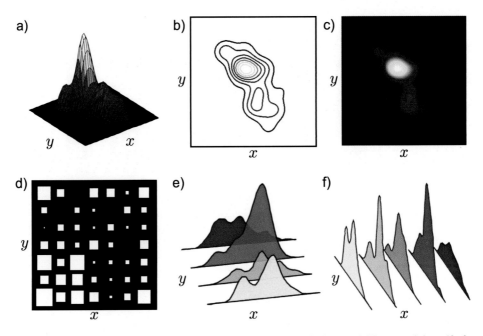

Figure 2.3 Joint probability distributions between variables x and y. a–c) The same joint pdf of two continuous variables represented as a surface, contour plot, and image, respectively. d) Joint distribution of two discrete variables represented as a 2D Hinton diagram. e) Joint distribution of a continuous variable x and discrete variable y. f) Joint distribution of a discrete variable x and continuous variable y.

we can recover the distributions $Pr(x)$ and $Pr(y)$ using the relations

$$Pr(x) = \int Pr(x,y)\,dy,$$
$$Pr(y) = \int Pr(x,y)\,dx. \tag{2.1}$$

The recovered distributions $Pr(x)$ and $Pr(y)$ are referred to as *marginal* distributions, and the process of integrating/summing over the other variables is called *marginalization*. Calculating the marginal distribution $Pr(x)$ from the joint distribution $Pr(x,y)$ by marginalizing over the variable y has a simple interpretation: we are finding the probability distribution of x regardless of (or in the absence of information about) the value of y.

In general, we can recover the joint probability of any subset of variables, by marginalizing over all of the others. For example, given variables, w,x,y,z, where w is discrete and z is continuous, we can recover $Pr(x,y)$ using

$$Pr(x,y) = \sum_w \int Pr(w,x,y,z)\,dz. \tag{2.2}$$

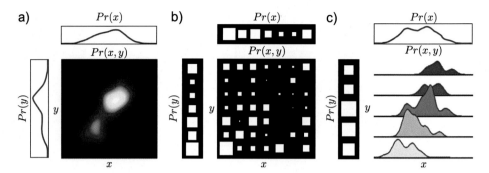

Figure 2.4 Joint and marginal probability distributions. The marginal probability $Pr(x)$ is found by summing over all values of y (discrete case) or integrating over y (continuous case) in the joint distribution $Pr(x,y)$. Similarly the marginal probability $Pr(y)$ is found by summing or integrating over x. Note that the plots for the marginal distributions have different scales from those for the joint distribution (on the same scale, the marginals would look larger as they sum all of the mass from one direction). a) Both x and y are continuous. b) Both x and y are discrete. c) The random variable x is continuous and the variable y is discrete.

2.4   Conditional probability

The conditional probability of x given that y takes value y^* tells us the relative propensity of the random variable x to take different outcomes given that the random variable y is fixed to value y^*. This conditional probability is written as $Pr(x|y = y^*)$. The vertical line "|" can be read as the English word "given."

The conditional probability $Pr(x|y = y^*)$ can be recovered from the joint distribution $Pr(x,y)$. In particular, we examine the appropriate slice $Pr(x, y = y^*)$ of the joint distribution (Figure 2.5). The values in the slice tell us about the relative probability that x takes various values having observed $y = y^*$, but they do not themselves form a valid probability distribution; they cannot sum to one as they constitute only a small part of the joint distribution which did itself sum to one. To calculate the conditional probability distribution, we hence normalize by the total probability in the slice

$$Pr(x|y = y^*) = \frac{Pr(x, y = y^*)}{\int Pr(x, y = y^*)dx} = \frac{Pr(x, y = y^*)}{Pr(y = y^*)}, \tag{2.3}$$

where we have used the marginal probability relation (Equation 2.1) to simplify the denominator. It is common to write the conditional probability relation without explicitly defining the value $y = y^*$ to give the more compact notation

$$Pr(x|y) = \frac{Pr(x,y)}{Pr(y)}. \tag{2.4}$$

This relationship can be rearranged to give

$$Pr(x,y) = Pr(x|y)Pr(y), \tag{2.5}$$

and by symmetry we also have

$$Pr(x,y) = Pr(y|x)Pr(x). \tag{2.6}$$

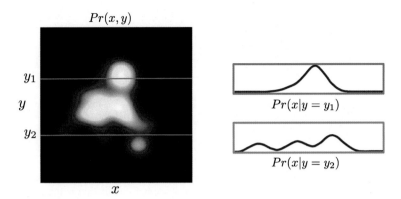

Figure 2.5 Conditional probability. Joint pdf of x and y and two conditional probability distributions $Pr(x|y=y_1)$ and $Pr(x|y=y_2)$. These are formed by extracting the appropriate slice from the joint pdf and normalizing so that the area is one. A similar operation can be performed for discrete distributions.

When we have more than two variables, we may repeatedly take conditional probabilities to divide up the joint probability distribution into a product of terms

$$
\begin{aligned}
Pr(w,x,y,z) &= Pr(w,x,y|z)Pr(z) \\
&= Pr(w,x|y,z)Pr(y|z)Pr(z) \\
&= Pr(w|x,y,z)Pr(x|y,z)Pr(y|z)Pr(z).
\end{aligned}
\tag{2.7}
$$

2.5   Bayes' rule

In Equations 2.5 and 2.6 we expressed the joint probability in two ways. We can combine these formulations to find a relationship between $Pr(x|y)$ and $Pr(y|x)$,

$$
Pr(y|x)Pr(x) = Pr(x|y)Pr(y),
\tag{2.8}
$$

or, rearranging, we have

$$
\begin{aligned}
Pr(y|x) &= \frac{Pr(x|y)Pr(y)}{Pr(x)} \\
&= \frac{Pr(x|y)Pr(y)}{\int Pr(x,y)\,dy} \\
&= \frac{Pr(x|y)Pr(y)}{\int Pr(x|y)Pr(y)\,dy},
\end{aligned}
\tag{2.9}
$$

where in the second and third lines we have expanded the denominator using the definitions of marginal and conditional probability, respectively. These three equations are all commonly referred to as *Bayes' rule*.

Each term in Bayes' rule has a name. The term $Pr(y|x)$ on the left-hand side is the *posterior*. It represents what we know about y given x. Conversely, the term $Pr(y)$ is the *prior* as it represents what is known about y before we consider x. The term $Pr(x|y)$ is the *likelihood*, and the denominator $Pr(x)$ is the *evidence*.

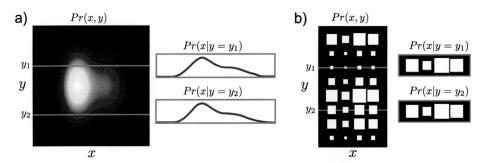

Figure 2.6 Independence. a) Joint pdf of continuous independent variables x and y. The independence of x and y means that every conditional distribution is the same: the value of y tells us nothing about x and vice versa. Compare this to Figure 2.5, which illustrated variables that were dependent. b) Joint distribution of discrete independent variables x and y. The conditional distributions of x given y are all the same.

In computer vision, we often describe the relationship between variables x and y in terms of the conditional probability $Pr(x|y)$. However, we may be primarily interested in the variable y, and in this situation Bayes' rule is exploited to compute the probability $Pr(y|x)$.

2.6 Independence

If knowing the value of variable x tells us nothing about variable y (and vice versa), then we say x and y are independent (Figure 2.6). Here, we can write

$$Pr(x|y) = Pr(x)$$
$$Pr(y|x) = Pr(y). \tag{2.10}$$

Substituting into Equation 2.5, we see that for independent variables the joint probability $Pr(x,y)$ is the product of the marginal probabilities $Pr(x)$ and $Pr(y)$,

$$Pr(x,y) = Pr(x|y)Pr(y) = Pr(x)Pr(y). \tag{2.11}$$

2.7 Expectation

Given a function $f[\bullet]$ that returns a value for each possible value x^* of the variable x and a probability $Pr(x = x^*)$ that each value of x occurs, we sometimes wish to calculate the *expected* output of the function. If we drew a very large number of samples from the probability distribution, calculated the function for each sample, and took the average of these values, the result would be the *expectation*. More precisely, the expected value of a function $f[\bullet]$ of a random variable x is defined as

$$\mathrm{E}[f[x]] = \sum_x f[x]Pr(x)$$
$$\mathrm{E}[f[x]] = \int f[x]Pr(x)\,dx, \tag{2.12}$$

Function $f[\bullet]$	Expectation
x	mean, μ_x
x^k	k^{th} moment about zero
$(x - \mu_x)^k$	k^{th} moment about the mean
$(x - \mu_x)^2$	variance
$(x - \mu_x)^3$	skew
$(x - \mu_x)^4$	kurtosis
$(x - \mu_x)(y - \mu_y)$	covariance of x and y

Table 2.1 Special cases of expectation. For some functions $f(x)$, the expectation $E[f(x)]$ is given a special name. Here we use the notation μ_x to represent the mean with respect to random variable x and μ_y the mean with respect to random variable y.

for the discrete and continuous cases, respectively. This idea generalizes to functions $f[\bullet]$ of more than one random variable so that, for example,

$$E[f[x,y]] = \int\int f[x,y] Pr(x,y) \, dx \, dy. \tag{2.13}$$

For some choices of the function $f[\bullet]$, the expectation is given a special name (Table 2.1). Such quantities are commonly used to summarize the properties of complex probability distributions.

There are four rules for manipulating expectations, which can be easily proved from the original definition (Equation 2.12):

1. The expected value of a constant κ with respect to the random variable x is just the constant itself:

$$E[\kappa] = \kappa. \tag{2.14}$$

2. The expected value of a constant κ times a function $f[x]$ of the random variable x is κ times the expected value of the function:

$$E[\kappa f[x]] = \kappa E[f[x]]. \tag{2.15}$$

3. The expected value of the sum of two functions of a random variable x is the sum of the individual expected values of the functions:

$$E[f[x] + g[x]] = E[f[x]] + E[g[x]]. \tag{2.16}$$

4. The expected value of the product of two functions $f[x]$ and $g[y]$ of random variables x and y is equal to the product of the individual expected values if the variables x and y are independent:

$$E[f[x]g[y]] = E[f[x]]E[g[y]], \qquad \text{if } x, y \text{ independent.} \tag{2.17}$$

Discussion

The rules of probability are remarkably compact and simple. The concepts of marginalization, joint and conditional probability, independence, and Bayes' rule will underpin all of the machine vision algorithms in this book. There is one remaining important concept related to probability, which is *conditional independence*. We discuss this at length in Chapter 10.

Notes

For a more formal discussion of probability, the reader is encouraged to investigate one of the many books on this topic (e.g., Papoulis 1991). For a view of probability from a machine learning perspective, consult the first chapter of Bishop (2006).

Problems

2.1 Give a real-world example of a joint distribution $Pr(x, y)$ where x is discrete and y is continuous.

2.2 What remains if I marginalize a joint distribution $Pr(v, w, x, y, z)$ over five variables with respect to variables w and y? What remains if I marginalize the resulting distribution with respect to v?

2.3 Show that the following relation is true:

$$Pr(w, x, y, z) = Pr(x, y)Pr(z|w, x, y)Pr(w|x, y).$$

2.4 In my pocket there are two coins. Coin 1 is unbiased, so the likelihood $Pr(h = 1|c = 1)$ of getting heads is 0.5 and the likelihood $Pr(h = 0|c = 1)$ of getting tails is also 0.5. Coin 2 is biased, so the likelihood $Pr(h = 1|c = 2)$ of getting heads is 0.8 and the likelihood $Pr(h = 0|c = 2)$ of getting tails is 0.2. I reach into my pocket and draw one of the coins at random. There is an equal prior probability I might have picked either coin. I flip the coin and observe a head. Use Bayes' rule to compute the posterior probability that I chose coin 2.

2.5 If variables x and y are independent and variables x and z are independent, does it follow that variables y and z are independent?

2.6 Use Equation 2.3 to show that when x and y are independent, the marginal distribution $Pr(x)$ is the same as the conditional distribution $Pr(x|y = y^*)$ for any y^*.

2.7 The joint probability $Pr(w, x, y, z)$ over four variables factorizes as

$$Pr(w, x, y, z) = Pr(w)Pr(z|y)Pr(y|x, w)Pr(x).$$

Demonstrate that x is independent of w by showing that $Pr(x, w) = Pr(x)Pr(w)$.

2.8 Consider a biased die where the probabilities of rolling sides $\{1, 2, 3, 4, 5, 6\}$ are $\{1/12, 1/12, 1/12, 1/12, 1/6, 1/2\}$, respectively. What is the expected value of the die? If I roll the die twice, what is the expected value of the sum of the two rolls?

2.9 Prove the four relations for manipulating expectations:

$$E[\kappa] = \kappa,$$
$$E[\kappa f[x]] = \kappa E[f[x]],$$
$$E[f[x] + g[x]] = E[f[x]] + E[g[x]],$$
$$E[f[x]g[y]] = E[f[x]]E[g[y]], \qquad \text{if } x, y \text{ independent.}$$

For the last case, you will need to use the definition of independence (see Section 2.6).

2.10 Use the relations from Problem 2.9 to prove the following relationship between the second moment around zero and the second moment about the mean (variance):

$$E\left[(x - \mu)^2\right] = E\left[x^2\right] - E[x]E[x].$$

Chapter 3

Common probability distributions

In Chapter 2 we introduced abstract rules for manipulating probabilities. To use these rules we will need to define some probability distributions. The choice of distribution $Pr(x)$ will depend on the *domain* of the data x that we are modeling (Table 3.1).

Data Type	Domain	Distribution
univariate, discrete, binary	$x \in \{0,1\}$	Bernoulli
univariate, discrete, multivalued	$x \in \{1,2,\ldots,K\}$	categorical
univariate, continuous, unbounded	$x \in \mathbb{R}$	univariate normal
univariate, continuous, bounded	$x \in [0,1]$	beta
multivariate, continuous, unbounded	$\mathbf{x} \in \mathbb{R}^K$	multivariate normal
multivariate, continuous, bounded, sums to one	$\mathbf{x} = [x_1, x_2, \ldots, x_K]^T$ $x_k \in [0,1], \sum_{k=1}^{K} x_k = 1$	Dirichlet
bivariate, continuous, x_1 unbounded, x_2 bounded below	$\mathbf{x} = [x_1, x_2]$ $x_1 \in \mathbb{R}$ $x_2 \in \mathbb{R}^+$	normal-scaled inverse gamma
vector $\mathbf{x}$ and matrix $\mathbf{X}$, $\mathbf{x}$ unbounded, $\mathbf{X}$ square, positive definite	$\mathbf{x} \in \mathbb{R}^K$ $\mathbf{X} \in \mathbb{R}^{K \times K}$ $\mathbf{z}^T \mathbf{X} \mathbf{z} > 0 \quad \forall \mathbf{z} \in \mathbb{R}^K$	normal inverse Wishart

Table 3.1 Common probability distributions: the choice of distribution depends on the type/ domain of data to be modeled.

Probability distributions such as the categorical and normal distributions are obviously useful for modeling visual data. However, the need for some of the other distributions is not so obvious; for example, the Dirichlet distribution models K positive numbers that sum to one. Visual data do not normally take this form.

Distribution	Domain	Parameters Modeled by
Bernoulli	$x \in \{0, 1\}$	beta
categorical	$x \in \{1, 2, \ldots, K\}$	Dirichlet
univariate normal	$x \in \mathbb{R}$	normal inverse gamma
multivariate normal	$\mathbf{x} \in \mathbb{R}^k$	normal inverse Wishart

Table 3.2 Common distributions used for modeling (left) and their associated domains (center). For each of these distributions, there is a second associated distribution over the parameters (right).

The explanation is as follows: when we fit probability models to data, we need to know how uncertain we are about the fit. This uncertainty is represented as a probability distribution over the parameters of the fitted model. So for each distribution used for modeling, there is a second distribution over the associated parameters (Table 3.2). For example, the Dirichlet is used to model the parameters of the categorical distribution. In this context, the parameters of the Dirichlet would be known as *hyperparameters*. More generally, the hyperparameters determine the shape of the distribution over the parameters of the original distribution.

We will now work through the distributions in Table 3.2 before looking more closely at the relationship between these pairs of distributions.

3.1   Bernoulli distribution

The *Bernoulli distribution* (Figure 3.1) is a discrete distribution that models binary trials: it describes the situation where there are only two possible outcomes $x \in \{0, 1\}$ which are referred to as "failure" and "success." In machine vision, the Bernoulli distribution could be used to model the data. For example, it might describe the probability of a pixel taking an intensity value of greater or less than 128. Alternatively, it could be used to model the state of the world. For example, it might describe the probability that a face is present or absent in the image.

The Bernoulli has a single parameter $\lambda \in [0, 1]$ which defines the probability of observing a success $x = 1$. The distribution is hence

$$Pr(x = 0) = 1 - \lambda$$
$$Pr(x = 1) = \lambda. \tag{3.1}$$

We can alternatively express this as

$$Pr(x) = \lambda^x (1 - \lambda)^{1-x}, \tag{3.2}$$

and we will sometimes use the equivalent notation

$$Pr(x) = \text{Bern}_x[\lambda]. \tag{3.3}$$

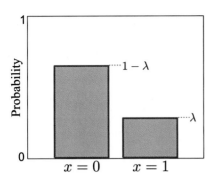

Figure 3.1 Bernoulli distribution. The Bernoulli distribution is a discrete distribution with two possible outcomes, $x \in \{0, 1\}$ which are referred to as failure and success, respectively. It is governed by a single parameter λ that determines the probability of success such that $Pr(x = 0) = 1 - \lambda$ and $Pr(x = 1) = \lambda$.

3.2 Beta distribution

The *beta distribution* (Figure 3.2) is a continuous distribution defined on single variable λ where $\lambda \in [0, 1]$. As such it is suitable for representing uncertainty in the parameter λ of the Bernoulli distribution.

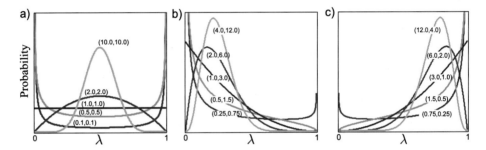

Figure 3.2 Beta distribution. The beta distribution is defined on $[0, 1]$ and has parameters (α, β) whose relative values determine the expected value so $E[\lambda] = \alpha/(\alpha + \beta)$ (numbers in parentheses show the α, β for each curve). As the absolute values of (α, β) increase, the concentration around $E[\lambda]$ increases. a) $E[\lambda] = 0.5$ for each curve, concentration varies. b) $E[\lambda] = 0.25$. c) $E[\lambda] = 0.75$.

The beta distribution has two parameters $\alpha, \beta \in [0, \infty]$, which both take positive values and affect the shape of the curve as indicated in Figure 3.2. Mathematically, the beta distribution has the form

$$Pr(\lambda) = \frac{\Gamma[\alpha + \beta]}{\Gamma[\alpha]\Gamma[\beta]} \lambda^{\alpha-1}(1 - \lambda)^{\beta-1}, \tag{3.4}$$

where $\Gamma[\bullet]$ is the *gamma function*.[1] For short, we abbreviate this to

$$Pr(\lambda) = \text{Beta}_\lambda[\alpha, \beta]. \tag{3.5}$$

3.3 Categorical distribution

The *categorical distribution* (Figure 3.3) is a discrete distribution that determines the probability of observing one of K possible outcomes. Hence, the Bernoulli distribution

---

[1]The gamma function is defined as $\Gamma[z] = \int_0^\infty t^{z-1}e^{-t}dt$ and is closely related to factorials, so that for positive integers $\Gamma[z] = (z - 1)!$ and $\Gamma[z + 1] = z\Gamma[z]$.

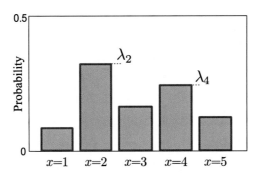

Figure 3.3 The categorical distribution is a discrete distribution with K possible outcomes, $x \in \{1, 2, \ldots, K\}$ and K parameters $\lambda_1, \lambda_2, \ldots, \lambda_K$ where $\lambda_k \geq 0$ and $\sum_k \lambda_k = 1$. Each parameter represents the probability of observing one of the outcomes, so that the probability of observing $x = k$ is given by λ_k. When the number of possible outcomes K is 2, the categorical reduces to the Bernoulli distribution.

is a special case of the categorical distribution when there are only two outcomes. In machine vision the intensity data at a pixel is usually quantized into discrete levels and so can be modeled with a categorical distribution. The state of the world may also take one of several discrete values. For example an image of a vehicle might be classified into {car,motorbike,van,truck} and our uncertainty over this state could be described by a categorical distribution.

The probabilities of observing the K outcomes are held in a $K \times 1$ parameter vector $\boldsymbol{\lambda} = [\lambda_1, \lambda_2, \ldots, \lambda_K]$, where $\lambda_k \in [0, 1]$ and $\sum_{k=1}^{K} \lambda_k = 1$. The categorical distribution can be visualized as a normalized histogram with K bins and can be written as

$$Pr(x = k) = \lambda_k. \tag{3.6}$$

For short, we use the notation

$$Pr(x) = \text{Cat}_x[\boldsymbol{\lambda}]. \tag{3.7}$$

Alternatively, we can think of the data as taking values $\mathbf{x} \in \{\mathbf{e}_1, \mathbf{e}_2, \ldots, \mathbf{e}_K\}$ where $\mathbf{e}_k$ is the kth unit vector; all elements of $\mathbf{e}_k$ are zero except the kth, which is one. Here we can write

$$Pr(\mathbf{x} = \mathbf{e}_k) = \prod_{j=1}^{K} \lambda_j^{x_j} = \lambda_k, \tag{3.8}$$

where x_j is the jth element of $\mathbf{x}$.

3.4   Dirichlet distribution

The *Dirichlet distribution* (Figure 3.4) is defined over K continuous values $\lambda_1 \ldots \lambda_K$ where $\lambda_k \in [0, 1]$ and $\sum_{k=1}^{K} \lambda_k = 1$. Hence it is suitable for defining a distribution over the parameters of the categorical distribution.

In K dimensions the Dirichlet distribution has K parameters $\alpha_1 \ldots \alpha_K$ each of which can take any positive value. The relative values of the parameters determine the expected values $E[\lambda_1] \ldots E[\lambda_k]$. The absolute values determine the concentration around the expected value. We write

$$Pr(\lambda_{1 \ldots K}) = \frac{\Gamma[\sum_{k=1}^{K} \alpha_k]}{\prod_{k=1}^{K} \Gamma[\alpha_k]} \prod_{k=1}^{K} \lambda_k^{\alpha_k - 1}, \tag{3.9}$$

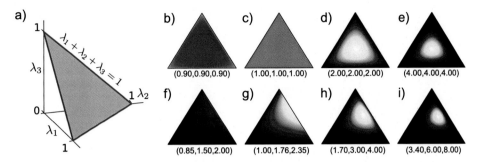

Figure 3.4 The Dirichlet distribution in K dimensions is defined on values $\lambda_1, \lambda_2, \ldots, \lambda_K$ such that $\sum_k \lambda_k = 1$ and $\lambda_k \in [0,1] \ \forall \ k \in \{1 \ldots K\}$. a) For K=3, this corresponds to a triangular section of the plane $\sum_k \lambda_k = 1$. In K dimensions, the Dirichlet is defined by K positive parameters $\alpha_{1 \ldots K}$. The ratio of the parameters determines the expected value for the distribution. The absolute values determine the concentration: the distribution is highly peaked around the expected value at high parameter values but pushed away from the expected value at low parameter values. b–e) Ratio of parameters is equal, absolute values increase. f–i) Ratio of parameters favors $\alpha_3 > \alpha_2 > \alpha_1$, absolute values increase.

or for short

$$Pr(\lambda_{1 \ldots K}) = \mathrm{Dir}_{\lambda_{1 \ldots K}}[\alpha_{1 \ldots K}]. \tag{3.10}$$

Just as the Bernoulli distribution was a special case of the categorical distribution with two possible outcomes, so the beta distribution is a special case of the Dirichlet distribution where the dimensionality is two.

3.5   Univariate normal distribution

The *univariate normal* or *Gaussian distribution* (Figure 3.5) is defined on continuous values $x \in [-\infty, \infty]$. In vision, it is common to ignore the fact that the intensity of a pixel is quantized and model it with the continuous normal distribution. The world state may also be described by the normal distribution. For example, the distance to an object could be represented in this way.

The normal distribution has two parameters, the mean μ and the variance σ^2. The parameter μ can take any value and determines the position of the peak. The parameter σ^2 takes only positive values and determines the width of the distribution. The normal distribution is defined as

$$Pr(x) = \frac{1}{\sqrt{2\pi\sigma^2}} \exp\left[-0.5\frac{(x-\mu)^2}{\sigma^2}\right], \tag{3.11}$$

and we will abbreviate this by writing

$$Pr(x) = \mathrm{Norm}_x[\mu, \sigma^2]. \tag{3.12}$$

3.6   Normal-scaled inverse gamma distribution

The *normal-scaled inverse gamma distribution* (Figure 3.6) is defined over a pair of continuous values μ, σ^2, the first of which can take any value and the second of which is

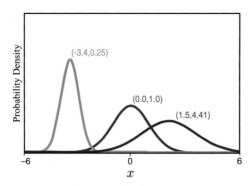

Figure 3.5 The univariate normal distribution is defined on $x \in \mathbb{R}$ and has two parameters $\{\mu, \sigma^2\}$. The mean parameter μ determines the expected value and the variance σ^2 determines the concentration about the mean so that as σ^2 increases, the distribution becomes wider and flatter.

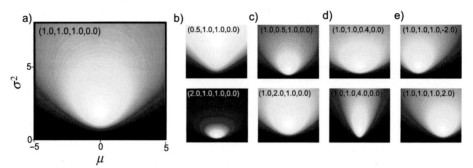

Figure 3.6 The normal-scaled inverse gamma distribution defines a probability distribution over bivariate continuous values μ, σ^2 where $\mu \in [-\infty, \infty]$ and $\sigma^2 \in [0, \infty]$. a) Distribution with parameters $[\alpha, \beta, \gamma, \delta] = [1, 1, 1, 0]$. b) Varying α. c) Varying β. d) Varying γ. e) Varying δ.

constrained to be positive. As such it can define a distribution over the mean and variance parameters of the normal distribution.

The normal-scaled inverse gamma has four parameters $\alpha, \beta, \gamma, \delta$ where α, β, and γ are positive real numbers but δ can take any value. It has pdf:

$$Pr(\mu, \sigma^2) = \frac{\sqrt{\gamma}}{\sigma\sqrt{2\pi}} \frac{\beta^\alpha}{\Gamma[\alpha]} \left(\frac{1}{\sigma^2}\right)^{\alpha+1} \exp\left[-\frac{2\beta + \gamma(\delta - \mu)^2}{2\sigma^2}\right], \qquad (3.13)$$

or for short

$$Pr(\mu, \sigma^2) = \text{NormInvGam}_{\mu, \sigma^2}[\alpha, \beta, \gamma, \delta]. \qquad (3.14)$$

3.7   Multivariate normal distribution

The *multivariate normal* or Gaussian distribution models D-dimensional variables $\mathbf{x}$ where each of the D elements $x_1 \ldots x_D$ is continuous and lies in the range $[-\infty, +\infty]$ (Figure 3.7). As such the univariate normal distribution is a special case of the multivariate normal where the number of elements D is one. In machine vision the multivariate normal might model the joint distribution of the intensities of D pixels within a region of the image. The state of the world might also be described by this distribution. For example, the multivariate normal might describe the joint uncertainty in the 3D position (x, y, z) of an object in the scene.

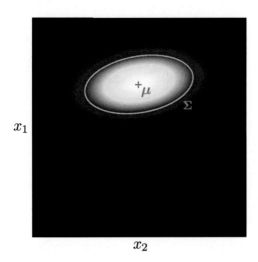

Figure 3.7 The multivariate normal distribution models D-dimensional variables $\mathbf{x} = [x_1 \dots x_D]^T$ where each dimension x_d is continuous and real. It is defined by a $D \times 1$ vector $\boldsymbol{\mu}$ defining the mean of the distribution and a $D \times D$ covariance matrix $\boldsymbol{\Sigma}$ which determines the shape. The isocontours of the distribution are ellipsoids where the center of the ellipsoid is determined by $\boldsymbol{\mu}$ and the shape by $\boldsymbol{\Sigma}$. This figure depicts a bivariate distribution, where the covariance is illustrated by drawing one of these ellipsoids.

The multivariate normal distribution has two parameters: the mean $\boldsymbol{\mu}$ and covariance $\boldsymbol{\Sigma}$. The mean $\boldsymbol{\mu}$ is a $D \times 1$ vector that describes the mean of the distribution. The covariance $\boldsymbol{\Sigma}$ is a symmetric $D \times D$ positive definite matrix so that $\mathbf{z}^T \boldsymbol{\Sigma} \mathbf{z}$ is positive for any real vector $\mathbf{z}$. The probability density function has the following form

$$Pr(\mathbf{x}) = \frac{1}{(2\pi)^{D/2}|\boldsymbol{\Sigma}|^{1/2}} \exp\left[-0.5(\mathbf{x} - \boldsymbol{\mu})^T \boldsymbol{\Sigma}^{-1}(\mathbf{x} - \boldsymbol{\mu})\right], \tag{3.15}$$

or for short

$$Pr(\mathbf{x}) = \text{Norm}_{\mathbf{x}}\left[\boldsymbol{\mu}, \boldsymbol{\Sigma}\right]. \tag{3.16}$$

The multivariate normal distribution will be used extensively throughout this book, and we devote the whole of Chapter 5 to describing its properties.

3.8   Normal inverse Wishart distribution

The *normal inverse Wishart distribution* defines a distribution over a $D \times 1$ vector $\boldsymbol{\mu}$ and a $D \times D$ positive definite matrix $\boldsymbol{\Sigma}$. As such it is suitable for describing uncertainty in the parameters of a multivariate normal distribution. The normal inverse Wishart has four parameters $\alpha, \boldsymbol{\Psi}, \gamma, \boldsymbol{\delta}$, where α and γ are positive scalars, $\boldsymbol{\delta}$ is a $D \times 1$ vector and $\boldsymbol{\Psi}$ is a positive definite $D \times D$ matrix

$$Pr(\boldsymbol{\mu}, \boldsymbol{\Sigma})$$
$$= \frac{\gamma^{D/2}|\boldsymbol{\Psi}|^{\alpha/2}|\boldsymbol{\Sigma}|^{-(\alpha+D+2)/2} \exp\left[-0.5\left(\text{Tr}[\boldsymbol{\Psi}\boldsymbol{\Sigma}^{-1}] + \gamma(\boldsymbol{\mu} - \boldsymbol{\delta})^T \boldsymbol{\Sigma}^{-1}(\boldsymbol{\mu} - \boldsymbol{\delta})\gamma^{D/2}\right)\right]}{2^{\alpha D/2}(2\pi)^{D/2}\Gamma_D[\alpha/2]},$$
$$\tag{3.17}$$

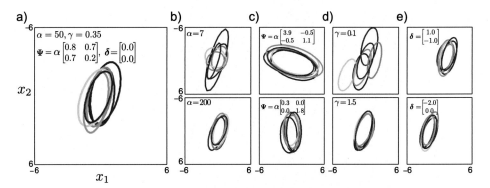

Figure 3.8 Sampling from 2D normal inverse Wishart distribution. a) Each sample consists of a mean vector and covariance matrix, here visualized with 2D ellipses illustrating the iso-contour of the associated Gaussian at a Mahalanobis distance of 2. b) Changing α modifies the dispersion of covariances observed. c) Changing $\boldsymbol{\Psi}$ modifies the average covariance. d) Changing γ modifies the dispersion of mean vectors observed. e) Changing $\boldsymbol{\delta}$ modifies the average value of the mean vectors.

where $\Gamma_D[\bullet]$ is the multivariate gamma function and $\text{Tr}[\boldsymbol{\Psi}]$ returns the trace of the matrix $\boldsymbol{\Psi}$ (see Appendix C.2.4). For short we will write

$$Pr(\boldsymbol{\mu}, \boldsymbol{\Sigma}) = \text{NorIWis}_{\boldsymbol{\mu}, \boldsymbol{\Sigma}}[\alpha, \boldsymbol{\Psi}, \gamma, \boldsymbol{\delta}]. \tag{3.18}$$

The mathematical form of the normal inverse Wishart distribution is rather opaque. However, it is just a function that produces a positive value for any valid mean vector $\boldsymbol{\mu}$ and covariance matrix $\boldsymbol{\Sigma}$, such that when we integrate over all possible values of $\boldsymbol{\mu}$ and $\boldsymbol{\Sigma}$, the answer is one. It is hard to visualize the normal inverse Wishart, but easy to draw samples and examine them: each sample is the mean and covariance of a normal distribution (Figure 3.8).

3.9 Conjugacy

We have argued that the beta distribution can represent probabilities over the parameters of the Bernoulli. Similarly the Dirichlet defines a distribution over the parameters of the categorical, and there are analogous relationships between the normal-scaled inverse gamma and univariate normal and the normal inverse Wishart and the multivariate normal.

These pairs were carefully chosen because they have a special relationship: in each case, the former distribution is *conjugate* to the latter: the beta is *conjugate* to the Bernoulli and the Dirichlet is conjugate to the categorical and so on. When we multiply a distribution with its conjugate, the result is proportional to a new distribution which has the same form as the conjugate. For example

$$\text{Bern}_x[\lambda] \cdot \text{Beta}_\lambda[\alpha, \beta] = \kappa(x, \alpha, \beta) \cdot \text{Beta}_\lambda\left[\tilde{\alpha}, \tilde{\beta}\right], \tag{3.19}$$

where κ is a scaling factor that is constant with respect to the variable of interest, λ. It is important to realize that this was not necessarily the case: if we had picked any distribution other than the beta, then this product would not have retained the same form. For this case, the relationship in Equation 3.19 is easy to prove

$$\text{Bern}_x[\lambda] \cdot \text{Beta}_\lambda[\alpha, \beta] = \lambda^x(1-\lambda)^{1-x}\frac{\Gamma[\alpha+\beta]}{\Gamma[\alpha]\Gamma[\beta]}\lambda^{\alpha-1}(1-\lambda)^{\beta-1}$$

$$= \frac{\Gamma[\alpha+\beta]}{\Gamma[\alpha]\Gamma[\beta]}\lambda^{x+\alpha-1}(1-\lambda)^{1-x+\beta-1}$$

$$= \frac{\Gamma[\alpha+\beta]}{\Gamma[\alpha]\Gamma[\beta]}\frac{\Gamma[x+\alpha]\Gamma[1-x+\beta]}{\Gamma[x+\alpha+1-x+\beta]}\text{Beta}_\lambda[x+\alpha, 1-x+\beta]$$

$$= \kappa(x, \alpha, \beta) \cdot \text{Beta}_\lambda\left[\tilde{\alpha}, \tilde{\beta}\right], \tag{3.20}$$

where in the third line we have both multiplied and divided by the constant associated with $\text{Beta}_\lambda[\tilde{\alpha}, \tilde{\beta}]$.

The conjugate relationship is important because we take products of distributions during both learning (fitting distributions) and evaluating the model (assessing the probability of new data under the fitted distribution). The conjugate relationship means that these products can both be computed neatly in closed form.

Summary

We use probability distributions to describe both the world state and the image data. We have presented four distributions (Bernoulli, categorical, univariate normal, multivariate normal) that are suited to this purpose. We also presented four other distributions (beta, Dirichlet, normal-scaled inverse gamma, normal inverse Wishart) that can be used to describe the uncertainty in parameters of the first; they can hence describe the uncertainty in the fitted model. These four pairs of distributions have a special relationship: each distribution from the second set is conjugate to one from the first set. As we shall see, the conjugate relationship makes it easier to fit these distributions to observed data and evaluate new data under the fitted model.

Notes

Throughout this book, I use rather esoteric terminology for discrete distributions. I distinguish between the *binomial distribution* (probability of getting M successes in N binary trials) and the *Bernoulli distribution* (the binary trial itself or probability of getting a success or failure in one trial) and talk exclusively about the latter distribution. I take a similar approach to discrete variables which can take K values. The *multinomial distribution* assigns a probability to observing the values $\{1, 2, \ldots, K\}$ with frequency $\{M_1, M_2, \ldots, M_K\}$ given N trials. The *categorical distribution* is a special case of this with $N = 1$. Most other authors do not make this distinction and would term this "multinomial" as well.

A more complete list of common probability distributions and details of their properties are given in Appendix B of Bishop (2006). Further information about conjugacy can be found in Chapter 2 of Bishop (2006) or any textbook on Bayesian methods, such as that of Gelman et al. (2004). Much more information about the normal distribution is provided in Chapter 5 of this book.

Problems

3.1 Consider a variable x which is Bernoulli distributed with parameter λ. Show that the mean $\text{E}[x]$ is λ and the variance $\text{E}[(x - \text{E}[x])^2]$ is $\lambda(1 - \lambda)$.

3.2 Calculate an expression for the mode (position of the peak) of the beta distribution with $\alpha, \beta > 1$ in terms of the parameters α and β.

3.3 The mean and variance of the beta distribution are given by the expressions

$$E[\lambda] = \mu = \frac{\alpha}{\alpha + \beta}$$

$$E[(\lambda - \mu)^2] = \sigma^2 = \frac{\alpha\beta}{(\alpha + \beta)^2(\alpha + \beta + 1)}.$$

We may wish to choose the parameters α and β so that the distribution has a particular mean μ and variance σ^2. Derive suitable expressions for α and β in terms of μ and σ^2.

3.4 All of the distributions in this chapter are members of the *exponential family* and can be written in the form

$$Pr(x|\boldsymbol{\theta}) = a[x]\exp[\mathbf{b}[\boldsymbol{\theta}]^T\mathbf{c}[x] - d[\boldsymbol{\theta}]],$$

where $a[x]$ and $\mathbf{c}[x]$ are functions of the data and $\mathbf{b}[\boldsymbol{\theta}]$ and $d[\boldsymbol{\theta}]$ are functions of the parameters. Find the functions $a[x], \mathbf{b}[\boldsymbol{\theta}], \mathbf{c}[x]$ and $d[\boldsymbol{\theta}]$ that allow the Beta distribution to be represented in the generalized form of the exponential family.

3.5 Use integration by parts to prove that if

$$\Gamma[z] = \int_0^\infty t^{z-1}e^{-t}dt,$$

then

$$\Gamma[z+1] = z\Gamma[z].$$

3.6 Consider a restricted family of univariate normal distributions where the variance is always 1, so that

$$Pr(x|\mu) = \frac{1}{\sqrt{2\pi}}\exp\left[-0.5(x-\mu)^2\right].$$

Show that a normal distribution over the parameter μ

$$Pr(\mu) = \text{Norm}_\mu[\mu_p, \sigma_p^2]$$

has a conjugate relationship to the restricted normal distribution.

3.7 For the normal distribution, find the functions $a[x], b[\theta], c[x]$, and $d[\theta]$ that allow it to be represented in the generalized form of the exponential family (see Problem 3.4).

3.8 Calculate an expression for the mode (position of the peak in μ, σ^2 space) of the normal-scaled inverse gamma distribution in terms of the parameters $\alpha, \beta, \gamma, \delta$.

3.9 Show that the more general form of the conjugate relation in which we multiply I Bernoulli distributions by the conjugate beta prior is given by

$$\prod_{i=1}^I \text{Bern}_{x_i}[\lambda] \cdot \text{Beta}_\lambda[\alpha, \beta] = \kappa \cdot \text{Beta}_\lambda[\tilde{\alpha}, \tilde{\beta}],$$

where

$$\kappa = \frac{\Gamma[\alpha+\beta]\Gamma[\alpha+\sum x_i]\Gamma[\beta+\sum(1-x_i)]}{\Gamma[\alpha+\beta+I]\Gamma[\alpha]\Gamma[\beta]}$$

$$\tilde{\alpha} = \alpha + \sum x_i$$

$$\tilde{\beta} = \beta + \sum(1-x_i).$$

3.10 Prove the conjugate relation

$$\prod_{i=1}^{I} \text{Cat}_{\mathbf{x}_i}[\lambda_{1\ldots K}] \cdot \text{Dir}_{\lambda_{1\ldots K}}[\alpha_{1\ldots K}] = \kappa \cdot \text{Dir}_{\lambda_{1\ldots K}}[\tilde{\alpha}_{1\ldots K}],$$

where

$$\tilde{\kappa} = \frac{\Gamma[\sum_{j=1}^{K} \alpha_j]}{\Gamma[I + \sum_{j=1}^{K} \alpha_j]} \cdot \frac{\prod_{j=1}^{K} \Gamma[\alpha_j + N_j]}{\prod_{j=1}^{K} \Gamma[\alpha_j]}$$

$$\tilde{\alpha}_{1\ldots K} = [\alpha_1 + N_1, \alpha_2 + N_2, \ldots, \alpha_K + N_K].$$

and N_k is the total number of times that the variable took the value k.

3.11 Show that the conjugate relation between the normal and normal inverse gamma is given by

$$\prod_{i=1}^{I} \text{Norm}_{x_i}[\mu, \sigma^2] \cdot \text{NormInvGam}_{\mu, \sigma^2}[\alpha, \beta, \gamma, \delta] = \kappa \cdot \text{NormInvGam}_{\mu, \sigma^2}[\tilde{\alpha}, \tilde{\beta}, \tilde{\gamma}, \tilde{\delta}],$$

where

$$\kappa = \frac{1}{(2\pi)^{I/2}} \frac{\sqrt{\gamma} \beta^\alpha}{\sqrt{\tilde{\gamma}} \tilde{\beta}^{\tilde{\alpha}}} \frac{\Gamma[\tilde{\alpha}]}{\Gamma[\alpha]}$$

$$\tilde{\alpha} = \alpha + I/2$$

$$\tilde{\beta} = \frac{\sum_i x_i^2}{2} + \beta + \frac{\gamma \delta^2}{2} - \frac{(\gamma \delta + \sum_i x_i)^2}{2(\gamma + I)}$$

$$\tilde{\gamma} = \gamma + I$$

$$\tilde{\delta} = \frac{\gamma \delta + \sum_i x_i}{\gamma + I}.$$

3.12 Show that the conjugate relationship between the multivariate normal and the normal inverse Wishart is given by

$$\prod_{i=1}^{I} \text{Norm}_{\mathbf{x}_i}[\boldsymbol{\mu}, \boldsymbol{\Sigma}] \cdot \text{NorIWis}_{\boldsymbol{\mu}, \boldsymbol{\Sigma}}[\alpha, \boldsymbol{\Psi}, \gamma, \boldsymbol{\delta}] = \kappa \cdot \text{NorIWis}\left[\tilde{\alpha}, \tilde{\boldsymbol{\Psi}}, \tilde{\gamma}, \tilde{\boldsymbol{\delta}}\right],$$

where

$$\kappa = \frac{1}{\pi^{ID/2}} \frac{\gamma^{D/2}}{\tilde{\gamma}^{D/2}} \frac{\boldsymbol{\Psi}^{\alpha/2}}{\tilde{\boldsymbol{\Psi}}^{\tilde{\alpha}/2}} \frac{\Gamma_D[\tilde{\alpha}/2]}{\Gamma_D[\alpha/2]}$$

$$\tilde{\alpha} = \alpha + I$$

$$\tilde{\boldsymbol{\Psi}} = \boldsymbol{\Psi} + \gamma \boldsymbol{\delta} \boldsymbol{\delta}^T + \sum_{i=1}^{I} \mathbf{x}_i \mathbf{x}_i^T - \frac{1}{(\gamma + I)} \left(\gamma \boldsymbol{\delta} + \sum_{i=1}^{I} \mathbf{x}_i\right) \left(\gamma \boldsymbol{\delta} + \sum_{i=1}^{I} \mathbf{x}_i\right)^T$$

$$\tilde{\gamma} = \gamma + I$$

$$\tilde{\boldsymbol{\delta}} = \frac{\gamma \boldsymbol{\delta} + \sum_{i=1}^{I} \mathbf{x}_i}{\gamma + I}.$$

You may need to use the relation $\text{Tr}\left[\mathbf{z}\mathbf{z}^T \mathbf{A}^{-1}\right] = \mathbf{z}^T \mathbf{A}^{-1} \mathbf{z}$.

Chapter 4

Fitting probability models

This chapter concerns fitting probability models to data $\{\mathbf{x}_i\}_{i=1}^{I}$. This process is referred to as *learning* because we learn about the parameters $\boldsymbol{\theta}$ of the model.[1] It also concerns calculating the probability of a new datum $\mathbf{x}^*$ under the resulting model. This is known as evaluating the *predictive distribution*. We consider three methods: *maximum likelihood*, *maximum a posteriori*, and the *Bayesian approach*.

4.1   Maximum likelihood

As the name suggests, the maximum likelihood (ML) method finds the set of parameters $\hat{\boldsymbol{\theta}}$ under which the data $\{\mathbf{x}_i\}_{i=1}^{I}$ are most likely. To calculate the likelihood function $Pr(\mathbf{x}_i|\boldsymbol{\theta})$ at a single data point $\mathbf{x}_i$, we simply evaluate the probability density function at $\mathbf{x}_i$. Assuming each data point was drawn independently from the distribution, the likelihood function $Pr(\mathbf{x}_{1...I}|\boldsymbol{\theta})$ for a set of points is the product of the individual likelihoods. Hence, the ML estimate of the parameters is

$$\hat{\boldsymbol{\theta}} = \underset{\boldsymbol{\theta}}{\operatorname{argmax}} \left[Pr(\mathbf{x}_{1...I}|\boldsymbol{\theta}) \right]$$

$$= \underset{\boldsymbol{\theta}}{\operatorname{argmax}} \left[\prod_{i=1}^{I} Pr(\mathbf{x}_i|\boldsymbol{\theta}) \right], \tag{4.1}$$

where $\operatorname{argmax}_{\boldsymbol{\theta}} f[\boldsymbol{\theta}]$ returns the value of $\boldsymbol{\theta}$ that maximizes the argument $f[\boldsymbol{\theta}]$.

To evaluate the predictive distribution for a new data point $\mathbf{x}^*$ (compute the probability that $\mathbf{x}^*$ belongs to the fitted model), we simply evaluate the probability density function $Pr(\mathbf{x}^*|\hat{\boldsymbol{\theta}})$ using the ML fitted parameters $\hat{\boldsymbol{\theta}}$.

4.2   Maximum a posteriori

In maximum a posteriori (MAP) fitting, we introduce *prior* information about the parameters $\boldsymbol{\theta}$. From previous experience we may know something about the possible parameter values. For example, in a time-sequence the values of the parameters at time t tell us a

---

[1] Here we adopt the notation $\boldsymbol{\theta}$ to represent a generic set of parameters when we have not specified the particular probability model.

lot about the possible values at time $t + 1$, and this information would be encoded in the prior distribution.

As the name suggests, maximum a posteriori estimation maximizes the posterior probability $Pr(\boldsymbol{\theta}|\mathbf{x}_{1...I})$ of the parameters

$$
\begin{aligned}
\hat{\boldsymbol{\theta}} &= \underset{\boldsymbol{\theta}}{\mathrm{argmax}}\,[Pr(\boldsymbol{\theta}|\mathbf{x}_{1...I})] \\
&= \underset{\boldsymbol{\theta}}{\mathrm{argmax}}\left[\frac{Pr(\mathbf{x}_{1...I}|\boldsymbol{\theta})Pr(\boldsymbol{\theta})}{Pr(\mathbf{x}_{1...I})}\right] \\
&= \underset{\boldsymbol{\theta}}{\mathrm{argmax}}\left[\frac{\prod_{i=1}^{I}Pr(\mathbf{x}_i|\boldsymbol{\theta})Pr(\boldsymbol{\theta})}{Pr(\mathbf{x}_{1...I})}\right],
\end{aligned}
\tag{4.2}
$$

where we have used Bayes' rule between the first two lines and subsequently assumed independence. In fact, we can discard the denominator as it is constant with respect to the parameters and so does not affect the position of the maximum, and we get

$$
\hat{\boldsymbol{\theta}} = \underset{\boldsymbol{\theta}}{\mathrm{argmax}}\left[\prod_{i=1}^{I}Pr(\mathbf{x}_i|\boldsymbol{\theta})Pr(\boldsymbol{\theta})\right].
\tag{4.3}
$$

Comparing this to the maximum likelihood criterion (Equation 4.1), we see that it is identical except for the additional prior term; maximum likelihood is a special case of maximum a posteriori where the prior is uninformative.

The predictive density (probability of a new datum $\mathbf{x}^*$ under the fitted model) is again calculated by evaluating the pdf $Pr(\mathbf{x}^*|\hat{\boldsymbol{\theta}})$ using the new parameters.

4.3   The Bayesian approach

In the Bayesian approach we stop trying to estimate single fixed values (*point estimates*) of the parameters $\boldsymbol{\theta}$ and admit what is obvious; there may be many values of the parameters that are compatible with the data. We compute a probability distribution $Pr(\boldsymbol{\theta}|\mathbf{x}_{1...I})$ over the parameters $\boldsymbol{\theta}$ based on data $\{\mathbf{x}_i\}_{i=1}^{I}$ using Bayes' rule so that

$$
Pr(\boldsymbol{\theta}|\mathbf{x}_{1...I}) = \frac{\prod_{i=1}^{I}Pr(\mathbf{x}_i|\boldsymbol{\theta})Pr(\boldsymbol{\theta})}{Pr(\mathbf{x}_{1...I})}.
\tag{4.4}
$$

Evaluating the predictive distribution is more difficult for the Bayesian case since we have not estimated a single model but have instead found a probability distribution over possible models. Hence, we calculate

$$
Pr(\mathbf{x}^*|\mathbf{x}_{1...I}) = \int Pr(\mathbf{x}^*|\boldsymbol{\theta})Pr(\boldsymbol{\theta}|\mathbf{x}_{1...I})\,d\boldsymbol{\theta},
\tag{4.5}
$$

which can be interpreted as follows: the term $Pr(\mathbf{x}^*|\boldsymbol{\theta})$ is the prediction for a given value of $\boldsymbol{\theta}$. So, the integral can be thought of as a weighted sum of the predictions given by different parameters $\boldsymbol{\theta}$, where the weighting is determined by the posterior probability distribution $Pr(\boldsymbol{\theta}|\mathbf{x}_{1...I})$ over the parameters (representing our confidence that different parameter values are correct).

The predictive density calculations for the Bayesian, MAP, and ML cases can be unified if we consider the ML and MAP estimates to be special probability distributions over the parameters where all of the density is at $\hat{\theta}$. More formally, we can consider them as *delta functions* centered at $\hat{\theta}$. A delta function $\delta[z]$ is a function that integrates to one, and that returns zero everywhere except at $z = 0$. We can now write

$$Pr(\mathbf{x}^*|\mathbf{x}_{1...I}) = \int Pr(\mathbf{x}^*|\boldsymbol{\theta})\delta[\boldsymbol{\theta} - \hat{\boldsymbol{\theta}}] \, d\boldsymbol{\theta}$$

$$= Pr(\mathbf{x}^*|\hat{\boldsymbol{\theta}}), \tag{4.6}$$

which is exactly the calculation we originally prescribed: we simply evaluate the probability of the data under the model with the estimated parameters.

4.4   Worked example 1: Univariate normal

To illustrate the above ideas, we will consider fitting a univariate normal model to scalar data $\{x_i\}_{i=1}^I$. Recall that the univariate normal model has pdf

$$Pr(x|\mu,\sigma^2) = \text{Norm}_x[\mu,\sigma^2] = \frac{1}{\sqrt{2\pi\sigma^2}} \exp\left[-0.5\frac{(x-\mu)^2}{\sigma^2}\right], \tag{4.7}$$

and has two parameters, the mean μ and the variance σ^2. Let us generate I independent data points $\{x_i\}_{i=1}^I$ from a univariate normal with $\mu = 1$ and $\sigma^2 = 1$. Our goal is to reestimate these parameters from the data.

4.4.1   Maximum likelihood estimation

The likelihood $Pr(x_{1...I}|\mu,\sigma^2)$ of the parameters $\{\mu,\sigma^2\}$ for observed data $\{x_i\}_{i=1}^I$ is computed by evaluating the pdf for each data point separately and taking the product:

$$Pr(x_{1...I}|\mu,\sigma^2) = \prod_{i=1}^I Pr(x_i|\mu,\sigma^2)$$

⚙ 4.1

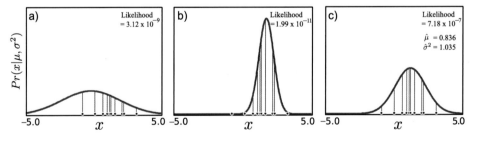

Figure 4.1 Maximum likelihood fitting. The likelihood of the parameters for a single datapoint is the height of the pdf evaluated at that point (blue vertical lines). The likelihood of a set of independently sampled data is the product of the individual likelihoods. a) The likelihood for this normal distribution is low because the large variance means the height of the pdf is low everywhere. b) The likelihood for this normal distribution is even lower as the left-most datum is very unlikely under the model. c) The maximum likelihood solution is the set of parameters for which the likelihood is maximized.

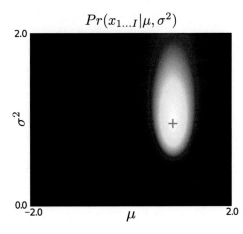

$$Pr(x_{1...I}|\mu,\sigma^2)$$

Figure 4.2 The likelihood function for a fixed set of observed data is a function of the mean μ and variance σ^2 parameters. The plot shows that there are many parameter settings which might plausibly be responsible for the ten data points from Figure 4.1. A sensible choice for the "best" parameter setting is the maximum likelihood solution (green cross), which corresponds to the maximum of this function.

$$= \prod_{i=1}^{I} \text{Norm}_{x_i}[\mu,\sigma^2]$$

$$= \frac{1}{(2\pi\sigma^2)^{I/2}} \exp\left[-0.5\sum_{i=1}^{I}\frac{(x_i-\mu)^2}{\sigma^2}\right]. \tag{4.8}$$

Obviously, the likelihood for some sets of parameters $\{\mu,\sigma^2\}$ will be higher than others (Figure 4.1), and it is possible to visualize this as a 2D function of the mean μ and variance σ^2 (Figure 4.2). The maximum likelihood solution $\hat{\mu},\hat{\sigma}$ will occur at the peak of this surface so that

$$\hat{\mu},\hat{\sigma}^2 = \underset{\mu,\sigma^2}{\text{argmax}}\left[Pr(x_{1...I}|\mu,\sigma^2)\right]. \tag{4.9}$$

In principle we can maximize this by taking the derivative of Equation 4.8 with respect to μ and σ^2, equating the result to zero and solving. In practice, however, the resulting equations are messy. To simplify things, we work instead with the logarithm of this expression (the log likelihood, L). Since the logarithm is a monotonic function (Figure 4.3), the position of the maximum in the transformed function remains the same. Algebraically, the logarithm turns the product of the likelihoods of the individual data points into a sum and so decouples the contribution of each. The ML parameters can now be calculated as

$$\hat{\mu},\hat{\sigma}^2 = \underset{\mu,\sigma^2}{\text{argmax}}\left[\sum_{i=1}^{I}\log\left[\text{Norm}_{x_i}[\mu,\sigma^2]\right]\right] \tag{4.10}$$

$$= \underset{\mu,\sigma^2}{\text{argmax}}\left[-0.5I\log[2\pi]-0.5I\log\sigma^2-0.5\sum_{i=1}^{I}\frac{(x_i-\mu)^2}{\sigma^2}\right].$$

To maximize, we differentiate this *log likelihood L* with respect to μ and equate the result to zero

$$\frac{\partial L}{\partial \mu} = \sum_{i=1}^{I}\frac{(x_i-\mu)}{\sigma^2}$$

$$= \frac{\sum_{i=1}^{I}x_i}{\sigma^2} - \frac{I\mu}{\sigma^2} = 0, \tag{4.11}$$

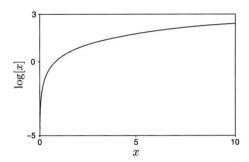

and rearranging, we see that

$$\hat{\mu} = \frac{\sum_{i=1}^{I} x_i}{I}.$$ (4.12)

By a similar process, the expression for the variance can be shown to be

$$\hat{\sigma}^2 = \sum_{i=1}^{I} \frac{(x_i - \hat{\mu})^2}{I}.$$ (4.13)

These expressions are hardly surprising, but the same idea can be used to estimate parameters in other distributions where the results are less familiar.

Figure 4.1 shows a set of data points and three possible fits to the data. The mean of the maximum likelihood fit is the mean of the data. The ML fit is neither too narrow (giving very low probabilities to the furthest data points from the mean) nor too wide (resulting in a flat distribution and giving low probability to all points).

Least squares fitting

As an aside, we note that many texts discuss fitting in terms of *least squares*. Consider fitting just the mean parameter μ of the normal distribution using maximum likelihood. Manipulating the cost function so that

$$\hat{\mu} = \underset{\mu}{\operatorname{argmax}} \left[-0.5 I \log[2\pi] - 0.5 I \log \sigma^2 - 0.5 \sum_{i=1}^{I} \frac{(x_i - \mu)^2}{\sigma^2} \right]$$

$$= \underset{\mu}{\operatorname{argmax}} \left[-\sum_{i=1}^{I} (x_i - \mu)^2 \right]$$

$$= \underset{\mu}{\operatorname{argmin}} \left[\sum_{i=1}^{I} (x_i - \mu)^2 \right]$$ (4.14)

leads to a formulation where we minimize the sum of squares. In other words, least squares fitting is equivalent to fitting the mean parameter of a normal distribution using the maximum likelihood method.

4.4.2   Maximum a posteriori estimation

Returning to the main thread, we will now demonstrate maximum a posteriori fitting of the parameters of the normal distribution. The cost function becomes

$$\hat{\mu}, \hat{\sigma}^2 = \underset{\mu,\sigma^2}{\operatorname{argmax}} \left[\prod_{i=1}^{I} Pr(x_i|\mu,\sigma^2) Pr(\mu,\sigma^2) \right]$$

$$= \underset{\mu,\sigma^2}{\operatorname{argmax}} \left[\prod_{i=1}^{I} \operatorname{Norm}_{x_i}[\mu,\sigma^2] \operatorname{NormInvGam}_{\mu,\sigma^2}[\alpha,\beta,\gamma,\delta] \right], \qquad (4.15)$$

where we have chosen normal inverse gamma prior with parameters $\alpha, \beta, \gamma, \delta$ (Figure 4.4) as this is conjugate to the normal distribution. The expression for the prior is

$$Pr(\mu,\sigma^2) = \frac{\sqrt{\gamma}}{\sigma\sqrt{2\pi}} \frac{\beta^\alpha}{\Gamma(\alpha)} \left(\frac{1}{\sigma^2}\right)^{\alpha+1} \exp\left[-\frac{2\beta + \gamma(\delta-\mu)^2}{2\sigma^2}\right]. \qquad (4.16)$$

The posterior distribution is proportional to the product of the likelihood and the prior (Figure 4.5), and has the highest density in regions that both agree with the data *and* were a priori plausible.

Like the ML case, it is easier to maximize the logarithm of Equation 4.15:

$$\hat{\mu}, \hat{\sigma}^2 = \underset{\mu,\sigma^2}{\operatorname{argmax}} \left[\sum_{i=1}^{I} \log[\operatorname{Norm}_{x_i}[\mu,\sigma^2]] + \log\left[\operatorname{NormInvGam}_{\mu,\sigma^2}[\alpha,\beta,\gamma,\delta]\right] \right].$$
$$(4.17)$$

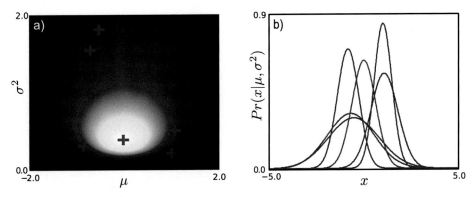

Figure 4.4 Prior over normal parameters. a) A normal inverse gamma with $\alpha, \beta, \gamma = 1$ and $\delta = 0$ gives a broad prior distribution over univariate normal parameters. The magenta cross indicates the peak of this prior distribution. The blue crosses are five samples randomly drawn from the distribution. b) The peak and the samples can be visualized by plotting the normal distributions that they represent.

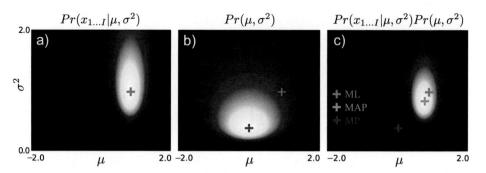

Figure 4.5 MAP inference for normal parameters. a) The likelihood function is multiplied by b) the prior probability to give a new function c) that is proportional to the posterior distribution. The maximum a posteriori (MAP) solution (cyan cross) is found at the peak of the posterior distribution. It lies between the maximum likelihood (ML) solution (green cross) and the maximum of the prior distribution (MP, magenta cross).

To find the MAP parameters, we substitute in the expressions, differentiate with respect to μ and σ, equate to zero, and rearrange to give

$$\hat{\mu} = \frac{\sum_{i=1}^{I} x_i + \gamma\delta}{I + \gamma} \quad \text{and} \quad \hat{\sigma}^2 = \frac{\sum_{i=1}^{I}(x_i - \hat{\mu})^2 + 2\beta + \gamma(\delta - \hat{\mu})^2}{I + 3 + 2\alpha}.$$

(4.18)

The formula for the mean can be more easily understood if we write it as

$$\hat{\mu} = \frac{I\bar{x} + \gamma\delta}{I + \gamma}.$$

(4.19)

This is a weighted sum of two terms. The first term is the data mean $\bar{x}$ and is weighted by the number of training examples I. The second term is δ, the value of μ favored by the prior, and is weighted by γ.

This gives some insight into the behavior of the MAP estimate (Figure 4.6). With a large amount of data, the first term dominates, and the MAP estimate $\hat{\mu}$ is very close to the data mean (and the ML estimate). With intermediate amounts of data, $\hat{\mu}$ is a weighted sum of the prediction from the data and the prediction from the prior. With no data at all, the estimate is completely governed by the prior. The hyperparameter (parameter of the prior) γ controls the concentration of the prior with respect to μ and determines the extent of its influence. Similar conclusions can be drawn about the MAP estimate of the variance.

Where there is a single data point (Figure 4.6e–f), the data tells us nothing about the variance and the maximum likelihood estimate $\hat{\sigma}^2$ is actually zero; the best fit is an infinitely thin and infinitely tall normal distribution centered on the one data point. This is unrealistic, not least because it accords the datum an infinite likelihood. However, MAP estimation is still valid as the prior ensures that sensible parameter values are chosen.

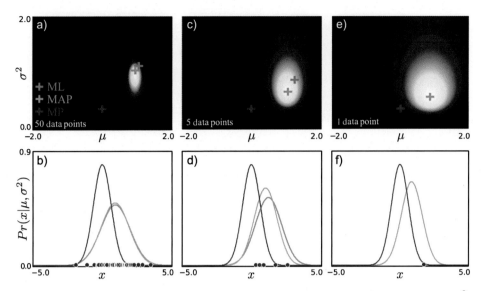

Figure 4.6 Maximum a posteriori estimation. a) Posterior distribution over parameters μ and σ^2. MAP solution (cyan cross) lies between ML (green cross) and the peak of the prior (purple cross). b) Normal distributions corresponding to MAP solution, ML solution and peak of prior. c–d) With fewer data points, the prior has a greater effect on the final solution. e–f) With only one data point, the maximum likelihood solution cannot be computed (you cannot calculate the variance of a single point). However, the MAP solution can still be calculated.

4.4.3   The Bayesian approach

In the Bayesian approach, we calculate a posterior distribution $Pr(\mu, \sigma^2|x_{1...I})$ over possible parameter values using Bayes' rule,

$$
\begin{aligned}
Pr(\mu, \sigma^2|x_{1...I}) &= \frac{\prod_{i=1}^{I} Pr(x_i|\mu, \sigma^2) Pr(\mu, \sigma^2)}{Pr(x_{1...I})} \\
&= \frac{\prod_{i=1}^{I} \text{Norm}_{x_i}[\mu, \sigma^2] \text{NormInvGam}_{\mu, \sigma^2}[\alpha, \beta, \gamma, \delta]}{Pr(x_{1...I})} \\
&= \frac{\kappa \text{NormInvGam}_{\mu, \sigma^2}[\tilde{\alpha}, \tilde{\beta}, \tilde{\gamma}, \tilde{\delta}]}{Pr(x_{1...I})},
\end{aligned}
\tag{4.20}
$$

where we have used the conjugate relationship between likelihood and prior (Section 3.9) and κ is the associated constant. The product of the normal likelihood and normal inverse gamma prior creates a posterior over μ and σ^2, which is a new normal inverse gamma distribution and can be shown to have parameters

$$
\tilde{\alpha} = \alpha + I/2, \qquad \tilde{\gamma} = \gamma + I \qquad \tilde{\delta} = \frac{\gamma\delta + \sum_i x_i}{\gamma + I}
$$

$$
\tilde{\beta} = \frac{\sum_i x_i^2}{2} + \beta + \frac{\gamma\delta^2}{2} - \frac{(\gamma\delta + \sum_i x_i)^2}{2(\gamma + I)}.
\tag{4.21}
$$

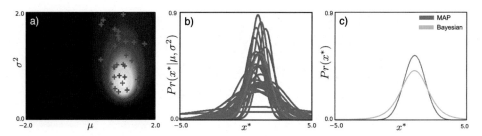

Figure 4.7 Bayesian predictions. a) Posterior probability distribution over parameters. b) Samples from posterior probability distribution correspond to normal distributions. c) The predictive distribution for the Bayesian case is the average of an infinite set of samples. Alternately, we can think of choosing the parameters from a uniform distribution and computing a weighted average where the weights correspond to the posterior distribution.

Note that the posterior (left-hand side of Equation 4.20) must be a valid probability distribution and sum to one, so the constant κ from the conjugate product and the denominator from the right-hand side must exactly cancel to give

$$Pr(\mu, \sigma^2 | x_{1...I}) = \text{NormInvGam}_{\mu, \sigma^2}[\tilde{\alpha}, \tilde{\beta}, \tilde{\gamma}, \tilde{\delta}]. \tag{4.22}$$

Now we see the major advantage of using a conjugate prior: we are guaranteed a closed form expression for the posterior distribution over the parameters.

This posterior distribution represents the relative plausibility of various parameter settings μ and σ^2 having created the data. At the peak of the distribution is the MAP estimate, but there are many other plausible configurations (Figure 4.6).

When data are plentiful (Figure 4.6a), the parameters are well specified, and the probability distribution is concentrated. In this case, placing all of the probability mass at the MAP estimate is a good approximation to the posterior. However, when data are scarce (Figure 4.6c), many possible parameters might have explained the data and the posterior is broad. In this case approximation with a point mass is inadequate.

Predictive density

For the maximum likelihood and MAP estimates, we evaluate the predictive density (probability that a new data point x^* belongs to the same model) by simply evaluating the normal pdf with the estimated parameters. For the Bayesian case, we compute a weighted average of the predictions for each possible parameter set, where the weighting is given by the posterior distribution over parameters (Figures 4.6a–c and 4.7),

$$Pr(x^* | x_{1...I}) = \iint Pr(x^* | \mu, \sigma^2) Pr(\mu, \sigma^2 | x_{1...I}) \, d\mu d\sigma \tag{4.23}$$

$$= \iint \text{Norm}_{x^*}[\mu, \sigma^2] \text{NormInvGam}_{\mu, \sigma^2}[\tilde{\alpha}, \tilde{\beta}, \tilde{\gamma}, \tilde{\delta}] \, d\mu d\sigma$$

$$= \iint \kappa(x^*, \tilde{\alpha}, \tilde{\beta}, \tilde{\gamma}, \tilde{\delta}) \text{NormInvGam}_{\mu, \sigma^2}[\breve{\alpha}, \breve{\beta}, \breve{\gamma}, \breve{\delta}] \, d\mu d\sigma.$$

Here we have used the conjugate relation for a second time. The integral contains a constant with respect to μ and σ^2 multiplied by a probability distribution. Taking the

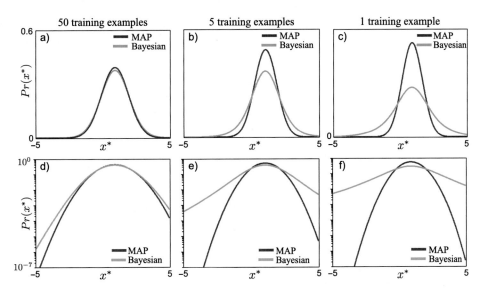

Figure 4.8 a–c) Predictive densities for MAP and Bayesian approaches with 50, 5, and 1 training examples. As the training data decreases, the Bayesian prediction becomes less certain but the MAP prediction is erroneously overconfident. d–f) This effect is even more clear on a log scale.

constant outside the integral, we get

$$Pr(x^*|x_{1...I}) = \kappa(x^*, \tilde{\alpha}, \tilde{\beta}, \tilde{\gamma}, \tilde{\delta}) \int\int \text{NormInvGam}_{\mu, \sigma^2}[\breve{\alpha}, \breve{\beta}, \breve{\gamma}, \breve{\delta}] \, d\mu d\sigma$$

$$= \kappa(x^*, \tilde{\alpha}, \tilde{\beta}, \tilde{\gamma}, \tilde{\delta}), \tag{4.24}$$

which follows because the integral of a pdf is one. It can be shown that the constant is given by

$$\kappa(x^*, \tilde{\alpha}, \tilde{\beta}, \tilde{\gamma}, \tilde{\delta}) = \frac{1}{\sqrt{2\pi}} \frac{\sqrt{\tilde{\gamma}} \tilde{\beta}^{\tilde{\alpha}}}{\sqrt{\breve{\gamma}} \breve{\beta}^{\breve{\alpha}}} \frac{\Gamma[\breve{\alpha}]}{\Gamma[\tilde{\alpha}]}, \tag{4.25}$$

where

$$\breve{\alpha} = \tilde{\alpha} + 1/2, \qquad \breve{\gamma} = \tilde{\gamma} + 1$$

$$\breve{\beta} = \frac{x^{*2}}{2} + \tilde{\beta} + \frac{\tilde{\gamma}\tilde{\delta}^2}{2} - \frac{(\tilde{\gamma}\tilde{\delta} + x^*)^2}{2(\tilde{\gamma} + 1)}. \tag{4.26}$$

Here, we see the second advantage of using the conjugate prior; it means that the integral can be computed, and so we get a nice closed form expression for the predictive density.

Figure 4.8 shows the predictive distribution for the Bayesian and MAP cases, for varying amounts of training data. With plenty of training data, they are quite similar but as the amount of data decreases, the Bayesian predictive distribution has a significantly longer tail. This is typical of Bayesian solutions: they are more moderate (less certain) in their predictions. In the MAP case, erroneously committing to a single estimate of μ and σ^2 causes overconfidence in our future predictions.

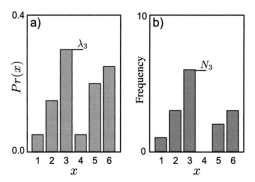

Figure 4.9 a) Categorical probability distribution over six discrete values with parameters $\{\lambda_k\}_{k=1}^6$ where $\sum_{k=1}^6 \lambda_k = 1$. This could be the relative probability of a biased die landing on its six sides. b) Fifteen observations $\{x_i\}_{i=1}^I$ randomly sampled from this distribution. We denote the number of times category k was observed by N_k so that here the total observations $\sum_{k=1}^6 N_k = 15$.

4.5 Worked example 2: Categorical distribution

As a second example, we consider discrete data $\{x_i\}_{i=1}^I$ where $x_i \in \{1, 2, \ldots, 6\}$ (Figure 4.9). This could represent observed rolls of a die with unknown bias. We will describe the data using a categorical distribution (normalized histogram) where

$$Pr(x = k | \lambda_{1\ldots K}) = \lambda_k. \tag{4.27}$$

For the ML and MAP techniques, we estimate the six parameters $\{\lambda_k\}_{k=1}^6$. For the Bayesian approach, we compute a probability distribution over the parameters.

4.5.1 Maximum Likelihood

To find the maximum likelihood solution, we maximize the product of the likelihoods for each individual data point with respect to the parameters $\lambda_{1\ldots 6}$.

$$
\begin{aligned}
\hat{\lambda}_{1\ldots 6} &= \underset{\lambda_{1\ldots 6}}{\operatorname{argmax}} \left[\prod_{i=1}^I Pr(x_i | \lambda_{1\ldots 6}) \right] && \text{s.t.} \sum_k \lambda_k = 1 \\
&= \underset{\lambda_{1\ldots 6}}{\operatorname{argmax}} \left[\prod_{i=1}^I \operatorname{Cat}_{x_i}[\lambda_{1\ldots 6}] \right] && \text{s.t.} \sum_k \lambda_k = 1 \\
&= \underset{\lambda_{1\ldots 6}}{\operatorname{argmax}} \left[\prod_{k=1}^6 \lambda_k^{N_k} \right] && \text{s.t.} \sum_k \lambda_k = 1, \tag{4.28}
\end{aligned}
$$

where N_k is the total number of times we observed bin k in the training data. As before, it is easier to maximize the log probability, and we use the criterion

$$L = \sum_{k=1}^6 N_k \log[\lambda_k] + \nu \left(\sum_{k=1}^6 \lambda_k - 1 \right), \tag{4.29}$$

where the second term uses the Lagrange multiplier ν to enforce the constraint on the parameters $\sum_{k=1}^6 \lambda_k = 1$. We differentiate L with respect to λ_k and ν, set the derivatives equal to zero, and solve for λ_k to obtain

$$\hat{\lambda}_k = \frac{N_k}{\sum_{m=1}^6 N_m}. \tag{4.30}$$

In other words, λ_k is the proportion of times that we observed bin k.

4.5.2 Maximum a posteriori

To find the maximum a posteriori solution we need to define a prior. We choose the Dirichlet distribution as it is conjugate to the categorical likelihood. This prior over the six categorical parameters is hard to visualize but samples can be drawn and examined (Figure 4.10a–e). The MAP solution is given by

$$
\begin{aligned}
\hat{\lambda}_{1\ldots 6} &= \operatorname*{argmax}_{\lambda_{1\ldots 6}} \left[\prod_{i=1}^{I} Pr(x_i|\lambda_{1\ldots 6}) Pr(\lambda_{1\ldots 6}) \right] \\
&= \operatorname*{argmax}_{\lambda_{1\ldots 6}} \left[\prod_{i=1}^{I} \mathrm{Cat}_{x_i}[\lambda_{1\ldots 6}] \mathrm{Dir}_{\lambda_{1\ldots 6}}[\alpha_{1\ldots 6}] \right] \\
&= \operatorname*{argmax}_{\lambda_{1\ldots 6}} \left[\prod_{k=1}^{6} \lambda_k^{N_k} \prod_{k=1}^{6} \lambda_k^{\alpha_k-1} \right] \\
&= \operatorname*{argmax}_{\lambda_{1\ldots 6}} \left[\prod_{k=1}^{6} \lambda_k^{N_k+\alpha_k-1} \right].
\end{aligned}
\tag{4.31}
$$

which is again subject to the constraint that $\sum_{k=1}^{6} \lambda_k = 1$. As in the maximum likelihood case, this constraint is enforced using a Lagrange multiplier. The MAP estimate of the parameters can be shown to be

$$
\hat{\lambda}_k = \frac{N_k + \alpha_k - 1}{\sum_{m=1}^{6}(N_m + \alpha_m - 1)},
\tag{4.32}
$$

where N_k is the number of times that observation k occurred in the training data. Note that if all the values α_k are set to one, the prior is uniform and this expression reverts to the maximum likelihood solution (Equation 4.30).

4.5.3 Bayesian Approach

In the Bayesian approach, we calculate a posterior over the parameters

$$
\begin{aligned}
Pr(\lambda_1 \ldots \lambda_6 | x_{1\ldots I}) &= \frac{\prod_{i=1}^{I} Pr(x_i|\lambda_{1\ldots 6}) Pr(\lambda_{1\ldots 6})}{Pr(x_{1\ldots I})} \\
&= \frac{\prod_{i=1}^{I} \mathrm{Cat}_{x_i}[\lambda_{1\ldots 6}] \mathrm{Dir}_{\lambda_{1\ldots 6}}[\alpha_{1\ldots 6}]}{Pr(x_{1\ldots I})} \\
&= \frac{\kappa(\alpha_{1\ldots 6}, x_{1\ldots I}) \mathrm{Dir}_{\lambda_{1\ldots 6}}[\tilde{\alpha}_{1\ldots 6}]}{Pr(x_{1\ldots I})} \\
&= \mathrm{Dir}_{\lambda_{1\ldots 6}}[\tilde{\alpha}_{1\ldots 6}],
\end{aligned}
\tag{4.33}
$$

where $\tilde{\alpha}_k = N_k + \alpha_k$. We have again exploited the conjugate relationship to yield a posterior distribution with the same form as the prior. The constant κ must again cancel with the denominator to ensure a valid probability distribution on the left-hand side. Samples from this distribution are shown in Figure 4.10f–j.

Predictive Density

For the ML and MAP estimates we compute the predictive density (probability that a new data point x^* belongs to the same model) by simply evaluating the categorical pdf

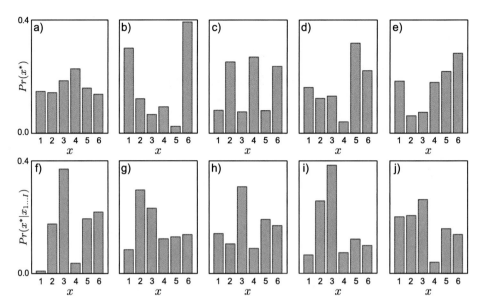

Figure 4.10 a–e) Five samples drawn from Dirichlet prior with hyperparameters $\alpha_{1...6} = 1$. This defines a uniform prior, so each sample looks like a random unstructured probability distribution. f–j) Five samples from Dirichlet posterior. The distribution favors histograms where bin three is larger and bin four is small as suggested by the data.

with the estimated parameters. With the uniform prior ($\alpha_{1...6} = 1$) the MAP and ML predictions are identical (Figure 4.11a) and both are exactly proportional to the frequencies of the observed data.

For the Bayesian case, we compute a weighted average of the predictions for each possible parameter set, where the weighting is given by the posterior distribution over parameters so that

$$Pr(x^*|x_{1...I}) = \int Pr(x^*|\lambda_{1...6})Pr(\lambda_{1...6}|x_{1...I})\, d\lambda_{1...6}$$

$$= \int \mathrm{Cat}_{x^*}[\lambda_{1...6}]\mathrm{Dir}_{\lambda_{1...6}}[\tilde{\alpha}_{1...6}]\, d\lambda_{1...6}$$

$$= \int \kappa(x^*, \tilde{\alpha}_{1...6})\mathrm{Dir}_{\lambda_{1...6}}[\breve{\alpha}_{1...6}]\, d\lambda_{1...6}$$

$$= \kappa(x^*, \tilde{\alpha}_{1...6}). \tag{4.34}$$

Here, we have again exploited the conjugate relationship to yield a constant multiplied by a probability distribution and the integral is simply the constant as the integral of the pdf is one. For this case, it can be shown that

$$Pr(x^* = k|x_{1...I}) = \kappa(x^*, \tilde{\alpha}_{1...6}) = \frac{N_k + \alpha_k}{\sum_{j=1}^{6}(N_j + \alpha_j)}. \tag{4.35}$$

This is illustrated in Figure 4.11b. It is notable that once more the Bayesian predictive density is less confident than the ML/MAP solutions. In particular, it does not allot zero probability to observing $x^* = 4$ despite the fact that this value was never observed in the training data. This is sensible; just because we have not drawn a 4 in 15 observations

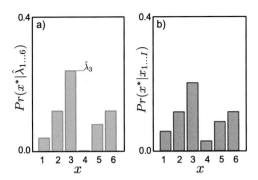

Figure 4.11 Predictive distributions with $\alpha_{1...6} = 1$ for a) maximum likelihood / maximum a posteriori approaches and b) Bayesian approach. The ML/MAP approaches predict the same distribution that exactly follows the data frequencies. The Bayesian approach predicts a more moderate distribution and allots some probability to the case $x = 4$ despite having seen no training examples in this category.

does not imply that it is inconceivable that we will ever see one. We may have just been unlucky. The Bayesian approach takes this into account and allots this category a small amount of probability.

Summary

We presented three ways to fit a probability distribution to data and to predict the probability of new points. Of the three methods discussed, the Bayesian approach is the most desirable. Here it is not necessary to find a point estimate of the (uncertain) parameters, and so errors are not introduced because this point estimate is inaccurate.

However, the Bayesian approach is only tractable when we have a conjugate prior, which makes it easy to calculate the posterior distribution over the parameters $Pr(\boldsymbol{\theta}|\mathbf{x}_{1...I})$ and also to evaluate the integral in the predictive density. When this is not the case, we will usually have to rely on maximum a posteriori estimates. Maximum likelihood estimates can be thought of as a special case of maximum a posteriori estimates in which the prior is uninformative.

Notes

For more information about the Bayesian approach to fitting distributions consult chapter 3 of Gelman et al. (2004). More information about Bayesian model selection (Problem 4.6), including an impassioned argument for its superiority as a method of hypothesis testing can be found in Mackay (2003).

Problems

4.1 Show that the maximum likelihood solution for the variance σ^2 of the normal distribution is given by

$$\sigma^2 = \sum_{i=1}^{I} \frac{(x_i - \hat{\mu})^2}{I}.$$

4.2 Show that the MAP solution for the mean μ and variance σ^2 of the normal distribution are given by

$$\hat{\mu} = \frac{\sum_{i=1}^{I} x_i + \gamma\delta}{I + \gamma} \quad \text{and} \quad \hat{\sigma}^2 = \frac{\sum_{i=1}^{I}(x_i - \hat{\mu})^2 + 2\beta + \gamma(\delta - \hat{\mu})^2}{I + 3 + 2\alpha},$$

when we use the conjugate normal-scaled inverse gamma prior

$$Pr(\mu, \sigma^2) = \frac{\sqrt{\gamma}}{\sigma\sqrt{2\pi}} \frac{\beta^\alpha}{\Gamma[\alpha]} \left(\frac{1}{\sigma^2}\right)^{\alpha+1} \exp\left[-\frac{2\beta + \gamma(\delta-\mu)^2}{2\sigma^2}\right].$$

4.3 Taking Equation 4.29 as a starting point, show that the maximum likelihood parameters for the categorical distribution are given by

$$\hat{\lambda}_k = \frac{N_k}{\sum_{m=1}^6 N_m},$$

where N_k is the number of times that category K was observed in the training data.

4.4 Show that the MAP estimate for the parameters $\{\lambda\}_{k=1}^K$ of the categorical distribution is given by

$$\hat{\lambda}_k = \frac{N_k + \alpha_k - 1}{\sum_{m=1}^6 (N_m + \alpha_m - 1)},$$

under the assumption of a Dirichlet prior with hyperparameters $\{\alpha_k\}_{k=1}^K$. The terms N_k again indicate the number of times that category k was observed in the training data.

4.5 The denominator of Bayes' rule

$$Pr(x_{1...I}) = \int \prod_{i=1}^I Pr(x_i|\theta)Pr(\theta)\,d\theta$$

is known as the *evidence*. It is a measure of how well the distribution fits *regardless* of the particular values of the parameters. Find an expression for the evidence term for (i) the normal distribution and (ii) the categorical distribution assuming conjugate priors in each case.

4.6 The evidence term can be used to compare models. Consider two sets of data $S_1 = \{0.1, -0.5, 0.2, 0.7\}$ and $S_2 = \{1.1, 2.0, 1.4, 2.3\}$. Let us pose the question of whether these two data sets came from the same normal distribution or from two different normal distributions.

Let model M_1 denote the case where all of the data comes from the one normal distribution. The evidence for this model is

$$Pr(S_1 \cup S_2|M_1) = \int \prod_{i \in S_1 \cup S_2} Pr(x_i|\boldsymbol{\theta})Pr(\boldsymbol{\theta})\,d\boldsymbol{\theta},$$

where $\boldsymbol{\theta} = \{\mu, \sigma^2\}$ contains the parameters of this normal distribution. Similarly, we will let M_2 denote the case where the two sets of data belong to different normal distributions

$$Pr(S_1 \cup S_2|M_2) = \int \prod_{i \in S_1} Pr(x_i|\boldsymbol{\theta}_1)Pr(\boldsymbol{\theta}_1)\,d\boldsymbol{\theta}_1 \int \prod_{i \in S_2} Pr(x_i|\boldsymbol{\theta}_2)Pr(\boldsymbol{\theta}_2)\,d\boldsymbol{\theta}_2,$$

where $\boldsymbol{\theta}_1 = \{\mu_1, \sigma_1^2\}$ and $\boldsymbol{\theta}_2 = \{\mu_2, \sigma_2^2\}$.

Now it is possible to compare the probability of the data under each of these two models using Bayes' rule

$$Pr(M_1|S_1 \cup S_2) = \frac{Pr(S_1 \cup S_2|M_1)Pr(M_1)}{\sum_{n=1}^2 Pr(S_1 \cup S_2|M_n)Pr(M_n)}$$

Use this expression to compute the posterior probability that the two datasets came from the same underlying normal distribution. You may assume normal-scaled inverse gamma priors over $\boldsymbol{\theta}, \boldsymbol{\theta}_1$, and $\boldsymbol{\theta}_2$ with parameters $\alpha = 1, \beta = 1, \gamma = 1, \delta = 0$.

Note that this is (roughly) a Bayesian version of the two-sample t-test, but it is much neater – we get a posterior probability distribution over the two hypotheses rather than the potentially misleading p value of the t-test. The process of comparing evidence terms in this way is known as *Bayesian model selection* or *the evidence framework*. It is rather clever in that two normal distributions fitted with maximum likelihood will *always* explain the data better than one; the additional parameters simply make the model more flexible. However because we have marginalized these parameters away here, it is valid to compare these models in the Bayesian case.

4.7 In the Bernoulli distribution, the likelihood $Pr(x_{1...I}|\lambda)$ of the data $\{x_i\}_{i=1}^I$ given parameter λ where $x_i \in \{0,1\}$ is

$$Pr(x_{1...I}|\lambda) = \prod_{i=1}^{I} \lambda^{x_i}(1-\lambda)^{1-x_i}.$$

Find an expression for the maximum likelihood estimate of the parameter λ.

4.8 Find an expression for the MAP estimate of the Bernoulli parameter λ (see Problem 4.7) assuming a beta distributed prior

$$Pr(\lambda) = \text{Beta}_\lambda[\alpha, \beta].$$

4.9 Now consider the Bayesian approach to fitting Bernoulli data, using a beta distributed prior. Find expressions for (i) the posterior probability distribution over the Bernoulli parameters given observed data $\{x_i\}_{i=1}^I$ and (ii) the predictive distribution for new data $\mathbf{x}^*$.

4.10 Staying with the Bernoulli distribution, consider observing data $0,0,0,0$ from four trials. Assuming a uniform beta prior ($\alpha = 1, \beta = 1$), compute the predictive distribution using the (i) maximum likelihood, (ii) maximum a posteriori, and (iii) Bayesian approaches. Comment on the results.

Chapter 5

The normal distribution

The most common representation for uncertainty in machine vision is the multivariate normal distribution. We devote this chapter to exploring its main properties, which will be used extensively throughout the rest of the book.

Recall from Chapter 3 that the multivariate normal distribution has two parameters: the mean $\boldsymbol{\mu}$ and covariance $\boldsymbol{\Sigma}$. The mean $\boldsymbol{\mu}$ is a $D \times 1$ vector that describes the position of the distribution. The covariance $\boldsymbol{\Sigma}$ is a symmetric $D \times D$ positive definite matrix (implying that $\mathbf{z}^T \boldsymbol{\Sigma} \mathbf{z}$ is positive for any real vector $\mathbf{z}$) and describes the shape of the distribution. The probability density function is

$$Pr(\mathbf{x}) = \frac{1}{(2\pi)^{D/2}|\boldsymbol{\Sigma}|^{1/2}} \exp\left[-0.5(\mathbf{x}-\boldsymbol{\mu})^T \boldsymbol{\Sigma}^{-1}(\mathbf{x}-\boldsymbol{\mu})\right], \tag{5.1}$$

or for short

$$Pr(\mathbf{x}) = \text{Norm}_{\mathbf{x}}\left[\boldsymbol{\mu}, \boldsymbol{\Sigma}\right]. \tag{5.2}$$

5.1 Types of covariance matrix

Covariance matrices in multivariate normals take three forms, termed *spherical*, *diagonal*, and *full* covariances. For the two-dimensional (bivariate) case, these are

$$\boldsymbol{\Sigma}_{spher} = \begin{bmatrix} \sigma^2 & 0 \\ 0 & \sigma^2 \end{bmatrix} \quad \boldsymbol{\Sigma}_{diag} = \begin{bmatrix} \sigma_1^2 & 0 \\ 0 & \sigma_2^2 \end{bmatrix} \quad \boldsymbol{\Sigma}_{full} = \begin{bmatrix} \sigma_{11}^2 & \sigma_{12}^2 \\ \sigma_{21}^2 & \sigma_{22}^2 \end{bmatrix}. \tag{5.3}$$

The spherical covariance matrix is a positive multiple of the identity matrix and so has the same value on all of the diagonal elements and zeros elsewhere. In the diagonal covariance matrix, each value on the diagonal has a different positive value. The full covariance matrix can have nonzero elements everywhere although the matrix is still constrained to be symmetric and positive definite so for the 2D example, $\sigma_{12}^2 = \sigma_{21}^2$.

For the bivariate case (Figure 5.1), spherical covariances produce circular iso-density contours. Diagonal covariances produce ellipsoidal iso-contours that are aligned with the coordinate axes. Full covariances also produce ellipsoidal iso-density contours, but these may now take an arbitrary orientation. More generally, in D dimensions, spherical covariances produce iso-contours that are D-spheres, diagonal covariances produce iso-contours that are D-dimensional ellipsoids aligned with the coordinate axes, and full covariances produce iso-contour that are D-dimensional ellipsoids in general position.

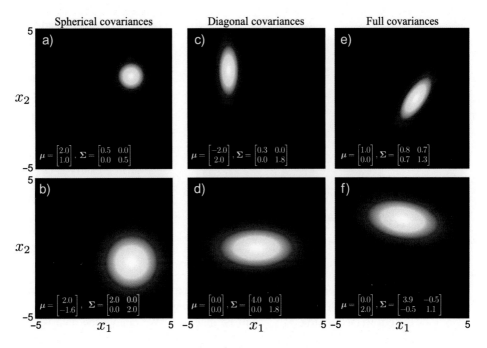

Figure 5.1 Covariance matrices take three forms.   a–b) Spherical covariance matrices are multiples of the identity. The variables are independent and the iso-probability surfaces are hyperspheres. c–d) Diagonal covariance matrices permit different nonzero entries on the diagonal, but have zero entries elsewhere. The variables are independent, but scaled differently and the iso-probability surfaces are hyperellipsoids (ellipses in 2D) whose principal axes are aligned to the coordinate axes. e–f) Full covariance matrices are symmetric and positive definite. Variables are dependent, and iso-probability surfaces are ellipsoids that are not aligned in any special way.

When the covariance is spherical or diagonal, the individual variables are independent. For example, for the bivariate diagonal case with zero mean, we have

$$
\begin{aligned}
Pr(x_1, x_2) &= \frac{1}{2\pi\sqrt{|\boldsymbol{\Sigma}|}} \exp\left[-0.5\begin{pmatrix} x_1 & x_2 \end{pmatrix} \boldsymbol{\Sigma}^{-1} \begin{pmatrix} x_1 \\ x_2 \end{pmatrix}\right] \\
&= \frac{1}{2\pi\sigma_1\sigma_2} \exp\left[-0.5\begin{pmatrix} x_1 & x_2 \end{pmatrix} \begin{pmatrix} \sigma_1^{-2} & 0 \\ 0 & \sigma_2^{-2} \end{pmatrix} \begin{pmatrix} x_1 \\ x_2 \end{pmatrix}\right] \\
&= \frac{1}{\sqrt{2\pi\sigma_1^2}} \exp\left[-\frac{x_1^2}{2\sigma_1^2}\right] \frac{1}{\sqrt{2\pi\sigma_2^2}} \exp\left[-\frac{x_2^2}{2\sigma_2^2}\right] \\
&= Pr(x_1)Pr(x_2).
\end{aligned}
\tag{5.4}
$$

5.2   Decomposition of covariance

We can use the foregoing geometrical intuitions to decompose the full covariance matrix $\boldsymbol{\Sigma}_{full}$. Given a normal distribution with mean zero and a full covariance matrix, we know that the iso-contours take an ellipsoidal form with the major and minor axes at arbitrary orientations.

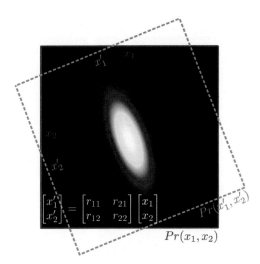

Figure 5.2 Decomposition of full covariance. For every bivariate normal distribution in variables x_1 and x_2 with full covariance matrix, there exists a coordinate system with variables x'_1 and x'_2 where the covariance is diagonal: the ellipsoidal iso-contours align with the coordinate axes x'_1 and x'_2 in this canonical coordinate frame. The two frames of reference are related by the rotation matrix $\mathbf{R}$ which maps (x'_1, x'_2) to (x_1, x_2). From this it follows (see text) that any covariance matrix $\boldsymbol{\Sigma}$ can be broken down into the product $\mathbf{R}^T \boldsymbol{\Sigma}'_{diag} \mathbf{R}$ of a rotation matrix $\mathbf{R}$ and a diagonal covariance matrix $\boldsymbol{\Sigma}'_{diag}$.

Now consider viewing the distribution in a new coordinate frame where the axes that *are* aligned with the axes of the normal (Figure 5.2): in this new frame of reference, the covariance matrix $\boldsymbol{\Sigma}'_{diag}$ will be diagonal. We denote the data vector in the new coordinate system by $\mathbf{x}' = [x'_1, x'_2]^T$ where the frames of reference are related by $\mathbf{x}' = \mathbf{R}\mathbf{x}$. We can write the probability distribution over $\mathbf{x}'$ as

$$Pr(\mathbf{x}') = \frac{1}{(2\pi)^{D/2}|\boldsymbol{\Sigma}'_{diag}|^{1/2}} \exp\left[-0.5\mathbf{x}'^T \boldsymbol{\Sigma}'^{-1}_{diag}\mathbf{x}'\right]. \tag{5.5}$$

We now convert back to the original axes by substituting in $\mathbf{x}' = \mathbf{R}\mathbf{x}$ to get

$$Pr(\mathbf{x}) = \frac{1}{(2\pi)^{D/2}|\boldsymbol{\Sigma}'_{diag}|^{1/2}} \exp\left[-0.5(\mathbf{R}\mathbf{x})^T \boldsymbol{\Sigma}'^{-1}_{diag}\mathbf{R}\mathbf{x}\right]$$

$$= \frac{1}{(2\pi)^{D/2}|\mathbf{R}^T\boldsymbol{\Sigma}'_{diag}\mathbf{R}|^{1/2}} \exp\left[-0.5\mathbf{x}^T(\mathbf{R}^T\boldsymbol{\Sigma}'_{diag}\mathbf{R})^{-1}\mathbf{x}\right], \tag{5.6}$$

where we have used $|\mathbf{R}^T\boldsymbol{\Sigma}'\mathbf{R}| = |\mathbf{R}^T|.|\boldsymbol{\Sigma}'|.|\mathbf{R}| = 1.|\boldsymbol{\Sigma}'|.1 = |\boldsymbol{\Sigma}'|$. Equation 5.6 is a multivariate normal with covariance

$$\boldsymbol{\Sigma}_{full} = \mathbf{R}^T\boldsymbol{\Sigma}'_{diag}\mathbf{R}. \tag{5.7}$$

We conclude that full covariance matrices are expressible as a product of this form involving a rotation matrix $\mathbf{R}$ and a diagonal covariance matrix $\boldsymbol{\Sigma}'_{diag}$. Having understood this, it is possible to retrieve these elements from an arbitrary valid covariance matrix $\boldsymbol{\Sigma}_{full}$ by decomposing it in this way using the singular value decomposition.

The matrix $\mathbf{R}$ contains the principal directions of the ellipsoid in its columns. The values on the diagonal of $\boldsymbol{\Sigma}'_{diag}$ encode the variance (and hence the width of the distribution) along each of these axes. Hence we can use the results of the singular value decomposition to answer questions about which directions in space are most and least certain.

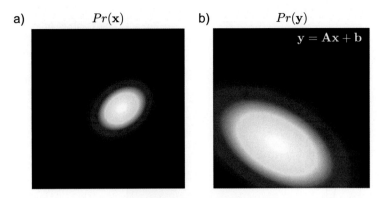

Figure 5.3 Transformation of normal variables. a) If $\mathbf{x}$ has a multivariate normal pdf and we apply a linear transformation to create new variable $\mathbf{y} = \mathbf{A}\mathbf{x} + \mathbf{b}$, then b) the distribution of $\mathbf{y}$ is also multivariate normal. The mean and covariance of $\mathbf{y}$ depend on the original mean and covariance of $\mathbf{x}$ and the parameters $\mathbf{A}$ and $\mathbf{b}$.

5.3   Linear transformations of variables

The form of the multivariate normal is preserved under linear transformations $\mathbf{y} = \mathbf{A}\mathbf{x} + \mathbf{b}$ (Figure 5.3). If the original distribution was

$$Pr(\mathbf{x}) = \text{Norm}_{\mathbf{x}}[\boldsymbol{\mu}, \boldsymbol{\Sigma}], \tag{5.8}$$

then the transformed variable $\mathbf{y}$ is distributed as

$$Pr(\mathbf{y}) = \text{Norm}_{\mathbf{y}}\left[\mathbf{A}\boldsymbol{\mu} + \mathbf{b}, \mathbf{A}\boldsymbol{\Sigma}\mathbf{A}^T\right]. \tag{5.9}$$

This relationship provides a simple method to draw samples from a normal distribution with mean $\boldsymbol{\mu}$ and covariance $\boldsymbol{\Sigma}$. We first draw a sample $\mathbf{x}$ from a standard normal distribution (with mean $\boldsymbol{\mu} = \mathbf{0}$ and covariance $\boldsymbol{\Sigma} = \mathbf{I}$) and then apply the transformation $\mathbf{y} = \boldsymbol{\Sigma}^{1/2}\mathbf{x} + \boldsymbol{\mu}$.

5.4   Marginal distributions

If we marginalize over any subset of random variables in a multivariate normal distribution, the remaining distribution is also normally distributed (Figure 5.4). If we partition the original random variable into two parts $\mathbf{x} = [\mathbf{x}_1^T, \mathbf{x}_2^T]^T$ so that

$$Pr(\mathbf{x}) = Pr\left(\begin{bmatrix} \mathbf{x}_1 \\ \mathbf{x}_2 \end{bmatrix}\right) = \text{Norm}_{\mathbf{x}}\left[\begin{bmatrix} \boldsymbol{\mu}_1 \\ \boldsymbol{\mu}_2 \end{bmatrix}, \begin{bmatrix} \boldsymbol{\Sigma}_{11} & \boldsymbol{\Sigma}_{21}^T \\ \boldsymbol{\Sigma}_{21} & \boldsymbol{\Sigma}_{22} \end{bmatrix}\right], \tag{5.10}$$

then

$$\begin{aligned} Pr(\mathbf{x}_1) &= \text{Norm}_{\mathbf{x}_1}[\boldsymbol{\mu}_1, \boldsymbol{\Sigma}_{11}] \\ Pr(\mathbf{x}_2) &= \text{Norm}_{\mathbf{x}_2}[\boldsymbol{\mu}_2, \boldsymbol{\Sigma}_{22}]. \end{aligned} \tag{5.11}$$

So, to find the mean and covariance of the marginal distribution of a subset of variables, we extract the relevant entries from the original mean and covariance.

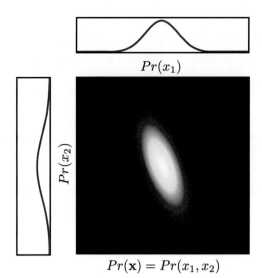

$$Pr(x_1)$$

$$Pr(x_2)$$

Figure 5.4 The marginal distribution of any subset of variables in a normal distribution is also normally distributed. In other words, if we sum over the distribution in any direction, the remaining quantity is also normally distributed. To find the mean and the covariance of the new distribution, we can simply extract the relevant entries from the original mean and covariance matrix.

$$Pr(\mathbf{x}) = Pr(x_1, x_2)$$

5.5   Conditional distributions

If the variable $\mathbf{x}$ is distributed as a multivariate normal, then the conditional distribution of a subset of variables $\mathbf{x}_1$ given known values for the remaining variables $\mathbf{x}_2$ is also distributed as a multivariate normal (Figure 5.5). If

$$Pr(\mathbf{x}) = Pr\left(\begin{bmatrix} \mathbf{x}_1 \\ \mathbf{x}_2 \end{bmatrix}\right) = \text{Norm}_{\mathbf{x}}\left[\begin{bmatrix} \boldsymbol{\mu}_1 \\ \boldsymbol{\mu}_2 \end{bmatrix}, \begin{bmatrix} \boldsymbol{\Sigma}_{11} & \boldsymbol{\Sigma}_{21}^T \\ \boldsymbol{\Sigma}_{21} & \boldsymbol{\Sigma}_{22} \end{bmatrix}\right], \tag{5.12}$$

then the conditional distributions are

$$Pr(\mathbf{x}_1|\mathbf{x}_2 = \mathbf{x}_2^*) = \text{Norm}_{\mathbf{x}_1}\left[\boldsymbol{\mu}_1 + \boldsymbol{\Sigma}_{21}^T\boldsymbol{\Sigma}_{22}^{-1}(\mathbf{x}_2^* - \boldsymbol{\mu}_2), \boldsymbol{\Sigma}_{11} - \boldsymbol{\Sigma}_{21}^T\boldsymbol{\Sigma}_{22}^{-1}\boldsymbol{\Sigma}_{21}\right] \tag{5.13}$$

$$Pr(\mathbf{x}_2|\mathbf{x}_1 = \mathbf{x}_1^*) = \text{Norm}_{\mathbf{x}_2}\left[\boldsymbol{\mu}_2 + \boldsymbol{\Sigma}_{21}\boldsymbol{\Sigma}_{11}^{-1}(\mathbf{x}_1^* - \boldsymbol{\mu}_1), \boldsymbol{\Sigma}_{22} - \boldsymbol{\Sigma}_{21}\boldsymbol{\Sigma}_{11}^{-1}\boldsymbol{\Sigma}_{21}^T\right].$$

5.6   Product of two normals

The product of two normal distributions is proportional to a third normal distribution (Figure 5.6). If the two original distributions have means $\mathbf{a}$ and $\mathbf{b}$ and covariances $\mathbf{A}$ and $\mathbf{B}$, respectively, then we find that

$$\text{Norm}_{\mathbf{x}}[\mathbf{a}, \mathbf{A}]\text{Norm}_{\mathbf{x}}[\mathbf{b}, \mathbf{B}] = \tag{5.14}$$
$$\kappa \cdot \text{Norm}_{\mathbf{x}}\left[\left(\mathbf{A}^{-1} + \mathbf{B}^{-1}\right)^{-1}\left(\mathbf{A}^{-1}\mathbf{a} + \mathbf{B}^{-1}\mathbf{b}\right), \left(\mathbf{A}^{-1} + \mathbf{B}^{-1}\right)^{-1}\right],$$

where the constant κ is itself a normal distribution,

$$\kappa = \text{Norm}_{\mathbf{a}}[\mathbf{b}, \mathbf{A} + \mathbf{B}] = \text{Norm}_{\mathbf{b}}[\mathbf{a}, \mathbf{A} + \mathbf{B}]. \tag{5.15}$$

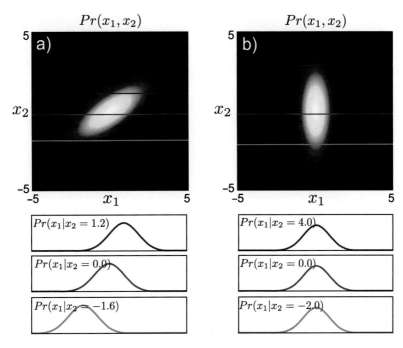

Figure 5.5 Conditional distributions of multivariate normal. a) If we take any multivariate normal distribution, fix a subset of the variables, and look at the distribution of the remaining variables, this distribution will also take the form of a normal. The mean of this new normal depends on the values that we fixed the subset to, but the covariance is always the same. b) If the original multivariate normal has spherical or diagonal covariance, both the mean and covariance of the resulting normal distributions are the same, regardless of the value we conditioned on: these forms of covariance matrix imply independence between the constituent variables.

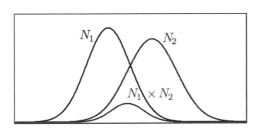

Figure 5.6 The product of any two normals N_1 and N_2 is proportional to a third normal distribution, with a mean between the two original means and a variance that is smaller than either of the original distributions.

5.6.1   Self-conjugacy

The preceding property can be used to demonstrate that the normal distribution is *self-conjugate* with respect to its mean μ. Consider taking a product of a normal distribution over data $\mathbf{x}$ and a second normal distribution over the mean vector μ of the first distribution. It is easy to show from Equation 5.14 that

$$\text{Norm}_\mathbf{x}[\mu, \Sigma]\text{Norm}_\mu[\mu_p, \Sigma_p] = \text{Norm}_\mu[\mathbf{x}, \Sigma]\text{Norm}_\mu[\mu_p, \Sigma_p]$$
$$= \kappa \cdot \text{Norm}_\mu[\tilde{\mu}, \tilde{\Sigma}], \qquad (5.16)$$

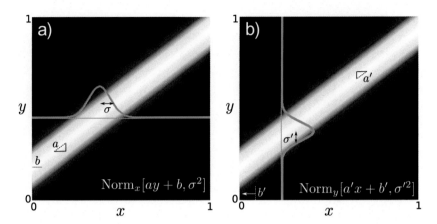

Figure 5.7 a) Consider a normal distribution in x whose variance σ^2 is constant, but whose mean is a linear function $ay + b$ of a second variable y. b) This is mathematically equivalent to a constant κ times a normal distribution in y whose variance σ'^2 is constant and whose mean is a linear function $a'x + b'$ of x.

which is the definition of conjugacy (see Section 3.9). The new parameters $\tilde{\mu}$ and $\tilde{\Sigma}$ are determined from Equation 5.14. This analysis assumes that the variance Σ is being treated as a fixed quantity. If we also treat this as uncertain, then we must use a normal inverse Wishart prior.

5.7   Change of variable

Consider a normal distribution in variable $\mathbf{x}$ whose mean is a linear function $\mathbf{Ay} + \mathbf{b}$ of a second variable $\mathbf{y}$. We can reexpress this in terms of a normal distribution in $\mathbf{y}$, which is a linear function $\mathbf{A'x} + \mathbf{b'}$ of $\mathbf{x}$ so that

$$\text{Norm}_{\mathbf{x}}[\mathbf{Ay} + \mathbf{b}, \Sigma] = \kappa \cdot \text{Norm}_{\mathbf{y}}[\mathbf{A'x} + \mathbf{b'}, \Sigma'], \tag{5.17}$$

where κ is a constant and the new parameters are given by

$$\begin{aligned}
\Sigma' &= (\mathbf{A}^T \Sigma^{-1} \mathbf{A})^{-1} \\
\mathbf{A}' &= (\mathbf{A}^T \Sigma^{-1} \mathbf{A})^{-1} \mathbf{A}^T \Sigma^{-1} \\
\mathbf{b}' &= -(\mathbf{A}^T \Sigma^{-1} \mathbf{A})^{-1} \mathbf{A}^T \Sigma^{-1} \mathbf{b}.
\end{aligned} \tag{5.18}$$

This relationship is mathematically opaque, but it is easy to understand visually when x and y are scalars (Figure 5.7). It is often used in the context of Bayes' rule where our goal is to move from $Pr(\mathbf{x}|\mathbf{y})$ to $Pr(\mathbf{y}|\mathbf{x})$.

Summary

In this chapter we have presented a number of properties of the multivariate normal distribution. The most important of these relates to the marginal and conditional distributions: when we marginalize or take the conditional distribution of a normal with respect to a subset of variables, the result is another normal. These properties are exploited in many vision algorithms.

Notes

The normal distribution has further interesting properties which are not discussed because they are not relevant for this book. For example, the convolution of a normal distribution with a second normal distribution produces a function that is proportional to a third normal, and the Fourier transform of a normal profile creates a normal profile in frequency space. For a different treatment of this topic the interested reader can consult chapter 2 of Bishop (2006).

Problems

5.1 Consider a multivariate normal distribution in variable $\mathbf{x}$ with mean $\boldsymbol{\mu}$ and covariance $\boldsymbol{\Sigma}$. Show that if we make the linear transformation $\mathbf{y} = \mathbf{A}\mathbf{x} + \mathbf{b}$, then the transformed variable $\mathbf{y}$ is distributed as

$$Pr(\mathbf{y}) = \text{Norm}_{\mathbf{y}} \left[\mathbf{A}\boldsymbol{\mu} + \mathbf{b}, \mathbf{A}\boldsymbol{\Sigma}\mathbf{A}^T \right].$$

5.2 Show that we can convert a normal distribution with mean $\boldsymbol{\mu}$ and covariance $\boldsymbol{\Sigma}$ to a new distribution with mean $\mathbf{0}$ and covariance $\mathbf{I}$ using the linear transformation $\mathbf{y} = \mathbf{A}\mathbf{x} + \mathbf{b}$ where

$$\mathbf{A} = \boldsymbol{\Sigma}^{-1/2}$$
$$\mathbf{b} = -\boldsymbol{\Sigma}^{-1/2}\boldsymbol{\mu}.$$

This is known as the *whitening* transformation.

5.3 Show that for multivariate normal distribution

$$Pr(\mathbf{x}) = Pr\left(\begin{bmatrix} \mathbf{x}_1 \\ \mathbf{x}_2 \end{bmatrix} \right) = \text{Norm}_{\mathbf{x}} \left[\begin{bmatrix} \boldsymbol{\mu}_1 \\ \boldsymbol{\mu}_2 \end{bmatrix}, \begin{bmatrix} \boldsymbol{\Sigma}_{11} & \boldsymbol{\Sigma}_{21}^T \\ \boldsymbol{\Sigma}_{21} & \boldsymbol{\Sigma}_{22} \end{bmatrix} \right],$$

the marginal distribution in $\mathbf{x}_1$ is

$$Pr(\mathbf{x}_1) = \text{Norm}_{\mathbf{x}_1} \left[\boldsymbol{\mu}_1, \boldsymbol{\Sigma}_{11} \right].$$

Hint: Apply the transformation $\mathbf{y} = [\mathbf{I}, \mathbf{0}]\mathbf{x}$.

5.4 The Schur complement identity states that inverse of a matrix in terms of its subblocks is

$$\begin{bmatrix} \mathbf{A} & \mathbf{B} \\ \mathbf{C} & \mathbf{D} \end{bmatrix}^{-1} = \begin{bmatrix} (\mathbf{A} - \mathbf{B}\mathbf{D}^{-1}\mathbf{C})^{-1} & -(\mathbf{A} - \mathbf{B}\mathbf{D}^{-1}\mathbf{C})^{-1}\mathbf{B}\mathbf{D}^{-1} \\ -\mathbf{D}^{-1}\mathbf{C}(\mathbf{A} - \mathbf{B}\mathbf{D}^{-1}\mathbf{C})^{-1} & \mathbf{D}^{-1} + \mathbf{D}^{-1}\mathbf{C}(\mathbf{A} - \mathbf{B}\mathbf{D}^{-1}\mathbf{C})^{-1}\mathbf{B}\mathbf{D}^{-1} \end{bmatrix}.$$

Show that this relation is true.

5.5 Prove the conditional distribution property for the normal distribution: if

$$Pr(\mathbf{x}) = Pr\left(\begin{bmatrix} \mathbf{x}_1 \\ \mathbf{x}_2 \end{bmatrix} \right) = \text{Norm}_{\mathbf{x}} \left[\begin{bmatrix} \boldsymbol{\mu}_1 \\ \boldsymbol{\mu}_2 \end{bmatrix}, \begin{bmatrix} \boldsymbol{\Sigma}_{11} & \boldsymbol{\Sigma}_{12}^T \\ \boldsymbol{\Sigma}_{12} & \boldsymbol{\Sigma}_{22} \end{bmatrix} \right],$$

then

$$Pr(\mathbf{x}_1|\mathbf{x}_2) = \text{Norm}_{\mathbf{x}_1} \left[\boldsymbol{\mu}_1 + \boldsymbol{\Sigma}_{12}^T\boldsymbol{\Sigma}_{22}^{-1}(\mathbf{x}_2 - \boldsymbol{\mu}_2), \boldsymbol{\Sigma}_{11} - \boldsymbol{\Sigma}_{12}^T\boldsymbol{\Sigma}_{22}^{-1}\boldsymbol{\Sigma}_{12} \right].$$

Hint: Use the Schur complement identity.

5.6 Use the conditional probability relation for the normal distribution to show that the conditional distribution $Pr(x_1|x_2 = k)$ is the same for all k when the covariance is diagonal and the variables are independent (see Figure 5.5b).

5.7 Show that

$$\text{Norm}_{\mathbf{x}}[\mathbf{a}, \mathbf{A}]\text{Norm}_{\mathbf{x}}[\mathbf{b}, \mathbf{B}] \propto \text{Norm}_{\mathbf{x}}[(\mathbf{A}^{-1} + \mathbf{B}^{-1})^{-1}(\mathbf{A}^{-1}\mathbf{a} + \mathbf{B}^{-1}\mathbf{b}), (\mathbf{A}^{-1} + \mathbf{B}^{-1})^{-1}].$$

5.8 For the 1D case, show that when we take the product of the two normal distributions with means μ_1, μ_2 and variances σ_1^2, σ_2^2, the new mean lies between the original two means and the new variance is smaller than either of the original variances.

5.9 Show that the constant of proportionality κ in the product relation in Problem 5.7 is also a normal distribution where

$$\kappa = \text{Norm}_{\mathbf{a}}[\mathbf{b}, \mathbf{A} + \mathbf{B}].$$

5.10 Prove the change of variable relation. Show that

$$\text{Norm}_{\mathbf{x}}[\mathbf{A}\mathbf{y} + \mathbf{b}, \boldsymbol{\Sigma}] = \kappa \cdot \text{Norm}_{\mathbf{y}}[\mathbf{A}'\mathbf{x} + \mathbf{b}', \boldsymbol{\Sigma}'],$$

and derive expressions for κ, $\mathbf{A}'$, $\mathbf{b}'$, and $\boldsymbol{\Sigma}'$. *Hint*: Write out the terms in the original exponential, extract quadratic and linear terms in $\mathbf{y}$, and complete the square.

Part II

Machine learning for machine vision

In the second part of this book (chapters 6–9), we treat vision as a machine learning problem and disregard everything we know about the creation of the image. For example, we will not exploit our understanding of perspective projection or light transport. Instead, we treat vision as pattern recognition; we interpret new image data based on prior experience of images in which the contents were known. We divide this process into two parts: in *learning* we model the relationship between the image data and the scene content. In *inference*, we exploit this relationship to predict the contents of new images.

To abandon useful knowledge about image creation may seem odd, but the logic is twofold. First, these same learning and inference techniques will also underpin our algorithms when image formation is taken into account. Second, it is possible to achieve a great deal with a pure learning approach to vision. For many tasks, knowledge of the image formation process is genuinely unnecessary.

The structure of Part II is as follows. In Chapter 6 we present a taxonomy of models that relate the measured image data and the actual scene content. In particular, we distinguish between *generative* models and *discriminative* models. For generative models, we build a probability model of the data and parameterize it by the scene content. For discriminative models, we build a probability model of the scene content and parameterize it by the data. In the subsequent three chapters, we elaborate our discussion of these models.

In Chapter 7 we consider generative models. In particular, we discuss how to use *hidden variables* to construct complex probability densities over visual data. As examples, we consider mixtures of Gaussians, t-distributions, and factor analyzers. Together, these three models allow us to build densities that are multi-modal, robust, and suitable for modeling high dimensional data.

In Chapter 8 we consider *regression* models: we aim to estimate a continuous quantity from continuous data. For example, we might want to predict the joint angles from an image of the human body. We start with linear regression and move to more complex nonlinear methods such as Gaussian process regression and relevance vector regression. In Chapter 9 we consider *classification* models: here we want to predict a discrete quantity from continuous data. For example, we might want to assign a label to a region of the image to indicate whether or not a face is present. We start with logistic regression and work toward more sophisticated methods such as Gaussian process classification, boosting, and classification trees.

Chapter 6

Learning and inference in vision

At an abstract level, the goal of computer vision problems is to use the observed image data to infer something about the world. For example, we might observe adjacent frames of a video sequence and infer the camera motion, or we might observe a facial image and infer the identity.

The aim of this chapter is to describe a mathematical framework for solving this type of problem and to organize the resulting models into useful subgroups, which will be explored in subsequent chapters.

6.1   Computer vision problems

In vision problems, we take visual data $\mathbf{x}$ and use them to infer the state of the world $\mathbf{w}$. The world state $\mathbf{w}$ may be continuous (the 3D pose of a body model) or discrete (the presence or absence of a particular object). When the state is continuous, we call this inference process *regression*. When the state is discrete, we call it *classification*.

Unfortunately, the measurements $\mathbf{x}$ may be compatible with more than one world state $\mathbf{w}$. The measurement process is noisy, and there is inherent ambiguity in visual data: a lump of coal viewed under bright light may produce the same luminance measurements as white paper in dim light. Similarly, a small object seen close-up may produce the same image as a larger object that is further away.

In the face of such ambiguity, the best that we can do is to return the *posterior probability distribution* $Pr(\mathbf{w}|\mathbf{x})$ over possible states $\mathbf{w}$. This describes everything we know about the state after observing the visual data. So, a more precise description of an abstract vision problem is that we wish to take observations $\mathbf{x}$ and return the whole posterior probability distribution $Pr(\mathbf{w}|\mathbf{x})$ over world states.

In practice, computing the posterior is not always tractable; we often have to settle for returning the world state $\hat{\mathbf{w}}$ at the peak of the posterior (the maximum a posteriori solution). Alternatively, we might draw samples from the posterior and use the collection of samples as an approximation to the full distribution.

6.1.1 Components of the solution

To solve a vision problem of this kind, we need three components.

- We need a *model* that mathematically relates the visual data $\mathbf{x}$ and the world state $\mathbf{w}$. The model specifies a family of possible relationships between $\mathbf{x}$ and $\mathbf{w}$ and the particular relationship is determined by the model parameters $\boldsymbol{\theta}$.
- We need a *learning algorithm* that allows us to fit the parameters $\boldsymbol{\theta}$ using paired training examples $\{\mathbf{x}_i, \mathbf{w}_i\}$, where we know both the measurements and the underlying state.
- We need an *inference algorithm* that takes a new observation $\mathbf{x}$ and uses the model to return the posterior $Pr(\mathbf{w}|\mathbf{x}, \boldsymbol{\theta})$ over the world state $\mathbf{w}$. Alternately, it might return the MAP solution or draw samples from the posterior.

The rest of this book is structured around these components: each chapter focusses on one model or one family of models, and discusses the associated learning and inference algorithms.

6.2 Types of model

The first and most important component of the solution is the model. Every model relating the data $\mathbf{x}$ to the world $\mathbf{w}$ falls into one of two categories. We either

1. Model the contingency of the world state on the data $Pr(\mathbf{w}|\mathbf{x})$ or
2. Model the contingency of the data on the world state $Pr(\mathbf{x}|\mathbf{w})$.

The first type of model is termed *discriminative*. The second is termed *generative*; here, we construct a probability model over the data and this can be used to generate (confabulate) new observations. Let us consider these two types of models in turn and discuss learning and inference in each.

6.2.1 Model contingency of world on data (discriminative)

To model $Pr(\mathbf{w}|\mathbf{x})$, we choose an appropriate form for the distribution $Pr(\mathbf{w})$ over the world state $\mathbf{w}$ and then make the distribution parameters a function of the data $\mathbf{x}$. So if the world state was continuous, we might model $Pr(\mathbf{w})$ with a normal distribution and make the mean $\boldsymbol{\mu}$ a function of the data $\mathbf{x}$.

The value that this function returns also depends on a set of parameters, $\boldsymbol{\theta}$. Since the distribution over the state depends on both the data and these parameters, we write it as $Pr(\mathbf{w}|\mathbf{x}, \boldsymbol{\theta})$ and refer to it as the *posterior distribution*.

The goal of the learning algorithm is to fit the parameters $\boldsymbol{\theta}$ using paired training data $\{\mathbf{x}_i, \mathbf{w}_i\}_{i=1}^{I}$. This can be done using the maximum likelihood (ML), maximum a posteriori (MAP), or Bayesian approaches (Chapter 4).

The goal of inference is to find a distribution over the possible world states $\mathbf{w}$ for a new observation $\mathbf{x}$. In this case, this is easy: we have already directly constructed an expression for the posterior distribution $Pr(\mathbf{w}|\mathbf{x}, \boldsymbol{\theta})$, and we simply evaluate it with the new data.

6.2.2 Model contingency of data on world (generative)

To model $Pr(\mathbf{x}|\mathbf{w})$, we choose the form for the distribution $Pr(\mathbf{x})$ over the data and make the distribution parameters a function of the world state $\mathbf{w}$. For example, if the data were discrete and multivalued then we might use a categorical distribution and make the parameter vector $\boldsymbol{\lambda}$ a function of the world state $\mathbf{w}$.

The value that this function returns also depends on a set of parameters $\boldsymbol{\theta}$. Since the distribution $Pr(\mathbf{x})$ now depends on both the world state and these parameters, we write it as $Pr(\mathbf{x}|\mathbf{w},\boldsymbol{\theta})$ and refer to it as the *likelihood*. The goal of learning is to fit the parameters $\boldsymbol{\theta}$ using paired training examples $\{\mathbf{x}_i, \mathbf{w}_i\}_{i=1}^{I}$.

In inference, we aim to compute the posterior distribution $Pr(\mathbf{w}|\mathbf{x})$. To this end we specify a prior $Pr(\mathbf{w})$ over the world state and then use Bayes' rule,

$$Pr(\mathbf{w}|\mathbf{x}) = \frac{Pr(\mathbf{x}|\mathbf{w})Pr(\mathbf{w})}{\int Pr(\mathbf{x}|\mathbf{w})Pr(\mathbf{w})d\mathbf{w}}. \tag{6.1}$$

Summary

We've seen that there are two distinct approaches to modeling the relationship between the world state $\mathbf{w}$ and the data $\mathbf{x}$, corresponding to modeling the posterior $Pr(\mathbf{w}|\mathbf{x})$ or the likelihood $Pr(\mathbf{x}|\mathbf{w})$.

The two model types result in different approaches to inference. For the discriminative model, we describe the posterior $Pr(\mathbf{w}|\mathbf{x})$ directly and there is no need for further work. For the generative model, we compute the posterior using Bayes' rule. This sometimes results in complex inference algorithms.

To make these ideas concrete, we now consider two toy examples. For each case, we will investigate using both generative and discriminative models. At this stage, we won't present the details of the learning and inference algorithms; these are presented in subsequent chapters anyway. The goal here is to introduce the main types of model used in computer vision, in their most simple form.

6.3 Example 1: Regression

Consider the situation where we make a univariate continuous measurement x and use this to predict a univariate continuous state w. For example, we might predict the distance to a car in a road scene based on the number of pixels in its silhouette.

6.3.1 Model contingency of world on data (discriminative)

We define a probability distribution over the world state w and make its parameters contingent on the data x. Since the world state is univariate and continuous, we chose the univariate normal. We fix the variance, σ^2 and make the mean μ a linear function $\phi_0 + \phi_1 x$ of the data. So we have

$$Pr(w|x,\boldsymbol{\theta}) = \text{Norm}_w\left[\phi_0 + \phi_1 x, \sigma^2\right], \tag{6.2}$$

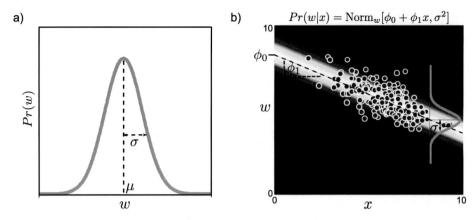

Figure 6.1 Regression by modeling the posterior $Pr(w|x)$ (discriminative). a) We model the world state w as a normal. b) We make the normal parameters a function of the observations x: The mean is a linear function $\mu = \phi_0 + \phi_1 x$ of the observations, and the variance σ^2 is fixed. The learning algorithm fits the parameters $\boldsymbol{\theta} = \{\phi_0, \phi_1, \sigma^2\}$ to example training pairs $\{x_i, w_i\}_{i=1}^I$ (blue dots). In inference, we take a new observation x and compute the posterior distribution $Pr(w|x)$ over the state.

where $\boldsymbol{\theta} = \{\phi_0, \phi_1, \sigma^2\}$ are the unknown parameters of the model (Figure 6.1). This model is referred to as *linear regression*.

The learning algorithm estimates the model parameters $\boldsymbol{\theta}$ from paired training examples $\{x_i, w_i\}_{i=1}^I$. For example, in the MAP approach, we seek

$$
\begin{aligned}
\hat{\boldsymbol{\theta}} &= \underset{\boldsymbol{\theta}}{\operatorname{argmax}} \left[Pr(\boldsymbol{\theta}|w_{1...I}, x_{1...I}) \right] \\
&= \underset{\boldsymbol{\theta}}{\operatorname{argmax}} \left[Pr(w_{1...I}|x_{1...I}, \boldsymbol{\theta}) Pr(\boldsymbol{\theta}) \right] \\
&= \underset{\boldsymbol{\theta}}{\operatorname{argmax}} \left[\prod_{i=1}^I Pr(w_i|x_i, \boldsymbol{\theta}) Pr(\boldsymbol{\theta}) \right],
\end{aligned}
\tag{6.3}
$$

where we have assumed that the I training pairs $\{x_i, w_i\}_{i=1}^I$ are independent, and defined a suitable prior $Pr(\boldsymbol{\theta})$.

We also need an *inference algorithm* that takes visual data x and returns the posterior distribution $Pr(w|x, \boldsymbol{\theta})$. Here this is very simple: we simply evaluate Equation 6.2 using the data x and the learned parameters $\hat{\boldsymbol{\theta}}$.

6.3.2 Model the contingency of data on world (generative)

In the generative formulation, we choose a probability distribution over the data x and make its parameters contingent on the world state w. Since the data are univariate and continuous, we will model the data as a normal distribution with fixed variance, σ^2 and a mean μ that is a linear function $\phi_0 + \phi_1 w$ of the world state (Figure 6.2) so that

$$
Pr(x|w, \boldsymbol{\theta}) = \operatorname{Norm}_x \left[\phi_0 + \phi_1 w, \sigma^2 \right].
\tag{6.4}
$$

We also need a prior $Pr(w)$ over the world states, which might also be normal so

$$
Pr(w) = \operatorname{Norm}_w [\mu_p, \sigma_p^2].
\tag{6.5}
$$

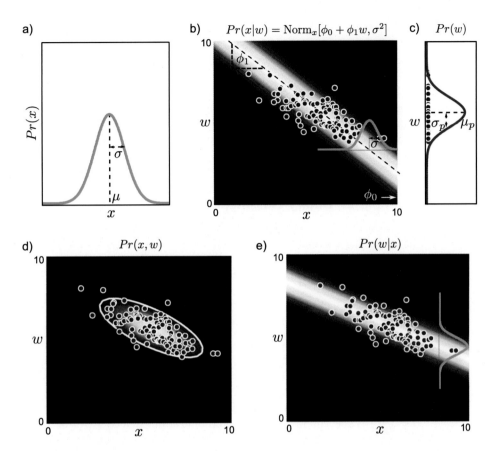

Figure 6.2 Regression by modeling likelihood $Pr(x|w)$ (generative). a) We represent the data x with a normal distribution. b) We make the normal parameters functions of the world state w. Here the mean is a linear function $\mu = \phi_0 + \phi_1 w$ of the world state and the variance σ^2 is fixed. The learning algorithm fits the parameters $\boldsymbol{\theta} = \{\phi_0, \phi_1, \sigma^2\}$ to example training pairs $\{x_i, w_i\}_{i=1}^{I}$ (blue dots). c) We also learn a prior distribution over the world state w (here modeled as a normal distribution with parameters $\boldsymbol{\theta}_p = \{\mu_p, \sigma_p\}$). In inference, we take a new datum x and compute the posterior $Pr(w|x)$ over the state. d) This can be done by computing the joint distribution $Pr(x, w) = Pr(x|w)Pr(w)$ (weighting each row of (b) by the appropriate value from the prior) and e) normalizing the columns $Pr(w|x) = Pr(x, w)/Pr(x)$. Together these operations implement Bayes' rule: $Pr(w|x) = Pr(x|w)Pr(w)/Pr(x)$.

The learning algorithm fits the parameters $\boldsymbol{\theta} = \{\phi_0, \phi_1, \sigma^2\}$ using paired training data $\{x_i, w_i\}_{i=1}^{I}$ and fits the parameters $\boldsymbol{\theta}_p = \{\mu_p, \sigma_p^2\}$ using the world states $\{w_i\}_{i=1}^{I}$. The inference algorithm takes a new datum x and returns the posterior $Pr(w|x)$ over the world state w using Bayes' rule

$$Pr(w|x) = \frac{Pr(x|w)Pr(w)}{Pr(x)} = \frac{Pr(x, w)}{Pr(x)}. \tag{6.6}$$

In this case, the posterior can be computed in closed form and is again normally distributed with fixed variance and a mean that is proportional to the data x.

Discussion

We have presented two models that can be used to estimate the world state w from an observed data example x, based on modeling the posterior $Pr(w|x)$ and the likelihood $Pr(x|w)$, respectively.

The models were carefully chosen so that they predict exactly the same posterior $P(w|x)$ over the world state (compare Figures 6.1b, and 6.2e). This is only the case with maximum likelihood learning: in the MAP approach we would have placed priors on the parameters, and because each model is parameterized differently, they would in general have different effects.

6.4   Example 2: Binary classification

As a second example, we will consider the case where the observed measurement x is univariate and continuous, but the world state w is discrete and can take one of two values. For example, we might wish to classify a pixel as belonging to a skin or non-skin region based on observing just the red channel.

6.4.1   Model contingency of world on data (discriminative)

We define a probability distribution over the world state $w \in \{0,1\}$ and make its parameters contingent on the data x. Since the world state is discrete and binary, we will use a Bernoulli distribution. This has a single parameter λ, which determines the probability of success so that $Pr(w=1) = \lambda$.

We make λ a function of the data x, but in doing so we must ensure the constraint $0 \leq \lambda \leq 1$ is obeyed. To this end, we form linear function $\phi_0 + \phi_1 x$ of the data x, which returns a value in the range $[-\infty \;\; \infty]$. We then pass the result through a function $\mathrm{sig}[\bullet]$ that maps $[-\infty \;\; \infty]$ to $[0 \;\; 1]$, so that

$$Pr(w|x) = \mathrm{Bern}_w\left[\mathrm{sig}[\phi_0 + \phi_1 x]\right] = \mathrm{Bern}_w\left[\frac{1}{1+\exp[-\phi_0 - \phi_1 x]}\right]. \qquad (6.7)$$

This produces a sigmoidal dependence of the distribution parameter λ on the data x (Figure 6.3). The function $\mathrm{sig}[\bullet]$ is called the *logistic sigmoid*. This model is confusingly termed *logistic regression* despite being used here for classification.

In learning, we aim to fit the parameters $\theta = \{\phi_0, \phi_1\}$ from paired training examples $\{x_i, w_i\}_{i=1}^I$. In inference, we simply substitute in the observed data value x into Equation 6.7 to retrieve the posterior distribution $Pr(w|x)$ over the state.

6.4.2   Model contingency of data on world (generative)

We choose a probability distribution over the data x and make its parameters contingent on the world state w. Since the data are univariate and continuous, we will choose a univariate normal and allow the variance σ^2 and the mean μ to be functions of the binary world state w (Figure 6.4) so that the likelihood is

$$Pr(x|w,\boldsymbol{\theta}) = \mathrm{Norm}_x\left[\mu_w, \sigma_w^2\right]. \qquad (6.8)$$

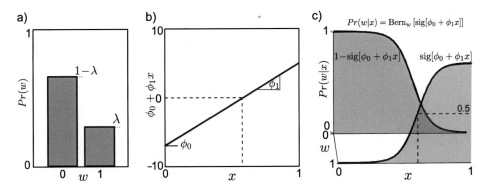

Figure 6.3 Classification by modeling posterior $Pr(w|x)$ (discriminative). a) We represent the world state w as a Bernoulli distribution. We make the Bernoulli parameter λ a function of the observations x. b) To this end, we form a linear function $\phi_0 + \phi_1 x$ of the observations. c) The Bernoulli parameter $\lambda = \text{sig}[\phi_0 + \phi_1 x]$ is formed by passing the linear function through the logistic sigmoid $\text{sig}[\bullet]$ to constrain the value to lie between 0 and 1, giving the characteristic sigmoid shape (red curve). In learning we fit parameters $\boldsymbol{\theta} = \{\phi_0, \phi_1\}$ using example training pairs $\{x_i, w_i\}_{i=1}^I$. In inference, we take a new datum x and evaluate the posterior $Pr(w|x)$ over the state.

In practice, this means that we have one set of parameters $\{\mu_0, \sigma_0^2\}$ when the state of the world is $w = 0$ and a different set $\{\mu_1, \sigma_1^2\}$ when the state is $w = 1$ so

$$Pr(x|w=0) = \text{Norm}_x\left[\mu_0, \sigma_0^2\right]$$
$$Pr(x|w=1) = \text{Norm}_x\left[\mu_1, \sigma_1^2\right]. \tag{6.9}$$

These are referred to as *class conditional density functions* as they model the density of the data for each class separately.

We also define a prior distribution $Pr(w)$ over the world state,

$$Pr(w) = \text{Bern}_w[\lambda_p], \tag{6.10}$$

where λ_p is the prior probability of observing the state $w = 1$.

In learning, we fit the parameters $\boldsymbol{\theta} = \{\mu_0, \sigma_0^2, \mu_1, \sigma_1^2, \lambda_p\}$ using paired training data $\{x_i, w_i\}_{i=1}^I$. In practice, this consists of fitting the parameters μ_0 and σ_0^2 of the first class-conditional density function $Pr(x|w=0)$ from just the data x where the state w was 0, and the parameters μ_1 and σ_1^2 of $P(x|w=1)$ from the data x where the state was 1. We learn the prior parameter λ_p from the training world states $\{w_i\}_{i=1}^I$.

The inference algorithm takes new datum x and returns the posterior distribution $Pr(w|x, \boldsymbol{\theta})$ over the world state w using Bayes' rule,

$$Pr(w|x) = \frac{Pr(x|w)Pr(w)}{\sum_{w=0}^1 Pr(x|w)Pr(w)}. \tag{6.11}$$

This is very easy to compute; we evaluate the two class-conditional density functions, weight each by the appropriate prior and normalize so that the two values sum to one.

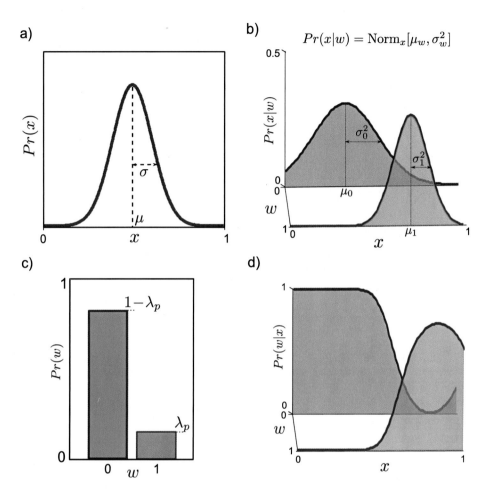

Figure 6.4 Classification by modeling the likelihood $Pr(x|w)$ (generative). a) We choose a normal distribution to represent the data x. b) We make the parameters $\{\mu, \sigma^2\}$ of this normal a function of the world state w. In practice, this means using one set of mean and variance parameters when the world state $w = 0$ and another when $w = 1$. The learning algorithm fits the parameters $\boldsymbol{\theta} = \{\mu_0, \mu_1, \sigma_0^2, \sigma_1^2\}$ to example training pairs $\{x_i, w_i\}_{i=1}^I$. c) We also model the prior probability of the world state w with a Bernoulli distribution with parameter λ_p. d) In inference, we take a new datum x and compute the posterior $Pr(w|x)$ over the state using Bayes' rule.

Discussion

For binary classification, there is an asymmetry between the world state, which is discrete, and the measurements, which are continuous. Consequently, the generative and discriminative models look quite different, and the posteriors over the world state w as a function of the data x have different shapes (compare Figure 6.3c with Figure 6.4d). For the discriminative model, this function is by definition sigmoidal, but for the generative case it has a more complex form that was implicitly defined by the normal likelihoods. In general, choosing to model $Pr(w|x)$ or $Pr(x|w)$ will affect the expressiveness of the final model.

6.5   Which type of model should we use?

We have established that there are two different types of model that relate the world state and the observed data. But when should we use each type of model? There is no definitive answer to this question, but some considerations are:

- Inference is generally simpler with *discriminative* models. They directly model the conditional probability distribution of the world $Pr(\mathbf{w}|\mathbf{x})$ given the data. In contrast, generative models calculate the posterior indirectly via Bayes' rule, and sometimes this requires a computationally expensive algorithm.
- *Generative methods* build probability models $Pr(\mathbf{x}|\mathbf{w})$ over the data, whereas *discriminative models* just build a probability model $Pr(\mathbf{w}|\mathbf{x})$ over the world state. The data (usually an image) are generally of much higher dimension than the world state (some aspect of a scene), and modeling it is costly. Moreover, there may be many aspects of the data which do not influence the state; we might devote parameters to describing whether data configuration 1 is more likely than data configuration 2 although they both imply the same world state (Figure 6.5).
- Modeling the likelihood $Pr(\mathbf{x}|\mathbf{w})$ mirrors the actual way that the data were created; the state of the world did create the observed data through some physical process (usually light being emitted from a source, interacting with the object and being captured by a camera). If we wish to build information about the generation process into our model, this approach is desirable. For example, we can account for phenomena such as perspective projection and occlusion. Using the other approaches, it is harder to exploit this knowledge: essentially we have to relearn these phenomena from the data.
- In some situations, some parts of the training or test data vector $\mathbf{x}$ may be missing. Here, generative models are preferred. They model the joint distribution over all of the data dimensions and can effectively interpolate the missing elements.

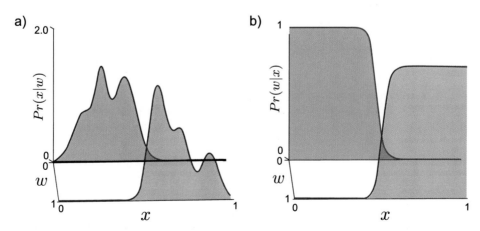

Figure 6.5 Generative vs. discriminative models. a) Generative approach: we separately model the probability density function $Pr(x|w)$ for each class. This may require a complex model with many parameters. b) Posterior probability distribution $Pr(w|x)$ computed via Bayes' rule with a uniform prior. Notice that the complicated structure of the individual class conditional density functions is hardly reflected in the posterior: In this case, it might have been more efficient to take a discriminative approach and model this posterior directly.

- A fundamental property of the generative approach is that it allows incorporation of expert knowledge in the form of a prior. It is harder to impose prior knowledge in a principled way in discriminative models.

It is notable that generative models are more common in vision applications. Consequently, most of the chapters in the rest of the book concern generative models.

6.6   Applications

The focus of this chapter, and indeed most of the chapters of this book, is on the models themselves and the learning and inference algorithms. From this point forward, we will devote a section at the end of each chapter to discussing practical applications of the relevant models in computer vision. For this chapter, only one of the models can actually be implemented based on the information presented so far. This is the generative classification model from Section 6.4.2. Consequently, we will focus the applications on variations of this model and return to the other models in subsequent chapters.

6.6.1   Skin detection

The goal of skin-detection algorithms is to infer a label $w \in \{0,1\}$ denoting the presence or absence of skin at a given pixel, based on the RGB measurements $\mathbf{x} = [x^R, x^G, x^B]$ at that pixel. This is a useful precursor to segmenting a face or hand, or it may be used as the basis of a crude method for detecting prurient content in Web images. Taking a generative approach, we describe the likelihoods as

$$Pr(\mathbf{x}|w = k) = \text{Norm}_{\mathbf{x}}[\boldsymbol{\mu}_k, \boldsymbol{\Sigma}_k] \tag{6.12}$$

and the prior probability over states as

$$Pr(w) = \text{Bern}_w[\lambda]. \tag{6.13}$$

In the learning algorithm, we estimate the parameters $\boldsymbol{\mu}_0, \boldsymbol{\mu}_1, \boldsymbol{\Sigma}_0, \boldsymbol{\Sigma}_1$ from training data pairs $\{w_i, \mathbf{x}_i\}_{i=1}^I$ where the pixels have been labeled by hand. In particular, we learn $\boldsymbol{\mu}_0$ and $\boldsymbol{\Sigma}_0$ from the subset of the training data where $w_i = 0$ and $\boldsymbol{\mu}_1$ and $\boldsymbol{\Sigma}_1$ from the subset where $w_i = 1$. The prior parameter is learned from the world states $\{w_i\}_{i=1}^I$ alone. In each case, this involves fitting a probability distribution to data using one of the techniques discussed in Chapter 4.

To classify a new data point $\mathbf{x}$ as skin or non-skin, we apply Bayes' rule

$$Pr(w = 1|\mathbf{x}) = \frac{Pr(\mathbf{x}|w = 1)Pr(w = 1)}{\sum_{k=0}^1 Pr(\mathbf{x}|w = k)Pr(w = k)}, \tag{6.14}$$

and denote this pixel as skin if $Pr(w = 1|\mathbf{x}) > 0.5$. Figure 6.6 shows the result of applying this model at each pixel independently in the image. Note that the classification is not perfect: there is genuinely an overlap between the skin and non-skin distributions, and this inevitably results in misclassified pixels. The results could be improved by exploiting the fact that skin areas tend to be contiguous regions without small holes. To do this, we must somehow connect together all of the per-pixel classifiers. This is the topic of chapters 11 and 12.

We briefly note that the RGB data are naturally discrete with $x^R, x^G, x^B \in \{0, 1, \ldots, 255\}$, and we could alternatively have based our skin detection model on

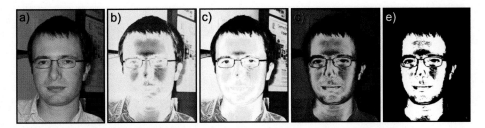

Figure 6.6 Skin detection. For each pixel we aim to infer a label $w \in \{0, 1\}$ denoting the absence or presence of skin based on the RGB triple $\mathbf{x}$. Here we modeled the class conditional density functions $Pr(\mathbf{x}|w)$ as normal distributions. a) Original image. b) Log likelihood (log of data assessed under class-conditional density function) for non-skin. c) Log likelihood for skin. d) Posterior probability of belonging to skin class. e) Thresholded posterior probability $Pr(w|\mathbf{x}) > 0.5$ gives estimate of w.

this assumption. For example, modeling the three color channels independently, the likelihoods become

$$Pr(\mathbf{x}|w = k) = \text{Cat}_{x^R}[\boldsymbol{\lambda}_k^R]\text{Cat}_{x^G}[\boldsymbol{\lambda}_k^G]\text{Cat}_{x^B}[\boldsymbol{\lambda}_k^B]. \tag{6.15}$$

We refer to the assumption that the elements of the data vector are independent as *naïve Bayes*. Of course, this assumption is not necessarily valid in the real world. To model the joint probability distribution of the R,G, and B components properly, we might combine them to form one variable with 256^3 entries and model this with a single categorical distribution. Unfortunately, this means we must learn 256^3 parameters for each categorical distribution, and so it is more practical to quantize each channel to fewer levels (say 8) before combining them together.

6.6.2 Background subtraction

A second application of the generative classification model is for background subtraction. Here, the goal is to infer a binary label $w_n \in \{0, 1\}$, which indicates whether the nth pixel in the image is part of a known background ($w = 0$) or whether a foreground object is occluding it ($w = 1$). As for the skin detection model, this is based on its RGB pixel data $\mathbf{x}_n$ at that pixel.

It is usual to have training data $\{\mathbf{x}_{in}\}_{i=1,n=1}^{I,N}$ that consists of a number of empty scenes where all pixels are known to be background. However, it is not typical to have examples of the foreground objects which are highly variable in appearance. For this reason, we model the class conditional distribution of the background as a normal distribution

$$Pr(\mathbf{x}_n|w = 0) = \text{Norm}_{\mathbf{x}_n}[\boldsymbol{\mu}_{n0}, \boldsymbol{\Sigma}_{n0}], \tag{6.16}$$

but model the foreground class as a uniform distribution

$$Pr(\mathbf{x}_n|w = 1) = \begin{cases} 1/255^3 & 0 < x_n^R, x_n^G, x_n^B < 255 \\ 0 & \text{otherwise} \end{cases}, \tag{6.17}$$

and again model the prior as a Bernoulli variable.

To compute the posterior distribution we once more apply Bayes' rule. Typical results are shown in Figure 6.7, which illustrates a common problem with this method: shadows

Figure 6.7 Background subtraction. For each pixel we aim to infer a label $w \in \{0, 1\}$ denoting the absence or presence of a foreground object. a) We learn a class conditional density model $Pr(\mathbf{x}|w)$ for the background from training examples of an empty scene. The foreground model is treated as uniform. b) For a new image, we then compute the posterior distribution using Bayes' rule. c) Posterior probability of being foreground $Pr(w = 1|\mathbf{x})$. Images from CAVIAR database.

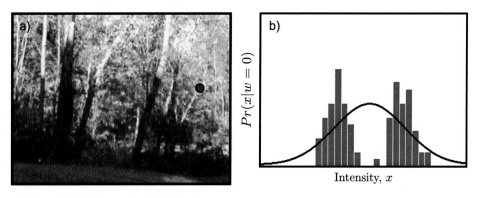

Figure 6.8 Background subtraction in deforming scene. a) The foliage is blowing in the wind in the training images. b) The distribution of RGB values at the pixel indicated by the circle in (a) is now bimodal and not well described by a normal density function (red channel only shown). Images from video by Terry Boult.

are often misclassified as foreground. A simple way to remedy this is to classify pixels based on the hue alone.

In some situations we need a more complex distribution to describe the background. For example, consider an outdoor scene in which trees are blowing in the wind (Figure 6.8). Certain pixels may have bimodal distributions where one part of the foliage intermittently moves in front of another. It is clear that the unimodal normal distribution cannot provide a good description of this data, and the resulting background segmentation result will be poor. We devote part of the next chapter to methods for describing more complex probability distributions of this type.

Summary

In this chapter, we have provided an overview of how abstract vision problems can be solved using machine learning techniques. We have illustrated these ideas with some simple examples. We did not provide the implementation level details of the learning and inference algorithms; these are presented in subsequent chapters.

	Model $Pr(w\|x)$	Model $Pr(x\|w)$
Regression $x \in [-\infty, \infty], w \in [-\infty, \infty]$	Linear regression	Linear regression
Classification $x \in [-\infty, \infty], w \in \{0, 1\}$	Logistic regression	Probability density function

Table 6.1 Example models in this chapter. These can be categorized into those that are based on modeling probability density functions, those that are based on linear regression, and those that are based on logistic regression.

The examples in this chapter are summarized in Table 6.1, where it can be seen that there are three distinct types of model. First, there are those that depend on building probability density functions (describing the class conditional density functions $Pr(x|w = k)$). In the following chapter, we investigate building complex probability density models. The second type of model is based on linear regression, and Chapter 8 investigates a family of related algorithms. Finally, the third type of model discussed in this chapter was logistic regression. We will elaborate on the logistic regression model in Chapter 9.

Notes

The goal of this chapter was to give a very compact view of learning and inference in vision. Alternative views of this material which are not particularly aimed at vision can be found in Bishop (2006) and Duda et al. (2001) and many other texts.

Skin Detection: Reviews of skin detection can be found in Kakumanu et al. (2007) and Vezhnevets et al. (2003). Pixel-based skin-segmentation algorithms have been variously used as the basis for face detection (Hsu et al. 2002), hand gesture analysis (Zhu et al. 2000) and filtering of pornographic images (Jones and Rehg 2002).

There are two main issues that affect the quality of the final results: the representation of the pixel color and the classification algorithm. With regard to the latter issue, various generative approaches have been investigated, including methods based on normal distributions (Hsu et al. 2002), mixtures of normal distributions (Jones and Rehg 2002), and categorical distributions (Jones and Rehg 2002) as well as discriminative methods such as the multilayer perceptron (Phung et al. 2005). There are several detailed empirical studies that compare the efficacy of the color representation and classification algorithm (Phung et al. 2005; Brand and Mason 2000; Schmugge et al. 2007).

Background Subtraction: Reviews of background subtraction techniques can be found in Piccardi (2004), Bouwmans et al. (2010), and Elgammal (2011). Background subtraction is a common first step in many vision systems as it quickly identifies regions of the image that are of interest. Generative classification systems have been built based on normal distributions (Wren et al. 1997), mixtures of normal distributions (Stauffer and Grimson 1999), and kernel density functions (Elgammal et al. 2000). Several systems (Friedman and Russell 1997; Horprasert et al. 2000) have incorporated an explicit label in the model to identify shadows.

Most recent research in this area has addressed the maintenance of the background model in changing environments. Many systems such as that of Stauffer and Grimson (1999) are adaptive and can incorporate new objects into the background model when the background changes. Other models compensate for lighting changes by exploiting the fact that all of the background pixels change together and describing this covariance with a subspace model (Oliver et al. 2000). It is also common now to abandon the per-pixel approach and to estimate the whole label field simultaneously using a technique based on Markov random fields (e.g., Sun et al. 2006).

Problems

6.1 Consider the following problems.

   i Determining the gender of an image of a face.

  ii Determining the pose of the human body given an image of the body.

 iii Determining which suit a playing card belongs to based on an image of that card.

  iv Determining whether two images of faces match (face verification).

   v Determining the 3D position of a point given the positions to which it projects in two cameras at different positions in the world (stereo reconstruction).

For each case, try to describe the contents of the world state $\mathbf{w}$ and the data $\mathbf{x}$. Is each discrete or continuous? If discrete, then how many values can it take? Which are regression problems and which are classification problems?

6.2 Describe a classifier that relates univariate discrete data $x \in \{1 \ldots K\}$ to a univariate discrete world state $w \in \{1 \ldots M\}$ for both discriminative and generative model types.

6.3 Describe a regression model that relates univariate binary discrete data $x \in \{0, 1\}$ to a univariate continuous world state $w \in [-\infty, \infty]$. Use a generative formulation in which $Pr(x|w)$ and $Pr(w)$ are modeled.

6.4 Describe a discriminative regression model that relates a continuous world state $w \in [0, 1]$ to univariate continuous data $x \in [-\infty, \infty]$. *Hint*: Base your classifier on the beta distribution. Ensure that the constraints on the parameters are obeyed.

6.5 Find expressions for the maximum likelihood estimates of the parameters in the discriminative linear regression model (Section 6.3.1). In other words find the parameters $\{\phi_0, \phi_1, \sigma^2\}$ that satisfy

$$
\begin{aligned}
\hat{\phi}_0, \hat{\phi}_1, \hat{\sigma}^2 &= \underset{\phi_0, \phi_1, \sigma^2}{\operatorname{argmax}} \left[\prod_{i=1}^{I} Pr(w_i | x_i, \phi_0, \phi_1, \sigma^2) \right] \\
&= \underset{\phi_0, \phi_1, \sigma^2}{\operatorname{argmax}} \left[\sum_{i=1}^{I} \log \left[Pr(w_i | x_i, \phi_0, \phi_1, \sigma^2) \right] \right] \\
&= \underset{\phi_0, \phi_1, \sigma^2}{\operatorname{argmax}} \left[\sum_{i=1}^{I} \log \left[\operatorname{Norm}_w \left[\phi_0 + \phi_1 x, \sigma^2 \right] \right] \right],
\end{aligned}
$$

where $\{w_i, x_i\}_{i=1}^{I}$ are paired training examples.

6.6 Consider a regression model which models the joint probability between the world w and the data x (Figure 6.9) as

$$Pr\left(\begin{bmatrix} w_i \\ x_i \end{bmatrix}\right) = \text{Norm}_{[w_i, x_i]^T}\left[\begin{bmatrix} \mu_w \\ \mu_x \end{bmatrix}, \begin{bmatrix} \sigma_{ww}^2 & \sigma_{xw}^2 \\ \sigma_{xw}^2 & \sigma_{xx} \end{bmatrix}\right]. \tag{6.18}$$

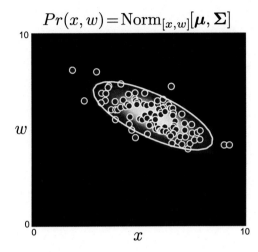

Figure 6.9 Regression model for Problem 6.6. An alternative generative approach to regression is to model the joint probability distribution $Pr(x, w)$, instead of modeling the likelihood $Pr(x|w)$ and the prior $Pr(w)$ separately. In this case, $Pr(x, w)$ is modelled as a joint normal distribution in the two variables. In inference, we compute the posterior distribution $Pr(w|x)$ over the world state using Bayes' rule $Pr(w|x) = Pr(x, w)/Pr(x)$.

Use the relation in Section 5.5 to compute the posterior distribution $Pr(w_i|x_i)$. Show that it has the form

$$Pr(w_i|x_i) = \text{Norm}_{w_i}[\phi_0 + \phi_1 x, \sigma^2], \tag{6.19}$$

and compute expressions for ϕ_0 and ϕ_1 in terms of the training data $\{w_i, x_i\}_{i=1}^I$ by substituting in explicit maximum likelihood estimates of the parameters $\{\mu_w, \mu_x, \sigma_{ww}^2, \sigma_{xw}^2, \sigma_{xx}^2\}$.

6.7 For a two-class problem, the *decision boundary* is the locus of world values w where the posterior probability $Pr(w = 1|x)$ is equal to 0.5. In other words, it represents the boundary between regions that would be classified as $w = 0$ and $w = 1$. Consider the generative classifier from section 6.4.2. Show that with equal priors $Pr(w = 0) = Pr(w = 1) = 0.5$ points on the decision boundary (the locus of points where $Pr(w = 0|x) = Pr(w = 1|x)$) obey a constraint of the form

$$ax^2 + bx + c = 0, \tag{6.20}$$

where and $\{a, b, c\}$ are scalars. Does the shape of the decision boundary for the logistic regression model from section 6.4.1 have the same form?

6.8 Consider a generative classification model for 1D data with likelihood terms

$$Pr(x_i|w_i = 0) = \text{Norm}_{x_i}\left[0, \sigma^2\right]$$
$$Pr(x_i|w_i = 1) = \text{Norm}_{x_i}\left[0, 1.5\sigma^2\right].$$

What is the decision boundary for this classifier with equal priors $Pr(w = 0) = Pr(w = 1) = 0.5$? Develop a discriminative classifier that can produce the same decision boundary. *Hint*: Base your classifier on a quadratic rather than a linear function.

6.9 Consider a generative binary classifier for multivariate data based on multivariate normal likelihood terms

$$Pr(\mathbf{x}_i|w_i = 0) = \text{Norm}_{\mathbf{x}_i}\left[\boldsymbol{\mu}_0, \boldsymbol{\Sigma}_0\right]$$
$$Pr(\mathbf{x}_i|w_i = 1) = \text{Norm}_{\mathbf{x}_i}\left[\boldsymbol{\mu}_1, \boldsymbol{\Sigma}_1\right]$$

and a discriminative classifier based on logistic regression for the same data

$$Pr(w_i|\mathbf{x}_i) = \text{Bern}_{w_i}\left[\text{sig}[\phi_0 + \boldsymbol{\phi}^T\mathbf{x}_i]\right].$$

where there is one entry in the gradient vector $\boldsymbol{\phi}$ for each entry of $\mathbf{x}_i$.

How many parameters does each model have as a function of the dimensionality of $\mathbf{x}_i$? What are the relative advantages and disadvantages of each model as the dimensionality increases?

6.10 One of the problems with the background subtraction method described is that it erroneously classifies shadows as foreground. Describe a model that could be used to classify pixels into three categories (foreground, background, and shadow).

Chapter 7

Modeling complex data densities

In the last chapter we showed that classification with generative models is based on building simple probability models. In particular, we build class-conditional density functions $Pr(\mathbf{x}|w = k)$ over the observed data $\mathbf{x}$ for each value of the world state w.

In Chapter 3 we introduced several probability distributions that could be used for this purpose, but these were quite limited in scope. For example, it is not realistic to assume that all of the complexities of visual data are well described by the normal distribution. In this chapter, we show how to construct complex probability density functions from elementary ones using the idea of a *hidden variable*.

As a representative problem we consider *face detection*; we observe a 60×60 RGB image patch, and we would like to decide whether it contains a face or not. To this end, we concatenate the RGB values to form the 10800×1 vector $\mathbf{x}$. Our goal is to take the vector $\mathbf{x}$ and return a label $w \in \{0, 1\}$ indicating whether it contains background $(w = 0)$ or a face $(w = 1)$. In a real face detection system, we would repeat this procedure for every possible subwindow of an image (Figure 7.1).

We will start with a basic generative approach in which we describe the likelihood of the data in the presence/absence of a face with a normal distribution. We will then extend this model to address its weaknesses. We emphasize though that state-of-the-art face detection algorithms are *not* based on generative methods such as these; they are usually tackled using the discriminative methods of Chapter 9. This application was selected for purely pedagogical reasons.

7.1 Normal classification model

We will take a generative approach to face detection; we will model the probability of the data $\mathbf{x}$ and parameterize this by the world state w. We will describe the data with a multivariate normal distribution so that

$$Pr(\mathbf{x}|w) = \text{Norm}_{\mathbf{x}}[\boldsymbol{\mu}_w, \boldsymbol{\Sigma}_w] \tag{7.1}$$

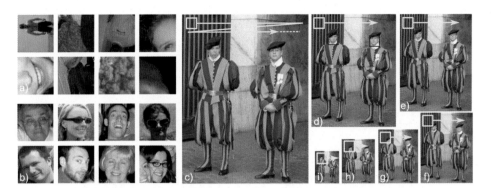

Figure 7.1 Face detection. Consider examining a small window of the image (here 60×60). We concatenate the RGB values in the window to make a data vector $\mathbf{x}$ of dimension 10800×1. The goal of face detection is to infer a label $w \in \{0,1\}$ indicating whether the window contains a) a background region ($w=0$) or b) an aligned face ($w=1$). c–i) We repeat this operation at every position and scale in the image by sweeping a fixed size window through a stack of resized images, estimating w at every point.

or treating the two possible values of the state w separately, we can explicitly write

$$Pr(\mathbf{x}|w=0) = \text{Norm}_{\mathbf{x}}[\boldsymbol{\mu}_0, \boldsymbol{\Sigma}_0]$$
$$Pr(\mathbf{x}|w=1) = \text{Norm}_{\mathbf{x}}[\boldsymbol{\mu}_1, \boldsymbol{\Sigma}_1]. \tag{7.2}$$

These expressions are examples of *class conditional density functions*. They describe the density of the data $\mathbf{x}$ conditional on the value of the world state w.

The goal of learning is to estimate the parameters $\boldsymbol{\theta} = \{\boldsymbol{\mu}_0, \boldsymbol{\Sigma}_0, \boldsymbol{\mu}_1, \boldsymbol{\Sigma}_1\}$ from example pairs of training data $\{\mathbf{x}_i, w_i\}_{i=1}^{I}$. Since parameters $\boldsymbol{\mu}_0$ and $\boldsymbol{\Sigma}_0$ are concerned exclusively with background regions (where $w=0$), we can learn them from the subset of training data $\mathcal{S}_0$ that belonged to the background. For example, using the maximum likelihood approach, we would seek

$$\hat{\boldsymbol{\mu}}_0, \hat{\boldsymbol{\Sigma}}_0 = \underset{\boldsymbol{\mu}_0, \boldsymbol{\Sigma}_0}{\operatorname{argmax}} \left[\prod_{i \in \mathcal{S}_0} Pr(\mathbf{x}_i | \boldsymbol{\mu}_0, \boldsymbol{\Sigma}_0) \right]$$
$$= \underset{\boldsymbol{\mu}_0, \boldsymbol{\Sigma}_0}{\operatorname{argmax}} \left[\prod_{i \in \mathcal{S}_0} \text{Norm}_{\mathbf{x}_i}[\boldsymbol{\mu}_0, \boldsymbol{\Sigma}_0] \right]. \tag{7.3}$$

Similarly, $\boldsymbol{\mu}_1$ and $\boldsymbol{\Sigma}_1$ are concerned exclusively with faces (where $w=1$) and can be learned from the subset $\mathcal{S}_1$ of training data which contained faces. Figure 7.2 shows the maximum likelihood estimates of the parameters where we have used the diagonal form of the covariance matrix.

The goal of the inference algorithm is to take a new facial image $\mathbf{x}$ and assign a label w to it. To this end, we define a prior over the values of the world state $Pr(w) = \text{Bern}_w[\lambda]$ and apply Bayes' rule

$$Pr(w=1|\mathbf{x}) = \frac{Pr(\mathbf{x}|w=1)Pr(w=1)}{\sum_{k=0}^{1} Pr(\mathbf{x}|w=k)Pr(w=k)}. \tag{7.4}$$

All of these terms are simple to compute, and so inference is very easy and will not be discussed further in this chapter.

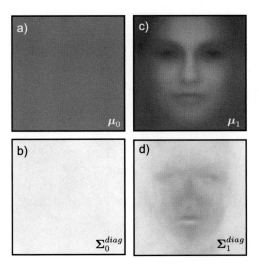

Figure 7.2 Class conditional density functions for normal model with diagonal covariance. Maximum likelihood fits based on 1000 training examples per class. a) Mean for background data μ_0 (reshaped from 10800×1 vector to 60×60 RGB image). b) Reshaped square root of diagonal covariance for background data Σ_0. c) Mean for face data μ_1. d) Covariance for face data Σ_1. The background model has little structure: the mean is uniform, and the variance is high everywhere. The mean of the face model clearly captures class-specific information. The covariance of the face is larger at the edges of the image, which usually contain hair or background.

7.1.1   Deficiencies of the multivariate normal model

Unfortunately, this model does not detect faces reliably. We will defer presenting experimental results until Section 7.9.1, but for now please take it on trust that while this model achieves above-chance performance, it doesn't come close to producing a state-of-the-art result. This is hardly surprising: the success of this classifier hinges on fitting the data with a normal distribution. Unfortunately, this fit is poor for three reasons (Figure 7.3).

- The normal distribution is unimodal; neither faces nor background regions are well represented by a pdf with a single peak.

- The normal distribution is not robust; a single outlier can dramatically affect the estimates of the mean and covariance.

- The normal distribution has too many parameters; here the data have $D = 10800$ dimensions. The full covariance matrix contains $D(D+1)/2$ parameters. With only 1000 training examples, we cannot even specify these parameters uniquely, so we were forced to use the diagonal form.

We devote the rest of this chapter to tackling these problems. To make the density multimodal, we introduce *mixture models*. To make the density robust, we replace the normal with the *t-distribution*. To cope with parameter estimation in high dimensions, we introduce *subspace models*.

The new models have much in common with each other. In each case, we introduce a *hidden* or *latent variable* $\mathbf{h}_i$ associated with each observed data point $\mathbf{x}_i$. The hidden variable induces the more complex properties of the resulting pdf. Moreover, because the structure of the models is similar, we can use a common approach to learn the parameters.

In the following section, we present an abstract discussion of how hidden variables can be used to model complex pdfs. In Section 7.3, we discuss how to learn the parameters of models with hidden variables. Then in Sections 7.4, 7.5, and 7.6, we will introduce mixture models, t-distributions, and factor analysis, respectively.

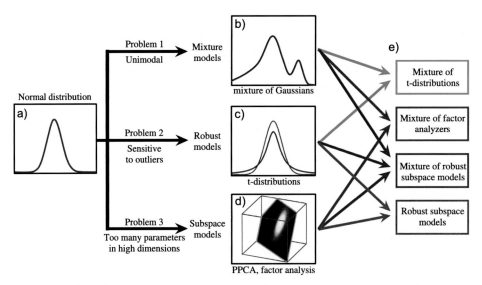

Figure 7.3 a) Problems with the multivariate normal density. b) Normal models are unimodal, but mixtures of Gaussians can model multimodal distributions. c) Normal distributions are not robust to outliers, but t-distributions can cope with unusual observations. d) Normal models need many parameters in high dimensions but subspace models reduce this requirement. e) These solutions can be combined to form hybrid models addressing several of these problems at once.

7.2   Hidden variables

To model a complex probability density function over the variable $\mathbf{x}$, we will introduce a *hidden* or *latent* variable $\mathbf{h}$, which may be discrete or continuous. We will discuss the continuous formulation, but all of the important concepts transfer to the discrete case.

To exploit the hidden variables, we describe the final density $Pr(\mathbf{x})$ as the marginalization of the joint density $Pr(\mathbf{x}, \mathbf{h})$ between $\mathbf{x}$ and $\mathbf{h}$ so that

$$Pr(\mathbf{x}) = \int Pr(\mathbf{x}, \mathbf{h}) \, d\mathbf{h}. \tag{7.5}$$

We now concentrate on describing the joint density $Pr(\mathbf{x}, \mathbf{h})$. We can choose this so that it is relatively simple to model but produces an expressive family of marginal distributions $Pr(\mathbf{x})$ when we integrate over $\mathbf{h}$ (see Figure 7.4).

Whatever form we choose for the joint distribution, it will have some parameters $\boldsymbol{\theta}$, and so really we should write

$$Pr(\mathbf{x}|\boldsymbol{\theta}) = \int Pr(\mathbf{x}, \mathbf{h}|\boldsymbol{\theta}) \, d\mathbf{h}. \tag{7.6}$$

There are two possible approaches to fitting the model to training data $\{\mathbf{x}_i\}_{i=1}^{I}$ using the maximum likelihood method. We could directly maximize the log likelihood of the distribution $Pr(\mathbf{x})$ from the left-hand side of Equation 7.6 so that

$$\hat{\boldsymbol{\theta}} = \underset{\boldsymbol{\theta}}{\operatorname{argmax}} \left[\sum_{i=1}^{I} \log \left[Pr(\mathbf{x}_i|\boldsymbol{\theta}) \right] \right]. \tag{7.7}$$

This formulation has the advantage that we don't need to involve the hidden variables at all. However, in the models that we will consider, it will not result in a neat closed

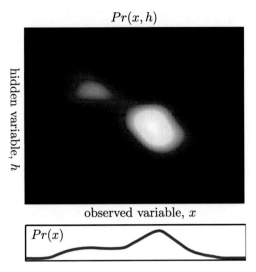

$Pr(x, h)$

hidden variable, h

observed variable, x

$Pr(x)$

Figure 7.4 Using hidden variables to help model complex densities. One way to model the density $Pr(x)$ is to consider the joint probability distribution $Pr(x,h)$ between the observed data x and a hidden variable h. The density $Pr(x)$ can be considered as the marginalization of (integral over) this distribution with respect to the hidden variable h. As we manipulate the parameters $\boldsymbol{\theta}$ of this joint distribution, the marginal distribution changes and the agreement with the observed data $\{x_i\}_{i=1}^I$ increases or decreases. Sometimes it is easier to fit the distribution in this indirect way than to directly manipulate $Pr(x)$.

form solution. Of course, we could apply a brute force nonlinear optimization technique (Appendix B), but there is an alternative approach: we use the *expectation maximization* algorithm, which works directly with the right-hand side of Equation 7.6 and seeks

$$\hat{\boldsymbol{\theta}} = \underset{\boldsymbol{\theta}}{\operatorname{argmax}} \left[\sum_{i=1}^I \log \left[\int Pr(\mathbf{x}_i, \mathbf{h}_i | \boldsymbol{\theta}) \, d\mathbf{h}_i \right] \right]. \tag{7.8}$$

7.3   Expectation maximization

In this section, we will present a brief description of the *expectation maximization (EM)* algorithm. The goal is to provide just enough information to use this technique for fitting models. We will return to a more detailed treatment in Section 7.8.

The EM algorithm is a general-purpose tool for fitting parameters $\boldsymbol{\theta}$ in models of the form of Equation 7.6 where

$$\hat{\boldsymbol{\theta}} = \underset{\boldsymbol{\theta}}{\operatorname{argmax}} \left[\sum_{i=1}^I \log \left[\int Pr(\mathbf{x}_i, \mathbf{h}_i | \boldsymbol{\theta}) \, d\mathbf{h}_i \right] \right]. \tag{7.9}$$

The EM algorithm works by defining a lower bound $\mathcal{B}\left[\{q_i(\mathbf{h}_i)\}, \boldsymbol{\theta}\right]$ on the log likelihood in Equation 7.9 and iteratively increasing this bound. The lower bound is simply a function that is parameterized by $\boldsymbol{\theta}$ and some other quantities and is guaranteed to always return a value that is less than or equal to the log likelihood $L[\boldsymbol{\theta}]$ for any given set of parameters $\boldsymbol{\theta}$ (Figure 7.5).

For the EM algorithm, the particular lower bound chosen is

$$\mathcal{B}\left[\{q_i(\mathbf{h}_i)\}, \boldsymbol{\theta}\right] = \sum_{i=1}^I \int q_i(\mathbf{h}_i) \log \left[\frac{Pr(\mathbf{x}_i, \mathbf{h}_i | \boldsymbol{\theta})}{q_i(\mathbf{h}_i)} \right] d\mathbf{h}_i \tag{7.10}$$

$$\leq \sum_{i=1}^I \log \left[\int Pr(\mathbf{x}_i, \mathbf{h}_i | \boldsymbol{\theta}) \, d\mathbf{h}_i \right].$$

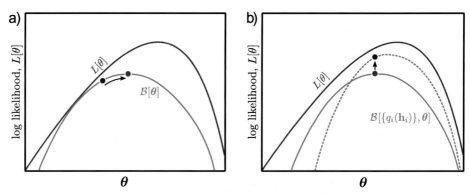

Figure 7.5 Manipulating the lower bound. a) Consider the log likelihood $L[\theta]$ of the data $\{\mathbf{x}\}_{i=1}^I$ as a function of the model parameters θ (red curve). In maximum likelihood learning, our goal is to find the parameters θ that maximize this function. A lower bound on the log likelihood is another function $\mathcal{B}[\theta]$ of the parameters θ that is everywhere lower or equal to the log likelihood (green curve). One way to improve the current estimate (blue dot) is to manipulate the parameters so that $\mathcal{B}[\theta]$ increases (pink dot). This is the goal of the maximization step of the EM algorithm. b) The lower bound $\mathcal{B}[\{q_i(\mathbf{h}_i)\}, \theta]$ also depends on a set of probability distributions $\{q_i(\mathbf{h}_i)\}_{i=1}^I$ over hidden variables $\{\mathbf{h}_i\}$. Manipulating these probability distributions changes the value that the lower bound returns for every θ (e.g., green curve). So a second way to improve the current estimate (pink dot) is to change the distributions in such a way that the curve increases for the current parameters (blue dot). This is the goal of the expectation step of the EM algorithm.

It is not obvious that this inequality is true, making this a valid lower bound; take this on trust for the moment and we will return to this in Section 7.8.

In addition to the parameters θ, the lower bound $\mathcal{B}[\{q_i(\mathbf{h}_i)\}, \theta]$ also depends on a set of I probability distributions $\{q_i(\mathbf{h}_i)\}_{i=1}^I$ over the hidden variables $\{\mathbf{h}_i\}_{i=1}^I$. When we vary these probability distributions, the value that the lower bound returns will change, but it will always remain less than or equal to the log likelihood.

The EM algorithm manipulates both the parameters θ and the distributions $\{q_i(\mathbf{h}_i)\}_{i=1}^I$ to increase the lower bound. It alternates between

- Updating the probability distributions $\{q_i(\mathbf{h}_i)\}_{i=1}^I$ to improve the bound in Equation 7.10. This is called the *expectation step* or *E-step* and
- Updating the parameters θ to improve the bound in Equation 7.10. This is called the *maximization step* or *M-step*.

In the E-step at iteration $t + 1$, we set each distribution $q_i(\mathbf{h}_i)$ to be the posterior distributions $Pr(\mathbf{h}_i|\mathbf{x}_i, \theta)$ over that hidden variable given the associated data example and the current parameters $\theta^{[t]}$. To compute these, we use Bayes' rule

$$\hat{q}_i(\mathbf{h}_i) = Pr(\mathbf{h}_i|\mathbf{x}_i, \theta^{[t]}) = \frac{Pr(\mathbf{x}_i|\mathbf{h}_i, \theta^{[t]})Pr(\mathbf{h}_i|\theta^{[t]})}{Pr(\mathbf{x}_i)}. \tag{7.11}$$

It can be shown that this choice maximizes the bound as much as possible.

In the M-step, we directly maximize the bound (Equation 7.10) with respect to the parameters θ. In practice, we can simplify the expression for the bound to eliminate terms that do not depend on θ and this yields

$$\hat{\theta}^{[t+1]} = \underset{\theta}{\operatorname{argmax}} \left[\sum_{i=1}^{I} \int \hat{q}_i(\mathbf{h}_i) \log \left[Pr(\mathbf{x}_i, \mathbf{h}_i|\theta) \right] d\mathbf{h}_i \right]. \tag{7.12}$$

Each of these steps is guaranteed to improve the bound, and iterating them alternately is guaranteed to find at least a local maximum with respect to $\boldsymbol{\theta}$.

This is a practical description of the EM algorithm, but there is a lot missing: we have not demonstrated that Equation 7.10 really is a bound on the log likelihood. We have not shown that the posterior distribution $Pr(\mathbf{h}_i|\mathbf{x}_i,\boldsymbol{\theta}^{[t]})$ is the optimal choice for $q_i(\mathbf{h}_i)$ in the E-step (Equation 7.11), and we have not demonstrated that the cost function for the M-step (Equation 7.12) improves the bound. For now we will assume that these things are true and proceed with the main thrust of the chapter. We will return to these issues in Section 7.8.

7.4   Mixture of Gaussians

The *mixture of Gaussians* (MoG) is a prototypical example of a model where learning is suited to the EM algorithm. The data are described as a weighted sum of K normal distributions

$$Pr(\mathbf{x}|\boldsymbol{\theta}) = \sum_{k=1}^{K} \lambda_k \text{Norm}_{\mathbf{x}}[\boldsymbol{\mu}_k, \boldsymbol{\Sigma}_k], \tag{7.13}$$

where $\boldsymbol{\mu}_{1...K}$ and $\boldsymbol{\Sigma}_{1...K}$ are the means and covariances of the normal distributions and $\lambda_{1...K}$ are positive valued weights that sum to one. The mixtures of Gaussians model describes complex multimodal probability densities by combining simpler constituent distributions (Figure 7.6).

To learn the parameters $\boldsymbol{\theta} = \{\boldsymbol{\mu}_k, \boldsymbol{\Sigma}_k, \lambda_k\}_{k=1}^{K}$ from training data $\{\mathbf{x}_i\}_{i=1}^{I}$, we could apply the straightforward maximum likelihood approach

$$\hat{\boldsymbol{\theta}} = \underset{\boldsymbol{\theta}}{\operatorname{argmax}} \left[\sum_{i=1}^{I} \log\left[Pr(\mathbf{x}_i|\boldsymbol{\theta})\right] \right]$$

$$= \underset{\boldsymbol{\theta}}{\operatorname{argmax}} \left[\sum_{i=1}^{I} \log\left[\sum_{k=1}^{K} \lambda_k \text{Norm}_{\mathbf{x}_i}[\boldsymbol{\mu}_k, \boldsymbol{\Sigma}_k] \right] \right]. \tag{7.14}$$

Unfortunately, if we take the derivative with respect to the parameters $\boldsymbol{\theta}$ and equate the resulting expression to zero, it is not possible to solve the resulting equations in closed form. The sticking point is the summation inside the logarithm, which precludes a simple

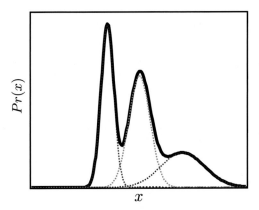

Figure 7.6 Mixture of Gaussians model in 1D. A complex multimodal probability density function (black solid curve) is created by taking a weighted sum or *mixture* of several constituent normal distributions with different means and variances (red, green, and blue dashed curves). To ensure that the final distribution is a valid density, the weights must be positive and sum to one.

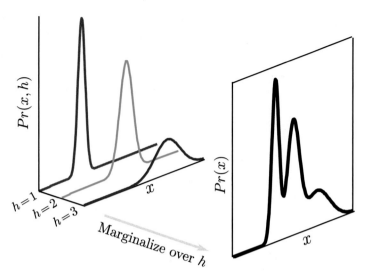

Figure 7.7 Mixture of Gaussians as a marginalization. The mixture of Gaussians can also be thought of in terms of a joint distribution $Pr(x,h)$ between the observed variable x and a discrete hidden variable h. To create the mixture density, we marginalize over h. The hidden variable has a straightforward interpretation: it is the index of the constituent normal distribution.

solution. Of course, we could use a nonlinear optimization approach, but this would be complex as we would have to maintain the constraints on the parameters; the weights $\boldsymbol{\lambda}$ must sum to one and the covariances $\{\boldsymbol{\Sigma}_k\}_{k=1}^K$ must be positive definite. For a simpler approach, we express the observed density as a marginalization and use the EM algorithm to learn the parameters.

7.4.1 Mixture of Gaussians as a marginalization

The mixture of Gaussians model can be expressed as the marginalization of a joint probability distribution between the observed data $\mathbf{x}$ and a discrete hidden variable h that takes values $h \in \{1 \ldots K\}$ (Figure 7.7). If we define

$$Pr(\mathbf{x}|h, \boldsymbol{\theta}) = \text{Norm}_{\mathbf{x}}[\boldsymbol{\mu}_h, \boldsymbol{\Sigma}_h]$$

$$Pr(h|\boldsymbol{\theta}) = \text{Cat}_h[\boldsymbol{\lambda}], \tag{7.15}$$

where $\boldsymbol{\lambda} = [\lambda_1 \ldots \lambda_K]$ are the parameters of the categorical distribution, then we can recover the original density using

$$Pr(\mathbf{x}|\boldsymbol{\theta}) = \sum_{k=1}^K Pr(\mathbf{x}, h = k|\boldsymbol{\theta})$$

$$= \sum_{k=1}^K Pr(\mathbf{x}|h = k, \boldsymbol{\theta})Pr(h = k|\boldsymbol{\theta})$$

$$= \sum_{k=1}^K \lambda_k \text{Norm}_{\mathbf{x}}[\boldsymbol{\mu}_k, \boldsymbol{\Sigma}_k]. \tag{7.16}$$

Interpreting the model in this way also provides a method to draw samples from a mixture of Gaussians: we sample from the joint distribution $Pr(\mathbf{x}, h)$ and then discard the hidden variable h to leave just a data sample $\mathbf{x}$. To sample from the joint distribution $Pr(\mathbf{x}, h)$, we first sample h from the categorical prior $Pr(h)$, then sample $\mathbf{x}$ from the normal distribution $Pr(\mathbf{x}|h)$ associated with the value of h. Notice that the hidden variable h has a clear interpretation in this procedure. It determines which of the constituent normal distributions is *responsible* for the observed data point $\mathbf{x}$.

7.4.2   Expectation maximization for fitting mixture models

To learn the MoG parameters $\boldsymbol{\theta} = \{\lambda_k, \boldsymbol{\mu}_k, \boldsymbol{\Sigma}_k\}_{k=1}^{K}$ from training data $\{\mathbf{x}_i\}_{i=1}^{I}$ we apply the EM algorithm. Following the recipe of Section 7.3, we initialize the parameters randomly and alternate between performing the E- and M-steps.

In the E-step, we maximize the bound with respect to the distributions $q_i(h_i)$ by finding the posterior probability distribution $Pr(h_i|\mathbf{x}_i)$ of each hidden variable h_i given the observation $\mathbf{x}_i$ and the current parameter settings,

$$
\begin{aligned}
q_i(h_i) = Pr(h_i = k|\mathbf{x}_i, \boldsymbol{\theta}^{[t]}) &= \frac{Pr(\mathbf{x}_i|h_i = k, \boldsymbol{\theta}^{[t]})Pr(h_i = k, \boldsymbol{\theta}^{[t]})}{\sum_{j=1}^{K} Pr(\mathbf{x}_i|h_i = j, \boldsymbol{\theta}^{[t]})Pr(h_i = j, \boldsymbol{\theta}^{[t]})} \\
&= \frac{\lambda_k \text{Norm}_{\mathbf{x}_i}[\boldsymbol{\mu}_k, \boldsymbol{\Sigma}_k]}{\sum_{j=1}^{K} \lambda_j \text{Norm}_{\mathbf{x}_i}[\boldsymbol{\mu}_j, \boldsymbol{\Sigma}_j]} \\
&= r_{ik}.
\end{aligned}
\tag{7.17}
$$

In other words we compute the probability $Pr(h_i = k|\mathbf{x}_i, \boldsymbol{\theta}^{[t]})$ that the kth normal distribution was responsible for the ith datapoint (Figure 7.8). We denote this *responsibility* by r_{ik} for short.

In the M-step, we maximize the bound with respect to the model parameters $\boldsymbol{\theta} = \{\lambda_k, \boldsymbol{\mu}_k, \boldsymbol{\Sigma}_k\}_{k=1}^{K}$ so that

$$
\begin{aligned}
\hat{\boldsymbol{\theta}}^{[t+1]} &= \underset{\boldsymbol{\theta}}{\text{argmax}} \left[\sum_{i=1}^{I} \sum_{k=1}^{K} \hat{q}_i(h_i = k) \log\left[Pr(\mathbf{x}_i, h_i = k|\boldsymbol{\theta})\right] \right] \\
&= \underset{\boldsymbol{\theta}}{\text{argmax}} \left[\sum_{i=1}^{I} \sum_{k=1}^{K} r_{ik} \log\left[\lambda_k \text{Norm}_{\mathbf{x}_i}[\boldsymbol{\mu}_k, \boldsymbol{\Sigma}_k]\right] \right].
\end{aligned}
\tag{7.18}
$$

This maximization can be performed by taking the derivative of the expression with respect to the parameters, equating the result to zero, and rearranging, taking care to enforce the constraint $\sum_k \lambda_k = 1$ using Lagrange multipliers. The procedure results in the update rules:

$$
\lambda_k^{[t+1]} = \frac{\sum_{i=1}^{I} r_{ik}}{\sum_{j=1}^{K} \sum_{i=1}^{I} r_{ij}}
\tag{7.19}
$$

$$
\boldsymbol{\mu}_k^{[t+1]} = \frac{\sum_{i=1}^{I} r_{ik}\mathbf{x}_i}{\sum_{i=1}^{I} r_{ik}}
$$

$$
\boldsymbol{\Sigma}_k^{[t+1]} = \frac{\sum_{i=1}^{I} r_{ik}(\mathbf{x}_i - \boldsymbol{\mu}_k^{[t+1]})(\mathbf{x}_i - \boldsymbol{\mu}_k^{[t+1]})^T}{\sum_{i=1}^{I} r_{ik}}.
$$

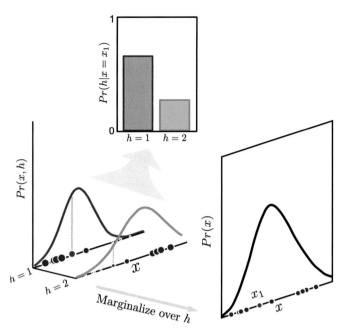

Figure 7.8 E-step for fitting the mixture of Gaussians model. For each of the I data points $\mathbf{x}_{1...I}$, we calculate the posterior distribution $Pr(h_i|\mathbf{x}_i)$ over the hidden variable h_i. The posterior probability $Pr(h_i = k|\mathbf{x}_i)$ that h_i takes value k can be understood as the responsibility of normal distribution k for data point x_i. For example, for data point x_1 (magenta circle), component 1 (red curve) is more than twice as likely to be responsible than component 2 (green curve). Note that in the joint distribution (left), the size of the projected data point indicates the responsibility.

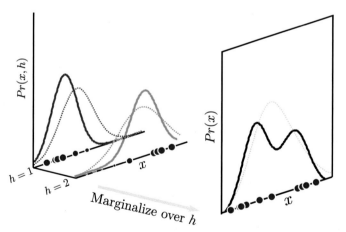

Figure 7.9 M-step for fitting the mixture of Gaussians model. For the kth constituent Gaussian, we update the parameters $\{\boldsymbol{\lambda}_k, \boldsymbol{\mu}_k, \boldsymbol{\Sigma}_k\}$. The ith data point $\mathbf{x}_i$ contributes to these updates according to the responsibility r_{ik} (indicated by size of point) assigned in the E-step; data points that are more associated with the kth component have more effect on the parameters. Dashed and solid lines represent fit before and after the update, respectively.

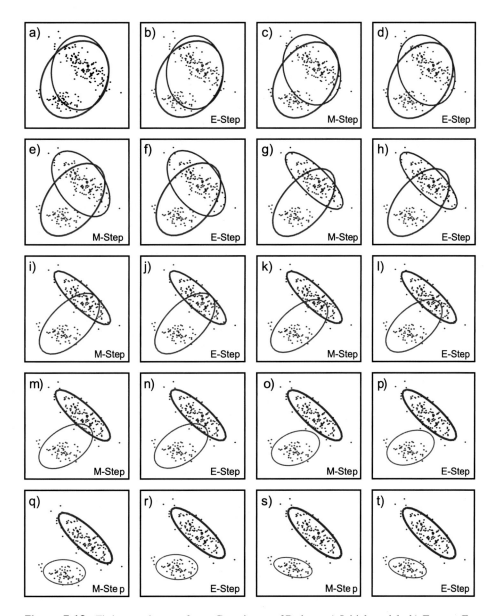

Figure 7.10 Fitting a mixture of two Gaussians to 2D data. a) Initial model. b) E-step. For each data point the posterior probability that is was generated from each Gaussian is calculated (indicated by color of point). c) M-step. The mean, variance and weight of each Gaussian is updated based on these posterior probabilities. Ellipse shows Mahalanobis distance of two. Weight (thickness) of ellipse indicates weight of Gaussian. d–t) Further E-step and M-step iterations.

These update rules can be easily understood (Figure 7.9): we update the weights $\{\lambda_k\}_{k=1}^K$ according to the relative total responsibility of each component for the data points. We update the cluster means $\{\boldsymbol{\mu}_k\}_{k=1}^K$ by computing the weighted mean over the datapoints where the weights are given by the responsibilities. If component k is mostly responsible for data point $\mathbf{x}_i$, then this data point has a high weight and affects the update more. The update rule for the covariances has a similar interpretation.

In practice the E- and M-steps are alternated until the bound on the data no longer increases and the parameters no longer change. The alternating E-steps and M-steps for a two-dimensional example are shown in Figure 7.10. Notice that the final fit identifies the two *clusters* in the data. The mixture of Gaussians is closely related to clustering techniques such as the *K-means* algorithm (Section 13.4.4).

The EM approach to estimating mixture models has three attractive features.

1. Both steps of the algorithm can be computed in closed form without the need for an optimization procedure.

2. The solution guarantees that the constraints on the parameters are respected: the weighting parameters $\{\lambda_k\}_{k=1}^K$ are guaranteed to be positive and sum to one, and the covariance matrices $\{\Sigma_k\}_{k=1}^K$ are guaranteed to be positive definite.

3. The method can cope with missing data. Imagine that some of the elements of training example $\mathbf{x}_i$ are missing. In the E-step, the remaining dimensions can still be used to establish a distribution over the hidden variable h. In the M-step, this datapoint would contribute only to the dimensions of $\{\boldsymbol{\mu}_k\}_{k=1}^K$ and $\{\Sigma_k\}_{k=1}^K$ where data were observed.

Figure 7.11 shows a mixture of five Gaussians that has been fit to a 2D data set. As for the basic multivariate normal model, it is possible to constrain the covariance matrices to be spherical or diagonal. We can also constrain the covariances to be the same for each component if desired. Figure 7.12 shows the mean vectors $\boldsymbol{\mu}_k$ for a ten-component model with diagonal covariances fitted to the face data set. The clusters represent different illumination conditions as well as changes in pose, expression, and background color.

In fitting mixtures of Gaussians, there are several things to consider. First, the EM algorithm does not guarantee to find a global solution to this non-convex optimization problem. Figure 7.13 shows three different solutions that were computed by starting the fitting algorithm with different initial random values for the parameters $\boldsymbol{\theta}$. The best we can do to circumvent this problem is to start fitting in different places and take the solution with the greatest log likelihood. Second, we must prespecify the number of mixing components. Unfortunately, we cannot decide the number of components by comparing the log likelihood; models with more parameters will inevitably describe the data better. There are methods to tackle this problem, but they are beyond the scope of this volume.

Finally, although we presented a maximum likelihood approach here, it is important in practice to include priors over model parameters $Pr(\boldsymbol{\theta})$ to prevent the scenario where one of the Gaussians becomes exclusively associated with a single datapoint. Without a prior, the variance of this component becomes progressively smaller and the likelihood increases without bound.

7.5   The t-distribution

The second significant problem with using the normal distribution to describe visual data is that it is not robust: the height of the normal pdf falls off very rapidly as we move into the tails. The effect of this is that outliers (unusually extreme observations)

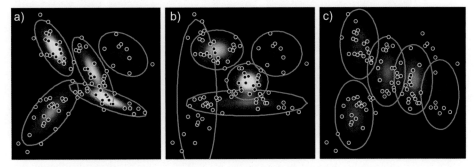

Figure 7.11   Covariance of components in mixture models. a) Full covariances. b) Diagonal covariances. c) Identical diagonal covariances.

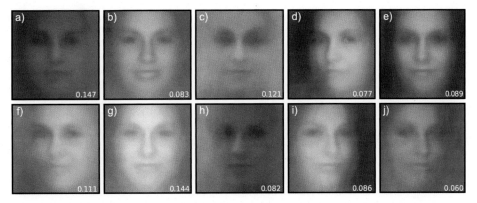

Figure 7.12   Mixtures of Gaussians model for face data. a–j) Mean vectors $\boldsymbol{\mu}_k$ for a mixture of ten Gaussians fitted to the face data set. The model has captured variation in the mean luminance and chromaticity of the face and other factors such as the pose and background color. Numbers indicate the weight λ_k of each component.

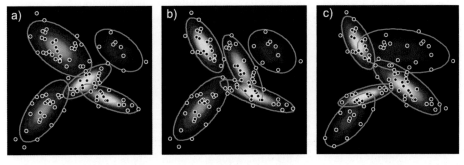

Figure 7.13   Local maxima. Repeated fitting of mixture of Gaussians model with different starting points results in different models as the fit converges to different local maxima. The log likelihoods are a) 98.76 b) 96.97 c) 94.35, respectively, indicating that (a) is the best fit.

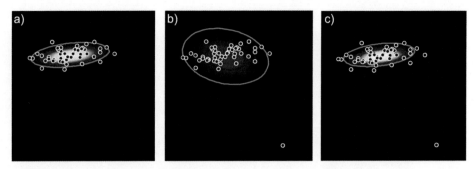

Figure 7.14 Motivation for t-distribution. a) The multivariate normal model fit to data. b) Adding a single outlier completely changes the fit. c) With the multivariate t-distribution the outlier does not have such a drastic effect.

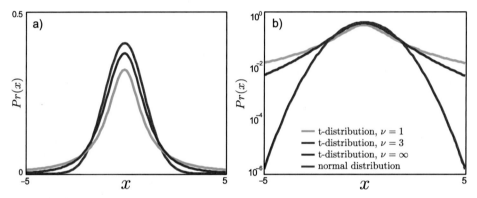

Figure 7.15 The univariate t-distribution. a) As well as the mean μ and scaling parameter σ^2, the t-distribution has a parameter ν which is termed the degrees of freedom. As ν decreases, the tails of the distribution become longer and the model becomes more robust. b) This is seen more clearly on a log scale.

drastically affect the estimated parameters (Figure 7.14). The t-distribution is a closely related distribution in which the length of the tails is parameterized.

The univariate t-distribution (Figure 7.15) has probability density function

$$Pr(x) = \text{Stud}_{\mathbf{x}}\left[\mu, \sigma^2, \nu\right]$$

$$= \frac{\Gamma\left[\frac{\nu+1}{2}\right]}{\sqrt{\nu\pi\sigma^2}\Gamma\left[\frac{\nu}{2}\right]}\left(1 + \frac{(x-\mu)^2}{\nu\sigma^2}\right)^{-\frac{\nu+1}{2}}, \tag{7.20}$$

where μ is the mean and σ^2 is the scale parameter. The degrees of freedom $\nu \in (0, \infty]$ controls the length of the tails: when ν is small there is considerable weight in the tails. For example, with $\mu = 0$ and $\sigma^2 = 1$ a datapoint at $x = -5$ is roughly $10^4 = 10000$ times more likely under the t-distribution with $\nu = 1$ than under the normal distribution. As ν tends to infinity, the distribution approximates a normal more and more closely and there is less weight in the tails. The variance of the distribution is given by $\sigma\nu/(\nu - 2)$ for $\nu > 2$ and infinite if $0 < \nu \leq 2$.

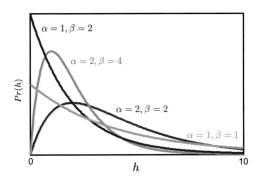

Figure 7.16 The gamma distribution is defined on positive real values and has two parameters α, β. The mean of the distribution is $E[h] = \alpha/\beta$ and the variance is $E[(h - E[h])^2] = \alpha/\beta^2$. The t-distribution can be thought of as a weighted sum of normal distributions with the same mean, but covariances that depend inversely on the gamma distribution.

The multivariate t-distribution has pdf

$$Pr(\mathbf{x}) = \text{Stud}_{\mathbf{x}}\left[\boldsymbol{\mu}, \boldsymbol{\Sigma}, \nu\right]$$

$$= \frac{\Gamma\left[\frac{\nu+D}{2}\right]}{(\nu\pi)^{D/2}|\boldsymbol{\Sigma}|^{1/2}\Gamma\left[\frac{\nu}{2}\right]}\left(1 + \frac{(\mathbf{x} - \boldsymbol{\mu})^T\boldsymbol{\Sigma}^{-1}(\mathbf{x} - \boldsymbol{\mu})}{\nu}\right)^{-\frac{\nu+D}{2}}, \quad (7.21)$$

where D is the dimensionality of the space, $\boldsymbol{\mu}$ is a $D \times 1$ mean vector, $\boldsymbol{\Sigma}$ is a $D \times D$ positive definite scale matrix, and $\nu \in [0, \infty]$ is the degrees of freedom. As for the multivariate normal distribution (Figure 5.1), the scale matrix can take full, diagonal or spherical forms. The covariance of the distribution is given by $\boldsymbol{\Sigma}\nu/(\nu - 2)$ for $\nu > 2$ and is infinite if $0 \le \nu \le 2$.

7.5.1   Student t-distribution as a marginalization

As for the mixtures of Gaussians, it is also possible to understand the t-distribution in terms of hidden variables. We define

$$Pr(\mathbf{x}|h) = \text{Norm}_x[\boldsymbol{\mu}, \boldsymbol{\Sigma}/h]$$
$$Pr(h) = \text{Gam}_h[\nu/2, \nu/2], \quad (7.22)$$

where h is a scalar hidden variable and $\text{Gam}[\alpha, \beta]$ is the gamma distribution with parameters α, β (Figure 7.16). The gamma distribution is a continuous probability distribution defined on the positive real axis with probability density function

$$\text{Gam}_h[\alpha, \beta] = \frac{\beta^\alpha}{\Gamma[\alpha]}\exp[-\beta h]h^{\alpha-1}, \quad (7.23)$$

where $\Gamma[\bullet]$ is the gamma function.

The t-distribution is the marginalization with respect to the hidden variable h of the joint distribution between the data $\mathbf{x}$ and h (Figure 7.17),

$$Pr(\mathbf{x}) = \int Pr(\mathbf{x}, h)dh = \int Pr(\mathbf{x}|h)Pr(h)dh$$

$$= \int \text{Norm}_x[\boldsymbol{\mu}, \boldsymbol{\Sigma}/h]\text{Gam}_h[\nu/2, \nu/2]dh$$

$$= \text{Stud}_{\mathbf{x}}[\boldsymbol{\mu}, \boldsymbol{\Sigma}, \nu]. \quad (7.24)$$

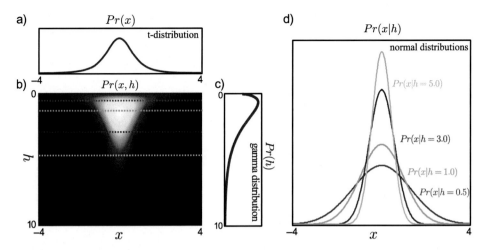

Figure 7.17 The t-distribution as a marginalization. a) The t-distribution has a similar form to the normal distribution but longer tails. b) The t-distribution is the marginalization of the joint distribution $Pr(x,h)$ between the observed variable x and a hidden variable h. c) The prior distribution over the hidden variable h has a gamma distribution. d) The conditional distribution $Pr(x|h)$ is normal with a variance that depends on h. So the t-distribution can be considered as an infinite weighted sum of normal distributions with variances determined by the gamma prior (equation 7.24).

This formulation also provides a method to generate data from the t-distribution. We first generate h from the gamma distribution and then generate $\mathbf{x}$ from the associated normal distribution $Pr(\mathbf{x}|h)$. Hence the hidden variable has a simple interpretation: it tells us which one of the continuous family of underlying normal distributions was responsible for this datapoint.

7.5.2 Expectation maximization for fitting t-distributions

Since the pdf takes the form of a marginalization of the joint distribution with a hidden variable (Equation 7.24), we can use the EM algorithm to learn the parameters $\boldsymbol{\theta} = \{\boldsymbol{\mu}, \boldsymbol{\Sigma}, \nu\}$ from a set of training data $\{\mathbf{x}_i\}_{i=1}^{I}$.

In the E-step (Figure 7.18a–b), we maximize the bound with respect to the distributions $q_i(h_i)$ by finding the posterior $Pr(h_i|\mathbf{x}_i, \boldsymbol{\theta}^{[t]})$ over each hidden variable h_i given associated observation $\mathbf{x}_i$ and the current parameter settings. By Bayes' rule, we get

$$
\begin{aligned}
q_i(h_i) = Pr(h_i|\mathbf{x}_i, \boldsymbol{\theta}^{[t]}) &= \frac{Pr(\mathbf{x}_i|h_i, \boldsymbol{\theta}^{[t]})Pr(h_i)}{Pr(\mathbf{x}_i|\boldsymbol{\theta}^{[t]})} \\
&= \frac{\text{Norm}_{\mathbf{x}_i}[\boldsymbol{\mu}, \boldsymbol{\Sigma}/h_i]\text{Gam}_{h_i}[\nu/2, \nu/2]}{Pr(\mathbf{x}_i)} \\
&= \text{Gam}_{h_i}\left[\frac{\nu+D}{2}, \frac{(\mathbf{x}_i - \boldsymbol{\mu})^T\boldsymbol{\Sigma}^{-1}(\mathbf{x}_i - \boldsymbol{\mu})}{2} + \frac{\nu}{2}\right],
\end{aligned}
\tag{7.25}
$$

where we have used the fact that the gamma distribution is conjugate to the scaling factor for the normal variance. The E-step can be understood as follows: we are treating each data point $\mathbf{x}_i$ as if it were generated from one of the normals in the infinite mixture where

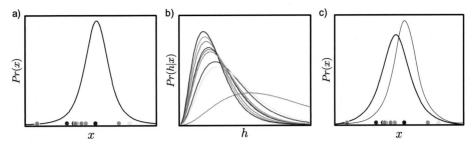

Figure 7.18 Expectation maximization for fitting t-distributions. a) Estimate of distribution before update. b) In the E-step, we calculate the posterior distribution $Pr(h_i|x_i)$ over the hidden variable h_i for each data point x_i. The color of each curve corresponds to that of the original data point in (a). c) In the M-step, we use these distributions over h to update the estimate of the parameters $\theta = \{\mu, \sigma^2, \nu\}$.

the hidden variable h_i determines which normal. So, the E-step computes a distribution over h_i, which hence determines a distribution over which normal created the data.

We now compute the following expectations (section 2.7) with respect to the distribution in Equation 7.25:

$$\mathrm{E}[h_i] = \frac{(\nu+D)}{\nu+(\mathbf{x}_i-\boldsymbol{\mu})^T\boldsymbol{\Sigma}^{-1}(\mathbf{x}_i-\boldsymbol{\mu})} \tag{7.26}$$

$$\mathrm{E}[\log[h_i]] = \Psi\left[\frac{\nu+D}{2}\right] - \log\left[\frac{\nu+(\mathbf{x}_i-\boldsymbol{\mu})^T\boldsymbol{\Sigma}^{-1}(\mathbf{x}_i-\boldsymbol{\mu})}{2}\right], \tag{7.27}$$

where $\Psi[\bullet])$ is the *digamma* function. These expectations will be needed in the M-step.

In the M-step (Figure 7.18c) we maximize the bound with respect to the parameters $\boldsymbol{\theta} = \{\boldsymbol{\mu}, \boldsymbol{\Sigma}, \nu\}$ so that

$$
\begin{aligned}
\hat{\boldsymbol{\theta}}^{[t+1]} &= \underset{\boldsymbol{\theta}}{\mathrm{argmax}}\left[\sum_{i=1}^{I}\int \hat{q}_i(h_i)\log\left[Pr(\mathbf{x}_i, h_i|\boldsymbol{\theta})\right]dh_i\right] \\
&= \underset{\boldsymbol{\theta}}{\mathrm{argmax}}\left[\sum_{i=1}^{I}\int \hat{q}_i(h_i)\left(\log\left[Pr(\mathbf{x}_i|h_i, \boldsymbol{\theta})\right] + \log\left[Pr(h_i)\right]\right)dh_i\right] \\
&= \underset{\boldsymbol{\theta}}{\mathrm{argmax}}\left[\sum_{i=1}^{I}\int Pr(h_i|\mathbf{x}_i, \boldsymbol{\theta}^{[t]})\left(\log\left[Pr(\mathbf{x}_i|h_i, \boldsymbol{\theta})\right] + \log\left[Pr(h_i)\right]\right)dh_i\right] \\
&= \underset{\boldsymbol{\theta}}{\mathrm{argmax}}\left[\sum_{i=1}^{I} E\left[\log\left[Pr(\mathbf{x}_i|h_i, \boldsymbol{\theta})\right]\right] + E\left[\log\left[Pr(h_i)\right]\right]\right], \tag{7.28}
\end{aligned}
$$

where the expectation is taken relative to the posterior distribution $Pr(h_i|\mathbf{x}_i, \boldsymbol{\theta}^{[t]})$. Substituting in the expressions for the normal likelihood $Pr(\mathbf{x}_i|h_i)$ and the gamma prior $Pr(h_i)$, we find that

$$E\left[\log\left[Pr(\mathbf{x}_i|h_i, \boldsymbol{\theta})\right]\right] = \frac{D\mathrm{E}[\log h_i] - D\log 2\pi - \log|\boldsymbol{\Sigma}| - (\mathbf{x}_i-\boldsymbol{\mu})^T\boldsymbol{\Sigma}^{-1}(\mathbf{x}_i-\boldsymbol{\mu})\mathrm{E}[h_i]}{2}$$

$$E\left[\log\left[Pr(h_i)\right]\right] = \frac{\nu}{2}\log\left[\frac{\nu}{2}\right] - \log\Gamma\left[\frac{\nu}{2}\right] + \left(\frac{\nu}{2} - 1\right)\mathrm{E}[\log h_i] - \frac{\nu}{2}\mathrm{E}[h_i]. \tag{7.29}$$

To optimize μ and Σ, we take derivatives of Equation 7.28, set the resulting expressions to zero and rearrange to yield update equations

$$\mu^{[t+1]} = \frac{\sum_{i=1}^{I} \mathrm{E}[h_i]\mathbf{x}_i}{\sum_{i=1}^{I} \mathrm{E}[h_i]}$$

$$\Sigma^{[t+1]} = \frac{\sum_{i=1}^{I} \mathrm{E}[h_i](\mathbf{x}_i - \mu^{[t+1]})(\mathbf{x}_i - \mu^{[t+1]})^T}{\sum_{i=1}^{I} \mathrm{E}[h_i]}. \tag{7.30}$$

These update equations have an intuitive form: for the mean, we are computing a weighted sum of the data. Outliers in the data set will tend to be explained best by the normal distributions in the infinite mixture which have larger covariances: for these distributions h is small (h scales the normal covariance inversely). Consequently, $\mathrm{E}[h]$ is small, and they are weighted less in the sum. The update for the Σ has a similar interpretation.

Unfortunately, there is no closed form solution for the degrees of freedom ν. We hence perform a one-dimensional line search to maximize Equation 7.28 having substituted in the updated values of μ and Σ, or use one of the optimization techniques described in Chapter 9.

When we fit a t-distribution with a diagonal scale matrix Σ to the face data set, the mean μ and scale matrix Σ (not shown) look visually similar to those for the normal model (Figure 7.2). However, the model is not the same. The fitted degrees of freedom ν is 6.6. This low value indicates that the distribution has significantly longer tails than the normal model.

In conclusion, the multivariate t-distribution provides an improved description of data with outliers (Figure 7.14). It has just one more parameter than the normal (the degrees of freedom, ν), and subsumes the normal as a special case (where ν becomes very large). However, this generality comes at a cost: there is no closed form solution for the maximum likelihood parameters and so we must resort to more complex approaches such as the EM algorithm to fit the distribution.

7.6 Factor analysis

We now address the final problem with the normal distribution. Visual data are often very high dimensional; in the face detection task, the data comes in the form of 60×60 RGB images and is hence characterized as a $60 \times 60 \times 3 = 10800$ dimensional vector. To model this data with the full multivariate normal distribution, we require a covariance matrix of dimensions 10800×10800: we would need a very large number of training examples to get good estimates of all of these parameters in the absence of prior information. Furthermore, to store the covariance matrix, we will need a large amount of memory, and there remains the problem of inverting this large matrix when we evaluate the normal likelihood (Equation 5.1).

Of course, we could just use the diagonal form of the covariance matrix, which contains only 10800 parameters. However, this is too great a simplification: we are assuming that each dimension of the data is independent and for face images this is clearly not true. For example, in the cheek region, the RGB values of neighboring pixels covary very closely. A good model should capture this information.

Factor analysis provides a compromise in which the covariance matrix is structured so that it contains fewer unknown parameters than the full matrix but more than the diagonal form. One way to think about the covariance of a factor analyzer is that it models part

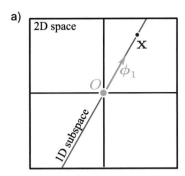 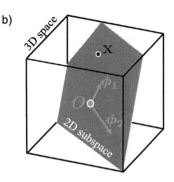

Figure 7.19 Linear subspaces. a) A one-dimensional subspace (a line through the origin, O) is embedded in a two-dimensional space. Any point $\mathbf{x}$ in the subspace can be reached by weighting the single basis vector $\boldsymbol{\phi}_1$ appropriately. b) A two-dimensional subspace (a plane through the origin, O) is embedded in a three dimensional space. Any point $\mathbf{x}$ in the subspace can be reached using a linear combination $\mathbf{x} = \alpha\boldsymbol{\phi}_1 + \beta\boldsymbol{\phi}_2$ of the two basis functions $\boldsymbol{\phi}_1, \boldsymbol{\phi}_2$ that describe the subspace. In general, a K-dimensional subspace can be described using K basis functions.

of the high-dimensional space with a full model and mops up remaining variation with a diagonal model.

More precisely, the factor analyzer describes a *linear subspace* with a full covariance model. A linear subspace is a subset of a high-dimensional space that can be reached by taking linear combinations (weighted sums) of a fixed set of basis functions (Figure 7.19). So, a line through the origin is a subspace in two dimensions as we can reach any point on it by weighting a single-basis vector. A line through the origin is also a subspace in three dimensions, but so is a plane through the origin: we can reach any point on the plane by taking linear combinations of two basis vectors. In general, a D-dimensional space contains subspaces of dimensions $1, 2, \ldots, D-1$.

The probability density function of a factor analyzer is given by

$$Pr(\mathbf{x}) = \text{Norm}_{\mathbf{x}}[\boldsymbol{\mu}, \boldsymbol{\Phi}\boldsymbol{\Phi}^T + \boldsymbol{\Sigma}], \tag{7.31}$$

where the covariance matrix $\boldsymbol{\Phi}\boldsymbol{\Phi}^T + \boldsymbol{\Sigma}$ contains a sum of two terms. The first term $\boldsymbol{\Phi}\boldsymbol{\Phi}^T$ describes a full covariance model over the subspace: the K columns of the portrait[1] rectangular matrix $\boldsymbol{\Phi} = [\boldsymbol{\phi}_1, \boldsymbol{\phi}_2, \ldots, \boldsymbol{\phi}_K]$ are termed *factors*. The factors are basis vectors that determine the subspace modeled. When we fit the model to data, the factors will span the set of directions where the data covary the most. The second term $\boldsymbol{\Sigma}$ is a diagonal matrix that accounts for all remaining variation.

Notice that this model has $K \times D$ parameters to describe $\boldsymbol{\Phi}$ and another D parameters to describe the diagonal matrix $\boldsymbol{\Sigma}$. If the number of factors K is much less than the dimensionality of the data D, then this model has fewer parameters than a normal with full covariance and hence can be learned from fewer training examples.

When $\boldsymbol{\Sigma}$ is a constant multiple of the identity matrix (i.e., models spherical covariance) the model is called *probabilistic principal component analysis*. This simpler model has slightly fewer parameters and can be fit in closed form (i.e., without the need for the EM algorithm), but otherwise it has no advantages over factor analysis (see Section 17.5.1 for more details). We will hence restrict ourselves to a discussion of the more general factor analysis model.

---

[1]That is, it is tall and thin as opposed to landscape, which would be short and wide.

7.6.1   Factor analysis as a marginalization

As for the mixtures of Gaussians and the t-distribution, it is possible to view the factor analysis model as a marginalization of a joint distribution between the observed data $\mathbf{x}$ and a K-dimensional hidden variable $\mathbf{h}$. We define

$$Pr(\mathbf{x}|\mathbf{h}) = \text{Norm}_{\mathbf{x}}[\boldsymbol{\mu} + \boldsymbol{\Phi}\mathbf{h}, \boldsymbol{\Sigma}]$$
$$Pr(\mathbf{h}) = \text{Norm}_{\mathbf{h}}[\mathbf{0}, \mathbf{I}], \tag{7.32}$$

where $\mathbf{I}$ represents the identity matrix. It can be shown (but is not obvious) that

$$Pr(\mathbf{x}) = \int Pr(\mathbf{x}, \mathbf{h}) d\mathbf{h} = \int Pr(\mathbf{x}|\mathbf{h}) Pr(\mathbf{h}) \, d\mathbf{h}$$

$$= \int \text{Norm}_{\mathbf{x}}[\boldsymbol{\mu} + \boldsymbol{\Phi}\mathbf{h}, \boldsymbol{\Sigma}] \text{Norm}_{\mathbf{h}}[\mathbf{0}, \mathbf{I}] \, d\mathbf{h}$$

$$= \text{Norm}_{\mathbf{x}}[\boldsymbol{\mu}, \boldsymbol{\Phi}\boldsymbol{\Phi}^{T} + \boldsymbol{\Sigma}], \tag{7.33}$$

which was the original definition of the factor analyzer (Equation 7.31).

Expressing factor analysis as a marginalization reveals a simple method to draw samples from the distribution. We first draw a hidden variable $\mathbf{h}$ from the normal prior. We then draw the sample $\mathbf{x}$ from a normal distribution with mean $\boldsymbol{\mu} + \boldsymbol{\Phi}\mathbf{h}$ and diagonal covariance $\boldsymbol{\Sigma}$ (see Equation 7.32).

This leads us to a simple interpretation of the hidden variable $\mathbf{h}$: each element h_k weights the associated basis function ϕ_k in the matrix $\boldsymbol{\Phi}$ and so $\mathbf{h}$ defines a point on the subspace (Figure 7.19). The final density (Equation 7.31) is hence an infinite weighted sum of normal distributions with the same diagonal covariance $\boldsymbol{\Sigma}$ and means $\boldsymbol{\mu} + \boldsymbol{\Phi}\mathbf{h}$ that are distributed over the subspace. The relationship between mixture models and factor analysis is explored further in Figure 7.20.

7.6.2   Expectation maximization for learning factor analyzers

Since the factor analyzer can be expressed as a marginalization of a joint distribution between the observed data $\mathbf{x}$ and a hidden variable $\mathbf{h}$ (Equation 7.33), it is possible to use the EM algorithm to learn the parameters $\boldsymbol{\theta} = \{\boldsymbol{\mu}, \boldsymbol{\Phi}, \boldsymbol{\Sigma}\}$. Once more, we follow the recipe described in Section 7.3.

In the E-step (Figure 7.21), we optimize the bound with respect to the distributions $q_i(\mathbf{h}_i)$. To do this we compute the posterior probability distribution $Pr(\mathbf{h}_i|\mathbf{x}_i)$ over each hidden variable $\mathbf{h}_i$ given the associated observed data $\mathbf{x}_i$ and the current values of the parameters $\boldsymbol{\theta}^{[t]}$. To this end we apply Bayes' rule:

$$\hat{q}(\mathbf{h}_i) = Pr(\mathbf{h}_i|\mathbf{x}_i, \boldsymbol{\theta}^{[t]}) \tag{7.34}$$

$$= \frac{Pr(\mathbf{x}_i|\mathbf{h}_i, \boldsymbol{\theta}^{[t]}) Pr(\mathbf{h}_i)}{Pr(\mathbf{x}_i|\boldsymbol{\theta}^{[t]})}$$

$$= \frac{\text{Norm}_{\mathbf{x}_i}[\boldsymbol{\mu} + \boldsymbol{\Phi}\mathbf{h}_i, \boldsymbol{\Sigma}] \text{Norm}_{\mathbf{h}_i}[\mathbf{0}, \mathbf{I}]}{Pr(\mathbf{x}_i|\boldsymbol{\theta}^{[t]})}$$

$$= \text{Norm}_{\mathbf{h}_i}[(\boldsymbol{\Phi}^{T}\boldsymbol{\Sigma}^{-1}\boldsymbol{\Phi} + \mathbf{I})^{-1}\boldsymbol{\Phi}^{T}\boldsymbol{\Sigma}^{-1}(\mathbf{x}_i - \boldsymbol{\mu}), (\boldsymbol{\Phi}^{T}\boldsymbol{\Sigma}^{-1}\boldsymbol{\Phi} + \mathbf{I})^{-1}],$$

where we have made use of the change of variables relation (Section 5.7) and then the fact that the product of two normals is proportional to a third normal (Section 5.6).

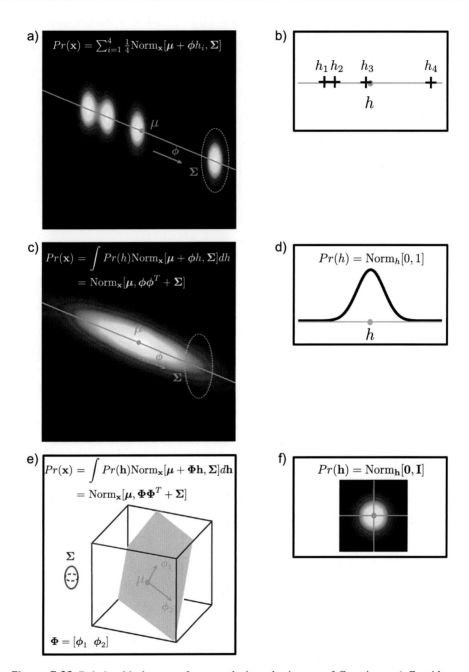

Figure 7.20 Relationship between factor analysis and mixtures of Gaussians. a) Consider an MoG model where each component has identical diagonal covariance $\boldsymbol{\Sigma}$. We could describe variation in a particular direction $\boldsymbol{\phi}$ by parameterizing the mean of each Gaussian as $\boldsymbol{\mu}_i = \boldsymbol{\mu} + \boldsymbol{\phi}h_i$. b) Different values of the scalar hidden variable h_i determine different positions along direction $\boldsymbol{\phi}$. c) Now we replace the MoG with an infinite sum (integral) over a continuous family of Gaussians, each of which is determined by a certain value of h. d) If we choose the prior over the hidden variable to be normal, this integral has a closed form solution and is a factor analyzer. e) More generally we want to describe variance in a set of directions $\boldsymbol{\Phi} = [\boldsymbol{\phi}_1, \boldsymbol{\phi}_2, \ldots, \boldsymbol{\phi}_K]$ in a high dimensional space. f) To this end we use a K-dimensional hidden variable $\mathbf{h}$ and an associated normal prior $Pr(\mathbf{h})$.

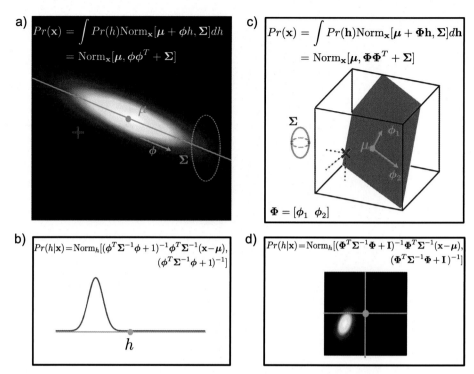

Figure 7.21 E-step for expectation maximization algorithm for factor analysis. a) Two-dimensional case with one factor. We are given a data point $\mathbf{x}$ (purple cross). b) In the E-step we seek a distribution over possible values of the associated hidden variable h. It can be shown that this posterior distribution over h is itself normally distributed. c) Three-dimensional case with two factors. Given a data point $\mathbf{x}$ (purple cross), we aim to find a distribution (d) over possible values of the associated hidden variable $\mathbf{h}$. Once more this posterior is normally distributed.

The resulting constant of proportionality exactly cancels out with the term $Pr(\mathbf{x})$ in the denominator, ensuring that the result is a valid probability distribution.

The E-step computes a probability distribution over the possible causes $\mathbf{h}$ for the observed data. This implicitly defines a probability distribution over the positions $\mathbf{\Phi h}$ on the subspace that might have generated this example.

We extract the following expectations from the posterior distribution (Equation 7.34) as they will be needed in the M-step:

$$
\begin{aligned}
\mathrm{E}[\mathbf{h}_i] &= (\mathbf{\Phi}^T \mathbf{\Sigma}^{-1} \mathbf{\Phi} + \mathbf{I})^{-1} \mathbf{\Phi}^T \mathbf{\Sigma}^{-1} (\mathbf{x}_i - \boldsymbol{\mu}) \\
\mathrm{E}[\mathbf{h}_i \mathbf{h}_i^T] &= E\left[(\mathbf{h}_i - \mathrm{E}[\mathbf{h}_i])(\mathbf{h}_i - \mathrm{E}[\mathbf{h}_i])^T\right] + \mathrm{E}[\mathbf{h}_i]\mathrm{E}[\mathbf{h}_i]^T \\
&= (\mathbf{\Phi}^T \mathbf{\Sigma}^{-1} \mathbf{\Phi} + \mathbf{I})^{-1} + \mathrm{E}[\mathbf{h}_i]\mathrm{E}[\mathbf{h}_i]^T.
\end{aligned} \tag{7.35}
$$

In the M-step, we optimize the bound with respect to the parameters $\boldsymbol{\theta} = \{\boldsymbol{\mu}, \mathbf{\Phi}, \mathbf{\Sigma}\}$ so that

$$
\hat{\boldsymbol{\theta}}^{[t+1]} = \underset{\boldsymbol{\theta}}{\mathrm{argmax}} \left[\sum_{i=1}^{I} \int \hat{q}_i(\mathbf{h}_i) \log\left[Pr(\mathbf{x}, \mathbf{h}_i, \boldsymbol{\theta})\right] d\mathbf{h}_i \right]
$$

$$= \underset{\boldsymbol{\theta}}{\operatorname{argmax}} \left[\sum_{i=1}^{I} \int \hat{q}_i(\mathbf{h}_i) \left[\log\left[Pr(\mathbf{x}|\mathbf{h}_i, \boldsymbol{\theta})\right] + \log\left[Pr(\mathbf{h}_i)\right] \right] d\mathbf{h}_i \right]$$

$$= \underset{\boldsymbol{\theta}}{\operatorname{argmax}} \left[\sum_{i=1}^{I} \int \hat{q}_i(\mathbf{h}_i) \log\left[Pr(\mathbf{x}|\mathbf{h}_i, \boldsymbol{\theta})\right] d\mathbf{h}_i \right]$$

$$= \underset{\boldsymbol{\theta}}{\operatorname{argmax}} \left[\sum_{i=1}^{I} E\left[\log Pr(\mathbf{x}|\mathbf{h}_i, \boldsymbol{\theta})\right] \right], \tag{7.36}$$

where we have removed the term $\log[Pr(\mathbf{h}_i)]$ as it is not dependent on the variables $\boldsymbol{\theta}$. The expectations $E[\bullet]$ are taken with respect to the relevant posterior distributions $\hat{q}_i(\mathbf{h}_i) = Pr(\mathbf{h}_i|\mathbf{x}_i, \boldsymbol{\theta}^{[t]})$. The expression for $\log[Pr(\mathbf{x}_i|\mathbf{h}_i)]$ is given by

$$\log Pr(\mathbf{x}_i|\mathbf{h}_i) = -\frac{D\log[2\pi] + \log[|\boldsymbol{\Sigma}|] + (\mathbf{x}_i - \boldsymbol{\mu} - \boldsymbol{\Phi}\mathbf{h}_i)^T \boldsymbol{\Sigma}^{-1}(\mathbf{x}_i - \boldsymbol{\mu} - \boldsymbol{\Phi}\mathbf{h}_i)}{2}. \tag{7.37}$$

We optimize Equation 7.36 by taking derivatives with respect to the parameters $\boldsymbol{\theta} = \{\boldsymbol{\mu}, \boldsymbol{\Phi}, \boldsymbol{\Sigma}\}$, equating the resulting expressions to zero and rearranging to yield

$$\hat{\boldsymbol{\mu}} = \frac{\sum_{i=1}^{I} \mathbf{x}_i}{I}$$

$$\hat{\boldsymbol{\Phi}} = \left(\sum_{i=1}^{I} (\mathbf{x}_i - \hat{\boldsymbol{\mu}}) E[\mathbf{h}_i]^T \right) \left(\sum_{i=1}^{I} E[\mathbf{h}_i \mathbf{h}_i^T] \right)^{-1}$$

$$\hat{\boldsymbol{\Sigma}} = \frac{1}{I} \sum_{i=1}^{I} \operatorname{diag}\left[(\mathbf{x}_i - \hat{\boldsymbol{\mu}})(\mathbf{x}_i - \hat{\boldsymbol{\mu}})^T - \hat{\boldsymbol{\Phi}} E[\mathbf{h}_i](\mathbf{x}_i - \hat{\boldsymbol{\mu}})^T \right], \tag{7.38}$$

where the function $\operatorname{diag}[\bullet]$ is the operation of setting all elements of the matrix argument to zero except those on the diagonal.

Figure 7.22 shows the parameters of a factor analysis model fitted to the face data using ten iterations of the EM algorithm. The different factors encode different *modes of variation* of the data set, which often have real-world interpretations such as changes in pose or lighting.

In conclusion, the factor analyzer is an efficient model for capturing the covariance in high-dimensional data. It devotes one set of parameters $\boldsymbol{\Phi}$ to describing the directions in which the data are most correlated and a second set $\boldsymbol{\Sigma}$ describes the remaining variation.

7.7   Combining models

The mixture of Gaussians, t-distribution, and factor analysis models are constructed similarly: each is a weighted sum or integral of a set of constituent normal distributions. Mixture of Gaussian models consist of a weighted sum of K normal distributions with different means and variances. The t-distribution consists of an infinite weighted sum of normal distributions with the same mean, but different covariances. Factor analysis models consist of an infinite weighted sum of normal distributions with different means, but the same diagonal covariance.

In light of these similarities, it is perhaps unsurprising then that the models can be easily combined. If we combine mixture models and factor analyzers, we get a *mixture*

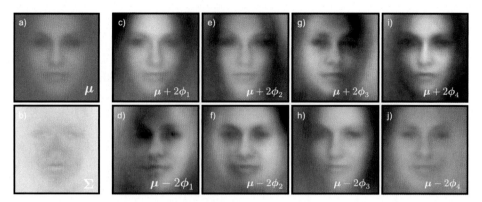

Figure 7.22 Factor analyzer with ten factors (four shown) for face classes. a) Mean μ for face model. b) Diagonal covariance component Σ for face model. To visualize the effect of the first factor ϕ_1 we add (c) or subtract (d) a multiple of it from the mean: we are moving along one axis of the 10D subspace that seems to encode mainly the mean intensity. Other factors (e–j) encode changes in the hue and the pose of the face.

of factor analyzers (MoFA) model. This is a weighted sum of factor analyzers, each of which has a different mean and allocates high probability density to a different subspace. Similarly, combining mixture models and t-distributions results in a *mixture of t-distributions* or *robust mixture model*. Combining t-distributions and factor analyzers, we can construct a *robust subspace model*, which models data that lie primarily in a subspace but is tolerant to outliers. Finally, combining all three models, we get a *mixture of robust subspace models*. This has the combined benefits of all three approaches (it is multimodal and robust and makes efficient use of parameters). The associated density function is

$$Pr(\mathbf{x}) = \sum_{k=1}^{K} \lambda_k \text{Stud}_\mathbf{x}\left[\boldsymbol{\mu}_k, \boldsymbol{\Phi}_k\boldsymbol{\Phi}_k^T + \Sigma_k, \nu_k\right], \tag{7.39}$$

where $\boldsymbol{\mu}_k, \boldsymbol{\Phi}_k$ and Σ_k represent the mean, factors and diagonal covariance matrix belonging to the kth component, λ_k represents the weighting of the kth component and ν_k represents the degrees of freedom of the kth component. To learn this model, we would use a series of interleaved expectation maximization algorithms.

7.8   Expectation maximization in detail

Throughout this chapter, we have employed the expectation maximization algorithm, using the recipe from Section 7.3. We now examine the EM algorithm in detail to understand why this recipe works.

The EM algorithm is used to find maximum likelihood or MAP estimates of model parameters $\boldsymbol{\theta}$ where the likelihood $Pr(\mathbf{x}|\boldsymbol{\theta})$ of the data $\mathbf{x}$ can be written as

$$Pr(\mathbf{x}|\boldsymbol{\theta}) = \sum_k Pr(\mathbf{x}, h = k|\boldsymbol{\theta}) = \sum_k Pr(\mathbf{x}|h = k, \boldsymbol{\theta})Pr(h = k) \tag{7.40}$$

and

$$Pr(\mathbf{x}|\boldsymbol{\theta}) = \int Pr(\mathbf{x}, \mathbf{h}|\boldsymbol{\theta}) \, d\mathbf{h} = \int Pr(\mathbf{x}|\mathbf{h}, \boldsymbol{\theta})Pr(\mathbf{h}) \, d\mathbf{h} \tag{7.41}$$

for discrete and continuous hidden variables, respectively. In other words, the likelihood $Pr(\mathbf{x}|\boldsymbol{\theta})$ is a marginalization of a joint distribution over the data and the hidden variables. We will work with the continuous case.

The EM algorithm relies on the idea of a lower bounding function (or *lower bound*), $\mathcal{B}[\boldsymbol{\theta}]$ on the log likelihood. This is a function of the parameters $\boldsymbol{\theta}$ that is always guaranteed to be equal to or lower than the log likelihood. The lower bound is carefully chosen so that it is easy to maximize with respect to the parameters.

This lower bound is also parameterized by a set of probability distributions $\{q_i(\mathbf{h}_i)\}_{i=1}^{I}$ over the hidden variables, so we write it as $\mathcal{B}[\{q_i(\mathbf{h}_i)\}, \boldsymbol{\theta}]$. Different probability distributions $q_i(\mathbf{h}_i)$ predict different lower bounds $\mathcal{B}[\{q_i(\mathbf{h}_i)\}, \boldsymbol{\theta}]$ and hence different functions of $\boldsymbol{\theta}$ that lie everywhere below the true log likelihood (Figure 7.5b).

In the EM algorithm, we alternate between expectation steps (E-steps) and maximization steps (M-steps) where

- in the E-step (Figure 7.23a) we fix $\boldsymbol{\theta}$ and find the best lower bound $\mathcal{B}[\{q_i(\mathbf{h}_i)\}, \boldsymbol{\theta}]$ with respect to the distributions $q_i(\mathbf{h}_i)$. In other words, at iteration t

$$q_i^{[t]}[\mathbf{h}_i] = \underset{q_i[\mathbf{h}_i]}{\operatorname{argmax}} \left[\mathcal{B}[\{q_i(\mathbf{h}_i)\}, \boldsymbol{\theta}^{[t-1]}] \right]. \tag{7.42}$$

The best lower bound will be a function that is as high as possible at the current parameter estimates $\boldsymbol{\theta}$. Since it must be everywhere equal to or lower than the log likelihood, the highest possible value is the log likelihood itself. So the bound touches the log-likelihood curve for the current parameters $\boldsymbol{\theta}$.

- in the M-step (Figure 7.23b), we fix $q_i(\mathbf{h}_i)$ and find the values of $\boldsymbol{\theta}$ that maximize this bounding function $\mathcal{B}[\{q_i(\mathbf{h}_i)\}, \boldsymbol{\theta}]$. In other words, we compute

$$\boldsymbol{\theta}^{[t]} = \underset{\boldsymbol{\theta}}{\operatorname{argmax}} \left[\mathcal{B}[\{q_i^{[t]}(\mathbf{h}_i)\}, \boldsymbol{\theta}] \right]. \tag{7.43}$$

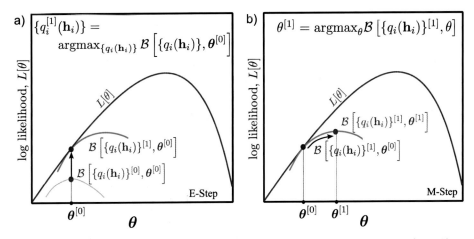

Figure 7.23 E-step and M-step. a) In the E-step, we manipulate the distributions $\{q_i(\mathbf{h}_i)\}$ to find the best new lower bound given parameters $\boldsymbol{\theta}$. This optimal lower bound will touch the log likelihood at the current parameter values $\boldsymbol{\theta}$ (we cannot do better than this!). b) In the M-step, we hold $\{q_i(\mathbf{h}_i)\}$ constant and optimize $\boldsymbol{\theta}$ with respect to the new bound.

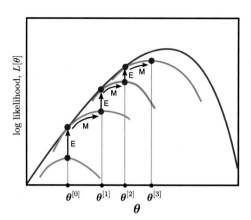

Figure 7.24 Expectation maximization algorithm. We iterate the expectation and maximization steps by alternately changing the distributions $q_i(\mathbf{h}_i)$ and the parameter $\boldsymbol{\theta}$ so that the bound increases. In the E-step, the bound is maximized with respect to $q_i(\mathbf{h}_i)$ for fixed parameters $\boldsymbol{\theta}$: the new function with respect to $\boldsymbol{\theta}$ touches the true log likelihood at $\boldsymbol{\theta}$. In the M-step, we find the maximum of this function. In this way we are guaranteed to reach a local maximum in the likelihood function.

By iterating these steps, the (local) maximum of the actual log likelihood is approached (Figure 7.24). To complete our picture of the EM algorithm, we must

- Define $\mathcal{B}[\{q_i(\mathbf{h}_i)\}, \boldsymbol{\theta}^{[t-1]}]$ and show that it always lies below the log likelihood,
- Show which probability distribution $q_i(\mathbf{h}_i)$ optimizes the bound in the E-step,
- Show how to optimize the bound with respect to $\boldsymbol{\theta}$ in the M-step.

These three issues are tackled in Sections 7.8.1, 7.8.2 and 7.8.3, respectively.

7.8.1 Lower bound for EM algorithm

We define the lower bound $\mathcal{B}[\{q_i(\mathbf{h}_i)\}, \boldsymbol{\theta}]$ to be

$$
\begin{aligned}
\mathcal{B}[\{q_i(\mathbf{h}_i)\}, \boldsymbol{\theta}] &= \sum_{i=1}^{I} \int q_i(\mathbf{h}_i) \log \left[\frac{Pr(\mathbf{x}_i, \mathbf{h}_i | \boldsymbol{\theta})}{q_i(\mathbf{h}_i)} \right] d\mathbf{h}_i \\
&\leq \sum_{i=1}^{I} \log \left[\int q_i(\mathbf{h}_i) \frac{Pr(\mathbf{x}_i, \mathbf{h}_i | \boldsymbol{\theta})}{q_i(\mathbf{h}_i)} d\mathbf{h}_i \right] \\
&= \sum_{i=1}^{I} \log \left[\int Pr(\mathbf{x}_i, \mathbf{h}_i | \boldsymbol{\theta}) \, d\mathbf{h}_i \right],
\end{aligned}
\tag{7.44}
$$

where we have used *Jensen's inequality* between the first and second lines. This states that because the logarithm is a concave function, we can write

$$
\int Pr(y) \log[y] dy \leq \log \left[\int y Pr(y) dy \right]
\tag{7.45}
$$

or $\mathrm{E}[\log[y]] \leq \log(\mathrm{E}[y])$. Figure 7.25 illustrates Jensen's inequality for a discrete variable.

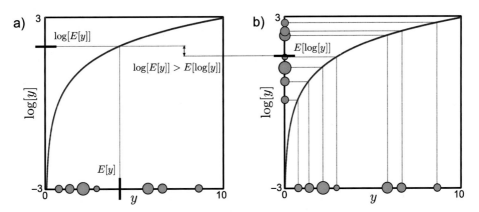

Figure 7.25 Jensen's inequality for the logarithmic function (discrete case). a) Taking a weighted average of examples E[y] and passing them through the log function. b) Passing the samples through the log function and taking a weighted average E[log[y]]. The latter case always produces a smaller value than the former (E[log[y]] $\leq$ log(E[y])): higher valued examples are relatively compressed by the concave log function.

7.8.2   The E-Step

In the E-step, we update the bound $\mathcal{B}[\{q_i(\mathbf{h}_i)\}, \boldsymbol{\theta}]$ with respect to the distributions $q_i(\mathbf{h}_i)$. To see how to do this, we manipulate the expression for the bound as follows:

$$
\begin{aligned}
\mathcal{B}[\{q_i(\mathbf{h}_i)\}, \boldsymbol{\theta}] &= \sum_{i=1}^{I} \int q_i(\mathbf{h}_i) \log \left[\frac{Pr(\mathbf{x}_i, \mathbf{h}_i | \boldsymbol{\theta})}{q_i(\mathbf{h}_i)} \right] d\mathbf{h}_i \\
&= \sum_{i=1}^{I} \int q_i(\mathbf{h}_i) \log \left[\frac{Pr(\mathbf{h}_i | \mathbf{x}_i, \boldsymbol{\theta}) Pr(\mathbf{x}_i | \boldsymbol{\theta})}{q_i(\mathbf{h}_i)} \right] d\mathbf{h}_i \\
&= \sum_{i=1}^{I} \int q_i(\mathbf{h}_i) \log \left[Pr(\mathbf{x}_i | \boldsymbol{\theta}) \right] d\mathbf{h}_i - \sum_{i=1}^{I} \int q_i(\mathbf{h}_i) \log \left[\frac{q_i(\mathbf{h}_i)}{Pr(\mathbf{h}_i | \mathbf{x}_i, \boldsymbol{\theta})} \right] d\mathbf{h}_i \\
&= \sum_{i=1}^{I} \log \left[Pr(\mathbf{x}_i | \boldsymbol{\theta}) \right] - \sum_{i=1}^{I} \int q_i(\mathbf{h}_i) \log \left[\frac{q_i(\mathbf{h}_i)}{Pr(\mathbf{h}_i | \mathbf{x}_i, \boldsymbol{\theta})} \right] d\mathbf{h}_i, \quad (7.46)
\end{aligned}
$$

where the hidden variables from the first term are integrated out between the last two lines. The first term in this expression is constant with respect to the distributions $q_i(\mathbf{h}_i)$, and so to optimize the bound we must find the distributions $\hat{q}_i(\mathbf{h}_i)$ that satisfy

$$
\begin{aligned}
\hat{q}_i(\mathbf{h}_i) &= \operatorname*{argmax}_{q_i(\mathbf{h}_i)} \left[-\int q_i(\mathbf{h}_i) \log \left[\frac{q_i(\mathbf{h}_i)}{Pr(\mathbf{h}_i | \mathbf{x}_i, \boldsymbol{\theta})} \right] d\mathbf{h}_i \right] \\
&= \operatorname*{argmax}_{q_i(\mathbf{h}_i)} \left[\int q_i(\mathbf{h}_i) \log \left[\frac{Pr(\mathbf{h}_i | \mathbf{x}_i, \boldsymbol{\theta})}{q_i(\mathbf{h}_i)} \right] d\mathbf{h}_i \right] \\
&= \operatorname*{argmin}_{q_i(\mathbf{h}_i)} \left[-\int q_i(\mathbf{h}_i) \log \left[\frac{Pr(\mathbf{h}_i | \mathbf{x}_i, \boldsymbol{\theta})}{q_i(\mathbf{h}_i)} \right] d\mathbf{h}_i \right]. \quad (7.47)
\end{aligned}
$$

This expression is known as the *Kullback-Leibler* divergence between $q_i(\mathbf{h}_i)$ and $Pr(\mathbf{h}_i | \mathbf{x}_i, \boldsymbol{\theta})$. It is a measure of distance between probability distributions. We can use the inequality $\log[y] \leq y - 1$ (plot the functions to convince yourself of this!) to show that this cost function (including the minus sign) is always positive,

$$\int q_i(\mathbf{h}_i) \log\left[\frac{Pr(\mathbf{h}_i|\mathbf{x}_i, \boldsymbol{\theta})}{q_i(\mathbf{h}_i)}\right] d\mathbf{h}_i \leq \int q_i(\mathbf{h}_i) \left(\frac{Pr(\mathbf{h}_i|\mathbf{x}_i, \boldsymbol{\theta})}{q_i(\mathbf{h}_i)} - 1\right) d\mathbf{h}_i$$
$$= \int Pr(\mathbf{h}_i|\mathbf{x}_i, \boldsymbol{\theta}) - q_i(\mathbf{h}_i) \, d\mathbf{h}_i$$
$$= 1 - 1 = 0, \tag{7.48}$$

implying that when we reintroduce the minus sign the cost function *must* be positive. So the criteria in Equation 7.46 will be maximized when the Kullback-Leibler divergence is zero. This value is reached when $q_i(\mathbf{h}_i) = Pr(\mathbf{h}_i|\mathbf{x}_i, \boldsymbol{\theta})$ so that

$$\int q_i(\mathbf{h}_i) \log\left[\frac{Pr(\mathbf{h}_i|\mathbf{x}_i, \boldsymbol{\theta})}{q_i(\mathbf{h}_i)}\right] d\mathbf{h}_i = \int Pr(\mathbf{h}_i|\mathbf{x}_i, \boldsymbol{\theta}) \log\left[\frac{Pr(\mathbf{h}_i|\mathbf{x}_i, \boldsymbol{\theta})}{Pr(\mathbf{h}_i|\mathbf{x}_i, \boldsymbol{\theta})}\right] d\mathbf{h}_i$$
$$= \int Pr(\mathbf{h}_i|\mathbf{x}_i, \boldsymbol{\theta}) \log[1] \, d\mathbf{h}_i = 0. \tag{7.49}$$

In other words, to maximize the bound with respect to $q_i(\mathbf{h}_i)$, we set this to be the posterior distribution $Pr(\mathbf{h}_i|\mathbf{x}_i, \boldsymbol{\theta})$ over the hidden variables $\mathbf{h}_i$ given the current set of parameters. In practice, this is computed using Bayes' rule,

$$Pr(\mathbf{h}_i|\mathbf{x}_i, \boldsymbol{\theta}) = \frac{Pr(\mathbf{x}_i|\mathbf{h}_i, \boldsymbol{\theta}) Pr(\mathbf{h}_i)}{Pr(\mathbf{x}_i)}. \tag{7.50}$$

So the E-step consists of computing the posterior distribution for each hidden variable using Bayes' rule.

7.8.3   The M-Step

In the M-step, we maximize the bound with respect to the parameters $\boldsymbol{\theta}$ so that

$$\boldsymbol{\theta}^{[t]} = \underset{\boldsymbol{\theta}}{\mathrm{argmax}} \left[\mathcal{B}[\{q_i^{[t]}(\mathbf{h}_i)\}, \boldsymbol{\theta}]\right]$$
$$= \underset{\boldsymbol{\theta}}{\mathrm{argmax}} \left[\sum_{i=1}^{I} \int q_i^{[t]}(\mathbf{h}_i) \log\left[\frac{Pr(\mathbf{x}_i, \mathbf{h}_i|\boldsymbol{\theta})}{q_i^{[t]}(\mathbf{h}_i)}\right] d\mathbf{h}_i\right]$$

$$= \operatorname*{argmax}_{\boldsymbol{\theta}} \left[\sum_{i=1}^{I} \int q_i^{[t]}(\mathbf{h}_i) \log \left[Pr(\mathbf{x}_i, \mathbf{h}_i | \boldsymbol{\theta}) \right] - q_i^{[t]}(\mathbf{h}_i) \log \left[q_i^{[t]}(\mathbf{h}_i) \right] d\mathbf{h}_i \right]$$

$$= \operatorname*{argmax}_{\boldsymbol{\theta}} \left[\sum_{i=1}^{I} \int q_i^{[t]}(\mathbf{h}_i) \log \left[Pr(\mathbf{x}_i, \mathbf{h}_i | \boldsymbol{\theta}) \right] d\mathbf{h}_i \right], \tag{7.51}$$

where we have omitted the second term as it does not depend on the parameters. If you look back at the algorithms in this chapter, you will see that we have maximized exactly this criterion.

7.9 Applications

The models in this chapter have many uses in computer vision. We now present a cross-section of applications. As an example of two-class classification using mixtures of Gaussians densities, we reconsider the face detection application that has been a running theme throughout this chapter. To illustrate multiclass classification, we describe an object recognition model based on t-distributions. We also describe a segmentation application which is an example of unsupervised learning: we do not have labeled training data to build our model.

To illustrate the use of the factor analyzer for classification, we present a face recognition example. To illustrate its use for regression, we consider the problem of changing a face image from one pose to another. Finally, we highlight the fact that hidden variables can take on real-world interpretations by considering a model that explains the weak spatial alignment of digits.

7.9.1 Face detection

In face detection, we attempt to infer a discrete label $w \in \{0, 1\}$ indicating whether a face is present or not based on observed data $\mathbf{x}$. We will describe the likelihood for each world state with a mixtures of Gaussians model, where the covariances of the Gaussian components are constrained to be diagonal so that

$$Pr(\mathbf{x}|w = m) = \sum_{k=1}^{K} \lambda_{km} \operatorname{Norm}_{\mathbf{x}}[\boldsymbol{\mu}_{km}, \boldsymbol{\Sigma}_{km}], \tag{7.52}$$

where m indexes the world state and k indexes the component of the mixture distribution.

We will assume that we have no prior knowledge about whether the face is present or not so that $Pr(w = 0) = Pr(w = 1) = 0.5$. We fit the two likelihood terms using a set of labeled training pairs $\{\mathbf{x}_i, w_i\}$. In practice this means learning one mixtures of Gaussians model for the non-faces based on the data where $w_i = 0$ and a separate model for the faces based on the data where $w = 1$.

For test data $\mathbf{x}^*$, we compute the posterior probability over w using Bayes' rule:

$$Pr(w^* = 1|\mathbf{x}^*) = \frac{Pr(\mathbf{x}^*|w^* = 1)Pr(w^* = 1)}{\sum_{k=0}^{1} Pr(\mathbf{x}^*|w^* = k)Pr(w^* = k)}. \tag{7.53}$$

Table 7.1 shows percent correct classification for 100 test examples The results are based on models learned from 1000 training examples of each class.

	Color	Grayscale	Equalized
Single Gaussian	76%	79%	80%
Mixture of 10 Gaussians	81%	85%	89%

Table 7.1 Percent correct classification rates for two different models and three different types of preprocessing. In each case, the data $\mathbf{x}^*$ was assigned to be a face if the posterior probability $Pr(w = 1|\mathbf{x}^*)$ was greater than 0.5.

The first column shows results where the data vector consists of the RGB values with a 24×24 region (the running example in this chapter used 60×60 pixel regions, but this is unnecessarily large). The results are compared to classification based on a single normal distribution. The subsequent columns of the table show results for systems trained and tested with grayscale 24×24 pixel regions and grayscale 24×24 regions that have been histogram equalized (Section 13.1.2).

There are two insights to be gleaned from these classification results. First, the choice of model does make a difference; the mixtures of Gaussians density always results in better classification performance than the single Gaussian model. Second, the choice of *preprocessing* is also critical to the final performance. This book concerns models for vision, but it is important to understand that this is not the only thing that determines the final performance of real-world systems. A brief summary of preprocessing methods is presented in Chapter 13.

The reader should not depart with the impression that this is a sensible approach to face detection. Even the best performance of 89% is far below what would be required in a real face detector: consider that in a single image we might classify patches at 10000 different positions and scales, so an 11% error rate will be unacceptable. Moreover, evaluating each patch under both class conditional density functions is too computationally expensive to be practical. In practice, face detection would normally be achieved using discriminative methods (see Chapter 9).

7.9.2 Object recognition

In object recognition, the goal is to assign a discrete world vector $w_i \in \{1, 2, \ldots, M\}$ indicating which of M categories is present based on observed data $\mathbf{x}_i$ from the ith image. To this end, Aeschliman et al. (2010) split each image into 100 10×10 pixel regions arranged in a regular grid. The grayscale pixel data $\mathbf{x}_{ij}$ from the jth region of the ith image were concatenated to form a 100×1 vector $\mathbf{x}_{ij}$. They treated the regions independently and described each with a t-distribution so that the class conditional density functions were

$$Pr(\mathbf{x}_i|w = m) = \prod_{j=1}^{J} \text{Stud}_{\mathbf{x}_{ij}}[\boldsymbol{\mu}_{jm}, \boldsymbol{\Sigma}_{jm}, \nu_{jm}]. \tag{7.54}$$

Figure 7.26 shows results based on training with 10 classes from the Amsterdam library of images (Guesebroek et al. 2005). Each class consists of 72 images taken at 5-degree intervals around the object. The data were divided randomly into 36 test images and 36 training images for each class. The prior probabilities of the classes were set to

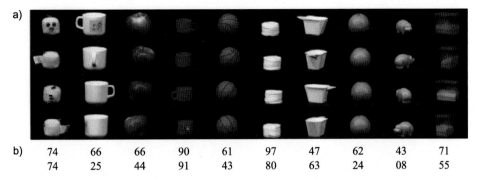

a)

b)

| 74 | 66 | 66 | 90 | 61 | 97 | 47 | 62 | 43 | 71 |
| 74 | 25 | 44 | 91 | 43 | 80 | 63 | 24 | 08 | 55 |

Figure 7.26 Object recognition. a) The training database consists of a series of different views of ten different objects. The goal is to learn a class-conditional density function for each object and classify new examples using Bayes' rule. b) Percent correct results for class conditional densities based on the t-distribution (top row) and the normal distributions (bottom row). The robust model performs better, especially on objects with specularities. Images from Amsterdam library (Guesebroek et al. 2005).

uniform, and the posterior distribution $Pr(w_i|\mathbf{x}_i)$ was calculated using Bayes' rule. A test object was classified according to the class with the highest posterior probability.

The results show the superiority of the t-distribution – for almost every class; the percent correct performance is better, and this is especially true for objects such as the china pig where the specularities act as outliers. By adding just one more parameter per patch, the performance increases from a mean of 51% to 68%.

7.9.3   Segmentation

The goal of segmentation is to assign a discrete label $\{w_n\}_{n=1}^N$ which takes one of K values $w_n \in \{1, 2, \ldots, K\}$ to each of the N pixels in the image so that regions that belong to the same object are assigned the same label. The segmentation model depends on observed data vectors $\{\mathbf{x}_n\}_{n=1}^N$ at each of the N pixels that would typically include the RGB pixel values, the (x, y) position of the pixel and other information characterizing local texture.

We will frame this problem as *unsupervised learning*. In other words, we do not have the luxury of having training images where the state of the world is known. We must both learn the parameters $\boldsymbol{\theta}$ and estimate the world states $\{w_i\}_{i=1}^I$ from the image data $\{\mathbf{x}_n\}_{n=1}^N$.

We will assume that the kth object is associated with a normal distribution with parameters $\boldsymbol{\mu}_k$ and $\boldsymbol{\Sigma}_k$ and prevalence λ_k so that

$$Pr(w_n) = \text{Cat}_{w_n}[\boldsymbol{\lambda}]$$
$$Pr(\mathbf{x}_i|w_i = k) = \text{Norm}_{\mathbf{x}_i}[\boldsymbol{\mu}_k, \boldsymbol{\Sigma}_k]. \tag{7.55}$$

Marginalizing out the world state w, we have

$$Pr(\mathbf{x}_{1\ldots N}) = \prod_{n=1}^N \sum_{k=1}^K \lambda_k \text{Norm}_{\mathbf{x}_n}[\boldsymbol{\mu}_k, \boldsymbol{\Sigma}_k]. \tag{7.56}$$

To fit this model, we find the parameters $\boldsymbol{\theta} = \{\lambda_k, \boldsymbol{\mu}_k, \boldsymbol{\Sigma}_k\}_{k=1}^K$ using the EM algorithm. To assign a class to each pixel, we then find the value of the world state that has

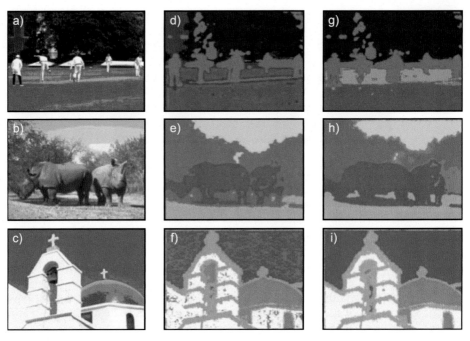

Figure 7.27 Segmentation. a–c) Original images. d–f) Segmentation results based on a mixture of five normal distributions. The pixels associated with the kth component are colored with the mean RGB values of the pixels that are assigned to this value. g–i) Segmentation results based on a mixture of K t-distributions. The segmentation here is less noisy than for the MoG model. Results from Sfikas et al. (2007). ©IEEE 2007.

the highest posterior probability given the observed data

$$\hat{w}_i = \underset{w_i}{\operatorname{argmax}} \left[Pr(w_i | \mathbf{x}_i) \right], \tag{7.57}$$

where the posterior is computed as in the E-step.

Figure 7.27 shows results from this model and a similar mixture model based on t-distributions from Sfikas et al. (2007). The mixture models manage to partition the image quite well into different regions. Unsurprisingly, the t-distribution results are rather less noisy than those based on the normal distribution.

7.9.4   Frontal face recognition

The goal of face identification (Figure 7.28) is to assign a label $w \in \{1 \ldots M\}$ indicating which of M possible identities the face belongs to based on a data vector $\mathbf{x}$. The model is learned from labeled training data $\{\mathbf{x}_i, w_i\}_{i=1}^{I}$ where the identity is known. In a simple system, the data vector might consist of the concatenated grayscale values from the face image, which should be reasonably large (say 50×50 pixels) to ensure that the identity is well represented.

Since the data are high-dimensional, a reasonable approach is to model each class conditional density function with a factor analyzer

$$Pr(\mathbf{x}_i | w_i = k) = \operatorname{Norm}_{\mathbf{x}_i}[\boldsymbol{\mu}_k, \boldsymbol{\Phi}_k \boldsymbol{\Phi}_k^T + \boldsymbol{\Sigma}_k], \tag{7.58}$$

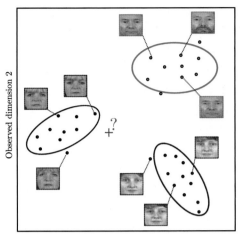

Observed dimension 2

Observed dimension 1

Figure 7.28 Face recognition. Our goal is to take the RGB values of a facial image **x** and assign a label $w \in \{1 \ldots K\}$ corresponding to the identity. Since the data are high-dimensional, we model the class conditional density function $Pr(\mathbf{x}|w = k)$ for each individual in the database as a factor analyzer. To classify a new face, we apply Bayes' rule with suitable priors $Pr(w)$ to compute the posterior distribution $Pr(w|\mathbf{x})$. We choose the label $\hat{w} = \text{argmax}_w [Pr(w = k|\mathbf{x})]$ that maximizes the posterior. This approach assumes that there are sufficient training examples to learn a factor analyzer for each class.

where the parameters for the kth identity $\boldsymbol{\theta}_k = \boldsymbol{\mu}_k, \boldsymbol{\Phi}_k, \boldsymbol{\Sigma}_k$ can be learned from the subset of data that belongs to that identity using the EM algorithm. We also assign priors $P(w = k)$ according to the prevalence of each identity in the database.

To perform recognition, we compute the posterior distribution $Pr(w^*|\mathbf{x}^*)$ for the new data example $\mathbf{x}^*$ using Bayes' rule. We assign the identity that maximizes this posterior distribution.

This approach works well if there are sufficient examples of each gallery individual to learn a factor analyzer, and if the poses of all of the faces are similar. In the next example, we develop a method to change the pose of faces, so that we can cope when the poses of the faces differ.

7.9.5   Changing face pose (regression)

To change the pose of the face, we predict the RGB values **w** of the face in the new pose given a face **x** in the old pose. This is different from the previous examples in that it is a regression problem: the output **w** is a continuous multidimensional variable rather than a class label.

We form a compound variable $\mathbf{z} = [\mathbf{x}^T \ \mathbf{w}^T]^T$ by concatenating the RGB values from the two poses together. We now model the joint density as $Pr(\mathbf{z}) = Pr(\mathbf{x}, \mathbf{w})$ with a factor analyzer

$$Pr(\mathbf{x}, \mathbf{w}) = Pr(\mathbf{z}) = \text{Norm}_{\mathbf{z}}[\boldsymbol{\mu}, \boldsymbol{\Phi}\boldsymbol{\Phi}^T + \boldsymbol{\Sigma}], \tag{7.59}$$

which we learn for paired training examples $\{\mathbf{x}_i, \mathbf{w}_i\}_{i=1}^I$ where the identity is known to be the same for each pair.

To find the non-frontal face $\mathbf{w}^*$ corresponding to a new frontal face $\mathbf{x}^*$ we use the approach of Section 6.3.2: the posterior over $\mathbf{w}^*$ is just the conditional distribution $Pr(\mathbf{w}|\mathbf{x})$. Since the joint distribution is normal, we can compute the posterior distribution in closed form using equation 5.5. Using the notation

$$\boldsymbol{\mu} = \begin{bmatrix} \boldsymbol{\mu}_{\mathbf{x}} \\ \boldsymbol{\mu}_{\mathbf{w}} \end{bmatrix} \text{ and } \boldsymbol{\Phi}\boldsymbol{\Phi}^T + \boldsymbol{\Sigma} = \begin{bmatrix} \boldsymbol{\Phi}_{\mathbf{x}}\boldsymbol{\Phi}_{\mathbf{x}}^T + \boldsymbol{\Sigma}_{\mathbf{x}} & \boldsymbol{\Phi}_{\mathbf{x}}\boldsymbol{\Phi}_{\mathbf{w}}^T \\ \boldsymbol{\Phi}_{\mathbf{w}}\boldsymbol{\Phi}_{\mathbf{x}}^T & \boldsymbol{\Phi}_{\mathbf{w}}\boldsymbol{\Phi}_{\mathbf{w}}^T + \boldsymbol{\Sigma}_{\mathbf{w}} \end{bmatrix}, \tag{7.60}$$

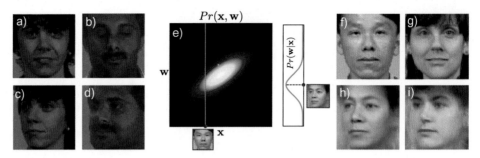

Figure 7.29 Regression example: we aim to predict quarter-left face image $\mathbf{w}$ from the frontal image $\mathbf{x}$. To this end, we take paired examples of frontal faces (a–b) and quarter-left faces (c–d) and learn a joint probability model $Pr(\mathbf{x}, \mathbf{w})$ by concatenating the variables to form $\mathbf{z} = [\mathbf{x}^T, \mathbf{w}^T]^T$ and fitting a factor analyzer to $\mathbf{z}$. e) Since the factor analyzer has a normal density (Equation 7.31), we can predict the conditional distribution $Pr(\mathbf{w}|\mathbf{x})$ of a quarter-left face given a frontal face which will also be normal (see section 5.5). f–g) Two frontal faces. h–i) MAP predictions for non-frontal faces (the mean of the normal distribution $Pr(\mathbf{w}|\mathbf{x})$).

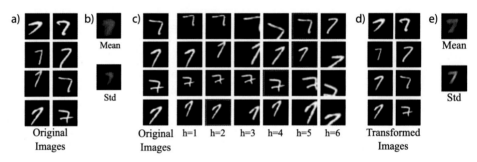

Figure 7.30 Modeling transformations with hidden variables. a) The original set of digit images are only weakly aligned. b) The mean and standard deviation images are consequently blurred out. The probability density model does not fit well. c) Each possible value of a discrete hidden variable represents a different transformation (here inverse transformations are shown). The red square highlights the most likely choice of hidden variable after ten iterations. d) The inversely transformed digits (based on most likely hidden variable). d) The new mean and standard deviation images are more focused: the probability density function fits better.

the posterior is given by

$$Pr(\mathbf{w}^*|\mathbf{x}^*) = \text{Norm}_{\mathbf{w}^*}[\boldsymbol{\mu}_{\mathbf{w}} + \boldsymbol{\Phi}_{\mathbf{w}}\boldsymbol{\Phi}_{\mathbf{x}}^T(\boldsymbol{\Phi}_{\mathbf{x}}\boldsymbol{\Phi}_{\mathbf{x}}^T + \boldsymbol{\Sigma}_{\mathbf{x}})^{-1}(\mathbf{x}^* - \boldsymbol{\mu}_{\mathbf{x}}), \qquad (7.61)$$
$$\boldsymbol{\Phi}_{\mathbf{w}}\boldsymbol{\Phi}_{\mathbf{w}}^T + \boldsymbol{\Sigma}_{\mathbf{w}} - \boldsymbol{\Phi}_{\mathbf{w}}\boldsymbol{\Phi}_{\mathbf{x}}^T(\boldsymbol{\Phi}_{\mathbf{x}}\boldsymbol{\Phi}_{\mathbf{x}}^T + \boldsymbol{\Sigma}_{\mathbf{x}})^{-1}\boldsymbol{\Phi}_{\mathbf{x}}\boldsymbol{\Phi}_{\mathbf{w}}^T],$$

and the most probable $\mathbf{w}^*$ is at the mean of this distribution.

7.9.6   Transformations as hidden variables

Finally, we consider a model that is closely related to the mixture of Gaussians, but where the hidden variables have a clear real-world interpretation. Consider the problem of building a density function for a set of poorly aligned images of digits (Figure 7.30). A simple normal distribution with diagonal covariance produces only a very poor representation of the data because most of the variation is due to the poor alignment.

We construct a generative model that first draws an *aligned* image $\mathbf{x}'$ from a normal distribution, and then translates it using one of a discrete set $\{\text{trans}_k[\bullet]\}_{k=1}^{K}$ of K possible transformations to explain the poorly aligned image $\mathbf{x}$. In mathematical terms, we have

$$Pr(\mathbf{x}') = \text{Norm}_{\mathbf{x}'}[\boldsymbol{\mu}, \boldsymbol{\Sigma}]$$
$$Pr(h) = \text{Cat}_h[\boldsymbol{\lambda}]$$
$$\mathbf{x} = \text{trans}_h[\mathbf{x}'], \tag{7.62}$$

where $h \in \{1, \ldots, K\}$ is a hidden variable that denotes which of the possible transformations warped this example.

This model can be learned using an EM-like procedure. In the E-step, we compute a probability distribution $Pr(h_i|\mathbf{x}_i)$ over the hidden variables by applying all of the inverse transformations to the each example and evaluating how likely the result is under the current parameters $\boldsymbol{\mu}$ and $\boldsymbol{\Sigma}$. In the M-step, we update these parameters by taking weighted sums of the inverse transformed images.

Summary

In this chapter we have introduced the idea of the *hidden variable* to induce structure in density models. The main approach to learning models of this kind is the expectation maximization algorithm. This is an iterative approach that is only guaranteed to find a local maximum. We have seen that although these models are more sophisticated than the normal distribution, they are still not really good representations of the density of high-dimensional visual data.

Notes

Expectation maximization: The EM algorithm was originally described by Dempster et al. (1977) although the presentation in this chapter owes more to the perspective espoused in Neal and Hinton (1999). A comprehensive summary of the EM algorithm and its extensions can be found in McLachlan and Krishnan (2008).

Mixtures of Gaussians: The mixtures of Gaussians model is closely related to the *K-means* algorithm (discussed in Section 13.4.4), which is a pure clustering algorithm, but does not have a probabilistic interpretation. Mixture models are used extensively in computer vision. Common applications include skin detection (e.g., Jones and Rehg 2002) and background subtraction (e.g., Stauffer and Grimson 1999).

t-distributions: General information about the t-distribution can be found in Kotz and Nadarajah (2004). The EM algorithm for fitting the t-distribution is given in Liu and Rubin (1995), and other fitting methods are discussed in Nadarajah and Kotz (2008) and Aeschliman et al. (2010). Applications of t-distributions in vision include object recognition (Aeschliman et al. 2010) and tracking (Loxam and Drummond 2008; Aeschliman et al. 2010), and they are also used as the building blocks of sparse image priors (Roth and Black 2009).

Subspace models: The EM algorithm to learn the factor analyzer is due to Rubin and Thayer (1982). Factor analysis is closely related to several other models including probabilistic principal component analysis (Tipping and Bishop 1999), which is discussed in Section 17.5.1, and principal component analysis, which is discussed in Section 13.4.2. Subspace models have been extended to the nonlinear case by Lawrence (2004). This is discussed in detail in Section 17.8. In Chapter 18, we present a series of models based on factor analysis which explicitly encode the identity and style of the object.

Combining models: Ghahramani and Hinton (1996c) introduced the mixtures of factor analyzers model. Peel and McLachlan (2000) present an algorithm for learning robust mixture models (mixtures of t-distributions). Khan and Dellaert (2004) and Zhao and Jiang (2006) both present subspace models based on the t-distribution. De Ridder and Franc (2003) combined mixture models, subspace models and t-distributions to create a distribution that is mutli-modal, robust and oriented along a subspace.

Face detection, face recognition, object recognition: Models based on subspace distributions were used in early methods for face and object recognition (e.g., Moghaddam and Pentland 1997; Murase and Nayar 1995). Modern face detection methods mainly rely on discriminative methods (Chapter 9), and the current state of the art in object recognition relies on bag of words approaches (chapter 20). Face recognition applications do not usually have the luxury of having many examples of each individual and so cannot build a separate density for each. However, modern approaches are still largely based on subspace methods (see Chapter 18).

Segmentation: Belongie et al. (1998) use a mixtures of Gaussians scheme similar to that described to segment the image as part of a content-based image retrieval system. A modern approach to segmentation based on the mixture of Gaussians model can be found in Ma et al. (2007). Sfikas et al. (2007) compared the segmentation performance of mixtures of Gaussians and mixtures of t-distributions.

Other uses for hidden variables: Frey and Jojic (1999a), (1999b) used hidden variables to model unseen transformations applied to data from mixture models and subspace models, respectively. Jojic and Frey (2001) used discrete hidden variables to represent the index of the layer in a multi-layered model of a video. Jojic et al. (2003) presented a structured mixture model, where the mean and variance parameters are represented as an image and the hidden variable indexes the starting position of subpatch from this image.

Problems

7.1 Consider a computer vision system for machine inspection of oranges in which the goal is to tell if the orange is ripe. For each image we separate the orange from the background and calculate the average color of the pixels, which we describe as a 3×1 vector $\mathbf{x}$. We are given training pairs $\{\mathbf{x}_i, w_i\}$ of these vectors, each with an associated binary variable $w \in \{0, 1\}$ that indicates that this training example was unripe ($w = 0$) or ripe ($w = 1$). Describe how to build a generative classifier that could classify new examples $\mathbf{x}^*$ as being ripe or unripe.

7.2 It turns out that a small subset of the training labels w_i in the previous example were wrong. How could you modify your classifier to cope with this situation?

7.3 Derive the M-step equations for the mixtures of Gaussians model (Equation 7.19).

7.4 Consider modeling some univariate continuous visual data $x \in [0, 1]$ using a *mixture of beta distributions*. Write down an equation for this model. Describe in words what will occur in (i) the E-step and (ii) the M-step.

7.5 Prove that the student t-distribution over x is the marginalization with respect to h of the joint distribution $Pr(x, h)$ between x and a hidden variable h where

$$\text{Stud}_x[\mu, \sigma^2, \nu] = \int \text{Norm}_x[\mu, \sigma^2/h]\text{Gam}_h[\nu/2, \nu/2]dh.$$

7.6 Show that the peak of the Gamma distribution $\text{Gam}_z[\alpha, \beta]$ is at

$$\hat{z} = \frac{\alpha - 1}{\beta}.$$

7.7 Show that the Gamma distribution is conjugate to the inverse scaling factor of the variance in a normal distribution so that

$$\text{Norm}_{\mathbf{x}_i}[\boldsymbol{\mu}, \boldsymbol{\Sigma}/h_i]\text{Gam}_{h_i}[\nu/2, \nu/2] = \kappa \text{Gam}_{h_i}[\alpha, \beta],$$

and find the constant of proportionality κ and the new parameters α and β.

7.8 The model for factor analysis can be written as

$$\mathbf{x}_i = \boldsymbol{\mu} + \boldsymbol{\Phi}\mathbf{h}_i + \boldsymbol{\epsilon}_i,$$

where $\mathbf{h}_i$ is distributed normally with mean zero and identity covariance and $\boldsymbol{\epsilon}_i$ is distributed normally with mean zero and covariance $\boldsymbol{\Sigma}$. Determine expressions for

1. $E[\mathbf{x}_i]$,
2. $E[(\mathbf{x}_i - E[\mathbf{x}_i])(\mathbf{x}_i - E[\mathbf{x}_i])^T]$.

7.9 Derive the E-step for factor analysis (Equation 7.34).

7.10 Derive the M-step for factor analysis (Equation 7.38).

Chapter 8

Regression models

This chapter concerns regression problems: the goal is to estimate a univariate world state w based on observed measurements $\mathbf{x}$. The discussion is limited to discriminative methods in which the distribution $Pr(w|\mathbf{x})$ of the world state is directly modeled. This contrasts with Chapter 7 where the focus was on generative models in which the likelihood $Pr(\mathbf{x}|w)$ of the observations is modeled.

To motivate the regression problem, consider *body pose estimation*: here the goal is to estimate the joint angles of a human body, based on an observed image of the person in an unknown pose (Figure 8.1). Such an analysis could form the first step toward activity recognition.

We assume that the image has already been preprocessed and a low-dimensional vector $\mathbf{x}$ that represents the shape of the contour has been extracted. Our goal is to use this data vector to predict a second vector containing the joint angles for each of the major body joints. In practice, we will estimate each joint angle separately; we can hence concentrate our discussion on how to estimate a univariate quantity w from continuous observed data $\mathbf{x}$. We begin by assuming that the relation between the world and the data is linear and that the uncertainty around this prediction is normally distributed with constant variance. This is the linear regression model.

8.1 Linear regression

The goal of linear regression is to predict the posterior distribution $Pr(w|\mathbf{x})$ over the world state w based on observed data $\mathbf{x}$. Since this is a discriminative model, we proceed by choosing a probability distribution over the world w and making the parameters dependent on the data $\mathbf{x}$. The world state w is univariate and continuous and so a suitable distribution is the univariate normal. In linear regression (Figure 8.2), we make the mean μ of this normal distribution a linear function $\phi_0 + \boldsymbol{\phi}^T\mathbf{x}_i$ of the data and treat the variance σ^2 as a constant so that

$$Pr(w_i|\mathbf{x}_i, \boldsymbol{\theta}) = \text{Norm}_{w_i}\left[\phi_0 + \boldsymbol{\phi}^T\mathbf{x}_i, \sigma^2\right], \tag{8.1}$$

where $\boldsymbol{\theta} = \{\phi_0, \boldsymbol{\phi}, \sigma^2\}$ are the model parameters. The term ϕ_0 can be interpreted as the y-intercept of a hyperplane and the entries of $\boldsymbol{\phi} = [\phi_1, \phi_2, \ldots, \phi_D]^T$ are its gradients with respect to each of the D data dimensions.

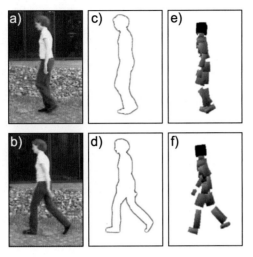

Figure 8.1 Body pose estimation. a–b) Human beings in unknown poses. c–d) The silhouette is found by segmenting the image and the contour extracted by tracing around the edge of the silhouette. A 100 dimensional measurement vector **x** is extracted that describes the contour shape based on the shape context descriptor (see Section 13.3.5). e–f) The goal is to estimate the vector **w** containing the major joint angles of the body. This is a regression problem as each element of the world state **w** is continuous. Adapted from Agarwal and Triggs (2006).

It is cumbersome to treat the y-intercept separately from the gradients, so we apply a trick that allows us to simplify the subsequent notation. We attach a 1 to the start of every data vector $\mathbf{x}_i \leftarrow [1 \quad \mathbf{x}_i^T]^T$ and attach the y-intercept ϕ_0 to the start of the gradient vector $\boldsymbol{\phi} \leftarrow [\phi_0 \quad \boldsymbol{\phi}^T]^T$ so that we can now equivalently write

$$Pr(w_i|\mathbf{x}_i,\boldsymbol{\theta}) = \text{Norm}_{w_i}\left[\boldsymbol{\phi}^T\mathbf{x}_i,\sigma^2\right]. \tag{8.2}$$

In fact, since each training data example is considered independent, we can write the probability $Pr(\mathbf{w}|\mathbf{X})$ of the entire training set as a single normal distribution with a diagonal covariance so that

$$Pr(\mathbf{w}|\mathbf{X}) = \text{Norm}_\mathbf{w}[\mathbf{X}^T\boldsymbol{\phi},\sigma^2\mathbf{I}], \tag{8.3}$$

where $\mathbf{X} = [\mathbf{x}_1,\mathbf{x}_2,\dots,\mathbf{x}_I]$ and $\mathbf{w} = [w_1,w_2,\dots,w_I]^T$.

Inference for this model is very simple: for a new datum $\mathbf{x}^*$ we simply evaluate Equation 8.2 to find the posterior distribution $Pr(w^*|\mathbf{x}^*)$ over the world state w^*. Hence we turn our main focus to learning.

8.1.1 Learning

The learning algorithm estimates the model parameters $\boldsymbol{\theta} = \{\boldsymbol{\phi},\sigma^2\}$ from paired training examples $\{\mathbf{x}_i,w_i\}_{i=1}^I$. In the maximum likelihood approach we seek

$$\hat{\boldsymbol{\theta}} = \underset{\boldsymbol{\theta}}{\text{argmax}}\left[Pr(\mathbf{w}|\mathbf{X},\boldsymbol{\theta})\right]$$
$$= \underset{\boldsymbol{\theta}}{\text{argmax}}\left[\log\left[Pr(\mathbf{w}|\mathbf{X},\boldsymbol{\theta})\right]\right], \tag{8.4}$$

where as usual we have taken the logarithm of the criterion. The logarithm is a monotonic transformation, and so it does not change the position of the maximum, but the resulting cost function is easier to optimize. Substituting in we find that

$$\hat{\boldsymbol{\phi}},\hat{\sigma}^2 = \underset{\boldsymbol{\phi},\sigma^2}{\text{argmax}}\left[-\frac{I\log[2\pi]}{2} - \frac{I\log[\sigma^2]}{2} - \frac{(\mathbf{w}-\mathbf{X}^T\boldsymbol{\phi})^T(\mathbf{w}-\mathbf{X}^T\boldsymbol{\phi})}{2\sigma^2}\right]. \tag{8.5}$$

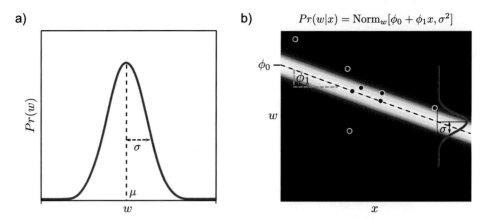

Figure 8.2 Linear regression model with univariate data x. a) We choose a univariate normal distribution over the world state w. b) The parameters of this distribution are now made to depend on the data x: the mean μ is a linear function $\phi_0 + \phi_1 x$ of the data and the variance σ^2 is constant. The parameters ϕ_0 and ϕ_1 represent the intercept and slope of the linear function, respectively.

We now take the derivatives with respect to ϕ and σ^2, equate the resulting expressions to zero and solve to find

$$\hat{\phi} = (\mathbf{XX}^T)^{-1}\mathbf{Xw}$$
$$\hat{\sigma}^2 = \frac{(\mathbf{w} - \mathbf{X}^T\phi)^T(\mathbf{w} - \mathbf{X}^T\phi)}{I}. \tag{8.6}$$

Figure 8.2b shows an example fit with univariate data x. In this case, the model describes the data reasonably well.

8.1.2 Problems with the linear regression model

There are three main limitations of the linear regression model.

- The predictions of the model are overconfident; for example, small changes in the estimated slope ϕ_1 make increasingly large changes in the predictions as we move further from the y-intercept ϕ_0. However, this increasing uncertainty is not reflected in the posterior distribution.

- We are limited to linear functions and usually there is no particular reason that the visual data and world state should be linearly related.

- When the observed data $\mathbf{x}$ is high-dimensional, it may be that many elements of this variable aren't useful for predicting the state of the world, and so the resulting model is unnecessarily complex.

We tackle each of these problems in turn. In the following section we address the overconfidence of the model by developing a Bayesian approach to the same problem. In Section 8.3, we generalize this model to fit nonlinear functions. In section 8.6, we introduce a sparse version of the regression model where most of the weighting coefficients ϕ are encouraged to be zero. The relationships between the models in this chapter are indicated in Figure 8.3.

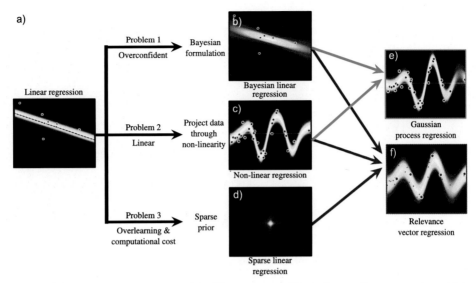

Figure 8.3 Family of regression models. There are several limitations to linear regression which we deal with in subsequent sections. The linear regression model with maximum likelihood learning is overconfident, and hence we develop a Bayesian version. It is unrealistic to always assume a linear relationship between the data and the world and to this end, we introduce a nonlinear version. The linear regression model has many parameters when the data dimension is high, and hence we consider a sparse version of the model. The ideas of Bayesian estimation, nonlinear functions and sparsity are variously combined to form the Gaussian process regression and relevance vector regression model.

8.2   Bayesian linear regression

In the Bayesian approach, we compute a probability distribution over possible values of the parameters ϕ (we will assume for now that σ^2 is known, see Section 8.2.2). When we evaluate the probability of new data, we take a weighted average of the predictions induced by the different possible values.

Since the gradient vector ϕ is multivariate and continuous, we model the prior $Pr(\phi)$ as normal with zero mean and spherical covariance,

$$Pr(\phi) = \text{Norm}_\phi[\mathbf{0}, \sigma_p^2 \mathbf{I}], \tag{8.7}$$

where σ_p^2 scales the prior covariance and $\mathbf{I}$ is the identity matrix. Typically σ_p^2 is set to a large value to reflect the fact that our prior knowledge is weak.

Given paired training examples $\{\mathbf{x}_i, w_i\}_{i=1}^{I}$, the posterior distribution over the parameters can be computed using Bayes' rule

$$Pr(\phi|\mathbf{X}, \mathbf{w}) = \frac{Pr(\mathbf{w}|\mathbf{X}, \phi)Pr(\phi)}{Pr(\mathbf{w}|\mathbf{X})}, \tag{8.8}$$

where, as before, the likelihood is given by

$$Pr(\mathbf{w}|\mathbf{X}, \boldsymbol{\theta}) = \text{Norm}_{\mathbf{w}}\left[\mathbf{X}^T \phi, \sigma^2 \mathbf{I}\right]. \tag{8.9}$$

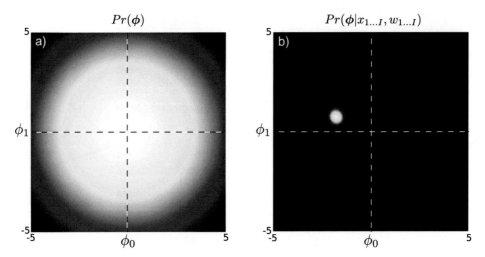

Figure 8.4 Bayesian linear regression. a) Prior $Pr(\phi)$ over intercept ϕ_0 and slope ϕ_1 parameters. This represents our knowledge about the parameters before we observe the data. b) Posterior distribution $Pr(\phi|\mathbf{X},\mathbf{w})$ over intercept and slope parameters. This represents our knowledge about the parameters after observing the data from Figure 8.2b: we are considerably more certain but there remain a range of possible parameter values.

The posterior distribution can be computed in closed form (using the relations in Sections 5.7 and 5.6) and is given by the expression:

$$Pr(\phi|\mathbf{X},\mathbf{w}) = \text{Norm}_{\phi}\left[\frac{1}{\sigma^2}\mathbf{A}^{-1}\mathbf{X}\mathbf{w}, \mathbf{A}^{-1}\right], \tag{8.10}$$

where

$$\mathbf{A} = \frac{1}{\sigma^2}\mathbf{X}\mathbf{X}^T + \frac{1}{\sigma_p^2}\mathbf{I}. \tag{8.11}$$

Note that the posterior distribution $Pr(\phi|\mathbf{X},\mathbf{w})$ is always narrower than the prior distribution $Pr(\phi)$ (Figure 8.4); the data provides information that refines our knowledge of the parameter values.

We now turn to the problem of computing the predictive distribution over the world state w^* for a new observed data vector $\mathbf{x}^*$. We take an infinite weighted sum (i.e., an integral) over the predictions $Pr(w^*|\mathbf{x}^*,\phi)$ implied by each possible ϕ where the weights are given by the posterior distribution $Pr(\phi|\mathbf{X},\mathbf{w})$.

$$\begin{aligned}
Pr(w^*|\mathbf{x}^*,\mathbf{X},\mathbf{w}) &= \int Pr(w^*|\mathbf{x}^*,\phi)Pr(\phi|\mathbf{X},\mathbf{w})d\phi \\
&= \int \text{Norm}_{w^*}[\phi^T\mathbf{x}^*,\sigma^2]\text{Norm}_{\phi}\left[\frac{1}{\sigma^2}\mathbf{A}^{-1}\mathbf{X}\mathbf{w}, \mathbf{A}^{-1}\right]d\phi \\
&= \text{Norm}_{w^*}\left[\frac{1}{\sigma^2}\mathbf{x}^{*T}\mathbf{A}^{-1}\mathbf{X}\mathbf{w}, \mathbf{x}^{*T}\mathbf{A}^{-1}\mathbf{x}^* + \sigma^2\right]. \tag{8.12}
\end{aligned}$$

To compute this, we reformulated the integrand using the relations from Sections 5.7 and 5.6 as the product of a normal distribution in ϕ and a constant with respect to ϕ. The

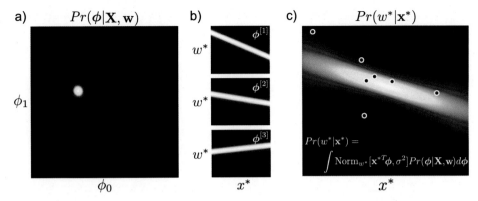

Figure 8.5 Bayesian linear regression. a) In learning we compute the posterior distribution $Pr(\phi|\mathbf{X}, \mathbf{w})$ over the intercept and slope parameters: there is a family of parameter settings that are compatible with the data. b) Three samples from the posterior, each of which corresponds to a different regression line. c) To form the predictive distribution we take an infinite weighted sum (integral) of the predictions from all of the possible parameter settings, where the weight is given by the posterior probability. The individual predictions vary more as we move from the centroid $\overline{\mathbf{x}}$ and this is reflected in the fact that the certainty is lower on either side of the plot.

integral of the normal distribution must be one, and so the final result is just the constant. This constant is itself a normal distribution in w^*.

This Bayesian formulation of linear regression (Figure 8.5) is less confident about its predictions, and the confidence decreases as the test data $\mathbf{x}^*$ departs from the mean $\overline{\mathbf{x}}$ of the observed data. This is because uncertainty in the gradient causes increasing uncertainty in the predictions as we move further away from the bulk of the data. This agrees with our intuitions: predictions ought to become less confident as we extrapolate further from the data.

8.2.1   Practical concerns

To implement this model we must compute the $D \times D$ matrix inverse $\mathbf{A}^{-1}$ (Equation 8.12). If the dimension D of the original data is large, then it will be difficult to compute this inverse directly.

Fortunately, the structure of $\mathbf{A}$ is such that it can be inverted far more efficiently. We exploit the Woodbury identity (see appendix C.8.4), to rewrite $\mathbf{A}^{-1}$ as

$$\mathbf{A}^{-1} = \left(\frac{1}{\sigma^2} \mathbf{X}\mathbf{X}^T + \frac{1}{\sigma_p^2} \mathbf{I}_D \right)^{-1}$$

$$= \sigma_p^2 \mathbf{I}_D - \sigma_p^2 \mathbf{X} \left(\mathbf{X}^T \mathbf{X} + \frac{\sigma^2}{\sigma_p^2} \mathbf{I}_I \right)^{-1} \mathbf{X}^T, \tag{8.13}$$

where we have explicitly noted the dimensionality of each of the identity matrices $\mathbf{I}$ as a subscript. This expression still includes an inversion, but now it is of size $I \times I$ where I is the number of examples: if the number of data examples I is smaller than the data dimensionality D, then this formulation is more practical. This formulation also demonstrates clearly that the posterior covariance is less than the prior; the posterior covariance is the prior covariance $\sigma_p^2 \mathbf{I}$ with a data-dependent term subtracted from it.

Substituting the new expression for $\mathbf{A}^{-1}$ into Equation 8.12, we derive a new expression for the predictive distribution,

$$Pr(w^*|\mathbf{x}^*, \mathbf{X}, \mathbf{w}) \tag{8.14}$$

$$= \text{Norm}_{w^*}\left[\frac{\sigma_p^2}{\sigma^2}\mathbf{x}^{*T}\mathbf{X}\mathbf{w} - \frac{\sigma_p^2}{\sigma^2}\mathbf{x}^{*T}\mathbf{X}\left(\mathbf{X}^T\mathbf{X} + \frac{\sigma^2}{\sigma_p^2}\mathbf{I}\right)^{-1}\mathbf{X}^T\mathbf{X}\mathbf{w},\right.$$

$$\left.\sigma_p^2\mathbf{x}^{*T}\mathbf{x}^* - \sigma_p^2\mathbf{x}^{*T}\mathbf{X}\left(\mathbf{X}^T\mathbf{X} + \frac{\sigma^2}{\sigma_p^2}\mathbf{I}\right)^{-1}\mathbf{X}^T\mathbf{x}^* + \sigma^2\right].$$

It is notable that only inner products of the data vectors (e.g., in the terms $\mathbf{X}^T\mathbf{x}^*$, or $\mathbf{X}^T\mathbf{X}$) are required to compute this expression. We will exploit this fact when we generalize these ideas to nonlinear regression (Section 8.3).

8.2.2   Fitting the variance

The previous analysis has concentrated exclusively on the slope parameters ϕ. In principle, we could have taken a Bayesian approach to estimating the variance parameter σ^2 as well. However, for simplicity we will compute a point estimate of σ^2 using the maximum likelihood approach. To this end, we optimize the *marginal likelihood*, which is the likelihood after marginalizing out ϕ and is given by

$$Pr(\mathbf{w}|\mathbf{X}, \sigma^2) = \int Pr(\mathbf{w}|\mathbf{X}, \phi, \sigma^2)Pr(\phi)\,d\phi$$

$$= \int \text{Norm}_{\mathbf{w}}[\mathbf{X}^T\phi, \sigma^2\mathbf{I}]\text{Norm}_{\phi}[\mathbf{0}, \sigma_p^2\mathbf{I}]\,d\phi$$

$$= \text{Norm}_{\mathbf{w}}[\mathbf{0}, \sigma_p^2\mathbf{X}^T\mathbf{X} + \sigma^2\mathbf{I}] \tag{8.15}$$

where the integral was solved using the same technique as that used in equation 8.12.

To estimate the variance, we maximize the log of this expression with respect to σ^2. Since the unknown is a scalar it is straightforward to optimize this function by simply evaluating the function over a range of values and choosing the maximum. Alternatively, we could use a general purpose nonlinear optimization technique (see Appendix B).

8.3   Nonlinear regression

It is unrealistic to assume that there is always a linear relationship between the world state w and the input data $\mathbf{x}$. In developing an approach to nonlinear regression, we would like to retain the mathematical convenience of the linear model while extending the class of functions that can be described.

Consequently, the approach that we describe is extremely simple: we first pass each data example through a nonlinear transformation

$$\mathbf{z}_i = \mathbf{f}[\mathbf{x}_i], \tag{8.16}$$

to create a new data vector $\mathbf{z}_i$ which is usually higher dimensional than the original data. Then we proceed as before: we describe the mean of the posterior distribution $Pr(w_i|\mathbf{x}_i)$ as a linear function $\phi^T\mathbf{z}_i$ of the transformed measurements so that

$$Pr(w_i|\mathbf{x}_i) = \text{Norm}_{w_i}[\phi^T\mathbf{z}_i, \sigma^2]. \tag{8.17}$$

For example, consider the case of 1D polynomial regression:

$$Pr(w_i|x_i) = \text{Norm}_{w_i}[\phi_0 + \phi_1 x_i + \phi_2 x_i^2 + \phi_3 x_i^3, \sigma^2]. \tag{8.18}$$

This model can be considered as computing the nonlinear transformation

$$\mathbf{z}_i = \begin{bmatrix} 1 \\ x_i \\ x_i^2 \\ x_i^3 \end{bmatrix}, \tag{8.19}$$

and so it has the general form of Equation 8.17.

8.3.1 Maximum likelihood

To find the maximum likelihood solution for the gradient vector, we first combine all of the transformed training data relations (Equation 8.17) into a single expression:

$$Pr(\mathbf{w}|\mathbf{X}) = \text{Norm}_{\mathbf{w}}[\mathbf{Z}^T\phi, \sigma^2\mathbf{I}]. \tag{8.20}$$

The optimal weights can now be computed as

$$\hat{\phi} = (\mathbf{Z}\mathbf{Z}^T)^{-1}\mathbf{Z}\mathbf{w}$$
$$\hat{\sigma}^2 = \frac{(\mathbf{w} - \mathbf{Z}^T\phi)^T(\mathbf{w} - \mathbf{Z}^T\phi)}{I}, \tag{8.21}$$

where the matrix $\mathbf{Z}$ contains the transformed vectors $\{\mathbf{z}_i\}_{i=1}^I$ in its columns. These equations were derived by replacing the original data term $\mathbf{X}$ by the transformed data $\mathbf{Z}$ in the equivalent linear expressions (Equation 8.6). For a new observed data example $\mathbf{x}^*$, we compute the vector $\mathbf{z}^*$ and then evaluate Equation 8.17.

Figures 8.6 and 8.7 provide two more examples of this approach. In Figure 8.6, the new vector $\mathbf{z}$ is computed by evaluating the data $\mathbf{x}$ under a set of radial basis functions:

$$\mathbf{z}_i = \begin{bmatrix} 1 \\ \exp\left[-(x_i - \alpha_1)^2/\lambda\right] \\ \exp\left[-(x_i - \alpha_2)^2/\lambda\right] \\ \exp\left[-(x_i - \alpha_3)^2/\lambda\right] \\ \exp\left[-(x_i - \alpha_4)^2/\lambda\right] \\ \exp\left[-(x_i - \alpha_5)^2/\lambda\right] \\ \exp\left[-(x_i - \alpha_6)^2/\lambda\right] \end{bmatrix}. \tag{8.22}$$

The term *radial basis functions* can be used to denote any spherically symmetric function, and here we have used the Gaussian. The parameters $\{\alpha_k\}_{k=1}^K$ are the centers of the functions, and λ is a scaling factor that determines their width. The functions themselves are shown in Figure 8.6b. Because they are spatially localized, each one accounts for a part of the original data space. We can approximate a function by taking weighted sums $\phi^T\mathbf{z}$ of these functions. For example, when they are weighted as in Figure 8.6c, they create the function in Figure 8.6a.

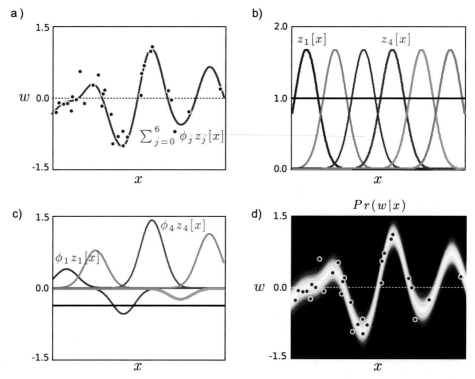

Figure 8.6 Nonlinear regression using radial basis functions. a) The relationship between the data x and world w is clearly not linear. b) We compute a new seven-dimensional vector $\mathbf{z}$ by evaluating the original observation x against each of six radial basis functions (Gaussians) and a constant function (black line). c) The mean of the predictive distribution (red line in (a)) can be formed by taking a linear sum $\boldsymbol{\phi}^T \mathbf{z}$ of these seven functions where the weights are as shown. The weights are estimated by maximum likelihood estimation of the linear regression model using the nonlinearly transformed data $\mathbf{z}$ instead of the original data $\mathbf{x}$. d) The final distribution $Pr(w|x)$ has a mean that is a sum of these functions and constant variance σ^2.

In Figure 8.7 we compute a different nonlinear transformation and regress against the same data. This time, the transformation is based on arc tangent functions so that

$$\mathbf{z}_i = \begin{bmatrix} \arctan[\lambda x_i - \alpha_1] \\ \arctan[\lambda x_i - \alpha_2] \\ \arctan[\lambda x_i - \alpha_3] \\ \arctan[\lambda x_i - \alpha_4] \\ \arctan[\lambda x_i - \alpha_5] \\ \arctan[\lambda x_i - \alpha_6] \\ \arctan[\lambda x_i - \alpha_7] \end{bmatrix}. \tag{8.23}$$

Here, the parameter λ controls the speed with which the function changes and the parameters $\{\alpha_m\}_{m=1}^7$ determine the horizontal offsets of the arc tangent functions.

In this case, it is harder to understand the role of each weighted arc tangent function in the final regression, but nonetheless they collectively approximate the function well.

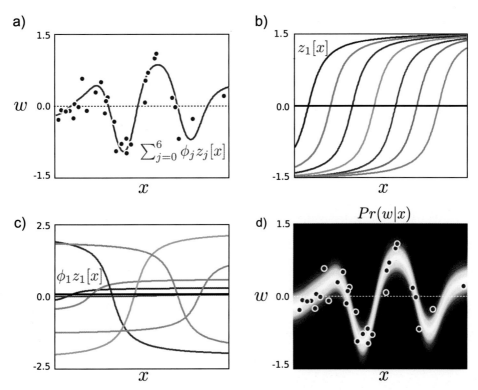

Figure 8.7 Nonlinear regression using arc tangent functions. a) The relationship between the data x and world w is not linear. b) We compute a new seven-dimensional vector $\mathbf{z}$ by evaluating the original observation x against each of seven arc tangent functions. c) The mean of the predictive distribution (red line in (a)) can be formed by taking a linear sum of these seven functions weighted as shown. The optimal weights were established using the maximum likelihood approach. d) The final distribution $Pr(w|x)$ has a mean that is a sum of these weighted functions and constant variance.

8.3.2   Bayesian nonlinear regression

In the Bayesian solution, the weights ϕ of the nonlinear basis functions are treated as uncertain: in learning we compute the posterior distribution over these weights. For a new observation $\mathbf{x}^*$, we compute the transformed vector $\mathbf{z}^*$ and compute an infinite weighted sum over the predictions due to the possible parameter values (Figure 8.8). The new expression for the predictive distribution is

$$Pr(w^*|\mathbf{z}^*, \mathbf{X}, \mathbf{w}) \tag{8.24}$$
$$= \text{Norm}_{w^*}\left[\frac{\sigma_p^2}{\sigma^2}\mathbf{z}^{*T}\mathbf{Z}\mathbf{w} - \frac{\sigma_p^2}{\sigma^2}\mathbf{z}^{*T}\mathbf{Z}\left(\mathbf{Z}^T\mathbf{Z} + \frac{\sigma^2}{\sigma_p^2}\mathbf{I}\right)^{-1}\mathbf{Z}^T\mathbf{Z}\mathbf{w}, \right.$$
$$\left. \sigma_p^2\mathbf{z}^{*T}\mathbf{z}^* - \sigma_p^2\mathbf{z}^{*T}\mathbf{Z}\left(\mathbf{Z}^T\mathbf{Z} + \frac{\sigma^2}{\sigma_p^2}\mathbf{I}\right)^{-1}\mathbf{Z}^T\mathbf{z}^* + \sigma^2 \right],$$

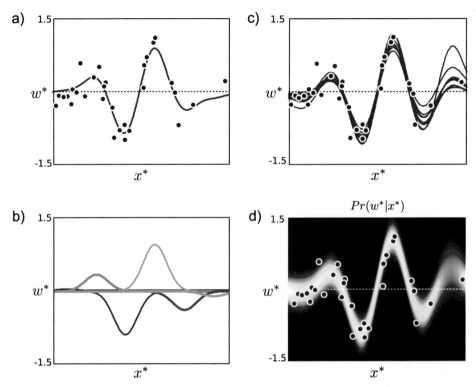

Figure 8.8 Bayesian nonlinear regression using radial basis functions. a) The relationship between the data and measurements is nonlinear. b) As in Figure 8.6, the mean of the predictive distribution is constructed as a weighted linear sum of radial basis functions. However, in the Bayesian approach we compute the posterior distribution over the weights ϕ of these basis functions. c) Different draws from this distribution of weight parameters result in different predictions. d) The final predictive distribution is formed from an infinite weighted average of these predictions where the weight is given by the posterior probability. The variance of the predictive distribution depends on both the mutual agreement of these predictions and the uncertainty due to the noise term σ^2. The uncertainty is greatest in the region on the right where there is little data and so the individual predictions vary widely.

where we have simply substituted the transformed vectors $\mathbf{z}$ for the original data $\mathbf{x}$ in Equation 8.14. The prediction variance depends on both the uncertainty in ϕ and the additive variance σ^2. The Bayesian solution is less confident than the maximum likelihood solution (compare Figures 8.8d and 7.7d), especially in regions where the data is sparse.

To compute the additive variance σ^2 we again optimize the marginal likelihood. The expression for this can be found by substituting $\mathbf{Z}$ for $\mathbf{X}$ in Equation 8.15.

8.4   Kernels and the kernel trick

The Bayesian approach to nonlinear regression described in the previous section is rarely used directly in practice: the final expression for the predictive distribution

(Equation 8.24) relies on computing inner products $\mathbf{z}_i^T \mathbf{z}_j$. However, when the transformed space is high-dimensional, it may be costly to compute the vectors $\mathbf{z}_i = \mathbf{f}[\mathbf{x}_i]$ and $\mathbf{z}_j = \mathbf{f}[\mathbf{x}_j]$ explicitly and then compute the inner product $\mathbf{z}_i^T \mathbf{z}_j$.

An alternative approach is to use *kernel substitution* in which we directly define a single *kernel function* $\mathrm{k}[\mathbf{x}_i, \mathbf{x}_j]$ as a replacement for the operation $\mathbf{f}[\mathbf{x}_i]^T \mathbf{f}[\mathbf{x}_j]$. For many transformations $\mathbf{f}[\bullet]$, it is more efficient to evaluate the kernel function directly than to transform the variables separately and then compute the dot product.

Taking this idea one step further, it is possible to choose a kernel function $\mathrm{k}[\mathbf{x}_i, \mathbf{x}_j]$ with no knowledge of what transformation $\mathbf{f}[\bullet]$ it corresponds to. When we use kernel functions, we no longer explicitly compute the transformed vector $\mathbf{z}$. One advantage of this is we can define kernel functions that correspond to projecting the data into very high-dimensional or even infinite spaces. This is sometimes called the *kernel trick*.

Clearly, the kernel function must be carefully chosen so that it does in fact correspond to computing some function $\mathbf{z} = \mathbf{f}[\mathbf{x}]$ for each data vector and taking the inner product of the resulting values: for example, since $\mathbf{z}_i^T \mathbf{z}_j = \mathbf{z}_j^T \mathbf{z}_i$ the kernel function must treat its arguments symmetrically so that $\mathrm{k}[\mathbf{x}_i, \mathbf{x}_j] = \mathrm{k}[\mathbf{x}_j, \mathbf{x}_i]$.

More precisely, *Mercer's theorem* states that a kernel function is valid when the kernel's arguments are in a measurable space, and the kernel is positive semi-definite so that

$$\sum_{ij} \mathrm{k}[\mathbf{x}_i, \mathbf{x}_j] a_i a_j \geq 0 \tag{8.25}$$

for any finite subset $\{\mathbf{x}_n\}_{n=1}^N$ of vectors in the space and any real numbers $\{a_n\}_{n=1}^N$. Examples of valid kernels include

- Linear

$$\mathrm{k}[\mathbf{x}_i, \mathbf{x}_j] = \mathbf{x}_i^T \mathbf{x}_j, \tag{8.26}$$

- Degree p polynomial

$$\mathrm{k}[\mathbf{x}_i, \mathbf{x}_j] = (\mathbf{x}_i^T \mathbf{x}_j + 1)^p, \tag{8.27}$$

- Radial basis function (RBF) or Gaussian

$$\mathrm{k}[\mathbf{x}_i, \mathbf{x}_j] = \exp\left[-0.5\left(\frac{(\mathbf{x}_i - \mathbf{x}_j)^T (\mathbf{x}_i - \mathbf{x}_j)}{\lambda^2}\right)\right]. \tag{8.28}$$

The last of these is particularly interesting. It can be shown that this kernel function corresponds to computing *infinite* length vectors $\mathbf{z}$ and taking their dot product. The entries of $\mathbf{z}$ correspond to evaluating a radial basis function (Figure 8.6b) at every possible point in the space of $\mathbf{x}$.

It is also possible to create new kernels by combining two or more existing kernels. For example, sums and products of valid kernels are guaranteed to be positive semidefinite and so are also valid kernels.

8.5   Gaussian process regression

We now replace the inner products $\mathbf{z}_i^T \mathbf{z}_j$ in the nonlinear regression algorithm (Equation 8.24) with kernel functions. The resulting model is termed *Gaussian process*

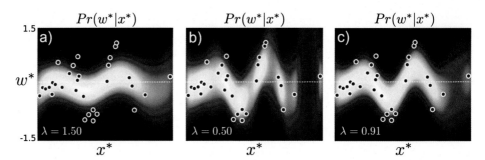

Figure 8.9 Gaussian process regression using an RBF kernel. a) When the length scale parameter λ is large, the function is too smooth. b) For small values of the length parameter the model does not successfully interpolate between the examples. c) The regression using the maximum likelihood length scale parameter is neither too smooth nor disjointed.

regression. The predictive distribution for a new datum $\mathbf{x}^*$ is

$$Pr(w^*|\mathbf{x}^*, \mathbf{X}, \mathbf{w}) \tag{8.29}$$

$$= \text{Norm}_{w^*}\left[\frac{\sigma_p^2}{\sigma^2}\mathbf{K}[\mathbf{x}^*, \mathbf{X}]\mathbf{w} - \frac{\sigma_p^2}{\sigma^2}\mathbf{K}[\mathbf{x}^*, \mathbf{X}]\left(\mathbf{K}[\mathbf{X}, \mathbf{X}] + \frac{\sigma^2}{\sigma_p^2}\mathbf{I}\right)^{-1}\mathbf{K}[\mathbf{X}, \mathbf{X}]\mathbf{w},\right.$$

$$\left.\sigma_p^2\mathbf{K}[\mathbf{x}^*, \mathbf{x}^*] - \sigma_p^2\mathbf{K}[\mathbf{x}^*, \mathbf{X}]\left(\mathbf{K}[\mathbf{X}, \mathbf{X}] + \frac{\sigma^2}{\sigma_p^2}\mathbf{I}\right)^{-1}\mathbf{K}[\mathbf{X}, \mathbf{x}^*] + \sigma^2\right].$$

where the notation $\mathbf{K}[\mathbf{X}, \mathbf{X}]$ represents a matrix of dot products where element (i, j) is given by $\text{k}[\mathbf{x}_i, \mathbf{x}_j]$.

Note that kernel functions may also contain parameters. For example, the RBF kernel (Equation 8.28) takes the parameter λ, which determines the width of the underlying RBF functions and hence the smoothness of the function (Figure 8.9). Kernel parameters such as λ can be learned by maximizing the marginal likelihood

$$\hat{\lambda} = \underset{\lambda}{\operatorname{argmax}}\left[Pr(\mathbf{w}|\mathbf{X}, \sigma^2)\right]$$

$$= \underset{\lambda}{\operatorname{argmax}}\left[\int Pr(\mathbf{w}|\mathbf{X}, \phi, \sigma^2)Pr(\phi)d\phi\right]$$

$$= \underset{\lambda}{\operatorname{argmax}}\left[\text{Norm}_{\mathbf{w}}[\mathbf{0}, \sigma_p^2\mathbf{K}[\mathbf{X}, \mathbf{X}] + \sigma^2\mathbf{I}]\right]. \tag{8.30}$$

This typically requires a nonlinear optimization procedure.

8.6 Sparse linear regression

8.4 We now turn our attention to the third potential disadvantage of linear regression. It is often the case that only a small subset of the dimensions of $\mathbf{x}$ are useful for predicting w. However, without modification, the linear regression algorithm will assign nonzero values to the gradient ϕ in these directions. The goal of *sparse* linear regression is to adapt the algorithm to find a gradient vector ϕ where most of the entries are zero. The resulting classifier will be faster, since we no longer even have to make all of the

$$Pr(\phi_1, \phi_2)$$

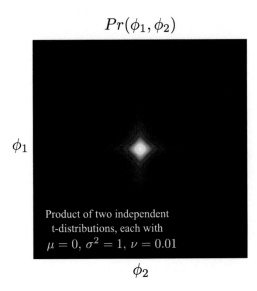

ϕ_1

Product of two independent
t-distributions, each with
$\mu = 0,\ \sigma^2 = 1,\ \nu = 0.01$

ϕ_2

Figure 8.10 A product of two 1D t-distributions where each has small degrees of freedom ν. This 2D distribution favors sparseness (where one or both variables are close to zero). In higher dimensions, the product of t-distributions encourages solutions where *most* variables are set to zero. Note that the product of 1D distributions is *not* the same as a multivariate t-distribution with a spherical covariance matrix, which looks like a multivariate normal distribution but with longer tails.

measurements. Furthermore, simpler models are preferable to complex ones; they capture the main trends in the data without overfitting to peculiarities of the training set and generalize better to new test examples.

To encourage sparse solutions, we impose a penalty for every nonzero weighted dimension. We replace the normal prior over the gradient parameters $\phi = [\phi_1, \phi_2, \ldots, \phi_D]^T$ with a product of one-dimensional t-distributions so that

$$Pr(\phi) = \prod_{d=1}^{D} \mathrm{Stud}_{\phi_d}[0, 1, \nu]$$

$$= \prod_{d=1}^{D} \frac{\Gamma\left(\frac{\nu+1}{2}\right)}{\sqrt{\nu\pi}\,\Gamma\left(\frac{\nu}{2}\right)} \left(1 + \frac{\phi_d^2}{\nu}\right)^{-(\nu+1)/2}. \tag{8.31}$$

The product of univariate t-distributions has ridges of high probability along the coordinate axes, which encourages sparseness (see Figure 8.10). We expect the final solution to be a trade-off between fitting the training data accurately and the sparseness of ϕ (and hence the number of training data dimensions that contribute to the solution).

Adopting the Bayesian approach, our aim is to compute the posterior distribution $Pr(\phi|\mathbf{X}, \mathbf{w}, \sigma^2)$ over the possible values of the gradient variable ϕ using this new prior so that

$$Pr(\phi|\mathbf{X}, \mathbf{w}, \sigma^2) = \frac{Pr(\mathbf{w}|\mathbf{X}, \phi, \sigma^2)Pr(\phi)}{Pr(\mathbf{w}|\mathbf{X}, \sigma^2)} \tag{8.32}$$

Unfortunately, there is no simple closed form expression for the posterior on the left-hand side. The prior is no longer normal, and the conjugacy relationship is lost.

To make progress, we reexpress each t-distribution as an infinite weighted sum of normal distributions where a hidden variable h_d determines the variance (Section 7.5), so that

$$Pr(\phi) = \prod_{d=1}^{D} \int \text{Norm}_{\phi_d}[0, 1/h_d] \text{Gam}_{h_d}[\nu/2, \nu/2] \, dh_d$$

$$= \int \text{Norm}_{\phi}[0, \mathbf{H}^{-1}] \prod_{d=1}^{D} \text{Gam}_{h_d}[\nu/2, \nu/2] \, d\mathbf{H}, \tag{8.33}$$

where the matrix $\mathbf{H}$ contains the hidden variables $\{h_d\}_{d=1}^{D}$ on its diagonal and zeros elsewhere. We now write out the expression for the marginal likelihood (likelihood after integrating over the gradient parameters ϕ) as

$$Pr(\mathbf{w}|\mathbf{X}, \sigma^2) = \int Pr(\mathbf{w}, \phi | \mathbf{X}, \sigma^2) \, d\phi$$

$$= \int Pr(\mathbf{w}|\mathbf{X}, \phi, \sigma^2) Pr(\phi) \, d\phi$$

$$= \int \text{Norm}_{\mathbf{w}}[\mathbf{X}^T \phi, \sigma^2 \mathbf{I}] \int \text{Norm}_{\phi}[0, \mathbf{H}^{-1}] \prod_{d=1}^{D} \text{Gam}_{h_d}[\nu/2, \nu/2] \, d\mathbf{H} d\phi$$

$$= \int\int \text{Norm}_{\mathbf{w}}[\mathbf{X}^T \phi, \sigma^2 \mathbf{I}] \text{Norm}_{\phi}[0, \mathbf{H}^{-1}] \prod_{d=1}^{D} \text{Gam}_{h_d}[\nu/2, \nu/2] \, d\mathbf{H} d\phi$$

$$= \int \text{Norm}_{\mathbf{w}}[0, \mathbf{X}^T \mathbf{H}^{-1} \mathbf{X} + \sigma^2 \mathbf{I}] \prod_{d=1}^{D} \text{Gam}_{h_d}[\nu/2, \nu/2] \, d\mathbf{H}, \tag{8.34}$$

where the integral over $\mathbf{\Phi}$ was computed using the same technique as used in Equation 8.12.

Unfortunately, we still cannot compute the remaining integral in closed form, so we instead take the approach of maximizing over hidden variables to give an approximate expression for the marginal likelihood

$$Pr(\mathbf{w}|\mathbf{X}, \sigma^2) \approx \max_{\mathbf{H}} \left[\text{Norm}_{\mathbf{w}}[0, \mathbf{X}^T \mathbf{H}^{-1} \mathbf{X} + \sigma^2 \mathbf{I}] \prod_{d=1}^{D} \text{Gam}_{h_d}[\nu/2, \nu/2] \right]. \tag{8.35}$$

As long as the true distribution over the hidden variables is concentrated tightly around the mode, this will be a reasonable approximation. When h_d takes a large value, the prior has a small variance $(1/h_d)$, and the associated coefficient ϕ_d will be forced to be close to zero: in effect, this means that the dth dimension of $\mathbf{x}$ does not contribute to the solution and can be dropped from the equations.

The general approach to fitting the model is now clear. There are two unknown quantities – the variance σ^2 and the hidden variables $\mathbf{h}$ and we alternately update each to maximize the log marginal likelihood.[1]

---

[1] More details about how these (nonobvious) update equations were generated can be found in Tipping (2001) and section 3.5 of Bishop (2006).

- To update the hidden variables, we take the derivative of the log of this expression with respect to $\mathbf{H}$, equate the result to zero, and rearrange to get the iteration

$$h_d^{new} = \frac{1 - h_d \Sigma_{dd} + \nu}{\mu_d^2 + \nu}, \tag{8.36}$$

where μ_d is the dth element of the mean $\boldsymbol{\mu}$ of the posterior distribution over the weights $\boldsymbol{\phi}$ and Σ_{dd} is the dth element of the diagonal of the covariance Σ of the posterior distribution over the weights (Equation 8.10) so that

$$\boldsymbol{\mu} = \frac{1}{\sigma^2} \mathbf{A}^{-1} \mathbf{X} \mathbf{w}$$
$$\Sigma = \mathbf{A}^{-1}, \tag{8.37}$$

and $\mathbf{A}$ is defined as

$$\mathbf{A} = \frac{1}{\sigma^2} \mathbf{X} \mathbf{X}^T + \mathbf{H}. \tag{8.38}$$

- To update the variance, we take the derivative of the log of this expression with respect to σ^2, equate the result to zero, and simplify to get

$$(\sigma^2)^{new} = \frac{1}{D - \sum_d (1 - h_d \Sigma_{dd})} (\mathbf{w} - \mathbf{X}\boldsymbol{\mu})^T (\mathbf{w} - \mathbf{X}\boldsymbol{\mu}) \tag{8.39}$$

Between each of these updates, the posterior mean $\boldsymbol{\mu}$ and variance Σ should be recalculated.

In practice, we choose a very small value for the degrees of freedom ($\nu < 10^{-3}$) to encourage sparseness. We may also restrict the maximum possible values of the hidden variables h_i to ensure numerical stability.

At the end of the training, all dimensions of $\boldsymbol{\phi}$ where the hidden variable h_d is large (say > 1000) are discarded. Figure 8.11 shows an example fit to some two-dimensional data. The sparse solution depends only on one of the two possible directions and so is twice as efficient.

In principle, a nonlinear version of this algorithm can be generated by transforming the input data $\mathbf{x}$ to create the vector $\mathbf{z} = \mathbf{f}[\mathbf{x}]$. However, if the transformed data $\mathbf{z}$ is very high-dimensional, we will need correspondingly more hidden variables h_d to cope with these dimensions. Obviously, this idea will not transfer to kernel functions where the dimensionality of the transformed data could be infinite.

To resolve this problem, we will develop the *relevance vector machine*. This model also imposes sparsity, but it does so in a way that makes the final prediction depend only on a sparse subset of the training data, rather than a sparse subset of the observed dimensions. Before we can investigate this model, we must develop a version of linear regression where there is one parameter per data example rather than one per observed dimension. This model is known as *dual linear regression*.

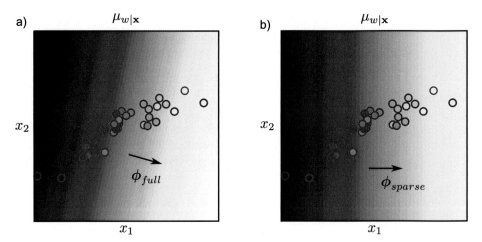

Figure 8.11 Sparse linear regression. a) Bayesian linear regression from two-dimensional data. The background color represents the mean $\mu_{w|\mathbf{x}}$ of the Gaussian prediction $Pr(w|\mathbf{x})$ for w. The variance of $Pr(w|\mathbf{x})$ is not shown. The color of the datapoints indicates the training value w, so for a perfect regression fit this should match exactly the surrounding color. Here the elements of ϕ take arbitrary values and so the gradient of the function points in an arbitrary direction. b) Sparse linear regression. Here, the elements of ϕ are encouraged to be zero where they are not necessary to explain the data. The algorithm has found a good fit where the second element of ϕ is zero and so there is no dependence on the vertical axis.

8.7   Dual linear regression

In the standard linear regression model the parameter vector ϕ contains D entries corresponding to each of the D dimensions of the (possibly transformed) input data. In the dual formulation, we reparameterize the model in terms of a vector ψ which has I entries where I is the number of training examples. This is more efficient in situations where we are training a model where the input data are high-dimensional, but the number of examples is small ($I < D$), and leads to other interesting models such as relevance vector regression.

8.7.1   Dual model

In the dual model, we retain the original linear dependence of the prediction w on the input data $\mathbf{x}$ so that

$$Pr(w_i|\mathbf{x}_i) = \text{Norm}_{\mathbf{x}_i}[\phi^T\mathbf{x}_i, \sigma^2]. \qquad (8.40)$$

However, we now represent the slope parameters ϕ as a weighted sum of the observed data points so that

$$\phi = \mathbf{X}\psi, \qquad (8.41)$$

where ψ is a $I \times 1$ vector representing the weights (Figure 8.12). We term this the *dual parameterization*. Notice that, if there are fewer data examples than data dimensions, then there will be fewer unknowns in this model than in the standard formulation of linear regression and hence learning and inference will be more efficient. Note that the term *dual* is heavily overloaded in computer science, and the reader should be careful not to confuse this use with its other meanings.

If the data dimensionality D is less than the number of examples I, then we can find parameters ψ to represent any gradient vector ϕ. However, if $D > I$ (often true in

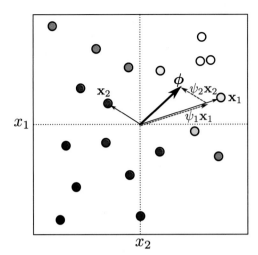

Figure 8.12 Dual variables. Two-dimensional training data $\{\mathbf{x}_i\}_{i=1}^{I}$ and associated world state $\{w_i\}_{i=1}^{I}$ (indicated by marker color). The linear regression parameter ϕ determines the direction in this 2D space in which w changes most quickly. We can alternately represent the gradient direction as a weighted sum of data examples. Here we show the case $\phi = \psi_1\mathbf{x}_1 + \psi_2\mathbf{x}_2$. In practical problems, the data dimensionality D is greater than the number of examples I so we take a weighted sum $\phi = \mathbf{X}\boldsymbol{\psi}$ of all the datapoints. This is the dual parameterization.

vision where measurements can be high-dimensional), then the vector $\mathbf{X}\boldsymbol{\psi}$ can only span a subspace of the possible gradient vectors. However, this is not a problem: if there was no variation in the data $\mathbf{X}$ in a given direction in space, then the gradient along that axis should be zero anyway since we have no information about how the world state w varies in this direction.

Making the substitution from Equation 8.41, the regression model becomes

$$Pr(w_i|\mathbf{x}_i,\boldsymbol{\theta}) = \text{Norm}_{w_i}[\boldsymbol{\psi}^T\mathbf{X}^T\mathbf{x}_i, \sigma^2], \tag{8.42}$$

or writing all of the data likelihoods in one term

$$Pr(\mathbf{w}|\mathbf{X},\boldsymbol{\theta}) = \text{Norm}_{\mathbf{w}}\left[\mathbf{X}^T\mathbf{X}\boldsymbol{\psi}, \sigma^2\mathbf{I}\right], \tag{8.43}$$

where the parameters of the model are $\boldsymbol{\theta} = \{\boldsymbol{\psi}, \sigma^2\}$. We now consider how to learn this model using both the maximum likelihood and Bayesian approaches.

Maximum likelihood solution

We apply the maximum likelihood method to estimate the parameters $\boldsymbol{\psi}$ in the dual formulation. To this end, we maximize the logarithm of the likelihood (Equation 8.43) with respect to $\boldsymbol{\psi}$ and σ^2 so that

$$\hat{\boldsymbol{\psi}}, \hat{\sigma}^2 = \underset{\boldsymbol{\psi}, \sigma^2}{\text{argmax}}\left[-\frac{I\log[2\pi]}{2} - \frac{I\log[\sigma^2]}{2} - \frac{(\mathbf{w} - \mathbf{X}^T\mathbf{X}\boldsymbol{\psi})^T(\mathbf{w} - \mathbf{X}^T\mathbf{X}\boldsymbol{\psi})}{2\sigma^2}\right]. \tag{8.44}$$

To maximize this expression, we take derivatives with respect to $\boldsymbol{\psi}$ and σ^2, equate the resulting expressions to zero, and solve to find

$$\hat{\boldsymbol{\psi}} = (\mathbf{X}^T\mathbf{X})^{-1}\mathbf{w}$$
$$\hat{\sigma}^2 = \frac{(\mathbf{w} - \mathbf{X}^T\mathbf{X}\boldsymbol{\psi})^T(\mathbf{w} - \mathbf{X}^T\mathbf{X}\boldsymbol{\psi})}{I} = 0. \tag{8.45}$$

where the variance will be zero when $D > I$.

When the matrix $\mathbf{X}$ is square and invertible, the solution is actually the same as for the original linear regression model (Equation 8.6). For example, if we substitute in the definition $\phi = \mathbf{X}\psi$,

$$\hat{\phi} = \mathbf{X}\hat{\psi} = \mathbf{X}(\mathbf{X}^T\mathbf{X})^{-1}\mathbf{w}$$
$$= (\mathbf{X}\mathbf{X}^T)^{-1}\mathbf{X}\mathbf{X}^T\mathbf{X}(\mathbf{X}^T\mathbf{X})^{-1}\mathbf{w}$$
$$= (\mathbf{X}\mathbf{X}^T)^{-1}\mathbf{X}\mathbf{w}, \tag{8.46}$$

which was the original maximum likelihood solution for ϕ.

Bayesian solution

We now explore the Bayesian approach to the dual regression model. As before, we treat the dual parameters ψ as uncertain, assuming that the noise σ^2 is known. Once again, we will estimate this separately using maximum likelihood.

The goal of the Bayesian approach is to compute the posterior distribution $Pr(\psi|\mathbf{X},\mathbf{w})$ over possible values of the parameters ψ given the training data pairs $\{\mathbf{x}_i, w_i\}_{i=1}^{I}$. We start by defining a prior $Pr(\psi)$ over the parameters. Since we have no particular prior knowledge, we choose a normal distribution with a large spherical covariance,

$$Pr(\psi) = \text{Norm}_{\psi}[\mathbf{0}, \sigma_p^2\mathbf{I}]. \tag{8.47}$$

We use Bayes' rule to compute the posterior distribution over the parameters

$$Pr(\psi|\mathbf{X},\mathbf{w},\sigma^2) = \frac{Pr(\mathbf{w}|\mathbf{X},\psi,\sigma^2)Pr(\psi)}{Pr(\mathbf{w}|\mathbf{X},\sigma^2)}, \tag{8.48}$$

which can be shown to yield the closed form expression

$$Pr(\psi|\mathbf{X},\mathbf{w},\sigma^2) = \text{Norm}_{\psi}\left[\frac{1}{\sigma^2}\mathbf{A}^{-1}\mathbf{X}^T\mathbf{X}\mathbf{w}, \mathbf{A}^{-1}\right], \tag{8.49}$$

where

$$\mathbf{A} = \frac{1}{\sigma^2}\mathbf{X}^T\mathbf{X}\mathbf{X}^T\mathbf{X} + \frac{1}{\sigma_p^2}\mathbf{I}. \tag{8.50}$$

To compute the predictive distribution $Pr(w^*|\mathbf{x}^*)$, we take an infinite weighted sum over the predictions of the model associated with each possible value of the parameters ψ,

$$Pr(w^*|\mathbf{x}^*,\mathbf{X},\mathbf{w}) = \int Pr(w^*|\mathbf{x}^*,\psi)Pr(\psi|\mathbf{X},\mathbf{w})\,d\psi \tag{8.51}$$

$$= \text{Norm}_{w^*}\left[\frac{1}{\sigma^2}\mathbf{x}^{*T}\mathbf{X}\mathbf{A}^{-1}\mathbf{X}^T\mathbf{X}\mathbf{w}, \mathbf{x}^{*T}\mathbf{X}\mathbf{A}^{-1}\mathbf{X}^T\mathbf{x}^* + \sigma^2\right].$$

⚙ 8.6   To generalize the model to the nonlinear case, we replace the training data $\mathbf{X} = [\mathbf{x}_1, \mathbf{x}_2, \ldots, \mathbf{x}_I]$ with the transformed data $\mathbf{Z} = [\mathbf{z}_1, \mathbf{z}_2, \ldots, \mathbf{z}_I]$ and the test data $\mathbf{x}^*$ with the transformed test data $\mathbf{z}^*$. Since the resulting expression depends only on inner products of the form $\mathbf{Z}^T\mathbf{Z}$ and $\mathbf{Z}^T\mathbf{z}^*$, it is directly amenable to kernelization.

As for the original regression model, the variance parameter σ^2 can be estimated by maximizing the log of the marginal likelihood which is given by

$$Pr(\mathbf{w}|\mathbf{X},\sigma^2) = \text{Norm}_{\mathbf{w}}[\mathbf{0}, \sigma_p^2\mathbf{X}^T\mathbf{X}\mathbf{X}^T\mathbf{X} + \sigma^2\mathbf{I}]. \tag{8.52}$$

8.8 Relevance vector regression

Having developed the dual approach to linear regression, we are now in a position to develop a model that depends only sparsely on the training data. To this end, we impose a penalty for every nonzero weighted training example. We achieve this by replacing the normal prior over the dual parameters ψ with a product of one-dimensional t-distributions so that

$$Pr(\psi) = \prod_{i=1}^{I} \text{Stud}_{\psi_i}[0, 1, \nu]. \tag{8.53}$$

This model is known as *relevance vector regression*.

This situation is exactly analogous to the sparse linear regression model (Section 8.6) except that now we are working with dual variables. As for the sparse model, it is not possible to marginalize over the variables ψ with the t-distributed prior. Our approach will again be to approximate the t-distributions by maximizing with respect to their hidden variables rather than marginalizing over them (Equation 8.35). By analogy with Section 8.6, the marginal likelihood becomes

$$Pr(\mathbf{w}|\mathbf{X}, \sigma^2) \approx \max_{\mathbf{H}} \left[\text{Norm}_{\mathbf{w}}[0, \mathbf{X}^T\mathbf{X}\mathbf{H}^{-1}\mathbf{X}^T\mathbf{X} + \sigma^2\mathbf{I}] \prod_{i=1}^{I} \text{Gam}_{h_i}[\nu/2, \nu/2] \right], \tag{8.54}$$

where the matrix $\mathbf{H}$ contains the hidden variables $\{h_i\}_{i=1}^{I}$ associated with the t-distribution on its diagonal and zeros elsewhere. Notice that this expression is similar to Equation 8.52 except that instead of every datapoint having the same prior variance σ_p^2, they now have individual variances that are determined by the hidden variables that form the elements of the diagonal matrix $\mathbf{H}$.

In relevance vector regression, we alternately (i) optimize the marginal likelihood with respect to the hidden variables and (ii) optimize the marginal likelihood with respect to the variance parameter σ^2 using

$$h_i^{new} = \frac{1 - h_i\Sigma_{ii} + \nu}{\mu_i^2 + \nu} \tag{8.55}$$

and

$$(\sigma^2)^{new} = \frac{1}{I - \sum_i(1 - h_i\Sigma_{ii})} \left(\mathbf{w} - \mathbf{X}^T\mathbf{X}\boldsymbol{\mu}\right)^T \left(\mathbf{w} - \mathbf{X}^T\mathbf{X}\boldsymbol{\mu}\right). \tag{8.56}$$

In between each step we update the mean $\boldsymbol{\mu}$ and variance $\boldsymbol{\Sigma}$ of the posterior distribution

$$\boldsymbol{\mu} = \frac{1}{\sigma^2}\mathbf{A}^{-1}\mathbf{X}^T\mathbf{X}\mathbf{w}$$

$$\boldsymbol{\Sigma} = \mathbf{A}^{-1}, \tag{8.57}$$

where $\mathbf{A}$ is defined as

$$\mathbf{A} = \frac{1}{\sigma^2}\mathbf{X}^T\mathbf{X}\mathbf{X}^T\mathbf{X} + \mathbf{H}. \tag{8.58}$$

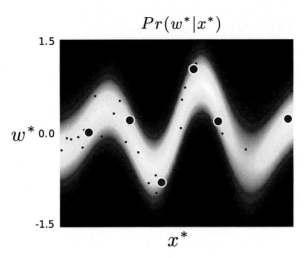

Figure 8.13 Relevance vector regression. A prior applying sparseness is applied to the dual parameters. This means that the final classifier only depends on a subset of the datapoints (indicated by the six larger points). The resulting regression function is considerably faster to evaluate and tends to be simpler: this means it is less likely to overfit to random statistical fluctuations in the training data and generalizes better to new data.

At the end of the training, all data examples where the hidden variable h_i is large (say > 1000) are discarded as here the coefficients ψ_i will be very small and contribute almost nothing to the solution.

Since this algorithm depends only on inner products, a nonlinear version of this algorithm can be generated by replacing the inner products with a kernel function $k[\mathbf{x}_i, \mathbf{x}_j]$. If the kernel itself contains parameters, these may be also be manipulated to improve the log marginal variance during the fitting procedure. Figure 8.13 shows an example fit using the RBF kernel. The final solution now only depends on six datapoints but nonetheless still captures the important aspects of the data.

8.9   Regression to multivariate data

Throughout this chapter we have discussed predicting a scalar value w_i from multivariate data $\mathbf{x}_i$. In real-world situations such as the pose regression problem, the world states $\mathbf{w}_i$ are multivariate. It is trivial to extend the models in this chapter: we simply construct a separate regressor for each dimension. The exception to this rule is the relevance vector machine: here we might want to ensure that the sparse structure is common for each of these models, so the efficiency gains are retained. To this end, we modify the model so that a single set of hidden variables is shared across the model for each world state dimension.

8.10   Applications

Regression methods are used less frequently in vision than classification, but nonetheless there are many useful applications. The majority of these involve estimating the position or pose of objects, since the unknowns in such problems are naturally treated as continuous.

8.10.1 Human body pose estimation

Agarwal and Triggs (2006) developed a system based on the relevance vector machine to predict body pose $\mathbf{w}$ from silhouette data $\mathbf{x}$. To encode the silhouette, they computed a 60-dimensional shape context feature (Section 13.3.5) at each of 400-500 points on the boundary of the object. To reduce the data dimensionality, they computed the similarity of each shape context feature to each of 100 different prototypes. Finally, they formed a 100-dimensional histogram containing the aggregated 100-dimensional similarities for all of the boundary points. This histogram was used as the data vector $\mathbf{x}$. The body pose was encoded by the 3 joint angles of each of the 18 major body joints and the overall azimuth (compass heading) of the body. The resulting 55-dimensional vector was used as the world state $\mathbf{w}$.

A relevance vector machine was trained using 2636 data vectors $\mathbf{x}_i$ extracted from silhouettes that were rendered using the commercial program POSER from known motion capture data $\mathbf{w}_i$. Using a radial basis function kernel, the relevance vector machine based its solution on just 6% of these training examples. The body pose angles of test data could be predicted to within an average of 6° error (Figure 8.14). They also demonstrated that the system worked reasonably well on silhouettes from real images (Figure 8.1).

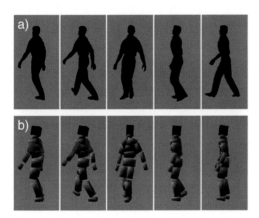

Figure 8.14 Body pose estimation results. a) Silhouettes of walking avatar. b) Estimated body pose based on silhouette using a relevance vector machine. The RVM used radial basis functions and constructed its final solution from just 156 of 2636 (6%) of the training examples. It produced a mean test error of 6.0^o averaged over the three joint angles for the 18 main body parts and the overall compass direction of the model. Adapted from Agarwal and Triggs (2006).

Silhouette information is by its nature ambiguous: it is very hard to tell which leg is in front of the other based on a single silhouette. Agarwal and Triggs (2006) partially circumvented this system by tracking the body pose $\mathbf{w}_i$ through a video sequence. Essentially, the ambiguity at a given frame is resolved by encouraging the estimated pose in adjacent frames in the sequence to be similar: information from frames where the pose vector is well defined is propagated through the sequence to resolve ambiguities in other parts (see Chapter 19).

However, the ambiguity of silhouette data is an argument for *not* using this type of classifier: the regression models in this chapter are designed to give a unimodal normal output. To effectively classify single frames of data, we should use a regression method that produces a multimodal prediction that can effectively describe the ambiguity.

8.10.2 Displacement experts

Regression models are also used to form *displacement experts* in tracking applications. The goal is to take a region of the image $\mathbf{x}$ and return a set of numbers $\mathbf{w}$ that indicate the

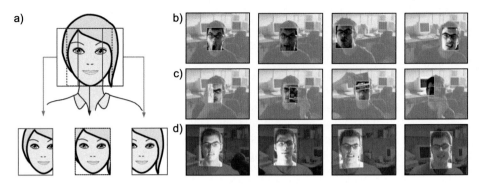

Figure 8.15 Tracking using displacement experts. The goal of the system is to predict a displacement vector indicating the motion of the object based on the pixel data at its last known position. a) The system is trained by perturbing the bounding box around the object to simulate the motion of the object. b) The system successfully tracks a face, even in the presence c) of partial occlusions. d) If the system is trained using gradient vectors rather than raw pixel values, it is also quite robust to changes in illumination. Adapted from Williams et al. (2005). ©2005 IEEE.

change in position of an object relative to the window. The world state $\mathbf{w}$ might simply contain the horizontal and vertical translation vectors or might contain parameters of a more complex 2D transformation (see Chapter 15). For simplicity, we will describe the former situation.

Training data are extracted as follows. A bounding box around the object of interest (car, face, etc.) is identified in a number of frames. For each of these frames, the bounding box is perturbed by a predetermined set of translation vectors, to simulate the object moving in the opposite direction (Figure 8.15a). In this way, we associate a translation vector $\mathbf{w}_i$ with each perturbation. The data from the perturbed bounding box are extracted and resized to a standard shape, and histogram equalized (Section 13.1.2) to induce a degree of invariance to illumination changes. The resulting values are then concatenated to form the data vector $\mathbf{x}_i$.

Williams et al. (2005) describe a system of this kind in which the elements of $\mathbf{w}$ were learned by a set of independent relevance vector machines. They initialize the position of the object using a standard object detector (see Chapter 9). In the subsequent frame, they compute a prediction for the displacement vector $\mathbf{w}$ using the relevance vector machines on the data $\mathbf{x}$ from the original position. This prediction is combined in a Kalman filter-like system (Chapter 19) that imposes prior knowledge about the continuity of the motion to create a robust method for tracking known objects in scenes. Figures 8.15b–d show a series of tracking results from this system.

Discussion

The goal of this chapter was to introduce discriminative approaches to regression. These have niche applications in vision related to predicting the pose and position of objects. However, the main reason for studying these models is that the concepts involved (sparsity, dual variables, kernelization) are all important for discriminative classification methods. These are very widely used but are rather more complex and are discussed in the following chapter.

Notes

Regression methods: Rasmussen and Williams (2006) is a comprehensive resource on Gaussian processes. The relevance vector machine was first introduced by Tipping (2001). Several innovations within the vision community have extended these models. Williams et al. (2006) presented a semisupervised method for Gaussian process regression in which the world state **w** is only known for a subset of examples. Ranganathan and Yang (2008) presented an efficient algorithm for online learning of Gaussian processes when the kernel matrix is sparse. Thayananthan et al. (2006) developed a multivariate version of the relevance vector machine.

Applications: Applications of regression in vision include head pose estimation (Williams et al. 2006; Ranganathan and Yang 2008; Rae and Ritter 1998), body tracking (Williams et al. 2006; Agarwal and Triggs 2006; Thayananthan et al. 2006), eye tracking (Williams et al. 2006), and tracking of other objects (Williams et al. 2005; Ranganathan and Yang 2008).

Multimodal posterior: One of the drawbacks of using the methods in this chapter is that they always produce a unimodal normally distributed posterior. For some problems (e.g., body pose estimation), the posterior probability over the world state may be genuinely multimodal – there is more than one interpretation of the data. One approach to this is to build many regressors that relate small parts of the world state to the data (Thayananthan et al. 2006). Alternatively, it is possible to use generative regression methods in which either the joint density is modeled directly (Navaratnam et al. 2007) or the likelihood and prior are modeled separately (Urtasun et al. 2006). In these methods, the posterior compute distribution over the world is multimodal. However, the cost of this is that it is intractable to compute the posterior exactly, and so we must rely on optimization techniques to find its modes.

Problems

8.1 Consider a regression problem where the world state w is known to be positive. To cope with this, we could construct a regression model in which the world state is modeled as a gamma distribution. We could constrain both parameters α, β of the gamma distribution to be the same so that $\alpha = \beta$ and make them a function of the data **x**. Describe a maximum likelihood approach to fitting this model.

8.2 Consider a robust regression model based on the t-distribution rather than the normal distribution. Define this model precisely in mathematical terms and sketch out a maximum likelihood approach to fitting the parameters.

8.3 Prove that the maximum likelihood solution for the gradient in the linear regression model is

$$\hat{\phi} = (\mathbf{X}\mathbf{X}^T)^{-1}\mathbf{X}\mathbf{w}.$$

8.4 For the Bayesian linear regression model (Section 8.2), show that the posterior distribution over the parameters ϕ is given by

$$Pr(\phi|\mathbf{X}, \mathbf{w}) = \text{Norm}_\phi \left[\frac{1}{\sigma^2} \mathbf{A}^{-1}\mathbf{X}\mathbf{w}, \mathbf{A}^{-1} \right],$$

where

$$\mathbf{A} = \frac{1}{\sigma^2}\mathbf{X}\mathbf{X}^T + \frac{1}{\sigma_p^2}\mathbf{I}.$$

8.5 For the Bayesian linear regression model (Section 8.2), show that the predictive distribution for a new data example $\mathbf{x}^*$ is given by

$$Pr(w^*|\mathbf{x}^*, \mathbf{X}, \mathbf{w}) = \text{Norm}_{w^*} \left[\frac{1}{\sigma^2}\mathbf{x}^{*T}\mathbf{A}^{-1}\mathbf{X}\mathbf{w}, \mathbf{x}^{*T}\mathbf{A}^{-1}\mathbf{x}^* + \sigma^2 \right].$$

8.6 Use the matrix inversion lemma (Appendix C.8.4) to show that

$$\mathbf{A}^{-1} = \left(\frac{1}{\sigma^2} \mathbf{X} \mathbf{X}^T + \frac{1}{\sigma_p^2} \mathbf{I}_D \right)^{-1} = \sigma_p^2 \mathbf{I}_D - \sigma_p^2 \mathbf{X} \left(\mathbf{X}^T \mathbf{X} + \frac{\sigma^2}{\sigma_p^2} \mathbf{I}_I \right)^{-1} \mathbf{X}^T.$$

8.7 Compute the derivative of the marginal likelihood

$$Pr(\mathbf{w}|\mathbf{X}, \sigma^2) = \text{Norm}_{\mathbf{w}}[\mathbf{0}, \sigma_p^2 \mathbf{X}^T \mathbf{X} + \sigma^2 \mathbf{I}],$$

with respect to the variance parameter σ^2.

8.8 Compute a closed form expression for the approximated t-distribution used to impose sparseness.

$$q(\phi) = \max_h \left[\text{Norm}_\phi[0, h^{-1}] \text{Gam}_h[\nu/2, \nu/2] \right].$$

Plot this function for $\nu = 2$. Plot the 2D function $[h_1, h_2] = q(\phi_1) q(\phi_2)$ for $\nu = 2$.

8.9 Describe maximum likelihood learning and inference algorithms for a nonlinear regression model based on polynomials where

$$Pr(w|x) = \text{Norm}_w[\phi_0 + \phi_1 x + \phi_2 x^2 + \phi_3 x^3, \sigma^2].$$

8.10 I wish to learn a linear regression model in which I predict the world w from I examples of $D \times 1$ data $\mathbf{x}$ using the maximum likelihood method. If $I > D$, is it more efficient to use the dual parameterization or the original linear regression model?

8.11 Show that the maximum likelihood estimate for the parameters $\boldsymbol{\psi}$ in the dual linear regression model (Section 8.7) is given by

$$\hat{\boldsymbol{\psi}} = (\mathbf{X}^T \mathbf{X})^{-1} \mathbf{w}.$$

Chapter 9

Classification models

This chapter concerns discriminative models for classification. The goal is to directly model the posterior probability distribution $Pr(w|\mathbf{x})$ over a discrete world state $w \in \{1, \ldots K\}$ given the continuous observed data vector $\mathbf{x}$. Models for classification are very closely related to those for regression and the reader should be familiar with the contents of Chapter 8 before proceeding.

To motivate the models in this chapter, we will consider *gender classification*: here we observe a 60×60 RGB image containing a face (Figure 9.1) and concatenate the RGB values to form the 10800×1 vector $\mathbf{x}$. Our goal is to take the vector $\mathbf{x}$ and return the probability distribution $Pr(w|\mathbf{x})$ over a label $w \in \{0, 1\}$ indicating whether the face is male ($w = 0$) or female ($w = 1$).

Gender classification is a *binary classification* task as there are only two possible values of the world state. Throughout most of this chapter, we will restrict our discussion to binary classification. We discuss how to extend these models to cope with an arbitrary number of classes in Section 9.9.

9.1 Logistic regression

We will start by considering *logistic regression*, which despite its name is a model that can be applied to classification. Logistic regression (Figure 9.2) is a discriminative model; we select a probability distribution over the world state $w \in \{0, 1\}$ and make its parameters contingent on the observed data $\mathbf{x}$. Since the world state is binary, we will describe it with a Bernoulli distribution, and we will make the single Bernoulli parameter λ (indicating the probability that the world state takes the value $w = 1$) a function of the measurements $\mathbf{x}$.

In contrast to the regression model, we cannot simply make the parameter λ a linear function $\phi_0 + \boldsymbol{\phi}^T\mathbf{x}$ of the measurements; a linear function can return any value, but the parameter λ must lie between 0 and 1. Consequently, we first compute the linear function and then pass this through the *logistic sigmoid function* sig[•] that maps the range $[-\infty, \infty]$ to $[0, 1]$. The final model is hence

$$Pr(w|\phi_0, \boldsymbol{\phi}, \mathbf{x}) = \text{Bern}_w\left[\text{sig}[a]\right], \tag{9.1}$$

where a is termed the *activation* and is given by the linear function

$$a = \phi_0 + \boldsymbol{\phi}^T\mathbf{x}. \tag{9.2}$$

a)
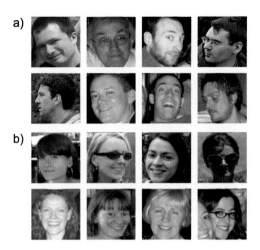
b)

Figure 9.1 Gender classification. Consider a 60×60 pixel image of a face. We concatenate the RGB values to make a 10800×1 data vector **x**. The goal of gender classification is to use the data **x** to infer a label $w \in \{0,1\}$ indicating whether the window contains a) a male or b) a female face. This is challenging because the differences are subtle and there is image variation due to changes in pose, lighting, and expression. Note that real systems would preprocess the image before classification by registering the faces more closely and compensating in some way for lighting variation (see Chapter 13).

The logistic sigmoid function sig[•] is given by

$$\text{sig}[a] = \frac{1}{1 + \exp[-a]}. \tag{9.3}$$

As the activation a tends to ∞ this function tends to one. As a tends to $-\infty$ it tends to zero. When a is zero, the logistic sigmoid function returns a value of one half.

For 1D data x, the overall effect of this transformation is to describe a sigmoid curve relating x to λ (Figures 9.2c and 9.3a). The horizontal position of the sigmoid is determined by the place that the linear function a crosses zero (i.e., the x-intercept) and the steepness of the sigmoid depends on the gradient ϕ_1.

In more than one dimension, the relationship between **x** and λ is more complex (Figure 9.3b). The predicted parameter λ has a sigmoid profile in the direction of the gradient vector ϕ but is constant in all perpendicular directions. This induces a linear *decision boundary*. This is the set of positions in data space $\{\mathbf{x} : Pr(w = 1|\mathbf{x}) = 0.5\}$ where the posterior probability is 0.5; the decision boundary separates the region where the world state w is more likely to be 0 from the region where it is more likely to be 1. For logistic regression, the decision boundary takes the form of a hyperplane with the normal vector in the direction of ϕ.

As for regression, we can simplify the notation by attaching the y-intercept ϕ_0 to the start of the parameter vector ϕ so that $\phi \leftarrow [\phi_0 \quad \phi^T]^T$ and attaching 1 to the start of the data vector **x** so that $\mathbf{x} \leftarrow [1 \quad \mathbf{x}^T]^T$. After these changes, the activation is now $a = \phi^T \mathbf{x}$, and the final model becomes

$$Pr(w|\phi, \mathbf{x}) = \text{Bern}_w \left[\frac{1}{1 + \exp[-\phi^T \mathbf{x}]} \right]. \tag{9.4}$$

Notice that this is very similar to the linear regression model (Section 8.1) except for the introduction of the nonlinear logistic sigmoid function sig[•] (explaining the unfortunate name "logistic regression"). However, this small change has serious implications:

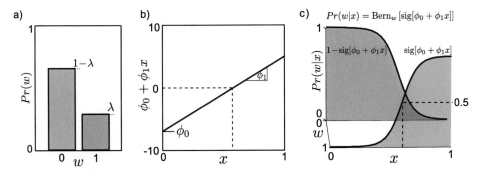

Figure 9.2 Logistic regression. a) We represent the world state w as a Bernoulli distribution and make the Bernoulli parameter λ a function of the observations x. b) We compute the activation a as a linear sum $a = \phi_0 + \phi_1 x$ of the observations. c) The Bernoulli parameter λ is formed by passing the activation through a logistic sigmoid function $\text{sig}[\bullet]$ to constrain the value to lie between 0 and 1, giving the characteristic sigmoid shape. In learning, we fit parameters $\boldsymbol{\theta} = \{\phi_0, \phi_1\}$ using training pairs $\{x_i, w_i\}$. In inference, we take a new datum x^* and evaluate the posterior $Pr(w^*|x^*)$ over the state.

maximum likelihood learning of the parameters ϕ is considerably harder than for linear regression and to adopt the Bayesian approach we will be forced to make approximations.

9.1.1 Learning: maximum likelihood

In maximum likelihood learning, we consider fitting the parameters ϕ using I paired examples of training data $\{\mathbf{x}_i, w_i\}_{i=1}^I$ (Figure 9.3). Assuming independence of the training pairs we have

$$
Pr(\mathbf{w}|\mathbf{X}, \boldsymbol{\phi}) = \prod_{i=1}^I \lambda^{w_i} (1-\lambda)^{1-w_i} \tag{9.5}
$$

$$
= \prod_{i=1}^I \left(\frac{1}{1+\exp[-\boldsymbol{\phi}^T \mathbf{x}_i]} \right)^{w_i} \left(\frac{\exp[-\boldsymbol{\phi}^T \mathbf{x}_i]}{1+\exp[-\boldsymbol{\phi}^T \mathbf{x}_i]} \right)^{1-w_i},
$$

where $\mathbf{X} = [\mathbf{x}_1, \mathbf{x}_2, \ldots, \mathbf{x}_I]$ is a matrix containing the measurements and $\mathbf{w} = [w_1, w_2, \ldots, w_I]^T$ is a vector containing all of the binary world states. The maximum likelihood method finds parameters ϕ, which maximize this expression.

As usual, however, it is simpler to maximize the logarithm L of this expression. Since the logarithm is a monotonic transformation, it does not change the position of the maximum with respect to ϕ. Applying the logarithm replaces the product with a sum so that

$$
L = \sum_{i=1}^I w_i \log \left[\frac{1}{1+\exp[-\boldsymbol{\phi}^T \mathbf{x}_i]} \right] + \sum_{i=1}^I (1-w_i) \log \left[\frac{\exp[-\boldsymbol{\phi}^T \mathbf{x}_i]}{1+\exp[-\boldsymbol{\phi}^T \mathbf{x}_i]} \right]. \tag{9.6}
$$

The derivative of the log likelihood L with respect to the parameters ϕ is

$$
\frac{\partial L}{\partial \boldsymbol{\phi}} = -\sum_{i=1}^I \left(\frac{1}{1+\exp[-\boldsymbol{\phi}^T \mathbf{x}_i]} - w_i \right) \mathbf{x}_i = -\sum_{i=1}^I \left(\text{sig}[a_i] - w_i \right) \mathbf{x}_i. \tag{9.7}
$$

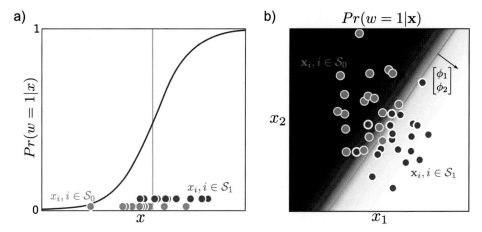

Figure 9.3 Logistic regression model fitted to two different data sets. a) One dimensional data. Green points denote set of examples $\mathcal{S}_0$ where $w = 0$. Pink points denote $\mathcal{S}_1$ where $w = 1$. Note that in this (and all future figures in this chapter), we have only plotted the probability $Pr(w = 1|x)$ (compare to Figure 9.2c). The probability $Pr(w = 0|x)$ can be computed as $1 - Pr(w = 1|\mathbf{x})$. b) Two-dimensional data. Here, the model has a sigmoid profile in the direction of the gradient ϕ and $Pr(w = 1|\mathbf{x})$ is constant in the orthogonal directions. The decision boundary (cyan line) is linear.

Unfortunately, when we equate this expression to zero, there is no way to re-arrange to get a closed form solution for the parameters ϕ. Instead, we must rely on a *nonlinear optimization* technique to find the maximum of this objective function. Optimization techniques are discussed in detail in Appendix B. In brief, we start with an initial estimate of the solution ϕ and iteratively improve it until no more progress can be made.

Here, we will apply the *Newton method*, in which we base the update of the parameters on the first and second derivatives of the function at the current position so that

$$\phi^{[t]} = \phi^{[t-1]} + \alpha \left(\frac{\partial^2 L}{\partial \phi^2} \right)^{-1} \frac{\partial L}{\partial \phi}, \tag{9.8}$$

where $\phi^{[t]}$ denotes the estimate of the parameters ϕ at iteration t and α determines how much we change this estimate and is usually chosen by an explicit search at each iteration.

For the logistic regression model, the $D \times 1$ vector of first derivatives and the $D \times D$ matrix of second derivatives are given by

$$\frac{\partial L}{\partial \phi} = -\sum_{i=1}^{I} (\text{sig}[a_i] - w_i)\mathbf{x}_i$$

$$\frac{\partial^2 L}{\partial \phi^2} = -\sum_{i=1}^{I} \text{sig}[a_i](1 - \text{sig}[a_i])\mathbf{x}_i\mathbf{x}_i^T. \tag{9.9}$$

These are known as the *gradient vector* and the *Hessian matrix*, respectively.[1]

---

[1]Note that these are the gradient and Hessian of the log likelihood that we aim to *maximize*. If this is implemented using a nonlinear minimization algorithm, we should multiply the objective function, gradient and Hessian by -1.

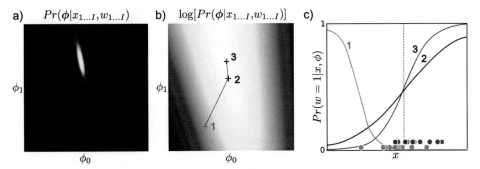

Figure 9.4 Parameter estimation for logistic regression with 1D data. a) In maximum likelihood learning, we seek the maximum of $Pr(\mathbf{w}|\mathbf{X}, \phi)$ with respect to ϕ. b) In practice, we instead maximize log likelihood: notice that the peak is in the same place. Crosses show results of two iterations of optimization using Newton's method. c) The logistic sigmoid functions associated with the parameters at each optimization step. As the log likelihood increases, the model fits the data more closely: the green points represent data where $w = 0$ and the purple points represent data where $w = 1$ and so we expect the best-fitting model to increase from left to right just like curve 3.

The expression for the gradient vector has an intuitive explanation. The contribution of each datapoint depends on the difference between the actual class w_i and the predicted probability $\lambda = \text{sig}[a_i]$ of being in class 1; points that are classified incorrectly contribute more to this expression and hence have more influence on the parameter values. Figure 9.4 shows maximum likelihood learning of the parameters ϕ for 1D data using a series of Newton steps.

For general functions, the Newton method only finds *local maxima*. At the end of the procedure, we cannot be certain that there is not a taller peak in the likelihood function elsewhere. However, the log likelihood for logistic regression has a special property. It is a *concave* function of the parameters ϕ. For concave functions there are never multiple maxima and gradient-based approaches are guaranteed to find the global maximum. It is possible to establish whether a function is concave or not by examining the Hessian matrix. If this is negative definite for all ϕ, then the function is concave. This is the case for logistic regression as the Hessian (Equation 9.9) consists of a negative weighted sum of outer products.[2]

9.1.2 Problems with the logistic regression model

The logistic regression model works well for simple data sets, but for more complex visual data it will not generally suffice. It is limited in the following ways.

1. It is overconfident as it was learned using maximum likelihood.
2. It can only describe linear decision boundaries.
3. It is inefficient and prone to overfitting in high dimensions.

In the remaining part of this chapter, we will extend this model to cope with these problems (Figure 9.5).

---

[2] When we are concerned with minimizing functions, we equivalently consider whether the function is *convex* and so only has a single local minimum. If the Hessian is positive definite everywhere then the function is convex.

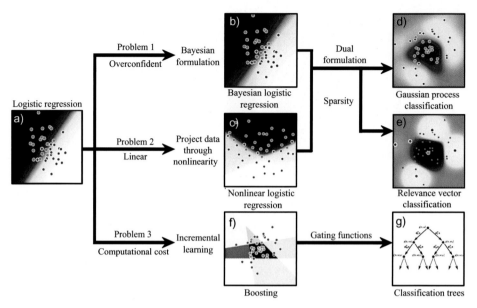

Figure 9.5 Family of classification models. a) In the remaining part of the chapter, we will address several of the limitations of logistic regression for binary classification. b) The logistic regression model with maximum likelihood learning is overconfident, and hence we develop a Bayesian version. c) It is unrealistic to always assume a linear relationship between the data and the world, and to this end we introduce a nonlinear version. d) Combining the Bayesian and nonlinear versions of regression leads to Gaussian process classification. e) The logistic regression model also has many parameters and may require considerable resources to learn when the data dimension is high, and so we develop relevance vector classification that encourages sparsity. f) We can also build a sparse model by incrementally adding parameters in a boosting scheme. g) Finally, we consider a very fast classification model based on a tree structure.

9.2   Bayesian logistic regression

In the Bayesian approach, we learn a distribution $Pr(\phi|\mathbf{X}, \mathbf{w})$ over the possible parameter values ϕ that are compatible with the training data. In inference, we observe a new data example $\mathbf{x}^*$ and use this distribution to weight the predictions for the world state w^* given by each possible estimate of ϕ. In linear regression (Section 8.2), there were closed form expressions for both of these steps. However, the nonlinear function $\text{sig}[\bullet]$ in logistic regression means that this is no longer the case. To get around this, we will approximate both steps so that we retain neat closed form expressions and the algorithm is tractable.

9.2.1   Learning

We start by defining a prior over the parameters ϕ. Unfortunately, there is no conjugate prior for the likelihood in the logistic regression model (Equation 9.1); this is why there won't be closed form expressions for the likelihood and predictive distribution. With nothing else to guide us, a reasonable choice for the prior over the continuous parameters

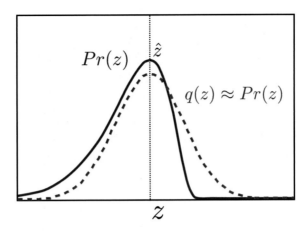

Figure 9.6 Laplace approximation. A probability density (blue curve) is approximated by a normal distribution (red curve). The mean of the normal (and hence the peak) is chosen to coincide with the peak of the original pdf. The variance of the normal is chosen so that its second derivatives at the mean match the second derivatives of the original pdf at the peak.

ϕ is a multivariate normal distribution with zero mean and a large spherical covariance so that

$$Pr(\phi) = \text{Norm}_\phi[\mathbf{0}, \sigma_p^2 \mathbf{I}]. \tag{9.10}$$

To compute the posterior probability distribution $Pr(\phi|\mathbf{X}, \mathbf{w})$ over the parameters ϕ given the training data pairs $\{\mathbf{x}_i, w_i\}$, we apply Bayes' rule,

$$Pr(\phi|\mathbf{X}, \mathbf{w}) = \frac{Pr(\mathbf{w}|\mathbf{X}, \phi) Pr(\phi)}{Pr(\mathbf{w}|\mathbf{X})}, \tag{9.11}$$

where the likelihood and prior are given by Equations 9.5 and 9.10, respectively. Since we are not using a conjugate prior, there is no simple closed form expression for this posterior and so we are forced to make an approximation of some kind.

One possibility is to use the *Laplace approximation* (Figure 9.6) which is a general method for approximating complex probability distributions. The goal is to approximate the posterior distribution by a multivariate normal. We select the parameters of this normal so that (i) the mean is at the peak of the posterior distribution (i.e., at the MAP estimate) and (ii) the covariance is such that the second derivatives at the peak match the second derivatives of the true posterior distribution at its peak.

Hence, to make the Laplace approximation, we first find the MAP estimate of the parameters $\hat{\phi}$, and to this end we use a nonlinear optimization technique such as Newton's method to maximize the criterion,

$$L = \sum_{i=1}^{I} \log[Pr(w_i|\mathbf{x}_i, \phi)] + \log[Pr(\phi)]. \tag{9.12}$$

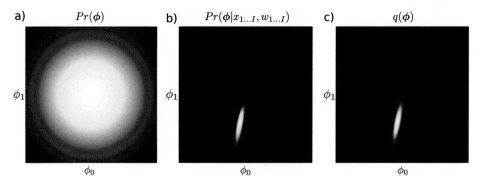

Figure 9.7 Laplace approximation for logistic regression. a) The prior $Pr(\phi)$ over the parameters is a normal distribution with mean zero and a large spherical covariance. b) The posterior distribution $Pr(\phi|\mathbf{X}, \mathbf{w})$ represents the refined state of our knowledge after observing the data. Unfortunately, this posterior cannot be expressed in closed form. c) We approximate the true posterior with a normal distribution $q(\phi) = \text{Norm}_\phi[\boldsymbol{\mu}, \boldsymbol{\Sigma}]$ whose mean is at the peak of the posterior and whose covariance is chosen so that the second derivatives at the peak of the true posterior match the second derivatives at the peak of the normal. This is termed the Laplace approximation.

Newton's method needs the derivatives of the log posterior which are

$$\frac{\partial L}{\partial \phi} = -\sum_{i=1}^{I} (\text{sig}[a_i] - w_i)\mathbf{x}_i - \frac{\phi}{\sigma_p^2}$$

$$\frac{\partial^2 L}{\partial \phi^2} = -\sum_{i=1}^{I} \text{sig}[a_i](1 - \text{sig}[a_i])\mathbf{x}_i\mathbf{x}_i^T - \frac{1}{\sigma_p^2}. \tag{9.13}$$

We then approximate the posterior by a multivariate normal so that

$$Pr(\phi|\mathbf{X}, \mathbf{w}) \approx q(\phi) = \text{Norm}_\phi[\boldsymbol{\mu}, \boldsymbol{\Sigma}], \tag{9.14}$$

where the mean $\boldsymbol{\mu}$ is set to the MAP estimate $\hat{\phi}$, and the covariance $\boldsymbol{\Sigma}$ is chosen so that the second derivatives of the normal match those of the log posterior at the MAP estimate (Figure 9.7) so that

$$\boldsymbol{\mu} = \hat{\phi}$$

$$\boldsymbol{\Sigma} = -\left(\frac{\partial^2 L}{\partial \phi^2}\right)^{-1}\Bigg|_{\phi=\hat{\phi}}. \tag{9.15}$$

9.2.2 Inference

In inference we aim to compute a posterior distribution $Pr(w^*|\mathbf{x}^*, \mathbf{X}, \mathbf{w})$ over the world state w^* given new observed data $\mathbf{x}^*$. To this end, we compute an infinite weighted sum (i.e., an integral) of the predictions $Pr(w^*|\mathbf{x}^*, \phi)$ given by each possible value of the parameters ϕ,

$$Pr(w^*|\mathbf{x}^*, \mathbf{X}, \mathbf{w}) = \int Pr(w^*|\mathbf{x}^*, \phi)Pr(\phi|\mathbf{X}, \mathbf{w})d\phi$$

$$\approx \int Pr(w^*|\mathbf{x}^*, \phi)q(\phi)d\phi, \tag{9.16}$$

where the weights $q(\phi)$ are given by the approximated posterior distribution over the parameters from the learning stage. Unfortunately, this integral cannot be computed in closed form either, and so we must make a further approximation.

We first note that the prediction $Pr(w^*|\mathbf{x}^*, \phi)$ depends only on a linear projection $a = \phi^T\mathbf{x}^*$ of the parameters (see Equation 9.4). Hence we could reexpress the prediction as

$$Pr(w^*|\mathbf{x}^*, \mathbf{X}, \mathbf{w}) \approx \int Pr(w^*|a)Pr(a)da. \tag{9.17}$$

The probability distribution $Pr(a)$ can be computed using the transformation property of the normal distribution (Section 5.3) and is given by

$$Pr(a) = Pr(\phi^T\mathbf{x}^*) = \text{Norm}_a[\boldsymbol{\mu}^T\mathbf{x}^*, \mathbf{x}^{*T}\boldsymbol{\Sigma}\mathbf{x}^*] \tag{9.18}$$

$$= \text{Norm}_a[\mu_a, \sigma_a^2],$$

where we have denoted the mean and variance of the activation by μ_a and σ_a^2, respectively. The one-dimensional integration in Equation 9.17 can now be computed using numerical integration over a, or we can approximate the result with a similar function such as

$$\int Pr(w^*|a)\text{Norm}_a[\mu_a, \sigma_a^2]da \approx \frac{1}{1 + \exp[-\mu_a/\sqrt{1 + \pi\sigma_a^2/8}]}. \tag{9.19}$$

It is not obvious by inspection that this function should approximate the integral well; however, Figure 9.8 demonstrates that the approximation is quite accurate.

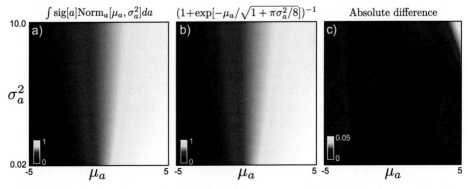

Figure 9.8 Approximation of activation integral (Equation 9.19). a) Actual result of integral as a function of μ_a and σ_a^2. b) The (nonobvious) approximation from Equation 9.19. c) The absolute difference between the actual result and the approximation is very small over a range of reasonable values.

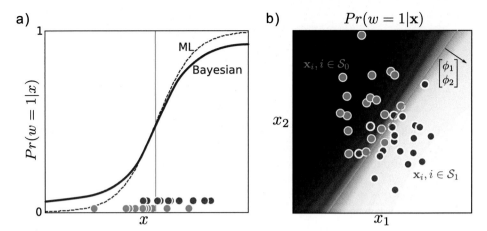

Figure 9.9 Bayesian logistic regression predictions. a) The Bayesian prediction for the class w is more moderate than the maximum likelihood prediction. b) In 2D the decision boundary in the Bayesian case (blue line) is still linear but iso-probability contours at levels other than 0.5 are curved (compare to maximum likelihood case in Figure 9.3b). Here too, the Bayesian solution makes more moderate predictions than the maximum likelihood model.

Figure 9.9 compares the classification predictions $Pr(w^*|\mathbf{x}^*)$ for the maximum likelihood and Bayesian approaches for logistic regression. The Bayesian approach makes more moderate predictions for the final class. This is particularly the case in regions of data space that are far from the mean.

9.3   Nonlinear logistic regression

The logistic regression model described previously can only create linear decision boundaries between classes. To create nonlinear decision boundaries, we adopt the same approach as we did for regression (Section 8.3): we compute a nonlinear transformation $\mathbf{z} = \mathbf{f}[\mathbf{x}]$ of the observed data and then build the logistic regression model substituting the original data $\mathbf{x}$ for the transformed data $\mathbf{z}$, so that

$$Pr(w = 1|\mathbf{x}, \boldsymbol{\phi}) = \text{Bern}_w\left[\text{sig}[\boldsymbol{\phi}^T\mathbf{z}]\right] = \text{Bern}_w\left[\text{sig}[\boldsymbol{\phi}^T\mathbf{f}[\mathbf{x}]]\right]. \qquad (9.20)$$

The logic of this approach is that arbitrary nonlinear activations can be built as a linear sum of nonlinear basis functions. Typical nonlinear transformations include

- Heaviside step functions of projections: $z_k = \text{heaviside}[\boldsymbol{\alpha}_k^T\mathbf{x}]$,
- Arc tangent functions of projections: $z_k = \arctan[\boldsymbol{\alpha}_k^T\mathbf{x}]$, and
- Radial basis functions: $z_k = \exp[-\frac{1}{\lambda_0}(\mathbf{x} - \boldsymbol{\alpha}_k)^T(\mathbf{x} - \boldsymbol{\alpha}_k)]$,

where z_k denotes the kth element of the transformed vector $\mathbf{z}$ and the function heaviside[$\bullet$] returns zero if its argument is less than zero and one otherwise. In the first two cases we have attached a 1 to the start of the observed data $\mathbf{x}$ where we use projections $\boldsymbol{\alpha}^T\mathbf{x}$ to avoid having a separate offset parameter. Figures 9.10 and 9.11 show examples of nonlinear classification using arc tangent functions for one and two-dimensional data, respectively.

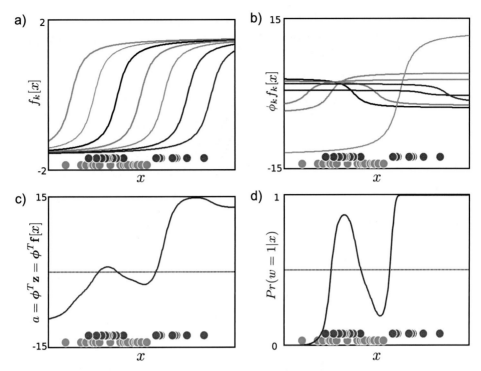

Figure 9.10 Nonlinear classification in 1D using arc tangent transformation. We consider a complex 1D data set (bottom of all panels) where the posterior $Pr(w = 1|x)$ cannot easily be described by a single sigmoid. Green circles represent data x_i where $w_i = 0$. Pink circles represent data x_i where $w_i = 1$. a) The seven dimensional transformed data vectors $z_1 \dots z_I$ are computed by evaluating each data example against seven predefined arc tangent functions $z_{ik} = f_k[x_i] = \arctan[\alpha_{0k} + \alpha_{1k}x_i]$. b) When we learn the parameters ϕ, we are learning weights for these nonlinear arc tangent functions. The functions are shown after applying the maximum likelihood weights $\hat{\phi}$. c) The final activation $a = \phi^T\mathbf{z}$ is a weighted sum of the nonlinear functions. d) The probability $Pr(w = 1|x)$ is computed by passing the activation a through the logistic sigmoid function.

Note that the basis functions also have parameters. For example, in the arc tangent example, there are the projection directions $\{\alpha_k\}_{k=1}^K$, each of which contains an offset and a set of gradients. These can also be optimized during the fitting procedure together with the weights ϕ. We form a new vector of unknowns $\boldsymbol{\theta} = [\phi^T, \alpha_1^T, \alpha_2^T, \dots, \alpha_K^T]^T$ and optimize the model with respect to all of these unknowns together. The gradient vector and the Hessian matrix depend on the chosen transformation $\mathbf{f}[\bullet]$ but can be computed using the expressions

$$\frac{\partial L}{\partial \boldsymbol{\theta}} = -\sum_{i=1}^I (w_i - \text{sig}[a_i])\frac{\partial a_i}{\partial \boldsymbol{\theta}}$$

$$\frac{\partial^2 L}{\partial \boldsymbol{\theta}^2} = -\sum_{i=1}^I \text{sig}[a_i](\text{sig}[a_i] - 1)\frac{\partial a_i}{\partial \boldsymbol{\theta}}\frac{\partial a_i}{\partial \boldsymbol{\theta}}^T - (w_i - \text{sig}[a_i])\frac{\partial^2 a_i}{\partial \boldsymbol{\theta}^2}, \qquad (9.21)$$

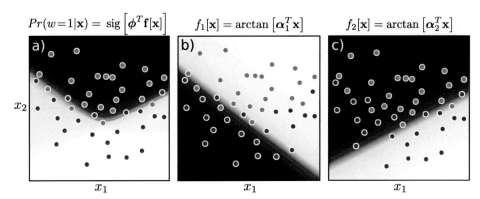

Figure 9.11 Nonlinear classification in 2D using arc tangent transform. a) These data have been successfully classified with nonlinear logistic regression. Note the nonlinear decision boundary (cyan line). To compute the posterior $Pr(w = 1|\mathbf{x})$, we transform the data to a new two-dimensional space $\mathbf{z} = \mathbf{f}[\mathbf{x}]$ where the elements of $\mathbf{z}$ are computed by evaluating $\mathbf{x}$ against the 1D arc tangent functions in b) and c). The arc tangent activations are weighted (the first by a negative number) and summed and the result is put through the logistic sigmoid to compute $Pr(w = 1|\mathbf{x})$.

where $a_i = \boldsymbol{\phi}^T \mathbf{f}[\mathbf{x}_i]$. These relations were established using the chain rules for derivatives. Unfortunately, this joint optimization problem is generally not convex and will be prone to terminating in local maxima. In the Bayesian case, it would be typical to marginalize over the parameters $\boldsymbol{\phi}$ but maximize over the function parameters.

9.4 Dual logistic regression

There is a potential problem with the logistic regression models as described earlier: in the original linear model, there is one element of the gradient vector $\boldsymbol{\phi}$ corresponding to each dimension of the observed data $\mathbf{x}$, and in the nonlinear extension there is one element corresponding to each transformed data dimension $\mathbf{z}$. If the relevant data $\mathbf{x}$ (or $\mathbf{z}$) is very high-dimensional, then the model will have a large number of parameters: this will render the Newton update slow or even intractable. To solve this problem, we switch to the *dual* representation. For simplicity, we will develop this model using the original data $\mathbf{x}$, but all of the ideas transfer directly to the nonlinear case where we use transformed data $\mathbf{z}$.

In the *dual* parameterization, we express the gradient parameters $\boldsymbol{\phi}$ as a weighted sum of the observed data (see Figure 8.12) so that

$$\boldsymbol{\phi} = \mathbf{X}\boldsymbol{\psi}, \tag{9.22}$$

where $\boldsymbol{\psi}$ is an $I \times 1$ variable in which each element weights one of the data examples. If the number of data points I is less than the dimensionality D of the data $\mathbf{x}$, then the number of parameters has been reduced.

The price that we pay for this reduction is that we can now only choose gradient vectors $\boldsymbol{\phi}$ that are in the space spanned by the data examples. However, the gradient vector represents the direction in which the final probability $Pr(w = 1|\mathbf{x})$ changes fastest, and this should not point in a direction in which there was no variation in the training data anyway, so this is not a limitation.

Substituting Equation 9.22 into the original logistic regression model leads to the dual logistic regression model,

$$Pr(\mathbf{w}|\mathbf{X}, \boldsymbol{\psi}) = \prod_{i=1}^{I} \mathrm{Bern}_{w_i} \left[\mathrm{sig}[a_i] \right] = \prod_{i=1}^{I} \mathrm{Bern}_{w_i} \left[\mathrm{sig}[\boldsymbol{\psi}^T \mathbf{X}^T \mathbf{x}_i] \right]. \qquad (9.23)$$

The resulting learning and inference algorithms are very similar to those for the original logistic regression model, and so we cover them only in brief:

- In the maximum likelihood method, we learn the parameters $\boldsymbol{\psi}$ by nonlinear optimization of the log likelihood $L = \log[Pr(\mathbf{w}|\mathbf{X}, \boldsymbol{\psi})]$ using the Newton method. This optimization requires the derivatives of the log likelihood, which are

$$\frac{\partial L}{\partial \boldsymbol{\psi}} = -\sum_{i=1}^{I} (\mathrm{sig}[a_i] - w_i) \mathbf{X}^T \mathbf{x}_i$$

$$\frac{\partial^2 L}{\partial \boldsymbol{\psi}^2} = -\sum_{i=1}^{I} \mathrm{sig}[a_i] (1 - \mathrm{sig}[a_i]) \mathbf{X}^T \mathbf{x}_i \mathbf{x}_i^T \mathbf{X}. \qquad (9.24)$$

- In the Bayesian approach, we use a normal prior over the parameters $\boldsymbol{\psi}$,

$$Pr(\boldsymbol{\psi}) = \mathrm{Norm}_{\boldsymbol{\psi}}[\mathbf{0}, \sigma_p^2 \mathbf{I}]. \qquad (9.25)$$

The posterior distribution $Pr(\boldsymbol{\psi}|\mathbf{X}, \mathbf{w})$ over the new parameters is found using Bayes' rule, and once more this cannot be written in closed form, so we apply the Laplace approximation. We find the MAP solution $\hat{\boldsymbol{\psi}}$ using nonlinear optimization, which requires the derivatives of the log posterior $L = \log[Pr(\boldsymbol{\psi}|\mathbf{X}, \mathbf{w})]$:

$$\frac{\partial L}{\partial \boldsymbol{\psi}} = -\sum_{i=1}^{I} (\mathrm{sig}[a_i] - w_i) \mathbf{X}^T \mathbf{x}_i - \frac{\boldsymbol{\psi}}{\sigma_p^2}$$

$$\frac{\partial^2 L}{\partial \boldsymbol{\psi}^2} = -\sum_{i=1}^{I} \mathrm{sig}[a_i] (1 - \mathrm{sig}[a_i]) \mathbf{X}^T \mathbf{x}_i \mathbf{x}_i^T \mathbf{X} - \frac{1}{\sigma_p^2}. \qquad (9.26)$$

The posterior is now approximated by a multivariate normal so that

$$Pr(\boldsymbol{\psi}|\mathbf{X}, \mathbf{w}) \approx q(\boldsymbol{\psi}) = \mathrm{Norm}_{\boldsymbol{\psi}}[\boldsymbol{\mu}, \boldsymbol{\Sigma}], \qquad (9.27)$$

where

$$\boldsymbol{\mu} = \hat{\boldsymbol{\psi}} \qquad (9.28)$$

$$\boldsymbol{\Sigma} = -\left(\frac{\partial^2 L}{\partial \boldsymbol{\psi}^2} \right)^{-1} \Bigg|_{\boldsymbol{\psi} = \hat{\boldsymbol{\psi}}}.$$

In inference, we compute the distribution over the activation

$$Pr(a) = Pr(\boldsymbol{\psi}^T \mathbf{X}^T \mathbf{x}^*) = \mathrm{Norm}_a[\mu_a, \sigma_a^2]$$
$$= \mathrm{Norm}_a[\boldsymbol{\mu}^T \mathbf{X}^T \mathbf{x}^*, \mathbf{x}^{*T} \mathbf{X} \boldsymbol{\Sigma} \mathbf{X}^T \mathbf{x}^*] \qquad (9.29)$$

and then approximate the predictive distribution using Equation 9.19.

Dual logistic regression gives identical results to the original logistic regression algorithm for the maximum likelihood case and very similar results in the Bayesian situation (where the difference results from the slightly different priors). However, the dual classification model is much faster to fit in high dimensions as the parameters are fewer.

9.5   Kernel logistic regression

We motivated the dual model by the reduction in the number of parameters ψ in the model when the data lies in a high-dimensional space. However, now that we have developed the model, a further advantage is easy to identify: both learning and inference in the dual model rely only on inner products $\mathbf{x}_i^T\mathbf{x}_j$ of that data. Equivalently, the nonlinear version of this algorithm depends only on inner products $\mathbf{z}_i^T\mathbf{z}_j$ of the transformed data vectors. This means that the algorithm is suitable for *kernelization* (see Section 8.4).

The idea of kernelization is to define a kernel function $k[\bullet,\bullet]$, which computes the quantity

$$k[\mathbf{x}_i,\mathbf{x}_j] = \mathbf{z}_i^T\mathbf{z}_j, \tag{9.30}$$

where $\mathbf{z}_i = \mathbf{f}[\mathbf{x}_i]$ and $\mathbf{z}_j = \mathbf{f}[\mathbf{x}_j]$ are the nonlinear transformations of the two data vectors. Replacing the inner products with the kernel function means that we do not have to explicitly calculate the transformed vectors $\mathbf{z}$, and hence they may be of very high, or even infinite dimensions. See Section 8.4 for a more detailed description of kernel functions.

The kernel logistic regression model (compare to Equation 9.23) is hence

$$Pr(\mathbf{w}|\mathbf{X},\psi) = \prod_{i=1}^{I}\mathrm{Bern}_{w_i}\left[\mathrm{sig}[a_i]\right] = \prod_{i=1}^{I}\mathrm{Bern}_{w_i}\left[\mathrm{sig}[\psi^T\mathbf{K}[\mathbf{X},\mathbf{x}_i]]\right], \tag{9.31}$$

where the notation $\mathbf{K}[\mathbf{X},\mathbf{x}]_i$ represents a column vector of dot products where element k is given by $k[\mathbf{x}_k,\mathbf{x}_i]$.

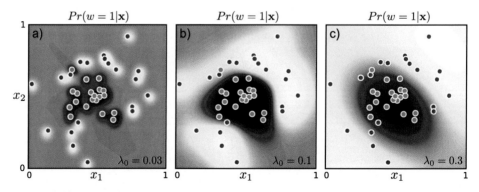

Figure 9.12 Kernel logistic regression using RBF kernel and maximum likelihood learning. a) With a small length scale λ, the model does not interpolate much from the data examples. b) With a reasonable length scale, the classifier does a good job of modeling the posterior $Pr(w = 1|\mathbf{x})$. c) With a large length scale, the estimated posterior is very smooth and the model interpolates confident decisions into regions such as the top-left where there is no data.

$$Pr(w = 1|\mathbf{x})$$

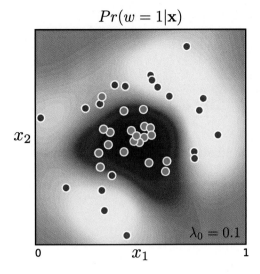

x_2

$\lambda_0 = 0.1$

0 x_1 1

Figure 9.13 Kernel logistic regression with RBF kernel in a Bayesian setting: we now take account of our uncertainty in the dual parameters ψ by approximating their posterior distribution using Laplace's method and marginalizing them out of the model. This produces a very similar result to the maximum likelihood case with the same length scale (Figure 9.12b). However, as is typical with Bayesian implementations, the confidence is (appropriately) somewhat lower.

For maximum likelihood learning, we simply optimize the log posterior probability L with respect to the parameters, which requires the derivatives:

$$\frac{\partial L}{\partial \psi} = -\sum_{i=1}^{I} \left(\text{sig}[a_i] - w_i \right) \mathbf{K}[\mathbf{X}, \mathbf{x}_i]$$

$$\frac{\partial^2 L}{\partial \psi^2} = -\sum_{i=1}^{I} \text{sig}[a_i] \left(1 - \text{sig}[a_i] \right) \mathbf{K}[\mathbf{X}, \mathbf{x}_i] \mathbf{K}[\mathbf{x}_i, \mathbf{X}]. \tag{9.32}$$

The Bayesian formulation of kernel logistic regression, which is sometimes known as *Gaussian process classification*, proceeds along similar lines; we follow the dual formulation, replacing each the dot products between data examples with the kernel function.

A very common example of a kernel function is the radial basis kernel in which the nonlinear transformation and inner product operations are replaced by

$$\text{k}[\mathbf{x}_i, \mathbf{x}_j] = \exp \left[-0.5 \left(\frac{(\mathbf{x}_i - \mathbf{x}_j)^T (\mathbf{x}_i - \mathbf{x}_j)}{\lambda^2} \right) \right]. \tag{9.33}$$

This is equivalent to computing transformed vectors $\mathbf{z}_i$ and $\mathbf{z}_j$ of infinite length, where each entry evaluates the data $\mathbf{x}$ against a radial basis function at a different position, and then computing the inner product $\mathbf{z}_i^T \mathbf{z}_j$. Examples of the kernel logistic regression with a radial basis kernel are shown in Figures 9.12 and 9.13.

9.6 Relevance vector classification

The Bayesian version of the kernel logistic regression model is powerful, but computationally expensive as it requires us to compute dot products between the new data example and the all of the training examples (in the kernel function in Equation 9.31).

It would be more efficient if the model depended only sparsely on the training data. To achieve this, we impose a penalty for every nonzero weighted training example. As in the relevance regression model (Section 8.8), we replace the normal prior over the dual parameters $\boldsymbol{\psi}$ (Equation 9.25) with a product of one-dimensional t-distributions so that

$$Pr(\boldsymbol{\psi}) = \prod_{i=1}^{I} \text{Stud}_{\psi_i}[0, 1, \nu]. \tag{9.34}$$

Applying the Bayesian approach to this model with respect to the parameters $\boldsymbol{\Psi}$ is known as *relevance vector classification*.

Following the argument of Section 8.6, we rewrite each student t-distribution as a marginalization of a joint distribution $Pr(\psi_i, h_i)$

$$Pr(\boldsymbol{\psi}) = \prod_{i=1}^{I} \int \text{Norm}_{\psi_i}\left[0, \frac{1}{h_i}\right] \text{Gam}_{h_i}\left[\frac{\nu}{2}, \frac{\nu}{2}\right] dh_i$$

$$= \int \text{Norm}_{\boldsymbol{\psi}}[0, \mathbf{H}^{-1}] \prod_{d=1}^{D} \text{Gam}_{h_d}[\nu/2, \nu/2] \, d\mathbf{H}, \tag{9.35}$$

where the matrix $\mathbf{H}$ contains the hidden variables $\{h_i\}_{i=1}^{I}$ on its diagonal and zeros elsewhere. Now we can write the model likelihood as

$$Pr(\mathbf{w}|\mathbf{X}) \tag{9.36}$$

$$= \int Pr(\mathbf{w}|\mathbf{X}, \boldsymbol{\psi}) Pr(\boldsymbol{\psi}) \, d\boldsymbol{\psi}$$

$$= \int\int \prod_{i=1}^{I} \text{Bern}_{w_i}\left[\text{sig}[\boldsymbol{\psi}^T \mathbf{K}[\mathbf{X}, \mathbf{x}_i]]\right] \text{Norm}_{\boldsymbol{\psi}}[0, \mathbf{H}^{-1}] \prod_{d=1}^{D} \text{Gam}_{h_d}[\nu/2, \nu/2] \, d\mathbf{H} d\boldsymbol{\psi}.$$

Now we make two approximations. First, we use the Laplace approximation to describe the first two terms in this integral as a normal distribution with mean $\boldsymbol{\mu}$ and covariance $\boldsymbol{\Sigma}$ centered at the MAP parameters, and use the following result for the integral over $\boldsymbol{\psi}$:

$$\int q(\boldsymbol{\psi}) \, d\boldsymbol{\psi} \approx q(\boldsymbol{\mu}) \int \exp\left[-\frac{1}{2}(\boldsymbol{\psi} - \boldsymbol{\mu})^T \boldsymbol{\Sigma}^{-1}(\boldsymbol{\psi} - \boldsymbol{\mu})\right] d\boldsymbol{\psi}$$

$$= q(\boldsymbol{\mu})(2\pi)^{D/2}|\boldsymbol{\Sigma}|^{1/2}. \tag{9.37}$$

This yields the expression

$$Pr(\mathbf{w}|\mathbf{X}) \approx \tag{9.38}$$

$$\int \prod_{i=1}^{I} (2\pi)^{I/2}|\boldsymbol{\Sigma}|^{0.5} \text{Bern}_{w_i}\left[\text{sig}[\boldsymbol{\mu}^T \mathbf{K}[\mathbf{X}, \mathbf{x}_i]]\right] \text{Norm}_{\boldsymbol{\mu}}[0, \mathbf{H}^{-1}] \text{Gam}_{h_i}\left[\frac{\nu}{2}, \frac{\nu}{2}\right] d\mathbf{H},$$

where the matrix $\mathbf{H}$ contains the hidden variables $\{h_i\}_{i=1}^{I}$ on the diagonal.

In the second approximation, we maximize over the hidden variables, rather than integrate over them. This yields the expression:

$$Pr(\mathbf{w}|\mathbf{X}) \approx \qquad (9.39)$$

$$\max_{\mathbf{H}} \left[\prod_{i=1}^{I} (2\pi)^{I/2} |\mathbf{\Sigma}|^{0.5} \text{Bern}_{w_i} \left[\text{sig}[\boldsymbol{\mu}^T \mathbf{K}[\mathbf{X}, \mathbf{x}_i]] \right] \text{Norm}_{\boldsymbol{\mu}}[0, \mathbf{H}^{-1}] \text{Gam}_{h_i} \left[\frac{\nu}{2}, \frac{\nu}{2} \right] \right].$$

To learn the model, we now alternate between updating the mean and variance $\boldsymbol{\mu}$ and $\mathbf{\Sigma}$ of the posterior distribution and updating the hidden variables $\{h_i\}$. To update the mean and variance parameters, we find the solution $\hat{\boldsymbol{\psi}}$ that maximizes

$$L = \sum_{i=1}^{I} \log \left[\text{Bern}_{w_i} \left[\text{sig}[\boldsymbol{\psi}^T \mathbf{K}[\mathbf{X}, \mathbf{x}_i]] \right] \right] + \log \left[\text{Norm}_{\boldsymbol{\psi}}[0, \mathbf{H}^{-1}] \right] \qquad (9.40)$$

using the derivatives

$$\frac{\partial L}{\partial \boldsymbol{\psi}} = -\sum_{i=1}^{I} (\text{sig}[a_i] - w_i) \mathbf{K}[\mathbf{X}, \mathbf{x}_i] - \mathbf{H}\boldsymbol{\psi}$$

$$\frac{\partial^2 L}{\partial \boldsymbol{\psi}^2} = -\sum_{i=1}^{I} \text{sig}[a_i] (1 - \text{sig}[a_i]) \mathbf{K}[\mathbf{X}, \mathbf{x}_i] \mathbf{K}[\mathbf{x}_i \mathbf{X}] - \mathbf{H}, \qquad (9.41)$$

and then set

$$\boldsymbol{\mu} = \hat{\boldsymbol{\psi}} \qquad (9.42)$$

$$\mathbf{\Sigma} = -\left(\frac{\partial^2 L}{\partial \boldsymbol{\psi}^2} \right)^{-1} \Bigg|_{\boldsymbol{\psi} = \hat{\boldsymbol{\psi}}}.$$

To update the hidden variables h_i we use the same expression as for relevance vector regression:

$$h_i^{new} = \frac{1 - h_i \Sigma_{ii} + \nu}{\mu_i^2 + \nu}. \qquad (9.43)$$

As this optimization proceeds, some of the hidden variables h_i will become very large. This means that the prior over the relevant parameter becomes very concentrated around zero and that the associated datapoints contribute nothing to the final solution. These can be removed, leaving a kernelized classifier that depends only sparsely on the data and can hence be evaluated very efficiently.

In inference, we aim to compute the distribution over the world state w^* given a new data example $\mathbf{x}^*$. We take the familiar strategy of approximating the posterior distribution over the activation as

$$Pr(a) = Pr(\boldsymbol{\psi}^T \mathbf{K}[\mathbf{X}, \mathbf{x}^*]) = \text{Norm}_a[\mu_a, \sigma_a^2] \qquad (9.44)$$
$$= \text{Norm}_a[\boldsymbol{\mu}^T \mathbf{K}[\mathbf{X}, \mathbf{x}], \mathbf{K}[\mathbf{x}^*, \mathbf{X}] \mathbf{\Sigma} \mathbf{K}[\mathbf{X}, \mathbf{x}^*]],$$

and then approximate the predictive distribution using Equation 9.19.

An example of relevance vector classification is shown in Figure 9.14, which shows that the data set can be discriminated based on 6 of the original 40 datapoints. This results in a considerable computational saving and the simpler solution guards against overfitting of the training set.

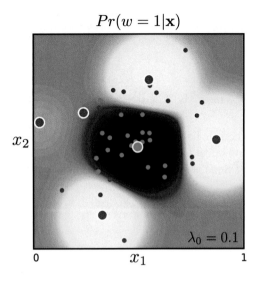

$$Pr(w = 1|\mathbf{x})$$

x_2

$\lambda_0 = 0.1$

0   x_1 1

Figure 9.14 Relevance vector regression with RBF kernel. We place a prior over the dual parameters ψ that encourages sparsity. After learning, the posterior distribution over most of the parameters is tightly centered around zero and they can be dropped from the model. Large points indicate data examples associated with nonzero dual parameters. The solution here can be computed from just 6 of the 40 datapoints but nonetheless classifies the data almost as well as the full kernel approach (Figure 9.13).

9.7   Incremental fitting and boosting

In the previous section, we developed the *relevance vector classification* model in which we applied a prior that encourages sparsity in the dual logistic regression parameters ψ and hence encouraged the model to depend on only a subset of the training data. It is similarly possible to develop a *sparse logistic regression method* by placing a prior that encourages sparsity in the original parameters ϕ and hence encourages the classifier to depend only on a subset of the data dimensions. This is left as an exercise to the reader.

In this section we will investigate a different approach to inducing sparsity; we will add one parameter at a time to the model in a greedy fashion; in other words, we add the parameter that improves the objective function most at each stage and then consider this fixed. As the most discriminative parts of the model are added first, it is possible to truncate this process after only a small fraction of the parameters are added and still achieve good results. The remaining, unused parameters can be considered as having a value of zero, and so this model also provides a sparse solution. We term this approach *incremental fitting*. We will work with the original formulation (so that the sparsity is over the data dimensions), although these ideas can equally be adapted to the dual case.

To describe the incremental fitting procedure, let us work with the nonlinear formulation of logistic regression (Section 9.3) where the probability of the class given the data was described as

$$Pr(w_i|\mathbf{x}_i) = \text{Bern}_{w_i}[\text{sig}[a_i]], \tag{9.45}$$

where $\text{sig}[\bullet]$ is the logistic sigmoid function and the activation a_i is given by

$$a_i = \phi^T \mathbf{z}_i = \phi^T \mathbf{f}[\mathbf{x}_i], \tag{9.46}$$

and $\mathbf{f}[\bullet]$ is a nonlinear transformation that returns the transformed vector $\mathbf{z}_i$.

To simplify the subsequent description, we will now write the activation term in a slightly different way so that the dot product is described explicitly as a weighted sum of individual nonlinear functions of the data

$$a_i = \phi_0 + \sum_{k=1}^{K} \phi_k f[\mathbf{x}_i, \boldsymbol{\xi}_k]. \tag{9.47}$$

Here $f[\bullet, \bullet]$ is a fixed nonlinear function that takes the data vector $\mathbf{x}_i$ and some parameters $\boldsymbol{\xi}_k$ and returns a scalar value. In other words, the kth entry of the transformed vector $\mathbf{z}$ arises by passing the data $\mathbf{x}$ through the function with the kth parameters $\boldsymbol{\xi}_k$. Example functions $f[\bullet, \bullet]$ might include:

- Arc tan functions, $\boldsymbol{\xi} = \{\boldsymbol{\alpha}\}$

$$f[\mathbf{x}, \boldsymbol{\xi}] = \arctan[\boldsymbol{\alpha}^T \mathbf{x}]. \tag{9.48}$$

- Radial basis functions, $\boldsymbol{\xi} = \{\boldsymbol{\alpha}, \lambda_0\}$

$$f[\mathbf{x}, \boldsymbol{\xi}] = \exp\left[-\frac{(\mathbf{x} - \boldsymbol{\alpha})^T (\mathbf{x} - \boldsymbol{\alpha})}{\lambda_0^2}\right]. \tag{9.49}$$

In incremental learning, we construct the activation term in Equation 9.47 piecewise. At each stage we add a new term, leaving all of the previous terms unchanged except the additive constant ϕ_0. So, at the first stage, we use the activation

$$a_i = \phi_0 + \phi_1 f[\mathbf{x}_i, \boldsymbol{\xi}_1] \tag{9.50}$$

and learn the parameters ϕ_0, ϕ_1, and $\boldsymbol{\xi}_1$ using the maximum likelihood approach. At the second stage, we fit the function

$$a_i = \phi_0 + \phi_1 f[\mathbf{x}_i, \boldsymbol{\xi}_1] + \phi_2 f[\mathbf{x}_i, \boldsymbol{\xi}_2] \tag{9.51}$$

and learn the parameters ϕ_0, ϕ_2, and $\boldsymbol{\xi}_2$, while keeping the remaining parameters ϕ_1 and $\boldsymbol{\xi}_1$ constant. At the Kth stage, we fit a model with activation

$$a_i = \phi_0 + \sum_{k=1}^{K} \phi_k f[\mathbf{x}_i, \boldsymbol{\xi}_k] \tag{9.52}$$

and learn the parameters ϕ_0, ϕ_K, and $\boldsymbol{\xi}_K$, while keeping the remaining parameters $\phi_1 \ldots \phi_{k-1}$ and $\boldsymbol{\xi}_1 \ldots \boldsymbol{\xi}_{k-1}$ constant.

At each stage, the learning is carried out using the maximum likelihood approach. We use a nonlinear optimization procedure to maximize the log posterior probability L with respect to the relevant parameters. The derivatives required by the optimization procedure depend on the choice of nonlinear function but can be computed using the chain rule relations (Equation 9.21).

This procedure is obviously suboptimal as we do not learn the parameters together or even revisit early parameters once they have been set. However, it has three nice properties.

1. It creates sparse models: the weights ϕ_k tend to decrease as we move through the sequence, and each subsequent basis function tends to have less influence on the model. Consequently, the series can be truncated to the desired length and the associated performance is likely to remain good.

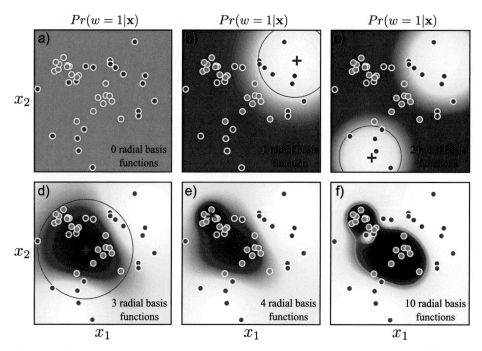

Figure 9.15 Incremental approach to fitting nonlinear logistic regression model with RBF functions. a) Before fitting, the activation (and hence the posterior probability) is uniform. b) Posterior probability after fitting one function (center and scale of RBF shown in blue). c–e) After fitting two, three, and four RBFs. f) After fitting ten RBGFs. The data are now all classified correctly as can be seen from the decision boundary (cyan line).

2. The previous logistic regression models have been suited to cases where either the dimensionality D of the data is small (original formulation) or the number of training examples I is small (dual formulation). However, it is quite possible that neither of these things is true. A strong advantage of incremental fitting is that it is still practical when the data are high-dimensional *and* there are a large number of training examples. During training, we do not need to hold all of the transformed vectors $\mathbf{z}$ in memory at once: at the Kth stage, we need only the Kth dimension of the transformed parameters $z_K = f[\mathbf{x}, \boldsymbol{\xi}_K]$ and the aggregate of the previous contributions to activation term $\sum_{k=1}^{K-1} \phi_k f[\mathbf{x}_i, \boldsymbol{\xi}_k]$.

3. Learning is relatively inexpensive because we only optimize a few parameters at each stage.

Figure 9.15 illustrates the incremental approach to learning a 2D data set using radial basis functions. Notice that even after only a few functions have been added to the sequence, the classification is substantially correct. Nonetheless, it is worth continuing to train this model even after the training data are classified correctly. Usually the model continues to improve and the classification performance on test data will continue to increase for some time.

9.7.1 Boosting

⚙ 9.7 There is a special case of the incremental approach to fitting nonlinear logistic regression that is commonly used in vision applications. Consider a logistic regression model based on a sum of step functions

$$a_i = \phi_0 + \sum_{k=1}^{K} \phi_k \text{heaviside}[\boldsymbol{\alpha}_k^T \mathbf{x}_i], \tag{9.53}$$

where the function heaviside[•] returns 0 if its argument is less than 0 and 1 otherwise. As usual, we have attached a 1 to the start of the data $\mathbf{x}$ so that the parameters $\boldsymbol{\alpha}_k$ contain both a direction $[\alpha_{k1}, \alpha_{k2}, \ldots, \alpha_{KD}]$ in the D-directional space (which determines the direction of the step function) and an offset α_{k0} (that determines where the step occurs).

One way to think about the step functions is as *weak classifiers*; they return 0 or 1 depending on the value of x_i so each classifies the data. The model combines these weak classifiers to compute a final *strong classifier*. Schemes for combining weak classifiers in this way are generically known as *boosting* and this particular model is called *logitboost*.

Unfortunately, we cannot simply fit this model using a gradient-based optimization approach because the derivative of the heaviside step function with respect to the parameters $\boldsymbol{\alpha}_k$ is not smooth. Consequently, it is usual to predefine a large set of J weak classifiers and assume that each parameter vector $\boldsymbol{\alpha}_k$ is taken from this set so that $\boldsymbol{\alpha}_k \in \{\boldsymbol{\alpha}^{(1)} \ldots \boldsymbol{\alpha}^{(J)}\}$.

As before, we learn the logitboost model incrementally by adding one term at a time to the activation (Equation 9.53). However, now we exhaustively search over the weak classifiers $\{\boldsymbol{\alpha}^{(1)} \ldots \boldsymbol{\alpha}^{(J)}\}$ and for each use nonlinear optimization to estimate the weights ϕ_0 and ϕ_k. We choose the combination $\{\boldsymbol{\alpha}_k, \phi_0, \phi_k\}$ that improves the log likelihood the most. This procedure may be made even more efficient (but more approximate) by choosing the weak classifier based on the log likelihood after just a single Newton or gradient descent step in the nonlinear optimization stage. When we have selected the best weak classifier $\boldsymbol{\alpha}_k$, we can return and perform the full optimization over the offset ϕ_0 and weight ϕ_k.

Note that after each classifier is added, the relative importance of each datapoint is effectively changed: the datapoints contribute to the derivative according to how well they are currently predicted (Equation 9.9). Consequently, the later weak classifiers become more specialized to the more difficult parts of the data set that are not well classified by the early ones. Usually, these are close to the final decision boundary.

Figure 9.16 shows several iterations of the boosting procedure. Because the model is composed from step functions, the final classification boundary is irregular and does not interpolate smoothly between the data examples. This is a potential disadvantage of this approach. In general, a classifier based on arc tangent functions (roughly smooth step functions) will have superior generalization and can also be fit using continuous optimization. It could be argued that the step function is faster to evaluate, but even this is illusory as more complex functions such as the arc tangent can be approximated with look-up tables.

9.8 Classification trees

In the nonlinear logistic regression model, we created complex decision boundaries using an activation function that is a linear combination $\phi^T \mathbf{z}$ of nonlinear functions $\mathbf{z} = \mathbf{f}[\mathbf{x}]$

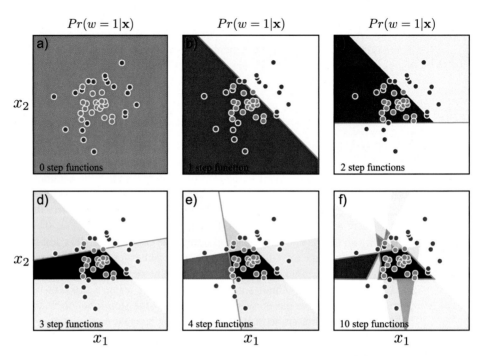

Figure 9.16 Boosting. a) We start with a uniform prediction $Pr(w = 1|\mathbf{x})$ and b) incrementally add a step function to the activation (green line indicates position of step). In this case the parameters of the step function were chosen greedily from a predetermined set containing 20 angles each with 40 offsets. c)-e) As subsequent functions are added the overall classification improves. f) However, the final decision surface (cyan line) is complex and does not interpolate smoothly between regions of high confidence.

of the data $\mathbf{x}$. We now investigate an alternative method to induce complex decision boundaries: we partition data space into distinct regions and apply a different classifier in each region.

The *branching logistic regression model* has activation,

$$a_i = (1 - g[\mathbf{x}_i, \boldsymbol{\omega}])\boldsymbol{\phi}_0^T\mathbf{x}_i + g[\mathbf{x}_i, \boldsymbol{\omega}]\boldsymbol{\phi}_1^T\mathbf{x}_i. \tag{9.54}$$

The term $g[\bullet, \bullet]$ is a *gating function* that returns a number between 0 and 1. If this gating function returns 0, then the activation will be $\boldsymbol{\phi}_0\mathbf{x}_i$, whereas if it returns 1, the activation will be $\boldsymbol{\phi}_1\mathbf{x}_i$. If the gating returns an intermediate value, then the activation will be a weighted sum of these two components. The gating function itself depends on the data $\mathbf{x}_i$ and takes parameters $\boldsymbol{\omega}$. This model induces a complex nonlinear decision boundary (Figure 9.17) where the two linear functions $\boldsymbol{\phi}_0\mathbf{x}_i$ and $\boldsymbol{\phi}_1\mathbf{x}_i$ are specialized to different regions of the data space. In this context, they are sometimes referred to as *experts*.

The gating function could take many forms, but an obvious possibility is to use a second logistic regression model. In other words, we compute a linear function $\boldsymbol{\omega}^T\mathbf{x}_i$ of the data that is passed through a logistic sigmoid so that

$$g[\mathbf{x}_i, \boldsymbol{\omega}] = \text{sig}[\boldsymbol{\omega}^T\mathbf{x}_i]. \tag{9.55}$$

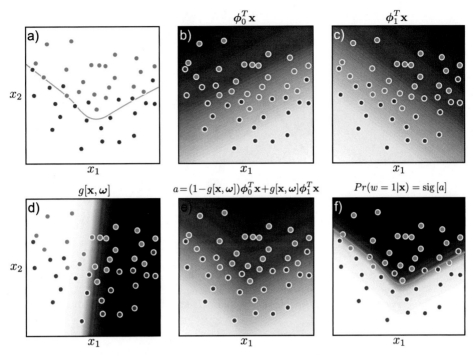

Figure 9.17 Branching logistic regression. a) This data set needs a nonlinear decision surface (cyan line) to classify the data reasonably. b) This linear activation is an *expert* that is specialized to describing the right-hand side of the data. c) This linear activation is an expert that describes the left-hand side of the data. d) A gating function takes the data vector $\mathbf{x}$ and returns a number between 0 and 1, which we will use to decide which expert contributes at each decision. e) The final activation consists of a weighted sum of the activation indicated by the two experts where the weight comes from the gating function. f) The final classifier predictions $Pr(w = 1|\mathbf{x})$ are generated by passing this activation through the logistic sigmoid function.

To learn this model we maximize the log probability $L = \sum_i \log[Pr(w_i|\mathbf{x}_i)]$ of the training data pairs $\{\mathbf{x}_i, w_i\}_{i=1}^I$ with respect to all of the parameters $\boldsymbol{\theta} = \{\boldsymbol{\phi}_0, \boldsymbol{\phi}_1, \boldsymbol{\omega}\}$. As usual this can be accomplished using a nonlinear optimization procedure. The parameters can be estimated simultaneously or using a coordinate ascent approach in which we update the three sets of parameters alternately.

We can extend this idea to create a hierarchical tree structure by nesting gating functions (Figure 9.18). For example, consider the activation

$$a_i = (1 - g[\mathbf{x}_i, \boldsymbol{\omega}]) \left[\boldsymbol{\phi}_0^T \mathbf{x}_i + (1 - g[\mathbf{x}_i, \boldsymbol{\omega}_0]) \boldsymbol{\phi}_{00}^T \mathbf{x}_i + g[\mathbf{x}_i, \boldsymbol{\omega}_0] \boldsymbol{\phi}_{01}^T \mathbf{x}_i \right] \quad (9.56)$$
$$+ g[\mathbf{x}_i, \boldsymbol{\omega}] \left[\boldsymbol{\phi}_1^T \mathbf{x}_i + (1 - g[\mathbf{x}_i, \boldsymbol{\omega}_1]) \boldsymbol{\phi}_{10}^T \mathbf{x}_i + g[\mathbf{x}_i, \boldsymbol{\omega}_1] \boldsymbol{\phi}_{11}^T \mathbf{x}_i \right].$$

This is an example of a *classification tree*.

To learn the parameters $\boldsymbol{\theta} = \{\boldsymbol{\phi}_0, \boldsymbol{\phi}_1, \boldsymbol{\phi}_{00}, \boldsymbol{\phi}_{01}, \boldsymbol{\phi}_{10}, \boldsymbol{\phi}_{11}, \boldsymbol{\omega}, \boldsymbol{\omega}_0, \boldsymbol{\omega}_1\}$, we could take an incremental approach. At the first stage, we fit the top part of the tree (Equation 9.54), setting parameters $\boldsymbol{\omega}, \boldsymbol{\phi}_0, \boldsymbol{\phi}_1$. Then we fit the left branch, setting parameters $\boldsymbol{\omega}_0, \boldsymbol{\phi}_{00}, \boldsymbol{\phi}_{01}$ and subsequently the right branch, setting parameters $\boldsymbol{\omega}_1, \boldsymbol{\phi}_{10}, \boldsymbol{\phi}_{11}$, and so on.

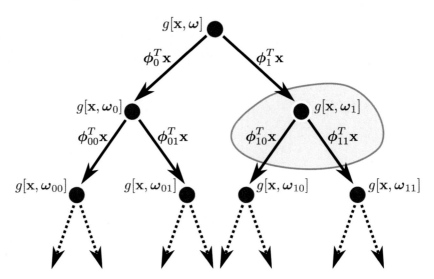

Figure 9.18 Logistic classification tree. Data flows from the root to the leaves. Each node is a gating function that weights the contributions of terms in the subbranches in the final activation. The gray region indicates variables that would be learned together in an incremental training approach.

The classification tree has the potential advantage of speed. If each gating function produces a binary output (like the heaviside step function), then each datapoint passes down just one of the outgoing edges from each node and ends up at a single leaf. When each branch in the tree is a linear operation (as in this example), these operations can be aggregated to a single linear operation at each leaf. Since each datapoint receives specialized processing, the tree need not usually be deep, and new data can be classified very efficiently.

9.9   Multiclass logistic regression

Throughout this chapter, we have discussed binary classification. We now discuss how to extend these models to handle $N > 2$ world states. One possibility is to build N *one-against-all* binary classifiers each of which computes the probability that the nth class is present as opposed to any of the other classes. The final label is assigned according to the one-against-all classifier with the highest probability.

The one-against-all approach works in practice but is not very elegant. A more principled way to cope with multiclass classification problems is to describe the the posterior $Pr(w|\mathbf{x})$ as a categorical distribution, where the parameters $\boldsymbol{\lambda} = [\lambda_1 \ldots \lambda_N]$ are functions of the data $\mathbf{x}$

$$Pr(w|\mathbf{x}) = \text{Cat}_w[\boldsymbol{\lambda}[\mathbf{x}]], \qquad (9.57)$$

where the parameters are in the range $\lambda_n \in [0,1]$ and sum to one, $\sum_n \lambda_n = 1$. In constructing the function $\boldsymbol{\lambda}[\mathbf{x}]$, we must ensure that we obey these constraints.

As for the two class logistic regression case, we will base the model on linear functions of the data $\mathbf{x}$ and pass these through a function that enforces the constraints. To this

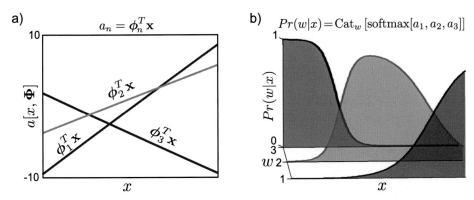

Figure 9.19 Multiclass logistic regression. a) We form one activation for each class based on linear functions of the data. b) We pass these activations through the softmax function to create the distribution $Pr(w|x)$ which is shown here as a function of x. The softmax function takes the three real-valued activations and returns three positive values that sum to one, ensuring that the distribution $Pr(w|x)$ is a valid probability distribution for all x.

end, we define N activations (one for each class),

$$a_n = \phi_n^T \mathbf{x}, \tag{9.58}$$

where $\{\phi_n\}_{n=1}^{N}$ are parameter vectors. We assume that as usual we have prepended a 1 to each of the data vectors $\mathbf{x}_i$ so that the first entry of each parameter vector ϕ_n represents an offset. The nth entry of the final categorical distribution is now defined by

$$\lambda_n = \text{softmax}_n[a_1, a_2 \ldots a_N] = \frac{\exp[a_n]}{\sum_{j=1}^{N} \exp[a_j]}. \tag{9.59}$$

The function **softmax**$[\bullet]$ takes the N activations $\{a_n\}_{n=1}^{N}$, which can take any real number, and maps them to the N parameters $\{\lambda_n\}_{n=1}^{N}$ of the categorical distribution, which are constrained to be positive and sum to one (Figure 9.19).

To learn the parameters $\boldsymbol{\theta} = \{\phi_n\}_{n=1}^{N}$ given training pairs $(w_i, \mathbf{x}_i)$ we optimize the log likelihood of the training data

$$L = \sum_{i=1}^{I} \log[Pr(w_i|\mathbf{x}_i)]. \tag{9.60}$$

As for the two-class case, there is no closed form expression for the maximum likelihood parameters. However, this is a convex function, and the maximum can be found using a nonlinear optimization technique such as the Newton method. These techniques require the first and second derivatives of the log likelihood with respect to the parameters, which are given by

$$\frac{\partial L}{\partial \phi_n} = -\sum_{i=1}^{I} (y_{in} - \delta[w_i - n])\mathbf{x}_i$$

$$\frac{\partial^2 L}{\partial \phi_m \phi_n} = -\sum_{i=1}^{I} y_{im}(\delta[m - n] - y_{in})\mathbf{x}_i \mathbf{x}_i^T, \tag{9.61}$$

where we define the term

$$y_{in} = Pr(w_i = n|\mathbf{x}_i) = \text{softmax}_n[a_{i1}, a_{i2} \ldots a_{iN}]. \tag{9.62}$$

It is possible to extend multiclass logistic regression in all of the ways that we extended the two-class model. We can construct Bayesian, nonlinear, dual and kernelized versions. It is possible to train incrementally and combine weak classifiers in a boosting framework. Here, we will consider tree-structured models as these are very common in modern vision applications.

9.10   Random trees, forests, and ferns

In Section 9.8 we introduced the idea of tree-structured classifiers, in which the processing for each data example is different and becomes steadily more specialized. This idea has recently become extremely popular for multiclass problems in the form of *random classification trees*.

As for the two-class case, the key idea is to construct a binary tree where at each node, the data are evaluated to determine whether it will pass to the left or the right branch. Unlike in Section 9.8, we will assume that each data point passes into just one branch. In a random classification tree, the data are evaluated against a function $q[\mathbf{x}]$ that was randomly chosen from a predefined family of possible functions. For example, this might be the response of a randomly chosen filter. The data point proceeds one way in the tree if the response of this function exceeds a threshold τ and the other way if not. While the functions are chosen randomly, the threshold is carefully selected.

We select the threshold that maximizes the log-likelihood L of the data:

$$L = \sum_{i=1}^{I}(1 - \text{heaviside}[q[\mathbf{x}_i] - \tau]) \log\left[\text{Cat}_{w_i}\left[\boldsymbol{\lambda}^{[l]}\right]\right] \tag{9.63}$$

$$+ \text{heaviside}[q[\mathbf{x}_i] - \tau] \log\left[\text{Cat}_{w_i}\left[\boldsymbol{\lambda}^{[r]}\right]\right].$$

Here the first term represents the contribution of the data that passes down the left branch, and the second term represents the contribution of the data that passes down the right branch. In each case, the data are evaluated against a categorical distribution with parameters $\boldsymbol{\lambda}^{[l]}$ and $\boldsymbol{\lambda}^{[r]}$, respectively. These parameters are set using maximum likelihood:

$$\lambda_k^{[l]} = \frac{\sum_{i=1}^{I} \delta[w_i - k](1 - \text{heaviside}[q[\mathbf{x}_i] - \tau])}{\sum_{i=1}^{I}(1 - \text{heaviside}[q[\mathbf{x}_i] - \tau])}$$

$$\lambda_k^{[r]} = \frac{\sum_{i=1}^{I} \delta[w_i - k](\text{heaviside}[q[\mathbf{x}_i] - \tau])}{\sum_{i=1}^{I}(\text{heaviside}[q[\mathbf{x}_i] - \tau])}. \tag{9.64}$$

The log likelihood is not a smooth function of the threshold τ, and so in practice we maximize the log likelihood by empirically trying a number of different threshold values and choosing the one that gives the best result.

We then perform this same procedure recursively; the data that pass to the left branch have a new randomly chosen classifier applied to them, and a new threshold that splits it again is chosen. This can be done without recourse to the data in the right branch. When we classify a new data example $\mathbf{x}^*$, we pass it down the tree until it reaches one of the leaves. The posterior distribution $Pr(w^*|\mathbf{x}^*)$ over the world state w^* is set to $\text{Cat}_{w^*}[\boldsymbol{\lambda}]$ where the parameters $\boldsymbol{\lambda}$ are the categorical parameters associated with this leaf during the training process.

The random classification tree is attractive because it is very fast to train – after all, most of its parameters are chosen randomly. It can also be trained with very large amounts of data as its complexity is linear in the number of data examples.

There are two important variations on this model:

1. A *fern* is a tree where the randomly chosen functions at each level of the tree are constrained to be the same. In other words, the data that pass through the left and right branches at any node are subsequently acted on by the same function (although the threshold level may optionally be different in each branch). In practice, this means that every datapoint is acted on by the same sequence of functions. This can make implementation extremely efficient when we are evaluating the classifier repeatedly.

2. A *random forest* is a collection of random trees, each of which uses a different randomly chosen set of functions. By averaging together the probabilities $Pr(w^*|\mathbf{x}^*)$ predicted by these trees, a more robust classifier is produced. One way to think of this is as approximating the Bayesian approach; we are constructing the final answer by taking a weighted sum of the predictions suggested by different sets of parameters.

9.11   Relation to non-probabilistic models

In this chapter, we have described a family of probabilistic algorithms for classification. Each is based on maximizing either the log Bernoulli probability of the training class labels given the data (two-class case) or the log categorical probability of the training class labels given the data (multiclass case).

However, it is more common in the computer vision literature to use non-probabilistic classification algorithms such as the multilayer perceptron, adaboost, or support vector classification. At their core, these algorithms optimize different objective functions and so are neither directly equivalent to each other, nor to the models in this chapter.

We chose to describe the less common probabilistic algorithms because

- They have no serious disadvantages relative to non-probabilistic techniques,
- They naturally produce estimates of certainty,
- They are easily extensible to the multiclass case, whereas non-probabilistic algorithms usually rely on one-against-all formulations, and
- They are more easily related to one another and to the rest of the book.

In short, it can reasonably be argued that the dominance of non-probabilistic approaches to classification is largely for historical reasons. We will now briefly describe the relationship between our models and common non-probabilistic approaches.

The *multilayer perceptron* (MLP) or *neural network* is very similar to our nonlinear logistic regression model in the special case where the nonlinear transformation consists of a set of sigmoid functions applied to linear projections of data (e.g., $z_k = \arctan[\boldsymbol{\alpha}_k^T \mathbf{x}]$). In the MLP, learning is known as *back propagation* and the transformed variable $\mathbf{z}$ is known as the *hidden layer*.

Adaboost is very closely related to the the logitboost model described in this chapter, but adaboost is not probabilistic. Performance of the two algorithms is similar.

The *support vector machine* (SVM) is similar to relevance vector classification; it is a kernelized classifier that depends sparsely on the data. It has the advantage that its objective function is convex, whereas the objective function in relevance vector classification is non-convex and only guarantees to converge to a local minimum. However, the SVM has several disadvantages: it does not assign certainty to its class predictions, it is not so easily extended to the multiclass case, it produces solutions that are less sparse than relevance vector classification, and it places more restrictions on the form of the kernel function. In practice, classification performance of the two models is again similar.

9.12   Applications

We now present a number of examples of the use of classification in computer vision from the research literature. In many of the examples, the method used was non-probabilistic (e.g., adaboost), but is very closely related to the algorithms in this chapter, and one would not expect the performance to differ significantly if these were substituted.

9.12.1   Gender classification

The algorithms in this chapter were motivated by the problem of gender detection in unconstrained facial images. The goal is to assign a label $w \in \{0, 1\}$ indicating whether a small patch of an image $\mathbf{x}$ contains a male or a female face. Prince and Aghajanian (2009) developed a system of this type. First, a bounding box around the face was identified using a face detector (see next section). The data within this bounding box were resized to 60×60, converted to grayscale and histogram equalized. The resulting image was convolved with a bank of Gabor functions, and the filtered images sampled at regular intervals that were proportionate to the wavelength to create a final feature vector of length 1064. Each dimension was whitened to have mean zero and unit standard deviation. Chapter 13 contains information about these and other preprocessing methods.

A training database of 32,000 examples was used to learn a nonlinear logistic regression model of the form

$$Pr(w_i|\mathbf{x}_i) = \text{Bern}_{w_i} \left[\frac{1}{1 + \exp\left[-\phi_0 - \sum_{k=1}^{K} \phi_k \text{f}[\mathbf{x}_i, \boldsymbol{\xi}_k]\right]} \right], \qquad (9.65)$$

where the nonlinear functions $\text{f}[\bullet]$ were arc tangents of linear projections of the data so that

$$\text{f}[\mathbf{x}_i, \boldsymbol{\xi}_k] = \arctan[\boldsymbol{\xi}_k^T \mathbf{x}_i]. \qquad (9.66)$$

As usual the data were augmented by prepending a 1 so the projection vectors $\{\boldsymbol{\xi}_k\}$ were of length $D + 1$. This model was learned using an incremental approach so that at each stage the parameters ϕ_0, ϕ_k and $\boldsymbol{\xi}_k$ were modified.

The system achieved 87.5 percent performance with $K = 300$ arc tangent functions on a challenging real-world database that contained large variations in scale, pose, lighting, and expression similar to the faces in Figure 9.1. Human observers managed only 95 percent performance on the same database using the resized face region alone.

9.12.2 Face and pedestrian detection

Before we can determine the gender of a face, we must first find it. In face detection (Figure 7.1), we assign a label $w \in \{0,1\}$ to a small region of the image $\mathbf{x}$ indicating whether a face is present ($w=1$) or not ($w=0$). To ensure that the face is found, this process is repeated at every position and scale in the image and consequently the classifier must be very fast.

Viola and Jones (2004) presented a face detection system based on *adaboost* (Figure 9.20). This is a non-probabilistic analogue of the boosting methods described in Section 9.7.1. The final classification is based on the sign of a sum of nonlinear functions of the data

$$a = \phi_0 + \sum_{k=1}^{K} \phi_k \mathrm{f}[\mathbf{x}, \boldsymbol{\xi}_k], \tag{9.67}$$

where the nonlinear functions $f[\bullet]$ are heaviside step functions of projections of the data (weak classifiers giving a response of zero or one for each possible data vector $\mathbf{x}$) so that

$$\mathrm{f}[\mathbf{x}, \boldsymbol{\xi}_k] = \mathrm{heaviside}[\boldsymbol{\xi}_k^T \mathbf{x}]. \tag{9.68}$$

As usual, the data vector $\mathbf{x}$ was prepended with a 1 to account for an offset.

The system was trained on 5,000 faces and 10,000 non-face regions, each of which were represented as a 24×24 image patch. Since the model is not smooth (due to the step function) gradient-based optimization is unsuitable, and so Viola and Jones (2004) exhaustively searched through a very large number of predefined projections $\boldsymbol{\xi}_k$.

There were two aspects of the design that ensured that the system ran quickly.

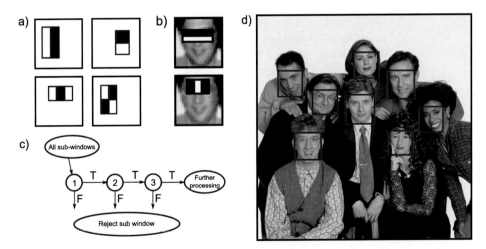

Figure 9.20 Fast face detection using a boosting method (Viola and Jones 2004). a) Each weak classifier consists of the response of the image to a Haar filter, which is then passed through a step function. b) The first two weak classifiers learned in this implementation have clear interpretations: The first responds to the dark horizontal region belonging to the eyes, and the second responds to the relative brightness of the bridge of the nose. c) The data passes through a cascade: most regions can be quickly rejected after evaluating only a few weak classifiers as they look nothing like faces. More ambiguous regions undergo further preprocessing. d) Example results. Adapted from Viola and Jones (2004).

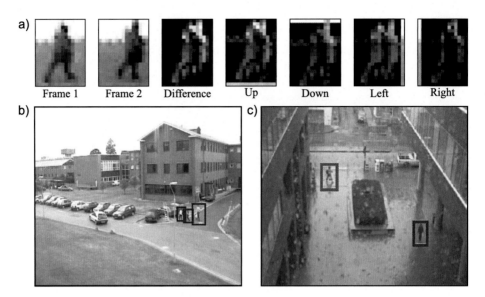

Figure 9.21 Boosting methods based on the thresholded responses of Haar functions have also been used for pedestrian detection in video footage. a) To improve detection rates two subsequent frames are used. The absolute difference between the frames is computed as is the difference when one of the frames is offset in each of four directions. The set of potential weak classifiers consists of Haar functions applied to all of these representations. b,c) Example results. Adapted from Viola et al. (2005). ©2005 Springer.

1. The structure of the classifier was exploited: training in boosting is incremental – the "weak classifiers" (nonlinear functions of the data) are incrementally added to create an increasingly sophisticated strong classifier. Viola and Jones (2004) exploited this structure when they ran the classifier: they reject regions that are very unlikely to be faces based on responses of the first few weak classifiers and only subject more ambiguous regions to further processing. This is known as a *cascade* structure. During training, the later stages of the cascade are trained with new negative examples that were not rejected by the earlier stages.

2. The projections ξ_k were carefully chosen so that they were very fast to evaluate: they consisted of Haar-like filters (Section 13.1.3), which require only a few operations to compute.

The final system consisted of 4297 weak classifiers divided into a 32-stage cascade. It found 91.1 percent of 507 frontal faces across 130 images, with a false positive rate of less than 1 per frame, and processed images in fractions of a second.

Viola et al. (2005) developed a similar system for detecting pedestrians in video sequences (Figure 9.21). The main modification was to extend the set of weak classifiers to encompass features that span more than one frame and hence select for the particular temporal patterns associated with human motion. To this end their system used not only the image data itself, but also the difference image between adjacent frames and similar difference images when taken after offsetting the frames in each of four directions. The final system achieved an 80 percent detection rate with a false alarm rate of 1/400,000 which corresponds to one false positive for every two frames.

9.12.3 Semantic segmentation

The goal of semantic segmentation is to assign a label $w \in \{1 \dots M\}$ to each pixel indicating which of M objects is present, based on the local image data $\mathbf{x}$. Shotton et al. (2009) developed a system known as *textonboost* that was based on a non-probabilistic boosting algorithm called *jointboost* (Torralba et al. 2007). The decision was based on a one-against-all strategy in which M binary classifiers are computed based on the weighted sums

$$a_m = \phi_{0m} + \sum_{k=1}^{K} \phi_{km} \mathbf{f}[\mathbf{x}, \boldsymbol{\xi}_k], \qquad (9.69)$$

where the nonlinear functions $\mathbf{f}[\bullet]$ were once more based on heaviside step functions. Note that the weighted sums associated with each object class share the same nonlinear functions but weight them differently. After computing these series, the decision is assigned based on the activation a_m that is the greatest.

Shotton et al. (2009) based the nonlinear functions on a *texton* representation of the image: each pixel in the image is replaced by a discrete index indicating the "type" of texture present at that position (see Section 13.1.5). Each nonlinear function considers one of these texton types and computes the number of times that it is found within a rectangular area. This area has a fixed spatial displacement from the pixel under consideration (Figures 9.22c–f). If this displacement is zero, then the function provides evidence about the pixel directly (e.g., it looks like grass). If the spatial displacement is larger, then the function provides evidence of the local context (e.g., there is grass nearby, so this pixel may belong to a cow).

For each nonlinear function, an offset is added to the texton count and the result is passed through a step function. The system was learned incrementally by assessing each of a set of a randomly chosen classifiers (defined by the choice of texton, rectangular region, and offset) and choosing the best at the current stage.

The full system also included a postprocessing step in which the result was refined using a conditional random field model (see Chapter 12). It achieved 72.2 percent performance on the challenging MRSC database that includes 21 diverse object classes including wiry objects such as bicycles and objects with a large degree of variation such as dogs.

9.12.4 Recovering surface layout

To recover the *surface layout* of a scene we assign a label $w \in \{1, 2, 3\}$ to each pixel in the image indicating whether the pixel contains a support object (e.g., floor), a vertical object (e.g., building), or the sky. This decision is based on local image data $\mathbf{x}$. Hoiem et al. (2007) constructed a system of this type using a one-against-all principle. Each of the three binary classifiers was based on logitboosted classification trees; different classification trees are treated as weak classifiers, and the results are weighted together to compute the final probability.

Hoiem et al. (2007) worked with the intermediate representation of *superpixels* – an oversegmentation of the scene into small homogeneous regions, which are assumed to belong to the same object. Each superpixel was assigned a label w using the classifier

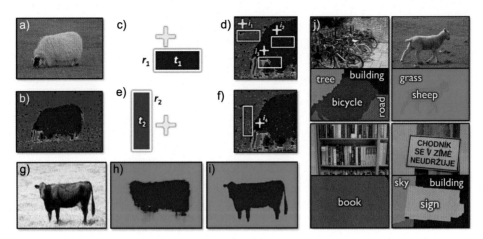

Figure 9.22 Semantic image labeling using "TextonBoost." a) Original image. b) Image converted to textons – a discrete value at each pixel indicating the type of texture that is present. c) The system was based on weak classifiers that count the number of textons of a certain type within a rectangle that is offset from the current position (yellow cross). d) This provides both information about the object itself (contains sheep-like textons) and nearby objects (near to grass-like textons). e,f) Another example of a weak classifier. g) Test image. h) Per-pixel classification is not very precise at the edges of objects and so i) a conditional random field is used to improve the result. j) Examples of results and ground truth. Adapted from Shotton et al. (2009). ©2009 Springer.

based on a data vector $\mathbf{x}$, which contained location, appearance, texture, and perspective information associated with the superpixel.

To mitigate against the possibility that the original superpixel segmentation was wrong, multiple segmentations were computed and the results merged to provide a final per-pixel classification (Figure 9.23). In the full system, regions that were classified as vertical were subclassified into left-facing planar surfaces, frontoparallel planar surfaces, or right-facing planar surfaces or nonplanar surfaces, which may be porous (e.g., trees) or solid. The system was trained and tested on a data set consisting of images collected from the Web including diverse environments (forests, cities, roads, etc.) and conditions (snowy, sunny, cloudy, etc.). The data set was pruned to remove photos where the horizon was not within the image.

The system correctly labeled 88.1 percent of pixels correctly with respect to the main three classes and 61.5 percent correctly with respect to the subclasses of the vertical surface. This algorithm was the basis of a remarkable system for creating a 3D model from a single 2D photograph (Hoiem et al. 2005).

9.12.5 Identifying human parts

Shotton et al. (2011) describe a system that assigns a discrete label $w \in \{1, \ldots, 31\}$, indicating which of 31 body parts is present at each pixel based on a depth image $\mathbf{x}$. The resulting distribution of labels is an intermediate representation in a system that proposes a possible configuration of the 3D joint positions in the Microsoft Kinect gaming system (Figure 9.24).

Input	Location	Colour	Texture	Perspective	All Cues

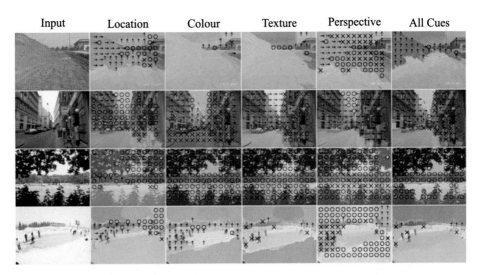

Figure 9.23 Recovering surface layout. The goal is to take an image and return a label indicating whether the pixel is part of a support surface (green pixels) vertical surface (red pixels) or the sky (blue pixels). Vertical surfaces were subclassified into planar objects at different orientations (left arrows, upward arrows and right arrows denote left-facing, frontoparrallel and right-facing surfaces) and nonplanar objects which can be porous (marked as "o") or nonporous (marked as "x". The final classification was based on (i) location cues (which include position in the image and position relative to the horizon), (ii) color cues, (iii) texture cues, and (iv) perspective cues which were based on the statistics of line segments in the region. The figure shows example classifications for each of these cues alone and when combined. Adapted from Hoiem et al. (2007). ©2007 Springer.

The classification was based on a *forest* of decision trees: the final probability $Pr(w|\mathbf{x})$ is an average (i.e., a mixture) of the predictions from a number of different classification trees. The goal is to mitigate against biases introduced by the greedy method with which a single tree is trained.

Within each tree, the decision about which branch a datapoint travels down is based on the difference in measured depths at two points, each of which is spatially offset from the current pixel. The offsets are inversely scaled by the distance to the pixel itself, which ensures that they address the same relative positions on the body when the person moves closer or further away to the depth camera.

The system was trained from a very large data set of 900,000 depth images, which were synthesized based on motion capture data and consisted of three trees of depth 20. Remarkably, the system is capable of assigning the correct label 59 percent of the time, and this provides a very solid basis for the subsequent joint proposals.

Discussion

In this chapter we have considered classification problems. We note that all of the ideas that were applied to regression models in Chapter 8 are also applicable to classification problems. However, for classification the model includes a nonlinear mapping between the data $\mathbf{x}$ and the parameters of the distribution $Pr(w|\mathbf{x})$ over the world w. This means

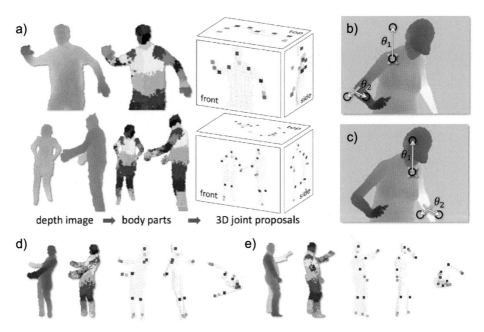

Figure 9.24 Identifying human parts. a) The goal of the system is to take a depth image $\mathbf{x}$ and assign a discrete label w to each pixel indicating which of 31 possible body parts is present. These depth labels are used to form proposals about the position of 3D joints. b) The classification is based on decision trees. At each point in the tree, the data are divided according to the relative depth at two points (red circles) offset relative to the current pixel (yellow crosses). In this example, this difference is large in both cases, whereas in c) this difference is small – hence these differences provide information about the pose. d,e) Two more examples of depth image, labeling and hypothesized pose. Adapted from Shotton et al. (2011). ©2011 IEEE.

that we cannot find the maximum likelihood solution in closed form (although the problem is still convex) and we cannot compute a full Bayesian solution without making approximations.

Classification techniques have many uses in machine vision. Notice though that these models have no domain-specific information about the problem other than that provided by the preprocessing of the data. This is both an advantage (they find many applications) and a disadvantage (they cannot take advantage of a priori information about the problem). In the remaining part of the book we will explore models that introduce increasing amounts of domain-specific information to the problem.

Notes

Classification in vision: Classification techniques such as those discussed in this chapter have been applied to many problems in vision including face detection (Viola and Jones 2004), surface layout estimation creation (Hoiem et al. 2007), boundary detection (Dollár et al. 2006), keypoint matching (Lepetit et al. 2005), body part classification (Hoiem et al. 2007), semantic segmentation (He et al. 2004), object recognition (Csurka et al. 2004), and gender classification (Kumar et al. 2008).

Probabilistic classification: More information about logistic regression can be found in Bishop (2006) and many other statistics textbooks. Kernel logistic regression (or Gaussian process regression) was presented in Williams and Barber (1998) and more information can be found in

Rasmussen and Williams (2006). A sparse version of kernel logistic regression (relevance vector classification) was presented by Tipping (2001) and a sparse multiclass variant was developed by Brishnapuram et al. (2005). Probabilistic interpretations of boosting were introduced by Friedman et al. (2000). Random forests of multinomial regressors were introduced in Prinzie and Van den Poel (2008).

Other classification schemes: In this chapter, we have presented a family of probabilistic classification models based on logistic regression. There are other non-probabilistic techniques for classification, and these include single and multilayer perceptrons (Rosenblatt 1958; Rumelhart et al. 1986), support vector machines (Vapnik 1995; Cristianini and Shawe-Taylor 2000), and adaboost (Freund and Schapire 1995). A critical difference between these techniques is the underlying objective function. Logistic regression models optimize the log Bernoulli probability, but the other models optimize different criteria, such as the hinge loss (support vector machines) or exponential error (adaboost). It is difficult to make general statements about the relative merits of these approaches, but it is probably fair to say that (i) there is no major disadvantage to using the probabilistic techniques in this chapter and (ii) the choice of classification method is usually less important in vision problems than the preprocessing of the data. Methods based on boosting and classification trees are particularly popular in vision because of their speed.

Boosting: Adaboost was introduced by Freund and Schapire (1995). Since then there have been a large number of variations, most of which have been used in computer vision. These include discrete adaboost (Freund and Schapire 1996), real adaboost (Schapire and Singer 1998), gentleboost (Friedman et al. 2000), logitboost (Friedman et al. 2000), floatboost (Li et al. 2003), KLBoost (Liu and Shum 2003), asymmetric boost (Viola and Jones 2002), and statboost (Pham and Cham 2007a). Boosting has also been applied to the multiclass case (Schapire and Singer 1998; Torralba et al. 2007) and for regression (Friedman 1999). A review of boosting approaches can be found in Meir and Mätsch (2003).

Classification trees: Classification trees have a long history in computer vision, dating back to at least Shepherd (1983). Modern interest was stimulated by Amit and Geman (1997) and Breiman (2001) who investigated the use of random forests. Since this time classification trees and forests have been applied to keypoint matching (Lepetit et al. 2005), segmentation (Yin et al. 2007), human pose detection (Rogez et al. 2006; Shotton et al. 2011), object detection (Bosch et al. 2007), image classification (Moosmann et al. 2006, 2008), deciding algorithm suitability (Mac Aodha et al., 2010), detection occlusions (Humayun et al. 2011), and semantic image segmentation (Shotton et al. 2009).

Gender classification: Automatic determination of gender from a facial image has variously been tackled with neural networks (Golomb et al. 1990), support vector machines (Moghaddam and Yang 2002), linear discriminant analysis (Bekios-Calfa et al. 2011) and both adaboost (Baluja and Rowley 2003), and logitboost (Prince and Aghajanian 2009). A review is provided by Mäkinen and Raisamo (2008b) and quantative comparisons are presented in Mäkinen and Raisamo (2008a). Representative examples of the state of the art can be found in Kumar et al. (2008) and Shan (2012).

Face detection: The application of boosting to face detection (Viola and Jones 2004) usurped earlier techniques (e.g., Osuna et al. 1997; Schneiderman and Kanade 2000). Since then, many boosting variants have been applied to the problem including floatboost (Li et al. 2002; Li and Zhang 2004), gentleboost (Lienhart et al. 2003), realboost (Huang et al. 2007a; Wu et al. 2007), asymboost (Pham and Cham 2007b; Viola and Jones 2002), and statboost (Pham and Cham 2007a). A recent review of this area can be found in Zhang and Zhang (2010).

Semantic segmentation: The authors of the system described in the text (Shotton et al. 2008b) subsequently presented a much faster system based on classification trees (Shotton et al. 2009). A recent comparison of quantitative performance can be found in Ranganathan (2009). Other work has investigated the imposition of prior knowledge such as the copresence of object classes (He et al. 2006) and likely spatial configurations of objects (He et al. 2004).

Problems

9.1 The logistic sigmoid function is defined as

$$\text{sig}[a] = \frac{1}{1 + \exp[-a]}.$$

Show that (i) $\text{sig}[-\infty] = 0$, (ii) $\text{sig}[0] = 0.5$, $\text{sig}[\infty] = 1$.

9.2 Show that the derivative of the log posterior probability for the logistic regression model

$$L = \sum_{i=1}^{I} w_i \log \left[\frac{1}{1 + \exp[-\boldsymbol{\phi}^T \mathbf{x}_i]} \right] + \sum_{i=1}^{I} (1 - w_i) \log \left[\frac{\exp[-\boldsymbol{\phi}^T \mathbf{x}_i]}{1 + \exp[-\boldsymbol{\phi}^T \mathbf{x}_i]} \right]$$

with respect to the parameters $\boldsymbol{\phi}$ is given by

$$\frac{\partial L}{\partial \boldsymbol{\phi}} = - \sum_{i=1}^{I} \left(\text{sig}[a_i] - w_i \right) \mathbf{x}_i.$$

9.3 Show that the second derivatives of the log likelihood of the logistic regression model is given by

$$\frac{\partial^2 L}{\partial \boldsymbol{\phi}^2} = - \sum_{i=1}^{I} \text{sig}[a_i](1 - \text{sig}[a_i]) \mathbf{x}_i \mathbf{x}_i^T.$$

9.4 Consider fitting a logistic regression model to 1D data x where the two classes are perfectly separable. For example, perhaps all the data x where the world state $w = 0$ takes values less than 0 and all the data x where the world state is $w = 1$ takes values greater than 1. Hence it is possible to classify the training data perfectly. What will happen to the parameters of the model during learning? How could you rectify this problem?

9.5 Compute the Laplace approximation to a beta distribution with parameters $\alpha = 1.0$, $\beta = 1.0$.

9.6 Show that the Laplace approximation to a univariate normal distribution with mean μ and variance σ^2 is the normal distribution itself.

9.7 Devise a method to choose the scale parameter λ_0 in the radial basis function in kernel logistic regression (Equation 9.33).

9.8 A *mixture of experts* (Jordan and Jacobs 1994) divides space into different regions, each of which receives specialized attention (Figure 9.25). For example, we could describe the data as a mixture of logistic classifiers so that

$$Pr(w_i | \mathbf{x}_i) = \sum_{k=1}^{K} \lambda_k [\mathbf{x}_i] \text{Bern}_{w_i} \left[\text{sig}[\boldsymbol{\phi}_k^T \mathbf{x}_i] \right].$$

Each logistic classifier is considered as an expert and the mixing weights decide the combination of experts that are applied to the data. The mixing weights, which are positive and sum to one, depend on the data $\mathbf{x}$: for a two-component model, they could be based on a second logistic regression model with activation $\boldsymbol{\omega}^T \mathbf{x}$. This model can be expressed as the marginalization of a joint distribution between $\mathbf{w}_i$ and a hidden variable h_i so that

$$Pr(w_i | \mathbf{x}_i) = \sum_{k=1}^{K} Pr(w_i, h_i = k | \mathbf{x}_i) = \sum_{k=1}^{K} Pr(w_i | h_i = k, \mathbf{x}_i) Pr(h_i = k | \mathbf{x}_i),$$

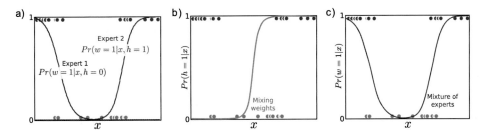

Figure 9.25 Mixture of two experts model for 1D data. Pink circles indicate positive examples. Green circles indicate negative examples. a) Two expert is specialized to model the left and right sides of the data respectively. b) The mixing weights change as a function of the data. c) The final output of the model is mixture of the two constituent experts and fits the data well.

where

$$Pr(w_i|h_i = k, \mathbf{x}_i) = \text{Bern}_{w_i}\left[\text{sig}[\boldsymbol{\phi}_k^T \mathbf{x}_i]\right]$$

$$Pr(h_i = k|\mathbf{x}_i) = \text{Bern}_{h_i}\left[\text{sig}[\boldsymbol{\omega}^T \mathbf{x}_i]\right].$$

How does this model differ from branching logistic regression (Section 9.8)? Devise a learning algorithm for this model.

9.9 The **softmax**[$\bullet, \bullet, \ldots, \bullet$] function is defined to return a multivariate quantity where the kth element is given by

$$s_k = \text{softmax}_k[a_1, a_2, \ldots a_K] = \frac{\exp[a_k]}{\sum_{j=1}^K \exp[a_j]}.$$

Show that $0 < s_k < 1$ and that $\sum_{k=1}^K s_k = 1$.

9.10 Show that the first derivative of the log-probability of the multiclass logistic regression model is given by Equation 9.61.

9.11 The classifiers in this chapter have all been based on continuous data $\mathbf{x}$. Devise a model that can distinguish between M world states $w \in \{1 \ldots M\}$ based on a discrete observation $x \in \{1 \ldots K\}$ and discuss potential learning algorithms.

Part III
Connecting local models

The models in chapters 6–9 describe the relationship between a set of measurements and the world state. They work well when the measurements and the world state are both low dimensional. However, there are many situations where this is not the case, and these models are unsuitable.

For example, consider the semantic image labeling problem in which we wish to assign a label that denotes the object class to each pixel in the image. For example, in a road scene we might wish to label pixels as 'road', 'sky', 'car', 'tree', 'building' or 'other'. For an image with $N = 10000$ pixels, this means we need to build a model relating the 10000 measured RGB triples to 6^{10000} possible world states. None of the models discussed so far can cope with this challenge: the number of parameters involved (and hence the amount of training data and the computational requirements of the learning and inference algorithms) is far beyond what current machines can handle.

One possible solution to this problem would be to build a set of independent local models: for example, we could build models that relate each pixel label separately to the nearby RGB data. However, this is not ideal as the image may be locally ambiguous. For example, a small blue image patch might result from a variety of semantically different classes: sky, water, a car door or a person's clothing. In general, it is insufficient to build independent local models.

The solution to this problem is to build local models that are *connected* to one another. Consider again the semantic labeling example: given the whole image, we can see that when the image patch is blue and is found above trees and mountains and alongside similar patches across the top of the image, then the correct class is probably sky. Hence, to solve this problem, we still model the relationship between the label and its local image region, but we also connect these models so that nearby elements can help to disambiguate one another.

In chapter 10 we introduce the idea of conditional independence, which is a way of characterizing redundancies in the model (i.e., the lack of direct dependence between variables). We show how conditional independence relations can be visualized with graphical models. We distinguish between directed and undirected graphical models. In chapter 11, we discuss models in which the local units are combined together to form chains or trees. In chapter 12, we extend this to the case where they have more general connections.

Chapter 10

Graphical models

The previous chapters discussed models that relate the observed measurements to some aspect of the world that we wish to estimate. In each case, this relationship depended on a set of parameters and for each model we presented a learning algorithm that estimated these parameters.

Unfortunately, the utility of these models is limited because every element of the model depends on every other. For example, in generative models we model the joint probability of the observations and the world state. In many problems both of these quantities may be high-dimensional. Consequently, the number of parameters required to characterize their joint density accurately is very large. Discriminative models suffer from the same pathology: if every element of the world state depends on every element of the data, a large number of parameters will be required to characterize this relationship. In practice, the required amount of training data and the computational burden of learning and inference reach impractical levels.

The solution to this problem is to reduce the dependencies between variables in the model by identifying (or asserting) some degree of redundancy. To this end, we introduce the idea of *conditional independence*, which is a way of characterizing these redundancies. We then introduce *graphical models* which are graph-based representations of the conditional independence relations. We discuss two different types of graphical models – directed and undirected – and we consider the implications for learning, inference, and drawing samples.

This chapter does not develop specific models or discuss vision applications. The goal is to provide the theoretical background for the models in subsequent chapters. We will illustrate the ideas with probability distributions where the constituent variables are discrete; however, almost all of the ideas transfer directly to the continuous case.

10.1 Conditional independence

When we first discussed probability distributions, we introduced the notion of independence (Section 2.6). Two variables x_1 and x_2 are independent if their joint probability distribution factorizes as $Pr(x_1, x_2) = Pr(x_1)Pr(x_2)$. In layman's terms, one variable provides no information about the other if they are independent.

With more than two random variables, independence relations become more complex. The variable x_1 is said to be *conditionally independent of variable x_3 given variable*

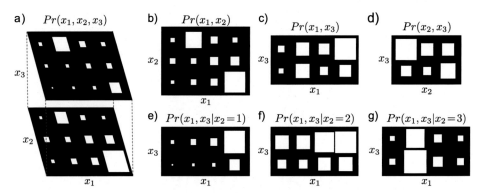

Figure 10.1 Conditional independence. a) Joint pdf of three discrete variables x_1, x_2, x_3, which take 4, 3, and 2 possible values, respectively. All 24 probability values sum to one. b) Marginalizing, we see that variables x_1 and x_2 are dependent; the conditional distribution of x_1 is different for different values of x_2 (the elements in each row are not in the same proportions)and vice versa. c) Variables x_1 and x_3 are also dependent. d) Variables x_2 and x_3 are also dependent. e–g) However, x_1 and x_3 are conditionally independent *given* x_2. For fixed x_2, x_1 tells us nothing more about x_3 and vice versa.

x_2 when x_1 and x_3 are independent for fixed x_2 (Figure 10.1). In mathematical terms, we have

$$Pr(x_1|x_2, x_3) = Pr(x_1|x_2)$$
$$Pr(x_3|x_1, x_2) = Pr(x_3|x_2). \tag{10.1}$$

Note that conditional independence relations are always symmetric; if x_1 is conditionally independent of x_3 given x_2, then it is also true that x_3 is independent of x_1 given x_2.

Confusingly, the conditional independence of x_1 and x_3 given x_2 does not mean that x_1 and x_3 are themselves independent. It merely implies that if we know variable x_2, then x_1 provides no further information about x_3 and vice versa. One way that this can occur is in a chain of events: if event x_1 causes event x_2 and x_2 causes x_3, then the dependence of x_3 on x_1 might be entirely mediated by x_2.

Now consider decomposing the joint probability distribution $Pr(x_1, x_2, x_3)$ into the product of conditional probabilities. When x_1 is independent of x_3 given x_2, we find that

$$Pr(x_1, x_2, x_3) = Pr(x_3|x_2, x_1)Pr(x_2|x_1)Pr(x_1)$$
$$= Pr(x_3|x_2)Pr(x_2|x_1)Pr(x_1). \tag{10.2}$$

The conditional independence relation means that the probability distribution factorizes in a certain way (and is hence redundant). This redundancy implies that we can describe the distribution with fewer parameters and so working with models with large numbers of variables becomes more tractable.

Throughout this chapter, we will explore the relationship between factorization of the distribution and conditional independence relations. To this end, we will introduce graphical models. These are graph-based representations that make both the factorization

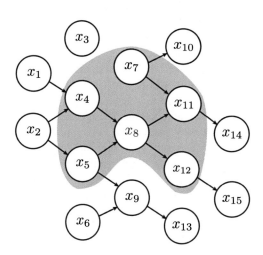

Figure 10.2 Example 1. A directed graphical model has one node per term in the factorization of the joint probability distribution. A node x_n with no incoming connections represents the term $Pr(x_n)$. A node x_n with incoming connections $x_{\text{pa}[n]}$ represents the term $Pr(x_n|x_{\text{pa}[n]})$. Variable x_n is conditionally independent of all of the others given its *Markov blanket*. This comprises its parents, its children, and other parents of its children. For example, the Markov blanket for variable x_8 is indicated by the shaded region.

and the conditional independence relations easy to establish. In this book we will consider two different types of graphical model – directed and undirected graphical models – each of which corresponds to a different type of factorization.

10.2   Directed graphical models

A *directed graphical model* or *Bayesian network* represents the factorization of the joint probability distribution into a product of conditional distributions that take the form of a directed acyclic graph (DAG) so that

$$Pr(x_{1...N}) = \prod_{n=1}^{N} Pr(x_n|x_{\text{pa}[n]}), \qquad (10.3)$$

where $\{x_n\}_{n=1}^{N}$ represent the constituent variables of the joint distribution and the function pa[n] returns the indices of variables that are parents of variable x_n.

We can visualize the factorization as a directed graphical model (Figure 10.2) by adding one node per random variable and drawing an arrow to each variable x_n from each of its parents $x_{\text{pa}[n]}$. This directed graphical model should never contain cycles. If it does, then the original factorization was not a valid probability distribution.

To retrieve the factorization from the graphical model, we introduce one factorization term per variable in the graph. If variable x_n is independent of all others (has no parents), then we write $Pr(x_n)$. Otherwise, we write $Pr(x_n|x_{\text{pa}[n]})$ where the parents $x_{\text{pa}[n]}$ consist of the set of variables with arrows that point to x_n.

10.2.1   Example 1

The graphical model in Figure 10.2 represents the factorization

$$
\begin{aligned}
Pr(x_1 \ldots x_{15}) = {} & Pr(x_1)Pr(x_2)Pr(x_3)Pr(x_4|x_1,x_2)Pr(x_5|x_2)Pr(x_6) \\
& \times Pr(x_7)Pr(x_8|x_4,x_5)Pr(x_9|x_5,x_6)Pr(x_{10}|x_7)Pr(x_{11}|x_7,x_8) \\
& \times Pr(x_{12}|x_8)Pr(x_{13}|x_9)Pr(x_{14}|x_{11})Pr(x_{15}|x_{12}). \qquad (10.4)
\end{aligned}
$$

The graphical model (or factorization) implies a set of independence and conditional independence relations between the variables. Some statements about these relations can be made based on a superficial look at the graph. First, if there is no directed path between two variables following the arrow directions and they have no common ancestors, then they are independent. So, variable x_3 in Figure 10.2 is independent of all of the other variables, and variables x_1 and x_2 are independent of each other. Variables x_4 and x_5 are not independent as they share an ancestor. Second, any variable is conditionally independent of all the other variables given its parents, children, and the other parents of its children (its *Markov blanket*). So, for example, variable x_8 in Figure 10.2 is conditionally independent of the remaining variables given those in the shaded area.

For vision applications, these rules are usually sufficient to gain an understanding of the main properties of a graphical model. However, occasionally we may wish to test whether one arbitrary set of nodes is independent of another given a third. This is not easily established by looking at the graph, but can be tested using the following criterion:

The variables in set $\mathcal{A}$ are conditionally independent of those in set $\mathcal{B}$ given set $\mathcal{C}$ if all routes from $\mathcal{A}$ to $\mathcal{B}$ are blocked. A route is blocked at a node if (i) this node is in $\mathcal{C}$ and the arrows meet head to tail or tail to tail or (ii) neither this node nor any of its descendants are in $\mathcal{C}$ and the arrows meet head to head.

See Koller and Friedman (2009) for more details of why this is the case.

10.2.2 Example 2

Figure 10.3 tells us that

$$Pr(x_1, x_2, x_3) = Pr(x_1)Pr(x_2|x_1)Pr(x_3|x_2). \tag{10.5}$$

In other words, this is the graphical model corresponding to the distribution in Figure 10.1.

If we condition on x_2, the only route from x_1 to x_3 is blocked at x_2 (the arrows meet head to tail here) and so x_1 must be conditionally independent of x_3 given x_2. We could have reached the same conclusion by noticing that the Markov blanket for variable x_1 is just variable x_2.

In this case, it is easy to prove this conditional independence relation algebraically. Writing out the conditional probability of x_1 given x_2 and x_3

$$
\begin{aligned}
Pr(x_1|x_2, x_3) &= \frac{Pr(x_1, x_2, x_3)}{Pr(x_2, x_3)} \\
&= \frac{Pr(x_1)Pr(x_2|x_1)Pr(x_3|x_2)}{\int Pr(x_1)Pr(x_2|x_1)Pr(x_3|x_2)dx_1} \\
&= \frac{Pr(x_1)Pr(x_2|x_1)}{\int Pr(x_1)Pr(x_2|x_1)dx_1},
\end{aligned} \tag{10.6}
$$

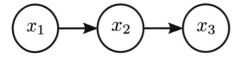

Figure 10.3 Example 2. Directed graphical model relating variables x_1, x_2, x_3 from Figure 10.1. This model implies that the joint probability can be broken down as $Pr(x_1, x_2, x_3) = Pr(x_1)Pr(x_2|x_1)Pr(x_3|x_2)$.

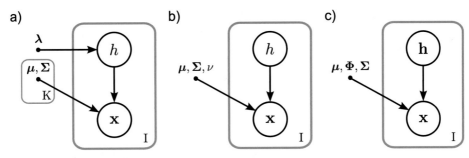

Figure 10.4 Example 3. Graphical models for a) mixture of Gaussians b) t-distribution and c) factor analysis. A node (black circle) represents a random variable. In a graphical model a bullet • represents a variable whose value is considered to be fixed. Each variable may be repeated many times, and this is indicated by a plate (blue rectangle) where the number of copies is indicated in the lower right corner. For example, in a) there are I data examples $\{\mathbf{x}_i\}_{i=1}^I$ and I hidden variables $\{h_i\}_{i=1}^I$. Similarly, there are K sets of parameters $\{\boldsymbol{\mu}_k, \boldsymbol{\Sigma}_k\}_{k=1}^K$, but just one weight vector $\boldsymbol{\lambda}$.

we see that the final expression does not depend on x_3 and so we deduce that x_1 is conditionally independent of x_3 given x_2 as required.

Notice that the factorized distribution is more efficient to represent than the full version. The original distribution $Pr(x_1, x_2, x_3)$ (figure 10.1a) contains $4 \times 3 \times 2 = 24$ entries. However, the terms $Pr(x_1)$, $Pr(x_2|x_1)$, and $Pr(x_3|x_2)$ contain 4, $4 \times 3 = 12$, and $3 \times 2 = 6$ entries, respectively, giving a total of 22 entries. In this case, this is not a dramatic reduction, but in more practical situations it would be. For example, if each variable took ten possible values, the full joint distribution would have $10 \times 10 \times 10 = 1000$ values, but the factorized distribution would have only $10 + 100 + 100 = 210$ values. For even larger systems, this can make a huge saving. One way to think about conditional independence relations is to consider them as redundancies in the full joint probability distribution.

10.2.3   Example 3

Finally, in Figure 10.4 we present graphical models for the mixture of Gaussians, t-distribution and factor analysis models from Chapter 7. These depictions immediately demonstrate that these models have very similar structures.

They also add several new features to the graphical representation. First, they include multidimensional variables. Second, they include variables that are considered as fixed and these are marked by a bullet •. We condition on the fixed variables, but do not define a probability distribution over them. Figure 10.4c depicts the factorization $Pr(\mathbf{h}_i, \mathbf{x}_i) = Pr(\mathbf{h}_i)Pr(\mathbf{x}_i|\mathbf{h}_i, \boldsymbol{\mu}, \boldsymbol{\Phi}, \boldsymbol{\Sigma})$.

Finally, we have also used *plate* notation. A plate is depicted as a rectangle with a number in the corner. It indicates that the quantities inside the rectangle should be repeated the given number of times. For example, in Figure 10.4c there are I copies $\{\mathbf{x}_i, \mathbf{h}_i\}_{i=1}^I$ of the variables $\mathbf{x}$ and $\mathbf{h}$ but only one set of parameters $\boldsymbol{\mu}, \boldsymbol{\Phi}$, and $\boldsymbol{\Sigma}$.

10.2.4   Summary

To summarize, we can think about the structure of the joint probability distribution in three ways. First, we can consider the way that the probability distribution factorizes.

Second, we can examine the directed graphical model. Third, we can think about the conditional independence relations.

There is a one-to-one mapping between directed graphical models (acyclic directed graphs of conditional probability relations) and factorizations. However, the relationship between the graphical model (or factorization) and the conditional independence relations is more complicated. A directed graphical model (or its equivalent factorization) determines a set of conditional independence relations. However, as we shall see later in this chapter, there are some sets of conditional independence relations that cannot be represented by directed graphical models.

10.3   Undirected graphical models

In this section we introduce a second family of graphical models. Undirected graphical models represent probability distributions over variables $\{x_n\}_{n=1}^{N}$ that take the form of a product of *potential functions* $\phi[x_{1...N}]$ so that

$$Pr(x_{1...N}) = \frac{1}{Z} \prod_{c=1}^{C} \phi_c[x_{1...N}], \tag{10.7}$$

where the potential function $\phi_c[x_{1...N}]$ always returns a positive number. Since the probability increases when $\phi_c[x_{1...N}]$ increases, each of these functions modulates the tendency for the variables $x_{1...N}$ to take certain values. The probability is greatest where all of the functions $\phi_{1...C}$ return high values. However, it should be emphasized that potential functions are *not* the same as conditional probabilities, and there is not usually a clear way to map from one to the other.

The term Z is known as the *partition function* and normalizes the product of these positive functions so that the total probability is one. In the discrete case, it would be computed as

$$Z = \sum_{x_1} \sum_{x_2} \cdots \sum_{x_N} \prod_{c=1}^{C} \phi_c[x_{1...N}]. \tag{10.8}$$

For realistically sized systems, this sum will be intractable; we will not be able to compute Z and hence will only be able to compute the overall probability up to an unknown scale factor.

We can equivalently write Equation 10.7 as

$$Pr(x_{1...N}) = \frac{1}{Z} \exp\left[-\sum_{c=1}^{C} \psi_c[x_{1...N}]\right], \tag{10.9}$$

where $\psi_c[x_{1...N}] = -\log[\phi_c[x_{1...N}]]$. When written in this form, the probability is referred to as a *Gibbs distribution*. The terms $\psi_c[x_{1...N}]$ are functions that may return any real number and can be thought of as representing a cost for every combination of labels $x_{1...N}$. As the cost increases, the probability decreases. The total cost $\sum_{c=1}^{C} \psi_c[x_{1...N}]$ is sometimes known as the *energy*, and the process of fitting the model (increasing the probability) is hence sometimes termed *energy minimization*.

When each potential function $\phi[\bullet]$ (or alternatively each cost function $\psi[\bullet]$) addresses all of the variables $x_{1...N}$, the undirected graphical model is known as a *product of experts*. However, in computer vision it is more common for each potential function to operate on a subset of the variables $\mathcal{S} \subset \{x_n\}_{n=1}^N$. These subsets are called *cliques* and it is the choice of these cliques that determines the conditional independence relations. Denoting the cth clique by $\mathcal{S}_c$ we can rewrite Equation 10.7 as

$$Pr(x_{1...N}) = \frac{1}{Z} \prod_{c=1}^C \phi_c[\mathcal{S}_c]. \tag{10.10}$$

In other words, the probability distribution is factorized into a product of terms, each of which only depends on a subset of variables. In this situation, the model is sometimes referred to as a *Markov random field*.

To visualize the undirected graphical model, we draw one node per random variable. Then, for every clique $\mathcal{S}_c$ we draw a connection from every member variable $x_i \in \mathcal{S}_c$ to every other member variable.

Moving in the opposite direction, we can take a graphical model and establish the underlying factorization using the following method. We add one term to the factorization per *maximal clique* (see Figure 10.6). A maximal clique is a fully connected subset of nodes (i.e., a subset where every node is connected to every other) where it is not possible to add another node and remain fully connected.

It is much easier to establish the conditional independence relations from an undirected graphical model than for directed graphical models. They can be found using the following property:

One set of nodes is conditionally independent of another given a third if the third set separates them (prevents a path from the first node to the second).

It follows that a node is conditionally independent of all other nodes given its set of immediate neighbors, and so these neighbors form the Markov blanket.

10.3.1   Example 1

Consider the graphical model in Figure 10.5. This represents the factorization

$$Pr(x_1, x_2, x_3) = \frac{1}{Z} \phi_1[x_1, x_2] \phi_2[x_2, x_3]. \tag{10.11}$$

We can immediately see that variable x_1 is conditionally independent of variable x_3 given x_2 because x_2 separates the other two variables: it blocks the path from x_1 to x_3. In this

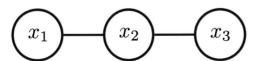

Figure 10.5 Example 1. Undirected graphical model relating variables x_1, x_2, and x_3. This model implies that the joint probability can be factorized as $Pr(x_1, x_2, x_3) = \frac{1}{Z} \phi_1[x_1, x_2] \phi_2[x_2, x_3]$.

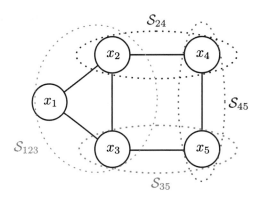

Figure 10.6 Example 2. Undirected graphical model representing variables $\{x_i\}_{i=1}^5$. The associated probability distribution factorizes into a product of one potential function per maximal clique. The clique $\mathcal{S}_{45} = \{x_4, x_5\}$ is a maximal clique as there is no other node that we can add that connects to every node in the clique. The clique $\mathcal{S}_{23} = \{x_2, x_3\}$ is not a maximal clique as it is possible to add node x_1, and all three nodes in the new clique are connected to each other.

case, the conditional independence relation is easy to prove:

$$
\begin{aligned}
Pr(x_1|x_2, x_3) &= \frac{Pr(x_1, x_2, x_3)}{Pr(x_2, x_3)} \\
&= \frac{\frac{1}{Z}\phi_1[x_1, x_2]\phi_2[x_2, x_3]}{\int \frac{1}{Z}\phi_1[x_1, x_2]\phi_2[x_2, x_3]dx_1} \\
&= \frac{\phi_1[x_1, x_2]}{\int \phi_1[x_1, x_2]dx_1}.
\end{aligned}
\tag{10.12}
$$

The final expression does not depend on x_3 and so we conclude that x_1 is conditionally independent of x_3 given x_2.

10.3.2 Example 2

Consider the graphical model in Figure 10.6. There are four maximal cliques in this graph, and so it represents the factorization

$$
Pr(x_{1\ldots5}) = \frac{1}{Z}\phi_1[x_1, x_2, x_3]\phi_2[x_2, x_4]\phi_3[x_3, x_5]\phi_4[x_4, x_5].
\tag{10.13}
$$

We can deduce various conditional independence relations from the graphical representation. For example, variable x_1 is conditionally independent of variables x_4 and x_5 given x_2 and x_3, and variable x_5 is independent of variables x_1 and x_2 given x_3 and x_4, and so on.

Note also that the factorization

$$
Pr(x_{1\ldots5}) = \frac{1}{Z}\left(\phi_1[x_1, x_2]\phi_2[x_2, x_3]\phi_3[x_1, x_3]\right)\phi_4[x_2, x_4]\phi_5[x_3, x_5]\phi_6[x_4, x_5].
\tag{10.14}
$$

creates the same graphical model: there is a many-to-one mapping from factorizations to undirected graphical models (as opposed to the one-to-one mapping for directed graphical models). When we compute a factorization from the graphical model based on the maximal cliques we do so in a conservative way. It is possible that there are further redundancies which were not made explicit by the undirected graphical model.

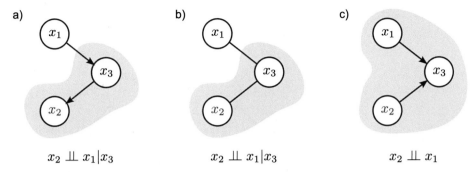

Figure 10.7 Directed versus undirected graphical models. a) Directed graphical model with three nodes. There is only one conditional independence relation implied by this model: the node x_3 is the Markov blanket of node x_2 (shaded area) and so $x_2 \perp\!\!\!\perp x_1 | x_3$, where the notation $\perp\!\!\!\perp$ can be read as "is independent of". b) This undirected graphical model implies the same conditional independence relation. c) Second directed graphical model. The relation $x_2 \perp\!\!\!\perp x_1 | x_3$ is no longer true, but x_1 and x_2 are independent if we don't condition on x_3 so we can write $x_2 \perp\!\!\!\perp x_1$. There is no undirected graphical model with three variables that has this pattern of independence and conditional independence.

10.4 Comparing directed and undirected graphical models

In Sections 10.2 and 10.3 we have discussed directed and undirected graphical models, respectively. Each graphical model represents a factorization of the probability distribution. We have presented methods to extract the conditional independence relations from each type of graphical model. The purpose of this section is to argue that these representations are not equivalent. There are patterns of conditional independence that can be represented by directed graphical models but not undirected graphical models and vice versa.

Figures 10.7a–b show an undirected and directed graphical model that do represent the same conditional independence relations. However, Figure 10.7c shows a directed graphical model for which there is no equivalent undirected graphical model. There is simply no way to induce the same pattern of independence and conditional independence with an undirected graphical model.

Conversely, Figure 10.8a shows an undirected graphical model that induces a pattern of conditional independence relations that cannot be replicated by any directed graphical model. Figure 10.8b shows a directed graphical model that is close, but still not equivalent; the Markov blanket of x_2 is different in each model and so are its conditional independence relations.

We conclude from this brief argument that directed and undirected graphical models do not represent the same subset of independence and conditional independence relations, and so we cannot eliminate one or the other from our consideration. In fact, there are other patterns of conditional independence that cannot be represented by either type of model. However, these will not be considered in this book. For further information concerning the families of distributions that can be represented by different types of graphical model, consult Barber (2012) or Koller and Friedman (2009).

10.5 Graphical models in computer vision

We will now introduce a number of common vision models and look at their associated graphical models. We will discuss each of these in detail in subsequent chapters. However, it is instructive to see them together.

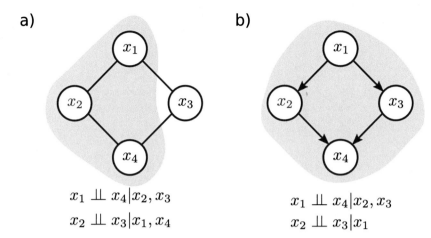

a)

b)

$$x_1 \perp\!\!\!\perp x_4 | x_2, x_3$$
$$x_2 \perp\!\!\!\perp x_3 | x_1, x_4$$

$$x_1 \perp\!\!\!\perp x_4 | x_2, x_3$$
$$x_2 \perp\!\!\!\perp x_3 | x_1$$

Figure 10.8 Directed versus undirected models. a) This undirected graphical model induces two conditional independence relations. However, there is no equivalent directed graphical model that produces the same pattern. b) This directed graphical model also induces two conditional independence relations, but they are not the same. In both cases, the shaded region represents the Markov blanket of variable x_2.

Figure 10.9a shows the graphical model for a *hidden Markov model* or *HMM*. We observe a sequence of measurements $\{\mathbf{x}_n\}_{n=1}^N$ each of which tells us something about the corresponding discrete world state $\{\mathbf{w}_n\}_{n=1}^N$. Adjacent world states are connected together so that the previous world state influences the current one and potentially resolves situations where the measurements are ambiguous. A prototypical application would be tracking sequences of sign language gestures (Figure 10.9b). There is information at each frame about which gesture is present, but it may be ambiguous. However, we can impose prior knowledge that certain signs are more likely to follow others using the HMM and get an improved result.

Figure 10.9c represents a *Markov tree*. Again we observe a number of measurements, each of which provides information about the associated discrete world state. However, the world states are now connected in a tree structure. A prototypical application would be human body fitting (Figure 10.9d) where each unknown world state represents a body part. The parts of the body naturally have a tree structure and so it makes sense to build a model that exploits this.

Figure 10.9e illustrates the use of a *Markov random field* or *MRF* as a prior. The MRF here describes the world state as a grid of undirected connections. Each node might correspond to a pixel. There is also a measurement variable associated with each world state variable. These pairs are connected with directed links, so overall this is a mixed model (partly directed and partly undirected). A prototypical application of an MRF in vision would be for semantic labeling (Figure 10.9f). The measurements constitute the RGB values at each position. The world state at each pixel is a discrete variable that determines the class of object present (i.e., cow versus grass). The Markov random field prior ties together all of the individual classifiers to help yield a solution that makes global sense.

Finally, Figure 10.9g shows the *Kalman filter*. This has the same graphical model as the hidden Markov model but in this case the world state is continuous rather than discrete. A prototypical application of the Kalman filter is for tracking objects through

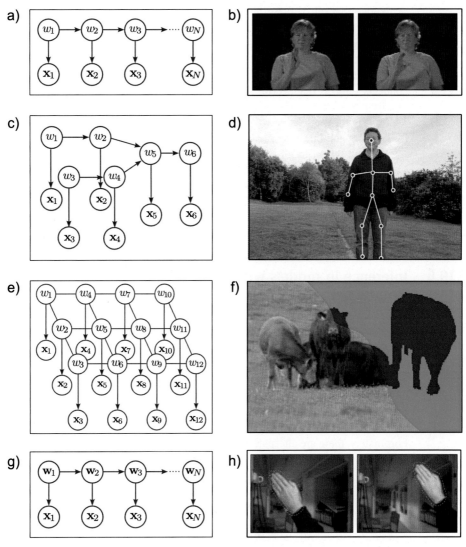

Figure 10.9 Commonly used graphical models in computer vision. a) Hidden Markov model. b) One possible application of the HMM is interpreting sign language sequences. The choice of sign at time n depends on the sign at time $n-1$. c) Markov tree. d) An example application is fitting a tree-structured body model e) Markov random field prior with independent observations. f) The MRF is often used as a prior distribution in semantic labeling tasks. Here the goal is to infer a binary label at each pixel determining whether it belongs to the cow or the grass. g) Kalman filter. An example application is tracking an object through a sequence. It has the same graphical model as the HMM, but the unknown quantities are continuous as opposed to discrete.

a time sequence (Figure 10.9h). At each time, we might want to know the 2D position, size, and orientation of the hand. However, in a given frame the measurements might be poor: the frame may be blurred or the object may be temporarily occluded. By building a model that connects the estimates from adjacent frames, we can increase the robustness to these factors; earlier frames can resolve the uncertainty in the current ambiguous frame.

Notice that all of these graphical models have directed links from the world $\mathbf{w}$ to the data $\mathbf{x}$ that indicate a relationship of the form $Pr(\mathbf{x}|\mathbf{w})$. Hence, they all construct a probability distribution over the data and are generative models. We will also consider discriminative models, but, historically speaking, generative models of this kind have been more important. Each model is quite sparsely connected: each data variable $\mathbf{x}$ connects only to one world state variable $\mathbf{w}$, and each world state variable connects to only a few others. The result of this is that there are many conditional independence relations in the model. We will exploit these redundancies to develop efficient algorithms for learning and inference.

We will return to all of these models later in the book. We investigate the hidden Markov model and the Markov tree in Chapter 11. We discuss the Markov random field in Chapter 12, and we will present the Kalman filter in Chapter 19. The remaining part of this chapter answers two questions: (i) How can we perform inference when there are a large number of unknown world variables? (ii) What are the implications of using a directed graphical model versus an undirected one?

10.6 Inference in models with many unknowns

We will now consider inference in these models. Ideally, we would compute the full posterior distribution $Pr(w_{1...N}|\mathbf{x}_{1...N})$ using Bayes' rule. However, the unknown world states in the preceding models are generally much larger than previously considered in this book and this makes inference challenging.

For example, consider the space of world states in the HMM example. If we are given 1000 frames of video and there are 500 common signs in the sign language, then there are 500^{1000} possible states. It is clearly not practical to compute and store the posterior probability associated with each. Even when the world states are continuous, computing and storing the parameters of a high-dimensional probability model is still problematic. Fortunately, there are alternative approaches to inference, which we now consider in turn.

10.6.1 Finding the MAP solution

One obvious possibility is to find the maximum a posteriori solution:

$$
\begin{aligned}
\hat{w}_{1...N} &= \underset{w_{1...N}}{\operatorname{argmax}} \left[Pr\left(w_{1...N}|\mathbf{x}_{1...N}\right) \right] \\
&= \underset{w_{1...N}}{\operatorname{argmax}} \left[Pr\left(\mathbf{x}_{1...N}|w_{1...N}\right) Pr\left(w_{1...N}\right) \right].
\end{aligned}
$$

This is still far from trivial. The number of world states is extremely large so we cannot possibly explore every one and take the maximum. We must employ intelligent and efficient algorithms that exploit the redundancies in the distribution to find the correct solution where possible. However, as we shall see, for some models there is no known polynomial algorithm to find the MAP solution.

10.6.2 Finding the marginal posterior distribution

An alternative strategy is to find the marginal posterior distributions:

$$
Pr(w_n|\mathbf{x}_{1...N}) = \int \int Pr(w_{1...N}|\mathbf{x}_{1...N}) dw_{1...n-1} \, dw_{n+1...N}. \tag{10.15}
$$

Since each of these distributions is over a single label, it is not implausible to compute and store each one separately. Obviously it is not possible to do this by directly computing the (extremely large) joint distribution and marginalizing it directly. We must use algorithms that exploit the conditional independence relations in the distribution to efficiently compute the marginals.

10.6.3   Maximum marginals

If we want a single estimate of the world state, we could return the maximum values of the marginal distributions, giving the criterion

$$\hat{w}_n = \underset{w_n}{\operatorname{argmax}} \left[Pr\left(w_n | \mathbf{x}_{1...N}\right) \right]. \tag{10.16}$$

This produces estimates of each world state that are individually most probable, but which may not reflect the joint statistics. For example, world state $w_n = 4$ might be the most probable value for the nth world state and $w_m = 6$ might be the most probable value for the mth world state, but it could be that the posterior probability for this configuration is zero: although the states are individually probable, they never co-occur (Figure 10.10).

10.6.4   Sampling the posterior

For some models, it is intractable to compute either the MAP solution or the marginal distributions. One possibility in this circumstance is to draw samples from the posterior distribution. Methods based on sampling the posterior would fall under the more general category of *approximate inference* as they do not normally return the true answer.

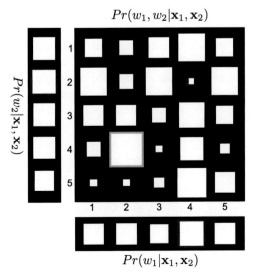

$Pr(w_1, w_2 | \mathbf{x}_1, \mathbf{x}_2)$

$Pr(w_1 | \mathbf{x}_1, \mathbf{x}_2)$

Figure 10.10 MAP solution versus max marginals solution. The main figure shows the joint posterior distribution $Pr(w_1, w_2 | \mathbf{x}_1, \mathbf{x}_2)$. The MAP solution is at the peak of this distribution at $w_1 = 2, w_2 = 4$ (highlighted in green). The figure also shows the two marginal distributions $Pr(w_1 | \mathbf{x}_1, \mathbf{x}_2)$ and $Pr(w_2 | \mathbf{x}_1, \mathbf{x}_2)$. The maximum marginals solution is computed by individually finding the maximum of each marginal distributions, which gives the solution $w_1 = 4, w_2 = 2$ (highlighted in red). For this distribution, this is very unrepresentative; although these labels are individually likely, they rarely co-occur and the joint posterior for this combination has low probability.

Having drawn a number of samples from the posterior, we can approximate the posterior probability distribution as a mixture of delta functions where there is one delta function at each of the sample positions. Alternatively, we could make estimates of marginal statistics such as the mean and variance based on the sampled values or select the sample with the highest posterior probability as an estimate of the MAP state; this latter approach has the advantage of being consistent with the full posterior distribution (as opposed to maximum marginals which is not) even if we cannot be sure that we have the correct answer.

An alternative way to compute a point estimate from a set of samples from the posterior is to compute the *empirical max-marginals*. We estimate the marginal probability distributions by looking at the marginal statistics of the samples. In other words, we consider one variable w_n at a time and look at the distribution of different values observed. For a discrete distribution, this information is captured in a histogram. For a continuous distribution, we could fit a univariate model such as a normal distribution to these values to summarize them.

10.7   Drawing samples

We have seen that some of the approaches to inference require us to draw samples from the posterior distribution. We will now discuss how to do this for both directed and undirected models and we will see that this is generally more straightforward in directed models.

10.7.1   Sampling from directed graphical models

Directed graphical models take the form of directed acyclic graphs of conditional probability relations that have the following algebraic form:

$$Pr(x_{1...N}) = \prod_{n=1}^{N} Pr(x_n | x_{\mathbf{pa}[n]}). \qquad (10.17)$$

It is relatively easy to sample from a directed graphical model using a technique known as *ancestral sampling*. The idea is to sample each variable in the network in turn, where the order is such that all parents of a node are sampled before the node itself. At each node, we condition on the observed sample values of the parents.

The simplest way to understand this is with an example. Consider the directed graphical model in Figure 10.11 whose probability distribution factorizes as

$$Pr(x_1, x_2, x_3, x_4, x_5) = Pr(x_1)Pr(x_2|x_1)Pr(x_3|x_4, x_2)Pr(x_4|x_2, x_1)Pr(x_5|x_3). \qquad (10.18)$$

To sample from this model we first identify x_1 as a node with no parents and draw a sample from the distribution $Pr(x_1)$. Let us say the observed sample at x_1 took value α_1.

We now turn to the remaining nodes. Node x_2 is the only node in the network where all of the parents have been processed, and so we turn our attention here next. We draw

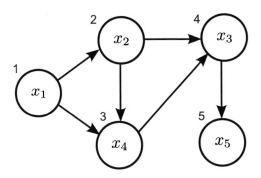

Figure 10.11 Ancestral sampling. We work our way through the graph in an order (red number) that guarantees that the parents of every node are visited before the node itself. At each step we draw a sample conditioned on the values of the samples at the parents. This is guaranteed to produce a valid sample from the full joint distribution.

a sample from the distribution $Pr(x_2|x_1 = \alpha_1)$ to yield a sample α_2. We now see that we are not yet ready to sample from x_3 as not all of its parents have been sampled, but we can sample x_4 from the distribution $Pr(x_4|x_1 = \alpha_1, x_2 = \alpha_2)$ to yield the value α_4. Continuing this process we draw x_3 from $Pr(x_3|x_2 = \alpha_2, x_4 = \alpha_4)$ and finally x_5 from $Pr(x_5|x_3 = \alpha_3)$.

The resulting vector $\mathbf{w}^* = [\alpha_1, \alpha_2, \alpha_3, \alpha_4, \alpha_5]$ is guaranteed to be a valid sample from the full joint distribution $Pr(x_1, x_2, x_3, x_4, x_5)$. An equivalent way to think about this algorithm is to consider it as working through the terms in the factorized joint distribution (right-hand side of Equation 10.18) sampling from each in turn conditioned on the previous values.

10.7.2   Sampling from undirected graphical models

Unfortunately, it is much harder to draw samples from undirected models except in certain special cases (e.g., where the variables are continuous and Gaussian or where the graph structure takes the form of a tree). In general graphs, we cannot use ancestral sampling because (i) there is no sense in which any variable is a parent to any other so we don't know which order to sample in and (ii) the terms $\phi[\bullet]$ in the factorization are not probability distributions anyway.

One way to generate samples from any complex high-dimensional probability distribution is to use a *Markov chain Monte Carlo* (MCMC) method. The principle is to generate a series (chain) of samples from the distribution, so that each sample depends directly on the previous one (hence "Markov"). However, the generation of the sample is not completely deterministic (hence "Monte Carlo").

One of the simplest MCMC methods is *Gibbs sampling*, which proceeds as follows. First, we randomly choose the initial state $\mathbf{x}^{[0]}$ using any method. We generate the next sample in the chain $\mathbf{x}^{[1]}$ by updating the state at each dimension $\{x_n\}_{n=1}^N$ in turn (in any order). To update the nth dimension x_n we fix the other $N-1$ dimensions and draw from the conditional distribution $Pr(x_n|x_{1...N\backslash n})$ where the set $x_{1...N\backslash n}$ denotes all of the N variables $x_1, x_2 \ldots x_N$ *except* x_n. Having modified every dimension in this way, we obtain the second sample in the chain. This idea is illustrated in Figure 10.12 for the multivariate normal distribution.

When this procedure is repeated a very large number of times, so that the initial conditions are forgotten, a sample from this sequence can be considered as a draw from the distribution $Pr(x_{1...N})$. Although this is not immediately obvious (and a proof is

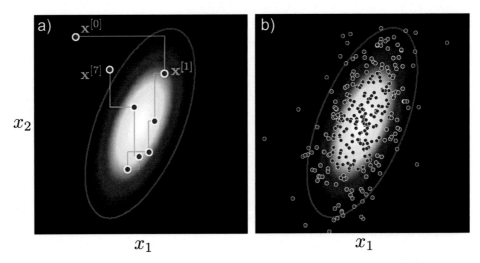

Figure 10.12 Gibbs sampling. We generate a chain of samples by cycling through each dimension in turn and drawing a sample from the conditional distribution of that dimension given that the others are fixed. a) For this 2D multivariate normal distribution, we start at a random position $\mathbf{x}^{[0]}$. We alternately draw samples from the conditional distribution of the first dimension keeping the second fixed (horizontal changes) and the second dimension keeping the first fixed (vertical changes). For the multivariate normal, these conditional distributions are themselves normal (Section 5.5). Each time we cycle through both of the dimensions, we create a new sample $\mathbf{x}^{[t]}$. b) Many samples generated using this method.

beyond the scope of this book), this procedure does clearly have some sensible properties: since we are sampling from the conditional probability distribution at each pixel, we are more likely to change the current value to one which has an overall higher probability. However, the stochastic update rule provides the possibility of (infrequently) visiting less probable regions of the space.

For undirected graphical models, the conditional distribution $Pr(x_n|x_{1...N\setminus n})$ can be quite efficient to evaluate because of the conditional independence properties: variable x_n is conditionally independent of the rest of the nodes given its immediate neighbors, and so computing this term only involves the immediate neighbors. However, overall this method is extremely inefficient: it requires a large amount of computational effort to generate even a single sample. Sampling from directed graphical models is far easier.

10.8 Learning

In Section 10.7 we argued that sampling from directed graphical models is considerably easier than sampling from undirected graphical models. In this section, we consider learning in each type of model and come to a similar conclusion. Note that we are not discussing the learning of the graph structure here; we are talking about learning the parameters of the model itself. For directed graphical models, these parameters would determine the conditional distributions $Pr(x_n|x_{\mathrm{pa}[n]})$ and for undirected graphical models they would determine the potential functions $\phi_c[\mathbf{x}_{1...N}]$.

10.8.1 Learning in directed graphical models

Any directed graphical model can be written in the factorized form

$$Pr(x_1 \ldots x_N) = \prod_{n=1}^{N} Pr(x_n | x_{\mathrm{pa}[n]}, \boldsymbol{\theta}), \qquad (10.19)$$

where the conditional probability relations form a directed acyclic graph, and $\boldsymbol{\theta}$ denotes the parameters of the model. For example, in the discrete distributions that we have focused on in this chapter, an individual conditional model might be

$$Pr(x_2 | x_1 = k) = \mathrm{Cat}_{x_2}[\boldsymbol{\lambda}_k] \qquad (10.20)$$

where the parameters here are $\{\boldsymbol{\lambda}_k\}_{k=1}^{K}$. In general, the parameters can be learned using the maximum likelihood method by finding

$$\hat{\boldsymbol{\theta}} = \operatorname*{argmax}_{\boldsymbol{\theta}} \left[\prod_{i=1}^{I} \prod_{n=1}^{N} Pr(x_{i,n} | x_{i,\mathrm{pa}[n]}, \boldsymbol{\theta}) \right] \qquad (10.21)$$

$$= \operatorname*{argmax}_{\boldsymbol{\theta}} \left[\sum_{i=1}^{I} \sum_{n=1}^{N} \log[Pr(x_{i,n} | x_{i,\mathrm{pa}[n]}, \boldsymbol{\theta})] \right], \qquad (10.22)$$

where $x_{i,n}$ represents the nth dimension of the ith training example. This criterion leads to simple learning algorithms, and often the maximum likelihood parameters can be computed in closed form.

10.8.2 Learning in undirected graphical models

An undirected graphical model is written as

$$Pr(\mathbf{x}) = \frac{1}{Z} \prod_{c=1}^{C} \phi_c[\mathbf{x}, \boldsymbol{\theta}], \qquad (10.23)$$

where $\mathbf{x} = [x_1, x_2, \ldots, x_N]$ and we have assumed that the training samples are independent. However, in this form we must constrain the parameters so that they ensure that each $\phi_c[\bullet]$ always returns a positive number. A more practical approach is to reparameterize the undirected graphical model in the form of the Gibbs distribution,

$$Pr(\mathbf{x}) = \frac{1}{Z} \exp \left[-\sum_{c=1}^{C} \psi_c[x_{1 \ldots N}, \boldsymbol{\theta}] \right] \qquad (10.24)$$

so that we do not have to worry about constraints on the parameters.

Given I training examples $\{\mathbf{x}_i\}_{i=1}^{I}$, we aim to fit parameters $\boldsymbol{\theta}$. Assuming that the training examples are independent, the maximum likelihood solution is

$$\hat{\boldsymbol{\theta}} = \operatorname*{argmax}_{\boldsymbol{\theta}} \left[\frac{1}{Z(\boldsymbol{\theta})^I} \exp \left[-\sum_{i=1}^{I} \sum_{c=1}^{C} \psi_c(\mathbf{x}_i, \boldsymbol{\theta}) \right] \right]$$

$$= \operatorname*{argmax}_{\boldsymbol{\theta}} \left[-I \log[Z(\boldsymbol{\theta})] - \sum_{i=1}^{I} \sum_{c=1}^{C} \psi_c(\mathbf{x}_i, \boldsymbol{\theta}) \right], \qquad (10.25)$$

where as usual we have taken the log to simplify the expression.

To maximize this expression we calculate the derivative of the log likelihood L with respect to the parameters $\boldsymbol{\theta}$:

$$\frac{\partial L}{\partial \boldsymbol{\theta}} = -I \frac{\partial \log[Z(\boldsymbol{\theta})]}{\partial \boldsymbol{\theta}} - \sum_{i=1}^{I} \sum_{c=1}^{C} \frac{\partial \psi_c(\mathbf{x}_i, \boldsymbol{\theta})}{\partial \boldsymbol{\theta}} \qquad (10.26)$$

$$= -I \frac{\partial \log \left[\sum_{\mathbf{x}_i} \exp \left[-\sum_{c=1}^{C} \psi_c(\mathbf{x}_i, \boldsymbol{\theta}) \right] \right]}{\partial \boldsymbol{\theta}} - \sum_{i=1}^{I} \sum_{c=1}^{C} \frac{\partial \psi_c(\mathbf{x}_i, \boldsymbol{\theta})}{\partial \boldsymbol{\theta}}.$$

The second term is readily computable but the first term involves an intractable sum over all possible values of the variable $\mathbf{x}$: we cannot compute the derivative with respect to the parameters for reasonable-sized models and so learning is difficult. Moreover, we cannot evaluate the original probability expression (Equation 10.23) as this too contains an intractable sum. Consequently, we can't compute the derivative using finite differences either.

In short, we can neither find an algebraic solution nor use a straightforward optimization technique as we cannot compute the gradient. The best that we can do is to approximate the gradient.

Contrastive divergence

One possible solution to this problem is the *contrastive divergence* algorithm. This is a method for approximating the gradient of the log likelihood with respect to parameters $\boldsymbol{\theta}$ for functions with the general form,

$$Pr(\mathbf{x}) = \frac{1}{Z(\boldsymbol{\theta})} f[\mathbf{x}, \boldsymbol{\theta}], \qquad (10.27)$$

where $Z(\boldsymbol{\theta}) = \sum_{\mathbf{x}} f[\mathbf{x}, \boldsymbol{\theta}]$ is the normalizing constant and the derivative of the log likelihood is

$$\frac{\partial \log[Pr(\mathbf{x})]}{\partial \boldsymbol{\theta}} = -\frac{\partial \log[Z(\boldsymbol{\theta})]}{\partial \boldsymbol{\theta}} + \frac{\partial \log[f[\mathbf{x}, \boldsymbol{\theta}]]}{\partial \boldsymbol{\theta}}. \qquad (10.28)$$

The main idea behind contrastive divergence follows from some algebraic manipulation of the first term:

$$\begin{aligned} \frac{\partial \log[Z(\boldsymbol{\theta})]}{\partial \boldsymbol{\theta}} &= \frac{1}{Z(\boldsymbol{\theta})} \frac{\partial Z(\boldsymbol{\theta})}{\partial \boldsymbol{\theta}} \\ &= \frac{1}{Z(\boldsymbol{\theta})} \frac{\partial \sum_{\mathbf{x}} f[\mathbf{x}, \boldsymbol{\theta}]}{\partial \boldsymbol{\theta}} \\ &= \frac{1}{Z(\boldsymbol{\theta})} \sum_{\mathbf{x}} \frac{\partial f[\mathbf{x}, \boldsymbol{\theta}]}{\partial \boldsymbol{\theta}} \\ &= \frac{1}{Z(\boldsymbol{\theta})} \sum_{\mathbf{x}} f[\mathbf{x}, \boldsymbol{\theta}] \frac{\partial \log[f[\mathbf{x}, \boldsymbol{\theta}]]}{\partial \boldsymbol{\theta}} \\ &= \sum_{\mathbf{x}} Pr(\mathbf{x}) \frac{\partial \log[f[\mathbf{x}, \boldsymbol{\theta}]]}{\partial \boldsymbol{\theta}}. \end{aligned} \qquad (10.29)$$

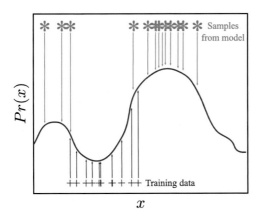

Figure 10.13 The contrastive divergence algorithm changes the parameters so that the unnormalized distribution increases at the observed data points (blue crosses) but decreases at sampled data points from the model (green stars). These two components counterbalance one another and ensure that the likelihood increases. When the model fits the data, these two forces will cancel out, and the parameters will remain constant.

where we have used the relation $\partial \log f[\mathbf{x}]/\partial x = (\partial f[\mathbf{x}]/\partial x)/f[\mathbf{x}]$ between the third and fourth lines.

The final term in Equation 10.29 is the expectation of the derivative of $\log[f[\mathbf{x},\boldsymbol{\theta}]]$. We cannot compute this exactly, but we can approximate it by drawing J independent samples $\mathbf{x}^*$ from the distribution to yield

$$\frac{\partial \log[Z(\boldsymbol{\theta})]}{\partial \boldsymbol{\theta}} = \sum_{\mathbf{x}} Pr(\mathbf{x}) \frac{\partial \log[f[\mathbf{x},\boldsymbol{\theta}]]}{\partial \boldsymbol{\theta}} \approx \frac{1}{J} \sum_{j=1}^{J} \frac{\partial \log[f[\mathbf{x}_j^*,\boldsymbol{\theta}]]}{\partial \boldsymbol{\theta}}. \qquad (10.30)$$

With I training examples $\{\mathbf{x}_i\}_{i=1}^{I}$, the gradient of the log likelihood L is hence

$$\frac{\partial L}{\partial \boldsymbol{\theta}} \approx -\frac{I}{J} \sum_{j=1}^{J} \frac{\partial \log[f(\mathbf{x}_j^*,\boldsymbol{\theta})]}{\partial \boldsymbol{\theta}} + \sum_{i=1}^{I} \frac{\partial \log[f(\mathbf{x}_i,\boldsymbol{\theta})]}{\partial \boldsymbol{\theta}}. \qquad (10.31)$$

A visual explanation of this expression is presented in Figure 10.13. The gradient points in a direction that (i) increases the logarithm of the unnormalized function at the data points $\mathbf{x}_i$ but (ii) decreases the same quantity in places where the model believes the density is high (i.e., the samples $\mathbf{x}_j^*$). When the model fits the data, these two forces cancel out, and the parameters will stop changing.

This algorithm requires us to draw samples $\mathbf{x}^*$ from the model at each iteration of the optimization procedure in order to compute the gradient. Unfortunately, the only way to draw samples from general undirected graphical models is to use costly Markov chain Monte Carlo methods such as Gibbs sampling (Section 10.7.2), and this is impractically time consuming. In practice it has been found that even approximate samples will do: one method is to restart $J = I$ samples at the data points at each iteration and do just a few MCMC steps. Surprisingly, this works well even with a single step. A second approach is to start with the samples from the previous iteration and perform a few MCMC steps so that the samples are free to wander without restarting. This technique is known as *persistent* contrastive divergence.

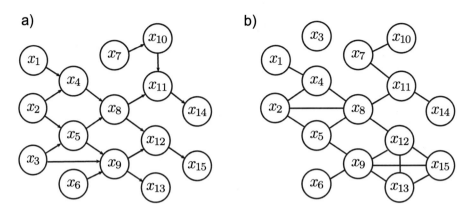

Figure 10.14 a) Graphical model for Problem 10.2. b) Graphical model for Problem 10.4

Discussion

In this chapter, we introduced directed and undirected graphical models. Each represents a different type of factorization of the joint distribution. A graphical model implies a set of independence and conditional independence relations. There are some sets that can only be represented by directed graphical models, others that can only be represented by undirected graphical models, some that can be represented by both, and some that cannot be represented by either.

We presented a number of common vision models and examined their graphical models. Each had sparse connections and hence many conditional independence relations. In subsequent chapters, we will exploit these redundancies to develop efficient learning and inference algorithms. Since the world state in these models is usually very high dimensional, we discussed alternative forms of inference including maximum marginals and sampling.

Finally, we looked at the implications of choosing directed or undirected graphical models for sampling and for learning. We concluded that it is generally more straightforward to draw samples from directed graphical models. Moreover, it is also easier to learn directed graphical models. The best-known learning algorithm for general undirected graphical models requires us to draw samples, which is itself challenging.

Notes

Graphical models: For a readable introduction to graphical models, consult Jordan (2004) or Bishop (2006). For a more comprehensive overview, I would recommend Barber (2012). For an even more encyclopaedic resource, consult Koller and Friedman (2009).

Contrastive divergence: The contrastive divergence algorithm was introduced by Hinton (2002). Further information about this technique can be found in Carreira-Perpiñán. and Hinton (2005) and Bengio and Delalleau (2009).

Problems

10.1 The joint probability model between variables $\{x_i\}_{i=1}^7$ factorizes as

$$Pr(x_1, x_2, x_3, x_4, x_5, x_6, x_7) =$$
$$Pr(x_1)Pr(x_3)Pr(x_7)Pr(x_2|x_1, x_3)Pr(x_5|x_7, x_2)Pr(x_4|x_2)Pr(x_6|x_5, x_4).$$

Draw a directed graphical model relating these variables. Which variables form the Markov blanket of variable x_2?

10.2 Write out the factorization corresponding to the directed graphical model in Figure 10.14a.

10.3 An undirected graphical model has the form

$$Pr(x_1 \ldots x_6) = \frac{1}{Z}\phi_1[x_1, x_2, x_5]\phi_2[x_2, x_3, x_4]\phi_3[x_1 x_5]\phi_4[x_5, x_6].$$

Draw the undirected graphical model that corresponds to this factorization.

10.4 Write out the factorization corresponding to the undirected graphical model in Figure 10.14b.

10.5 Consider the undirected graphical model defined over binary values $\{x_i\}_{i=1}^4 \in \{0,1\}$ defined by

$$Pr(x_1, x_2, x_3, x_4) = \frac{1}{Z}\phi(x_1, x_2)\phi(x_2, x_3)\phi(x_3, x_4)\phi(x_4, x_1),$$

where the function ϕ is defined by

$$\phi(0,0) = 1 \qquad \phi(1,1) = 2$$
$$\phi(0,1) = 0.1 \qquad \phi(1,0) = 0.1$$

Compute the probability of each of the 16 possible states of this system.

10.6 What is the Markov blanket for each of the variables in Figures 10.7 and 10.8?

10.7 Show that the stated patterns of independence and conditional independence in Figures 10.7 and 10.8 are true.

10.8 A *factor graph* is a third type of graphical model that depicts the factorization of a joint probability. As usual it contains a single node per variable, but it also contains one node per factor (usually indicated by a solid square). Each factor variable is connected to all of the variables that are contained in the associated term in the factorization by undirected links. For example, the factor node corresponding to the term $Pr(x_1|x_2, x_3)$ in a directed model would connect to all three variables x_1, x_2, and x_3. Similarly, the factor node corresponding to the term $\phi_{12}[x_1, x_2]$ in an undirected model would connect variables x_1 and x_2. Figure 10.15 shows two examples of factor graphs.

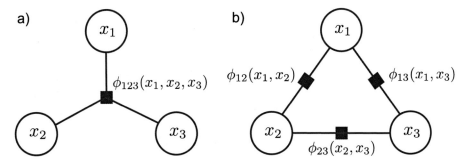

Figure 10.15 Factor graphs contain one node (square) per factor in the joint pdf as well as one node (circle) per variable. Each factor node is connected to all of the variables that belong to that factor. This type of graphical model can distinguish between the undirected graphical models a) $Pr(x_1, x_2, x_3) = \frac{1}{Z}\phi_{123}[x_1, x_2, x_3]$ and b) $Pr(x_1, x_2, x_3) = \frac{1}{Z}\phi_{12}[x_1, x_2]\phi_{23}[x_2, x_3]\phi_{13}[x_1, x_3]$.

Draw the factor graphs corresponding to the graphical models in Figures 10.7 and 10.8. You must first establish the factorized joint distribution associated with each graph.

10.9 What is the Markov blanket of variable w_2 in Figure 10.9c?

10.10 What is the Markov blanket of variable w_8 in Figure 10.9e?

Chapter 11

Models for chains and trees

In this chapter, we model the relationship between a multidimensional set of measurements $\{\mathbf{x}_n\}_{n=1}^N$ and an associated multidimensional world state $\{w_n\}_{n=1}^N$. When N is large, it is not practical to describe the full set of dependencies between all of these variables, as the number of model parameters will be too great. Instead, we construct models where we only directly describe the probabilistic dependence between variables in small neighborhoods. In particular, we will consider models in which the world variables $\{w_n\}_{n=1}^N$ are structured as chains or trees.

We define a *chain model* to be one in which the world state variables $\{w_n\}_{n=1}^N$ are connected to only the previous variable and the subsequent variable in the associated graphical model (as in Figure 11.2). We define a *tree model* to be one in which the world variables have more complex connections, but so there are no *loops* in the resulting graphical model. Importantly, we disregard the directionality of the connections when we assess whether a directed model is a tree. Hence, our definition of a tree differs from the standard computer science usage.

We will also make the following assumptions:

- The world states w_n are discrete.
- There is an observed data variable $\mathbf{x}_n$ associated with each world state w_n.
- The nth data variable $\mathbf{x}_n$ is conditionally independent of all other data variables and world states given the associated world state w_n.

These assumptions are not critical for the development of the ideas in this chapter but are typical for the type of computer vision applications that we consider. We will show that both maximum a posteriori and maximum marginals inference are tractable for this subclass of models, and we will discuss why this is not the case when the states are not organized as a chain or a tree.

To motivate these models, consider the problem of *gesture tracking*. Here, the goal is to automatically interpret sign language from a video sequence (Figure 11.1). We observe N frames $\{\mathbf{x}_n\}_{n=1}^N$ of a video sequence and wish to infer the N discrete variables $\{w_n\}_{n=1}^N$ that encode which sign is present in each of the N frames. The data at time n tells us something about the sign at time n but may be insufficient to specify it accurately. Consequently, we also model dependencies between adjacent world states: we know that the signs are more likely to appear in some orders than others and we exploit this knowledge to help disambiguate the sequence. Since we model probabilistic connections only between adjacent states in the time series, this has the form of a chain model.

Figure 11.1 Interpreting sign language. We observe a sequence of images of a person using sign language. In each frame we extract a vector $\mathbf{x}_n$ describing the shape and position of the hands. The goal is to infer the sign w_n that is present. Unfortunately, the visual data in a single frame may be ambiguous. We improve matters by describing probabilistic connections between adjacent states w_n and w_{n-1}. We impose knowledge about the likely sequence of signs, and this helps disambiguate any individual frame. Images from Purdue RVL-SLLL ASL database (Wilbur and Kak 2006).

11.1 Models for chains

In this section, we will describe both a directed and an undirected model for describing chain structure and show that these two models are equivalent.

11.1.1 Directed model for chains

The directed model describes the joint probability of a set of continuous measurements $\{\mathbf{x}_n\}_{n=1}^{N}$ and a set of discrete world states $\{w_n\}_{n=1}^{N}$ with the graphical model shown in Figure 11.2a. The tendency to observe the measurements $\mathbf{x}_n$ given that state w_n takes value k is encoded in the likelihood $Pr(\mathbf{x}_n|w_n = k)$. The prior probability of the first state w_1 is explicitly encoded in the discrete distribution $Pr(w_1)$, but for simplicity we assume that this is uniform and omit it from most of the ensuing discussion. The remaining states are each dependent on the previous one, and this information is captured in the distribution $Pr(w_n|w_{n-1})$. This is sometimes termed the *Markov assumption*.

Hence, the overall joint probability is

$$Pr(\mathbf{x}_{1...N}, w_{1...N}) = \left(\prod_{n=1}^{N} Pr(\mathbf{x}_n|w_n)\right)\left(\prod_{n=2}^{N} Pr(w_n|w_{n-1})\right). \qquad (11.1)$$

This is known as a *hidden Markov model* (HMM). The world states $\{w_n\}_{n=1}^{N}$ in the directed model have the form of a chain, and the overall model has the form of a tree. As we shall see, these properties are critical to our ability to perform inference.

11.1.2 Undirected model for chains

The undirected model (see Section 10.3) describes the joint probability of the measurements $\{\mathbf{x}_n\}_{n=1}^{N}$ and the world states $\{w_n\}_{n=1}^{N}$ with the graphical model shown in Figure 11.2b. The tendency for the measurements and the data to take certain values is encoded in the potential function $\phi[\mathbf{x}_n, w_n]$. This function always returns positive values and returns larger values when the measurements and the world state are more compatible. The tendency for adjacent states to take certain values is encoded in a second potential function $\zeta[w_n, w_{n-1}]$ which returns larger values when the adjacent states are more

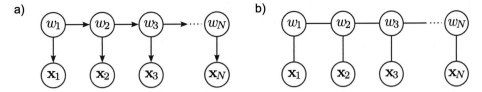

Figure 11.2 Models for chains. a) Directed model. There is one observation variable $\mathbf{x}_n$ for each state variable w_n and these are related by the conditional probability $Pr(\mathbf{x}_n|w_n)$ (downward arrows). Each state w_n is related to the previous one by the conditional probability $Pr(w_n|w_{n-1})$ (horizontal arrows). b) Undirected model. Here, each observed variable $\mathbf{x}_n$ is related to its associated state variable w_n via the potential function $\phi[\mathbf{x}_n, w_n]$ and the neighboring states are connected via the potential function $\zeta[w_n, w_{n-1}]$.

compatible. Hence, the overall probability is

$$Pr(\mathbf{x}_{1...N}, w_{1...N}) = \frac{1}{Z} \left(\prod_{n=1}^{N} \phi[\mathbf{x}_n, w_n] \right) \left(\prod_{n=2}^{N} \zeta[w_n, w_{n-1}] \right). \tag{11.2}$$

Once more the states form a chain and the overall model has the form of a tree; there are no loops.

11.1.3   Equivalence of models

When we take a directed model and make the edges undirected, we usually create a different model. However, comparing Equations 11.1 and 11.2 reveals that these two models represent the same factorization of the joint probability density; in this special case, the two models are equivalent. This equivalence becomes even more apparent if we make the substitutions

$$Pr(\mathbf{x}_n|w_n) = \frac{1}{z_n} \phi[\mathbf{x}_n, w_n]$$

$$Pr(w_n|w_{n-1}) = \frac{1}{z_n'} \zeta[w_n, w_{n-1}], \tag{11.3}$$

where z_n and z_n' are normalizing factors which form the partition function:

$$Z = \left(\prod_{n=1}^{N} z_n \right) \left(\prod_{n=2}^{N} z_n' \right). \tag{11.4}$$

Since the directed and undirected versions of the chain model are equivalent, we will continue our discussion in terms of the directed model alone.

11.1.4   Hidden Markov model for sign language application

We will now briefly describe how this directed model relates to the sign language application. We preprocess the video frame to create a vector $\mathbf{x}_n$ that represents the shape of the hands. For example, we might just extract a window of pixels around each hand and concatenate their RGB pixel values.

We now model the likelihood $Pr(\mathbf{x}_n|w_n = k)$ of observing this measurement vector given that the sign w_n in this image takes value k. A very simple model might assume that the measurements have a normal distribution with parameters that are contingent on which sign is present so that

$$Pr(\mathbf{x}_n|w_n=k) = \text{Norm}_{\mathbf{x}_n}[\boldsymbol{\mu}_k, \boldsymbol{\Sigma}_k]. \tag{11.5}$$

We model the sign w_n as a being categorically distributed, where the parameters depend on the previous sign w_{n-1} so that

$$Pr(w_n|w_{n-1}=k) = \text{Cat}_{w_n}[\boldsymbol{\lambda}_k]. \tag{11.6}$$

This hidden Markov model has parameters $\{\boldsymbol{\mu}_k, \boldsymbol{\Sigma}_k, \boldsymbol{\lambda}_k\}_{k=1}^K$. For most of this chapter, we will assume that these parameters are known, but we return briefly to the issue of learning in Section 11.6. We now turn our focus to inference in this type of model.

11.2   MAP inference for chains

Consider a chain with N unknown variables $\{w_n\}_{n=1}^N$, each of which can take K possible values. Here, there are K^N possible states of the world. For real-world problems, this means that there are far too many states to evaluate exhaustively; we can neither compute the full posterior distribution nor search directly through all of the states to find the maximum a posteriori estimate.

Fortunately, the factorization of the joint probability distribution (the conditional independence structure) can be exploited to find more efficient algorithms for MAP inference than brute force search. The MAP solution is given by

$$\begin{aligned}
\hat{w}_{1\ldots N} &= \underset{w_{1\ldots N}}{\text{argmax}}\left[Pr(w_{1\ldots N}|\mathbf{x}_{1\ldots N})\right] \\
&= \underset{w_{1\ldots N}}{\text{argmax}}\left[Pr(\mathbf{x}_{1\ldots N}, w_{1\ldots N})\right] \\
&= \underset{w_{1\ldots N}}{\text{argmin}}\left[-\log\left[Pr(\mathbf{x}_{1\ldots N}, w_{1\ldots N})\right]\right],
\end{aligned} \tag{11.7}$$

where line 2 follows from Bayes' rule. We have reformulated this as a minimization problem in line 3.

Substituting in the expression for the log probability (Equation 11.1), we get

$$\hat{w}_{1\ldots N} = \underset{w_{1\ldots N}}{\text{argmin}}\left[-\sum_{n=1}^N \log\left[Pr(\mathbf{x}_n|w_n)\right] - \sum_{n=2}^N \log\left[Pr(w_n|w_{n-1})\right]\right], \tag{11.8}$$

which has the general form

$$\hat{w}_{1\ldots N} = \underset{w_{1\ldots N}}{\text{argmin}}\left[\sum_{n=1}^N U_n(w_n) + \sum_{n=2}^N P_n(w_n, w_{n-1})\right], \tag{11.9}$$

where U_n is a *unary* term and depends only on a single variable w_n and P_n is a *pairwise* term, depending on two variables w_n and w_{n-1}. In this instance, the unary and pairwise terms can be defined as

$$\begin{aligned}
U_n(w_n) &= -\log[Pr(\mathbf{x}_n|w_n)] \\
P_n(w_n, w_{n-1}) &= -\log[Pr(w_n|w_{n-1})].
\end{aligned} \tag{11.10}$$

Any problem that has the form of Equation 11.9 can be solved in polynomial time using the *Viterbi algorithm* which is an example of *dynamic programming*.

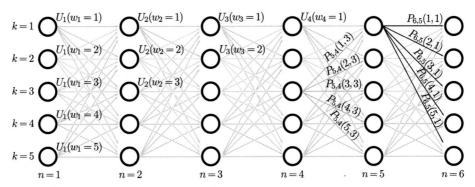

Figure 11.3 Dynamic programming formulation. Each solution is equated with a particular path from left-to-right through an acyclic directed graph. The N columns of the graph represent variables $w_{1...N}$ and the K rows represent possible states $1...K$. The nodes and edges of the graph have costs associated with the unary and pairwise terms, respectively. Any path from left to right through the graph has a cost that is the sum of the costs at all of the nodes and edges that it passes through. Optimizing the function is now equivalent to finding the path with the least cost.

11.2.1   Dynamic programming (Viterbi algorithm)

To optimize the cost function in Equation 11.9, we first visualize the problem with a 2D graph with vertices $\{V_{n,k}\}_{n=1,k=1}^{N,K}$. The vertex $V_{n,k}$ represents choosing the kth world state at the nth variable (Figure 11.3). Vertex $V_{n,k}$ is connected by a directed edge to each of the vertices $\{V_{n+1,k}\}_{k=1}^{K}$ at the next pixel position. Hence, the organization of the graph is such that each valid horizontal path from left to right represents a possible solution to the problem; it corresponds to assigning one value $k \in [1...K]$ to each variable w_n.

We now attach the costs $U_n(w_n = k)$ to the vertices $V_{n,k}$. We also attach the costs $P_n(w_n = k, w_{n-1} = l)$ to the edges joining vertices $V_{n-1,l}$ to $V_{n,k}$. We define the total cost of a path from left to right as the sum of the costs of the edges and vertices that make up the path. Now, every horizontal path represents a solution and the cost of that path is the cost for that solution; we have reformulated the problem as finding the minimum cost path from left to right across the graph.

Finding the minimum cost

The approach to finding the minimum cost path is simple. We work through the graph from left to right, computing at each vertex the minimum possible cumulative cost $S_{n,k}$ to arrive at this point *by any route*. When we reach the right-hand side, we compare the K values $S_{N,\bullet}$ and choose the minimum. This is the lowest possible cost for traversing the graph. We now retrace the route we took to reach this point, using information that was cached during the forward pass.

The easiest way to understand this method is with a concrete example (Figures 11.4 and 11.5) and the reader is encouraged to scrutinize these figures before continuing.

A more formal description is as follows. Our goal is to assign the minimum possible cumulative cost $S_{n,k}$ for reaching vertex $V_{n,k}$. Starting at the left-hand side, we set the first column of vertices to the unary costs for the first variable:

$$S_{1,k} = U_1(w_1 = k). \tag{11.11}$$

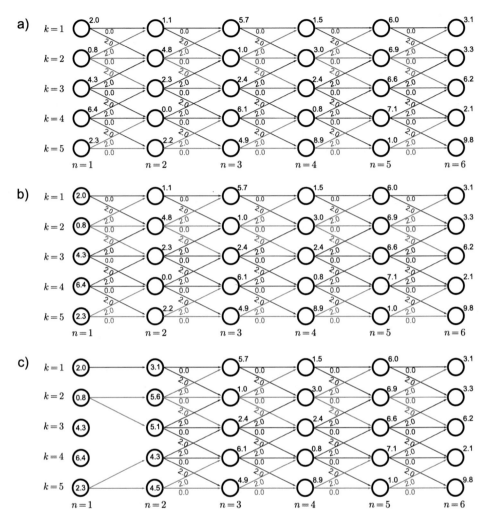

Figure 11.4 Dynamic programming. a) The unary cost $U_n(w_n = k)$ is given by the number above and to the right of each node. The pairwise costs $P_n(w_n, w_{n-1})$ are zero if $w_n = w_{n-1}$ (horizontal), two if $|w_n - w_{n-1}| = 1$, and ∞ otherwise. This favors a solution that is mostly constant but can also vary smoothly. For clarity, we have removed the edges with infinite cost as they cannot become part of the solution. We now work from left to right, computing the minimum cost $S_{n,k}$ for arriving at vertex $V_{n,k}$ by any route. b) For vertices $\{V_{1,k}\}_{k=1}^K$, the minimum cost is just the unary cost associated with that vertex. We have stored the values $S_{1,1} \ldots S_{1,5}$ inside the circle representing the respective vertex. c) To compute the minimum cost $S_{2,1}$ at vertex $(n = 2, k = 1)$, we must consider two possible routes. The path could have traveled horizontally from vertex $(1,1)$ giving a total cost of $2.0 + 0.0 + 1.1 = 3.1$, or it may have come diagonally upward from vertex $(1,2)$ with cost $0.8 + 2.0 + 1.1 = 3.9$. Since the former route is cheaper, we use this cost, store $S_{2,1} = 3.1$ at the vertex, and also remember the path used to get here. Now, we repeat this procedure at vertex $(2,2)$ where there are three possible routes from vertices $(1,1)$, $(1,2)$ and $(1,3)$. Here it turns out that the best route is from $(1,2)$ and has total cumulative cost of $S_{2,2} = 5.6$. Example continued in Figure 11.5.

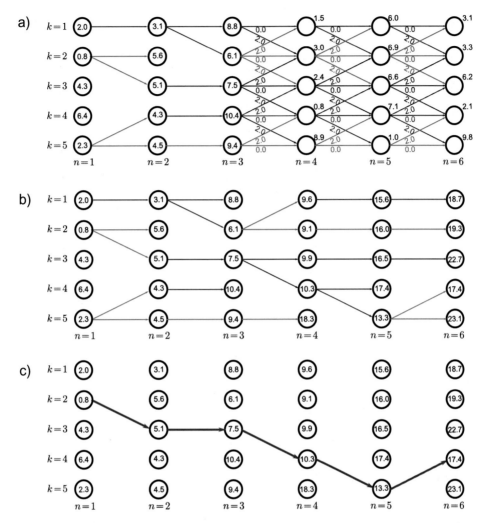

Figure 11.5 Dynamic programming worked example (continued from Figure 11.4). a) Having updated the vertices at pixel $n=2$, we carry out the same procedure at pixel $n=3$, accumulating at each vertex the minimum total cost to reach this point. b) We continue updating the minimum cumulative costs $S_{n,k}$ to arrive at pixel n in state k until we reach the right hand side. c) We identify the minimum cost among the right-most vertices. In this case, it is vertex (6,4), which has cost $S_{6,4} = 17.4$. This is the minimum possible cost for traversing the graph. By tracing back the route that we used to arrive here (red arrows), we find the world state at each pixel that was responsible for this cost.

The cumulative total $S_{2,k}$ for the kth vertex in the second column should represent the minimum possible cumulative cost to reach this point. To calculate this, we consider the K possible predecessors and compute the cost for reaching this vertex by each possible route. We set $S_{2,k}$ to the minimum of these values and store the route by which we reached this vertex so that

$$S_{2,k} = U_2(w_2 = k) + \min_l \left[S_{1,l} + P_2(w_2 = k, w_1 = l) \right]. \qquad (11.12)$$

More generally, to calculate the cumulative totals $S_{n,k}$, we use the recursion

$$S_{n,k} = U_n(w_n = k) + \min_l \left[S_{n-1,l} + P_n(w_n = k, w_{n-1} = l) \right], \qquad (11.13)$$

and we also cache the route by which this minimum was achieved at each stage. When we reach the right-hand side, we find the value of the final variable w_n that minimizes the total cost

$$\hat{w}_N = \underset{k}{\operatorname{argmin}} \left[S_{N,k} \right], \qquad (11.14)$$

and set the remaining labels $\{\hat{w}_n\}_{n=1}^{N-1}$ according to the route that we followed to get to this value.

This method exploits the factorization structure of the joint probability between the observations and the states to make vast computational savings. The cost of this procedure is $\mathcal{O}(NK^2)$, as opposed to $\mathcal{O}(K^N)$ for a brute force search through every possible solution.

11.3   MAP inference for trees

To show how MAP inference works in tree-structured models, consider the model in Figure 11.6. For this graph, the prior probability over the states factorizes as

$$Pr(w_{1...6}) = Pr(w_1)Pr(w_3)Pr(w_2|w_1)Pr(w_4|w_3)Pr(w_5|w_2, w_4)Pr(w_6|w_5), \qquad (11.15)$$

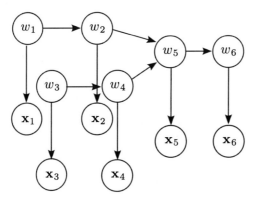

Figure 11.6 Tree-based models. As before, there is one observation $\mathbf{x}_n$ for each world state w_n, and these are related by the conditional probability $Pr(\mathbf{x}_n|w_n)$. However, disregarding the directionality of the edges, the world states are now connected as a tree. Vertex w_5 has two incoming connections, which means that there is a 'three-wise' term $Pr(w_5|w_2, w_4)$ in the factorization. The tree structure means it is possible to perform MAP and max-marginals inference efficiently.

and the world states have the structure of a tree (disregarding the directionality of the edges).

Once more, we can exploit this factorization to compute the MAP solution efficiently. Our goal is to find

$$\hat{w}_{1...6} = \underset{w_{1...6}}{\mathrm{argmax}} \left[\sum_{n=1}^{6} \log[Pr(\mathbf{x}_n|w_n)] + \log[Pr(w_{1...6})] \right].$$ (11.16)

By a similar process to that in Section 11.2, we can rewrite this as a minimization problem with the following cost function:

$$\hat{w}_{1...6} = \underset{w_{1...6}}{\mathrm{argmin}} \left[\sum_{n=1}^{6} U_n(w_n) + P_2(w_2, w_1) + P_4(w_4, w_3) \right.$$

$$\left. + P_6(w_6, w_5) + T_5(w_5, w_2, w_4) \right].$$ (11.17)

As before, we reformulate this cost function in terms of finding a route through a graph (see Figure 11.7). The unary costs U_n are associated with each vertex. The pairwise costs P_m are associated with edges between pairs of adjacent vertices. The three-wise cost T_5 is associated with the combination of states at the point where the tree branches. Our goal now is to find the least cost path from all of the leaves simultaneously to the root.

We work from the leaves to the root of the tree, at each stage computing $S_{n,k}$, the cumulative cost for arriving at this vertex (see worked example in Figure 11.7). For the first four vertices, we proceed as in standard dynamic programming:

$$S_{1,k} = U_1(w_1 = k)$$
$$S_{2,k} = U_2(w_2 = k) + \min_l [S_{1,l} + P_2(w_2 = k, w_1 = l)]$$
$$S_{3,k} = U_3(w_3 = k)$$
$$S_{4,k} = U_4(w_4 = k) + \min_l [S_{3,1} + P_4(w_4 = k, w_3 = l)].$$ (11.18)

When we come to the branch in the tree, we try to find the best combination of routes to reach the nodes for variable 5; we must now minimize over both variables to compute the next term. In other words,

$$S_{5,k} = U_5(w_5 = k) + \min_{l,m} [S_{2,l} + S_{4,m} + T_5(w_5 = k, w_2 = l, w_4 = m)].$$ (11.19)

Finally, we compute the last terms as normal so that

$$S_{6,k} = U_6(w_6 = k) + \min_l [S_{5,l} + P_6(w_6 = k, w_5 = l)].$$ (11.20)

Now we find the world state associated with the minimum of this final sum and trace back the route that we came by as before, splitting the route appropriately at junctions in the tree.

Dynamic programming in this tree has a greater computational complexity than dynamic programming in a chain with the same number of variables as we must minimize over two variables at the junction in the tree. The overall complexity is proportional to K^W, where W is the maximum number of variables over which we must minimize.

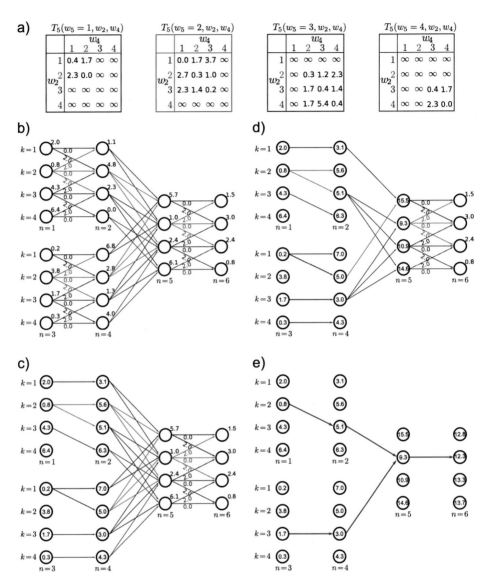

Figure 11.7 Dynamic programming example for tree model in Figure 11.6. a) Table of three-wise costs at vertex 5. This is a $K \times K \times K$ table consisting of the costs associated with $Pr(w_5 | w_2, w_4)$. Pairwise costs are as for the example in Figure 11.4. b) Tree-structured model with unary and pairwise costs attached. c) We work from the leaves, finding the minimal possible cost $S_{n,k}$ to reach vertex n in state k as in the original dynamic programming formulation. d) When we reach the vertex above a branch (here, vertex 5), we find the minimal possible cost, considering every combination of the incoming states. e) We continue until we reach the root. There, we find the minimum overall cost and trace back, making sure to split at the junction according to which pair of states was chosen.

For directed models, W is equal to the largest number of incoming connections at any vertex. For undirected models, W will be the size of the largest clique. It should be noted that for undirected models, the critical property that allows dynamic programming solutions is that the cliques themselves form a tree (see Figure 11.11).

11.4 Marginal posterior inference for chains

In Section 11.3, we demonstrated that it is possible to perform MAP inference in chain models efficiently using dynamic programming. In this section, we will consider a different form of inference: we will aim to calculate the marginal distribution $Pr(w_n|\mathbf{x}_{1...N})$ over each state variable w_n separately.

Consider computing the marginal distribution over the variable w_N. By Bayes' rule we have

$$Pr(w_N|\mathbf{x}_{1...N}) = \frac{Pr(w_N, \mathbf{x}_{1...N})}{Pr(\mathbf{x}_{1...N})} \propto Pr(w_N, \mathbf{x}_{1...N}). \tag{11.21}$$

The right-hand side of this equation is computed by marginalizing over all of the other state variables except w_N so we have

$$Pr(w_N, \mathbf{x}_{1...N}) \propto \sum_{w_1} \sum_{w_2} \cdots \sum_{w_{N-1}} Pr(w_{1...N}, \mathbf{x}_{1...N}) \tag{11.22}$$

$$\propto \sum_{w_1} \sum_{w_2} \cdots \sum_{w_{N-1}} \left(\prod_{n=1}^{N} Pr(\mathbf{x}_n|w_n) \right) Pr(w_1) \left(\prod_{n=2}^{N} Pr(w_n|w_{n-1}) \right).$$

Unfortunately, in its most basic form, this marginalization involves summing over $N-1$ dimensions of the N dimensional probability distribution. Since this discrete probability distribution contains K^N entries, computing this summation directly is not practical for realistic-sized problems. To make progress, we must again exploit the structured factorization of this distribution.

11.4.1 Computing one marginal distribution

We will first discuss how to compute the marginal distribution $Pr(w_N|\mathbf{x}_{1...N})$ for the last variable in the chain w_N. In the following section, we will exploit these ideas to compute all of the marginal distributions $Pr(w_n|\mathbf{x}_{1...N})$ simultaneously.

We observe that not every term in the product in Equation 11.22 is relevant to every summation. We can rearrange the summation terms so that only the variables over which they sum are to the right

$$Pr(w_N|\mathbf{x}_{1...N}) \propto \tag{11.23}$$
$$Pr(\mathbf{x}_N|w_N) \sum_{w_{N-1}} \cdots \sum_{w_2} Pr(w_3|w_2) Pr(\mathbf{x}_2|w_2) \sum_{w_1} Pr(w_2|w_1) Pr(\mathbf{x}_1|w_1) Pr(w_1).$$

Then, we proceed from right to left, computing each summation in turn. This technique is known as *variable elimination*. Let us denote the rightmost two terms as

$$\mathbf{f}_1[w_1] = Pr(\mathbf{x}_1|w_1) Pr(w_1). \tag{11.24}$$

Then we sum over w_1 to compute the function

$$\mathbf{f}_2[w_2] = Pr(\mathbf{x}_2|w_2)\sum_{w_1} Pr(w_2|w_1)\mathbf{f}_1[w_1]. \qquad (11.25)$$

At the nth stage, we compute

$$\mathbf{f}_n[w_n] = Pr(\mathbf{x}_n|w_n)\sum_{w_{n-1}} Pr(w_n|w_{n-1})\mathbf{f}_{n-1}[w_{n-1}], \qquad (11.26)$$

and we repeat this process until we have computed the full expression. We then normalize the result to find the marginal posterior $Pr(w_N|\mathbf{x}_{1...N})$ (Equation 11.21).

This solution consists of $N-1$ summations over K values; it is much more efficient to compute than explicitly computing all K^N solutions and marginalizing over $N-1$ dimensions.

11.4.2 Forward-backward algorithm

In the previous section, we showed an algorithm that could compute the marginal posterior distribution $Pr(w_N|\mathbf{x}_{1...N})$ for the last world state w_N. It is easy to adapt this method to compute the marginal posterior $Pr(w_n|\mathbf{x}_{1...N})$ over any other variable w_n. However, we usually want all of the marginal distributions, and it is inefficient to compute each separately as much of the effort is replicated. The goal of this section is to develop a single procedure that computes the marginal posteriors for *all* of the variables simultaneously and efficiently using a technique known as the *forward-backward algorithm*.

The principle is to decompose the marginal posterior into two terms

$$\begin{aligned} Pr(w_n|\mathbf{x}_{1...N}) &\propto Pr(w_n, \mathbf{x}_{1...N}) \\ &= Pr(w_n, \mathbf{x}_{1...n})Pr(\mathbf{x}_{n+1...N}|w_n, \mathbf{x}_{1...n}) \\ &= Pr(w_n, \mathbf{x}_{1...n})Pr(\mathbf{x}_{n+1...N}|w_n), \end{aligned} \qquad (11.27)$$

where the relation between the second and third line is true because $\mathbf{x}_{1...n}$ and $\mathbf{x}_{n+1...N}$ are conditionally independent given w_n (as can be gleaned from Figure 11.2). We will now focus on finding efficient ways to calculate each of these two terms.

Forward recursion

Let us consider the first term $Pr(w_n, \mathbf{x}_{1...n})$. We can exploit the recursion

$$\begin{aligned} & Pr(w_n, \mathbf{x}_{1...n}) \\ &= \sum_{w_{n-1}} Pr(w_n, w_{n-1}, \mathbf{x}_{1...n}) \\ &= \sum_{w_{n-1}} Pr(w_n, \mathbf{x}_n|w_{n-1}, \mathbf{x}_{1...n-1})Pr(w_{n-1}, \mathbf{x}_{1...n-1}) \\ &= \sum_{w_{n-1}} Pr(\mathbf{x}_n|w_n, w_{n-1}, \mathbf{x}_{1...n-1})Pr(w_n|w_{n-1}, \mathbf{x}_{1...n-1})Pr(w_{n-1}, \mathbf{x}_{1...n-1}) \\ &= \sum_{w_{n-1}} Pr(\mathbf{x}_n|w_n)Pr(w_n|w_{n-1})Pr(w_{n-1}, \mathbf{x}_{1...n-1}), \qquad (11.28) \end{aligned}$$

where we have again applied the conditional independence relations implied by the graphical model between the last two lines.

The term $Pr(w_n, \mathbf{x}_{1...n})$ is exactly the intermediate function $\mathbf{f}_n[w_n]$ that we calculated in the solution for the single marginal distribution in the previous section; we have reproduced the recursion

$$\mathbf{f}_n[w_n] = Pr(\mathbf{x}_n|w_n) \sum_{w_{n-1}} Pr(w_n|w_{n-1})\mathbf{f}_{n-1}[w_{n-1}], \tag{11.29}$$

but this time, we based the argument on conditional independence rather than the factorization of the probability distribution. Using this recursion, we can efficiently compute the first term of Equation 11.27 for all n; in fact, we were already doing this in our solution for the single marginal distribution $Pr(w_N|\mathbf{x}_{1...N})$.

Backward recursion

Now consider the second term $Pr(\mathbf{x}_{n+1...N}|w_n)$ from Equation 11.27. Our goal is to develop a recursive relation for this quantity so that we can compute it efficiently for all n. This time the recursion works backwards from the end of the chain to the front, so our goal is to establish an expression for $Pr(\mathbf{x}_{n...N}|w_{n-1})$ in terms of $Pr(\mathbf{x}_{n+1...N}|w_n)$:

$$
\begin{aligned}
Pr(\mathbf{x}_{n...N}&|w_{n-1})\\
&= \sum_{w_n} Pr(\mathbf{x}_{n...N}, w_n|w_{n-1})\\
&= \sum_{w_n} Pr(\mathbf{x}_{n...N}|w_n, w_{n-1})Pr(w_n|w_{n-1})\\
&= \sum_{w_n} Pr(\mathbf{x}_{n+1...N}|\mathbf{x}_n, w_n, w_{n-1})Pr(\mathbf{x}_n|w_n, w_{n-1})Pr(w_n|w_{n-1})\\
&= \sum_{w_n} Pr(\mathbf{x}_{n+1...N}|w_n)Pr(\mathbf{x}_n|w_n)Pr(w_n|w_{n-1}). \tag{11.30}
\end{aligned}
$$

Here we have again applied the conditional independence relations implied by the graphical model between the last two lines. Denoting the probability $Pr(x_{n+1...N}|w_n)$ as $\mathbf{b}_n[w_n]$, we see that we have the recursive relation

$$\mathbf{b}_{n-1}[w_{n-1}] = \sum_{w_n} Pr(\mathbf{x}_n|w_n)Pr(w_n|w_{n-1})\mathbf{b}_n[w_n]. \tag{11.31}$$

We can use this to compute the second term in Equation 11.27 efficiently for all n.

Forward-backward algorithm

We can now summarize the forward-backward algorithm to compute the marginal posterior probability distribution for all n. First, we observe (Equation 11.27) that the marginal distribution can be computed as

$$Pr(w_n|\mathbf{x}_{1...N}) \propto Pr(w_n, \mathbf{x}_{1...n})Pr(\mathbf{x}_{n+1...N}|w_n) = \mathbf{f}_n[w_n]\mathbf{b}_n[w_n]. \tag{11.32}$$

We recursively compute the forward terms using the relation

$$\mathbf{f}_n[w_n] = Pr(\mathbf{x}_n|w_n) \sum_{w_{n-1}} Pr(w_n|w_{n-1})\mathbf{f}_{n-1}[w_{n-1}], \tag{11.33}$$

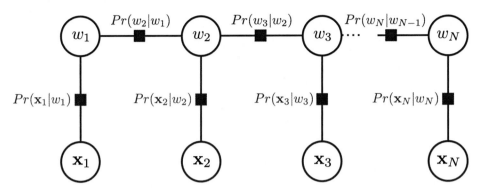

Figure 11.8 Factor graph for chain model. There is one node per variable (circles) and one function node per term in the factorization (squares). Each function node connects to all of the variables associated with this term.

where we set $\mathbf{f}_1[w_1] = Pr(\mathbf{x}_1|w_1)Pr(w_1)$. We recursively compute the backward terms using the relation

$$\mathbf{b}_{n-1}[w_{n-1}] = \sum_{w_n} Pr(\mathbf{x}_n|w_n)Pr(w_n|w_{n-1})\mathbf{b}_n[w_n], \qquad (11.34)$$

where we set $\mathbf{b}_N[w_N]$ to the constant value $1/K$.

Finally, to compute the nth marginal posterior distribution, we take the product of the associated forward and backward terms and normalize.

11.4.3 Belief propagation

The forward-backward algorithm can be considered a special case of a more general technique called *belief propagation*. Here, the intermediate functions $\mathbf{f}[\bullet]$ and $\mathbf{b}[\bullet]$ are considered as messages that convey information about the variables. In this section, we describe a version of belief propagation known as the *sum-product algorithm*. This does not compute the marginal posteriors any faster than the forward-backward algorithm, but it is much easier to see how to extend it to models based on trees.

The sum-product algorithm operates on a factor graph. A factor graph is a new type of graphical model that makes the factorization of the joint probability more explicit. It is very simple to convert directed and undirected graphical models to factor graphs. As usual, we introduce one node per variable; for example variables w_1, w_2, and w_3 all have a variable node associated with them. We also introduce one *function node* per term in the factorized joint probability distribution; in a directed model this would represent a conditional probability term such as $Pr(w_1|w_2, w_3)$, and in an undirected model it would represent a potential function such as $\phi[w_1, w_2, w_3]$. We then connect each function node to all of the variable nodes relevant to that term with undirected links. So, in a directed model, a term like $Pr(\mathbf{x}_1|w_1, w_2)$ would result in a function node that connects to $\mathbf{x}_1$, w_1, and w_2. In an undirected model, a term like $\phi_{12}(w_1, w_2)$ would result in a function node that connects to w_1 and w_2. Figure 11.8 shows the factor graph for the chain model.

Sum-product algorithm

The sum product algorithm proceeds in two phases: a forward pass and a backward pass. The forward pass distributes evidence through the graph and the backward pass collates this evidence. Both the distribution and collation of evidence are accomplished by passing messages from node to node in the factor graph. Every edge in the graph is connected to exactly one variable node, and each message is defined over the domain of this variable. There are three types of messages:

1. A message $\mathbf{m}_{\mathbf{z}_p \to g_q}$ from an unobserved variable $\mathbf{z}_p$ to a function node g_q is given by

$$\mathbf{m}_{\mathbf{z}_p \to g_q} = \prod_{r \in \mathrm{ne}[p] \backslash q} \mathbf{m}_{g_r \to \mathbf{z}_p}, \tag{11.35}$$

where $\mathrm{ne}[p]$ returns the set of the neighbors of $\mathbf{z}_p$ in the graph and so the expression $\mathrm{ne}[p] \backslash q$ denotes all of the neighbors except q. In other words, the message from a variable to a function node is the pointwise product of all other incoming messages to the variable; it is the combination of other beliefs.

2. A message $\mathbf{m}_{z_p \to g_q}$ from an observed variable $\mathbf{z}_p = \mathbf{z}_p^*$ to a function node g_q is given by

$$\mathbf{m}_{z_p \to g_q} = \delta[\mathbf{z}_p^*]. \tag{11.36}$$

In other words, the message from an observed node to a function conveys the certain belief that this node took the observed value.

3. A message $\mathbf{m}_{g_p \to \mathbf{z}_q}$ from a function node g_p to a recipient variable $\mathbf{z}_q$ is defined as

$$\mathbf{m}_{g_p \to \mathbf{z}_q} = \sum_{\mathrm{ne}[p] \backslash q} g_p[\mathrm{ne}[p]] \prod_{r \in \mathrm{ne}[p] \backslash q} m_{\mathbf{z}_r \to g_p}. \tag{11.37}$$

This takes beliefs from all variables connected to the function except the recipient variable and uses the function $g_p[\bullet]$ to convert these to a belief about the recipient variable.

In the forward phase, the message passing can proceed in any order, as long as the outgoing message from any variable or function is not sent until all the other incoming messages have arrived. In the backward pass, the messages are sent in the opposite order to the forward pass.

Finally, the marginal distribution at node $\mathbf{z}_p$ can be computed from a product of all of the incoming messages from both the forward and reverse passes so that

$$Pr(\mathbf{z}_p) \propto \prod_{r \in \mathrm{ne}[p]} \mathbf{m}_{g_r \to \mathbf{z}_p}. \tag{11.38}$$

A proof that this algorithm is correct is beyond the scope of this book. However, to make this at least partially convincing (and more concrete), we will work through these rules for the case of the chain model (Figure 11.8), and we will show that exactly the same computation occurs as for the forward-backward algorithm.

11.4.4   Sum-product algorithm for chain model

The factor graph for the chain solution annotated with messages is shown in Figure 11.9. We will now describe the sum-product algorithm for the chain model.

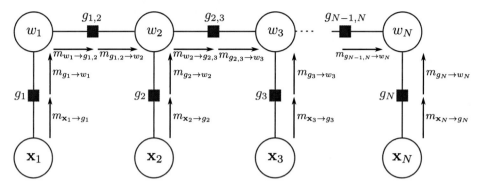

Figure 11.9 Sum product algorithm for chain model (forward pass). The sum-product algorithm has two phases. In the forward phase, messages are passed through the graph in an order such that a message cannot be sent until all incoming messages are received at the source node. So, the message $\mathbf{m}_{w_2 \to g_{23}}$ cannot be sent until the messages $\mathbf{m}_{g_2 \to w_2}$ and $\mathbf{m}_{g_{1,2} \to w_2}$ have been received.

Forward pass

We start by passing a message $\mathbf{m}_{\mathbf{x}_1 \to g_1}$ from node $\mathbf{x}_1$ to the function node g_1. Using rule 2, this message is a delta function at the observed value $\mathbf{x}_1^*$, so that

$$\mathbf{m}_{\mathbf{x}_1 \to g_1} = \delta[\mathbf{x}_1^*]. \tag{11.39}$$

Now we pass a message from function g_1 to node w_1. Using rule 3, we have

$$\mathbf{m}_{g_1 \to w_1} = \int Pr(\mathbf{x}_1|w_1)\delta[\mathbf{x}_1^*]d\mathbf{x}_1 = Pr(\mathbf{x}_1 = \mathbf{x}_1^*|w_1). \tag{11.40}$$

By rule 1, the message from node w_1 to function $g_{1,2}$ is simply the product of the incoming nodes, and since there is only one incoming node, this is just

$$\mathbf{m}_{w_1 \to g_{12}} = Pr(\mathbf{x}_1 = \mathbf{x}_1^*|w_1). \tag{11.41}$$

By rule 3, the message from function $g_{1,2}$ to node w_2 is computed as

$$\mathbf{m}_{g_{1,2} \to w_2} = \sum_{w_1} Pr(w_2|w_1)Pr(\mathbf{x}_1 = \mathbf{x}_1^*|w_1). \tag{11.42}$$

Continuing this process, the messages from $\mathbf{x}_2$ to g_2 and g_2 to w_2 are

$$\mathbf{m}_{\mathbf{x}_2 \to g_2} = \delta[\mathbf{x}_2^*]$$
$$\mathbf{m}_{g_2 \to w_2} = Pr(\mathbf{x}_2 = \mathbf{x}_2^*|w_2), \tag{11.43}$$

and the message from w_2 to $g_{2,3}$ is

$$\mathbf{m}_{w_2 \to g_{2,3}} = Pr(\mathbf{x}_2 = \mathbf{x}_2^*|w_2) \sum_{w_1} Pr(w_2|w_1)Pr(\mathbf{x}_1 = \mathbf{x}_1^*|w_1). \tag{11.44}$$

A clear pattern is emerging; the message from node w_n to function $g_{n,n+1}$ is equal to the forward term from the forward-backward algorithm:

$$\mathbf{m}_{w_n \to g_{n,n+1}} = \mathbf{f}_n[w_n] = Pr(w_n, \mathbf{x}_{1\ldots n}). \tag{11.45}$$

In other words, the sum-product algorithm is performing exactly the same computations as the forward pass of the forward-backward algorithm.

Backward pass

When we reach the end of the forward pass of the belief propagation, we initiate the backward pass. There is no need to pass messages toward the observed variables $\mathbf{x}_n$ since we already know their values for certain. Hence, we concentrate on the horizontal connections between the unobserved variables (i.e., along the spine of the model). The message from node w_N to function $g_{N,N-1}$ is given by

$$\mathbf{m}_{w_N \to g_{N,N-1}} = Pr(\mathbf{x}_N = \mathbf{x}_N^* | w_N), \tag{11.46}$$

and the message from $g_{N,N-1}$ to w_{N-1} is given by

$$\mathbf{m}_{g_{N,N-1} \to w_{N-1}} = \sum_{w_N} Pr(w_N | w_{N-1}) Pr(\mathbf{x}_N = \mathbf{x}_N^* | w_N). \tag{11.47}$$

In general, we have

$$\mathbf{m}_{g_{n,n-1} \to w_{n-1}} = \sum_{w_n} Pr(w_n | w_{n-1}) Pr(\mathbf{x}_n | w_n) \mathbf{m}_{g_{n+1,n} \to w_n}$$
$$= \mathbf{b}_{n-1}[w_{n-1}], \tag{11.48}$$

which is exactly the backward recursion from the forward-backward algorithm.

Collating evidence

Finally, to compute the marginal probabilities, we use the relation

$$Pr(w_n | \mathbf{x}_{1...N}) \propto \prod_{m \in \mathbf{ne}[n]} \mathbf{m}_{g_m \to \mathbf{w}_n}, \tag{11.49}$$

and for the general case, this consists of three terms:

$$Pr(w_n | \mathbf{x}_{1...N}) \propto \mathbf{m}_{g_{n-1,n} \to w_n} \mathbf{m}_{g_n \to w_n} \mathbf{m}_{g_{n,n+1} \to w_n}$$
$$= \mathbf{m}_{w_n \to g_{n,n+1}} \mathbf{m}_{g_{n,n+1} \to w_n}$$
$$= \mathbf{f}_n[w_n] \mathbf{b}_n[w_n], \tag{11.50}$$

where in the second line we have used the fact that the outgoing message from a variable node is the product of the incoming messages. We conclude that the sum-product algorithm computes the posterior marginals in exactly the same way as the forward backward algorithm.

11.5   Marginal posterior inference for trees

To compute the marginals in tree-structured models we simply apply the sum product algorithm to the new graph structure. The factor graph for the tree in Figure 11.6 is shown in Figure 11.10. The only slight complication is that we must ensure that the first two incoming messages to the function relating variables w_2, w_4, and w_5 have arrived before sending the outgoing message. This is very similar to the order of operations in the dynamic programming algorithm.

For undirected graphs, the key property is that the cliques, not the nodes, form a tree. For example, there is clearly a loop in the undirected model in Figure 11.11a, but when we convert this to a factor graph the structure is a tree (Figure 11.11b). For models with only pairwise cliques, the cliques always form a tree if there are no loops in the original graphical model.

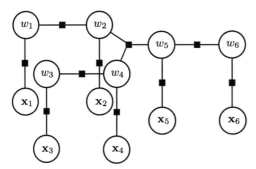

Figure 11.10 Factor graph corresponding to tree model in Figure 11.6. There is one function node connecting each world state variable to its associated measurement and these correspond to the terms $Pr(\mathbf{x}_n|w_n)$. There is one function node for each of the three pairwise terms $Pr(w_2|w_1)$, $Pr(w_4|w_3)$ and $Pr(w_6|w_5)$ and this is connected to both contributing variables. The function node corresponding to the three-wise term $Pr(w_5|w_2,w_4)$ has three neighbors, w_5, w_2, and w_4.

11.6 Learning in chains and trees

So far, we have only discussed inference for these models. Here, we briefly discuss learning which can be done in a *supervised* or *unsupervised* context. In the supervised case, we are given a training set of I matched sets of states $\{w_{in}\}_{i=1,n=1}^{I,N}$ and data $\{\mathbf{x}_{in}\}_{i=1,n=1}^{I,N}$. In the unsupervised case, we only observe the data $\{\mathbf{x}_{in}\}_{i=1,n=1}^{I,N}$.

Supervised learning for directed models is relatively simple. We first isolate the part of the model that we want to learn. For example, we might learn the parameters $\boldsymbol{\theta}$ of $Pr(\mathbf{x}_n|w_n,\boldsymbol{\theta})$ from paired examples of $\mathbf{x}_n$ and w_n. We can then learn these parameters in isolation using the ML, MAP, or Bayesian methods.

Unsupervised learning is more challenging; the states w_n are treated as hidden variables and the EM algorithm is applied. In the E-step, we compute the posterior marginals over the states using the forward backward algorithm. In the M-step we use these marginals to update the model parameters. For the hidden Markov model (the chain model), this is known as the *Baum-Welch* algorithm.

As we saw in the previous chapter, learning in undirected models can be challenging; we cannot generally compute the normalization constant Z and this in turn prevents us from computing the derivative with respect to the parameters. However, for the special case of tree and chain models, it is possible to compute Z efficiently and learning is tractable. To see why this is the case, consider the undirected model from Figure 11.2b, which we will treat here as representing the conditional distribution

$$Pr(w_{1...N}|\mathbf{x}_{1...N}) = \frac{1}{Z}\left(\prod_{n=1}^{N}\phi[\mathbf{x}_n,w_n]\right)\left(\prod_{n=2}^{N}\zeta[w_n,w_{n-1}]\right), \qquad (11.51)$$

since the data nodes $\{\mathbf{x}_n\}_{n=1}^{N}$ are fixed. This model is known as a *1D conditional random field*. The unknown constant Z now has the form

$$Z = \sum_{w_1}\sum_{w_2}\cdots\sum_{w_N}\left(\prod_{n=1}^{N}\phi[\mathbf{x}_n,w_n]\right)\left(\prod_{n=2}^{N}\zeta[w_n,w_{n-1}]\right). \qquad (11.52)$$

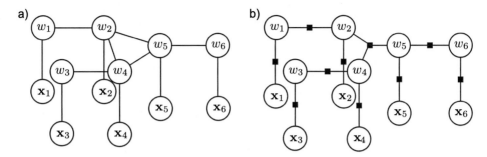

Figure 11.11 Converting an undirected model to a factor graph. a) Undirected model. b) Corresponding factor graph. There is one function node for each maximal clique (each clique which is not a subset of another clique). Although there was clearly a loop in the original graph, there is no loop in the factor graph and so the sum-product algorithm is still applicable.

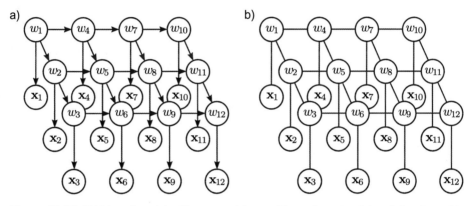

Figure 11.12 Grid-based models. For many vision problems, the natural description is a grid-based model. We observe a grid of pixel values $\{\mathbf{x}_n\}_{n=1}^N$ and wish to infer an unknown world state $\{w_n\}_{n=1}^N$ associated with each site. Each world state is connected to its neighbors. These connections are usually applied to ensure a smooth or piecewise smooth solution. a) Directed grid model. b) Undirected grid model (2D conditional random field).

We have already seen that it is possible to compute this type of sum efficiently, using a recursion (Equation 11.26). Hence, Z can be evaluated and maximum likelihood learning can be performed in this model without the need for contrastive divergence.

11.7 Beyond chains and trees

Unfortunately, there are many models in computer vision that do not take the form of a chain or a tree. Of particular importance are models that are structured to have one unknown w_n for each RGB pixel $\mathbf{x}_n$ in the image. These models are naturally structured as *grids* and the world states are each connected to their four pixel neighbors in the graphical model (Figure 11.12). Stereo vision, segmentation, denoising, superresolution, and many other vision problems can all be framed in this way.

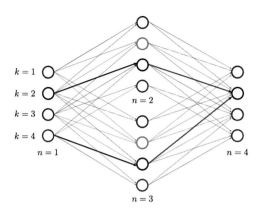

$k = 1$
$k = 2$
$k = 3$
$k = 4$
$n = 1$
$n = 2$
$n = 4$
$n = 3$

Figure 11.13 Dynamic programming fails when there are undirected loops. Here, we show a 2×2 image where we have performed a naïve forward pass through the variables. On retracing the route, we see that the two branches disagree over which state the first variable took. For a coherent solution the cumulative minimum costs at node 4, we should have forced the two paths to have common ancestors. With a large number of ancestors this is too computationally expensive to be practical.

We devote the whole of the next chapter to grid-based problems, but we will briefly take the time to examine why the methods developed in this chapter are not suitable. Consider a simple model based on a 2×2 grid. Figure 11.13 illustrates why we cannot blindly use dynamic programming to compute the MAP solution. To compute the minimum cumulative cost S_n at each node, we might naïvely proceed as normal:

$$S_{1,k} = U_1(w_1 = k)$$
$$S_{2,k} = U_2(w_2 = k) + \min_l [S_1(w_1 = l) + P_2(w_2 = k, w_1 = l)]$$
$$S_{3,k} = U_3(w_3 = k) + \min_l [S_1(w_1 = l) + P_2(w_3 = k, w_1 = l)]. \qquad (11.53)$$

Now consider the fourth term. Unfortunately,

$$S_{4,k} \neq U_4(w_k = 4) + \min_{l,m} [S_2(w_2 = l) + S_3(w_3 = m) + T(w_4 = k, w_2 = l, w_3 = m)].$$
$$\qquad (11.54)$$

The reason for this is that the partial cumulative sums S_2 and S_3 at the two previous vertices both rely on minimizing over the same variable w_1. However, they did not necessarily choose the same value at w_1. If we were to trace back the paths we took, the two routes back to vertex one might predict a different answer. To properly calculate the minimum cumulative cost at node $S_{4,k}$, we would have to take account of all three ancestors: the recursion is no longer valid, and the problem becomes intractable once more.

Similarly, we cannot perform belief propagation on this graph: the algorithm requires us to send a message from a node only when all other incoming messages have been received. However, the nodes w_1, w_2, w_3, and w_4 all simultaneously require messages from one another and so this is not possible.

11.7.1 Inference in graphs with loops

Although the methods of this chapter are not suitable for models based on graphs with loops, there are a number of ways to proceed:

1. **Prune the graph.** An obvious idea is to prune the graph by removing edges until what is left has a tree structure (Figure 11.14). The choice of which edges to prune will depend on the real-world problem.

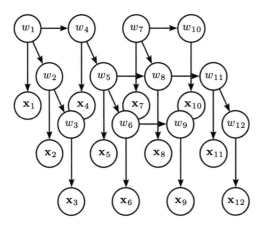

Figure 11.14 Pruning graphs with loops. One approach to dealing with models with loops is simply to prune the connections until the loops are removed. This graphical model is the model from Figure 11.12a after such a pruning process. Most of the connections are retained but now the remaining structure is a tree. The usual approach to pruning is to associate a strength with each edge so that weaker edges are more desirable. Then we compute the minimum spanning tree based in these strengths and discard any connections that do not form part of the tree.

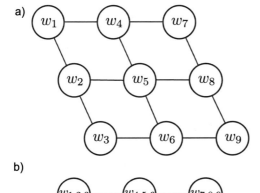

Figure 11.15 Combining variables. a) This graphical model contains loops. b) We form three compound variables, each of which consists of all of the variables in one of the original columns. These are now connected by a chain structure. However, the price we pay is that if there were K states for each original variable, the compound variables now have K^3 states.

2. **Combine variables.** A second approach is to combine variables together until what remains has the structure of a chain or tree. For example, in Figure 11.15 we combine the variables w_1, w_2, and w_3, to make a new variable w_{123} and the variables w_4, w_5, and w_6 to form w_{456}. Continuing in this way, we form a model that has a chain structure. If each of the original variables had K states, then the compound variables will have K^3 states, and so inference will be more expensive. In general the merging of variables can be automated using the *junction tree* algorithm. Unfortunately, this example illustrates why this approach will not work for large grid models: we must merge together so many variables that the resulting compound variable has too many states to work with.

3. **Loopy belief propagation.** Another idea is to simply apply belief propagation regardless of the loops. All messages are initialized to uniform and then the messages are repeatedly passed in some order according to the normal rules. This algorithm is not guaranteed to converge to the correct solution for the marginals

(or indeed to converge at all) but in practice it produces useful results in many situations.

4. **Sampling approaches.** For directed graphical models, it is usually easy to draw samples from the posterior. These can then be aggregated to compute an empirical estimate of the marginal distributions.

5. **Other approaches:** There are several other approaches for exact or approximate inference in graphs, including *tree reweighted message passing* and *graph cuts*. The latter is a particularly important class of algorithms, and we devote most of Chapter 12 to describing it.

11.8 Applications

The models in this chapter are attractive because they permit exact MAP inference. They have been applied to a number of problems in which there are assumed spatial or temporal connections between parts of a model.

11.8.1 Gesture tracking

The goal of gesture tracking is to classify the position $\{w_n\}_{n=1}^N$ of the hands within each of the N captured frames from a video sequence into a discrete set of possible gestures, $w_n \in \{1, 2, \ldots, K\}$ based on extracted data $\{\mathbf{x}_n\}_{n=1}^N$ from those frames. Starner et al. (1998) presented a wearable system for automatically interpreting sign language gestures. A camera mounted in the user's hat captured a top-down view of their hands (Figure 11.16). The positions of the hands were identified by using a per-pixel skin segmentation technique (see Section 6.6.1). The state of each hand was characterized in terms of the position and shape of a bounding ellipse around the associated skin region. The final eight-dimensional data vector $\mathbf{x}$ concatenated these measurements from each hand.

To describe the time sequences of these measurements, Starner et al. (1998) developed a hidden Markov model-based system in which the states w_n each represented a part of a sign language word. Each of these words was represented by a progression through four values of the state variable w, representing the various stages in the associated gesture for that word. The progression through these states might last any number of time steps (each state can be followed by itself so it can cycle indefinitely) but must come in the required order. They trained the system using 400 training sentences. They used a dynamic programming method to estimate the most likely states w and achieved recognition accuracy of 97.8 percent using a 40-word lexicon with a test set of 100 sentences. They found that performance was further improved if they imposed knowledge about the fixed grammar of each phrase (pronoun, verb, noun, adjective, pronoun). Remarkably, the system worked at a rate of 10 frames a second.

11.8.2 Stereo vision

In dense stereo vision, we are given two images of the same scene taken from slightly different positions. For our purposes, we will assume that they have been preprocessed so that for each pixel in image 1, the corresponding pixel is on the same scanline in image 2 (a process known as *rectification*; see Chapter 16). The horizontal offset or *disparity* between corresponding points depends on the depth. Our goal is to find the discrete

Figure 11.16 Gesture tracking from Starner et al. (1998). A camera was mounted on a baseball cap (inset) looking down at the users hands. The camera image (main figure) was used to track the hands in a HMM-based system that could accurately classify a 40-word lexicon and worked in real time. Each word was associated with four states in the HMM. The system was based on a compact description of the hand position and orientation within each frame. Adapted from Starner et al. (1998), ©1998 Springer.

disparity field $\mathbf{w}$ given the observed images $\mathbf{x}^{(1)}$ and $\mathbf{x}^{(2)}$, from which the depth of each pixel can be recovered (Figure 11.17).

We assume that the pixel in image 1 should closely resemble the pixel at the appropriate offset (disparity) in image 2 and any remaining small differences are treated as noise so that

$$Pr(\mathbf{x}_{m,n}^{(1)}|w_{m,n}=k) = \text{Norm}_{\mathbf{x}_{m,n}^{(1)}}\left[\mathbf{x}_{m,n+k}^{(2)}, \sigma^2 \mathbf{I}\right], \tag{11.55}$$

where $w_{m,n}$ is the disparity at pixel (m,n) of image 1, $\mathbf{x}_{m,n}^{(1)}$ is the RGB vector from pixel (m,n) of image 1 and $\mathbf{x}_{m,n}^{(2)}$ is the RGB vector from pixel (m,n) of image 2.

Unfortunately, if we compute the maximum likelihood disparities $w_{m,n}$ at each pixel separately, the result is extremely noisy (Figure 11.18a). As Figure 11.17 illustrates, the choice of disparity is ambiguous in regions of the image where there are few visual changes. In layman's terms, if the nearby pixels are all similar, it is difficult to establish with certainty which corresponds to a given position in the other image. To resolve this ambiguity, we introduce a prior $Pr(\mathbf{w})$ that encourages piecewise smoothness in the disparity map; we are exploiting the fact that we know that the scene mainly consists of smooth surfaces, with occasional jumps in disparity at the edge of objects.

One possible approach (attributed originally to Ohta and Kanade 1985) to recovering the disparity is to use an independent prior for each scanline so that

$$Pr(\mathbf{w}) = \prod_{m=1}^{M} Pr(\mathbf{w}_m), \tag{11.56}$$

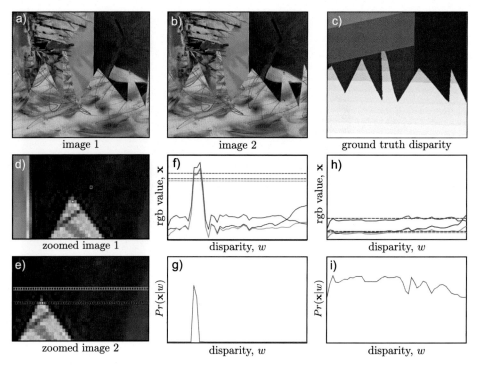

Figure 11.17 Dense stereo vision. a–b) Two images taken from slightly different positions. The corresponding point for every pixel in the first image is somewhere on the same scanline in the second image. The horizontal offset is known as the disparity and is inversely related to depth. c) Ground truth disparity map for this image. d) Close-up of part of first image with two pixels highlighted. e) Close-up of second image with potential corresponding pixels highlighted. f) RGB values for red pixel (dashed lines) in first image and as a function of the position in second image (solid lines). At the correct disparity, there is very little difference between the RGB values in the two images and so g) the likelihood that this disparity is correct is large. h–i) For the green pixel (which is in a smoothly changing region of the image), there are many positions where the RGB values in the second image are similar and hence many disparities have high likelihoods; the solution is ambiguous.

where each scanline was organized into a chain model (Figure 11.2) so that

$$Pr(\mathbf{w}_m) = Pr(w_{m,1}) \prod_{n=2}^{N} Pr(w_{m,n}|w_{m,n-1}). \tag{11.57}$$

The distributions $Pr(w_{m,n}|w_{m,n-1})$ are chosen so that they allot a high probability when adjacent disparities are the same, an intermediate probability when adjacent disparities change by a single value, and a low probability if they take values that are more widely separated. Hence, we encourage piecewise smoothness.

MAP inference can be performed within each scanline separately using the dynamic programming approach and the results combined to form the full disparity field $\mathbf{w}$. Whereas this definitely improves the fidelity of the solution, it results in a characteristic "streaky" result (Figure 11.18b). These artifacts are due to the (erroneous) assumption that the scanlines are independent. To get an improved solution, we should smooth in the

 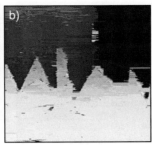 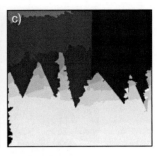

Figure 11.18 Dense stereo results. Recovered disparity maps for a) independent pixels model, b) independent scanlines model, and c) tree-based model of Veksler (2005).

vertical direction as well, but the resulting grid-based model will contain loops, making MAP inference problematic.

Veksler (2005) addressed this problem by pruning the full grid-based model until it formed a tree. Each edge was characterized by a cost that increased if the associated pixels were close to large changes in the image; at these positions, either there is texture in the image (and so the disparity is relatively well defined) or there is an edge between two objects in the scene. In either case, there is no need to apply a smoothing prior here. Hence, the minimum spanning tree tends to retain edges in regions where they are most needed. The minimum spanning tree can be computed using a standard method such as Prim's algorithm (see Cormen et al. 2001).

The results of MAP inference using this model are shown in Figure 11.18c. The solution is piecewise smooth in both directions and is clearly superior to either the independent pixels model or the independent scanline approach. However, even this model is an unnecessary approximation; we would ideally like the variables to be fully connected in a grid structure, but this would obviously contain loops. In Chapter 12, we consider models of this sort and revisit stereo vision.

11.8.3 Pictorial Structures

Pictorial structures are models for object classes that consist of a number of individual parts that are connected together by spring-like connections. A typical example would be a face model (Figure 11.19), which might consist of a nose, eyes, and mouth. The spring-like connections encourage the relative positions of these features to take sensible values. For example, the mouth is strongly encouraged to be below the nose. Pictorial structures have a long history in computer vision but were revived in a modern form by Felzenszwalb and Huttenlocher (2005) who identified that if the connections between parts take the form of an acyclic graph (a tree), then they can be fit to images in polynomial time.

The goal of matching a pictorial structure to an image is to identify the positions $\{w_n\}_{n=1}^{N}$ of the N parts based on data $\{\mathbf{x}_n\}$ associated with each. For example, a simple system might assign a likelihood $Pr(\mathbf{x}|w_n = k)$ that is a normal distribution over a patch of the image at position k. The relative positions of the parts are encoded using distributions of the form $Pr(w_n|w_{pa[n]})$. MAP inference in this system can be achieved using a dynamic programming technique.

Figure 11.19 shows a pictorial structure for a face. This model is something of a compromise in that it would be preferable if the features had more dense connections:

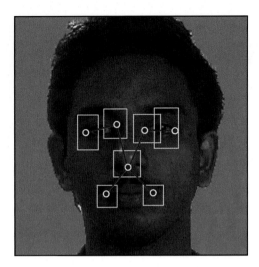

Figure 11.19 Pictorial structure. This face model consists of seven parts (red dots), which are connected together in a tree-like structure (red lines). The possible positions of each part are indicated by the yellow boxes. Although each part can take several hundred pixel positions, the MAP positions can be inferred efficiently by exploiting the tree-structure of the graph using a dynamic programming approach. Localizing facial features is a common element of many face recognition pipelines.

for example the left eye provides information about the position of the right eye as well as the nose. Nonetheless, this type of model can reliably find features on frontal faces.

A second application is for fitting articulated models such as human bodies (Figure 11.20). These naturally have the form of a tree and so the structure is determined by the problem itself. Felzenszwalb and Huttenlocher (2005) developed a system of this sort in which each state w_n represented a part of the model (e.g., the right forearm). Each state could take K possible values representing different possible positions and shapes of the object part.

The image was preclassified into foreground and background using a background subtraction technique. The likelihood $Pr(\mathbf{x}_n|w = k)$ for a particular part position was evaluated using this binary image. In particular, the likelihood was chosen so that it increased if the area within the rectangle was considered foreground and the area surrounding it was considered background.

Unfortunately, MAP inference in this model is somewhat unreliable: a common failure mode is for more than one part of the body to become associated with the same part of the binary image. This is technically possible as the limbs may occlude each other, but it can also happen erroneously if one limb dominates and supports the rectangle model significantly more than the others. Felzenszwalb and Huttenlocher (2005) dealt with this problem by drawing samples from the posterior distribution $Pr(w_{1...N}|\mathbf{x}_{1...N})$ over the positions of the parts of the model and using a more complex criterion to choose the most promising sample.

11.8.4 Segmentation

In Section 7.9.3, we considered segmentation as the problem of labeling pixels according to the object to which they belong. A different approach to segmentation is to infer the position of a closed contour that delineates two objects. In inference, the goal is usually to infer the positions of a set of points $\{w_n\}$ on the boundary of this contour based on the image data $\mathbf{x}$. As we update these points during an attempt to find the MAP solution, the contour moves across the image, and for this reason this type of model is referred to as an active contour or snake model.

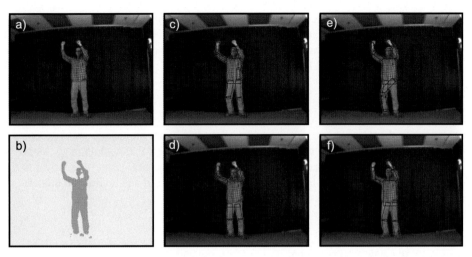

Figure 11.20 Pictorial structure for human body. a) Original image. b) After background subtraction. c–f) Four samples from the posterior distribution over part positions. Each part position is represented by a rectangle of fixed aspect ratio and characterized by its position, size, and angle. Adapted from Felzenszwalb and Huttenlocher (2005). ©2005 Springer.

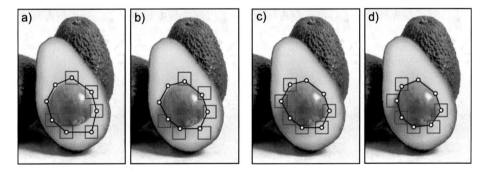

Figure 11.21 Segmentation using snakes. a) Two points are fixed, but the remaining points can take any position within their respective boxes. The posterior distribution favors positions that are on image contours (due to the likelihood term) and positions that are close to other points (due to the pairwise connections). b) Results of inference. c) Two other points are considered fixed. d) Result of inference. In this way, a closed contour in the image is identified. Adapted from Felzenszwalb and Zabih (2011). ©2011 IEEE.

Figure 11.21 shows an example of fitting this type of model. At each iteration, the positions $\{w_n\}$ of all of the points except two are updated and can take any position within small region surrounding their previous position. The likelihood of taking a particular value $w_n = k$ is high at positions in the image where the intensity changes rapidly (i.e., the edges) and low in constant regions. In addition, neighboring points are connected and have an attractive force: they are more likely to be close to one another. As usual, inference can be carried out using the dynamic programming method. During inference, the points tend to become closer together (due to their mutual attraction) but get stuck on the edge of an object.

In the full system, this process is repeated, but with a different pair of adjacent points chosen to be fixed at each step. Hence, the dynamic programming is a component step of a larger inference problem. As the inference procedure continues, the contour moves across the image and eventually fixes onto the boundary of an object. For this reason, these models are known as *snakes* or *active contour models*. They are considered in more detail in Chapter 17.

Discussion

In this chapter, we have considered models based on acyclic graphs (chains and trees). In Chapter 12, we will consider grid-based models that contain many loops. We will see that MAP inference is only tractable in a few special cases. In contrast to this chapter, we will also see a large difference between directed and undirected models.

Notes

Dynamic programming: Dynamic programming is used in many vision algorithms, including those where there is not necessarily a clear probabilistic interpretation. It is an attractive approach when it is applicable because of its speed, and some efforts have been made to improve this further (Raphael 2001). Interesting examples include image retargeting (Avidan and Shamir 2007), contour completion (Sha'ashua and Ullman 1988), fitting of deformable templates (Amit and Kong 1996; Coughlan et al. 2000), shape matching (Basri et al. 1998), the computation of superpixels (Moore et al. 2008) and semantic labeling of scenes with tiered structure (Felzenszwalb and Veksler 2010) as well as the applications described in this chapter. Felzenszwalb and Zabih (2011) provide a recent review of dynamic programming and other graph algorithms in computer vision.

Stereo vision: Dynamic programming was variously applied to stereo vision by Baker and Binford (1981), Ohta and Kanade (1985) (who use a model based on edges) and Geiger et al. (1992) (who used a model based on intensities). Birchfield and Tomasi (1998) improved the speed by removing unlikely search nodes from the dynamic programming solution and introduced a mechanism that made depth discontinuities more likely where there was intensity variation. Torr and Criminisi (2004) developed a system that integrated dynamic programming with known constraints such as matched keypoints. Gong and Yang (2005) developed a dynamic programming algorithm that ran on a graphics processing unit (GPU). Kim et al. (2005) introduced a method for identifying disparity candidates at each pixel using spatial filters and a two-pass method that performed optimization both along and across the scanlines. Veksler (2005) used dynamic programming in a tree to solve for the whole image at once, and this idea has subsequently been used in a method based on line segments (Deng and Lin 2006). A recent quantitative comparison of dynamic programming algorithms in computer vision can be found in Salmen et al. (2009). Alternative approaches to stereo vision, which are not based on dynamic programming, are considered in Chapter 12.

Pictorial structures: Pictorial structures were originally introduced by Fischler and Erschlager (1973) but recent interest was stimulated by the work of Felzenszwalb and Huttenlocher (2005) who introduced efficient methods of inference based on dynamic programming. There have been a number of attempts to improve the appearance (likelihood) term of the model (Kumar et al. 2004; Eichner and Ferrari 2009; Andriluka et al. 2009; Felzenszwalb et al. 2010). Models that do not conform to a tree structure have also been introduced (Kumar et al. 2004; Sigal and Black 2006; Ren et al. 2005; Jiang and Martin 2008) and here alternative methods such as loopy propagation must be used for inference. These more general structures are particularly important for addressing problems associated with occlusions in human body models. Other authors have based their model on a mixture of trees (Everingham et al. 2006; Felzenszwalb et al. 2010). In terms of applications, Ramanan et al. (2008) have developed a notable system for tracking humans in video sequences based on pictorial structures, Everingham et al. (2006) have developed a widely used system for locating facial features, and Felzenszwalb et al. (2010) have presented a system that is used for detecting more general objects.

Hidden Markov models: Hidden Markov models are essentially chain-based models that are applied to quantities evolving in time. Good tutorials on the subject including details of how to learn them in the unsupervised case can be found in Rabiner (1989) and Ghahramani (2001). Their most common application in vision is for gesture recognition (Starner et al. 1998; Rigoll et al. 1998; and see Moni and Ali 2009 for a recent review), but they have also been used in other contexts such as modeling interactions of pedestrians (Oliver et al. 2000). Some recent work (e.g., Bor Wang et al. 2006) uses a related discriminative model for tracking objects in time known as a *conditional random field* (see Chapter 12).

Snakes: The idea of a contour evolving over the surface of an image is due to Kass et al. (1987). Both Amini et al. (1990) and Geiger et al. (1995) describe dynamic programming approaches to this problem. These models are considered further in Chapter 17.

Belief propagation: The sum-product algorithm (Kschischang et al. 2001) is a development of earlier work on belief propagation by Pearl (1988). The factor graph representation is due to Frey et al. (1997). The use of belief propagation for finding marginal posteriors and MAP solutions in graphs with loops has been investigated by Murphy et al. (1999) and Weiss and Freeman (2001), respectively. Notable applications of loopy belief propagation in vision include stereo vision (Sun et al. 2003) and superresolving images (Freeman et al. 2000). More information about belief propagation can be found in machine learning textbooks such as Bishop (2006), Barber (2012), and Koller and Friedman (2009).

Problems

11.1 Compute by hand the lowest possible cost for traversing the graph in Figure 11.22 using the dynamic programming method.

11.2 MAP inference in chain models can also be performed by running Djikstra's algorithm on the graph in Figure 11.23, starting from the node on the left-hand side and terminating when we first reach the node on the right-hand side. If there are N variables, each of which takes K values, what is the best and worst case complexity of the algorithm? Describe a situation where Djikstra's algorithm outperforms dynamic programming.

11.3 Consider the graphical model in Figure 11.24a. Write out the cost function for MAP estimation in the form of Equation 11.17. Discuss the difference between your answer and Equation 11.17.

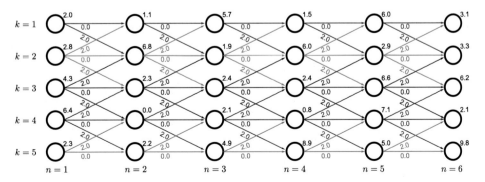

Figure 11.22 Dynamic programming example for Problem 11.1.

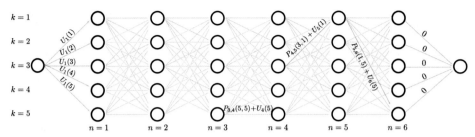

Figure 11.23 Graph construction for Problem 11.2. This is the same as the dynamic programming graph (Figure 11.3) except that: (i) there are two extra nodes at the start and the end of the graph. (ii) There are no vertex costs. (iii) The costs associated with the leftmost edges are $U_1(k)$ and the costs associated with the rightmost edges are 0. The general edge cost for passing from label a and node n to label b at node $n+1$ is given by $P_{n,n+1}(a,b) + U_{n+1}(b)$.

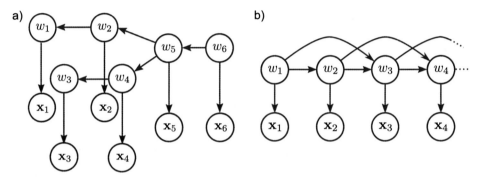

Figure 11.24 a) Graphical model for Problem 11.3. b) Graphical model for Problem 11.10. The unknown variables $w_3, w_4, \ldots$ in this model receive connections from the two preceding variables and so the graph contains loops.

11.4 Compute the solution (minimum cost path) to the dynamic programming problem on the tree in Figure 11.25 (which corresponds to the graphical model from figure 11.6).

11.5 MAP inference for the chain model can be expressed as

$$\hat{w}_N = \underset{w_N}{\operatorname{argmax}} \left[\underset{w_1}{\max} \left[\underset{w_2}{\max} \left[\ldots \underset{w_{N-1}}{\max} \left[\sum_{n=1}^{N} \log[Pr(\mathbf{x}_n|w_n)] + \sum_{n=2}^{N} \log[Pr(w_n|w_{n-1})] \right] \ldots \right] \right] \right].$$

Show that it is possible to compute this expression piecewise by moving the maximization terms through the summation sequence in a manner similar to that described in Section 11.4.1.

11.6 Develop an algorithm that can compute the marginal distribution for an arbitrary variable w_n in a chain model.

11.7 Develop an algorithm that computes the joint marginal distribution of any two variables w_m and w_n in a chain model.

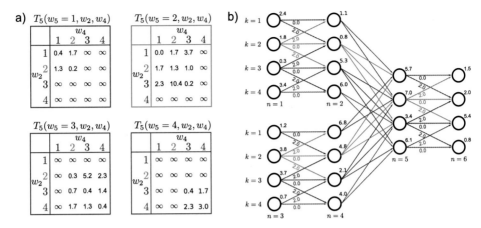

Figure 11.25 Dynamic programming example for Problem 11.4.

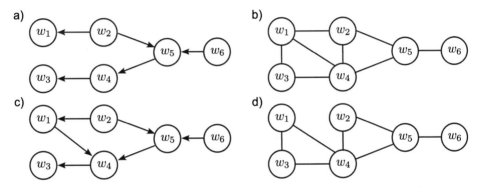

Figure 11.26 Graphical models for Problem 11.9.

11.8 Consider the following two distributions over three variables x_1, x_2, and x_3:

$$Pr(x_1, x_2, x_3) = \frac{1}{Z_1} \phi_{12}[x_1, x_2] \phi_{23}[x_2, x_3] \phi_{31}[x_3, x_1]$$

$$Pr(x_1, x_2, x_3) = \frac{1}{Z_2} \phi_{123}[x_1, x_2, x_3].$$

Draw (i) an undirected model and (ii) a factor graph for each distribution. What do you conclude?

11.9 Convert each of the graphical models in Figure 11.26 into the form of a factor graph. Which of the resulting factor graphs take the form of a chain?

11.10 Figure 11.24b shows a chain model in which each unknown variable w depends on its two predecessors. Describe a dynamic programming approach to finding the MAP solution. (*Hint:* You need to combine variables). If there are N variables in the chain and each takes K values, what is the overall complexity of your algorithm?

11.11 In the stereo vision problem, the solution was very poor when the pixels are treated independently (Figure 11.18a). Suggest some improvements to this method (while keeping the pixels independent).

11.12 Consider a variant on the segmentation application (Figure 11.21) in which we update all of the contour positions at once. The graphical model for this problem is a loop (i.e., a chain where there is also a edge between w_N and w_1). Devise an approach to finding the exact MAP solution in this model. If there are N variables each of which can take K values, what is the complexity of your algorithm?

Chapter 12

Models for grids

In Chapter 11, we discussed models that were structured as chains or trees. In this chapter, we consider models that associate a label with each pixel of an image. Since the unknown quantities are defined on the pixel lattice, models defined on a grid structure are appropriate. In particular, we will consider graphical models in which each label has a direct probabilistic connection to each of its four neighbors. Critically, this means that there are loops in the underlying graphical model and so the dynamic programming and belief propagation approaches of the previous chapter are no longer applicable.

These grid models are predicated on the idea that the pixel provides only very ambiguous information about the associated label. However, certain spatial configurations of labels are known to be more common than others, and we aim to exploit this knowledge to resolve the ambiguity. In this chapter, we describe the relative preference for different configurations of labels with a pairwise *Markov random field* or MRF. As we shall see, maximum a posteriori inference for pairwise MRFs is tractable in some circumstances using a family of approaches known collectively as *graph cuts*.

To motivate the grid models, we introduce a representative application. In *image denoising* we observe a corrupted image in which the intensities at a certain proportion of pixels have been randomly changed to another value according to a uniform distribution (Figure 12.1). Our goal is to recover the original clean image. We note two important aspects of the problem.

1. Most of the pixels are uncorrupted, so the data usually tell us which intensity value to pick.
2. The uncorrupted image is mainly smooth, with few changes between intensity levels.

Consequently, our strategy will be to construct a generative model where the MAP solution is an image that is mostly the same as the noisy version, but is smoother. As part of this solution, we need to define a probability distribution over images that favor smoothness. In this chapter, we will use a discrete formulation of a Markov random field to fulfill this role.

Figure 12.1 Image denoising. a) Original binary image. b) Observed image created by randomly flipping the polarity of a fixed proportion of pixels. Our goal is to recover the original image from the corrupted one. c) Original grayscale image. d) Observed corrupted image is created by setting a certain proportion of the pixels to values drawn from a uniform distribution. Once more, we aim to recover the original image.

12.1   Markov random fields

A *Markov random field* is formally determined by

- A set of sites $\mathcal{S} = \{1 \ldots N\}$. These will correspond to the N pixel locations.
- A set of random variables $\{w_n\}_{n=1}^{N}$ associated with each of the sites.
- A set of neighbors $\{\mathcal{N}_n\}_{n=1}^{N}$ at each of the N sites.

To be a Markov random field, the model must obey the Markov property:

$$Pr(w_n|w_{\mathcal{S}\setminus n}) = Pr(w_n|w_{\mathcal{N}_n}). \tag{12.1}$$

In other words, the model should be conditionally independent of all of the other variables given its neighbors. This property should sound familiar: this is exactly how conditional independence works in an undirected graphical model.

Consequently, we can consider a Markov random field as an undirected model (Section 10.3) that describes the joint probability of the variables as a product of potential functions so that

$$Pr(\mathbf{w}) = \frac{1}{Z} \prod_{j=1}^{J} \phi_j[\mathbf{w}_{\mathcal{C}_j}], \tag{12.2}$$

where $\phi_j[\bullet]$ is the jth potential function and always returns a nonnegative value. This value depends on the state of the subset of variables $\mathcal{C}_j \subset \{1, \ldots, N\}$. In this context, this subset is known as a *clique*. The term Z is called the partition function and is a normalizing constant that ensures that the result is a valid probability distribution.

Alternatively, we can rewrite the model as a Gibbs distribution:

$$Pr(\mathbf{w}) = \frac{1}{Z} \exp\left[-\sum_{j=1}^{J} \psi_j[\mathbf{w}_{\mathcal{C}_j}]\right], \tag{12.3}$$

where $\psi[\bullet] = -\log[\phi[\bullet]]$ is known as a cost function and returns either positive or negative values.

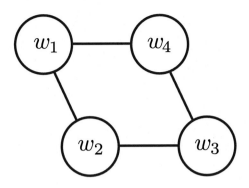

Figure 12.2 Graphical model for worked MRF example. The variables form a 2×2 grid. This is an undirected model where each link represents a potential function defined over the two variables that it connects. Each potential returns a positive number that indicates the tendency of the two variables to take these particular values.

12.1.1   Grid example

In a Markov random field, each potential function $\phi[\bullet]$ (or cost function $\psi[\bullet]$) addresses only a small subset of the variables. In this chapter, we will mainly be concerned with *pairwise Markov random fields* in which the cliques (subsets) consist of only neighboring pairs in a regular grid structure.

To see how the pairwise MRF can be used to encourage smoothness in an image, consider the graphical model for a 2×2 image (Figure 12.2). Here, we have defined the probability $Pr(w_{1\ldots4})$ over the associated discrete states as a normalized product of pairwise terms:

$$Pr(\mathbf{w}) = \frac{1}{Z}\phi_{12}(w_1,w_2)\phi_{23}(w_2,w_3)\phi_{34}(w_3,w_4)\phi_{41}(w_4,w_1), \qquad (12.4)$$

where $\phi_{mn}(w_m,w_n)$ is a potential function that takes the two states w_m and w_n and returns a positive number.

Let us consider the situation where the world state w_n at each pixel is binary and so takes a value of 0 or 1. The function ϕ_{mn} will now return four possible values depending on which of the four configurations $\{00,01,10,11\}$ of w_m and w_n is present. For simplicity, we will assume that the functions $\phi_{12},\phi_{23},\phi_{34}$ and ϕ_{41} are identical and that for each:

$$\begin{aligned}
\phi_{mn}(0,0) &= 1.0 & \phi_{mn}(0,1) &= 0.1 \\
\phi_{mn}(1,0) &= 0.1 & \phi_{mn}(1,1) &= 1.0.
\end{aligned} \qquad (12.5)$$

Since there are only four binary states, we can calculate the constant Z explicitly by computing the unnormalized probabilities for each of the 16 possible combinations and taking the sum. The resulting probabilities for each of the 16 possible states are:

$w_{1\ldots4}$	$Pr(w_{1\ldots4})$	$w_{1\ldots4}$	$Pr(w_{1\ldots4})$	$w_{1\ldots4}$	$Pr(w_{1\ldots4})$	$w_{1\ldots4}$	$Pr(w_{1\ldots4})$
0000	0.47176	0100	0.00471	1000	0.00471	1100	0.00471
0001	0.00471	0101	0.00005	1001	0.00471	1101	0.00471
0010	0.00471	0110	0.00471	1010	0.00005	1110	0.00471
0011	0.00471	0111	0.00471	1011	0.00471	1111	0.47176

The potential functions in Equation 12.5 encourage smoothness: the functions ϕ_{mn} return higher values when the neighbors take the same state and lower values when they differ, and this is reflected in the resulting probabilities.

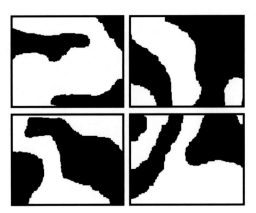

Figure 12.3 Samples from Markov random field prior. Four samples from the MRF prior which were generated using a Gibbs sampling procedure (see Section 10.7.2). Each sample is a binary image that is smooth almost everywhere; there are only very occasional changes from black to white and vice-versa. This prior encourages smooth solutions (like the original image in the denoising problems) and discourages isolated changes in label (as are present in the noise).

We can visualize this by scaling this model up to a larger image-sized grid where there is one node per pixel and drawing samples from the resulting probability distribution (Figure 12.3). The resulting binary images are mostly smooth, with only occasional changes between the two values.

It should be noted that for this more realistically sized model, we cannot compute the normalizing constant Z by brute force as for the 2×2 case. For example, with 10000 pixels each taking a binary value, the normalizing constant is the sum of 2^{10000} terms. In general we will have to cope with only knowing the probabilities up to an unknown scaling factor.

12.1.2 Image denoising with discrete pairwise MRFs

Now we will apply the pairwise Markov random field model to the denoising task. Our goal is to recover the original image pixel values from the observed noisy image.

More precisely, the observed image $\mathbf{x} = \{x_1, x_2, \ldots, x_N\}$ is assumed to consist of discrete variables where the different possible values (labels) represent different intensities. Our goal is to recover the original uncorrupted image $\mathbf{w} = \{w_1, w_2, \ldots, w_N\}$, which also consists of discrete variables representing the intensity. We will initially restrict our discussion to generative models and compute the posterior probability over the unknown world state $\mathbf{w}$ using Bayes' rule

$$Pr(w_{1\ldots N}|x_{1\ldots N}) = \frac{\prod_{n=1}^{N} Pr(x_n|w_n)Pr(w_{1\ldots N})}{Pr(x_{1\ldots N})}, \tag{12.6}$$

where we have assumed that the conditional probability $Pr(x_{1\ldots N}|w_{1\ldots N})$ factorizes into a product of individual terms associated with each pixel. We will first consider denoising binary images in which the noise process flips the pixel polarity with probability ρ so that

$$Pr(x_n|w_n = 0) = \text{Bern}_{x_n}[\rho]$$
$$Pr(x_n|w_n = 1) = \text{Bern}_{x_n}[1 - \rho]. \tag{12.7}$$

We subsequently consider gray level denoising where the observed pixel is replaced with probability ρ by a draw from a uniform distribution.

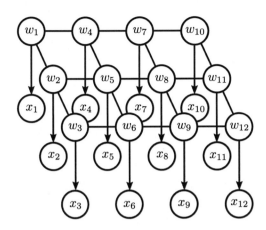

Figure 12.4 Denoising model. The observed data $\mathbf{x}_n$ at pixel n is conditionally dependent on the associated world state w_n (red directed edges). Each world state w_n has undirected edges to its four-connected neighbors (blue undirected edges). This is hence a mixed model: it contains both directed and undirected elements. Together the world states are connected in a Markov random field with cliques that consist of neighboring pairs of variables. For example variable w_5 contributes to cliques $\mathcal{C}_{25}, \mathcal{C}_{45}, \mathcal{C}_{65}, \mathcal{C}_{85}$.

We now define a prior that encourages the labels w_n to be smooth: we want them to mostly agree with the observed image, but to discourage configurations with isolated changes in label. To this end, we model the prior as a pairwise MRF. Each pair of four-connected neighboring pixels contributes one clique so that

$$Pr(w_{1...N}) = \frac{1}{Z} \exp\left[-\sum_{(m,n)\in\mathcal{C}} \psi[w_m, w_n, \boldsymbol{\theta}] \right], \tag{12.8}$$

where we have assumed that the clique costs $\psi[\bullet]$ are the same for every (w_m, w_n). The parameters $\boldsymbol{\theta}$ define the costs $\psi[\bullet]$ for each combination of neighboring pairwise values,

$$\psi[w_m = j, w_n = k, \boldsymbol{\theta}] = \theta_{jk}, \tag{12.9}$$

so when the first variable w_m in the clique takes label j and the second variable w_n takes label k we pay a price of θ_{jk}. As before, we will choose these values so that there is a small cost when neighboring labels are the same (so θ_{00} and θ_{11} are small) and a larger one when the neighboring labels differ (so θ_{01} and θ_{10} are large). This has the effect of encouraging solutions that are mostly smooth.

The associated graphical model is illustrated in Figure 12.4. It is a mixed model, containing both directed and undirected links. The likelihood terms (equation 12.7) contribute the red directed links between the observed data and the denoised image at each pixel, and the MRF prior (Equation 12.8) contributes the blue grid that connects the pixels together.

12.2 MAP inference for binary pairwise MRFs

To denoise the image, we estimate the variables $\{w_n\}_{n=1}^N$ using MAP inference; we aim to find the set of world states $\{w_n\}_{n=1}^N$ that maximizes the posterior probability

$Pr(w_{1...N}|\mathbf{x}_{1...N})$ so that

$$
\begin{aligned}
\hat{w}_{1...N} &= \underset{w_{1...N}}{\operatorname{argmax}}\left[Pr(w_{1...N}|\mathbf{x}_{1...N})\right] \\
&= \underset{w_{1...N}}{\operatorname{argmax}}\left[\prod_{n=1}^{N}Pr(x_n|w_n)Pr(w_{1...N})\right] \\
&= \underset{w_{1...N}}{\operatorname{argmax}}\left[\sum_{n=1}^{N}\log[Pr(x_n|w_n)]+\log[Pr(w_{1...N})]\right],
\end{aligned}
\tag{12.10}
$$

where we have applied Bayes' rule and transformed to the log domain. Because the prior is an MRF with pairwise connections, we can express this as

$$
\begin{aligned}
\hat{w}_{1...N} &= \underset{w_{1...N}}{\operatorname{argmax}}\left[\sum_{n=1}^{N}\log[Pr(x_n|w_n)]-\sum_{(m,n)\in\mathcal{C}}\psi[w_m,w_n,\boldsymbol{\theta}]\right] \\
&= \underset{w_{1...N}}{\operatorname{argmin}}\left[\sum_{n=1}^{N}-\log[Pr(x_n|w_n)]+\sum_{(m,n)\in\mathcal{C}}\psi[w_m,w_n,\boldsymbol{\theta}]\right] \\
&= \underset{w_{1...N}}{\operatorname{argmin}}\left[\sum_{n=1}^{N}U_n(w_n)+\sum_{(m,n)\in\mathcal{C}}P_{mn}(w_m,w_n)\right],
\end{aligned}
\tag{12.11}
$$

where $U_n(w_n)$ denotes the *unary* term at pixel n. This is a cost for observing the data at pixel n given state w_n and is the negative log-likelihood term. Similarly, $P_{mn}(w_m,w_n)$ denotes the *pairwise* term. This is a cost for placing labels w_m and w_n at neighboring locations m and n and is due to the clique costs $\psi[w_m,w_n,\boldsymbol{\theta}]$ from the MRF prior. Note that we have omitted the term $-\log[Z]$ from the MRF definition as it is constant with respect to the states $\{w_n\}_{n=1}^{N}$ and hence does not affect the optimal solution.

The cost function in Equation 12.11 can be optimized using a set of techniques known collectively as *graph cuts*. We will consider three cases:

- Binary MRFs (i.e., $w_i \in \{0,1\}$) where the costs for different combinations of adjacent labels are "submodular" (we will explain what this means later in the chapter). Exact MAP inference is tractable here.

- Multilabel MRFs (i.e., $w_i \in \{1,2,\ldots,K\}$) where the costs are "submodular." Once more, exact MAP inference is possible.

- Multilabel MRFs where the costs are more general. Exact MAP inference is intractable, but good approximate solutions can be found in some cases.

To solve these MAP inference tasks, we will translate them into the form of *maximum flow* (or *max-flow*) problems. Max-flow problems are well-studied, and exact polynomial time algorithms exist. In the following section, we describe the max-flow problem and its solution. In subsequent parts of the chapter, we describe how to translate MAP inference in Markov random fields into a max-flow problem.

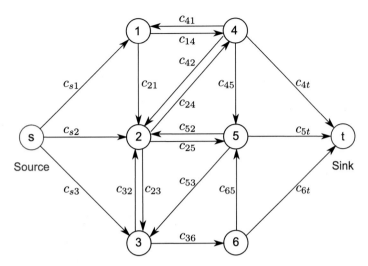

Figure 12.5 Max-flow problem: we are given a network of vertices connected by directed edges, each of which has a nonnegative capacity c_{mn}. There are two special vertices s and t termed the source and sink, respectively. In the max-flow problem, we seek to push as much 'flow' from source to sink while respecting the capacities of the edges.

12.2.1   Max-flow/Min-cut

Consider a graph $\mathbf{G} = (\mathcal{V}, \mathcal{E})$ with vertices $\mathcal{V}$ and directed edges $\mathcal{E}$ connecting them (Figure 12.5). Each edge has a nonnegative *capacity* so that the edge between vertices m and n has capacity c_{mn}. Two of the vertices are treated as special and are termed the *source* and the *sink*.

Consider transferring some quantity ("flow") through the network from the source to the sink. The goal of the max-flow algorithm is to compute the maximum amount of flow that can be transferred across the network without exceeding any of the edge capacities.

When the maximum possible flow is being transferred – the so-called *max-flow* solution – every path from source to sink must include a saturated edge (one where the capacity is reached). If not, then we could push more flow down this path, and so by definition this is not the maximum flow solution.

It follows that an alternate way to think about the problem is to consider the edges that saturate. We define a *cut* on the graph to be a minimal set of edges that separate the source from the sink. In other words, when these edges are removed, there is no path from the source to the sink. More precisely, a cut partitions the vertices into two groups: vertices that can be reached by some path from the source, but cannot reach the sink, and vertices that cannot be reached from the source, but can reach the sink via some path. For short, we will refer to a cut as "separating" the source from the sink. Every cut is given an associated cost, which is the sum of the capacities of the excised edges.

Since the saturated edges in the max-flow solution separate the source from the sink, they form a cut. In fact, this particular choice of cut has the minimum possible cost and is referred to as the *min-cut* solution. Hence, the maximum flow and minimum cut problems can be considered interchangeably.

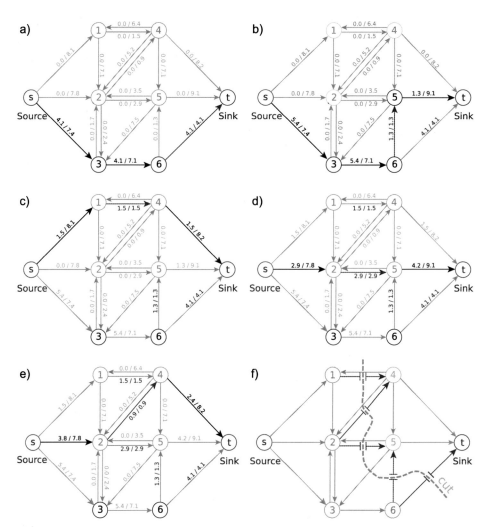

Figure 12.6 Augmenting paths algorithm for max-flow. The numbers attached to the edges correspond to current flow/capacity. a) We choose any path from source to sink with spare capacity and push as much flow as possible along this path. The edge with the smallest capacity (here edge 6-t) saturates. b) We then choose another path where there is still spare capacity and push as much flow as possible. Now edge 6-5 saturates. c–e) We repeat this until there is no path from source to sink that does not contain a saturated edge. The total flow pushed is the maximum flow. f) In the min-cut problem, we seek a set of edges that separate the source from the sink and have minimal total capacity. The min-cut (dashed line) consists of the saturated edges in the max-flow problem. In this example, the paths were chosen arbitrarily, but to ensure that this algorithm converges in the general case, we should choose the remaining path with the greatest capacity at each step.

Augmenting paths algorithm for maximum flow

There are many algorithms to compute the maximum flow, and to describe them properly is beyond the scope of this volume. However, for completeness, we present a sketch of the *augmenting paths* algorithm (Figure 12.6).

Consider choosing any path from the source to the sink and pushing the maximum possible amount of flow along it. This flow will be limited by the edge on that path that has the smallest capacity that will duly saturate. We remove this amount of flow from the capacities of all of the edges along the path, causing the saturated edge to have a new capacity of zero. We repeat this procedure, finding a second path from source to sink, pushing as much flow as possible along it and updating the capacities. We continue this process until there is no path from source to sink without at least one saturated edge. The total flow that we have transferred is the maximum flow, and the saturated edges form the minimum cut.

In the full algorithm, there are some extra complications: for example, if there is already some flow along edge $i-j$, it may be that there is a remaining path from source to sink that includes the edge $j-i$. In this situation, we reduce the flow in $i-j$ before adding flow to $j-i$. The reader should consult a specialized text on graph-based algorithms for more details.

If we choose the path with the greatest remaining capacity at each step, the algorithm is guaranteed to converge and has complexity $O(|\mathcal{E}|^2|\mathcal{V}|)$ where $|\mathcal{E}|$ is the number of edges and $|\mathcal{V}|$ the number of vertices in the graph. From now on we will assume that the max-flow/min-cut problem can be solved and concentrate on how to convert MAP estimation problems with MRFs into this form.

12.2.2   MAP inference: binary variables

Recall that to find the MAP solution we must find

$$\hat{w}_{1...N} = \underset{w_{1...N}}{\mathrm{argmin}} \left[\sum_{n=1}^{N} U_n(w_n) + \sum_{(m,n)\in\mathcal{C}} P_{mn}(w_m,w_n) \right], \qquad (12.12)$$

where $U_n(w_n)$ denotes the *unary* term and $P_{mn}(w_m,w_n)$ denotes the *pairwise* term.

For pedagogical reasons, we will first consider cases where the unary terms are positive and the pairwise terms have the following zero-diagonal form

$$P_{mn}(0,0) = 0 \qquad\qquad P_{mn}(1,0) = \theta_{10}$$
$$P_{mn}(0,1) = \theta_{01} \qquad\qquad P_{mn}(1,1) = 0,$$

where $\theta_{01}, \theta_{10} > 0$. We discuss the more general case later in this section.

The key idea will be to set up a directed graph $\mathcal{G} = \{\mathcal{V}, \mathcal{E}\}$ and attach weights to the edges, so that the minimum cut on this graph corresponds to the maximum a posteriori solution. In particular, we construct a graph with one vertex per pixel, and a pair of directed edges between adjacent vertices in the pixel grid. In addition, there is a directed edge from the source to every vertex and a directed edge from every vertex to the sink (Figure 12.7).

Now consider a cut on the graph. In any cut we must either remove the edge that connects the source to a pixel vertex, or the edge that connects the pixel vertex to the sink, or both. If we do not do this, then there will still be a path from source to sink and it is not a valid cut. For the minimum cut, we will never cut both (assuming the general case where the two edges have different capacities) – this is unnecessary and will inevitably incur a greater cost than cutting one or the other. We will label pixels where the edge to the source was cut as $w_n = 0$ and pixels where the edge to the sink was

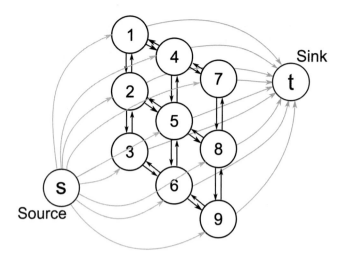

Figure 12.7 Graph structure for finding MAP solution for a MRF with binary labels and pairwise connections in a 3×3 image. There is one vertex per pixel, and neighbors in the pixel grid are connected by reciprocal pairs of directed edges. Each pixel vertex receives a connection from the source and sends a connection to the sink. To separate source from sink, the cut must include one of these two edges for each vertex. The choice of which edge is cut will determine which of two labels is assigned to the pixel.

cut as having label $w_n = 1$. So each plausible minimum cut is associated with a pixel labeling.

Our goal is now to assign capacities to the edges, so the cost of each cut matches the cost of the associated labeling as prescribed in Equation 12.12. For simplicity, we illustrate this with a 1D image with three pixels (Figure 12.8), but we stress that all the ideas are also valid for 2D images and higher dimensional constructions.

We attach the unary costs $U_n(0)$ and $U_n(1)$ to the edges from the pixel to the source and sink, respectively. If we cut the edge from the source to a given pixel (and hence assign $w_n = 0$), we pay the cost $U_n(0)$. Conversely, if we cut the edge from the pixel to the sink (and hence assign $w_n = 1$), we pay the cost $U_n(1)$.

We attach the pairwise costs $P_{mn}(1,0)$ and $P_{mn}(0,1)$ to the pairs of edges between adjacent pixels. Now if one pixel is attached to the source and the other to the sink, we pay either $P_{mn}(0,1) = \theta_{01}$ or $P_{mn}(1,0) = \theta_{10}$ as appropriate to separate source from sink. The cuts corresponding to all eight possible configurations of the three-pixel model and their costs are illustrated in Figure 12.9.

Any cut on the graph in which each pixel is either separated from the source or the sink now has the appropriate cost from Equation 12.12. It follows that the minimum cut on this graph will have the minimum cost and the associated labeling $w_{1...N}$ will correspond to the maximum a posteriori solution.

General pairwise costs

Now let us consider how to use the more general pairwise costs:

$$
\begin{aligned}
P_{mn}(0,0) &= \theta_{00} & P_{mn}(1,0) &= \theta_{10} \\
P_{mn}(0,1) &= \theta_{01} & P_{mn}(1,1) &= \theta_{11}.
\end{aligned}
\tag{12.13}
$$

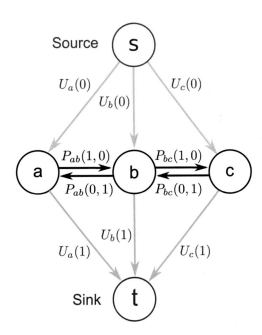

Figure 12.8 Graph construction for binary MRF with diagonal pairwise terms using simple 1D example. After the cut, vertices attached to the source are given label 1 and vertices attached to the sink are given label 0. We hence attach the appropriate unary costs to the links between the sink/source and the pixel vertices. The pairwise costs are attached to the horizontal links between pixels as shown. This arrangement ensures that the correct cost is paid for each of the eight possible solutions (Figure 12.9).

To illustrate this, we use an even simpler graph with only two pixels (Figure 12.10). Notice that we have added the pairwise cost $P_{ab}(0,0)$ to the edge $s - b$. We will have to pay this cost appropriately in the configuration where $w_a = 0$ and $w_b = 0$. Unfortunately, we would also pay it in the case where $w_a = 1$ and $w_b = 0$. Hence, we subtract the same cost from the edge $a - b$, which must also be cut in this solution. By a similar logic, we add $P_{ab}(1,1)$ to the edge $a - t$ and subtract it from edge $a - b$. In this way, we associate the correct costs with each labeling.

Reparameterization

The preceding discussion assumed that the edge costs are all nonnegative and can be valid capacities in the max-flow problem. If they are not, then it is not possible to compute the MAP solution. Unfortunately, it is often the case that they are negative; even if the original unary and pairwise terms were positive, the edge $a - b$ in Figure 12.10 with cost $P_{ab}(1,0) - P_{ab}(1,1) - P_{ab}(0,0)$ could be negative. The solution to this problem is *reparameterization*.

The goal of reparameterization is to modify the costs associated with the edges in the graph in such a way that the MAP solution is not changed. In particular, we will adjust the edge capacities so that every possible solution has a constant cost added to it. This does not change which solution has the minimum cost, and so the MAP labeling will be unchanged.

We consider two reparameterizations (Figure 12.11). First, consider adding a constant cost α to the edge from a given pixel to the source and the edge from the same pixel to the sink. Since any solution cuts exactly one of these edges, the overall cost of every solution increases by α. We can use this to ensure that none of the edges connecting the pixels to the source and sink have negative costs: we simply add a sufficiently large positive value α to make them all nonnegative.

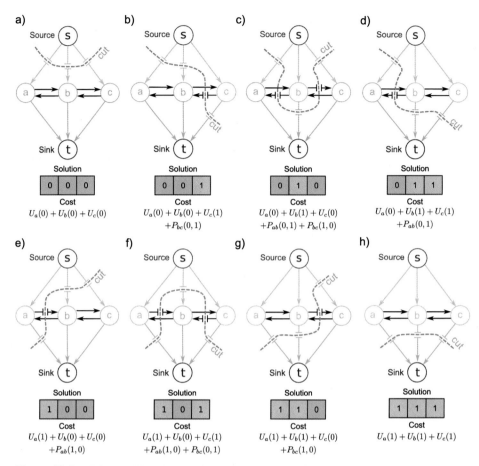

Figure 12.9 Eight possible solutions for the three-pixel example. When we set the costs as in Figure 12.8, each solution has the appropriate cost. a) For example, the solution $(a = 0, b = 0, c = 0)$ requires us to cut edges $s - a$, $s - b$, $s - c$ and pay the cost $U_a(0) + U_b(0) + U_c(0)$. b) For the solution $(a = 0, b = 0, c = 1)$ we must cut edges $s - a$, $s - b$, $c - t$, and $c - b$ (to prevent flow through the path $s - c - b - t$). This incurs a total cost of $U_a(0) + U_b(0) + U_c(1) + P_{bc}(0, 1)$. c) Similarly, in this example with $(a = 0, b = 1, c = 0)$, we pay the appropriate cost $U_a(0) + U_b(1) + U_c(0) + P_{ab}(0, 1) + P_{bc}(1, 0)$. d–h) The other five possible configurations.

A more subtle type of reparameterization is illustrated in Figure 12.11c. By changing the costs in this way, we increase the cost of each possible solution by β. For example, in the assignment $(w_a = 0, w_b = 1)$, we must cut the links $s - a$, $b - a$, and $b - t$ giving a total cost of $U_a(0) + U_b(1) + P_{ab}(0, 1) + \beta$.

Applying the reparameterization in Figure 12.11c to the general construction in Figure 2.10, we must ensure that the capacities on edges between pixel nodes are nonnegative so that

$$\theta_{10} - \theta_{11} - \theta_{00} - \beta \geq 0 \tag{12.14}$$

$$\theta_{01} + \beta \geq 0. \tag{12.15}$$

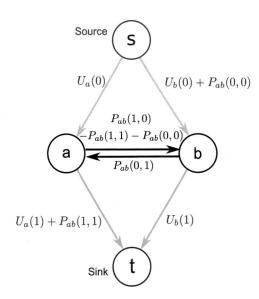

Figure 12.10 Graph structure for general (i.e., non-diagonal) pairwise costs. Consider the solution $(a = 0, b = 0)$. We must break the edges $s - a$ and $s - b$ giving a total cost of $U_a(0) + U_b(0) + P_{ab}(0, 0)$. For the solution $(a = 1, b = 0)$, we must break the edges $a - t, a - b$, and $s - b$ giving a total cost of $U_a(1) + U_b(0) + P_{ab}(1, 0)$. Similarly, the cuts corresponding to the solutions $(a = 0, b = 1)$ and $(a = 1, b = 1)$ on this graph have pairwise costs $P_{ab}(0, 1)$ and $P_{ab}(1, 1)$, respectively.

Adding these equations together, we can eliminate β to get a single inequality

$$\theta_{01} + \theta_{10} - \theta_{11} - \theta_{00} \geq 0. \tag{12.16}$$

If this condition holds, the problem is termed *submodular*, and the graph can be reparameterized to have only nonnegative costs. It can then be solved in polynomial time using the max-flow algorithm. If the condition does not hold, then this approach cannot be used, and in general the problem is NP hard. Fortunately, the former case is common for vision problems; we generally favor smooth solutions where neighboring labels are the same and hence the costs θ_{01}, θ_{10} for labels differing are naturally greater than the costs θ_{00}, θ_{11} for the labels agreeing.

Figure 12.12 shows the MAP solutions to the binary denoising problem with an MRF prior as we increase the strength of the cost for having adjacent labels that differ. Here we have assumed that the costs for adjacent labels being different are the same ($\theta_{01} = \theta_{10}$) and that there is no cost when neighboring labels are the same ($\theta_{00}, \theta_{11} = 0$); we are in the "zero-diagonal" regimen. When the MRF costs are small, the solution is dominated by the unary terms and the MAP solution looks like the noisy image. As the costs increase, the solution ceases to tolerate isolated regions, and most of the noise is removed. When the costs become larger, details such as the center of the "0" in "10" are lost and eventually nearby regions are connected together. With very high pairwise costs, the MAP solution is a uniform field of labels: the overall cost is dominated by the pairwise terms from the MRF and the unary terms merely determine the polarity.

12.3   **MAP inference for multilabel pairwise MRFs**

We now investigate MAP inference using MRF priors with pairwise connections when the world state w_n at each pixel can take multiple labels $\{1, 2, \ldots, K\}$. To solve the multilabel problem, we change the graph construction (Figure 12.13a). With K labels and N pixels, we introduce $(K+1)N$ vertices into the graph.

For each pixel, the $K + 1$ associated vertices are stacked. The top and bottom of the stack are connected to the source and sink by edges with infinite capacity. Between the

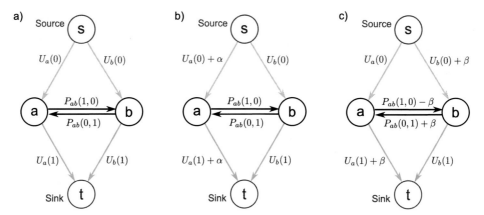

Figure 12.11 Reparameterization. a) Original graph construction. b) Reparameterization 1. Adding a constant cost α to the connections from a pixel vertex to both the source and sink results in a problem with the same MAP solution. Since we must cut either, but not both of these edges, every solution increases in cost by α, and the minimum cost solution remains the same. c) Reparameterization 2. Manipulating the edge capacities in this way results in a constant β being added to every solution and so the choice of minimum cost solution is unaffected.

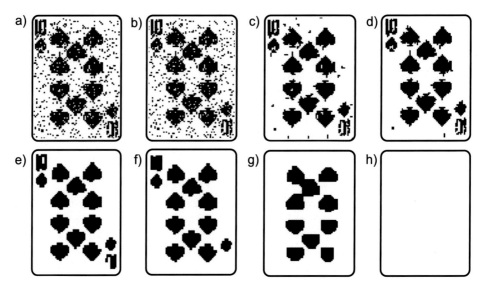

Figure 12.12 Denoising results. a) Observed noisy image. b–h) Maximum a posteriori solution as we increase zero-diagonal pairwise costs. When the pairwise costs are low, the unary terms dominate and the MAP solution is the same as the observed image. As the pairwise costs increase, the image gets more and more smooth until eventually it becomes uniform.

$K+1$ vertices in the stack are K edges forming a path from source to sink. These edges are associated with the K unary costs $U_n(1)\ldots U_n(K)$. To separate the source from the sink, we must cut at least one of the K edges in this chain. We will interpret a cut at the kth edge in this chain as indicating that the pixel takes label k and this incurs the appropriate cost of $U_n(k)$.

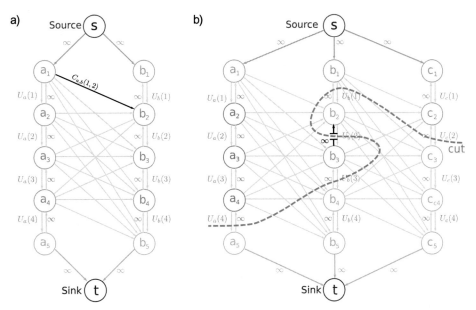

Figure 12.13 a) Graph setup for multilabel case for two pixels (a, b) and four labels $(1, 2, 3, 4)$. There is a chain of five vertices associated with each pixel. The four vertical edges between these vertices are assigned the unary costs for the four labels. The minimum cut must break this chain to separate source from sink, and the label is assigned according to where the chain is broken. Vertical constraint edges of infinite capacity run between the four vertices in the opposite direction. There are also diagonal edges between the ith vertex of pixel a and the jth vertex of pixel b with assigned costs $C_{ab}(i, j)$ (see text). b) The vertical constraint edges prevent solutions like this example with three pixels. Here, the chain of vertices associated with the central pixel is cut in more than one place and so the labeling has no clear interpretation. However, for this to happen a constraint link must be cut and hence this solution has an infinite cost.

To ensure that only a single edge from the chain is part of the minimum cut (and hence that each cut corresponds to one valid labeling), we add *constraint edges*. These are edges of infinite capacity that are strategically placed to prevent certain cuts occurring. In this case, the constraint edges connect the vertices backwards along each chain. Any cut that crosses the chain more than once must cut one of these edges and will never be the minimum cut solution (Figure 12.13b).

In Figure 12.13a, there are also diagonal interpixel edges from the vertices associated with pixel a to those associated with pixel b. These are assigned costs $C_{ab}(i, j)$, where i indexes the vertex associated with pixel a and j indexes the vertex associated with pixel b. We choose the edge costs to be

$$C_{ab}(i, j) = P_{ab}(i, j-1) + P_{ab}(i-1, j) - P_{ab}(i, j) - P_{ab}(i-1, j-1), \quad (12.17)$$

where we define any superfluous pairwise costs associated with the nonexistent labels 0 or $K+1$ to be zero, so that

$$P_{ab}(i, 0) = 0 \quad P_{ab}(i, K+1) = 0 \quad \forall \ i \in \{0 \ldots K+1\}$$
$$P_{ab}(0, j) = 0 \quad P_{ab}(K+1, j) = 0 \quad \forall \ j \in \{0 \ldots K+1\}. \quad (12.18)$$

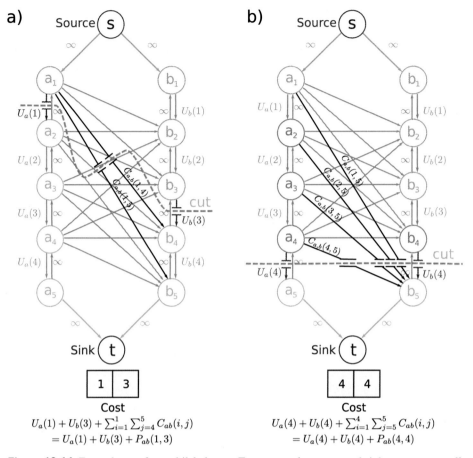

Figure 12.14 Example cuts for multilabel case. To separate the source and sink, we must cut all of the links that pass from above the chosen label for pixel a to below the chosen label for pixel b. a) Pixel a is set to label 1 and pixel b is set to label 3 meaning we must cut the links from vertex a_1 to nodes b_4 and b_5. b) Pixel a takes label 4 and pixel b takes label 4.

When label I is assigned to pixel a and label J to pixel b, we must cut all of the links from vertices $a_1 \ldots a_I$ to the vertices $b_{J+1} \ldots b_{K+1}$ to separate the source from the sink (Figure 12.14). So, the total cost due to the interpixel edges for assigning label I to pixel a and label J to pixel b is

$$\sum_{i=1}^{I}\sum_{j=J+1}^{K+1} C_{ab}(i,j) = \sum_{i=1}^{I}\sum_{j=J+1}^{K+1} P_{ab}(i,j-1)+P_{ab}(i-1,j)-P_{ab}(i,j)-P_{ab}(i-1,j-1)$$
$$= P_{ab}(I,J)+P_{ab}(0,J)-P_{ab}(I,K+1)-P_{ab}(0,K+1)$$
$$= P_{ab}(I,J). \tag{12.19}$$

Adding the unary terms, the total cost is $U_a(I)+U_b(J)+P_{ab}(I,J)$ as required.

Once more, we have implicitly made the assumption that the costs associated with edges are nonnegative. If the vertical (intrapixel) edge terms have negative costs, it is

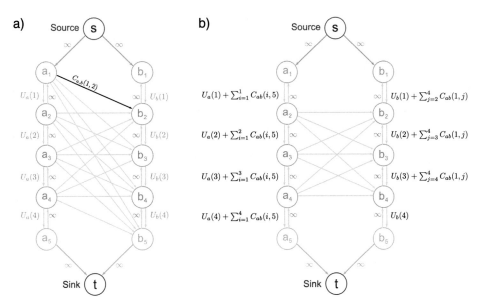

Figure 12.15 Reparameterization for multilabel graph cuts. The original construction (a) is equivalent to construction (b). The label at pixel b determines which edges that leave node a_1 are cut. Hence, we can remove these edges and add the extra costs to the vertical links associated with pixel b. Similarly, the costs of the edges passing into node b_5 can be added to the vertical edges associated with pixel a. If any of the resulting vertical edges associated with a pixel are negative, we can add a constant α to each: since exactly one is broken, the total cost increases by α, but the MAP solution remains the same.

possible to reparameterize the graph by adding a constant α to all of the unary terms. Since the final cost includes exactly one unary term per pixel, every possible solution increases by α and the MAP solution is unaffected.

The diagonal interpixel edges are more problematic. It is possible to remove the edges that leave node a_1 and the edges that arrive at b_{K+1} by adding terms to the intrapixel edges associated with the unary terms (Figure 12.15). These intrapixel edges can then be reparameterized as described above if necessary. Unfortunately, we can neither remove nor reparameterize the remaining interpixel edges so we require that

$$C_{ab}(i,j) = P_{ab}(i,j-1) + P_{ab}(i-1,j) - P_{ab}(i,j) - P_{ab}(i-1,j-1) \geq 0. \quad (12.20)$$

By mathematical induction, we get the more general result (Figure 12.16),

$$P_{ab}(\beta,\gamma) + P_{ab}(\alpha,\delta) - P_{ab}(\beta,\delta) - P_{ab}(\alpha,\gamma) \geq 0, \quad (12.21)$$

where $\alpha, \beta, \gamma, \delta$ are any four values of the state y such that $\beta > \alpha$ and $\delta > \gamma$. This is the multilabel generalization of the submodularity condition (Equation 12.16). An important class of pairwise costs that are submodular are those that are convex in the absolute difference $|w_i - w_j|$ between the labels at adjacent pixels (Figure 12.17a). Here, smoothness is encouraged; the penalty becomes increasingly stringent as the jumps between labels increase.

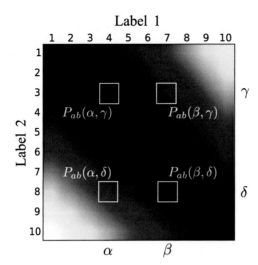

Figure 12.16 Submodularity constraint for multilabel case. Color at position (m,n) indicates pairwise costs $P_{ab}(m,n)$. For all edges in the graph to be positive, we require that the pairwise terms obey $P_{ab}(\beta,\gamma) + P_{ab}(\alpha,\delta) - P_{ab}(\beta,\delta) - P_{ab}(\alpha,\gamma) \geq 0$ for all $\alpha,\beta,\gamma,\delta$ such that $\beta > \alpha$ and $\delta > \gamma$. In other words, for any four positions arranged in a square configuration as in the figure, the sum of the two costs on the diagonal from top-left to bottom-right must be less than the sum on the off diagonal. If this condition holds, the problem can be solved in polynomial time.

12.4 Multilabel MRFs with non-convex potentials

Unfortunately, convex potentials are not always appropriate. For example, in the denoising task we might expect the image to be piecewise smooth: there are smooth regions (corresponding to objects) followed by abrupt jumps (corresponding to the boundaries between objects). A convex potential function cannot describe this situation because it penalizes large jumps much more than smaller ones. The result is that the MAP solution smooths over the sharp edges changing the label by several smaller amounts rather than one large jump (Figure 12.18).

To solve this problem, we need to work with interactions that are non-convex in the absolute label difference, such as the truncated quadratic function or the Potts model (Figures 12.17b–c). These favor small changes in the label and penalize large changes equally or nearly equally. This reflects the fact that the exact size of an abrupt jump in label is relatively unimportant. Unfortunately, these pairwise costs do not satisfy the submodularity constraint (Equation 12.21). Here, the MAP solution cannot in general be found exactly with the method described previously, and the problem is NP-hard. Fortunately, there are good approximate methods for optimizing such problems, one of which is the alpha-expansion algorithm.

12.4.1 Inference: alpha-expansion

The *alpha-expansion* algorithm works by breaking the solution down into a series of binary problems, each of which can be solved exactly. At each iteration, we choose one label value α, and for each pixel we consider either retaining the current label, or switching it to α. The name "alpha-expansion" derives from the fact that the space occupied by label α in the solution expands at each iteration (Figure 12.19). The process is iterated until no choice of α causes any change. Each expansion move is guaranteed to lower the overall objective function, although the final result is not guaranteed to be the global minimum.

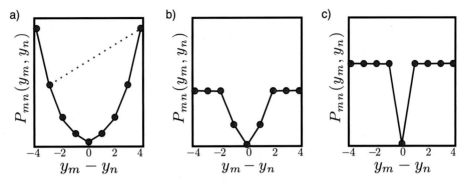

Figure 12.17 Convex vs. non-convex potentials. The method for MAP inference for multivalued variables depends on whether the costs are a convex or non-convex function of the difference in labels. a) Quadratic function (convex), $P_{mn}(w_m, w_n) = \kappa(w_m - w_n)^2$. For convex functions, it is possible to draw a chord between any two points on the function without intersecting the function elsewhere (e.g., dotted blue line). b) Truncated quadratic function (non-convex), $P_{mn}(w_m, w_n) = \min(\kappa_1, \kappa_2(w_m - w_n)^2)$. c) Potts model (non-convex), $P_{mn}(w_m, w_n) = \kappa(1 - \delta(w_m - w_n))$.

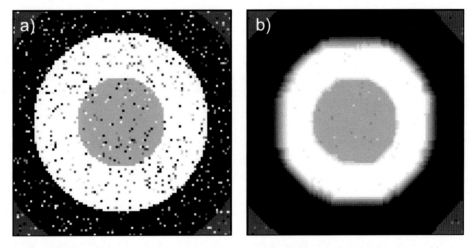

Figure 12.18 Denoising results with convex (quadratic) pairwise costs. a) Noisy observed image. b) Denoised image has artifacts where there are large intensity changes in the original image. Convex costs imply that there is a lower cost for a number of small changes rather than a single large one.

For the alpha-expansion algorithm to work, we require that the edge costs form a metric. In other words, we require that

$$P(\alpha, \beta) = 0 \Leftrightarrow \alpha = \beta$$
$$P(\alpha, \beta) = P(\beta, \alpha) \geq 0$$
$$P(\alpha, \beta) \leq P(\alpha, \gamma) + P(\gamma, \beta). \tag{12.22}$$

These assumptions are reasonable for many applications in vision, and allow us to model non-convex priors.

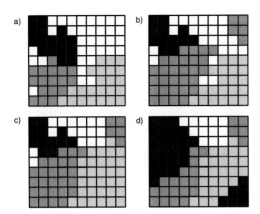

Figure 12.19 The alpha-expansion algorithm breaks the problem down into a series of binary subproblems. At each step, we choose a label α and we *expand*: for each pixel we either leave the label as it is or replace it with α. This subproblem is solved in such a way that it is guaranteed to decrease the multilabel cost function. a) Initial labeling. b) Orange label is expanded: each label stays the same or becomes orange. c) Yellow label is expanded. d) Red label is expanded.

In the alpha-expansion graph construction (Figure 12.20), there is one vertex associated with each pixel. Each of these vertices is connected to the source (representing keeping the original label or $\overline{\alpha}$) and the sink (representing the label α). To separate source from sink, we must cut one of these two edges at each pixel. The choice of edge will determine whether we keep the original label or set it to α. Accordingly, we associate the unary costs for each edge being set to α or its original label with the two links from each pixel. If the pixel already has label α, then we set the cost of being set to $\overline{\alpha}$ to ∞.

The remaining structure of the graph is dynamic: it changes at each iteration depending on the choice of α and the current labels. There are four possible relationships between adjacent pixels:

- Pixel i has label α and the pixel j has label α. Here, the final configuration is inevitably $\alpha-\alpha$, and so the pairwise cost is zero and there is no need to add further edges connecting nodes i and j in the graph. Pixels a and b in Figure 12.20 have this relationship.

- The first pixel has label α but the second pixel has a different label β. Here the final solution may be $\alpha-\alpha$ with zero cost or $\alpha-\beta$ with pairwise cost $P_{ij}(\alpha,\beta)$. Here we add a single edge connecting pixel j to pixel i with pairwise cost $P_{ij}(\alpha,\beta)$. Pixels b and c in Figure 12.20 have this relationship.

- Both pixels i and j have the same label β. Here the final solution may be $\alpha-\alpha$ with zero pairwise cost, $\beta-\beta$ with zero pairwise cost, $\alpha-\beta$ with pairwise cost $P_{ij}(\alpha,\beta)$ or $\beta-\alpha$ with pairwise cost $P_{ij}(\beta,\alpha)$. We add two edges between the pixels representing the two nonzero pairwise costs. Pixels c and d in Figure 12.20 have this relationship.

- Pixel i has label β and pixel j has a second label γ. Here the final solution may be $\alpha-\alpha$ with zero pairwise cost, $\beta-\gamma$ with pairwise cost $P_{ij}(\beta,\gamma)$, $\beta-\alpha$ with pairwise cost $P_{ij}(\beta,\alpha)$, or $\alpha-\gamma$ with pairwise cost $P_{ij}(\alpha,\gamma)$. We add a new vertex k between vertices i and j and add the three nonzero pairwise costs to edges $k-\alpha$, $i-k$, and $j-k$, respectively. Pixels d and e in Figure 12.20 have this relationship.

Three example cuts are shown in Figure 12.21.

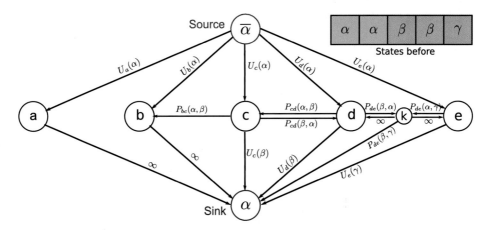

Figure 12.20 Alpha-expansion graph setup. Each pixel node (a,b,c,d,e) is connected to the source and the sink by edges with costs $U_\bullet(\overline{\alpha})$ and $U_\bullet(\alpha)$, respectively. In the minimum cut, exactly one of these links will be cut. The nodes and vertices describing the relationship between neighboring pixels depend on their current labels, which may be $\alpha-\alpha$ as for pixels a and b, $\alpha-\beta$ as for pixels b and c, $\beta-\beta$ as for pixels c and d or $\beta-\gamma$ as for pixels d and e. For the last case, an auxiliary node k must be added to the graph.

Note that this construction critically relies on the triangle inequality (Equation 12.22). For example, consider pixels d and e in Figure 12.21a. If the triangle inequality does not hold so that $P_{de}(\beta,\gamma) > P_{de}(\beta,\alpha) + P_{de}(\alpha,\gamma)$, then the wrong costs will be assigned; rather than the link $k-\alpha$, the two links $d-k$ and $e-k$ will both be cut, and the wrong cost will be used. In practice, it is sometimes possible to ignore this constraint by *truncating* the offending cost $P_{ij}(\beta,\gamma)$ and running the algorithm as normal. After the cut is done, the true objective function (sum of the unary and pairwise costs) can be computed for the new label map and the answer accepted if the cost has decreased.

It should be emphasized that although each step optimally updates the objective function with respect to expanding α, this algorithm is not guaranteed to converge to the overall global minimum. However, it can be proven that the result is within a factor of two of the minimum and often it behaves much better.

Figure 12.22 shows an example of multilabel denoising using the alpha-expansion algorithm. On each iteration, one of the labels is chosen and expanded, and the appropriate region is denoised. Sometimes the label is not supported at all by the unary costs and nothing happens. The algorithm terminates when no choice of α causes any further change.

12.5   Conditional random fields

In the models presented in this chapter, the Markov random fields have described the prior $Pr(\mathbf{w})$ in a generative model of the image data. We could alternatively describe the joint probability distribution $Pr(\mathbf{w},\mathbf{x})$ with the undirected model

$$Pr(\mathbf{w},\mathbf{x}) = \frac{1}{Z}\exp\left[-\sum_c \psi_C[\mathbf{w}] - \sum_d \zeta[\mathbf{w},\mathbf{x}]\right], \qquad (12.23)$$

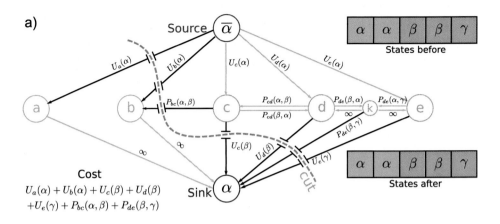

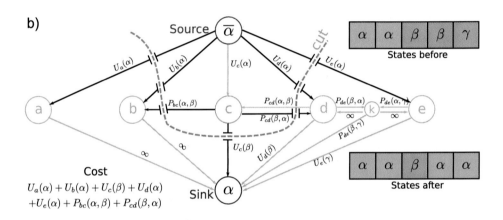

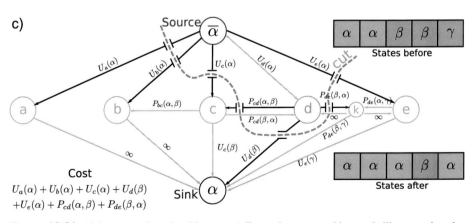

Figure 12.21 Alpha-expansion algorithm. a–c) Example cuts on this graph illustrate that the appropriate unary and pairwise costs are always paid.

Figure 12.22 Alpha-expansion algorithm for denoising task. a) Observed noisy image. b) Label 1 (black) is expanded, removing noise from the hair. c-f) Subsequent iterations in which the labels corresponding to the boots, trousers, skin and background are expanded, respectively.

where the functions $\psi[\bullet]$ encourage certain configurations of the label field and the functions $\zeta[\bullet, \bullet]$ encourage agreement between the data and the label field. If we now condition on the data (i.e., assume that it is fixed), then we can use the relation $Pr(\mathbf{w}|\mathbf{x}) \propto Pr(\mathbf{w}, \mathbf{x})$ to write

$$Pr(\mathbf{w}|\mathbf{x}) = \frac{1}{Z_2} \exp \left[-\sum_c \psi_C[\mathbf{w}] - \sum_d \zeta[\mathbf{w}, \mathbf{x}] \right], \qquad (12.24)$$

where $Z_2 = Z Pr(\mathbf{x})$. This discriminative model is known as a *conditional random field* or *CRF*.

We can choose the functions $\zeta[\bullet, \bullet]$ so that they each determine the compatibility of one label w_n to its associated measurement x_n. If the functions $\psi[\bullet]$ are used to encourage smoothness between neighboring labels, then the negative log posterior probability will again be the sum of unary and pairwise terms. The maximum a posteriori labels $\hat{\mathbf{w}}$

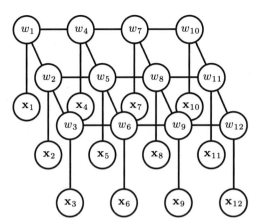

Figure 12.23 Graphical model for conditional random field (compare to Figure 12.4). The posterior probability of the labels **w** is a Markov random field for fixed data **x**. In this model, the two sets of cliques relate (i) neighboring labels and (ii) each label to its associated measurement. Since this model only includes unary and pairwise interactions between the labels, the unknown labels $\{w_n\}_{n=1}^{N}$ can be optimized using graph cut techniques.

can hence be found by minimizing a cost function of the form

$$\hat{\mathbf{w}} = \underset{w_{1\ldots N}}{\operatorname{argmin}} \left[\sum_{n=1}^{N} U_n(w_n) + \sum_{(m,n) \in \mathcal{C}} P_{mn}(w_m, w_n) \right], \qquad (12.25)$$

and the graphical model will be as in Figure 12.23. This cost function can be minimized using the graph cuts techniques described throughout this chapter.

12.6 Higher order models

The models that we have discussed so far have only connected immediate neighbors. However, these only allow us to model relatively simple statistical properties of the label field. One way to improve this situation is to consider each variable $w_n \in \{1 \ldots K\}$ as representing the index of a square patch of labels from a predefined library. The pairwise MRF now encodes the affinity of neighboring patches for each other. Unfortunately, the resulting costs are less likely to be submodular, or even obey the triangle inequality, and the number K of patches in the library is usually very large, making graph cut algorithms inefficient.

A second approach to modeling more complex statistical properties of the label field is to increase the number of the connections. For the undirected models (CRF, MRF) this would mean introducing larger cliques. For example, to model local texture, we might connect all of the variables in every 5×5 region of the image. Unfortunately, inference is hard in these models; optimizing the resulting complex cost functions is still an open research topic.

12.7 Directed models for grids

The Markov random field and conditional random field models are attractive because we can use graph-cuts approaches to search for the MAP solution. However, they have the drawback that it is very hard to learn the parameters of the model because they are based on undirected models. An obvious alternative is to use a similar directed model (Figure 12.24). Here, learning is relatively easy, but it turns out that MAP inference using graph cuts is not generally possible.

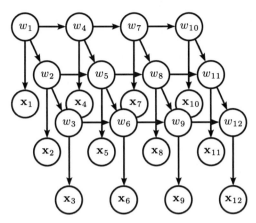

Figure 12.24 Directed graphical model for grid. Although this model appears similar to the pairwise Markov random field model, it represents a different factorization of the joint probability. In particular the factorization contains terms involving three variables such as $Pr(w_5|w_2, w_4)$. This means that the resulting cost function for MAP inference is no longer amenable to exact solution using graph-cut methods. In this case, an attractive alternative is to use sampling based methods as it is easy to generate samples from this directed model.

To see this, consider the cost function for MAP inference in this model,

$$\hat{w}_{1...N} = \underset{w_{1...N}}{\operatorname{argmax}} \left[\log[Pr(\mathbf{x}_{1...N}|w_{1...N})] + \log[Pr(w_{1...N})] \right] \tag{12.26}$$

$$= \underset{w_{1...N}}{\operatorname{argmax}} \left[\sum_{n=1}^{N} \log[Pr(\mathbf{x}_n|w_n)] + \sum_{n=1}^{N} \log[Pr(w_n|w_{pa[n]})] \right]$$

$$= \underset{w_{1...N}}{\operatorname{argmin}} \left[\sum_{n=1}^{N} -\log[Pr(\mathbf{x}_n|w_n)] - \sum_{n=1}^{N} \log[Pr(w_n|w_{pa[n]})] \right],$$

where we have multiplied the objective function by minus one and now seek the minimum. This minimization problem now has the general form

$$\hat{w}_{1...N} = \underset{w_{1...N}}{\operatorname{argmin}} \left[\sum_{n=1}^{N} U_n(w_n) + \sum_{n=1}^{N} T_n(w_n, w_{pa_1[n]}, w_{pa_2[n]}) \right], \tag{12.27}$$

where $U_n(w_n)$ is called a *unary term* reflecting the fact that it only depends on a single element w_n of the label field and $T_n(w_n, w_{pa_1[n]}, w_{pa_2[n]})$ is called a *three-wise term* reflecting the fact in general the label at a pixel is conditioned on the two parents $pa_1[n]$ and $pa_2[n]$ above and to the left of the current position.

Notice that this cost function is fundamentally different from the cost function for MAP inference in a pairwise MRF (Equation 12.11): it includes three-wise terms and there is no known polynomial algorithm to optimize this criterion. However, since this model is a directed graphical model, it is easy to generate samples from this model, and this can be exploited for approximate inference methods such as computing the empirical max marginals.

12.8 Applications

The models and algorithms in this chapter are used in a large number of computer vision applications, including stereo vision, motion estimation, background subtraction, interactive segmentation, semantic segmentation, image editing, image denoising, image superresolution, and building 3D models. Here, we review a few key examples. We consider background subtraction, which is a simple application with binary labels and interactive segmentation which uses binary labels in a system that simultaneously estimates the parameters in the likelihood terms. Then we consider stereo, motion estimation, and image editing, all of which are multilabel graph cut problems. We consider superresolution which is a multilabel problem where the units are patches rather than pixels and which there are so many labels that the alpha-expansion algorithm is not suitable. Finally, we consider drawing samples from directed grid models to generate novel images.

12.8.1 Background subtraction

First, let us revisit the background subtraction algorithm that we first encountered in Section 6.6.2. In background subtraction, the goal is to associate a binary label $\{w_n\}_{n=1}^{N}$ with each of the N pixels in the image, indicating whether this pixel belongs to the foreground or background based on the observed RGB data $\{\mathbf{x}_n\}_{n=1}^{N}$ at each pixel. When the pixel is background ($w_n = 0$), the data are assumed to be generated from a normal distribution with known mean $\boldsymbol{\mu}_n$ and covariance $\boldsymbol{\Sigma}_n$. When the pixel is foreground ($w_n = 1$), a uniform distribution over the data are assumed so that

$$
\begin{aligned}
Pr(\mathbf{x}_n|w=0) &= \text{Norm}_{\mathbf{x}_n}[\boldsymbol{\mu}_n, \boldsymbol{\Sigma}_n] \\
Pr(\mathbf{x}_n|w=1) &= \kappa,
\end{aligned}
\tag{12.28}
$$

where κ is a constant.

In the original description, we assumed that the models at each pixel were independent, and when we inferred the labels, the results were noisy (Figure 12.25b). We now place a Markov random field prior over the binary labels where the pairwise cliques are organized as a grid (as in most of the models in this chapter) and where the potential functions encourage smoothness. Figure 12.25 illustrates the results of performing inference in this model using the graph-cuts algorithm. There are now far fewer isolated foreground regions and fewer holes in the foreground object. The model has still erroneously discovered the shadow; a more sophisticated model would be required to deal with this problem.

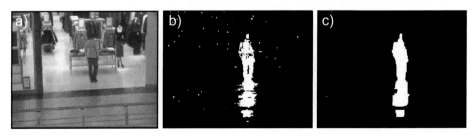

Figure 12.25 Background subtraction revisited. a) Original image. b) MAP solution of background subtraction model with independent pixels. The solution contains noise. c) MAP solution of background subtraction model with Markov random field prior. This smoothed solution has eliminated most of the noise.

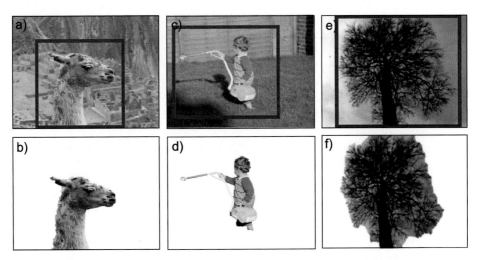

Figure 12.26 Grab Cut. a) The user draws a bounding box around the object of interest. b) The algorithm segments the foreground from the background by alternating between building color models and segmenting the image. c–d) A second example. e–f) Failure mode. This algorithm does not segment "wiry" objects well as the pairwise costs for tracing around all the boundaries are prohibitive. Adapted from Rother et al. (2005). ©2005 ACM.

12.8.2 Interactive segmentation (GrabCut)

The goal of interactive segmentation is to cut out the foreground object in a photo, based on some input from the user (Figure 12.26). More precisely, we aim to associate a binary label $\{w_n\}_{n=1}^{N}$ to each of the N pixels in the image, indicating whether this pixel belongs to the foreground or background, based on the observed RGB data $\{\mathbf{x}_n\}_{n=1}^{N}$ at each pixel. However, unlike background subtraction, we do not have any prior knowledge of either the foreground or the background.

In the GrabCut system of Rother et al. (2005) the likelihoods of observing the background ($w = 0$) and foreground ($w = 1$) are each modeled as a mixture of K Gaussians so that

$$Pr(\mathbf{x}_n|w = j) = \sum_{k=1}^{K} \lambda_{jk} \text{Norm}_{\mathbf{x}_n}[\boldsymbol{\mu}_{jk}, \boldsymbol{\Sigma}_{jk}], \tag{12.29}$$

and the prior over the labels is modeled as a pairwise connected Markov random field with the potentials chosen to encourage smoothness.

In this application, the image may have a wide variety of content, and so there is no suitable training data from which to learn the parameters $\{\boldsymbol{\lambda}_{jk}, \boldsymbol{\mu}_{jk}, \boldsymbol{\Sigma}_{jk}\}_{j=1,k=1}^{2,K}$ of the foreground and background color models. However, we note that (i) if we knew the color models, we could perform the segmentation via MAP inference with the graph cuts algorithm and (ii) if we knew the segmentation, then we could compute the foreground and background color models based on the pixels assigned to each category. This observation leads to an alternating approach to inference in this model, in which the segmentation and parameters are computed in turn until the system converges.

In the *Grabcut* algorithm, the user draws a bounding box around the desired object to be segmented. This effectively defines a rough segmentation (pixels within the box are foreground and pixels outside are background) from which the system is initialized. If the segmentation is not correct after the alternating optimization algorithm converges, the user may "paint" regions of the image with a foreground or background brush, indicating that these *must* belong to the appropriate class in the final solution. In practice, this means that the unary costs are set to ensure that these take the appropriate values, and the alternating solution is run again from this point until convergence. Example results are shown in Figure 12.26.

To improve the performance of this algorithm, it is possible to modify the MRF so that the pairwise cost for changing from foreground to background label is less where there is an edge in the image. This is referred to as using *geodesic distance*. From a pure probabilistic viewpoint, this is somewhat dubious as the MRF prior should embody what we know about the task before seeing the data, and hence cannot depend on the image. However, this is largely a philosophical objection, and the method works well in practice for a wide variety of objects. A notable failure mode is in segmenting "wiry" objects such as trees. Here, the model is not prepared to pay the extensive pairwise costs to cut exactly around the many edges of the object and so the segmentation is poor.

12.8.3 Stereo vision

In stereo vision, the goal is to infer a discrete multivalued label $\{w_n\}_{n=1}^N$ representing the disparity (horizontal shift) at each pixel in the image given the observed image data $\{\mathbf{x}_n\}_{n=1}^N$. More details about the likelihood terms in this problem can be found in Section 11.8.2, where we described tree-based priors for the unknown disparities. A more suitable approach is to use an MRF prior.

As for the denoising example, it is undesirable to use an MRF prior where the costs are a convex function of the difference in neighboring labels. This results in a MAP solution where the edges of objects are smoothed. Hence, it is usual to use a non-convex prior such as the Potts function, which embodies the idea that the scene consists of smooth surfaces, with sudden jumps in depth between them where the size of the jump is unimportant.

Boykov et al. (1999) used the alpha-expansion algorithm to perform approximate inference in a model of this sort (Figure 12.27). The performance of this algorithm is good, but errors are found where there is no true match in the other image (i.e., where

Figure 12.27 Stereo vision. a) One image of the original stereo pair. b) Disparity estimated using the method of Boykov et al. (1999). c) Ground truth disparity. Blue pixels indicate regions which are occluded in the second image and so do not have a valid match or disparity. The algorithm does not take account of this fact and produces noisy estimates in these regions. Adapted from Boykov et al. (1999).

the corresponding point is occluded by another object). Kolmogorov and Zabih (2001) subsequently developed a bespoke graph for dealing with occlusions in stereo vision and an alpha-expansion algorithm for optimizing the associated cost function. These methods can also be applied to *optical flow* in which we attempt to identify pixel correspondences between adjacent frames in a video sequence. Unlike in stereo vision, there is no guarantee that these matches will be on the same scanline, but other than this, the problem is very similar.

12.8.4 Rearranging Images

Markov random field models can also be used for rearranging images; we are given an original image $I^{(1)}$ and wish to create a new image $I^{(2)}$ by rearranging the pixels from $I^{(1)}$ in some way. Depending on the application, we may wish to change the dimensions of the original image (termed *image retargeting*), remove an object or move an object from one place to another.

Pritch et al. (2009) constructed a model with variables $\mathbf{w} = \{w_1 \ldots w_N\}$ at each of the N pixels of $I^{(2)}$. Each possible value of $w_n \in \{1 \ldots K\}$ represents a 2D relative offset to image $I^{(1)}$ that tells us which pixel from image $I^{(1)}$ will appear at the nth pixel of the new image. The label map $\mathbf{w}$ is hence termed a shift map as it represents 2D shifts to the original image. Each possible shift-map defines a different output image $I^{(2)}$ (Figure 12.28).

Pritch et al. (2009) model the shift-map $\mathbf{w}$ as an MRF with pairwise costs that encourage smoothness. The result of this is that only shift-maps that are piecewise constant have high probability: in other words, new images, which consist of large chunks of the original image that have been copied verbatim, are favored. They modify the pairwise costs so that they are lower when adjacent labels encode offsets with similar surrounding regions. This means that where the label does change, it does so in such a way that there is no visible seam in the output image.

The remainder of the model depends on the application (Figure 12.29):

- To *move* an object, we specify unary costs in the new region that ensure that we copy the desired object here. The remainder of the shifts are left free to vary but

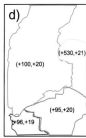

Figure 12.28 Shift maps for image retargeting to reduce width. a) New image $I^{(2)}$ is created from b) the original image $I^{(1)}$ by copying piecewise regions (five regions shown). c) These regions are carefully chosen to produce a seamless result. d) The underlying representation is a shiftmap – a label at each pixel of the new image that specifies the 2D offset to the position in the original image that will be copied from. An MRF encourages the labels to be piecewise constant, and hence the result tends to consist of large chunks copied verbatim. Figure shows method of Pritch et al. (2009).

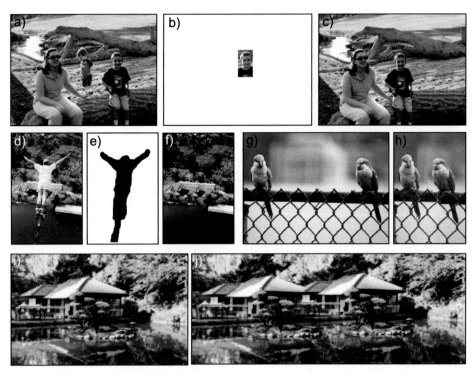

Figure 12.29 Applications of shift maps. Shift maps can be used to a) take an object from the original image b) move it to a new position and c) then fill in the remaining pixels to produce a new picture. d) They can also be used to remove an undesirable object e) specified by a mask from an image by f) filling in the missing area. g–h) Finally they can be used to retarget an original image to a smaller size, or i-j) to retarget an original image to a larger size. Results from method of Pritch et al. (2009).

favor small offsets so that parts of the scene that are far from the change tend to be unperturbed.

- To *replace* an area of the image, we specify unary costs so that the remainder of the image must have a shift of zero (verbatim copying), and the shift in the missing region must be such that it copies from outside the region.

- To *retarget* an image to larger width, we set the unary costs so that the left and right edges of the new image are forced to have shifts that correspond to the left and right of the original image. We also use the unary costs to specify that vertical shifts must be small.

- To *retarget* an image to a smaller width (Figure 12.28), we additionally specify that the horizontal offset can only increase as we move from left to right across the image. This ensures that the new image does not contain replicated objects and that their horizontal order remains constant.

In each case the best solution can be found using the alpha-expansion algorithm. Since the pairwise terms do not form a metric here, it is necessary to truncate the offending costs (see Section 12.4.1). In practice there are many labels and so Pritch et al. (2009) introduce a *coarse-to-fine* scheme in which a low resolution version of the image is initially synthesized and the result of this is used to guide further refinements at higher resolutions.

12.8.5 Superresolution

Image *superresolution* can also be framed as inference within a Markov random field model. Here, the basic unit of currency is an image patch rather than a pixel. For example, consider dividing the original image into a regular grid of N low resolution 3×3 patches $\{\mathbf{x}_n\}_{n=1}^N$. The goal is to infer a set of corresponding labels $\{w_n\}_{n=1}^N$ at each position in the grid. Each label can take one of K values, each of which corresponds to a different possible high resolution 7×7 patch. These patches are extracted from training images.

The pairwise cost for placing high-resolution patches together is determined by the agreement at the abutting edge. The unary cost for choosing a patch at a given position depends on the agreement between the proposed high-resolution patch and the observed low-resolution patch. This can be computed by downsampling the high-resolution patch to 3×3 pixels and then using a normal noise model.

In principle we could perform inference in this model with a graph cut formulation, but there are two problems. First, the resulting cost function is not submodular. Second, the number of possible high-resolution patches must be very large and so the alpha-expansion algorithm (which chooses these in turn) would be extremely inefficient.

Freeman et al. (2000) used loopy belief propagation to perform approximate inference in a model similar to this. To make this relatively fast, they used only a subset of $J \ll K$ possible patches at each position where these were chosen so that they were the J patches which agreed best with the observed data (and so had the lowest unary costs). Although the results (Figure 12.30) are quite convincing, they are sadly far from the feats demonstrated in modern TV crime drama.

12.8.6 Texture synthesis

The applications so far have all been based on performing inference in the undirected Markov random field model. We now consider the directed model. Inference is difficult

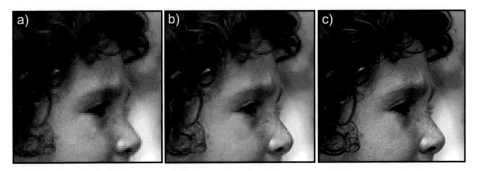

Figure 12.30 Superresolution. a) The observed image, which is broken down into a regular grid of low-resolution patches. b) We infer a regular grid of labels, each of which corresponds to a high-resolution patch, and "quilt" these together to form the superresolved image. c) Ground truth. Adapted from Freeman et al. (2000). ©2000 Springer.

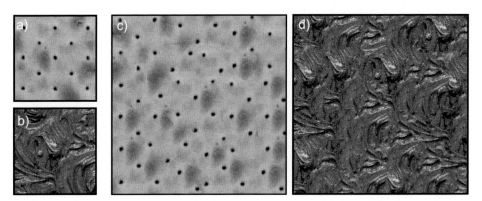

Figure 12.31 Texture synthesis. a,b) Original texture samples. c,d) Synthesized textures using *image quilting*. Adapted from Efros and Freeman (2001).

in this model due to the presence of three-wise terms in the associated cost function (see Section 12.7). However, generation from this model is relatively easy; since this is a directed model, we can use an ancestral sampling technique to generate examples. One possible application of this technique is for *texture synthesis*.

The goal of texture synthesis is to learn a generative model from a small patch of texture such that when we draw samples from the model they look like extended examples of the same texture (Figure 12.31). The particular technique that we describe here is known as *image quilting* and was originally described by Efros and Freeman (2001). We will first describe the algorithm as it was initially conceived, and then relate it to the directed model for grids.

The first step (see Figure 12.32) is to extract all possible patches of a given size from the input texture to form a *patch library*. The synthesized image will consist of a regular grid of these library patches such that each overlaps its neighbors by a few pixels. A new texture is synthesized starting in the top-left of this grid and proceeding to the bottom-right. At each position, a library patch is chosen such that it is visually consistent with the patches that have previously been placed above and to the left.

For the top-left position, we randomly choose a patch from the library. We then consider placing a second patch to the right of the first patch, such that they overlap by roughly $1/6$ of their width. We search through the library for the J patches where the squared RGB intensity difference in the overlapping region is smallest. We choose one of these J patches randomly and place it into the image at the second position. We continue in this way, synthesizing the top row of patches in the image. When we reach the second row, we must consider the overlap with the patches to the left and above in deciding whether a candidate library patch is suitable: we choose the J patches where the total RGB difference between the overlapping portions of the candidate patch and the previously chosen patches is minimal. This process continues until we reach the bottom-right of the image.

In this way, we synthesize a new example of the texture (Figure 12.32a-f). By forcing the overlapping regions to be similar, we enforce visual consistency between adjacent patches. By choosing randomly from the J best patches, we ensure that the result is stochastic: if we always chose the most visually consistent patch, we would replicate the original texture verbatim. At the end of this process, it is common to blend

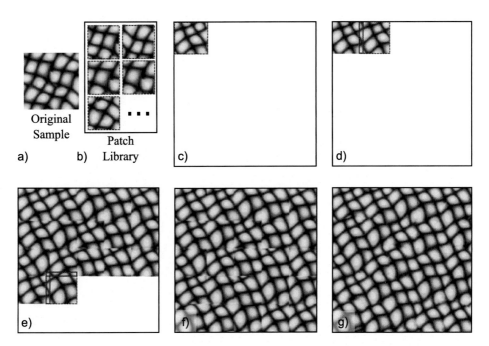

Figure 12.32 Image quilting. a) Original texture sample. b) Library of all overlapping patches from the original texture sample. c) The first patch is chosen randomly from the library. d) The second patch is chosen randomly from the k library patches that are most similar in the overlapping region. e) In subsequent rows, patches are chosen so that the overlapping region agrees with the previously placed patches to the left and above. f) This continues until we reach the bottom-right of the image. g) The patches are then blended together to give the final results.

the resulting patches together to remove remaining artifacts in the overlapping region (Figure 12.32g).

Image quilting can be thought of as ancestral sampling from the directed model for images (Figure 12.33). The observed data $\{\mathbf{x}_n\}_{n=1}^N$ are the output patches, and the hidden labels $\{w_n\}_{n=1}^N$ represent the patch index. The labels are conditioned on their parents with a probability distribution that allots a constant probability if the overlapping region is one of the J closest and zero otherwise. The only real change is that the relationship between label and observed data is now deterministic: a given label always produces exactly the same output patch.

12.8.7 Synthesizing novel faces

Mohammed et al. (2009) presented a related technique to synthesize more complex objects such as frontal faces (Figure 12.34), based on a large database of weakly aligned training examples. Faces have a distinct spatial structure, and we must ensure that our model enforces these constraints. To this end, we build a separate library of patches for each position in the image. This ensures that the features have roughly the correct spatial relations: the nose always appears in the center and the chin at the bottom.

In principle we could now apply a standard image quilting approach by synthesizing patches starting in the top-left and moving to the bottom-right. Unfortunately, the resulting faces can drift in appearance (e.g., from male to female) as we move through

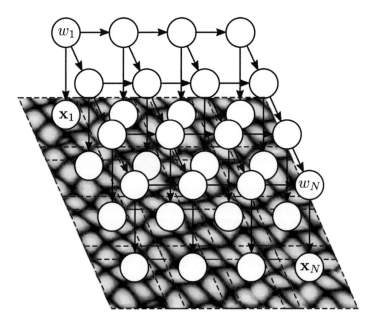

Figure 12.33 Image quilting as ancestral sampling from a graphical model. When we synthesize images we are effectively ancestral sampling from a directed grid model where each hidden node represents a patch index and each observed variable represents the patch data.

the image. To prevent this from happening, we condition the patch synthesis on a draw from a factor analysis model (Section 7.6), which has been trained with frontal faces. A sample from this model looks like a blurry, but globally coherent face. Now when we choose potential patches, they must agree with both the previously placed patches to the left and above, but also be similar to the appropriate part of the blurry sample from the subspace model. The generated images from this model look like highly realistic human faces.

In terms of probability, the labels $\{w_n\}_{n=1}^N$ in this model are conditioned not only on their ancestors w_{pa} but also on the hidden variable in the subspace model $\mathbf{h}$ (see Figure 12.35). This hidden variable connects to every patch label $\{w_n\}_{n=1}^N$ and gives the resulting image a greater visual coherence than the Markov connections of the patches alone.

Discussion

Models for grids are ubiquitous in vision: they occur in almost all applications that attempt to associate a label with each position in the image. Depending on the application, this label may indicate the depth, object type, segmentation mask, or motion at that pixel. Unfortunately, most problems of this type are NP hard, and so we must resort to efficient approximate inference techniques such as the alpha-expansion algorithm.

Notes

MRFs and CRFs: Markov random fields were first investigated in computer vision by Geman and Geman (1984), although much of the early work dealt with continuous variables rather than the

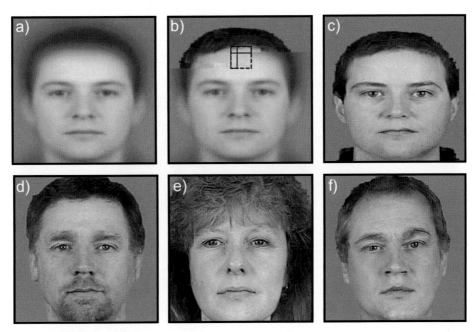

Figure 12.34 Synthesizing novel faces. a) A sample is drawn from a subspace model (see Chapter 7) that has been trained on facial images. b) Texture synthesis now proceeds but with two differences from before. First, the choice of patch must now agree with the sample from the subspace model as well as the previously placed patches. Second, the library patches are now different at each position: in this way we ensure that a nose patch is always chosen in the center and so on. c) After completing the synthesis and blending together the patches. d-f) Three more examples of synthesized faces. Adapted from Mohammed et al. (2009). ©2009 ACM.

discrete case as discussed in this chapter. A good review can be found in Li (2010). Conditional random fields were first used in computer vision by Kumar and Hebert (2003). An overview can be found in Sutton and McCallum (2011).

Applications: Grid-based models and graph cuts are used extensively in vision and graphics. A partial list of applications includes stereo vision (Kolmogorov and Zabih 2001; Woodford et al. 2009), optical flow (Kolmogorov and Zabih 2001), texture synthesis (Kwatra et al. 2003), photomontage (Agarwala et al. 2004), summarizing photo collections with collages (Rother et al. 2005, 2006), bilayer segmentation (Kolmogorov et al. 2006), interactive segmentation (Rother et al. 2004; Boykov et al. 2001), superresolution (Freeman et al. 2000), image retargeting (Pritch et al. 2009), denoising (Greig et al. 1989), oversegmentation (Moore et al. 2010; Veksler et al. 2010), image colorization (Levin et al. 2004), segmantic segmentation (Shotton et al. 2009), multi-view reconstruction (Kolmogorov and Zabih 2002; Vogiatzis et al. 2007), and matching image points (Isack and Boykov 2012).

Graph cuts: The first application of graph cuts to inference in an MRF is due to Greig et al. (1989) who investigated binary denoising. However, it was not until the work of Boykov et al. (2001) that this result was rediscovered and graph cuts became widely used. Ishikawa (2003) presented the exact solution for multilabel graph cuts with convex potentials, and this was generalized by Schlesinger and Flach (2006). The presentation in this chapter is a hybrid of these two methods. Boykov et al. (2001) introduced the idea of optimizing non-convex multilabel energies via a series of binary problems. They proposed two algorithms of this kind: the alpha-beta

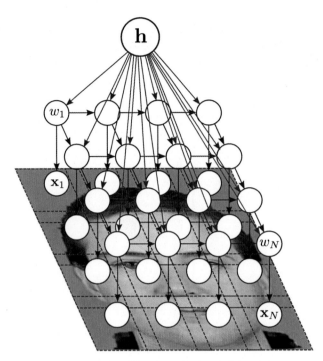

Figure 12.35 Graphical model for synthesizing novel faces. When we generate a new image we are ancestral sampling from a directed grid model, where each variable **w** is conditioned on the hidden variable **h** of the subspace model. Adapted from Mohammed et al. (2009) ©2009 ACM.

swap in which pairs of labels are exchanged for one another and the alpha-expansion algorithm. They also proved that the alpha-expansion solution is guaranteed to be within a factor of two of the true solution. In the same spirit, Lempitsky et al. (2010) and Kumar et al. (2011) have proposed more complex "moves". Tarlow et al. (2011) elucidates the conection between graph-cut methods and max-product belief propagation. For more detailed overviews of graph cut methods, consult Boykov and Veksler (2006), Felzenszwalb and Zabih (2011), and Blake et al. (2011).

Max-flow: Graph-cut methods rely on algorithms for computing maximum flow. The most common of these are the augmenting paths method of Ford and Fulkerson (1962) and the push-relabel method of Goldberg and Tarjan (1988). Details of these and other approaches to the same problem can be found in any standard textbook on algorithms such as Cormen et al. (2001). The most common technique in computer vision is a modified version of the augmented paths algorithm due to Boykov and Kolmogorov (2004) that has been demonstrated to have very good performance for vision problems. Kohli and Torr (2005), Juan and Boykov (2006), and Alahari et al. (2008) have all investigated methods for improving the efficiency of graph-cuts by reusing solutions to similar graph-cut problems (e.g., based on the solution to the previous frames in a time-sequence).

Cost functions and optimization: Kolmogorov and Zabih (2004) provide a summary of the cost functions that can be optimized using the basic graph-cuts max-flow formulation with binary variables. Kolmogorov and Rother (2007) summarize graph-cut approaches to non-submodular energies. Rother et al. (2007) and Komodakis et al. (2008) present algorithms that can approximately optimize more general cost functions.

Constraint edges: Recent work has investigated bespoke graph constructions that make heavy use of constraint edges (edges of infinite strength) to ensure that the solution conforms to a certain structure. For example, Delong and Boykov (2009) devised a method that forced certain labels to surround others, and Moore et al. (2010) described a method that forces the label field to conform to a lattice. See also Felzenszwalb and Veksler (2010) for a related scheme based on dynamic programming.

Higher-order cliques: All of the methods discussed in this chapter assume pairwise connections; the cliques include only two discrete variables. However, to model more complex statistics of the label field, it is necessary to include more than two variables in the cliques, and these are known as *higher-order* models. Roth and Black (2009) demonstrated good denoising and inpainting results with a continuous MRF model of this kind, and Domke et al. (2008) demonstrated the efficacy of a directed model in which each variable was conditioned on a number of variables above and to the right in the image. There has recently been considerable interest in developing algorithms for MAP estimation in models with discrete variables and higher-order cliques (Ishikawa 2009; Kohli et al. 2009a, 2009b; Rother et al. 2009).

Other approaches to MAP estimation: There are many other contemporary approaches to MAP estimation in MRFs and CRFs. These include loopy belief propagation (Weiss and Freeman 2001), quadratic pseudo-boolean optimization that is used in non-submodular cost functions (Kolmogorov and Rother 2007), random walks (Grady 2006), and linear programming (LP) relaxations (Weiss et al. 2011) and various approaches to maximize the LP lower bound such as tree reweighted message passing (Wainright et al. 2005; Kolmogorov 2006). An experimental comparison between different energy minimization methods for MRFs can be found in Szeliski et al. (2008).

Texture synthesis: Texture synthesis was originally investigated as a continuous problem and the focus was on modeling the joint statistics of the RGB values in a small patch (Heeger and Bergen 1995; Portilla and Simoncelli 2000). Although texture synthesis as a continuous problem is still an active research area (e.g., Heess et al. 2009), these early methods were displaced by methods that represented the texture in terms of discrete variables (either by quantizing the RGB values, indexing patches or using a shift-map representation). The resulting algorithms (e.g., Efros and Leung 1999; Wei and Levoy 2000; Efros and Freeman 2001; Kwatra et al. 2003) were originally described as heuristic approaches to generating textures, but can also be interpreted as exact or approximate ways to draw samples from directed or undirected grid models.

Interactive segmentation: The use of graph cuts for interactive segmentation algorithms was pioneered by Boykov and Jolly (2001). In early works (Boykov and Jolly 2001; Boykov and Funka Lea 2006; Li et al. 2004) the user interacted with the image by placing marks indicating foreground and background regions. Grab cut (Rother et al. 2004) allowed the user to draw a box around the object in question. More recent systems (Liu et al. 2009) are fast enough to allow the user to interactively "paint" the selection onto the images. Current interest in graph cut – based segmentation is mainly focused on developing novel priors over the shape that improve performance (e.g., Malcolm et al. 2007; Veksler 2008; Chittajallu et al. 2010; Freiman et al. 2010). To this end, Kumar et al. (2005) introduced a method for imposing high-level knowledge about the articulation of the object, Vicente et al. (2008) developed an algorithm that is suited for cutting out elongated objects, and Lempitsky et al. (2008) used a prior based on a bounding box around the object.

Stereo vision: Most state-of-the-art stereo vision algorithms rely on MRFs or CRFs and are solved using either graph cuts (e.g., Kolmogorov and Zabih 2001) or belief propagation (e.g., Sun et al. 2003). Comparisons of these approaches can be found in Tappen and Freeman (2003) and Szeliski et al. (2008). An active area of research in dense stereo vision is the formulation of the compatibility of the two images given a certain disparity offset (e.g., Bleyer and Chambon 2010; Hirschmüller and Scharstein 2009), which is rarely based on single pixels in practice (see Yoon and Kweon 2006; Tombari et al. 2008).

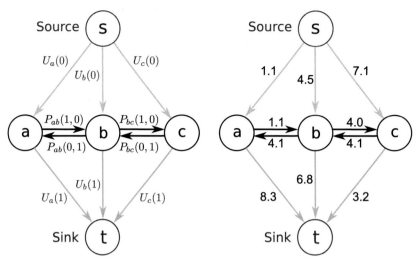

Figure 12.36 Graph for Problem 12.2.

For more information about stereo vision, see the reviews by Scharstein and Szeliski (2002) and Brown et al. (2003) or consult Szeliski (2010), which contains a good modern summary. Chapter 11 of this book summarizes dynamic programming approaches. Notable stereo implementations include the region growing approach of Lhuillier and Quan (2002); the systems of Zitnick and Kanade (2000) and Hirschmüller (2005), both of which are available online; and the extremely efficient GPU-based system of Sizintsev and Wildes (2010). For an up-to-date quantitative comparison of the latest stereo vision algorithms, consult the Middlebury stereo vision Web site (*http://vision.middlebury.edu/stereo/*).

Problems

12.1 Consider a Markov random field with the structure

$$Pr(x_1, x_2, x_3, x_4) = \frac{1}{Z}\phi[x_1, x_2]\phi[x_2, x_3]\phi[x_3, x_4]\phi[x_4, x_1]$$

but where the variables x_1, x_2, x_3, and x_4 are continuous and the potentials are defined as

$$\phi[a, b] = \exp\left[-(a-b)^2\right].$$

This is known as a *Gaussian Markov random field*. Show that the joint probability is a normal distribution, and find the information matrix (inverse covariance matrix).

12.2 Compute the MAP solution to the three-pixel graph-cut problem in Figure 12.36 by (i) computing the cost of all eight possible solutions explicitly and finding the one with the minimum cost (ii) running the augmenting paths algorithm on this graph by hand and interpreting the minimum cut.

12.3 Explicitly compute the costs associated with the four possible minimum cuts of the graph in Figure 12.10.

12.4 Compute the cost for each the four possible cuts of the graph in Figure 12.11c.

12.5 Consider the graph construction in Figure 12.37a, which contains a number of constraint edges of infinite cost (capacity). There are 25 possible minimum cuts on this graph, each of which corresponds to one possible labeling of the two pixels. Write out the cost for each labeling. Which solutions have finite cost for this graph construction?

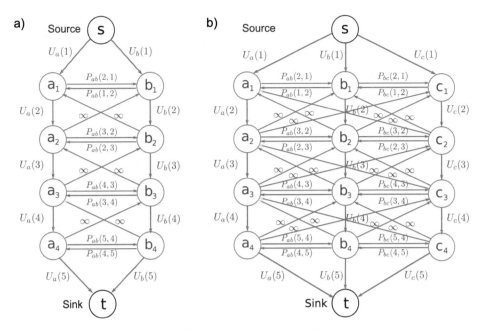

Figure 12.37 Alternative multilabel graph constructions. Each of these these graphs has extra *constraint links* with infinite weight. These have the effect of giving an infinite cost to a subset of the possible solutions.

12.6 Which of the possible minimum cuts of the graph in Figure 12.37b have a finite cost?

12.7 Confirm that the costs of the cuts in Figure 12.14 are as claimed by explicitly performing the summation over the relevant terms C_{ij}.

12.8 Show that the Potts model (Figure 12.17c) is not submodular by providing a counterexample to the required criterion:

$$P_{ab}(\beta,\gamma) + P_{ab}(\alpha,\delta) - P_{ab}(\beta,\delta) - P_{ab}(\alpha,\gamma) \geq 0.$$

12.9 An alternative to the alpha-expansion algorithm is the alpha-beta swap. Here, a multilabel MRF with non-convex potentials is optimized by repeatedly choosing pairs of labels α, β and performing a binary graph cut that allows them to swap in such a way that the overall cost function decreases. Devise a graph structure that can be used to perform this operation. *Hint*: consider separate cases for neighboring labels (α,α), (β,β), (β,γ), (α,γ) and (γ,γ) where γ is a label that is neither α nor β.

Part IV

Preprocessing

The main focus of this book is on statistical models for computer vision; the previous chapters concern models that relate visual measurements $\mathbf{x}$ to the world $\mathbf{w}$. However, there has been little discussion of how the measurement vector $\mathbf{x}$ was created, and it has often been implied that it contains concatenated RGB pixel values. In state-of-the-art vision systems, the image pixel data are almost always *preprocessed* to form the measurement vector.

We define preprocessing to be any transformation of the pixel data *prior to* building the model that relates the data to the world. Such transformations are often ad hoc heuristics: their parameters are not learned from training data, but they are chosen based on experience of what works well. The philosophy behind image preprocessing is easy to understand; the image data may be contingent on many aspects of the real world that do not pertain to the task at hand. For example, in an object detection task, the RGB values will change depending on the camera gain, illumination, object pose and particular instance of the object. The goal of image preprocessing is to remove as much of this unwanted variation as possible while retaining the aspects of the image that are critical to the final decision.

In a sense, the need for preprocessing represents a failure; we are admitting that we cannot directly model the relationship between the RGB values and the world state. Inevitably, we must pay a price for this. Although the variation due to extraneous factors is jettisoned, it is very probable that some of the task-related information is also discarded. Fortunately, in these nascent years of computer vision, this rarely seems to be the limiting factor that governs the overall performance.

We devote the single chapter in this section to discussing a variety of preprocessing techniques. Although the treatment here is not extensive, it should be emphasized that preprocessing is very important; in practice the choice of preprocessing technique can influence the performance of vision systems at least as much as the choice of model.

Chapter 13

Image preprocessing and feature extraction

This chapter provides a brief overview of modern preprocessing methods for computer vision. In Section 13.1 we introduce methods in which we replace each pixel in the image with a new value. Section 13.2 considers the problem of finding and characterizing edges, corners and interest points in images. In Section 13.3 we discuss visual descriptors; these are low-dimensional vectors that attempt to characterize the interesting aspects of an image region in a compact way. Finally, in Section 13.4 we discuss methods for dimensionality reduction.

13.1 Per-pixel transformations

We start our discussion of preprocessing with *per-pixel operations*: these methods return a single value corresponding to each pixel of the input image. We denote the original 2D array of pixel data as $\mathbf{P}$, where p_{ij} is the element at the ith of I rows and the jth of J columns. The element p_{ij} is a scalar representing the grayscale intensity. Per-pixel operations return a new 2D array $\mathbf{X}$ of the same size as $\mathbf{P}$ containing elements x_{ij}.

13.1.1 Whitening

The goal of whitening (Figure 13.1) is to provide invariance to fluctuations in the mean intensity level and contrast of the image. Such variation may arise because of a change in ambient lighting intensity, the object reflectance, or the camera gain. To compensate for these factors, the image is transformed so that the resulting pixel values have zero mean and unit variance. To this end, we compute the mean μ and variance σ^2 of the original grayscale image $\mathbf{P}$:

$$
\mu = \frac{\sum_{i=1}^{I}\sum_{j=1}^{J} p_{ij}}{IJ}
$$

$$
\sigma^2 = \frac{\sum_{i=1}^{I}\sum_{j=1}^{J} (p_{ij} - \mu)^2}{IJ}. \tag{13.1}
$$

Figure 13.1 Whitening and histogram equalization. a) A number of faces which have been captured with widely varying contrasts and mean levels. b) After whitening, the images have the same mean and variance. c) After histogram equalization, all of the moments of the images are approximately the same. Both of these transformations reduce the amount of variation due to contrast and intensity changes.

These statistics are used to transform each pixel value separately so that

$$x_{ij} = \frac{p_{ij} - \mu}{\sigma}. \tag{13.2}$$

For color images, this operation may be carried out by computing the statistics μ and σ^2 from all three channels or by separately transforming each of the RGB channels based on their own statistics.

Note that even this simple transformation has the potential to hamper subsequent inference about the scene: depending on the task, the absolute intensities may or may not contain critical information. Even the simplest preprocessing methods must be applied with care.

13.1.2 Histogram equalization

The goal of histogram equalization (Figure 13.1c) is to modify the statistics of the intensity values so that *all* of their moments take predefined values. To this end, a nonlinear transformation is applied that forces the distribution of pixel intensities to be flat.

We first compute the histogram of the original intensities $\mathbf{h}$ where the kth of K entries is given by

$$h_k = \sum_{i=1}^{I}\sum_{j=1}^{J} \delta[p_{ij} - k], \tag{13.3}$$

where the operation $\delta[\bullet]$ returns one if the argument is zero and zero otherwise. We then cumulatively sum this histogram and normalize by the total number of pixels to compute the cumulative proportion c of pixels that are less than or equal to each intensity level:

$$c_k = \frac{\sum_{l=1}^{k} h_l}{IJ}. \tag{13.4}$$

Finally, we use the cumulative histogram as a look up table to compute the transformed value so that

$$x_{ij} = K c_{p_{ij}}. \tag{13.5}$$

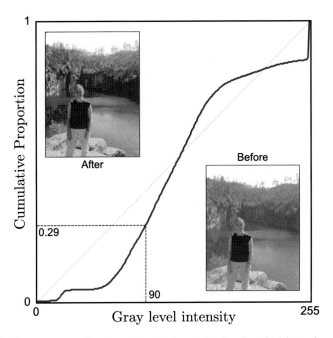

Figure 13.2 Histogram equalization. The abscissa indicates the pixel intensity. The ordinate indicates the proportion of intensities that were less than or equal to this value. This plot can be used as a look-up table for histogram equalizing the intensities. For a given intensity value on the abscissa, we choose the new intensity to be the maximum output intensity K times the value on the ordinate. After this transformation, the intensities are equally distributed. In the example image, many of the pixels are bright. Histogram equalization spreads these bright values out over a larger intensity range, and so has the effect of increasing the contrast in the brighter regions.

For example, in Figure 13.2 the value 90 will be mapped to $K \times 0.29$ where K is the maximum intensity (usually 255). The result is a continuous number rather than a discretized pixel intensity but is in the same range as the original data. The result can be rounded to the nearest integer if subsequent processing demands.

13.1.3 Linear filtering

After filtering an image, the new pixel value x_{ij} consists of a weighted sum of the intensities of pixels in the surrounding area of the original image $\mathbf{P}$. The weights are stored in a filter kernel $\mathbf{F}$, which has entries $f_{m,n}$, where $m \in \{-M \ldots M\}$ and $n \in \{-N \ldots N\}$.

More formally, when we apply a filter, we *convolve* the $\mathbf{P}$ with the filter $\mathbf{F}$, where two-dimensional convolution is defined as

$$x_{ij} = \sum_{m=-M}^{M} \sum_{n=-N}^{N} p_{i-m,j-n} f_{m,n}. \tag{13.6}$$

Notice that by convention, the filter is flipped in both directions so the top left of the filter $f_{-M,-N}$ weights the pixel $p_{i+M,j+N}$ to the right and below the current point in $\mathbf{P}$. Many filters used in vision are symmetric in such a way that this flipping makes no practical difference.

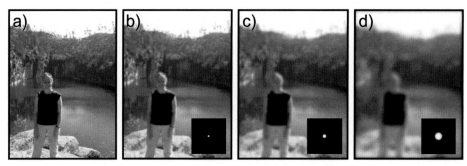

Figure 13.3 Image blurring. a) Original image. b) Result of convolving with a Gaussian filter (filter shown in bottom right of image). Each pixel in this image is a weighted sum of the surrounding pixels in the original image, where the weights are given by the filter. The result is that the image is slightly blurred. c–d) Convolving with a filter of increasing standard deviation causes the resulting image to be increasingly blurred.

Without further modification, this formulation will run into problems near the borders of the image: it needs to access points that are outside the image. One way to deal with this is to use *zero padding* in which it is assumed that the value of P is 0 outside the defined image region.

We now consider a number of common types of filter.

Gaussian (blurring) filter

To blur an image, we convolve it with a 2D Gaussian,

$$f(m,n) = \frac{1}{2\pi\sigma^2} \exp\left[-\frac{m^2 + n^2}{2\sigma^2}\right]. \tag{13.7}$$

Each pixel in the resulting image is a weighted sum of the surrounding pixels, where the weights depend on the Gaussian profile: nearer pixels contribute relatively more to the final output. This process blurs the image, where the degree of blurring is dependent on the standard deviation σ of the Gaussian filter (Figure 13.3). This is a simple method to reduce noise in images taken at very low light levels.

First derivative filters and edge filters

A second use for image filtering is to locate places in the image where the intensity changes abruptly. Consider taking the first derivative of the image along the rows. We could approximate this operation by simply computing the difference between two offset pixels along the row. This operation can be accomplished by filtering with the operator $\mathbf{F} = [-1 \ 0 \ 1]$. This filter gives zero response when the image is flat in the horizontal direction: it is hence invariant to constant additive luminance changes. It gives a negative response when the image values are increasing as we move in a horizontal direction and a positive response when they are decreasing (recall that convolution flips the filter by $180°$). As such, it is selective for edges in the image.

The response to the filter $\mathbf{F} = [-1 \ 0 \ 1]$ is noisy because of its limited spatial extent. Consequently, slightly more sophisticated filters are used to find edges in practice. Examples include the Prewitt operators (Figures 13.4b–c)

$$\mathbf{F}_x = \begin{bmatrix} 1 & 0 & -1 \\ 1 & 0 & -1 \\ 1 & 0 & -1 \end{bmatrix}, \qquad \mathbf{F}_y = \begin{bmatrix} 1 & 1 & 1 \\ 0 & 0 & 0 \\ -1 & -1 & -1 \end{bmatrix}, \tag{13.8}$$

and the Sobel operators

$$\mathbf{F}_x = \begin{bmatrix} 1 & 0 & -1 \\ 2 & 0 & -2 \\ 1 & 0 & -1 \end{bmatrix}, \qquad \mathbf{F}_y = \begin{bmatrix} 1 & 2 & 1 \\ 0 & 0 & 0 \\ -1 & -2 & -1 \end{bmatrix}, \tag{13.9}$$

where in each case the filter $\mathbf{F}_x$ is a filter selective for edges in the horizontal direction, and $\mathbf{F}_y$ is a filter selective for edges in the vertical direction.

Laplacian filters

The Laplacian filter is the discrete two-dimensional approximation to the Laplacian operator ∇^2 and is given by

$$\mathbf{F} = \begin{bmatrix} 0 & -1 & 0 \\ -1 & 4 & -1 \\ 0 & -1 & 0 \end{bmatrix}. \tag{13.10}$$

Applying the discretized filter $\mathbf{F}$ to an image results in a response of high magnitude where the image is changing, regardless of the direction of that change (Figure 13.4d): the response is zero in regions that are flat and significant where edges occur in the image. It is hence invariant to constant additive changes in luminance and useful for identifying interesting regions of the image.

Laplacian of Gaussian filters

In practice the Laplacian operator produces noisy results. A superior approach is to first smooth the image with a Gaussian filter and then apply the Laplacian. Due to the associative property of convolution, we can equivalently convolve the Laplacian filter by a Gaussian and apply the resulting *Laplacian of Gaussian* filter to the image (Figure 13.4e). This Laplacian of Gaussian has the advantage that it can be tuned to be selective for changes at different scales, depending on the scale of the Gaussian component.

Difference of Gaussians

The Laplacian of Gaussian filter is very well approximated by the difference of Gaussians filter (compare Figures 13.4e and 13.4f). As the name implies, this filter is created by taking the difference of two Gaussians at nearby scales. The same result can be achieved by filtering the image with the two Gaussians separately and taking the difference between the results. Again, this filter responds strongly in regions of the image that are changing at a predetermined scale.

Gabor filters

Gabor filters are selective for both scale and orientation. The 2D Gabor function is the product of a 2D Gaussian with a 2D sinusoid. It is parameterized by the covariance of the Gaussian and the phase ϕ, orientation ω, and wavelength λ of the sine wave. If the Gaussian component is spherical, it is defined by

$$f_{mn} = \frac{1}{2\pi\sigma^2} \exp\left[-\frac{m^2 + n^2}{2\sigma^2}\right] \sin\left[\frac{2\pi(\cos[\omega]m + \sin[\omega]n)}{\lambda} + \phi\right], \tag{13.11}$$

where σ controls the scale of the spherical Gaussian. It is typical to make the wavelength proportional to the scale σ of the Gaussian so a constant number of cycles is visible.

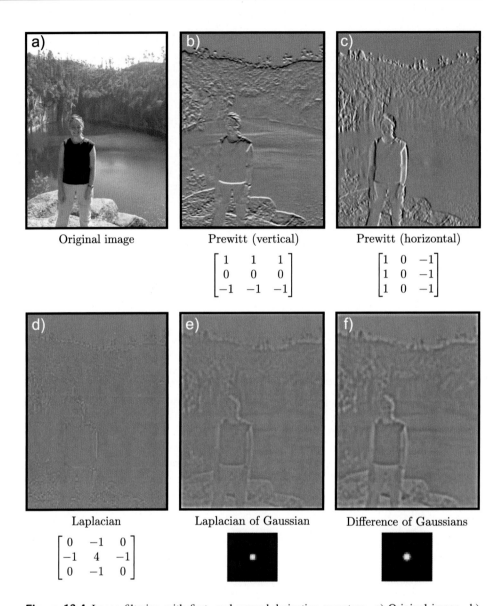

Figure 13.4 Image filtering with first- and second-derivative operators. a) Original image. b) Convolving with the vertical Prewitt filter produces a response that is proportional to the size and polarity of edges in the vertical direction. c) The horizontal Prewitt filter produces a response to edges in the horizontal direction. d) The Laplacian filter gives a significant response where the image changes rapidly regardless of direction. e) The Laplacian of Gaussian filter produces similar results but the output is smoothed and hence less noisy. f) The difference of Gaussians filter is a common approximation to the Laplacian of Gaussian.

The Gabor filter is selective for elements within the image at a certain frequency and orientation band and with a certain phase (Figure 13.5). It is invariant to constant additive changes in luminance when the sinusoidal component is asymmetric relative to the Gaussian. This is also nearly true for symmetric Gabor functions, as long as several cycles of the sinusoid are visible. A response that is independent of phase can easily be

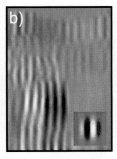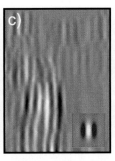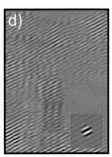

Figure 13.5 Filtering with Gabor functions. a) Original image. b) After filtering with horizontal asymmetric Gabor function at a large scale (filter shown bottom right). c) Result of filtering with horizontal symmetric Gabor function at a large scale. d) Response to diagonal Gabor filter (responds to diagonal changes).

generated by squaring and summing the responses of two Gabor features with the same frequency, orientation, and scale, but with phases that are $\pi/2$ radians apart. The resulting quantity is termed the *Gabor energy* and is somewhat invariant to small displacements of the image.

Filtering with Gabor functions is motivated by mammalian visual perception: this is one of the first processing operations applied to visual data in the brain. Moreover, it is known from psychological studies that certain tasks (e.g., face detection) are predominantly dependent on information at intermediate frequencies. This may be because high-frequency filters see only a small image region and are hence noisy and relatively uninformative, and low-frequency filters act over a large region and respond disproportionately to slow changes due to lighting.

Haar-like filters

Haar-like filters consist of adjacent rectangular regions that are balanced so that the average filter value is zero, and they are invariant to constant luminance changes. Depending on the configuration of these regions, they may be similar to derivative or Gabor filters (Figure 13.6).

However, Haar-like filters are noisier than the filters they approximate: they have sharp edges between positive and negative regions and so moving by a single pixel near an edge may change the response significantly. This drawback is compensated for by the relative speed with which Haar functions can be computed.

To compute Haar-like functions rapidly, we first form the *integral image* (Figure 13.6g). This is an intermediate representation in which each pixel contains the sum of all of the intensity values above and to the left of the current position. So the value in the top-left corner is the original pixel value at that position and the value in the bottom-right corner is the sum of all of the pixel values in the image. The values in the other parts of the integral image are between these extremes.

Given the integral image **I**, it is possible to compute the sum of the intensities in any rectangular region with just four operations, regardless of how large this region is. Consider the region is defined by the range $[i_0, i_1]$ down the columns and $[j_0, j_1]$ along the rows. The sum S of the internal pixel intensities is

$$S = \mathbf{I}_{i_1,j_1} + \mathbf{I}_{i_0,j_0} - \mathbf{I}_{i_1,j_0} - \mathbf{I}_{i_0,j_1}. \tag{13.12}$$

The logic behind this calculation is illustrated in Figure 13.6f–i.

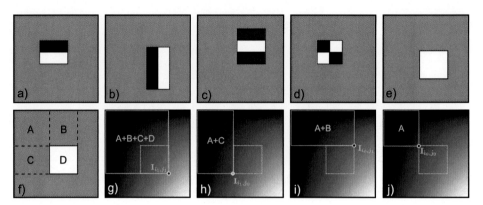

Figure 13.6 Haar-like filters. a–d) Haar-like filters consist of rectangular regions. Convolution with Haar-like filters can be done in constant time. e) To see why, consider the problem of filtering with this single rectangular region. f) We denote the sum of the pixel values in these four regions as A, B, C, and D. Our goal is to compute D. g) The integral image has a value that is the sum of the intensities of the pixels above and to the left of the current position. The integral image at position (i_1, j_1) hence has value $A + B + C + D$. h) The integral image at (i_1, j_0) has value $A + C$. i) The integral image at (i_0, j_1) has value $A + B$. j) The integral image at (i_0, j_0) has value A. The sum of the pixels in region D can now be computed as $\mathbf{I}_{i_1,j_1} + \mathbf{I}_{i_0,j_0} - \mathbf{I}_{i_1,j_0} - \mathbf{I}_{i_0,j_1} = (A + B + C + D) + A - (A + C) - (A + B) = D$. This requires just four operations regardless of the size of the original square region.

Since Haar-like filters are composed of rectangular regions, they can be computed using a similar trick. For a filter with two adjacent rectangular regions, six operations are required. With three adjacent rectangular regions, eight operations are required. When the filter dimensions M and N are large, this approach compares very favorably to a naïve implementation of conventional filtering which requires $O(MN)$ operations to compute the filter response due to a $M \times N$ kernel. Haar filters are often used in real-time applications such as face detection because of the speed with which they can be computed.

13.1.4 Local binary patterns

The local binary patterns (LBP) operator returns a discrete value at each pixel that characterizes the local texture in a way that is partially invariant to luminance changes. For this reason, features based on local binary patterns are commonly used as a substrate for face recognition algorithms.

The basic LBP operator compares the eight neighboring pixel intensities to the center pixel intensity, assigning a 0 or a 1 to each neighbor depending on whether they are less than or greater than the center value. These binary values are then concatenated in a predetermined order and converted to a single decimal number that represents the "type" of local image structure (Figure 13.7).

With further processing, the LBP operator can be made orientation invariant: the binary representation is repeatedly subjected to bitwise shifts to create eight new binary values and the minimum of these values is chosen. This reduces the number of possible LBP values to 36. In practice, it has been found that the distribution over these 36 LBP values is dominated by those that are relatively *uniform*. In other words, binary strings where transitions are absent (e.g., 00000000, 11111111) or infrequent (e.g., 00001111,

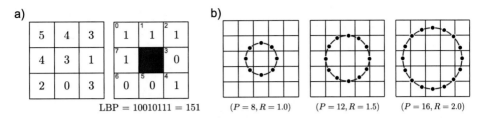

Figure 13.7 Local binary patterns. a) The local binary pattern is computed by comparing the central pixel to each of its eight neighbors. The binary value associated with each position is set to one if that neighbor is greater than or equal to the central pixel. The eight binary values can be read out and combined to make a single 8-bit number. b) Local binary patterns can be computed over larger areas by comparing the current pixels to the (interpolated) image at positions on a circle. This type of LBP is characterized by the number of samples P and the radius of the circle R.

00111111) occur most frequently. The number of texture classes can be further reduced by aggregating all of the nonuniform LBPs into a single class. Now the local image structure is categorized into nine LBP types (eight rotationally invariant uniform patterns and one nonuniform class).

The LBP operator can be extended to use neighborhoods of different sizes: the central pixel is compared to positions in a circular pattern (Figure 13.7b). In general, these positions do not exactly coincide with the pixel grid, and the intensity at these positions must be estimated using bilinear interpolation. This extended LBP operator can capture texture at different scales in the image.

13.1.5   Texton maps

The term texton stems from the study of human perception and refers to a primitive perceptual element of texture. In other words, it roughly occupies the role that a phoneme takes in speech recognition. In a machine vision context a texton is a discrete variable that designates which one of a finite number of possible texture classes is present in a region surrounding the current pixel. A texton map is an image in which the texton is computed at every pixel (Figure 13.8).

Texton assignment depends on training data. A bank of N filters is convolved with a set of training images. The responses are concatenated to form one $N \times 1$ vector for each pixel position in each training image. These vectors are then clustered into K classes using the K-means algorithm (Section 13.4.4). Textons are computed for a new image by convolving it with the same filter bank. For each pixel, the texton is assigned by noting which cluster mean is closest to the $N \times 1$ filter output vector associated with the current position.

The choice of filter bank seems to be relatively unimportant. One approach has been to use Gaussians at scales $\sigma, 2\sigma$, and 4σ to filter all three color channels, and derivatives of Gaussians at scales 2σ and 4σ and Laplacians of Gaussians at scales $\sigma, 2\sigma, 4\sigma$, and 8σ to filter the luminance (Figure 13.9a). In this way, both color and texture information is captured.

It may be desirable to compute textons that are invariant to orientation. One way of achieving this is to choose rotationally invariant filters to form the filter bank (Figure 13.9b). However, these have the undesirable property of not responding at all to oriented structures in the image. The Maximum Response (MR8) filter bank is designed

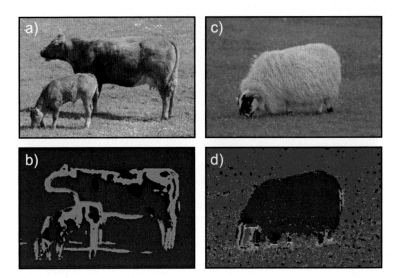

Figure 13.8 Texton maps. In a texton map each pixel is replaced by the texton index. This index characterizes the texture in the surrounding region. a) Original image. b) Associated texton map. Note how similar regions are assigned the same texton index (indicated by color). c) Original image. d) Associated texton map (using different filter bank from (b)). Texton maps are often used in semantic image segmentation. Adapted from Shotton et al. (2009). ©2009 Springer.

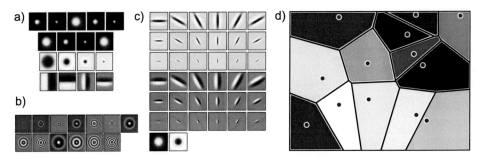

Figure 13.9 Textons. The image is convolved with a filter bank to yield an $N \times 1$ vector of filter responses at each position. Possible choices for the filter bank include a) a combination of Gaussians, derivatives of Gaussians, and Laplacians of Gaussians; b) rotationally invariant filters; and c) the maximum response (MR8) database. d) In training, the $N \times 1$ filter response vectors are clustered using K-means. For new data, the texton index is assigned based on the nearest of these clusters. Thus, the filter space is effectively partitioned into Voronoi regions.

to provide a rotationally invariant measure of local texture, which does not discard this information. The MR8 filter bank (Figure 13.9c) consists of a Gaussian and a Laplacian of Gaussian filter, an edge filter at three scales and a bar filter (a symmetric oriented filter) at the same three scales. The edge and bar filter are replicated at six orientations at each scale, giving a total of 38 filters. To induce rotational invariance only the *maximum* filter response over orientation is used. Hence the final vector of filter responses consists of eight numbers, corresponding to the Gaussian and Laplacian filters (already invariant) and the maximum responses over orientation of the edge and bar filters at each of the three scales.

13.2 Edges, corners, and interest points

In this section, we consider methods that aim to identify informative parts of the image. In *edge detection* the goal is to return a binary image where a nonzero value denotes the presence of an edge in the image. Edge detectors optionally also return other information such as the orientation and scale associated with the edge. Edge maps are a highly compact representation of an image, and it has been shown that it is possible to reconstruct an image very accurately with just information about the edges in the scene (Figure 13.10).

Corners are positions in the image that contain rich visual information and can be found reproducibly in different images of the same object (Figure 13.12). There are many schemes to find corners, but they all aim to identify points that are locally unique. Corner detection algorithms were originally developed for geometric computer vision problems such as wide baseline image matching; here we see the same scene from two different angles and wish to identify which points correspond to which. In recent years, corners have also been used in object recognition algorithms (where they are usually referred to as *interest points*). The idea here is that the regions surrounding interest points contain information about which object class is present.

13.2.1 Canny edge detector

To compute edges with the Canny edge detector (Figure 13.11), the image $\mathbf{P}$ is first blurred and then convolved with a pair of orthogonal derivative filters such as Prewitt filters to create images $\mathbf{H}$ and $\mathbf{V}$ containing derivatives in the horizontal and vertical directions, respectively. For pixel (i,j), the orientation θ_{ij} and magnitude a_{ij} of the gradient is computed using

$$\theta_{ij} = \arctan[v_{ij}/h_{ij}]$$
$$a_{ij} = \sqrt{h_{ij}^2 + v_{ij}^2}. \tag{13.13}$$

A simple approach would be to assign an edge to position (i,j) if the amplitude there exceeds a critical value. This is termed *thresholding*. Unfortunately, it produces poor results: the amplitude map takes high values on the edge, but also at adjacent positions. The Canny edge detector eliminates these unwanted responses using a method known as *non-maximum suppression*.

Figure 13.10 Reconstruction from edges. a) Original image. b) Edge map. Each edge pixel has associated scale and orientation information as well as a record of the luminance levels at either side. c) The image can be reconstructed almost perfectly from the edges and their associated information. Adapted from Elder (1999). ©1999 Springer.

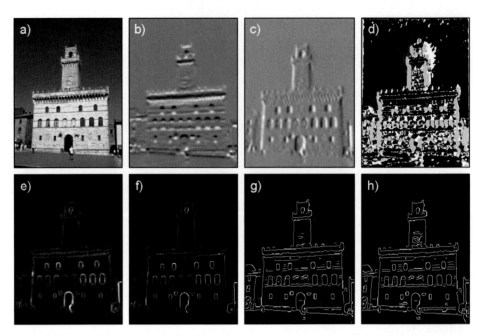

Figure 13.11 Canny edge detection. a) Original image. b) Result of vertical Prewitt filter. c) Results of horizontal Prewitt filter. d) Quantized orientation map. e) Gradient amplitude map. f) Amplitudes after non-maximum suppression. g) Thresholding at two levels: the white pixels are above the higher threshold. The red pixels are above the lower threshold but below the higher one. h) Final edge map after hysteresis thresholding contains all of the white pixels from (g) and those red pixels that connect to them.

In non-maximum suppression the gradient orientation is quantized into one of four angles $\{0^o, 45^o, 90^o, 135^o\}$, where angles 180° apart are treated as equivalent. The pixels associated with each angle are now treated separately. For each pixel, the amplitude is set to zero if either of the neighboring two pixels *perpendicular* to the gradient have higher values. For example, for a pixel where the gradient orientation is vertical (the image is changing in the horizontal direction), the pixels to the left and right are examined and the amplitude is set to zero if either of these are greater than the current value. In this way, the gradients at the maximum of the edge amplitude profile are retained, and those away from this maximum are suppressed.

A binary edge map can now be computed by comparing the remaining nonzero amplitudes to a fixed threshold. However, for any given threshold there will be misses (places where there are real edges, but their amplitude falls below the threshold) and false positives (pixels labeled as edges where none exist in the original image). To decrease these undesirable phenomena, knowledge about the continuity of real-world edges is exploited. Two thresholds are defined. All of the pixels whose amplitude is above the higher threshold are labeled as edges, and this threshold is chosen so that there are few false positives. To try to decrease the number of misses, pixels that are above the lower amplitude threshold *and* are connected to an existing edge pixel are also labeled as edges. By iterating this last step, it is possible to trace along weaker parts of strong contours. This technique is known as *hysteresis thresholding*.

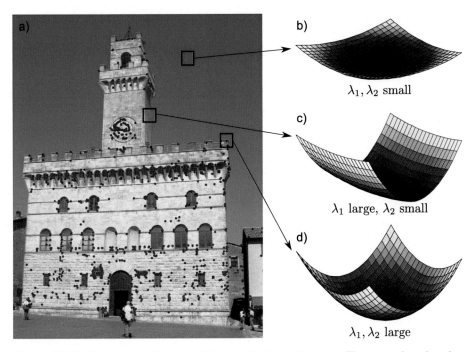

Figure 13.12 Harris corner detector. a) Image with detected corners. The corner detection algorithm is based on the image structure tensor that captures information about the distribution of gradients around the point. b) In flat regions, both singular values of the image structure tensor are small. c) On edges, one is small and the other large. d) At corners, both are large indicating that the image is changing quickly in both directions.

13.2.2 Harris corner detector

The Harris corner detector (Figure 13.12) considers the local gradients in the horizontal and vertical directions around each point. The goal is to find points in the image where the image intensity is varying in both directions (a corner) rather than in one direction (an edge) or neither (a flat region). The Harris corner detector bases this decision on the *image structure tensor*

$$\mathbf{S}_{ij} = \sum_{m=i-D}^{i+D} \sum_{n=j-D}^{j+D} w_{mn} \begin{bmatrix} h_{mn}^2 & h_{mn}v_{mn} \\ h_{mn}v_{mn} & v_{mn}^2 \end{bmatrix}, \tag{13.14}$$

where $\mathbf{S}_{ij}$ is the image structure tensor at position (i,j), which is computed over a square region of size $(2D+1) \times (2D+1)$ around the current position. The term h_{mn} denotes the response of a horizontal derivative filter (such as the Sobel) at position (m,n) and the term v_{mn} denotes the response of a vertical derivative filter. The term w_{mn} is a weight that diminishes the contribution of positions that are far from the central pixel (i,j).

To identify whether a corner is present, the Harris corner detector considers the singular values λ_1, λ_2 of the image structure tensor. If both singular values are small, then the region around the point is smooth and this position is not chosen. If one singular value is large but the other small, then the image is changing in one direction but not the other, and point lies on or near an edge. However, if both singular values are large, then this image is changing rapidly in both directions in this region and the position is deemed to be a corner.

In fact the Harris detector does not directly compute the singular values, but evaluates a criterion which accomplishes the same thing more efficiently:

$$c_{ij} = \lambda_1 \lambda_2 - \kappa(\lambda_1^2 + \lambda_2^2) = \det[\mathbf{S}_{ij}] - \kappa \cdot \text{trace}[\mathbf{S}_{ij}], \qquad (13.15)$$

where κ is a constant (values between 0.04 and 0.15 are sensible). If the value of c_{ij} is greater than a predetermined threshold, then a corner may be assigned. There is usually an additional non-maximum suppression stage similar to that in the Canny edge detector to ensure that only peaks in the function c_{ij} are retained.

13.2.3 SIFT detector

The scale invariant feature transform (SIFT) detector is a second method for identifying interest points. Unlike the Harris corner detector, it associates a scale and orientation to each of the resulting interest points. To find the interest points a number of operations are performed in turn.

The intensity image is filtered with a difference of Gaussian kernel at a series of K increasingly coarse scales (Figure 13.13). Then the filtered images are stacked to make a 3D volume of size $I \times J \times K$, where I and J are the vertical and horizontal size of the image. *Extrema* are identified within this volume: these are positions where the 26 3D voxel neighbors (from a $3 \times 3 \times 3$ block) are either all greater than or all less than the current value.

These extrema are localized to subvoxel accuracy, by applying a local quadratic approximation and returning the position of the peak or trough. The quadratic approximation is made by taking a Taylor expansion about the current point. This provides a position estimate that has subpixel resolution and an estimate of the scale that is more accurate than the resolution of the scale sampling. Finally, the image structure tensor $\mathbf{S}_{ij}$ (Equation 13.14) is computed at the location and scale of each point. Candidate points in smooth regions and on edges are removed by considering the singular values of $\mathbf{S}_{ij}$ as in the Harris corner detector (Figure 13.14).

This procedure returns a set of interest points that are localized to subpixel accuracy and associated accurately with a particular scale. Finally, a unique orientation is also assigned to each interest point. To this end, the amplitude and orientation of the local gradients are computed (Equations 13.13) in a region surrounding the interest point whose size is proportional to the identified scale. An orientation histogram is then computed over this region with 36 bins covering all 360° of orientation. The contribution to the histogram depends on the gradient amplitude and is weighted by a Gaussian profile centered at the location of the interest point, so that nearby regions contribute more. The orientation of the interest point is assigned to be the peak of this histogram. If there is a second peak within 80 percent of the maximum, we may choose to compute descriptors at two orientations at this point. The final detected points are hence associated with a particular orientation and scale (Figure 13.15).

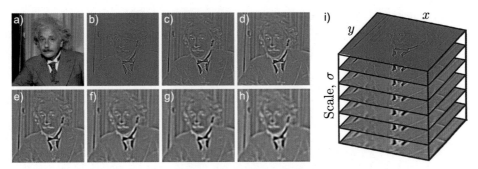

Figure 13.13 The SIFT detector. a) Original image. b–h) The image is filtered with difference of Gaussian kernels at a range of increasing scales. i) The resulting images are stacked to create a 3D volume. Points that are local extrema in the filtered image volume (i.e., are either greater than or less than all 26 3D neighbors) are considered to be candidates for interest points.

Figure 13.14 Refinement of SIFT detector candidates. a) Positions of extrema in the filtered image volume (Figure 13.13i). Note that the scale is not shown. These are considered candidates to be interest points. b) Remaining candidates after eliminating those in smooth regions. c) Remaining candidate points after removing those on edges using the image structure tensor.

13.3 Descriptors

In this section, we consider *descriptors*. These are compact representations that summarize the contents of an image region.

13.3.1 Histograms

The simplest approach to aggregating information over a large image region is to compute a histogram of the responses in this area. For example, we might collate RGB pixel intensities, filter responses, local binary patterns, or textons into a histogram depending on the application. The histogram entries can be treated as discrete and modeled with a categorical distribution, or treated as a continuous vector quantity.

For continuous quantities such as filter responses, the level of quantization is critical. Quantizing the responses into many bins potentially allows fine discrimination between responses. However, if data are scarce, then many of these bins will be empty, and it is harder to reliably determine the statistics of the descriptor. One approach is to use an adaptive clustering method such as K-means (Section 13.4.4) to automatically determine the bin sizes and shapes.

Figure 13.15 Results of SIFT detector. Each final interest point is indicated using an arrow. The length of the arrow indicates the scale with which the interest point is identified and the angle of the arrow indicates the associated orientation. Notice that there are some positions in the image where the orientation was not unique and here two interest points are used, one associated with each orientation. An example of this is on the right shirt collar. Subsequent descriptors that characterize the structure of the image around the interest points are computed relative to this scale and orientation and hence inherit some invariance to these factors.

Histogramming is a useful approach for tasks where spatial resolution is not paramount: for example, to classify a large region of texture, it makes sense to pool information. However, this approach is largely unsuitable for characterizing structured objects: the spatial layout of the object is important for identification. We now introduce two representations for image regions that retain some spatial information but also pool information locally and thus provide invariance to small displacements and warps of the image. Both the SIFT descriptor (Section 13.3.2) and the HOG descriptor (Section 13.3.3) concatenate several histograms that were computed over spatially distinct blocks.

13.3.2 SIFT descriptors

The scale invariant feature transform descriptor (Figure 13.16) characterizes the image region around a given point. It is usually used in conjunction with interest points that were found using the SIFT detector. These interest points are associated with a particular scale and rotation, and the SIFT descriptor would typically be computed over a square region that is transformed by these values. The goal is to characterize the image region in a way that is partially invariant to intensity and contrast changes and small geometric deformations.

To compute the SIFT descriptor, we first compute gradient orientation and amplitude maps (Equation 13.13) as for the Canny edge detector over a 16×16 pixel region around the interest point. The resulting orientation is quantized into eight bins spread over the range 0°–360°. Then the 16×16 detector region is divided into a regular grid of nonoverlapping 4×4 cells. Within each of these cells, an eight-dimensional histogram of the image orientations is computed. Each contribution to the histogram is weighted by the associated gradient amplitude and by distance so that positions further from the interest point contribute less. The $4 \times 4 = 16$ histograms are concatenated to make a single 128×1 vector, which is then normalized.

The descriptor is invariant to constant intensity changes as it is based on gradients. The final normalization provides some invariance to contrast. Small deformations do not affect the descriptor too much as it pools information within each cell. However, by keeping the information from each cell separate, some spatial information is retained.

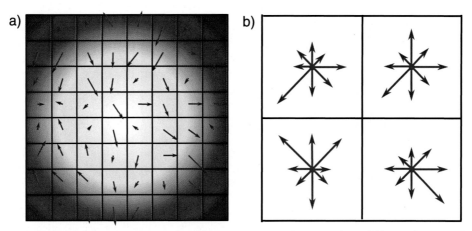

Figure 13.16 SIFT descriptor. a) Gradients are computed for every pixel within a region around the interest point. b) This region is subdivided into cells. Information is pooled within these cells to form an 8D histogram. These histograms are concatenated to provide a final descriptor that pools locally to provide invariance to small deformations but also retains some spatial information about the image gradients. In this figure, information from an 8×8 pixel patch has been divided to make a 2×2 grid of cells. In the original implementation of the SIFT detector, a 16×16 patch was divided into at 4×4 grid of cells.

13.3.3   Histogram of oriented gradients

The Histogram of Oriented Gradients (HOG) descriptor attempts to construct a more detailed characterization of the spatial structure with a small image window. It is a useful preprocessing step for algorithms that detect objects with quasi-regular structure such as pedestrians. Like the SIFT descriptor, the HOG descriptor consists of a collection of normalized histograms computed over spatially offset patches; the result is a descriptor that captures coarse spatial structure, but is invariant to small local deformations.

The process of computing a HOG descriptor suitable for pedestrian detection consists of the following stages. First, the orientation and amplitude of the image gradients are computed at every pixel in a 64×128 window using Equation 13.13. The orientation is quantized into nine bins spread over the range 0°–180°. The 64×128 detector region is divided into a regular grid of overlapping 6×6 cells. A 9D orientation histogram is computed within each cell, where the contribution to the histogram is weighted by the gradient amplitude and the distance from the center of the cell so that more central pixels contribute more. For each 3×3 block of cells, the descriptors are concatenated and normalized to form a block descriptor. All of the block descriptors are concatenated to form the final HOG descriptor.

The final descriptor contains spatially pooled information about local gradients (within each cell), but maintains some spatial resolution (as there are many cells). It creates invariance to contrast polarity by only using the gradient magnitudes. It creates invariance to local contrast strength by normalizing relative to each block. The HOG descriptor is similar in spirit to the SIFT descriptor but is distinguished by being invariant to contrast polarity, having a higher spatial resolution of computed histograms and performing normalization more locally.

13.3.4   Bag of words descriptor

The descriptors discussed thus far have been intended to characterize small regions of images. Often these regions have been connected to interest points. The bag of words

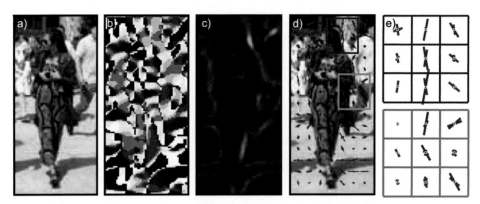

Figure 13.17 HOG descriptor. a) Original image. b) Gradient orientation, quantized into nine bins from $0°$ to $180°$. c) Gradient magnitude. d) Cell descriptors are 9D orientation histograms that are computed within 6×6 pixel regions. e) Block descriptors are computed by concatenating 3×3 blocks of cell descriptors. The block descriptors are normalized. The final HOG descriptor consists of the concatenated block descriptors.

representation attempts to characterize a larger region or an entire image by summarizing the statistics of the descriptors (e.g., SIFT) associated with all of the interest points in a region.

Each observed descriptor is considered to be one of a finite vocabulary of possible descriptors (termed *visual words*). Collectively, this vocabulary is known as a *dictionary*. The bag of words descriptor is simply a histogram describing the frequency of observing these words giving no regard to their position. To compute the dictionary, interest points are found in a large number of images and the associated descriptor is computed. These descriptors are clustered using K-means (Section 13.4.4). To compute the bag of words representation, each descriptor is assigned to the nearest word in this dictionary.

The bag of words representation is a remarkably good substrate for object recognition. This is somewhat surprising given that it surrenders any knowledge about the spatial configuration about the object. Of course, the drawback of approaches based on the bag of words is that it is very hard to localize the object after we have identified its presence or to decide how many instances are present using the same model.

13.3.5 Shape context descriptor

For certain vision tasks, the silhouette of the object contains much more information than the RGB values themselves. Consider, for example, the problem of body pose estimation: given an image of a human being, the goal is to estimate the 3D joint angles of the body. Unfortunately, the RGB values of the image depend on the person's clothing and are relatively uninformative. In such situations, it is wiser to attempt to characterize the shape of the object.

The shape context descriptor is a fixed length vector that characterizes the object contour. Essentially, it encodes the relative position of points on the contour. In common with the SIFT and HOG descriptors, it pools information locally over space to provide a representation that can capture the overall structure of the object but is not affected too much by small spatial variations.

To compute the shape context descriptor (Figure 13.18), a discrete set of points is sampled along the contour of the object. A fixed length vector is associated with each

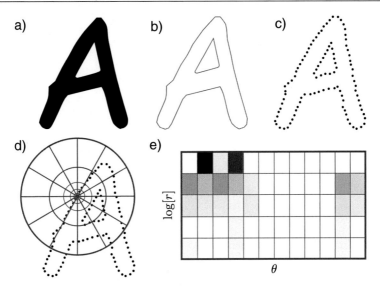

Figure 13.18 Shape context descriptor. a) Object silhouette. b) Contour of silhouette. c) Points are placed at equally spaced intervals around the silhouette. d) A log polar sampling array is centered at each point. e) The shape of the object relative to this point is captured by the histogram over the bins of the log polar array. The final descriptor would consist of a concatenation of the values from histograms from multiple points around the edge of the object.

point that characterizes the relative position of the other points. To this end, a log polar sampling array is centered on the current point. A histogram is then computed where each bin contains the number of the other points on the silhouette that fell into each bin of the log-polar array. The choice of the log-polar scheme means that the descriptor is very sensitive to local changes in the shape, but only captures the approximate configuration of distant parts.

The collection of histograms for all of the points on this image captures the shape. However, to directly match to another shape, the point correspondence must be established. It is possible to make this descriptor invariant to orientation by evaluating the orientation of the contour at each point and rotating the log polar sampling scheme so that it is aligned with this orientation.

13.4 Dimensionality reduction

It is often desirable to reduce the dimensionality of either the original or pre-processed image data. If we can do this without losing too much information, then the resulting models will require fewer parameters and be faster to learn and to use for inference.

Dimensionality reduction is possible because a given type of image data (e.g., RGB values from face images) usually lie in a tiny subset of the possible data space; not all sets of RGB values look like real images, and not all real images look like faces. We refer to the subset of the space occupied by a given dataset as a *manifold*. Dimensionality reduction can hence be thought of as a change of variables: we move from the original coordinate system to the (reduced) coordinate system within the manifold.

Our goal is hence to find a low-dimensional (or hidden) representation $\mathbf{h}$, which can approximately explain the data $\mathbf{x}$, so that

$$\mathbf{x} \approx f[\mathbf{h}, \boldsymbol{\theta}], \tag{13.16}$$

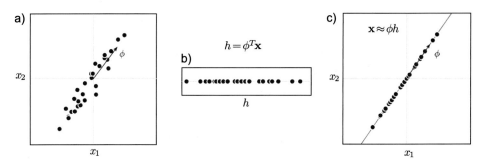

Figure 13.19 Reduction to a single dimension. a) Original data and direction ϕ of maximum variance. b) The data are projected onto ϕ to produce a one-dimensional representation. c) To reconstruct the data, we remultiply by ϕ. Most of the original variation is retained. PCA extends this model to project high-dimensional data onto the K orthogonal dimensions with the most variance, to produce a K-dimensional representation.

where $f[\bullet, \bullet]$ is a function that takes the hidden variable and a set of parameters $\boldsymbol{\theta}$. We would like the lower-dimensional representation to capture all of the relevant variation in the original data. Hence, one possible criterion for choosing the parameters is to minimize the least squares *reconstruction error* so that

$$\hat{\boldsymbol{\theta}}, \hat{\mathbf{h}}_{1...I} = \underset{\boldsymbol{\theta}, \mathbf{h}_{1...I}}{\operatorname{argmin}} \left[\sum_{i=1}^{I} (\mathbf{x}_i - f[\mathbf{h}_i, \boldsymbol{\theta}])^T (\mathbf{x}_i - f[\mathbf{h}_i, \boldsymbol{\theta}]) \right], \qquad (13.17)$$

where $\mathbf{x}_i$ is the ith of I training examples. In other words, we aim to find a set of low-dimensional variables $\{\mathbf{h}_i\}_{i=1}^{I}$ and a mapping from $\mathbf{h}$ to $\mathbf{x}$ so that it reconstructs the original data as closely as possible in a least squares sense.

13.4.1 Approximation with a single number

Let us first consider a very simple model in which we attempt to represent each observed datum with a single number (Figure 13.19) so that

$$\mathbf{x}_i \approx \phi h_i + \boldsymbol{\mu}, \qquad (13.18)$$

where the parameter $\boldsymbol{\mu}$ is the mean of the data is zero and the parameter ϕ is a basis vector mapping the low-dimensional representation $\mathbf{h}$ back to the original data space $\mathbf{x}$. For simplicity, we will assume from now on that the mean of the $\mathbf{x}_i \approx \phi h_i$. This can be achieved by computing the empirical mean $\boldsymbol{\mu}$ and subtracting it from every example $\mathbf{x}_i$.

The learning algorithm optimizes the criterion

$$\hat{\phi}, \hat{h}_{1...I} = \underset{\phi, h_{1...I}}{\operatorname{argmin}} [E] = \underset{\phi, h_{1...I}}{\operatorname{argmin}} \left[\sum_{i=1}^{I} (\mathbf{x}_i - \phi h_i)^T (\mathbf{x}_i - \phi h_i) \right]. \qquad (13.19)$$

Careful consideration of the cost function (Equation 13.19) reveals an immediate problem: the solution is ambiguous as we can multiply the basis function ϕ by any constant k and divide each of the hidden variables $\{h_i\}_{i=1}^{I}$ by the same number to yield exactly the same cost. To resolve this problem, we force the vector ϕ to have unit length. This is accomplished by adding in a Lagrange multiplier λ so that the cost function becomes

$$E = \sum_{i=1}^{I} (\mathbf{x}_i - \phi h_i)^T (\mathbf{x}_i - \phi h_i) + \lambda(\phi^T \phi - 1)$$

$$= \sum_{i=1}^{I} \mathbf{x}_i^T \mathbf{x}_i - 2h_i \phi^T \mathbf{x}_i + h_i^2 + \lambda(\phi^T \phi - 1). \tag{13.20}$$

To minimize the function, we first take the derivative with respect to h_i and then equate the resulting expression to zero to yield

$$\hat{h}_i = \hat{\phi}^T \mathbf{x}_i. \tag{13.21}$$

In other words, to find the reduced dimension representation h_i we simply project the observed data onto the vector ϕ.

We now take the derivative of Equation 13.20 with respect to ϕ, substitute in the solution for h_i, equate the result to zero, and rearrange to get

$$\sum_{i=1}^{I} \mathbf{x}_i \mathbf{x}_i^T \hat{\phi} = \lambda \hat{\phi}, \tag{13.22}$$

or in matrix form

$$\mathbf{X}\mathbf{X}^T \hat{\phi} = \lambda \hat{\phi}, \tag{13.23}$$

where the matrix $\mathbf{X} = [\mathbf{x}_1, \mathbf{x}_2, \ldots, \mathbf{x}_I]$ contains the data examples in its columns. This is an eigenvalue problem. To find the optimal vector, we compute the SVD $\mathbf{U}\mathbf{L}\mathbf{V}^T = \mathbf{X}\mathbf{X}^T$ and choose the first column of $\mathbf{U}$.

The scatter matrix $\mathbf{X}\mathbf{X}^T$ is a constant multiple of the covariance matrix, and so this has a simple geometric interpretation. The optimal vector ϕ to project onto corresponds to the principal direction of the covariance ellipse. This makes intuitive sense; we retain information from the direction in space where the data vary most.

13.4.2 Principal component analysis

Principal component analysis (PCA) generalizes the above model. Instead of finding a scalar variable h_i that represents the ith data example $\mathbf{x}_i$, we now seek a K-dimensional vector $\mathbf{h}_i$. The relation between the hidden and observed spaces is

$$\mathbf{x}_i \approx \mathbf{\Phi}\mathbf{h}_i, \tag{13.24}$$

where the matrix $\mathbf{\Phi} = [\phi_1, \phi_2, \ldots, \phi_K]$ contains K basis functions or *principal components*; the observed data are modeled as a weighted sum of the principal components, where the kth dimension of $\mathbf{h}_i$ weights the kth component.

The solution for the unknowns $\mathbf{\Phi}$ and $\mathbf{h}_{1...I}$ can now be written as

$$\mathbf{\Phi}, \hat{\mathbf{h}}_{1...I} = \operatorname*{argmin}_{\mathbf{\Phi}, \mathbf{h}_{1...I}} [E] = \operatorname*{argmin}_{\mathbf{\Phi}, \mathbf{h}_{1...I}} \left[\sum_{i=1}^{I} (\mathbf{x}_i - \mathbf{\Phi}\mathbf{h}_i)^T (\mathbf{x}_i - \mathbf{\Phi}\mathbf{h}_i) \right]. \tag{13.25}$$

Once more, the solution to this is nonunique as we can postmultiply $\mathbf{\Phi}$ by any matrix $\mathbf{A}$ and premultiply each hidden variable $\mathbf{h}_i$ by the inverse $\mathbf{A}^{-1}$ and still get the same cost. To (partially) resolve this problem, we add the extra constraint that $\mathbf{\Phi}^T\mathbf{\Phi} = \mathbf{I}$. In other words, we force the principal components to be orthogonal and length one. This gives a modified cost function of

$$E = \sum_{i=1}^{I}(\mathbf{x}_i - \mathbf{\Phi}\mathbf{h}_i)^T(\mathbf{x}_i - \mathbf{\Phi}\mathbf{h}_i) + \lambda(\mathbf{\Phi}^T\mathbf{\Phi} - \mathbf{I}), \tag{13.26}$$

where λ is a Lagrange multiplier. We now minimize this expression with respect to $\mathbf{\Phi}, \mathbf{h}_{1...I}$ and λ. The expression for the hidden variables becomes

$$\mathbf{h}_i = \mathbf{\Phi}^T\mathbf{x}_i, \tag{13.27}$$

The K principal components $\mathbf{\Phi} = [\phi_1, \phi_2, \ldots, \phi_K]$ are now found by computing the singular value decomposition $\mathbf{U}\mathbf{L}\mathbf{V}^T = \mathbf{X}\mathbf{X}^T$ and taking the first K columns of $\mathbf{U}$. In other words, to reduce the dimensionality, we project the data $\mathbf{x}_i$ onto a hyperplane defined by the K largest axes of the covariance ellipsoid.

This algorithm is very closely related to probabilistic principal component analysis (Section 17.5.1). Probabilistic PCA additionally models the noise that accounts for the inexact approximation in Equation 13.24. Factor analysis (Section 7.6) is also very similar, but constructs a more sophisticated model of this noise.

13.4.3 Dual principal component analysis

The method outlined in Section 13.4.2 requires us to compute the SVD of the scatter matrix $\mathbf{X}\mathbf{X}^T$. Unfortunately, if the data had dimension D, then this is a $D \times D$ matrix, which may be very large. We can sidestep this problem by using dual variables. We define $\mathbf{\Phi}$ as a weighted sum of the original datapoints so that

$$\mathbf{\Phi} = \mathbf{X}\mathbf{\Psi}, \tag{13.28}$$

where $\mathbf{\Psi} = [\psi_1, \psi_2, \ldots, \psi_K]$ is a $I \times K$ matrix representing these weights. The associated cost function now becomes

$$E = \sum_{i=1}^{I}(\mathbf{x}_i - \mathbf{X}\mathbf{\Psi}\mathbf{h}_i)^T(\mathbf{x}_i - \mathbf{X}\mathbf{\Psi}\mathbf{h}_i) + \lambda(\mathbf{\Psi}^T\mathbf{X}^T\mathbf{X}\mathbf{\Psi} - \mathbf{I}). \tag{13.29}$$

The solution for the hidden variables becomes

$$\mathbf{h}_i = \mathbf{\Psi}^T\mathbf{X}^T\mathbf{x}_i = \mathbf{\Phi}^T\mathbf{x}_i, \tag{13.30}$$

and the K dual principal components $\mathbf{\Psi} = [\psi_1, \psi_2 \ldots, \psi_K]$ are extracted from the matrix $\mathbf{U}$ in the SVD $\mathbf{U}\mathbf{L}\mathbf{V}^T = \mathbf{X}^T\mathbf{X}$. This is a smaller problem of size $I \times I$ and so is more efficient when the number of data examples I is less than the dimensionality of the observed space D.

Notice that this algorithm does not require the original datapoints: it only requires the inner products between them and so is amenable to kernelization. This resulting method is known as kernel PCA.

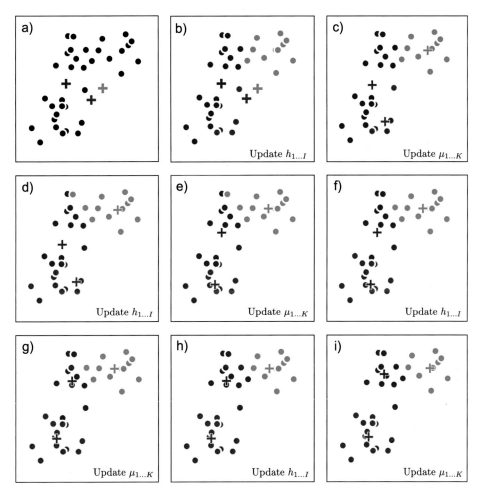

Figure 13.20 K-means algorithm for $K = 3$ clusters. a) We initialize the three prototype vectors (crosses) to random positions. We alternately b) assign the data to the nearest prototype vector and c) update the prototype vectors to be equal to the mean of the points assigned to them. d–i) We repeat these steps until there is no further change.

13.4.4   The K-means algorithm

A second common approach to dimensionality reduction is to abandon a continuous representation altogether and represent the each datapoint using one of a limited set of prototype vectors. In this model, the data are approximated as

$$\mathbf{x}_i \approx \boldsymbol{\mu}_{h_i}, \tag{13.31}$$

where $h_i \in \{1, 2, \ldots, K\}$ is an index that identifies which of the K prototype vectors $\{\boldsymbol{\mu}_k\}_{k=1}^{K}$ approximates the ith example.

To find the assignment indices and the prototype vectors (Figure 13.20), we optimize

$$\hat{\boldsymbol{\mu}}_{1\ldots K}, \hat{h}_{1\ldots I} = \underset{\boldsymbol{\mu}, h}{\operatorname{argmin}} \left[\sum_{i=1}^{I} \left(\mathbf{x}_i - \boldsymbol{\mu}_{h_i} \right)^T \left(\mathbf{x}_i - \boldsymbol{\mu}_{h_i} \right) \right]. \tag{13.32}$$

In the K-means algorithm, this cost function is minimized using an alternating strategy in which we first assign each datapoint to the nearest prototype

$$\hat{h}_i = \underset{h_i}{\operatorname{argmin}} \left[\left(\mathbf{x}_i - \boldsymbol{\mu}_{h_i} \right)^T \left(\mathbf{x}_i - \boldsymbol{\mu}_{h_i} \right) \right], \tag{13.33}$$

and then update the prototypes

$$\hat{\boldsymbol{\mu}}_k = \underset{\boldsymbol{\mu}_k}{\operatorname{argmin}} \left[\sum_{i=1}^{I} \left[\left(\mathbf{x}_i - \boldsymbol{\mu}_{h_i} \right)^T \left(\mathbf{x}_i - \boldsymbol{\mu}_{h_i} \right) \right] \right]$$
$$= \frac{\sum_{i=1}^{I} \mathbf{x}_i \delta[h_i - k]}{\sum_{i=1}^{I} \delta[h_i - k]}, \tag{13.34}$$

where $\delta[\bullet]$ is a function that returns one when its argument is zero and zero otherwise. In other words, the new prototype $\hat{\boldsymbol{\mu}}_k$ is simply the average of the datapoints that are assigned to this cluster. This algorithm is not guaranteed to converge to the global minimum and so it requires sensible starting conditions.

The K-means algorithm is very closely related to the mixtures of Gaussians model (Section 7.4). The main differences are that the mixtures of Gaussians model is probabilistic and defines a density over the data space. It also assigns weights to the clusters and describes their covariance.

Conclusion

Careful reading of the information in this chapter should convince you that there are certain recurring ideas in image preprocessing. To make a descriptor invariant to intensity changes we *filter* the image and *normalize* the filter responses over the region. A unique descriptor orientation and scale can be computed by *maximizing* over responses at different orientations and scales. To create invariance to small spatial changes, local responses are *pooled*. Despite the simplicity of these ideas, it is remarkable how much impact they have on the performance of real systems.

Notes

Image Processing: There are numerous texts on image processing which contain far more information than I could include in this chapter. I would particularly recommend the books by O'Gorman et al. (2008), Gonzalez and Woods (2002), Pratt (2007), and Nixon and Aguado (2008). A comprehensive recent summary of local image features can be found in Li and Allinson (2008).

Edge and corner detection: The Canny edge detector was first described in Canny (1986). Elder (1999) investigated whether it was possible to reconstruct an image based on edge information alone. Nowadays, it is common to use machine learning methods to identify object boundaries in images (e.g., Dollár et al. 2006)

Early work in corner detection (interest point detection) includes that of Moravec (1983), Förstner (1986), and the Harris corner detector (Harris and Stephens 1988), which we described in this chapter. Other more recent efforts to identify stable points and regions include the SUSAN corner detector (Smith and Brady 1997), a saliency-based descriptor (Kadir and Brady 2001), maximally stable extremal regions (Matas et al. 2002), the SIFT detector (Lowe 2004), and the FAST detector (Rosten and Drummond 2006). There has been considerable recent interest in *affine invariant* interest point detection, which aims to find features that are stable under affine transformations of the image (e.g., Schaffalitzky and Zisserman 2002; Mikolajczyk and Schmid 2002, 2004). Mikolajczyk et al. (2005) present a quantitative comparison of different affine region detectors. A recent review of this area can be found in Tuytelaars and Mikolajczyk (2007).

Image descriptors: For robust object recognition and image matching, it is crucial to characterize the region around the detected interest point in a way that is compact and stable to changes in the image. To this end, Lowe (2004) developed the SIFT descriptor, Dalal and Triggs (2005) developed the HOG descriptor, and Forssén and Lowe (2007) developed a descriptor for use with maximally stable extremal regions. Bay et al. (2008) developed a very efficient version of SIFT features known as SURF. Mikolajczyk and Schmid (2005) present a quantitative comparison of region descriptors. Recent work on image descriptors has applied machine learning techniques to optimize their performance (Brown et al. 2011; Philbin et al. 2010).

More information about local binary patterns can be found in Ojala et al. (2002). More information about the shape context descriptor can be found in Belongie et al. (2002).

Dimensionality reduction: Principal components analysis is a linear dimensionality reduction method. However, there are also many nonlinear approaches that describe a manifold of images in high dimensions with fewer parameters. Notable methods include kernel PCA (Schölkopf et al. 1997), ISOMAP (Tenenbaum et al. 2000), local linear embedding (Roweis and Saul 2000), charting (Brand 2002), the Gaussian process latent variable model (Lawrence 2004), and Laplacian eigenmaps (Belkin and Niyogi 2001). Recent reviews of dimensionality reduction can be found in Burgess (2010) and De La Torre (2011).

Problems

13.1 Consider an eight-bit image in which the pixel values are evenly distributed in the range 0–127, with no pixels taking a value of 128 or larger. Draw the cumulative histogram for this image (see Figure 13.2). What will the histogram of pixel intensities look like after applying histogram equalization?

13.2 Consider a continuous image $p[i,j]$ and a continuous filter $f[m,n]$ In the continuous domain, the operation $f \otimes p$ of convolving an image with the filter is defined as

$$f \otimes p = \int_{-\infty}^{\infty} \int_{-\infty}^{\infty} p[i-m, j-n] f[m,n] \, dm dn.$$

Now consider two filters f and g. Prove that convolving the image first with f and then with g has the same effect as convolving f with g and then convolving the image with the result. In other words:

$$g \otimes (f \otimes p) = (g \otimes f) \otimes p.$$

Does this result extend to discrete images?

13.3 Describe the series of operations that would be required to compute the Haar filters in Figures 13.6a–d from an integral image. How many points from the integral image are needed to compute each?

13.4 Consider a blurring filter where each pixel in an image is replaced by a weighted average of local intensity values, but the the weights decrease if these intensity values differ markedly from the central pixel. What effect would this *bilateral filter* have when applied to an image?

13.5 Define a 3×3 filter that is specialized to detecting luminance changes at a 45° angle and gives a positive response where the image intensity increases from the bottom left to the bottom right of the image.

13.6 Define a 3×3 filter that responds to the second derivative in the horizontal direction but is invariant to the gradient and absolute intensity in the horizontal direction and invariant to all changes in the vertical direction.

13.7 Why are most local binary patterns in a natural image typically uniform or near-uniform?

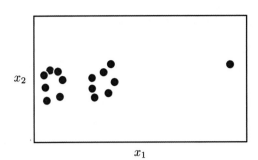

Figure 13.21 Clustering with the K-means algorithm in the presence of outliers (Problem 13.9). This data set contains two clusters and a single outlier (the point on the right-hand side). The outlier causes problems for the K-means algorithm when $K = 2$ clusters are used due to the implicit assumption that the clusters can be modeled as normal distributions with spherical covariance.

13.8 Give one example of a 2D data set where the mixtures of Gaussians model will succeed in clustering the data, but the K-means algorithm will fail.

13.9 Consider the data in Figure 13.21. What do you expect to happen if we run the K-means algorithm with $K = 2$ clusters on this data set? Suggest a way to resolve this problem.

13.10 An alternative approach to clustering the data would be to find modes (peaks) in the density of the points. This potentially has the advantage of also automatically selecting the number of clusters. Propose an algorithm to find these modes.

Part V
Models for geometry

In Part V, we finally acknowledge the process by which real-world images are formed. Light is emitted from one or more sources and travels through the scene, interacting with the materials via physical processes such as reflection, refraction, and scattering. Some of this light enters the camera and is measured. We have a very good understanding of this forward model. Given known geometry, light sources, and material properties, computer graphics techniques can simulate what will be seen by the camera very accurately.

The ultimate goal for a vision algorithm would be a complete *reconstruction*, in which we aim to invert this forward model and estimate the light sources, materials, and geometry from the image. Here, we aim to capture a structural description of the world: we seek an understanding of where things are and to measure their optical properties, rather than a semantic understanding. Such a structural description can be exploited to navigate around the environment or build 3D models for computer graphics.

Unfortunately, full visual reconstruction is very challenging. For one thing, the solution is nonunique. For example, if the light source intensity increases, but the object reflectance decreases commensurately, the image will remain unchanged. Of course, we could make the problem unique by imposing prior knowledge, but even then reconstruction remains difficult; it is hard to effectively parameterize the scene, and the problem is highly non-convex.

In this part of the book, we consider a family of models that approximate both the 3D scene and the observed image with sparse sets of visual primitives (points). The forward model that maps the proxy representation of the world (3D points) to the proxy representation of the image (2D points) is much simpler than the full light transport model, and is called the *projective pinhole camera*. We investigate the properties of this model in Chapter 14.

In Chapter 15, we consider the situation where the pinhole camera views a plane in the world; there is now a one-to-one mapping between points on the plane and points in the image, and we characterize this mapping with a family of 2D transformations. In Chapter 16, we will further exploit the pinhole camera model to recover a sparse geometric model of the scene.

Chapter 14

The pinhole camera

This chapter introduces the pinhole or projective camera. This is a purely geometric model that describes the process whereby points in the world are projected into the image. Clearly, the position in the image depends on the position in the world, and the pinhole camera model captures this relationship.

To motivate this model, we will consider the problem of *sparse stereo reconstruction* (Figure 14.1). We are given two images of a rigid object taken from different positions. Let us assume that we can identify corresponding 2D features between the two images – points that are projected versions of the same position in the 3D world. The goal now is to establish this 3D position using the observed 2D feature points. The resulting 3D information could be used by a robot to help it navigate through the scene, or to facilitate object recognition.

14.1 The pinhole camera

In real life, a pinhole camera consists of a chamber[1] with a small hole (the pinhole) in the front (Figure 14.2). Rays from an object in the world pass through this hole to form an inverted image on the back face of the box, or *image plane*. Our goal is to build a mathematical model of this process.

It is slightly inconvenient that the image from the pinhole camera is upside-down. Hence, we instead consider the *virtual image* that would result from placing the image plane *in front of* the pinhole. Of course, it is not physically possible to build a camera this way, but it is mathematically equivalent to the true pinhole model (except that the image is the right way up) and it is easier to think about. From now on, we will always draw the image plane in front of the pinhole.

Figure 14.3 illustrates the pinhole camera model and defines some terminology. The pinhole itself (the point at which the rays converge) is called the *optical center*. We will assume for now that the optical center is at the origin of the 3D world coordinate system, in which points are represented as $\mathbf{w} = [u, v, w]^T$. The virtual image is created on the *image plane*, which is displaced from the optical center along the w-axis or *optical axis*. The point where the optical axis strikes the image plane is known as the *principal point*. The distance between the principal point and the optical center (i.e., the distance between the image plane and the pinhole) is known as the *focal length*.

---

[1] This is not an accidental choice of word. The term *camera* is derived from the Latin word for 'chamber.'

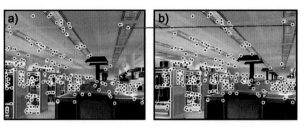 

Figure 14.1 Sparse stereo reconstruction. a,b) We are given two images of the same scene taken from different positions, and a set of I pairs of points in these images that are known to correspond to the same points in the world (e.g., the points connected by the red line are a corresponding pair). c) Our goal is to establish the 3D position of each of the world points. Here, the depth is encoded by color so that closer points are red and more distant points are blue.

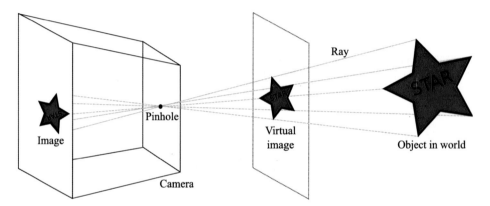

Figure 14.2 The pinhole camera model. Rays from an object in the world pass through the pinhole in the front of the camera and form an image on the back plane (the image plane). This image is upside-down, so we can alternatively consider the virtual image that would have been created if the image plane was in front of the pinhole. This is not physically possible, but it is more convenient to work with.

The pinhole camera model is a generative model that describes the likelihood $Pr(\mathbf{x}|\mathbf{w})$ of observing a feature at position $\mathbf{x} = [x, y]^T$ in the image given that it is the projection of a 3D point $\mathbf{w} = [u, v, w]^T$ in the world. Although light transport is essentially deterministic, we will nonetheless build a probability model; there is noise in the sensor, and unmodeled factors in the feature detection process can also affect the measured image position. However, for pedagogical reasons we will defer a discussion of this uncertainty until later, and temporarily treat the imaging process as if it were deterministic.

Our task then is to establish the position $\mathbf{x} = [x, y]^T$ where the 3D point $\mathbf{w} = [u, v, w]^T$ is imaged. Considering Figure 14.3 it is clear how to do this. We connect a ray between $\mathbf{w}$ and the optical center. The image position $\mathbf{x}$ can be found by observing where this ray strikes the image plane. This process is called *perspective projection*. In the next few sections, we will build a more precise mathematical model of this process. We will start with a very simple camera model (the normalized camera) and build up to a full camera parameterization.

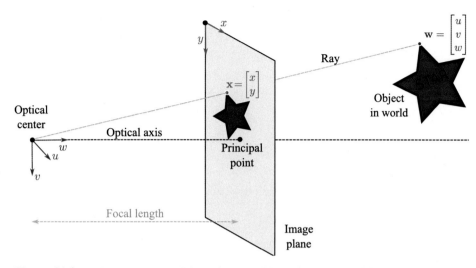

Figure 14.3 Pin-hole camera model terminology. The optical center (pinhole) is placed at the origin of the 3D world coordinate system (u, v, w) and the image plane (where the virtual image is formed) is displaced along the w-axis, which is also known as the optical axis. The position where the optical axis strikes the image plane is called the principal point. The distance between the image plane and the optical center is called the focal length.

14.1.1 The normalized camera

In the *normalized camera*, the focal length is one, and it is assumed that the origin of the 2D coordinate system (x, y) on the image plane is centered at the principal point. Figure 14.4 shows a 2D slice of the geometry of this system (the u- and x-axes now point upward out of the page and cannot be seen). By similar triangles, it can easily be seen that the y-position in the image of the world point at $\mathbf{w} = [u, v, w]^T$ is given by v/w. More generally, in the normalized camera, a 3D point $\mathbf{w} = [u, v, w]^T$ is projected into the image at $\mathbf{x} = [x, y]^T$ using the relations

$$x = \frac{u}{w}$$
$$y = \frac{v}{w},$$
(14.1)

where x, y, u, v, and w are measured in the same real-world units (e.g., mm).

14.1.2 Focal length parameters

The normalized camera is unrealistic; for one thing, in a real camera, there is no particular reason why the focal length should be one. Moreover, the final position in the image is measured in pixels, not physical distance, and so the model must take into account the photoreceptor spacing. Both of these factors have the effect of changing the mapping between points $\mathbf{w} = [u, v, w]^T$ in the 3D world and their 2D positions $\mathbf{x} = [x, y]^T$ in the

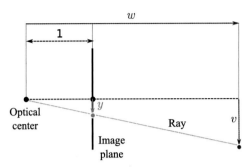

Figure 14.4 Normalized camera. The focal length is one, and the 2D image coordinate system (x, y) is centered on the principal point (only y-axis shown). By similar triangles, the y position in the image of a point at (u, v, w) is given by v/w. This corresponds to our intuition: as an object gets more distant, its projection becomes closer to the center of the image.

image plane by a constant scaling factor ϕ (Figure 14.5) so that

$$x = \frac{\phi u}{w}$$
$$y = \frac{\phi v}{w}. \tag{14.2}$$

To add a further complication, the spacing of the photoreceptors may differ in the x- and y-directions, so the scaling may be different in each direction, giving the relations

$$x = \frac{\phi_x u}{w}$$
$$y = \frac{\phi_y v}{w}, \tag{14.3}$$

where ϕ_x and ϕ_y are separate scaling factors for the x- and y-directions. These parameters are known as the *focal length parameters* in the x- and y-directions, but this name is somewhat misleading – they account for not just the distance between the optical center and the principal point (the true focal length) but also the photoreceptor spacing.

14.1.3 Offset and skew parameters

The model so far is still incomplete in that pixel position $\mathbf{x} = [0, 0]^T$ is at the principal point (where the w-axis intersects the image plane). In most imaging systems, the pixel position $\mathbf{x} = [0, 0]^T$ is at the top-left of the image rather than the center. To cope with this, we add *offset parameters* δ_x and δ_y so that

$$x = \frac{\phi_x u}{w} + \delta_x$$
$$y = \frac{\phi_y v}{w} + \delta_y, \tag{14.4}$$

where δ_x and δ_y are the offsets in pixels from the top-left corner of the image to the position where the w-axis strikes the image plane. Another way to think about this is that the vector $[\delta_x, \delta_y]^T$ is the position of the principal point in pixels.

If the image plane is exactly centered on the w-axis, these offset parameters should be half the image size: for a 640×480 VGA image δ_x and δ_y would be 320 and 240, respectively. However, in practice it is difficult and superfluous to manufacture cameras with

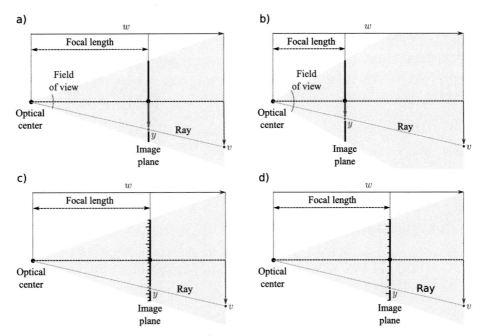

Figure 14.5 Focal length and photoreceptor spacing. a–b) Changing the distance between the optical center and the image plane (the focal length) changes the relationship between the 3D world point $\mathbf{w} = [u, v, w]^T$ and the 2D image point $\mathbf{x} = [x, y]^T$. In particular, if we take the original focal length (a) and halve it (b), the 2D image coordinate is also halved. The *field of view* of the camera is the total angular range that is imaged (usually different in the x- and y-directions). When the focal length decreases, the field of view increases. c–d) The position in the image $\mathbf{x} = [x, y]^T$ is usually measured in pixels. Hence, the position $\mathbf{x}$ depends on the density of the receptors on the image plane. If we take the original photoreceptor density (c) and halve it (d), then the 2D image coordinate is also halved. Hence, the photoreceptor spacing and focal length both change the mapping from rays to pixels in the same way.

the imaging sensor perfectly centered, and so we treat the offset parameters as unknown quantities.

We also introduce a *skew* term γ that moderates the projected position x as a function of the height v in the world. This parameter has no clear physical interpretation but can help explain the projection of points into the image in practice. The resulting camera model is

$$x = \frac{\phi_x u + \gamma v}{w} + \delta_x$$

$$y = \frac{\phi_y v}{w} + \delta_y. \tag{14.5}$$

14.1.4 Position and orientation of camera

Finally, we must account for the fact that the camera is not always conveniently centered at the origin of the world coordinate system with the optical axis exactly aligned with the w-axis. In general, we may want to define an arbitrary world coordinate system that may be common to more than one camera. To this end, we express the world points $\mathbf{w}$ in the coordinate system of the camera before they are passed through the projection model, using the coordinate transformation:

$$
\begin{bmatrix} u' \\ v' \\ w' \end{bmatrix} = \begin{bmatrix} \omega_{11} & \omega_{12} & \omega_{13} \\ \omega_{21} & \omega_{22} & \omega_{23} \\ \omega_{31} & \omega_{32} & \omega_{33} \end{bmatrix} \begin{bmatrix} u \\ v \\ w \end{bmatrix} + \begin{bmatrix} \tau_x \\ \tau_y \\ \tau_z \end{bmatrix}, \tag{14.6}
$$

or

$$
\mathbf{w}' = \mathbf{\Omega}\mathbf{w} + \boldsymbol{\tau}, \tag{14.7}
$$

where $\mathbf{w}'$ is the transformed point, $\mathbf{\Omega}$ is a 3×3 rotation matrix, and $\boldsymbol{\tau}$ is a 3×1 translation vector.

14.1.5 Full pinhole camera model

We are now in a position to describe the full camera model, by combining Equations 14.5 and 14.6. A 3D point $\mathbf{w} = [u, v, w]^T$ is projected to a 2D point $\mathbf{x} = [x, y]^T$ by the relations

$$
\begin{aligned}
x &= \frac{\phi_x(\omega_{11}u + \omega_{12}v + \omega_{13}w + \tau_x) + \gamma(\omega_{21}u + \omega_{22}v + \omega_{23}w + \tau_y)}{\omega_{31}u + \omega_{32}v + \omega_{33}w + \tau_z} + \delta_x \\
y &= \frac{\phi_y(\omega_{21}u + \omega_{22}v + \omega_{23}w + \tau_y)}{\omega_{31}u + \omega_{32}v + \omega_{33}w + \tau_z} + \delta_y.
\end{aligned} \tag{14.8}
$$

There are two sets of parameters in this model. The *intrinsic* or *camera parameters* $\{\phi_x, \phi_y, \gamma, \delta_x, \delta_y\}$ describe the camera itself, and the *extrinsic parameters* $\{\mathbf{\Omega}, \boldsymbol{\tau}\}$ describe the position and orientation of the camera in the world. For reasons that will become clear in Section 14.3.1, we will store the intrinsic parameters in the *intrinsic matrix* $\mathbf{\Lambda}$ where

$$
\mathbf{\Lambda} = \begin{bmatrix} \phi_x & \gamma & \delta_x \\ 0 & \phi_y & \delta_y \\ 0 & 0 & 1 \end{bmatrix}. \tag{14.9}
$$

We can now abbreviate the full projection model (Equations 14.8) by just writing

$$
\mathbf{x} = \mathbf{pinhole}[\mathbf{w}, \mathbf{\Lambda}, \mathbf{\Omega}, \boldsymbol{\tau}]. \tag{14.10}
$$

Finally, we must account for the fact that the estimated position of a feature in the image may differ from our predictions. There are a number of reasons for this, including noise in the sensor, sampling issues, and the fact that the detected position in the image may change at different viewpoints. We model these factors with additive noise that is normally distributed with a spherical covariance to give the final relation

$$
Pr(\mathbf{x}|\mathbf{w}, \mathbf{\Lambda}, \mathbf{\Omega}, \boldsymbol{\tau}) = \text{Norm}_{\mathbf{x}}\left[\mathbf{pinhole}[\mathbf{w}, \mathbf{\Lambda}, \mathbf{\Omega}, \boldsymbol{\tau}], \sigma^2\mathbf{I}\right], \tag{14.11}
$$

where σ^2 is the variance of the noise.

Note that the pinhole camera is a *generative model*. We are describing the likelihood $Pr(\mathbf{x}|\mathbf{w}, \mathbf{\Lambda}, \mathbf{\Omega}, \boldsymbol{\tau})$ of observing a 2D image point $\mathbf{x}$ given the 3D world point $\mathbf{w}$ and the parameters $\{\mathbf{\Lambda}, \mathbf{\Omega}, \boldsymbol{\tau}\}$.

Figure 14.6 Radial distortion. The pinhole model is only an approximation of the true imaging process. One important deviation from this model is a 2D warping in which points deviate from their expected positions by moving along radial lines from the center of the image by an amount that depends on the distance from the center. This is known as radial distortion. a) An image that suffers from radial distortion is easily spotted because lines that were straight in the world are mapped to curves in the image (e.g., red dotted line). b) After applying the inverse radial distortion model, straight lines in the world now correctly map to straight lines in the image. The distortion caused the magenta point to move along the red radial line to the position of the yellow point.

14.1.6   Radial distortion

In the previous section, we introduced the pinhole camera model. However, it has probably not escaped your attention that real-world cameras are rarely based on the pinhole: they have a lens (or possibly a system of several lenses) that collects light from a larger area and refocuses it on the image plane. In practice, this leads to a number of deviations from the pinhole model. For example, some parts of the image may be out of focus, which essentially means that the assumption that a point in the world $\mathbf{w}$ maps to a single point in the image $\mathbf{x}$ is no longer valid. There are more complex mathematical models for cameras that deal effectively with this situation, but they are not discussed here.

However, there is one deviation from the pinhole model that must be addressed. *Radial distortion* is a nonlinear warping of the image that depends on the distance from the center of the image. In practice, this occurs when the field of view of the lens system is large. It can easily be detected in an image because straight lines in the world no longer project to straight lines in the image (Figure 14.6).

Radial distortion is commonly modeled as a polynomial function of the distance r from the center of the image. In the normalized camera, the final image positions (x', y') are expressed as functions of the original positions (x, y) by

$$x' = x(1 + \beta_1 r^2 + \beta_2 r^4)$$
$$y' = y(1 + \beta_1 r^2 + \beta_2 r^4), \tag{14.12}$$

where the parameters β_1 and β_2 control the degree of distortion. These relations describe a family of possible distortions that approximate the true distortion closely for most common lenses.

This distortion is implemented after perspective projection (division by w) but before the effect of the intrinsic parameters (focal length, offset, etc.), so the warping is relative to the optical axis and not the origin of the pixel coordinate system. We will not discuss radial distortion further in this volume. However, it is important to realize that for accurate results, all of the algorithms in this and Chapters 15 and 16 should account for radial distortion. When the field of view is large, it is particularly critical to incorporate this into the pinhole camera model.

14.2   Three geometric problems

Now that we have described the pinhole camera model, we will consider three important geometric problems. Each is an instance of learning or inference within this model. We will first describe the problems themselves, and then tackle them one by one later in the chapter.

14.2.1   Problem 1: Learning extrinsic parameters

We aim to recover the position and orientation of the camera relative to a known scene. This is sometimes known as the *perspective-n-point (PnP)* problem or the *exterior orientation* problem. One common application is augmented reality, where we need to know this relationship to render virtual objects that appear to be stable parts of the real scene.

The problem can be stated more formally as follows: we are given a known object, with I distinct 3D points $\{\mathbf{w}_i\}_{i=1}^{I}$, their corresponding projections in the image $\{\mathbf{x}_i\}_{i=1}^{I}$, and known intrinsic parameters $\boldsymbol{\Lambda}$. Our goal is to estimate the rotation $\boldsymbol{\Omega}$ and translation $\boldsymbol{\tau}$ that map points in the coordinate system of the object to points in the coordinate system of the camera so that

$$\hat{\boldsymbol{\Omega}}, \hat{\boldsymbol{\tau}} = \underset{\boldsymbol{\Omega}, \boldsymbol{\tau}}{\operatorname{argmax}} \left[\sum_{i=1}^{I} \log \left[Pr(\mathbf{x}_i | \mathbf{w}_i, \boldsymbol{\Lambda}, \boldsymbol{\Omega}, \boldsymbol{\tau}) \right] \right]. \tag{14.13}$$

This is a maximum likelihood learning problem, in which we aim to find parameters $\boldsymbol{\Omega}, \boldsymbol{\tau}$ that make the predictions **pinhole**$[\mathbf{w}_i, \boldsymbol{\Lambda}, \boldsymbol{\Omega}, \boldsymbol{\tau}]$ of the model agree with the observed 2D points $\mathbf{x}_i$ (Figure 14.7).

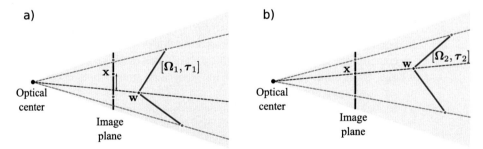

Figure 14.7 Problem 1 – Learning extrinsic parameters (exterior orientation problem). Given points $\{\mathbf{w}_i\}_{i=1}^{I}$ on a known object (blue lines), their positions $\{\mathbf{x}_i\}_{i=1}^{I}$ in the image (circles on image plane), and known intrinsic parameters $\boldsymbol{\Lambda}$, find the rotation $\boldsymbol{\Omega}$ and translation $\boldsymbol{\tau}$ relating the camera and the object. a) When the rotation or translation are wrong, the image points predicted by the model (where the rays strike the image plane) do not agree well with the observed points $\mathbf{x}_i$. b) When the rotation and translation are correct, they agree well and the likelihood $Pr(\mathbf{x}_i | \mathbf{w}, \boldsymbol{\Lambda}, \boldsymbol{\Omega}, \boldsymbol{\tau})$ will be high.

14.2.2   Problem 2: Learning intrinsic parameters

We aim to estimate the intrinsic parameters $\boldsymbol{\Lambda}$ that relate the direction of rays through the optical center to coordinates on the image plane. This estimation process is known

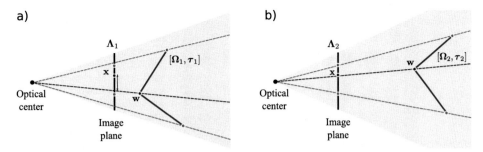

Figure 14.8 Problem 2 – Learning intrinsic parameters. Given a set of points $\{\mathbf{w}_i\}_{i=1}^I$ on a known object in the world (blue lines) and the 2D positions $\{\mathbf{x}\}_{i=1}^I$ of these points in an image, find the intrinsic parameters $\boldsymbol{\Lambda}$. To do this, we must also simultaneously estimate the extrinsic parameters $\boldsymbol{\Omega}, \boldsymbol{\tau}$. a) When the intrinsic or extrinsic parameters are wrong, the prediction of the pinhole camera (where rays strike the image plane) will deviate significantly from the observed 2D points. b) When the intrinsic and extrinsic parameters are correct, the prediction of the model will agree with the observed image.

as *calibration*. Knowledge of the intrinsic parameters is critical if we want to use the camera to build 3D models of the world.

The calibration problem can be stated more formally as follows: given a known 3D object, with I distinct 3D points $\{\mathbf{w}_i\}_{i=1}^I$ and their corresponding projections in the image $\{\mathbf{x}_i\}_{i=1}^I$, estimate the intrinsic parameters:

$$\hat{\boldsymbol{\Lambda}} = \underset{\boldsymbol{\Lambda}}{\operatorname{argmax}} \left[\underset{\boldsymbol{\Omega}, \boldsymbol{\tau}}{\max} \left[\sum_{i=1}^I \log\left[Pr(\mathbf{x}_i | \mathbf{w}_i, \boldsymbol{\Lambda}, \boldsymbol{\Omega}, \boldsymbol{\tau}) \right] \right] \right]. \tag{14.14}$$

Once more this is a maximum likelihood learning problem in which we aim to find parameters $\boldsymbol{\Lambda}, \boldsymbol{\Omega}, \boldsymbol{\tau}$ that make the predictions of the model **pinhole**$[\mathbf{w}_i, \boldsymbol{\Lambda}, \boldsymbol{\Omega}, \boldsymbol{\tau}]$ agree with the observed 2D points $\mathbf{x}_i$ (Figure 14.8). We do not particularly care about the extrinsic parameters $\boldsymbol{\Omega}, \boldsymbol{\tau}$; finding these is just a means to the end of estimating the intrinsic parameters $\boldsymbol{\Lambda}$.

The calibration process requires a known 3D object, on which distinct points can be identified, and their corresponding projections in the image found. A common approach is to construct a bespoke 3D *calibration target*[2] that achieves these goals (Figure 14.9).

14.2.3 Problem 3: Inferring 3D world points

We aim to estimate the 3D position of a point $\mathbf{w}$ in the scene, given its projections $\{\mathbf{x}_j\}_{j=1}^J$ in $J \geq 2$ calibrated cameras. When $J = 2$, this is known as *calibrated stereo reconstruction*. With $J > 2$ calibrated cameras, it is known to as *multiview reconstruction*. If we repeat this process for many points, the result is a sparse 3D point cloud. This could be used to help an autonomous vehicle navigate through the environment or to generate an image of the scene from a new viewpoint.

More formally, the multiview reconstruction problem can be stated as follows: given J calibrated cameras in known positions (i.e., cameras with known $\boldsymbol{\Lambda}, \boldsymbol{\Omega}, \boldsymbol{\tau}$) viewing the same 3D point $\mathbf{w}$ and knowing the corresponding 2D projections $\{\mathbf{x}_j\}_{j=1}^J$, in the J

---

[2]It should be noted that in practice calibration is more usually based on a number of views of a known 2D planar object (see Section 15.4.2).

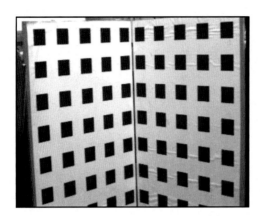

Figure 14.9 Camera calibration target. One way to calibrate the camera (estimate its intrinsic parameters) is to view a 3D object (a camera calibration target) for which the geometry is known. The marks on the surface are at known 3D positions in the frame of reference of the object and are easy to locate in the image using basic image-processing techniques. It is now possible to find the intrinsic and extrinsic parameters that optimally map the known 3D positions to their 2D projections in the image. Image from Hartley and Zisserman (2004).

images establish the 3D position $\mathbf{w}$ of the point in the world:

$$\hat{\mathbf{w}} = \underset{\mathbf{w}}{\operatorname{argmax}} \left[\sum_{j=1}^{J} \log[Pr(\mathbf{x}_j|\mathbf{w}, \mathbf{\Lambda}_j, \mathbf{\Omega}_j, \boldsymbol{\tau}_j)] \right]. \qquad (14.15)$$

The form of this inference problem is similar to that of the preceding learning problems: we perform an optimization in which we manipulate the variable of interest $\mathbf{w}$ until the predictions $\mathbf{pinhole}[\mathbf{w}, \mathbf{\Lambda}_j, \mathbf{\Omega}_j, \boldsymbol{\tau}_j]$ of the pinhole camera models agree with the data $\mathbf{x}_j$ (Figure 14.10). For obvious reasons, the principle behind reconstruction is known as *triangulation*.

14.2.4 Solving the problems

We have introduced three geometric problems, each of which took the form of a learning or inference problem using the pinhole camera model. We formulated each in terms of maximum likelihood estimation, and in each case this results in an optimization problem.

Unfortunately, none of the resulting objective functions can be optimized in closed form; each solution requires the use of nonlinear optimization. In each case, it is critical to have a good initial estimate of the unknown quantities to ensure that the optimization process converges to the global maximum. In the remaining part of this chapter, we develop algorithms that provide these initial estimates. The general approach is to choose new objective functions that can be optimized in closed form, and where the solution is close to the solution of the true problem.

14.3   Homogeneous coordinates

To get good initial estimates of the geometric quantities in the preceding optimization problems, we play a simple trick: we change the representation of both the 2D image points and 3D world points so that the projection equations become linear. After this change, it is possible to find solutions for the unknown quantities in closed form. However, it should be emphasized that these solutions *do not* directly address the original optimization criteria: they minimize more abstract objective functions based on *algebraic error* whose solutions are not guaranteed to be the same as those for the original problem. However, they are generally close enough to provide a good starting point for a nonlinear optimization of the true cost function.

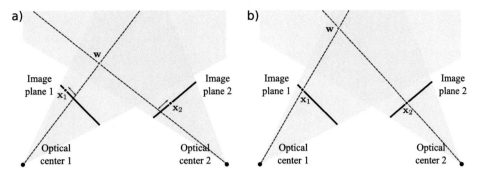

Figure 14.10 Problem 3 – Inferring 3D world points. Given two cameras with known position and orientation, and the projections $\mathbf{x}_1$ and $\mathbf{x}_2$ of the same 3D point in each image, the goal of calibrated stereo reconstruction is to infer the 3D position $\mathbf{w}$ of the world point. a) When the estimate of the world point (red circle) is wrong, the predictions of the pinhole camera model (where rays strike the image plane) will deviate from the observed data (brown circles on image plane). b) When the estimate of $\mathbf{w}$ is correct, the predictions of the model agree with the observed data.

We convert the original Cartesian representation of the 2D image points $\mathbf{x}$ to a 3D *homogeneous* coordinate $\tilde{\mathbf{x}}$ so that

$$\tilde{\mathbf{x}} = \lambda \begin{bmatrix} x \\ y \\ 1 \end{bmatrix}, \tag{14.16}$$

where λ is an arbitrary scaling factor. This is a redundant representation in that any scalar multiple λ represents the same 2D point. For example, the homogeneous vectors $\tilde{\mathbf{x}} = [2, 4, 2]^T$ and $\tilde{\mathbf{x}} = [3, 6, 3]^T$ both represent the Cartesian 2D point $\mathbf{x} = [1, 2]^T$, where scaling factors $\lambda = 2$ and $\lambda = 3$ have been used, respectively.

Converting between homogeneous and Cartesian coordinates is easy. To move to homogeneous coordinates, we choose $\lambda = 1$ and simply append a 1 to the original 2D Cartesian coordinate. To recover the Cartesian coordinates, we divide the first two entries of the homogeneous 3-vector by the third, so that if we observe the homogeneous vector $\tilde{\mathbf{x}} = [\tilde{x}, \tilde{y}, \tilde{z}]^T$, then we can recover the Cartesian coordinate $\mathbf{x} = [x, y]^T$ as

$$x = \frac{\tilde{x}}{\tilde{z}}$$
$$y = \frac{\tilde{y}}{\tilde{z}}. \tag{14.17}$$

Further insight into the relationship between the two representations is given in Figure 14.11.

It is similarly possible to represent the 3D world point $\mathbf{w}$ as a homogenous 4D vector $\tilde{\mathbf{w}}$ so that

$$\tilde{\mathbf{w}} = \lambda \begin{bmatrix} u \\ v \\ w \\ 1 \end{bmatrix}, \tag{14.18}$$

where λ is again an arbitrary scaling factor. Once more, the conversion from Cartesian to homogeneous coordinates can be achieved by appending a 1 to the original 3D vector $\mathbf{w}$.

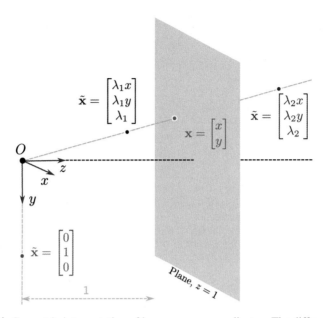

Figure 14.11 Geometric interpretation of homogeneous coordinates. The different scalar multiples λ of the homogeneous 3-vector $\tilde{\mathbf{x}}$ define a ray through the origin of a coordinate space. The corresponding 2D image point $\mathbf{x}$ can be found by considering the 2D point that this ray strikes on the plane $z = 1$. An interesting side-effect of this representation is that it is possible to represent points at infinity (known as *ideal points*). For example, the homogeneous coordinate $[0, 1, 0]^T$ defines a ray that is parallel to $z = 1$ and so never intersects the plane. It represents the point at infinity in direction $[0, 1]^T$.

The conversion from homogeneous to Cartesian coordinates is achieved by dividing each of the first three entries by the last.

14.3.1 Camera model in homogeneous coordinates

It is hard to see the point of converting the 2D image points to homogeneous 3-vectors and converting the 3D world point to homogeneous 4-vectors until we reexamine the pinhole projection equations,

$$
\begin{aligned}
x &= \frac{\phi_x u + \gamma v}{w} + \delta_x \\
y &= \frac{\phi_y v}{w} + \delta_y,
\end{aligned}
\tag{14.19}
$$

where we have temporarily assumed that the world point $\mathbf{w} = [u, v, w]^T$ is in the same coordinate system as the camera.

In homogeneous coordinates, these relationships can be expressed as a set of linear equations

$$
\lambda \begin{bmatrix} x \\ y \\ 1 \end{bmatrix} = \begin{bmatrix} \phi_x & \gamma & \delta_x & 0 \\ 0 & \phi_y & \delta_y & 0 \\ 0 & 0 & 1 & 0 \end{bmatrix} \begin{bmatrix} u \\ v \\ w \\ 1 \end{bmatrix}.
\tag{14.20}
$$

To convince ourselves of this, let us write these relations explicitly:

$$\lambda x = \phi_x u + \gamma v + \delta_x w$$
$$\lambda y = \phi_y v + \delta_y w$$
$$\lambda = w. \tag{14.21}$$

We solve for x and y by converting back to Cartesian coordinates: we divide the first two relations by the third to yield the original pinhole model (Equation 14.19).

Let us summarize what has happened: the original mapping from 3D Cartesian world points to 2D Cartesian image points is nonlinear (due to the division by w). However, the mapping from 4D homogeneous world points to 3D homogeneous image points is linear. In the homogeneous representation, the nonlinear component of the projection process (division by w) has been side-stepped: this operation still occurs, but it is in the final conversion back to 2D Cartesian coordinates, and thus does not trouble the homogeneous camera equations.

To complete the model, we add the extrinsic parameters $\{\Omega, \tau\}$ that relate the world coordinate system and the camera coordinate system, so that

$$\lambda \begin{bmatrix} x \\ y \\ 1 \end{bmatrix} = \begin{bmatrix} \phi_x & \gamma & \delta_x & 0 \\ 0 & \phi_y & \delta_y & 0 \\ 0 & 0 & 1 & 0 \end{bmatrix} \begin{bmatrix} \omega_{11} & \omega_{12} & \omega_{13} & \tau_x \\ \omega_{21} & \omega_{22} & \omega_{23} & \tau_y \\ \omega_{31} & \omega_{32} & \omega_{33} & \tau_z \\ 0 & 0 & 0 & 1 \end{bmatrix} \begin{bmatrix} u \\ v \\ w \\ 1 \end{bmatrix}, \tag{14.22}$$

or in matrix form

$$\lambda \tilde{x} = \begin{bmatrix} \Lambda & 0 \end{bmatrix} \begin{bmatrix} \Omega & \tau \\ 0^T & 1 \end{bmatrix} \tilde{w}, \tag{14.23}$$

where $0 = [0, 0, 0]^T$. The same relations can be simplified to

$$\lambda \tilde{x} = \Lambda \begin{bmatrix} \Omega & \tau \end{bmatrix} \tilde{w}. \tag{14.24}$$

In the next three sections, we revisit the three geometric problems introduced in Section 14.2. In each case, we will use algorithms based on homogeneous coordinates to compute good initial estimates of the variable of interest. These estimates can then be improved using nonlinear optimization.

14.4   Learning extrinsic parameters

Given a known object, with I distinct 3D points $\{w_i\}_{i=1}^I$, their corresponding projections in the image $\{x_i\}_{i=1}^I$, and known intrinsic parameters Λ, estimate the geometric relationship between the camera and the object determined by the rotation Ω and the translation τ:

$$\hat{\Omega}, \hat{\tau} = \underset{\Omega, \tau}{\operatorname{argmax}} \left[\sum_{i=1}^I \log \left[Pr(x_i | w_i, \Lambda, \Omega, \tau) \right] \right]. \tag{14.25}$$

This is a non-convex problem, so we make progress by expressing it in homogeneous coordinates. The relationship between the ith homogeneous world point $\tilde{w}_i$ and the ith corresponding homogeneous image point $\tilde{x}_i$ is

$$\lambda_i \begin{bmatrix} x_i \\ y_i \\ 1 \end{bmatrix} = \begin{bmatrix} \phi_x & \gamma & \delta_x \\ 0 & \phi_y & \delta_y \\ 0 & 0 & 1 \end{bmatrix} \begin{bmatrix} \omega_{11} & \omega_{12} & \omega_{13} & \tau_x \\ \omega_{21} & \omega_{22} & \omega_{23} & \tau_y \\ \omega_{31} & \omega_{32} & \omega_{33} & \tau_z \end{bmatrix} \begin{bmatrix} u_i \\ v_i \\ w_i \\ 1 \end{bmatrix}. \tag{14.26}$$

We would like to discard the effect of the (known) intrinsic parameters Λ. To this end, we premultiply both sides of the equation by the inverse of the intrinsic matrix Λ to yield

$$
\lambda_i \begin{bmatrix} x'_i \\ y'_i \\ 1 \end{bmatrix} = \begin{bmatrix} \omega_{11} & \omega_{12} & \omega_{13} & \tau_x \\ \omega_{21} & \omega_{22} & \omega_{23} & \tau_y \\ \omega_{31} & \omega_{32} & \omega_{33} & \tau_z \end{bmatrix} \begin{bmatrix} u_i \\ v_i \\ w_i \\ 1 \end{bmatrix} . \tag{14.27}
$$

The transformed coordinates $\tilde{\mathbf{x}}' = \Lambda^{-1}\tilde{\mathbf{x}}$ are known as *normalized image coordinates*: they are the coordinates that would have resulted if we had used a normalized camera. In effect, premultiplying by Λ^{-1} compensates for the idiosyncrasies of this particular camera.

We now note that the last of these three equations allows us to solve for the constant λ_i, so that

$$
\lambda_i = \omega_{31} u_i + \omega_{32} v_i + \omega_{33} w_i + \tau_z, \tag{14.28}
$$

and we can now substitute this back into the first two equations to get the relations

$$
\begin{bmatrix} (\omega_{31} u_i + \omega_{32} v_i + \omega_{33} w_i + \tau_z) x'_i \\ (\omega_{31} u_i + \omega_{32} v_i + \omega_{33} w_i + \tau_z) y'_i \end{bmatrix} = \begin{bmatrix} \omega_{11} & \omega_{12} & \omega_{13} & \tau_x \\ \omega_{21} & \omega_{22} & \omega_{23} & \tau_y \end{bmatrix} \begin{bmatrix} u_i \\ v_i \\ w_i \\ 1 \end{bmatrix} . \tag{14.29}
$$

These are two linear equations with respect to the unknown quantities Ω and τ. We can take the two equations provided by each of the I pairs of points in the world $\mathbf{w}$ and the image $\mathbf{x}$ to form the system of equations

$$
\begin{bmatrix} u_1 & v_1 & w_1 & 1 & 0 & 0 & 0 & 0 & -u_1 x'_1 & -v_1 x'_1 & -w_1 x'_1 & -x'_1 \\ 0 & 0 & 0 & 0 & u_1 & v_1 & w_1 & 1 & -u_1 y'_1 & -v_1 y'_1 & -w_1 y'_1 & -y'_1 \\ u_2 & v_2 & w_2 & 1 & 0 & 0 & 0 & 0 & -u_2 x'_2 & -v_2 x'_2 & -w_2 x'_2 & -x'_2 \\ 0 & 0 & 0 & 0 & u_2 & v_2 & w_2 & 1 & -u_2 y'_2 & -v_2 y'_2 & -w_2 y'_2 & -y'_2 \\ \vdots & \vdots & \vdots & \vdots & \vdots & \vdots & \vdots & \vdots & \vdots & \vdots & \vdots & \vdots \\ u_I & v_I & w_I & 1 & 0 & 0 & 0 & 0 & -u_I x'_I & -v_I x'_I & -w_I x'_I & -x'_I \\ 0 & 0 & 0 & 0 & u_I & v_I & w_I & 1 & -u_I y'_I & -v_I y'_I & -w_I y'_I & -y'_I \end{bmatrix} \begin{bmatrix} \omega_{11} \\ \omega_{12} \\ \omega_{13} \\ \tau_x \\ \omega_{21} \\ \omega_{22} \\ \omega_{23} \\ \tau_y \\ \omega_{31} \\ \omega_{32} \\ \omega_{33} \\ \tau_z \end{bmatrix} = \mathbf{0}. \tag{14.30}
$$

This problem is now in the standard form $\mathbf{Ab} = \mathbf{0}$ of a *minimum direction problem*. We seek the value of $\mathbf{b}$ that minimizes $|\mathbf{Ab}|^2$ subject to the constraint $|\mathbf{b}| = 1$ (to avoid the uninteresting solution $\mathbf{b} = \mathbf{0}$). The solution can be found by computing the singular value decomposition $\mathbf{A} = \mathbf{ULV}^T$ and setting $\hat{\mathbf{b}}$ to be the last column of $\mathbf{V}$ (see Appendix C.7.2).

The estimates of Ω and τ that we extract from $\mathbf{b}$ have had an arbitrary scale imposed on them, and we must find the correct scaling factor. This is possible because the rotation Ω has a predefined scale (its rows and columns must all have norm one). In practice, we first find the closest true rotation matrix to Ω, which also forces our estimate to be a valid orthogonal matrix. This is an instance of the *orthogonal Procrustes problem* (Appendix C.7.3). The solution is found by computing the singular value decomposition $\boldsymbol{\Omega} = \mathbf{ULV}^T$ and setting $\hat{\boldsymbol{\Omega}} = \mathbf{UV}^T$. Now, we rescale the translation $\boldsymbol{\tau}$. The scaling factor can be estimated by taking the average ratio of the nine entries of our initial estimate of $\boldsymbol{\Omega}$ to the final one, $\hat{\boldsymbol{\Omega}}$ so that

$$\hat{\boldsymbol{\tau}} = \sum_{m=1}^{3} \sum_{n=1}^{3} \frac{\hat{\Omega}_{mn}}{\Omega_{mn}} \boldsymbol{\tau}/9. \tag{14.31}$$

Finally, we must check that the sign of τ_z is positive, indicating that the object is in front of the camera. If this is not the case, then we multiply both $\hat{\boldsymbol{\tau}}$ and $\hat{\boldsymbol{\Omega}}$ by minus 1.

This scrappy algorithm is typical of methods that use homogeneous coordinates. The resulting estimates $\hat{\boldsymbol{\tau}}$ and $\hat{\boldsymbol{\Omega}}$ can be quite inaccurate in the presence of noise in the measured image positions. However, they usually suffice as a reasonable starting point for the subsequent nonlinear optimization of the true objective function (Equation 14.25) for this problem. This optimization must be carried out while ensuring that $\boldsymbol{\Omega}$ remains a valid rotation matrix (see Appendix B.4).

Note that this algorithm requires a minimum of 11 equations to solve the minimum direction problem. Since each point contributes two equations, this means we require $I = 6$ points for a unique solution. However, there are only really six unknowns (rotation and translation in 3D), so a minimal solution would require only $I = 3$ points. Minimal solutions for this problem have been developed and are discussed in the notes at the end of the chapter.

14.5 Learning intrinsic parameters

We now address the second problem. In *camera calibration* we attempt to learn the intrinsic parameters based on viewing a known object or *calibration target*. More precisely, we are given a known object, with I distinct 3D points $\{\mathbf{w}_i\}_{i=1}^I$ and their corresponding 2D projections in the image $\{\mathbf{x}_i\}_{i=1}^I$, and aim to form maximum likelihood estimates of the intrinsic parameters $\boldsymbol{\Lambda}$,

$$\hat{\boldsymbol{\Lambda}} = \underset{\boldsymbol{\Lambda}}{\operatorname{argmax}} \left[\underset{\boldsymbol{\Omega}, \boldsymbol{\tau}}{\max} \left[\sum_{i=1}^I \log\left[Pr(\mathbf{x}_i|\mathbf{w}_i, \boldsymbol{\Lambda}, \boldsymbol{\Omega}, \boldsymbol{\tau})\right] \right] \right]. \tag{14.32}$$

A simple (but inefficient) approach to this problem is to use a coordinate ascent method in which we alternately

- Estimate the extrinsic parameters for fixed intrinsic parameters (problem 1),

$$\hat{\boldsymbol{\Omega}}, \hat{\boldsymbol{\tau}} = \underset{\boldsymbol{\Omega}, \boldsymbol{\tau}}{\operatorname{argmax}} \left[\sum_{i=1}^I \log\left[Pr(\mathbf{x}_i|\mathbf{w}_i, \boldsymbol{\Lambda}, \boldsymbol{\Omega}, \boldsymbol{\tau})\right] \right], \tag{14.33}$$

using the procedure described in Section 14.4, and then
- Estimate the intrinsic parameters for fixed extrinsic parameters,

$$\hat{\boldsymbol{\Lambda}} = \underset{\boldsymbol{\Lambda}}{\operatorname{argmax}} \left[\sum_{i=1}^I \log\left[Pr(\mathbf{x}_i|\mathbf{w}_i, \boldsymbol{\Lambda}, \boldsymbol{\Omega}, \boldsymbol{\tau})\right] \right]. \tag{14.34}$$

By iterating these two steps, we will get closer and closer to the correct solution. Since we already know how to solve the first of these two subproblems, we now concentrate on solving the second. Happily there is a closed form solution that does not even require homogeneous coordinates.

Given known world points $\{\mathbf{w}_i\}_{i=1}^I$, their projections $\{\mathbf{x}_i\}_{i=1}^I$, and known extrinsic parameters $\{\mathbf{\Omega}, \mathbf{\tau}\}$, our goal is now to compute the intrinsic matrix $\mathbf{\Lambda}$, which contains the intrinsic parameters $\{\phi_x, \phi_y, \gamma, \delta_x, \delta_y\}$. We will apply the maximum likelihood method

$$\hat{\mathbf{\Lambda}} = \underset{\mathbf{\Lambda}}{\operatorname{argmax}} \left[\sum_{i=1}^{I} \log \left[\operatorname{Norm}_{\mathbf{x}_i} \left[\mathbf{pinhole}[\mathbf{w}_i, \mathbf{\Lambda}, \mathbf{\Omega}, \mathbf{\tau}], \sigma^2 \mathbf{I} \right] \right] \right] \qquad (14.35)$$

$$= \underset{\mathbf{\Lambda}}{\operatorname{argmin}} \left[\sum_{i=1}^{I} (\mathbf{x}_i - \mathbf{pinhole}[\mathbf{w}_i, \mathbf{\Lambda}, \mathbf{\Omega}, \mathbf{\tau}])^T (\mathbf{x}_i - \mathbf{pinhole}[\mathbf{w}_i, \mathbf{\Lambda}, \mathbf{\Omega}, \mathbf{\tau}]) \right],$$

which results in a least squares problem (see Section 4.4.1).

Now we note that the projection function $\mathbf{pinhole}[\bullet, \bullet, \bullet, \bullet]$ (Equation 14.8) is linear with respect to the intrinsic parameters, and can be written as $\mathbf{A}_i \mathbf{h}$ where

$$\mathbf{A}_i = \begin{bmatrix} \frac{\omega_{11}u_i + \omega_{12}v_i + \omega_{13}w_i + \tau_x}{\omega_{31}u_i + \omega_{32}v_i + \omega_{33}w_i + \tau_z} & \frac{\omega_{21}u_i + \omega_{22}v_i + \omega_{23}w_i + \tau_x}{\omega_{31}u_i + \omega_{32}v_i + \omega_{33}w_i + \tau_z} & 1 & 0 & 0 \\ 0 & 0 & 0 & \frac{\omega_{21}u_i + \omega_{22}v_i + \omega_{23}w_i + \tau_y}{\omega_{31}u_i + \omega_{32}v_i + \omega_{33}w_i + \tau_z} & 1 \end{bmatrix}$$

$$(14.36)$$

and $\mathbf{h} = [\phi_x, \gamma, \delta_x, \phi_y, \delta_y]^T$. Consequently, the problem has the form

$$\hat{\mathbf{h}} = \underset{\mathbf{h}}{\operatorname{argmin}} \left[\sum_{i=1}^{I} (\mathbf{A}_i \mathbf{h} - \mathbf{x}_i)^T (\mathbf{A}_i \mathbf{h} - \mathbf{x}_i) \right], \qquad (14.37)$$

which we recognize as a least squares problem that can be solved in closed form (Appendix C.7.1).

We have described this alternating approach for pedagogical reasons; it is simple to understand and implement. However, we emphasize that this is not really a practical method as the convergence will be very slow. A better approach would be to perform a couple of iterations of this method and then optimize both the intrinsic and extrinsic parameters simultaneously using a nonlinear optimization technique such as the Gauss-Newton method (Appendix B.2.3) with the original criterion (Equation 14.32). This optimization must be done while ensuring that the extrinsic parameter $\mathbf{\Omega}$ remains a valid rotation matrix (see Appendix B.4).

14.6   Inferring three-dimensional world points

⚙ 14.3   Finally, we consider the multiview reconstruction problem. Given J calibrated cameras in known positions (i.e., cameras with known $\mathbf{\Lambda}, \mathbf{\Omega}, \mathbf{\tau}$), viewing the same 3D point $\mathbf{w}$ and knowing the corresponding projections in the images $\{\mathbf{x}_j\}_{j=1}^J$, establish the position of the point in the world.

$$\hat{\mathbf{w}} = \underset{\mathbf{w}}{\operatorname{argmax}} \left[\left(\sum_{j=1}^{J} \log[Pr(\mathbf{x}_j | \mathbf{w}, \mathbf{\Lambda}_j, \mathbf{\Omega}_j, \mathbf{\tau}_j)] \right) \right]. \qquad (14.38)$$

This cannot be solved in closed form and so we move to homogeneous coordinates where we can solve for a good initial estimate in closed form. The relationship between the homogeneous world point $\tilde{\mathbf{w}}$ and the jth corresponding homogeneous image point $\tilde{\mathbf{x}}_j$ is

$$
\lambda_j \begin{bmatrix} x_j \\ y_j \\ 1 \end{bmatrix} = \begin{bmatrix} \phi_{xj} & \gamma_j & \delta_{xj} \\ 0 & \phi_{yj} & \delta_{yj} \\ 0 & 0 & 1 \end{bmatrix} \begin{bmatrix} \omega_{11j} & \omega_{12j} & \omega_{13j} & \tau_{xj} \\ \omega_{21j} & \omega_{22j} & \omega_{23j} & \tau_{yj} \\ \omega_{31j} & \omega_{32j} & \omega_{33j} & \tau_{zj} \end{bmatrix} \begin{bmatrix} u \\ v \\ w \\ 1 \end{bmatrix}, \quad (14.39)
$$

where we have appended the index j to the intrinsic and extrinsic parameters to denote the fact that they belong to the jth camera. Premultiplying both sides by the intrinsic matrix $\boldsymbol{\Lambda}_j^{-1}$ to convert to normalized image coordinates gives

$$
\lambda_j \begin{bmatrix} x'_j \\ y'_j \\ 1 \end{bmatrix} = \begin{bmatrix} \omega_{11j} & \omega_{12j} & \omega_{13j} & \tau_{xj} \\ \omega_{21j} & \omega_{22j} & \omega_{23j} & \tau_{yj} \\ \omega_{31j} & \omega_{32j} & \omega_{33j} & \tau_{zj} \end{bmatrix} \begin{bmatrix} u \\ v \\ w \\ 1 \end{bmatrix}, \quad (14.40)
$$

where x'_j and y'_j denote the normalized image coordinates in the jth camera.

We use the third equation to establish that $\lambda_j = \omega_{31j}u + \omega_{32j}v + \omega_{33j}w + \tau_{zj}$. Substituting into the first two equations, we get

$$
\begin{bmatrix} (\omega_{31j}u + \omega_{32j}v + \omega_{33j}w + \tau_{zj})x'_j \\ (\omega_{31j}u + \omega_{32j}v + \omega_{33j}w + \tau_{zj})y'_j \end{bmatrix} = \begin{bmatrix} \omega_{11j} & \omega_{12j} & \omega_{13j} & \tau_{xj} \\ \omega_{21j} & \omega_{22j} & \omega_{23j} & \tau_{yj} \end{bmatrix} \begin{bmatrix} u \\ v \\ w \\ 1 \end{bmatrix}. \quad (14.41)
$$

These equations can be rearranged to provide two linear constraints on the three unknown quantities in $\mathbf{w} = [u, v, w]^T$:

$$
\begin{bmatrix} \omega_{31j}x'_j - \omega_{11j} & \omega_{32j}x'_j - \omega_{12j} & \omega_{33j}x'_j - \omega_{13j} \\ \omega_{31j}y'_j - \omega_{21j} & \omega_{32j}y'_j - \omega_{22j} & \omega_{33j}y'_j - \omega_{23j} \end{bmatrix} \begin{bmatrix} u \\ v \\ w \end{bmatrix} = \begin{bmatrix} \tau_{xj} - \tau_{zj}x'_j \\ \tau_{yj} - \tau_{zj}y'_j \end{bmatrix}. \quad (14.42)
$$

With multiple cameras, we can build a larger system of equations and solve for $\mathbf{w}$ in a least squares sense (Appendix C.7.1). This typically provides a good starting point for the subsequent nonlinear optimization of the criterion in Equation 14.38.

This calibrated reconstruction algorithm is the basis for methods that construct 3D models. However, there are several parts missing from the argument.

- The method requires us to have found the points $\{\mathbf{x}_j\}_{j=1}^J$ that correspond to the same world point $\mathbf{w}$ in each of the J images. This process is called *correspondence* and is discussed in Chapters 15 and 16.

- The method requires the intrinsic and extrinsic parameters. Of course, these could be computed from a calibration target using the method of Section 14.5. However, it is still possible to perform reconstruction when the system is uncalibrated; this is known as projective reconstruction as the result is ambiguous up to a 3D projective transformation. Furthermore, if a single camera was used to take all of the images, it is possible to estimate the single intrinsic matrix and extrinsic parameters from a sequence, and reconstruct points in a scene up to a constant scaling factor. Chapter 16 presents an extended discussion of this method.

14.7   Applications

We discuss two applications for the techniques in this chapter. We consider a method to construct 3D models based on projecting structured light onto the object, and a method for generating novel views of an object based on an approximate model built from the silhouettes of the object.

14.7.1 Depth from structured light

In Section 14.6 we showed how to compute the depth of a point given its position in two or more calibrated cameras. However, we did not discuss how to find matching points in the two images. We defer a full answer to this question to Chapter 16, but here we will develop a method that circumvents this problem. This method will be based on a projector and a camera, rather than two cameras.

It is crucial to understand that the geometry of a projector is exactly the same as that of a camera: the projector has an optical center and has a regular pixel array that is analogous to the sensor in the camera. Each pixel in the projector corresponds to a direction in space (a ray) through the optical center, and this relationship can be captured by a set of intrinsic parameters. The major difference is that a projector sends outgoing light along these rays, whereas the camera captures incoming light along them.

Consider a system that comprises a single camera and a projector that are displaced relative to one another but that point at the same object (Figure 14.12). For simplicity, we will assume that the system is calibrated (i.e., the intrinsic matrices and the relative positions of the camera and projector are known). It is now easy to estimate the depth of the scene: we illuminate the scene using the projector *one pixel at a time*, and find the corresponding pixel in the camera by observing which part of the image gets brighter. We now have two corresponding points and can compute the depth using the method of Section 14.6. In practice, this technique is very time consuming as a separate image must be captured for each pixel in the projector. Scharstein and Szeliski (2003) used a more practical technique using *structured light* in which a series of horizontal and vertical stripe patterns is projected onto the scene that allow the mapping between pixels in the projector and those in the camera to be computed.

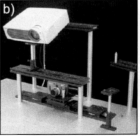

Figure 14.12 Depth maps from structured light. a) A three-dimensional scene that we wish to capture. b) The capture hardware consists of a projector and a camera, which both view the scene from different positions. c) The projector is used to illuminate the scene, and the camera records the pattern of illumination from its viewpoint. The resulting images contain information that can be used to compute a 3D reconstruction. Adapted from Scharstein and Szeliski (2003). ©2003 IEEE.

To understand how this works, consider a projector image in which the top half is light and the bottom half is dark. We capture two images I_1 and I_2 of the scene corresponding to when the projector shows this pattern and when it shows its inverse. We then take the difference $I_1 - I_2$ between the images. Pixels in the camera image where the difference is positive must now belong to the top half of the projector image, and pixels where the difference is negative must belong to the bottom half of the image. We now illuminate the image with a second pattern, which divides the images into four horizontally oriented black and white stripes. By capturing the image illuminated by this second pattern and its inverse, we can hence deduce whether each pixel is in the top or bottom half of the region determined by the first pattern. We continue in this way with successively finer patterns, refining the estimated position at each pixel until we know it accurately. The whole procedure is repeated with vertical striped patterns to estimate the horizontal position.

In practice, more sophisticated coding schemes are used as the sequence described in the preceding section; for example, this sequence means that there is always a boundary between black and white in the center of the projector image. It may be hard to establish the correspondence for a camera pixel, which always straddles this boundary. One solution is to base the sequences on *Gray codes* which have a more complex structure and avoid this problem (Figure 14.13). The estimated depth map of the scene in Figure 14.12 is shown in Figure 14.14.

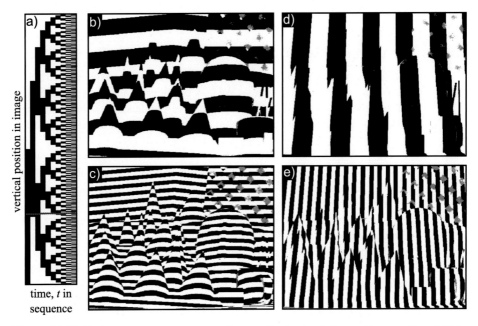

Figure 14.13 Projector to camera correspondence with structured light patterns. a) To establish the vertical position in the projector image, we present a sequence of horizontally striped patterns. Each height in the projected image receives a unique sequence of black and white values, so we can determine the height (e.g., red line) by measuring this sequence. b–c) Two examples of these horizontally striped patterns. d–e) Two examples of vertically striped patterns that are part of a sequence designed to estimate the horizontal position in the projector pattern. Adapted from Scharstein and Szeliski (2003). ©2003 IEEE.

Figure 14.14 Recovered depth map for scene in Figure 14.12 using the structured light method. Pixels marked as blue are places where the depth is uncertain: these include positions in the image that were occluded with respect to the projector, so no light was cast onto them. Scharstein and Szeliski (2003) also captured the scene with two cameras under normal illumination; they subsequently used the depth map from the structured light as ground truth data for assessing stereo vision algorithms. Adapted from Scharstein and Szeliski (2003). ©2003 IEEE.

14.7.2 Shape from silhouette

The preceding system computed a 3D model of a scene based on explicit correspondences between a projector and a camera. We now consider an alternative method for computing 3D models that does not require explicit correspondence. As the name suggests, *shape from silhouette* estimates the shape of an object based on its silhouette in a number of images.

The principle is illustrated in Figure 14.15. Given a single camera, we know that an object must lie somewhere within the bundle of rays that fall within its silhouette. Now consider adding a second camera. We also know that the object must lie somewhere within the bundle of rays corresponding to the silhouette in this image. Hence, we can refine our estimate of the shape to the 3D intersection of these two ray bundles. As we add more cameras, the possible region of space that the object can lie in is reduced.

This procedure is attractive because the silhouettes can be computed robustly and quickly using a background subtraction approach. However, there is also a downside; even if we have an infinite number of cameras viewing the object, some aspects of the shape will not be present in the resulting 3D region. For example, the concave region at the back of the seat of the chair in Figure 14.15a cannot be recovered as it is not represented in the silhouettes. In general, the "best possible" shape estimate is known as the *visual hull*.

We will now develop an algorithm based on shape from silhouette that can be used to generate images of an object from novel poses. One application of this is for augmented reality systems in which we wish to superimpose an object over a real image in such a way that it looks like it is a stable part of the scene. This can be accomplished by establishing the position and pose of the camera relative to the scene (Section 14.4) and then generating a novel image of the object from the same viewpoint. Figure 14.16

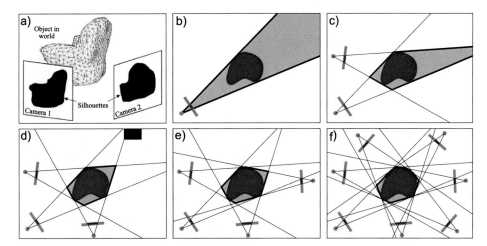

Figure 14.15 Shape from silhouette. a) The goal is to recover information about the shape of the object based on the silhouettes in a number of cameras. b) Consider a single camera viewing an object (2D slice shown). We know that the object must lie somewhere within the shaded region defined by the silhouette. c) When we add a second camera, we know that the object must lie within the intersection of the regions determined by the silhouettes (gray region). d–f) As we add more cameras, the approximation to the true shape becomes closer and closer. Unfortunately, we can never capture the concave region, no matter how many cameras we add.

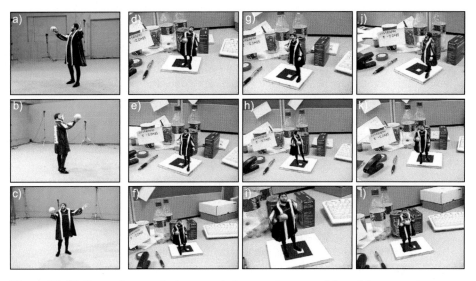

Figure 14.16 Generating novel views. a–c) An actor is captured from 15 cameras in a green screen studio. d-l) Novel views of the actor are now generated and superimposed on the scene. The novel view is carefully chosen so that it matches the direction that the camera views the desktop giving the impression that the actor is a stable part of the scene. Adapted from Prince et al. (2002). ©2002 IEEE.

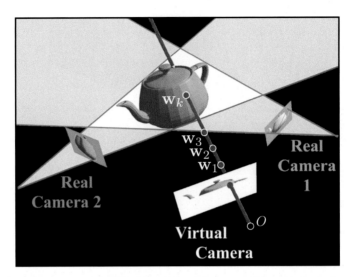

Figure 14.17 Novel view generation. A new image is generated one pixel at a time by testing a sequence of points $w_1, w_2, \ldots$ along the ray through the pixel. Each point is tested to see if it is within the visual hull by projecting it into the real images. If it lies within the silhouette in every real image, then it is within the visual hull and the search stops. In this case, point w_k is the first point on the surface. To establish the color for the pixel, this point is projected into a nearby real image, and the color is copied. Adapted from Prince et al. (2002). ©2002 IEEE.

depicts an example application of this kind, in which the performance of an actor is captured and rebroadcast as if he is standing on the desk.

Prince et al. (2002) described a method to generate a novel image from a virtual camera with intrinsic matrix $\mathbf{\Lambda}$ and extrinsic parameters $\{\mathbf{\Omega}, \boldsymbol{\tau}\}$. They considered each pixel in the virtual camera in turn, and computed the direction of the ray $\mathbf{r}$ passing through this point. With respect to the virtual camera itself, this ray has a direction

$$\mathbf{r} = \mathbf{\Lambda}^{-1} \tilde{\mathbf{x}}, \tag{14.43}$$

where $\tilde{\mathbf{x}} = [x, y, 1]^T$ is the position of the point in the image expressed in homogeneous coordinates. With respect to the global coordinate system, a point $\mathbf{w}$ that is κ units along the ray can be expressed as

$$\mathbf{w} = \boldsymbol{\tau} + \kappa \mathbf{\Omega} \mathbf{r}. \tag{14.44}$$

The depth of the object at this pixel is then computed by exploring along this direction; it is determined by an explicit search starting at the virtual camera projection center and proceeding outward along the ray corresponding to the pixel center (Figure 14.17). Each candidate 3D point along this ray is evaluated for potential occupancy. A candidate point is unoccupied if its projection into any of the real images is marked as background. When the first point is found for which all of the projected positions are marked as foreground, this is considered the depth with respect to the virtual object and the search stops.

The 3D point where the ray through the current virtual pixel meets the visual hull is now known. To establish the color of this pixel in the virtual image, the point is projected into the closest real image, and the color is copied. In general, the projection will not be exactly centered on a pixel, and to remedy this, the color value is estimated using bilinear or bicubic interpolation.

This procedure can be accomplished very quickly; the system of Prince et al. (2002) depicted in Figure 14.16 ran at interactive speeds, but the quality is limited to the extent that the visual hull is a reasonable approximation of the true shape. If this approximation is bad, the wrong depth will be estimated, the projections into the real images will be inaccurate, and the wrong color will be sampled.

Discussion

In this chapter, we have introduced a model for a pinhole camera and discussed learning and inference algorithms for this model. In the next chapter, we consider what happens when this camera views a planar scene; here there is a one-to-one mapping between points in the scene and points in the image. In Chapter 16, we return to the pinhole camera model and consider reconstruction of a scene from multiple cameras in unknown positions.

Notes

Camera geometry: There are detailed treatments of camera geometry in Hartley and Zisserman (2004), Ma et al. (2004), and Faugeras et al. (2001). Aloimonos (1990) and Mundy and Zisserman (1992) developed a hierarchy of camera models (see Problem 14.3). Tsai (1987) and Faugeras (1993) both present algorithms for camera calibration from a 3D object. However, it is now more usual to calibrate cameras from multiple images of a planar object (see Section 15.4) due to the difficulties associated with accurately machining a 3D object. For a recent summary of camera models and geometric computer vision, consult Sturm et al. (2011).

The projective pinhole camera discussed in this chapter is by no means the only camera model used in computer vision; there are specialized models for the pushbroom camera (Hartley and Gupta 1994), fish-eye lenses (Devernay and Faugeras 2001; Claus and Fitzgibbon 2005), catadioptric sensors (Geyer and Daniilidis 2001; Mičušík and Pajdla 2003; Claus and Fitzgibbon 2005), and perspective cameras imaging through an interface into a medium (Treibitz et al. 2008).

Estimating extrinsic parameters: A large body of work addresses the PnP problem of estimating the geometric relation between the camera and a rigid object. Lepetit et al. (2009) present a recent approach that has low complexity with respect to the number of points used and provides a quantitative comparison with other approaches. Quan and Lan (1999) and Gao et al. (2003) present minimal solutions based on three points.

Structured light: The structured light method discussed in this chapter is due to Scharstein and Szeliski (2003), although the main goal of their paper was to generate ground truth for stereo vision applications. The use of structured light has a long history in computer vision (e.g., Vuylsteke and Oosterlinck 1990), with the main research issue being the choice of pattern to project (Salvi et al. 2004; Batlle et al. 1998; Horn and Kiryati 1999).

Shape from silhouette: The recovery of shape from multiple silhouettes of an object dates back to at least Baumgart (1974). Laurentini (1994) introduced the concept of the visual hull and described its properties. The shape from silhouette algorithm discussed in this chapter was by Prince et al. (2002) and is closely related to earlier work by Matusik et al. (2000) but rather simpler to explain. Recent work in this area has considered a probabilistic approach to pixel occupancy (Franco and Boyer 2005), the application of human silhouette priors (Grauman et al. 2003), the use of temporal sequences of silhouettes (Cheung et al. 2004), and approaches that characterize the intrinsic projective features of the visual hull.

Human performance capture: Modern interest in human performance capture was stimulated by Kanade et al. (1997). More recent work in this area includes that of Starck et al. (2009), Theobalt et al. (2007), Vlasic et al. (2008), de Aguiar et al. (2008), and Ballan and Cortelazzo (2008).

Problems

14.1 A pinhole camera has a sensor that is $1\,\text{cm} \times 1\,\text{cm}$ and a horizontal field of view of 60°. What is the distance between the optical center and the sensor? The same camera has a resolution of 100 pixels in the horizontal direction and 200 pixels in the vertical direction (i.e., the pixels are not square). What are the focal length parameters f_x and f_y from the intrinsic matrix?

14.2 We can use the pinhole camera model to understand a famous movie effect. *Dolly zoom* was first used in Alfred Hitchcock's *Vertigo*. As the protagonist looks down a stairwell, it appears to deform (Figure 14.18) in a strange way. The background seems to move away from the camera, while the foreground remains at a constant position.

In terms of the camera model, two things occur simultaneously during the dolly zoom sequence: the camera moves along the w-axis, and the focal distance of the camera changes. The distance moved and the change of focal length are carefully chosen so that objects in a predefined plane

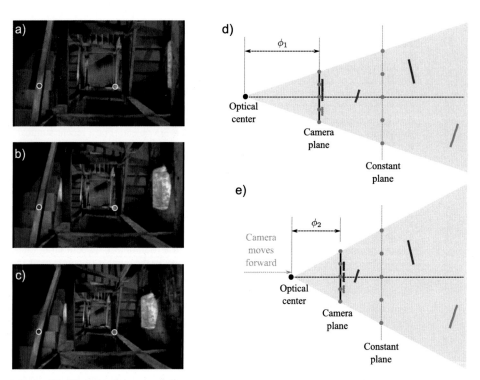

Figure 14.18 Dolly zoom. a–c) Three frames from *Vertigo* in which the stairwell appears to distort. Nearby objects remain in roughly the same place whereas object further away systematically move through the sequence. To see this, consider the red and green circles which are at the same (x, y) position in each frame. The red circle remains on the near bannister, but the green circle is on the floor of the stairwell in the first image but halfway up the stairs in the last image. d) To understand this effect consider a camera viewing a scene that consists of several green points at the same depth and some other surfaces (colored lines). e) We move the camera along the w-axis but simultaneously change the focal length so that the green points are imaged at the same position. Under these changes, objects in the plane of the green points are static, but other parts of the scene move and may even occlude one another.

a)   b)

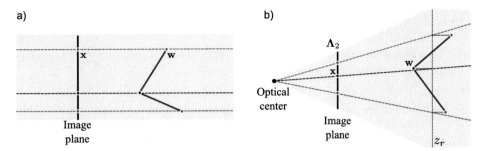

Figure 14.19 Alternative camera models. a) Orthographic camera. Rays are parallel and orthogonal to image plane. b) Weak perspective model. Points are projected orthogonally onto a reference plane at distance z_r from the camera and then pass to the image plane by perspective projection.

remain at the same position. However, objects out of this plane move relative to one another (Figures 14.18d–e).

I want to capture two pictures of a scene at either end of a dolly zoom. Before the zoom, the camera is at $w = 0$, the distance between the optical center and the image plane is 1 cm, and the image plane is 1 cm × 1 cm. After the zoom, the camera is at $w = 100$ cm. I want the plane at $w = 500$ cm to be stable after the camera movement. What should the new distance between the optical center and the image plane be?

14.3 Figure 14.19 shows two different camera models: the orthographic and weak perspective cameras. For each camera, devise the relationship between the homogeneous world points and homogeneous image points. You may assume that the world coordinate system and the camera coordinate system coincide, so there is no need to introduce the extrinsic matrix.

14.4 A 2D line can be as expressed as $ax + by + c = 0$ or in homogeneous terms

$$\mathbf{l}\tilde{\mathbf{x}} = 0,$$

where $\mathbf{l} = [a, b, c]$. Find the point where the homogeneous lines $\mathbf{l}_1$ and $\mathbf{l}_2$ join where:

1. $\mathbf{l}_1 = [3, 1, 1]$, and $\mathbf{l}_2 = [-1, 0, 1]$
2. $\mathbf{l}_1 = [1, 0, 1]$, and $\mathbf{l}_2 = [3, 0, 1]$

Hint: the 3×1 homogeneous point vector $\tilde{\mathbf{x}}$ must satisfy both $\mathbf{l}_1\tilde{\mathbf{x}} = 0$ and $\mathbf{l}_2\tilde{\mathbf{x}} = 0$. In other words it should be orthogonal to both $\mathbf{l}_1$ and $\mathbf{l}_2$.

14.5 Find the line joining the homogeneous points $\tilde{\mathbf{x}}_1$ and $\tilde{\mathbf{x}}_2$ where

$$\tilde{\mathbf{x}}_1 = [2, 2, 1]^T, \tilde{\mathbf{x}}_2 = [-2, -2, 1]^T.$$

14.6 A conic $\mathbf{C}$ is a geometric structure that can represent ellipses and circles in the 2D image. The condition for a point to lie on a conic is given by

$$\begin{bmatrix} x & y & 1 \end{bmatrix} \begin{bmatrix} a & b & c \\ b & d & e \\ c & e & f \end{bmatrix} \begin{bmatrix} x \\ y \\ 1 \end{bmatrix} = 0,$$

or

$$\tilde{\mathbf{x}}^T \mathbf{C} \tilde{\mathbf{x}} = 0.$$

Describe an algorithm to estimate the parameters a, b, c, d, e, f given several points $\mathbf{x}_1, \mathbf{x}_2, \ldots, \mathbf{x}_n$ that are known to lie on the conic. What is the minimum number of points that your algorithm requires to be successful?

14.7 Devise a method to find the intrinsic matrix of a projector using a camera and known calibration object.

14.8 What is the minimum number of binary striped light patterns of the type illustrated in Figure 14.13 required to estimate the camera-projector correspondences for a projector image of size $H \times W$?

14.9 There is a potential problem with the shape from silhouette algorithm as described; the point that we have found on the surface of the object may be occluded by another part of the object with respect to the nearest camera. Consequently, when we copy the color, we will get the wrong value. Propose a method to circumvent this problem.

14.10 In the augmented reality application (Figure 14.16), the realism might be enhanced if the object had a shadow. Propose an algorithm that could establish whether a point on the desktop (assumed planar) is shadowed by the object with respect to a point light source at a known position.

Chapter 15

Models for transformations

In this chapter, we consider a pinhole camera viewing a plane in the world. In these circumstances, the camera equations simplify to reflect the fact that there is a one-to-one mapping between points on this plane and points in the image.

Mappings between the plane and the image can be described using a family of 2D geometric transformations. In this chapter, we characterize these transformations and show how to estimate their parameters from data. We revisit the three geometric problems from Chapter 14 for the special case of a planar scene.

To motivate the ideas of this chapter, consider an augmented reality application in which we wish to superimpose 3D content onto a planar marker (Figure 15.1). To do this, we must establish the rotation and translation of the plane relative to the camera. We will do this in two stages. First, we will estimate the 2D transformation between points on the marker and points in the image. Second, we will extract the rotation and translation from the transformation parameters.

15.1 Two-dimensional transformation models

In this section, we consider a family of 2D transformations, starting with the simplest and working toward the most general. We will motivate each by considering viewing a planar scene under different viewing conditions.

15.1.1 Euclidean transformation model

Consider a calibrated camera viewing a fronto-parallel plane at known distance, D (i.e., a plane whose normal corresponds to the w-axis of the camera). This may seem like a contrived situation, but it is exactly what happens in machine inspection applications: an overhead camera views a conveyor belt and examines objects that contain little or no depth variation.

We assume that a position on the plane can be described by a 3D position $\mathbf{w} = [u, v, 0]^T$, measured in real-world units such as millimeters. The w-coordinate represents directions perpendicular to the plane, and is hence always zero. Consequently, we will sometimes treat $\mathbf{w} = [u, v]^T$ as a 2D coordinate.

Applying the pinhole camera model to this situation gives

$$\lambda \tilde{\mathbf{x}} = \mathbf{\Lambda}[\mathbf{\Omega}, \boldsymbol{\tau}]\tilde{\mathbf{w}}, \tag{15.1}$$

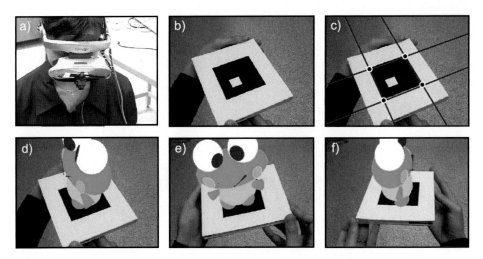

Figure 15.1 Video see-through augmented reality with a planar scene. a) The user views the world through a head mounted display with a camera attached to the front. The images from the camera are analyzed and augmented in near-real time and displayed to the user. b) Here, the world consists of a planar 2D marker. c) The marker corners are found by fitting edges to its sides and finding their intersections. d) The geometric transformation between the 2D positions of the corners on the marker surface and the corresponding positions in the image is computed. This transformation is analyzed to find the rotation and translation of the camera relative to the marker. This allows us to superimpose a 3D object as if it were rigidly attached to the surface of the image. e–f) As the marker is manipulated the superimposed object changes pose appropriately.

where $\tilde{\mathbf{x}}$ is the 2D observed image position represented as a homogeneous 3-vector and $\tilde{\mathbf{w}}$ is the 3D point in the world represented as a homogeneous 4-vector. Writing this out explicitly, we have

$$
\lambda \begin{bmatrix} x \\ y \\ 1 \end{bmatrix} = \begin{bmatrix} \phi_x & \gamma & \delta_x \\ 0 & \phi_y & \delta_y \\ 0 & 0 & 1 \end{bmatrix} \begin{bmatrix} \omega_{11} & \omega_{12} & 0 & \tau_x \\ \omega_{21} & \omega_{22} & 0 & \tau_y \\ 0 & 0 & 1 & D \end{bmatrix} \begin{bmatrix} u \\ v \\ 0 \\ 1 \end{bmatrix}
$$

$$
= \begin{bmatrix} \phi_x & \gamma & \delta_x \\ 0 & \phi_y & \delta_y \\ 0 & 0 & 1 \end{bmatrix} \begin{bmatrix} \omega_{11} & \omega_{12} & \tau_x \\ \omega_{21} & \omega_{22} & \tau_y \\ 0 & 0 & D \end{bmatrix} \begin{bmatrix} u \\ v \\ 1 \end{bmatrix}, \tag{15.2}
$$

where the 3D rotation matrix $\mathbf{\Omega}$ takes a special form with only four unknowns, reflecting the fact that the plane is known to be fronto-parallel.

We can move the distance parameter D into the intrinsic matrix without changing the last of these three equations and equivalently write

$$
\lambda \begin{bmatrix} x \\ y \\ 1 \end{bmatrix} = \begin{bmatrix} \phi_x & \gamma & \delta_x \\ 0 & \phi_y & \delta_y \\ 0 & 0 & D \end{bmatrix} \begin{bmatrix} \omega_{11} & \omega_{12} & \tau_x \\ \omega_{21} & \omega_{22} & \tau_y \\ 0 & 0 & 1 \end{bmatrix} \begin{bmatrix} u \\ v \\ 1 \end{bmatrix}. \tag{15.3}
$$

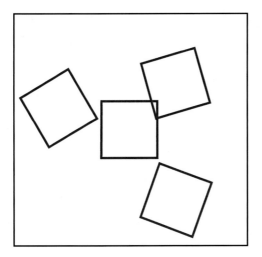

Figure 15.2 The 2D Euclidean transformation describes 2D rigid rotations and translations. The blue squares are all Euclidean transformations of the original red square. The transformation has three parameters: the rotation angle and the translations in the x- and y-directions. When a camera views a fronto-parallel plane at a known distance, the relation between the normalized camera coordinates and the 2D positions on the plane is a Euclidean transformation.

If we now eliminate the effect of this modified intrinsic matrix, by premultiplying both left and right by its inverse we get

$$\lambda \begin{bmatrix} x' \\ y' \\ 1 \end{bmatrix} = \begin{bmatrix} \omega_{11} & \omega_{12} & \tau_x \\ \omega_{21} & \omega_{22} & \tau_y \\ 0 & 0 & 1 \end{bmatrix} \begin{bmatrix} u \\ v \\ 1 \end{bmatrix}, \tag{15.4}$$

where x' and y' are camera coordinates that are normalized with respect to this modified intrinsic matrix.

The mapping in Equation 15.4 is known as a *Euclidean transformation*. It can be equivalently written in Cartesian coordinates as

$$\begin{bmatrix} x' \\ y' \end{bmatrix} = \begin{bmatrix} \omega_{11} & \omega_{12} \\ \omega_{21} & \omega_{22} \end{bmatrix} \begin{bmatrix} u \\ v \end{bmatrix} + \begin{bmatrix} \tau_x \\ \tau_y \end{bmatrix}, \tag{15.5}$$

or for short we may write

$$\mathbf{x}' = \mathbf{euc}[\mathbf{w}, \boldsymbol{\Omega}, \boldsymbol{\tau}], \tag{15.6}$$

where $\mathbf{x}' = [x', y']^T$ contains the normalized camera coordinates and $\mathbf{w} = [u, v]^T$ is the real-world position on the plane.

The Euclidean transformation describes rigid rotations and translations in the plane (Figure 15.2). Although this transformation appears to take six separate parameters, the rotation matrix $\boldsymbol{\Omega}$ can be reexpressed in terms of the rotation angle θ,

$$\begin{bmatrix} \omega_{11} & \omega_{12} \\ \omega_{21} & \omega_{22} \end{bmatrix} = \begin{bmatrix} \cos[\theta] & \sin[\theta] \\ -\sin[\theta] & \cos[\theta] \end{bmatrix}, \tag{15.7}$$

and hence the actual number of parameters is three (the two offsets τ_x and τ_y, and the rotation, θ).

15.1.2 Similarity transformation model

Now consider a calibrated camera viewing a fronto-parallel plane at *unknown* distance D. The relationship between image points $\mathbf{x} = [x, y]^T$ and points $\mathbf{w} = [u, v, 0]^T$ on the plane is once more given by Equation 15.2. Converting to normalized image coordinates by premultiplying both sides by the inverse of the intrinsic matrix gives

$$\lambda \begin{bmatrix} x' \\ y' \\ 1 \end{bmatrix} = \begin{bmatrix} \omega_{11} & \omega_{12} & 0 & \tau_x \\ \omega_{21} & \omega_{22} & 0 & \tau_y \\ 0 & 0 & 1 & D \end{bmatrix} \begin{bmatrix} u \\ v \\ 0 \\ 1 \end{bmatrix} = \begin{bmatrix} \omega_{11} & \omega_{12} & \tau_x \\ \omega_{21} & \omega_{22} & \tau_y \\ 0 & 0 & D \end{bmatrix} \begin{bmatrix} u \\ v \\ 1 \end{bmatrix}. \tag{15.8}$$

We now multiply each of these three equations by $\rho = 1/D$ to get

$$\rho\lambda \begin{bmatrix} x' \\ y' \\ 1 \end{bmatrix} = \begin{bmatrix} \rho\omega_{11} & \rho\omega_{12} & \rho\tau_x \\ \rho\omega_{21} & \rho\omega_{22} & \rho\tau_y \\ 0 & 0 & 1 \end{bmatrix} \begin{bmatrix} u \\ v \\ 1 \end{bmatrix}. \tag{15.9}$$

This is the homogeneous representation of the *similarity transformation*. However it is usual to incorporate ρ into the constant λ on the left-hand side so that $\lambda \leftarrow \rho\lambda$ and into the translation parameters so that $\tau_x \leftarrow \rho\tau_x$ and $\tau_y \leftarrow \rho\tau_y$ on the right-hand side to yield

$$\lambda \begin{bmatrix} x' \\ y' \\ 1 \end{bmatrix} = \begin{bmatrix} \rho\omega_{11} & \rho\omega_{12} & \tau_x \\ \rho\omega_{21} & \rho\omega_{22} & \tau_y \\ 0 & 0 & 1 \end{bmatrix} \begin{bmatrix} u \\ v \\ 1 \end{bmatrix}. \tag{15.10}$$

Converting to Cartesian coordinates, we have

$$\begin{bmatrix} x' \\ y' \end{bmatrix} = \begin{bmatrix} \rho\omega_{11} & \rho\omega_{12} \\ \rho\omega_{21} & \rho\omega_{22} \end{bmatrix} \begin{bmatrix} u \\ v \end{bmatrix} + \begin{bmatrix} \tau_x \\ \tau_y \end{bmatrix}, \tag{15.11}$$

or for short,

$$\mathbf{x}' = \mathbf{sim}[\mathbf{w}, \mathbf{\Omega}, \boldsymbol{\tau}, \rho]. \tag{15.12}$$

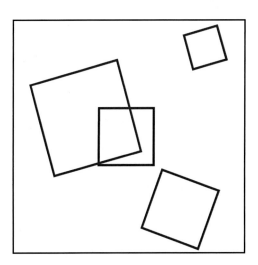

Figure 15.3 The similarity transformation describes rotations, translations, and isotropic scalings. The blue quadrilaterals are all similarity transformations of the original red square. The transformation has four parameters: the rotation angle, the scaling and the translations in the x- and y-directions. When a camera views a fronto-parallel plane at unknown distance, the relation between the normalized camera coordinates and positions on the plane is a similarity.

The similarity transformation is a Euclidean transformation with a scaling (Figure 15.3) and has four parameters: the rotation, the scaling, and two translations.

15.1.3 Affine transformation model

We motivated each of the previous transformations by considering a camera viewing a fronto-parallel plane. Ultimately, we wish to describe the relationship between image points and points on a plane in general position. As an intermediate step, let us generalize the transformations in Equations 15.4 and 15.10 to

$$\lambda \begin{bmatrix} x' \\ y' \\ 1 \end{bmatrix} = \begin{bmatrix} \phi_{11} & \phi_{12} & \tau_x \\ \phi_{21} & \phi_{22} & \tau_y \\ 0 & 0 & 1 \end{bmatrix} \begin{bmatrix} u \\ v \\ 1 \end{bmatrix},$$ (15.13)

where $\phi_{11}, \phi_{12}, \phi_{21}$, and ϕ_{22} are now unconstrained and can take arbitrary values. This is known as an *affine transformation*. In Cartesian coordinates, we have

$$\begin{bmatrix} x' \\ y' \end{bmatrix} = \begin{bmatrix} \phi_{11} & \phi_{12} \\ \phi_{21} & \phi_{22} \end{bmatrix} \begin{bmatrix} u \\ v \end{bmatrix} + \begin{bmatrix} \tau_x \\ \tau_y, \end{bmatrix}$$ (15.14)

or for short we might write

$$\mathbf{x}' = \mathbf{aff}[\mathbf{w}, \boldsymbol{\Phi}, \boldsymbol{\tau}].$$ (15.15)

Note that the camera calibration matrix $\boldsymbol{\Lambda}$ also has the form of an affine transformation (i.e., a 3×3 matrix with two zeros in the bottom row). The product of two affine transformations is a third affine transformation, so if Equation 15.15 is true, then there is also an affine transformation between points on the plane and the original (unnormalized) pixel positions.

The affine transformation encompasses both Euclidean and similarity transformations, but also includes *shears* (Figure 15.4). However, it is far from general, and a notable restriction is that parallel lines are always mapped to other parallel lines. It has six unknown parameters, each of which can take any value.

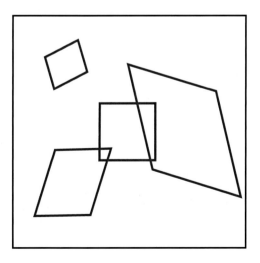

Figure 15.4 The affine transformation describes rotations, translations, scalings, and shears. The blue quadrilaterals are all affine transformations of the original red square. The affine transformation has six parameters: the translations in the x- and y-directions, and four parameters that determine the other effects. Notice that lines that were originally parallel remain parallel after the affine transformation is applied, so in each case the square becomes a parallelogram.

Figure 15.5 Approximating projection of a plane. a) A planar object viewed with a camera with a narrow field of view (long focal length) from a large distance. The depth variation within the object is small compared to the distance from the camera to the plane. Here, perspective distortion is small, and the relationship between points in the image and points on the surface is well approximated by an affine transformation. b) The same planar object viewed with a wide field of view (short focal length) from a short distance. The depth variation within the object is comparable to the average distance from the camera to the plane. An affine transformation cannot describe this situation well. c) However, a projective transformation (homography) captures the relationship between points on the surface and points in this image.

The question remains as to whether the affine transformation really does provide a good mapping between points on a plane and their positions in the image. This is indeed the case when the depth variation of the plane as seen by the camera is small relative to the mean distance from the camera. In practice, this occurs when the viewing angle is not too oblique, the camera is distant, and the field of view is small (Figure 15.5a). In more general situations, the affine transformation is not a good approximation. A simple counterexample is the convergence of parallel train tracks in an image as they become more distant. The affine transformation cannot describe this situation as it can only map parallel lines on the object to parallel lines in the image.

15.1.4 Projective transformation model

Finally, we investigate what really happens when a pinhole camera views a plane from an arbitrary viewpoint. The relationship between a point $\mathbf{w} = [u, v, 0]^T$ on the plane and the position $\mathbf{x} = [x, y]^T$ to which it is projected is

$$
\lambda \begin{bmatrix} x \\ y \\ 1 \end{bmatrix} = \begin{bmatrix} \phi_x & \gamma & \delta_x \\ 0 & \phi_y & \delta_y \\ 0 & 0 & 1 \end{bmatrix} \begin{bmatrix} \omega_{11} & \omega_{12} & \omega_{13} & \tau_x \\ \omega_{21} & \omega_{22} & \omega_{23} & \tau_y \\ \omega_{31} & \omega_{32} & \omega_{33} & \tau_z \end{bmatrix} \begin{bmatrix} u \\ v \\ 0 \\ 1 \end{bmatrix}
$$

$$
= \begin{bmatrix} \phi_x & \gamma & \delta_x \\ 0 & \phi_y & \delta_y \\ 0 & 0 & 1 \end{bmatrix} \begin{bmatrix} \omega_{11} & \omega_{12} & \tau_x \\ \omega_{21} & \omega_{22} & \tau_y \\ \omega_{31} & \omega_{32} & \tau_z \end{bmatrix} \begin{bmatrix} u \\ v \\ 1 \end{bmatrix}. \tag{15.16}
$$

Combining the two 3×3 matrices by multiplying them together, the result is a transformation with the general form

$$
\lambda \begin{bmatrix} x \\ y \\ 1 \end{bmatrix} = \begin{bmatrix} \phi_{11} & \phi_{12} & \phi_{13} \\ \phi_{21} & \phi_{22} & \phi_{23} \\ \phi_{31} & \phi_{32} & \phi_{33} \end{bmatrix} \begin{bmatrix} u \\ v \\ 1 \end{bmatrix} \tag{15.17}
$$

Figure 15.6 The projective transformation (also known as a collinearity or homography) can map any four points in the plane to any other four points. Rotations, translations, scalings, and shears and are all special cases. The blue quadrilaterals are all projective transformations of the original red square. The projective transformation has eight parameters. Lines that were parallel are not constrained to remain parallel after the projective transformation is applied.

and is variously known as a *projective transformation*, a *collinearity*, or a *homography*. In Cartesian coordinates the homography is written as

$$x = \frac{\phi_{11}u + \phi_{12}v + \phi_{13}}{\phi_{31}u + \phi_{32}v + \phi_{33}}$$
$$y = \frac{\phi_{21}u + \phi_{22}v + \phi_{23}}{\phi_{31}u + \phi_{32}v + \phi_{33}}, \tag{15.18}$$

or for short

$$\mathbf{x} = \mathbf{hom}[\mathbf{w}, \mathbf{\Phi}]. \tag{15.19}$$

The homography can map any four points in the plane to any other four points (Figure 15.6). It is a linear transformation in homogenous coordinates (Equation 15.17) but is nonlinear in Cartesian coordinates (Equation 15.18). It subsumes the Euclidean, similarity, and affine transformations as special cases. It exactly describes the mapping between the 2D coordinates of points on a plane in the real world and their positions in an image of that plane (Figure 15.5c).

Although there are nine entries in the matrix $\mathbf{\Phi}$, the homography only contains eight degrees of freedom; the entries are redundant with respect to scale. It is easy to see that a constant rescaling of all nine values produces the same transformation, as the scaling factor cancels out of the numerator and denominator in Equation 15.18. The properties of the homography are discussed further in Section 15.5.1.

15.1.5   Adding uncertainty

The four geometric models presented in the preceding sections are deterministic. However, in a real system, the measured positions of features in the image are subject to noise, and we need to incorporate this uncertainty into our models. In particular, we will assume that the positions $\mathbf{x}_i$ in the image are corrupted by normally distributed noise with

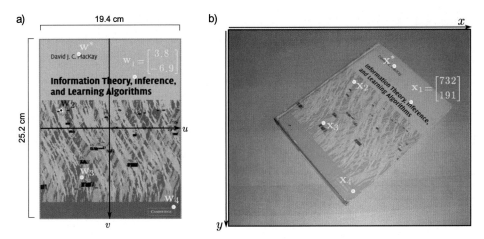

Figure 15.7 Learning and inference for transformation models. a) Planar object surface (position measured in cm). b) Image (position measured in pixels). In learning, we estimate the parameters of the mapping from points $\mathbf{w}$ on the object surface to image positions $\mathbf{x}_i$ based on pairs $\{\mathbf{x}_i, \mathbf{w}_i\}_{i=1}^{I}$ of known correspondences. We can use this mapping to find the position $\mathbf{x}^*$ in the image to which a point $\mathbf{w}^*$ on the object surface will project. In inference, we reverse this process: given a position $\mathbf{x}^*$ in the image, the goal is to establish the corresponding position $\mathbf{w}^*$ on the object surface.

spherical covariance so that, for example, the likelihood for the homography becomes

$$Pr(\mathbf{x}|\mathbf{w}) = \mathrm{Norm}_{\mathbf{x}}\left[\mathbf{hom}[\mathbf{w}, \boldsymbol{\Phi}], \sigma^2 \mathbf{I}\right]. \tag{15.20}$$

This is a generative model for the 2D image data $\mathbf{x}$. It can be thought of as a simplified version of the pinhole camera model that is specialized for viewing planar scenes; it is a recipe that tells us how to find the position in the image $\mathbf{x}$ corresponding to a point $\mathbf{w}$ on the surface of the planar object in the world.

The learning and inference problems in this model (Figure 15.7) are

- **Learning**: we are given pairs of points $\{\mathbf{x}_i, \mathbf{w}_i\}_{i=1}^{I}$ where $\mathbf{x}_i$ is a position in the image and $\mathbf{w}_i$ is the corresponding position on the plane in the world. The goal is to use these to establish the parameters $\boldsymbol{\theta}$ of the transformation. For example, in the case of the homography, the parameters $\boldsymbol{\theta}$ would comprise the nine entries of the matrix $\boldsymbol{\Phi}$.
- **Inference**: we are given a new point in the image $\mathbf{x}^*$, and our goal is to find the position on the plane $\mathbf{w}^*$ that projected to it.

We consider these two problems in the following sections.

15.2 Learning in transformation models

We are given a set of I 2D positions $\mathbf{w}_i = [u_i, v_i]^T$ on the surface of the plane and the I corresponding 2D image positions $\mathbf{x}_i = [x_i, y_i]^T$ in the image. We select a transformation class of the form $\mathbf{trans}[\mathbf{w}_i, \boldsymbol{\theta}]$. The goal of the learning algorithm is then to estimate the parameters $\boldsymbol{\theta}$ that best map the points $\mathbf{w}_i$ to the image positions $\mathbf{x}_i$.

Adopting the maximum likelihood approach, we have

$$\hat{\boldsymbol{\theta}} = \underset{\boldsymbol{\theta}}{\operatorname{argmax}} \left[\prod_{i=1}^{I} \mathrm{Norm}_{\mathbf{x}_i} \left[\mathbf{trans}[\mathbf{w}_i, \boldsymbol{\theta}], \sigma^2 \mathbf{I} \right] \right]$$

$$= \underset{\boldsymbol{\theta}}{\operatorname{argmax}} \left[\sum_{i=1}^{I} \log \left[\mathrm{Norm}_{\mathbf{x}_i} \left[\mathbf{trans}[\mathbf{w}_i, \boldsymbol{\theta}], \sigma^2 \mathbf{I} \right] \right] \right], \qquad (15.21)$$

where, as usual, we have taken the logarithm which is a monotonic transformation and hence does not affect the position of the maximum. Substituting in the expression for the normal distribution and simplifying, we get the least squares problem

$$\hat{\boldsymbol{\theta}} = \underset{\boldsymbol{\theta}}{\operatorname{argmin}} \left[\sum_{i=1}^{I} (\mathbf{x}_i - \mathbf{trans}[\mathbf{w}_i, \boldsymbol{\theta}])^T (\mathbf{x}_i - \mathbf{trans}[\mathbf{w}_i, \boldsymbol{\theta}]) \right]. \qquad (15.22)$$

The solutions to this least squares problem for each of the four transformation types are presented in Sections 15.2.1–15.2.4. The details differ in each case, but they have the common approach of reducing the problem into a standard form for which the solution is known. The algorithms are somewhat involved, and these sections can be skipped on first reading.

15.2.1   Learning Euclidean parameters

The Euclidean transformation is determined by a 2×2 rotation matrix $\boldsymbol{\Omega}$ and a 2×1 translation vector $\boldsymbol{\tau} = [\tau_x, \tau_y]^T$ (Equations 15.4 and 15.5). Each pair of matching points $\{\mathbf{x}_i, \mathbf{w}_i\}$ contributes two constraints to the solution (deriving from the x- and y-coordinates). Since there are three underlying degrees of freedom, we will require at least $I = 2$ pairs of points to get a unique estimate.

Our goal is to solve the problem

$$\hat{\boldsymbol{\Omega}}, \hat{\boldsymbol{\tau}} = \underset{\boldsymbol{\Omega}, \boldsymbol{\tau}}{\operatorname{argmin}} \left[\sum_{i=1}^{I} (\mathbf{x}_i - \mathbf{euc}[\mathbf{w}_i, \boldsymbol{\Omega}, \boldsymbol{\tau}])^T (\mathbf{x}_i - \mathbf{euc}[\mathbf{w}_i, \boldsymbol{\Omega}, \boldsymbol{\tau}]) \right]$$

$$= \underset{\boldsymbol{\Omega}, \boldsymbol{\tau}}{\operatorname{argmin}} \left[\sum_{i=1}^{I} (\mathbf{x}_i - \boldsymbol{\Omega}\mathbf{w}_i - \boldsymbol{\tau})^T (\mathbf{x}_i - \boldsymbol{\Omega}\mathbf{w}_i - \boldsymbol{\tau}) \right], \qquad (15.23)$$

with the constraint that $\boldsymbol{\Omega}$ is a rotation matrix so that $\boldsymbol{\Omega}\boldsymbol{\Omega}^T = \mathbf{I}$ and $|\boldsymbol{\Omega}| = 1$.

An expression for the translation vector can be found by taking the derivative of the objective function with respect to $\boldsymbol{\tau}$, setting the result to zero and simplifying. The result is the mean difference vector between the two sets of points after the rotation has been applied

$$\hat{\boldsymbol{\tau}} = \frac{\sum_{i=1}^{I} \mathbf{x}_i - \boldsymbol{\Omega}\mathbf{w}_i}{I} = \boldsymbol{\mu}_x - \boldsymbol{\Omega}\boldsymbol{\mu}_w, \qquad (15.24)$$

where $\boldsymbol{\mu}_x$ is the mean of the points $\{\mathbf{x}_i\}$ and $\boldsymbol{\mu}_w$ is the mean of the points $\{\mathbf{w}_i\}$. Substituting this result into the original criterion, we get

$$\hat{\boldsymbol{\Omega}} = \underset{\boldsymbol{\Omega}}{\operatorname{argmin}} \left[\sum_{i=1}^{I} ((\mathbf{x}_i - \boldsymbol{\mu}_x) - \boldsymbol{\Omega}(\mathbf{w}_i - \boldsymbol{\mu}_w))^T ((\mathbf{x}_i - \boldsymbol{\mu}_x) - \boldsymbol{\Omega}(\mathbf{w}_i - \boldsymbol{\mu}_w)) \right]. \quad (15.25)$$

Defining matrices $\mathbf{B} = [\mathbf{x}_1 - \boldsymbol{\mu}_x, \mathbf{x}_2 - \boldsymbol{\mu}_x, \ldots, \mathbf{x}_I - \boldsymbol{\mu}_x]$ and $\mathbf{A} = [\mathbf{w}_1 - \boldsymbol{\mu}_w, \mathbf{w}_2 - \boldsymbol{\mu}_w, \ldots, \mathbf{w}_I - \boldsymbol{\mu}_w]$, we can rewrite the objective function for the best rotation $\boldsymbol{\Omega}$ as

$$\hat{\boldsymbol{\Omega}} = \underset{\boldsymbol{\Omega}}{\operatorname{argmin}} \left[\|\mathbf{B} - \boldsymbol{\Omega}\mathbf{A}\|_F \right] \qquad \text{subject to } \boldsymbol{\Omega}\boldsymbol{\Omega}^T = \mathbf{I}, |\boldsymbol{\Omega}| = 1, \qquad (15.26)$$

where $|\bullet|_F$ denotes the Frobenius norm. This is an example of an *orthogonal Procrustes problem*. A closed form solution can be found by computing the SVD $\mathbf{ULV}^T = \mathbf{BA}^T$, and then choosing $\hat{\boldsymbol{\Omega}} = \mathbf{VU}^T$ (see Appendix C.7.3).

15.2.2 Learning similarity parameters

The similarity transformation is determined by a 2×2 rotation matrix $\boldsymbol{\Omega}$, a 2×1 translation vector $\boldsymbol{\tau}$, and a scaling factor ρ (Equations 15.10 and 15.11). There are four underlying degrees of freedom, so we will require at least $I = 2$ pairs of matching points $\{\mathbf{x}_i, \mathbf{w}_i\}$ to guarantee a unique solution.

The objective function for maximum likelihood fitting of the parameters is

$$\hat{\boldsymbol{\Omega}}, \hat{\boldsymbol{\tau}}, \hat{\rho} = \underset{\boldsymbol{\Omega}, \boldsymbol{\tau}, \rho}{\operatorname{argmin}} \left[\sum_{i=1}^{I} (\mathbf{x}_i - \mathbf{sim}[\mathbf{w}_i, \boldsymbol{\Omega}, \boldsymbol{\tau}, \rho])^T (\mathbf{x}_i - \mathbf{sim}[\mathbf{w}_i, \boldsymbol{\Omega}, \boldsymbol{\tau}, \rho]) \right]$$
$$= \underset{\boldsymbol{\Omega}, \boldsymbol{\tau}, \rho}{\operatorname{argmin}} \left[\sum_{i=1}^{I} (\mathbf{x}_i - \rho\boldsymbol{\Omega}\mathbf{w}_i - \boldsymbol{\tau})^T (\mathbf{x}_i - \rho\boldsymbol{\Omega}\mathbf{w}_i - \boldsymbol{\tau}) \right], \qquad (15.27)$$

with the constraint that $\boldsymbol{\Omega}$ is a rotation matrix so that $\boldsymbol{\Omega}\boldsymbol{\Omega}^T = \mathbf{I}$ and $|\boldsymbol{\Omega}| = 1$.

To optimize this criterion, we compute $\boldsymbol{\Omega}$ exactly as for the Euclidean transformation. The maximum likelihood solution for the scaling factor is given by

$$\hat{\rho} = \frac{\sum_{i=1}^{I} (\mathbf{x}_i - \boldsymbol{\mu}_x)^T \hat{\boldsymbol{\Omega}} (\mathbf{w}_i - \boldsymbol{\mu}_w)}{\sum_{i=1}^{I} (\mathbf{w}_i - \boldsymbol{\mu}_w)^T (\mathbf{w}_i - \boldsymbol{\mu}_w)}, \qquad (15.28)$$

and the translation can be found using

$$\hat{\boldsymbol{\tau}} = \frac{\sum_{i=1}^{I} (\mathbf{x}_i - \hat{\rho}\hat{\boldsymbol{\Omega}}\mathbf{w}_i)}{I}. \qquad (15.29)$$

15.2.3 Learning affine parameters

The affine transformation is parameterized by an unconstrained 2×2 matrix $\boldsymbol{\Phi}$ and a 2×1 translation vector $\boldsymbol{\tau}$ (Equations 15.13 and 15.14). There are six unknowns, and so we need a minimum of $I = 3$ pairs of matching points $\{\mathbf{x}_i, \mathbf{w}_i\}$ to guarantee a unique solution. The learning problem can be stated as

$$\hat{\boldsymbol{\Phi}}, \hat{\boldsymbol{\tau}} = \underset{\boldsymbol{\Phi}, \boldsymbol{\tau}}{\operatorname{argmin}} \left[\sum_{i=1}^{I} (\mathbf{x}_i - \mathbf{aff}[\mathbf{w}_i, \boldsymbol{\Phi}, \boldsymbol{\tau}])^T (\mathbf{x}_i - \mathbf{aff}[\mathbf{w}_i, \boldsymbol{\Phi}, \boldsymbol{\tau}]) \right]$$
$$= \underset{\boldsymbol{\Phi}, \boldsymbol{\tau}}{\operatorname{argmin}} \left[\sum_{i=1}^{I} (\mathbf{x}_i - \boldsymbol{\Phi}\mathbf{w}_i - \boldsymbol{\tau})^T (\mathbf{x}_i - \boldsymbol{\Phi}\mathbf{w}_i - \boldsymbol{\tau}) \right]. \qquad (15.30)$$

To solve this problem, observe that we can reexpress $\boldsymbol{\Phi}\mathbf{w}_i + \boldsymbol{\tau}$ as a linear function of the unknown elements of $\boldsymbol{\Phi}$ and $\boldsymbol{\tau}$

$$\boldsymbol{\Phi}\mathbf{w}_i + \boldsymbol{\tau} = \begin{bmatrix} u_i & v_i & 1 & 0 & 0 & 0 \\ 0 & 0 & 0 & u_i & v_i & 1 \end{bmatrix} \begin{bmatrix} \phi_{11} \\ \phi_{12} \\ \tau_x \\ \phi_{21} \\ \phi_{22} \\ \tau_y \end{bmatrix} = \mathbf{A}_i \mathbf{b}, \tag{15.31}$$

where $\mathbf{A}_i$ is a 2×6 matrix based on the point $\mathbf{w}_i$, and $\mathbf{b}$ contains the unknown parameters. The problem can now be written as

$$\hat{\mathbf{b}} = \underset{\mathbf{b}}{\operatorname{argmin}} \left[\sum_{i=1}^{I} (\mathbf{x}_i - \mathbf{A}_i \mathbf{b})^T (\mathbf{x}_i - \mathbf{A}_i \mathbf{b}) \right], \tag{15.32}$$

which is a linear least squares problem and can be solved easily (Appendix C.7.1).

15.2.4 Learning projective parameters

The projective transformation or homography is parameterized by a 3×3 matrix $\boldsymbol{\Phi}$ (Equations 15.17 and 15.18), which is ambiguous up to scale, giving a total of eight degrees of freedom. Consequently, we need a minimum of $I = 4$ pairs of corresponding points for a unique solution. This neatly matches our expectations: a homography can map any four points in the plane to any other four points, and so it is reasonable that we should need at least four pairs of points to determine it.

The learning problem can be stated as

$$\hat{\boldsymbol{\Phi}} = \underset{\boldsymbol{\Phi}}{\operatorname{argmin}} \left[\sum_{i=1}^{I} (\mathbf{x}_i - \mathbf{hom}[\mathbf{w}_i, \boldsymbol{\Phi}])^T (\mathbf{x}_i - \mathbf{hom}[\mathbf{w}_i, \boldsymbol{\Phi}]) \right] \tag{15.33}$$

$$= \underset{\boldsymbol{\Phi}}{\operatorname{argmin}} \left[\sum_{i=1}^{I} \left(x_i - \frac{\phi_{11}u_i + \phi_{12}v_i + \phi_{13}}{\phi_{31}u_i + \phi_{32}v_i + \phi_{33}} \right)^2 + \left(y_i - \frac{\phi_{21}u_i + \phi_{22}v_i + \phi_{23}}{\phi_{31}u_i + \phi_{32}v_i + \phi_{33}} \right)^2 \right].$$

Unfortunately, there is no closed form solution to this nonlinear problem and to find the answer we must rely on gradient-based optimization techniques. Since there is a scale ambiguity, this optimization would normally be carried out under the constraint that the sum of the squares of the elements of $\boldsymbol{\Phi}$ is one.

A successful optimization procedure depends on a good initial starting point, and for this we use the *direct linear transformation* or *DLT* algorithm. The DLT algorithm uses homogeneous coordinates where the homography is a linear transformation and finds a closed form solution for the algebraic error. This is not the same as optimizing the true objective function (Equation 15.33), but provides a result that is usually very close to the true answer and can be used as a starting point for the nonlinear optimization of the true criterion. In homogeneous coordinates we have

$$\lambda \begin{bmatrix} x_i \\ y_i \\ 1 \end{bmatrix} = \begin{bmatrix} \phi_{11} & \phi_{12} & \phi_{13} \\ \phi_{21} & \phi_{22} & \phi_{23} \\ \phi_{31} & \phi_{32} & \phi_{33} \end{bmatrix} \begin{bmatrix} u_i \\ v_i \\ 1 \end{bmatrix}. \tag{15.34}$$

Each homogeneous coordinate can be considered as a direction in 3D space (Figure 14.11). So, this equation states that the left-hand side $\tilde{\mathbf{x}}_i$ represents the same direction in space as the right-hand side, $\boldsymbol{\Phi}\tilde{\mathbf{w}}_i$. If this is the case, their cross product must be zero, so that

$$\tilde{\mathbf{x}} \times \boldsymbol{\Phi}\tilde{\mathbf{w}} = \mathbf{0}. \tag{15.35}$$

Writing this constraint in full gives the relations

$$\begin{bmatrix} y(\phi_{31}u + \phi_{32}v + \phi_{33}) - (\phi_{21}u + \phi_{22}v + \phi_{23}) \\ (\phi_{11}u + \phi_{12}v + \phi_{13}) - x(\phi_{31}u + \phi_{32}v + \phi_{33}) \\ x(\phi_{21}u + \phi_{22}v + \phi_{23}) - y(\phi_{11}u + \phi_{12}v + \phi_{13}) \end{bmatrix} = \mathbf{0}. \tag{15.36}$$

This appears to provide three linear constraints on the elements of $\boldsymbol{\Phi}$. However, only two of these three equations are independent, so we discard the third. We now stack the first two constraints from each of the I pairs of points $\{\mathbf{x}_i, \mathbf{w}_i\}$ to form the system

$$\begin{bmatrix} 0 & 0 & 0 & -u_1 & -v_1 & -1 & y_1u_1 & y_1v_1 & y_1 \\ u_1 & v_1 & 1 & 0 & 0 & 0 & -x_1u_1 & -x_1v_1 & -x_1 \\ 0 & 0 & 0 & -u_2 & -v_2 & -1 & y_2u_2 & y_2v_2 & y_2 \\ u_2 & v_2 & 1 & 0 & 0 & 0 & -x_2u_2 & -x_2v_2 & -x_2 \\ \vdots & \vdots & \vdots & \vdots & \vdots & \vdots & \vdots & \vdots & \vdots \\ 0 & 0 & 0 & -u_I & -v_I & -1 & y_Iu_I & y_Iv_I & y_I \\ u_I & v_I & 1 & 0 & 0 & 0 & -x_Iu_I & -x_Iv_I & -x_I \end{bmatrix} \begin{bmatrix} \phi_{11} \\ \phi_{12} \\ \phi_{13} \\ \phi_{21} \\ \phi_{22} \\ \phi_{23} \\ \phi_{31} \\ \phi_{32} \\ \phi_{33} \end{bmatrix} = \mathbf{0}, \tag{15.37}$$

which has the form $\mathbf{A}\boldsymbol{\phi} = \mathbf{0}$.

We solve this system of equations in a least squares sense with the constraint $\boldsymbol{\phi}^T\boldsymbol{\phi} = 1$ to prevent the trivial solution $\boldsymbol{\phi} = \mathbf{0}$. This is a standard problem (see Appendix C.7.2). To find the solution, we compute the SVD $\mathbf{A} = \mathbf{U}\mathbf{L}\mathbf{V}^T$ and choose $\boldsymbol{\phi}$ to be the last column of $\mathbf{V}$. This is reshaped into a 3×3 matrix $\boldsymbol{\Phi}$ and used as a starting point for the nonlinear optimization of the true criterion (Equation 15.33).

15.3   Inference in transformation models

⚙ 15.5

We have introduced four transformations (Euclidean, similarity, affine, projective) that relate positions $\mathbf{w}$ on a real-world plane to their projected positions $\mathbf{x}$ in the image and discussed how to learn their parameters. In each case, the transformation took the form of a generative model $Pr(\mathbf{x}|\mathbf{w})$. In this section, we consider how to infer the world position $\mathbf{w}$ from the image position $\mathbf{x}$.

For simplicity, we will take a maximum likelihood approach to this problem. For the generic transformation $\mathbf{trans}[\mathbf{w}_i, \boldsymbol{\theta}]$, we seek

$$\hat{\mathbf{w}} = \underset{\mathbf{w}}{\operatorname{argmax}} \left[\log\left[\text{Norm}_{\mathbf{x}}\left[\mathbf{trans}[\mathbf{w}, \boldsymbol{\theta}], \sigma^2\mathbf{I}\right]\right]\right]$$

$$= \underset{\mathbf{w}}{\operatorname{argmin}} \left[(\mathbf{x} - \mathbf{trans}[\mathbf{w}, \boldsymbol{\theta}])^T (\mathbf{x} - \mathbf{trans}[\mathbf{w}, \boldsymbol{\theta}])\right]. \tag{15.38}$$

It is clear that this will be achieved when the image point and the predicted image point agree exactly so that

$$\mathbf{x} = \mathbf{trans}[\mathbf{w}, \boldsymbol{\theta}]. \tag{15.39}$$

We can find the $\mathbf{w} = [u, v]^T$ that makes this true by moving to homogeneous coordinates. Each of the four transformations can be written in the form

$$\lambda \begin{bmatrix} x \\ y \\ 1 \end{bmatrix} = \begin{bmatrix} \phi_{11} & \phi_{12} & \phi_{13} \\ \phi_{21} & \phi_{22} & \phi_{23} \\ \phi_{31} & \phi_{32} & \phi_{33} \end{bmatrix} \begin{bmatrix} u \\ v \\ 1 \end{bmatrix}, \tag{15.40}$$

where the exact expressions are given by Equations 15.4, 15.10, 15.13, and 15.17.

To find the position $\mathbf{w} = [u, v]^T$, we simply premultiply by the inverse of the transformation matrix to yield

$$\lambda' \begin{bmatrix} u \\ v \\ 1 \end{bmatrix} = \begin{bmatrix} \phi_{11} & \phi_{12} & \phi_{13} \\ \phi_{21} & \phi_{22} & \phi_{23} \\ \phi_{31} & \phi_{32} & \phi_{33} \end{bmatrix}^{-1} \begin{bmatrix} x \\ y \\ 1 \end{bmatrix}, \tag{15.41}$$

and then recover u and v by converting back to Cartesian coordinates.

15.4   Three geometric problems for planes

We have introduced transformation models that mapped from 2D coordinates on the plane to 2D coordinates in the image, the most general of which was the homography. Now we relate this model back to the full pinhole camera and revisit the three geometric problems from Chapter 14 for the special case of a planar scene. We will show how to

- learn the extrinsic parameters (compute the geometric relationship between the plane and the camera),
- learn the intrinsic parameters (calibrate from a plane), and
- infer the 3D coordinates of a point in the plane relative to the camera, given its image position.

These three problems are illustrated in Figures 15.8, 15.9, and 15.11, respectively.

15.4.1 Problem 1: learning extrinsic parameters

Given I 3D points $\{\mathbf{w}_i\}_{i=1}^{I}$ *that lie on a plane* so that $w_i = 0$, their corresponding projections in the image $\{\mathbf{x}_i\}_{i=1}^{I}$ and known intrinsic matrix $\mathbf{\Lambda}$, estimate the extrinsic parameters

$$\hat{\mathbf{\Omega}}, \hat{\boldsymbol{\tau}} = \underset{\mathbf{\Omega}, \boldsymbol{\tau}}{\operatorname{argmax}} \left[\sum_{i=1}^{I} \log \left[Pr(\mathbf{x}_i | \mathbf{w}_i, \mathbf{\Lambda}, \mathbf{\Omega}, \boldsymbol{\tau}) \right] \right]$$

$$= \underset{\mathbf{\Omega}, \boldsymbol{\tau}}{\operatorname{argmax}} \left[\sum_{i=1}^{I} \log \left[\operatorname{Norm}_{\mathbf{x}_i} [\mathbf{pinhole}[\mathbf{w}_i, \mathbf{\Lambda}, \mathbf{\Omega}, \boldsymbol{\tau}], \sigma^2 \mathbf{I}] \right] \right], \tag{15.42}$$

where $\mathbf{\Omega}$ is a 3×3 rotation matrix and $\boldsymbol{\tau}$ is a 3×1 translation vector (Figure 15.8). The extrinsic parameters transform points $\mathbf{w} = [u, v, 0]$ on the plane into the coordinate system of the camera. Unfortunately, this problem (still) cannot be solved in closed form and requires nonlinear optimization. As usual, it is possible to get a good initial estimate for the parameters using a closed form algebraic solution based on homogeneous coordinates.

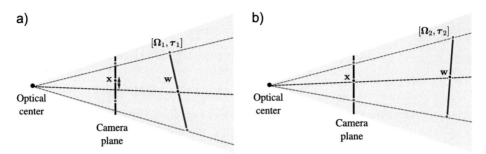

Figure 15.8 Problem 1 – Learning extrinsic parameters. Given points $\{\mathbf{w}_i\}_{i=1}^{I}$ on a plane, their positions $\{\mathbf{x}\}_{i=1}^{I}$ in the image and intrinsic parameters $\mathbf{\Lambda}$, find the rotation $\mathbf{\Omega}$ and translation $\boldsymbol{\tau}$ relating the camera and the plane. a) When the rotation and translation are wrong, the image points predicted by the model (where the rays strike the image plane) do not agree well with the observed points $\mathbf{x}$. b) When the rotation and translation are correct, they agree well and the likelihood $Pr(\mathbf{x}|\mathbf{w},\mathbf{\Lambda},\mathbf{\Omega},\boldsymbol{\tau})$ will be high.

From Equation 15.16, the relation between a homogeneous point on the plane and its projection in the image is

$$\lambda \begin{bmatrix} x \\ y \\ 1 \end{bmatrix} = \lambda' \begin{bmatrix} \phi_x & \gamma & \delta_x \\ 0 & \phi_y & \delta_y \\ 0 & 0 & D \end{bmatrix} \begin{bmatrix} \omega_{11} & \omega_{12} & \tau_x \\ \omega_{21} & \omega_{22} & \tau_y \\ \omega_{31} & \omega_{32} & \tau_z \end{bmatrix} \begin{bmatrix} u \\ v \\ 1 \end{bmatrix} = \begin{bmatrix} \phi_{11} & \phi_{12} & \phi_{13} \\ \phi_{21} & \phi_{22} & \phi_{23} \\ \phi_{31} & \phi_{32} & \phi_{33} \end{bmatrix} \begin{bmatrix} u \\ v \\ 1 \end{bmatrix}. \quad (15.43)$$

Our approach is to (i) calculate the homography $\mathbf{\Phi}$ between the points $\mathbf{w} = [u,v]^T$ on the plane and the points $\mathbf{x} = [x,y]^T$ in the image using the method of Section 15.2.4 and then (ii) decompose this homography to recover the rotation matrix $\mathbf{\Omega}$ and translation vector $\boldsymbol{\tau}$.

As a first step toward this decomposition, we eliminate the effect of the intrinsic parameters by premultiplying the estimated homography by the inverse of the intrinsic matrix $\mathbf{\Lambda}$. This gives a new homography $\mathbf{\Phi}' = \mathbf{\Lambda}^{-1}\mathbf{\Phi}$ such that

$$\begin{bmatrix} \phi'_{11} & \phi'_{12} & \phi'_{13} \\ \phi'_{21} & \phi'_{22} & \phi'_{23} \\ \phi'_{31} & \phi'_{32} & \phi'_{33} \end{bmatrix} = \lambda' \begin{bmatrix} \omega_{11} & \omega_{12} & \tau_x \\ \omega_{21} & \omega_{22} & \tau_y \\ \omega_{31} & \omega_{32} & \tau_z \end{bmatrix}. \quad (15.44)$$

To estimate the first two columns of the rotation matrix $\mathbf{\Omega}$, we compute the SVD of the first two columns of $\mathbf{\Phi}'$

$$\begin{bmatrix} \phi'_{11} & \phi'_{12} \\ \phi'_{21} & \phi'_{22} \\ \phi'_{31} & \phi'_{32} \end{bmatrix} = \mathbf{ULV}^T, \quad (15.45)$$

and then set

$$\begin{bmatrix} \omega_{11} & \omega_{12} \\ \omega_{21} & \omega_{22} \\ \omega_{31} & \omega_{32} \end{bmatrix} = \mathbf{U} \begin{bmatrix} 1 & 0 \\ 0 & 1 \\ 0 & 0 \end{bmatrix} \mathbf{V}^T. \quad (15.46)$$

These operations find the closest valid first two columns of a rotation matrix to the first two columns of $\mathbf{\Phi}'$ in a least squares sense. This approach is very closely related to the solution to the orthogonal Procrustes problem (Appendix C.7.3).

We then compute the last column $[\omega_{13}, \omega_{23}, \omega_{33}]^T$ of the rotation matrix by taking the cross product of the first two columns: this guarantees a vector that is also length one and is perpendicular to the first two columns, but the sign may still be wrong: we test the determinant of the resulting rotation matrix $\boldsymbol{\Omega}$, and if it is -1, we multiply the last column by -1.

We can now estimate the scaling factor λ' by taking the average of the scaling factors between these six elements

$$\lambda' = \frac{\sum_{m=1}^{3} \sum_{n=1}^{2} \phi'_{mn}/\omega_{mn}}{6}, \tag{15.47}$$

and this allows us to estimate the translation vector as $\boldsymbol{\tau} = [\phi'_{13}, \phi'_{23}, \phi'_{33}]^T / \lambda'$. The result of this algorithm is a very good initial estimate of the extrinsic matrix $[\boldsymbol{\Omega}, \boldsymbol{\tau}]$, which can be improved by optimizing the correct objective function (Equation 15.42).

15.4.2 Problem 2: learning intrinsic parameters

In this section, we revisit the problem of learning the intrinsic parameters of the camera (Figure 15.9). This is referred to as *camera calibration*. In Section 14.5, we developed a method based on viewing a special 3D calibration target. In practice, it is hard to manufacture a three-dimensional object with easy-to-find visual features at precisely known locations. However, it is easy to manufacture a 2D object of this kind. For example, it is possible to print out a checkerboard pattern and attach this to a flat surface (Figure 15.10). Unfortunately, a single view of a 2D calibration object is not sufficient to uniquely identify the intrinsic parameters. However, observing the same pattern from several different viewpoints does suffice.

Hence, the calibration problem can be reformulated as follows: given a planar object, with I distinct 3D points $\{\mathbf{w}_i\}_{i=1}^{I}$ on the surface and the corresponding projections in J images $\{\mathbf{x}_{ij}\}_{i=1,j=1}^{I,J}$, establish the intrinsic parameters in the form of the intrinsic

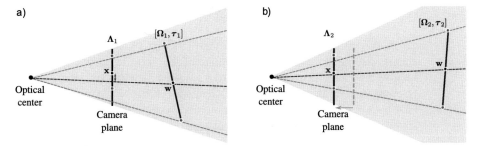

Figure 15.9 Problem 2 – Learning intrinsic parameters. Given a set of points $\{\mathbf{w}_i\}_{i=1}^{I}$ on a plane in the world (blue line) and the 2D positions $\{\mathbf{x}_i\}_{i=1}^{I}$ of these points in an image, find the intrinsic parameters $\boldsymbol{\Lambda}$. To do this, we must also simultaneously estimate the extrinsic parameters $\boldsymbol{\Omega}, \boldsymbol{\tau}$. a) When the intrinsic and extrinsic parameters are wrong, the prediction of the pinhole camera (where rays strike the image plane) deviates significantly from the known 2D points. b) When they are correct, the prediction of the model will agree with the observed image. To make the solution unique, the plane must be seen from several different angles.

Figure 15.10 Calibration from a plane. It is considerably easier to make a 2D calibration target than to machine an accurate 3D object. Consequently, calibration is usually based on viewing planes such as this checkerboard. Unfortunately, a single view of a plane is not sufficient to uniquely determine the intrinsic parameters. Therefore cameras are usually calibrated using several images of the same plane, where the plane has a different pose relative to the camera in each image.

matrix $\mathbf{\Lambda}$:

$$\hat{\mathbf{\Lambda}} = \underset{\mathbf{\Lambda}}{\operatorname{argmax}} \left[\max_{\mathbf{\Omega}_{1\ldots J}, \boldsymbol{\tau}_{1\ldots J}} \left[\sum_{i=1}^{I} \sum_{j=1}^{J} \log\left[Pr(\mathbf{x}_{ij} | \mathbf{w}_i, \mathbf{\Lambda}, \mathbf{\Omega}_j, \boldsymbol{\tau}_j) \right] \right] \right]. \tag{15.48}$$

A simple approach to this problem is to use a coordinate ascent technique in which we alternately

- Estimate the J extrinsic matrices relating the object frame of reference to the camera frame of reference in each of the J images,

$$\hat{\mathbf{\Omega}}_j, \hat{\boldsymbol{\tau}}_j = \underset{\mathbf{\Omega}_j, \boldsymbol{\tau}_j}{\operatorname{argmax}} \left[\sum_{i=1}^{I} \log\left[Pr(\mathbf{x}_{ij} | \mathbf{w}_i, \mathbf{\Lambda}, \mathbf{\Omega}_j, \boldsymbol{\tau}_j) \right] \right], \tag{15.49}$$

using the method of the previous section and then,

- Estimate the intrinsic parameters using a minor variation of the method described in Section 14.5:

$$\hat{\mathbf{\Lambda}} = \underset{\mathbf{\Lambda}}{\operatorname{argmax}} \left[\sum_{i=1}^{I} \sum_{j=1}^{J} \log\left[Pr(\mathbf{x}_{ij} | \mathbf{w}_i, \mathbf{\Lambda}, \mathbf{\Omega}_j, \boldsymbol{\tau}_j) \right] \right]. \tag{15.50}$$

As for the original calibration method (Section 14.5), a few iterations of this procedure will yield a useful initial estimate of the intrinsic parameters and these can be improved by directly optimizing the true objective function (Equation 15.48). It should be noted that this method is quite inefficient and is described for pedagogical reasons; it is easy both to understand and to implement. A modern implementation would use a more sophisticated technique to find the intrinsic parameters (see Hartley and Zisserman 2004).

15.4.3 Problem 3: inferring 3D position relative to camera

Given a calibrated camera (i.e., camera with known $\mathbf{\Lambda}$) that is known to be related to a planar scene by extrinsic parameters $\mathbf{\Omega}, \boldsymbol{\tau}$, find the 3D point $\mathbf{w}$ that is responsible for a given 2D position $\mathbf{x}$ in the image.

When the scene is planar there is normally a one-to-one relationship between points in the 3D world and points in the image. To compute the 3D point corresponding to a point $\mathbf{x}$, we initiallty infer the position $\mathbf{w} = [u, v, 0]^T$ on the plane. We exploit our knowledge of the intrinsic and extrinsic parameters to compute the homography $\mathbf{\Phi}$ mapping

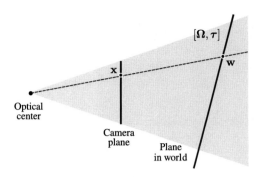

Figure 15.11 Inferring a 3D position relative to the camera. When the object is planar (blue line), there is a one-to-one mapping between points **x** in the image and points **w** on the plane. If we know the intrinsic matrix, and the rotation and translation of the plane relative to the camera, we can infer the 3D position **w** from the observed 2D image point **x**.

from points in the world to points in the image,

$$\mathbf{T} = \begin{bmatrix} \phi_{11} & \phi_{12} & \phi_{13} \\ \phi_{21} & \phi_{22} & \phi_{23} \\ \phi_{31} & \phi_{32} & \phi_{33} \end{bmatrix} = \begin{bmatrix} \phi_x & \gamma & \delta_x \\ 0 & \phi_y & \delta_y \\ 0 & 0 & D \end{bmatrix} \begin{bmatrix} \omega_{11} & \omega_{12} & \tau_x \\ \omega_{21} & \omega_{22} & \tau_y \\ \omega_{31} & \omega_{32} & \tau_z \end{bmatrix}. \tag{15.51}$$

We then infer the coordinates $\mathbf{w} = [u, v, 0]^T$ on the plane by inverting this transformation

$$\tilde{\mathbf{w}} = \mathbf{T}^{-1}\tilde{\mathbf{x}}. \tag{15.52}$$

Finally, we transfer the coordinates back to the frame of reference of the camera to give

$$\mathbf{w}' = \mathbf{\Omega}\mathbf{w} + \boldsymbol{\tau}. \tag{15.53}$$

15.5   Transformations between images

So far, we have considered transformations between a plane in the world and its image in the camera. We now consider two cameras viewing the same planar scene. The one-to-one mapping from positions on the plane to the positions in the first camera can be described by a homography. Similarly, the one-to-one mapping from positions on the plane to the positions in the second camera can be described by a second homography. It follows that there is a one-to-one mapping from the position in the first camera to the position in the second camera. This can also be described by a homography. The same logic follows for the other transformation types. Consequently, it is very common to find pairs of real-world images that are geometrically related by one of these transformations. For example, the image of the photograph in Figure 15.5a is related by a homography to that in 15.5b.

Let us denote the 3×3 matrix mapping points on the plane to points in the first image by $\mathbf{T}_1$. Similarly, we denote the 3×3 matrix mapping points on the plane to points in the second image by $\mathbf{T}_2$. To map from image 1 to image 2, we first apply the transformation from image 1 to the plane itself. By the argument of the previous section, this is $\mathbf{T}_1^{-1}$. Then we apply the transformation from the plane to image 2, which is $\mathbf{T}_2$. The mapping $\mathbf{T}_3$ from image 1 to image 2 is the concatenation of these operations and is hence $\mathbf{T}_3 = \mathbf{T}_2\mathbf{T}_1^{-1}$ (Figure 15.12).

15.5.1   Geometric properties of the homography

We've seen that transformations between planes in the world and the image plane are described by homographies, and so are transformations between multiple images of a real-world plane. There is another important family of images where the images are

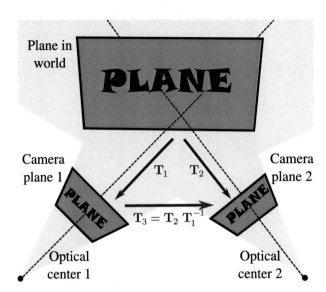

Figure 15.12 Transformations between images. Two cameras view the same planar scene. The relations between the 2D points on this plane and the two images are captured by the 3×3 transformation matrices $\mathbf{T}_1$ and $\mathbf{T}_2$, respectively. It follows that the transformation from the first image to the points on the plane is given by $\mathbf{T}^{-1}$. We can compute the transformation $\mathbf{T}_3$ from the first image to the second image by transforming from the first image to the plane and then transforming from the plane to the second image, giving the final result $\mathbf{T}_3 = \mathbf{T}_2 \mathbf{T}_1^{-1}$.

related to one another by the homography. Recall that the homography mapping point $\mathbf{x}_1$ to point $\mathbf{x}_2$ is linear in homogeneous coordinates:

$$\lambda \begin{bmatrix} x_1 \\ y_1 \\ 1 \end{bmatrix} = \begin{bmatrix} \phi_{11} & \phi_{12} & \phi_{13} \\ \phi_{21} & \phi_{22} & \phi_{23} \\ \phi_{31} & \phi_{32} & \phi_{33} \end{bmatrix} \begin{bmatrix} x_2 \\ y_2 \\ 1 \end{bmatrix}. \tag{15.54}$$

The homogeneous coordinates represent 2D points as directions or rays in a 3D space (Figure 14.11). When we apply a homography to a set of 2D points, we can think of this as applying a linear transformation (rotation, scaling, and shearing) to a bundle of rays in 3D. The positions where the transformed rays strike the plane at $w = 1$ determine the final 2D positions.

We could yield the same results by keeping the rays fixed and applying the inverse transformation to the plane so that it cuts the rays in a different way. Since any plane can be mapped to any other plane by a linear transformation, it follows that the images created by cutting a ray bundle with different planes are all related to one another by homographies (Figure 15.13). In other words, the images seen by different cameras *with the pinhole in the same place* are related by homographies. So, for example, if a camera zooms (the focal length increases), then the images before and after the zoom are related by a homography.

This relationship encompasses an important special case (Figure 15.14). If the camera rotates *but does not translate*, then the image plane still intersects the same set of rays. It follows that the projected points $\mathbf{x}_1$ before the rotation and the projected points $\mathbf{x}_2$ after the rotation are related by a homography. It can be shown that the homography

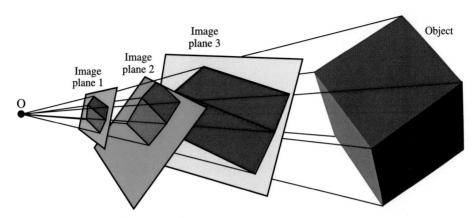

Figure 15.13 Geometric interpretation of homography. A ray bundle is formed by connecting rays from an optical center to points on a real-world object (the cube). A set of planes cut the ray bundle, forming a series of images of the cube. Each of these images is related to every other by a homography.

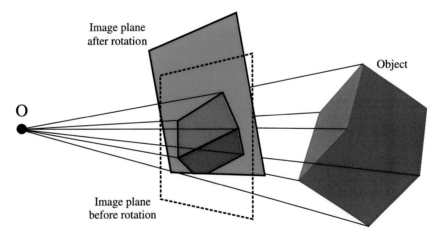

Figure 15.14 Images under pure camera rotation. When the camera rotates but does not translate, the bundle of rays remains the same, but is cut by a different plane. It follows that the two images are related by a homography.

$\boldsymbol{\Phi}$ mapping from image 1 to image 2 is given by

$$\boldsymbol{\Phi} = \boldsymbol{\Lambda}\boldsymbol{\Omega}_2\boldsymbol{\Lambda}^{-1}, \tag{15.55}$$

where $\boldsymbol{\Lambda}$ is the intrinsic matrix and $\boldsymbol{\Omega}_2$ is the rotation matrix that maps the coordinate system of the second camera to the first. This relationship is exploited when we stitch together images to form panoramas (Section 15.7.2).

In conclusion, the homography maps between

- Points on a plane in the world and their positions in an image,
- Points in two different images of the same plane, and
- Two images of a 3D object where the camera has rotated but not translated.

15.5.2 Computing transformations between images

In the previous sections we have argued that it is common for two images to be related to one another by a homography. If we denote the points in image 1 by $\mathbf{x}_i$ and their corresponding positions in image 2 as $\mathbf{y}_i$, then we could for example describe the mapping as a homography

$$Pr(\mathbf{x}_i|\mathbf{y}_i) = \text{Norm}_{\mathbf{x}_i}\left[\mathbf{hom}[\mathbf{y}_i, \mathbf{\Phi}], \sigma^2\mathbf{I}\right]. \tag{15.56}$$

This method ascribes all of the noise to the first image and it should be noted that it is not quite correct: we should really build a model that explains both sets of image data with a set of hidden variables representing the original 3D points so that the estimated point positions in each image are subject to noise. Nonetheless, the model in Equation 15.56 works well in practice. It is possible to learn the parameters using the technique of Section 15.2.

15.6   Robust learning of transformations

We have discussed transformation models that can be used either to (i) map the positions of points on a real-world plane to their projections in the image or (ii) map the positions of points in one image to their corresponding positions in another. Until now, we have assumed that we know a set of corresponding points from which to learn the parameters of the transformation model. However, establishing these correspondences automatically is a challenging task in itself.

Let us consider the case where we wish to compute a transformation between two images. A simple method to establish correspondences would be to compute interest points in each image and to characterize the region around each point using a region descriptor such as the SIFT descriptor (Section 13.3.2). We could then greedily associate points based on the similarity of the region descriptors (as in Figure 15.17c–d). Depending on the scene, this is likely to produce a set of matches that are 70–90% correct. Unfortunately the remaining erroneous correspondences (which we will call *outliers*) can severely hamper our ability to compute the transformation between the images. To cope with this problem, we need robust learning methods.

15.6.1 RANSAC

Random sample consensus or *RANSAC* is a general method for fitting models to data where the data are corrupted by outliers. These outliers violate the assumptions of the underlying probability model (usually a normal distribution) and can cause the estimated parameters to deviate significantly from their correct values.

For pedagogical reasons, we will describe RANSAC using the example of linear regression. We will subsequently return to the problem of learning parameters in transformation models. The linear regression model is

$$Pr(y|x) = \text{Norm}_y[ax + b, \sigma^2] \tag{15.57}$$

and was discussed at length in Section 8.1. Figure 15.15 shows an example of the predicted mean for y when we fit the model to data with two outliers. The fit has been unduly influenced by the outliers and no longer describes the data well.

The goal of RANSAC is to identify which points are outliers and to eliminate them from the final fit. This is a chicken and egg problem: if we had the final fit, then it would

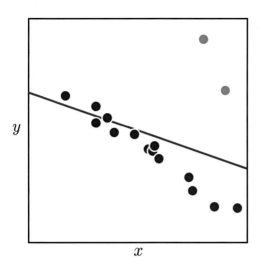

Figure 15.15 Motivation for random sample consensus (RANSAC). The majority of this data set (blue points) can be explained well by a linear regression model, but there are two outliers (green points). Unfortunately, if we fit the linear regression model to all of this data, the mean prediction (red line) is dragged toward the outliers and no longer describes the majority of the data well. The RANSAC algorithm circumvents this problem by establishing which datapoints are outliers and fitting the model to the remaining data.

be easy to identify the outliers (they are not well described by the model), and if we knew which points were outliers, it would be easy to compute the final fit.

RANSAC works by repeatedly fitting models based on random subsets of the data. The hope is that sooner or later, there will be no outliers in the chosen subset, and so we will fit a good model. To enhance the probability of this happening, RANSAC chooses subsets of the minimal size required to uniquely fit the model. For example, in the case of the line, it would choose subsets of size two.

Having chosen a minimal subset of datapoints and fitted the model, RANSAC assesses its quality. It does this by classifying points as inliers or outliers. This requires some knowledge about the expected amount of variation around the true model. For linear regression this means we need some prior knowledge of the variance parameter σ^2. If a datapoint exceeds the expected variation (perhaps two standard deviations from the mean), then it is classified as an outlier. Otherwise, it is an inlier. For each minimal subset of data, we count the number of inliers.

We repeat this procedure a number of times: on each iteration we choose a random minimal subset of points, fit a model, and count the number of datapoints that agree (the inliers). After a predetermined number of iterations, we then choose the model that had the most inliers and refit the model from these alone.

The complete RANSAC algorithm hence proceeds as follows (Figure 15.16):

1. Randomly choose a minimal subset of data.
2. Use this subset to estimate the parameters.
3. Compute the number of inliers for this model.
4. Repeat steps 1–3 a fixed number of times.
5. Reestimate model using inliers from the best fit.

If we know the degree to which our data are polluted with outliers, it is possible to estimate the number of iterations that provide any given chance of finding the correct answer.

Now let us return to the question of how to apply the model to fitting geometric 15.8 transformations. We will use the example of a homography (Equation 15.56). Here we

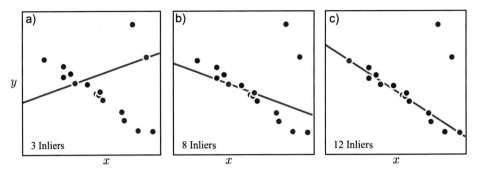

Figure 15.16 RANSAC procedure. a) We select a random minimal subset of points to fit the line (red points). We fit the line to these points and count how many of the other points agree with this solution (blue points). These are termed inliers. Here there are only three inliers. b,c) This procedure is repeated with different minimal subsets of points. After a number of iterations we choose the fit that had the most inliers. We refit the line using only the inliers from this fit.

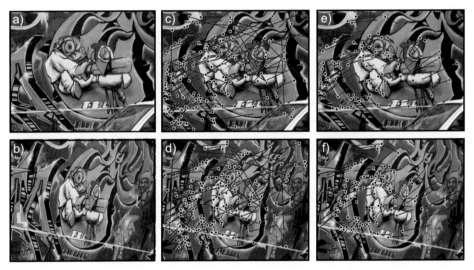

Figure 15.17 Fitting a homography with RANSAC. a,b) Original images of a textured plane. c,d) 162 strongest matches selected by greedy method. In each case the associated line travels from the interest point to the position of its match in the other image. These matches are clearly polluted by outliers. e,f) Model fitted from 102 inliers identified by applying 100 iterations of RANSAC. These matches form a coherent pattern as they are all described by a homography.

repeatedly choose subsets of hypothesized matches between the two images. The size of the subset is chosen to be four as this is the minimum number of pairs of points that are needed to uniquely identify the eight degrees of freedom of the homography.

For each subset, we count the number of inliers by evaluating Equation 15.56 and selecting those where the likelihood exceeds some predetermined value. In practice, this means measuring the distance between the points $\mathbf{x}_i$ in the first image and the mapped position $\mathbf{hom}[\mathbf{y}, \boldsymbol{\Phi}]$ of the points from the second image. After repeating this many times, we identify the trial with the most inliers (Figure 15.17) and recompute the model from these inliers alone.

Figure 15.18 Piecewise planarity. a) Although this scene is clearly not well described by a plane, it is well described by a set of planes. b) Consequently, the mapping to this second image of the same scene can be described by a set of homographies. Images from Oxford Colleges dataset.

15.6.2 Sequential RANSAC

Now let us look at a more challenging task. So far, we assumed that one set of points could be mapped to another using a single transformation model. However, many scenes containing man-made objects are piecewise planar (Figure 15.18). It follows that images of such scenes are related by piecewise homographies. In this section, we will consider methods for fitting this type of model.

The first approach is *sequential RANSAC*. The idea is simple: we fit a single homography to the scene using the RANSAC method. In principle this will correctly fit a model to one of the planes in the image and reject all the other points as outliers. We then remove the points that belong to this plane (i.e., the inliers to the final homography) and repeat the procedure on the remaining points. Ideally, each iteration will identify a new plane in the image.

Unfortunately, this method does not work well in practice (Figure 15.19) for two reasons. First, the algorithm is greedy: any matches that are erroneously incorporated into, or missed by one of the earlier models cannot be correctly assigned later. Second, the model has no notion of spatial coherence, ignoring the intuition that nearby points are more likely to belong to the same plane.

15.6.3 PEaRL

The *Propose, Expand and Re-Learn* or *PEaRL* algorithm solves both of these problems. In the "propose" stage, K hypothetical models are generated where K is usually of the order of several thousand. This can be achieved by using a RANSAC type procedure in which minimal subsets of points are chosen, a model is fitted, and the inliers are counted. This is done repeatedly until we have several thousand models $\{\mathbf{\Phi}_k\}_{k=1}^K$ that each have a reasonable degree of support.

In the "expand" stage, we model the assignment of matched pairs to the proposed models as a multilabel Markov random field. We associate a label $l_i \in [1, 2, \ldots, K]$ to each match $\{\mathbf{x}_i, \mathbf{y}_i\}$ where the value of the label determines which one of the K models is present at this point. The likelihood of each data pair $\{\mathbf{x}_i, \mathbf{y}_i\}$ under the kth model is given by

$$Pr(\mathbf{x}_i|\mathbf{y}_i, l_i = k) = \text{Norm}_{\mathbf{x}_i}\left[\mathbf{hom}[\mathbf{y}_i, \mathbf{\Phi}_k], \sigma^2\mathbf{I}\right]. \tag{15.58}$$

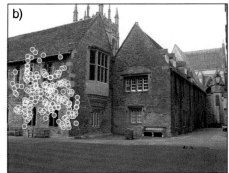
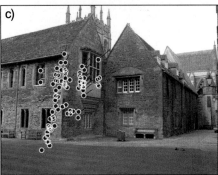

Figure 15.19 Sequential fitting of homographies mapping between images in Figure 15.18 using RANSAC. a) Running the RANSAC fitting procedure once identifies a set of points that all lie on the same plane in the image. b) Running the RANSAC procedure again on the points that were not explained by the first plane identifies a second set of points that lie on a different plane. c) Third iteration. The plane discovered does not correspond to a real plane in the scene. d) Fourth iteration. The model erroneously associates parts of the image which are quite separate. This sequential approach fails for two reasons. First, it is greedy and cannot recover from earlier errors. Second, it does not encourage spatial smoothness (nearby points should belong to the same model).

To incorporate spatial coherence, we choose a prior over the labels that encourages neighbors to take similar values. In particular, we choose an MRF with a Potts model potential

$$Pr(\mathbf{l}) = \frac{1}{Z} \exp\left[-\sum_{i,j \in \mathcal{N}_p} w_{ij} \delta[l_i - l_j] \right], \tag{15.59}$$

where Z is the constant partition function, w_{ij} is a weight associated with the pair of matches i and j, and $\delta[\bullet]$ is a function that returns 1 when the argument is zero and returns 0 otherwise. The neighborhood $\mathcal{N}_i$ of each point must be chosen in advance. One simple technique is to compute the K-nearest neighbors for each point in the first image and declare two points to be neighbors if either is in the other's set of closest neighbors. The weights w_{ij} are chosen so that points that are close in the image are more tightly coupled than points that are distant.

The goal of the "expand" stage is then to infer the labels l_i and hence the association between models and datapoints. This can be accomplished using the alpha expansion algorithm (Section 12.4.1). Finally, having associated each datapoint with

Figure 15.20 Results of the PEaRL algorithm. It formulates the problem as inference in a multi-label MRF. The MRF label associated with each matching pair denotes the index of one of a set of possible models. Inferring these labels is alternated with refining the parameters of the proposed models. The colored points denote different labels in the final solution. The algorithm has successfully identified many of the surfaces in the scene. Adapted from Isack and Boykov (2012). ©2012 Springer.

one of the models, we move to the "re-learn" stage. Here, we reestimate the parameters of each model based on the data that was associated with it. The "expand" and "re-learn" stages are iterated until no further progress is made. At the end of this process, we throw away any models that do not have sufficient support in the final solution (Figure 15.20).

15.7 Applications

In this section we present two examples of the techniques in this chapter. First, we discuss augmented reality in which we attempt to render an object onto a plane in the scene. This application exploits the fact that there is a homography between the image of the plane and the original object surface and uses the method of Section 15.4.1 to decompose this homography to find the relative position of the camera and the plane. Second, we discuss creating visual panoramas. The method exploits the fact that multiple images taken from a camera that has rotated but not translated are all related by homographies.

15.7.1 Augmented reality tracking

Figure 15.1 shows an example of augmented reality tracking. To accomplish this, the following steps were taken. First, the four corners of the marker are found as in Figure 15.1c; the marker was designed so that the corners can be easily identified using a set of image-processing operations. In brief, the image is thresholded, and then connected dark regions are found. The pixels around the edge of each region are identified. Then four 2D lines are fit to the edge pixels using sequential RANSAC. Regions that are not well explained by four lines are discarded. The only remaining region in this case is the square marker.

The positions where the fitted lines intersect provides four points $\{\mathbf{x}_i\}_{i=1}^4$ in the image, and we know the corresponding positions $\{\mathbf{w}_i\}_{i=1}^4$ in cm that occur on the surface of the planar marker. It is assumed that the camera is calibrated, and so we know the intrinsic matrix Λ. We can now compute the extrinsic parameters Ω, τ using the algorithm from Section 15.4.1.

To render the graphical object, we first set up a viewing frustum (the graphics equivalent of the "camera") so that it has the same field of view as specified by the intrinsic parameters. Then we render the model from the appropriate perspective using the extrinsic parameters as the *modelview matrix*. The result is that the object appears to be attached rigidly to the scene.

In this system, the points on the marker were found using a sequence of image-processing operations. However, this method is rather outdated. It is now possible to reliably identify natural features on an object so there is no need to use a marker with any special characteristics. One way to do this is to match SIFT features between a reference image of the object and the current scene. These interest point descriptors are invariant to image scaling and rotation, and for textured objects it is usually possible to generate a high percentage of correct matches. RANSAC is used to eliminate any mismatched pairs.

However, SIFT features are themselves relatively slow to compute. Lepetit et al. (2005) described a system that applies machine learning techniques to identify objects at interactive speeds (Figure 15.21). They first identify K stable keypoints (e.g., Harris corners) on the object to be tracked. They then create a training set for each keypoint by subjecting the region around it to a large number of random affine transformations. Finally, they train a multiclass classification tree that takes a new keypoint and assigns it to match one of the K original points. At each branch of the tree, the decision is made by

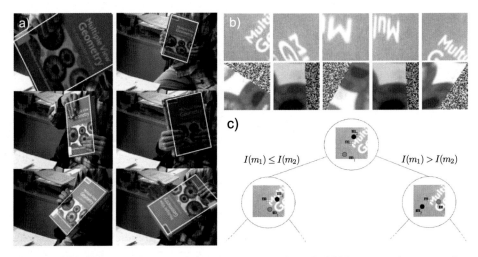

Figure 15.21 Robust tracking using keypoints. a) Lepetit et al. (2005) presented a system that automatically tracked objects such as this book. b) In the learning stage, the regions around the keypoints were subjected to a number of random affine transformations. c) Keypoints in the image were classified as belonging to a known keypoint on the object, using a tree-based classifier that compared the intensity at nearby points. Adapted from Lepetit et al. (2005). ©2005 IEEE.

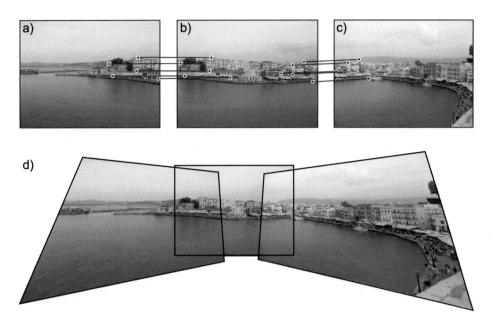

Figure 15.22 Computing visual panoramas. a–c) Three images of the same scene where the camera has rotated but not translated. Five matching points have been identified by hand between each pair. d) A panorama can be created by mapping the first and third images into the frame of reference of the second image.

a pairwise intensity comparison. This system works very quickly and reliably matches most of the feature points. Once more, RANSAC can be used to eliminate any erroneous matches.

15.7.2 Visual panoramas

A second application of the ideas of this chapter is the computation of visual panoramas. Recall that a set of pictures that are taken by rotating a camera about the optical center are all related by homographies. Hence, if we take pictures of this kind that are partially overlapping, it is possible to map them all into one large image. This process is known as *image mosaicing*.

An example is shown in Figure 15.22. This was constructed by placing the second (middle) photo into the center of a much larger empty image. Then 5 matches were identified by hand between this expanded second image and the first image and the homography from the expanded second image to the first image was computed. For each empty pixel in the expanded second image we compute the position in the first image using this homography. If this falls within the image boundaries, we copy the pixel value.

This process can be completely automated by finding features and fitting a homography to each pair of images using a robust technique such as RANSAC. In a real system, the final result is typically projected onto a cylinder and unrolled to give a more visually pleasing result.

Discussion

This chapter has presented a number of important ideas. First, we discussed a family of transformations and how each can be related to a camera viewing the scene under special conditions. These transformations are used widely within machine vision and we will see them exploited in Chapters 17–19. Second, we discussed a more practical method for camera calibration based on viewing a plane at a number of different orientations. Finally, we have also presented RANSAC, which is a robust method to fit models, even in the presence of noisy observations.

Notes

Transformations: For more information concerning the hierarchy of 2D transformations, consult Hartley and Zisserman (2004). The closed form solutions for the rotation and similarity transformations are special cases of *Procrustes problems*. Many more details about this type of problem can be found in Gower and Dijksterhuis (2004). The direct linear transformation algorithm for estimating the homography dates back to at least Sutherland (1963). Hartley and Zisserman (2004) present a detailed discussion of different objective functions for estimating homographies. In this chapter, we have discussed the estimation of transformations from point matches. However, it is also possible to compute transformations from other geometric primitives. For example, methods exist to compute the homography from matched lines (see Problem 15.3), a combination of points and lines (Murino et al. 2002), or conics (Sugimoto 2000).

Robust estimation: The RANSAC algorithm is due to Fischler and Bolles (1981). It has spawned many variants, the most notable of which is MLESAC (Torr and Zisserman 2000) which puts this fitting method on a sound probabilistic footing (see Problem 15.13 for a related model). Chum et al. (2005) and Frahm and Pollefeys (2006) present variants of RANSAC that can cope with degenerate data (where the model is nonunique). Torr (1998) and Vincent and Laganiere (2001) used RANSAC to estimate multiple geometric entities sequentially. Both Raguram et al. (2008) and Choi et al. (2009) present recent quantitative comparisons of variations of the RANSAC algorithm. The PEaRL algorithm is due to Isack and Boykov (2012). In the original paper, they also include an extra cost, which encourages parsimony (to describe the data with as few models as possible). Other approaches to robust estimation include (i) the use of long-tailed distributions such as the t-distribution (Section 7.5), (ii) M-estimators (Huber 2009), which replace the least-squares criterion with another function that penalizes large deviations less stringently, and (iii) the self-explanatory least median of squares regression (Rousseeuw 1984).

Augmented reality: Pose estimation methods for augmented reality initially relied on detecting special patterns in the scene known as fiducial markers. Early examples used circular patterns (e.g. Cho et al. 1998; State et al. 1996), but these were largely supplanted by square markers (e.g., Rekimoto 1998; Kato et al. 2000; Kato and Billinghurst 1999; Koller et al. 1997). The system described in the text is ARToolkit (Kato and Billinghurst 1999; Kato et al. 2000) and can be downloaded from *http://www.hitl.washington.edu/artoolkit/*.

Other systems have used "natural image features." For example, Harris (1992) estimated the pose of an object using line segments. Simon et al. (2000) and Simon and Berger (2002) estimated the pose of planes in the image using the results of a corner detector. More information about computing the pose of a plane can be found in Sturm (2000).

More recent systems have used interest point detectors such as SIFT features, which are robust to changes in illumination and pose (e.g. Skrypnyk and Lowe 2004). To increase the speed of systems, features are matched using machine learning techniques (Lepetit and Fua 2006; Özuysal et al. 2010), and current systems can now operate at interactive speeds on mobile hardware (Wagner et al. 2008). A review of methods to estimate and track the pose of rigid objects can be found in Lepetit and Fua (2005).

Calibration from a plane: Algorithms for calibration from several views of a plane can be found in Sturm and Maybank (1999) and Zhang (2000). They are now used much more frequently than calibration based on 3D objects, for the simple reason that accurate 3D objects are harder to manufacture.

Image mosaics: The presented method for computing a panorama by creating a mosaic of images is naïve in a number of ways. First, it is more sensible to explicitly estimate the rotation matrix and calibration parameters rather than the homography (Szeliski and Shum 1997; Shum and Szeliski 2000; Brown and Lowe 2007). Second, the method that we describe projects all of the images onto a single plane, but this does not work well when the panorama is too wide as the images become increasingly distorted. A more sensible approach is to project images onto a cylinder (Szeliski 1996; Chen 1995) which is then unrolled and displayed as an image. Third, the method to blend together images is not discussed. This is particularly important if there are moving objects in the image. A good review of these and other issues can be found in Szeliski (2006) and chapter 9 of Szeliski (2010).

Problems

15.1 The 2D point $\mathbf{x}_2$ is created by a rotating point $\mathbf{x}_1$ using the rotation matrix $\mathbf{\Omega}_1$ and then translating it by the translation vector $\boldsymbol{\tau}_1$ so that

$$\mathbf{x}_2 = \mathbf{\Omega}_1\mathbf{x}_1 + \boldsymbol{\tau}_1.$$

Find the parameters $\mathbf{\Omega}_2$ and $\boldsymbol{\tau}_2$ of the inverse transformation

$$\mathbf{x}_1 = \mathbf{\Omega}_2\mathbf{x}_2 + \boldsymbol{\tau}_2$$

in terms of the original parameters $\mathbf{\Omega}_1$ and $\boldsymbol{\tau}_1$.

15.2 A 2D line can be as expressed as $ax + by + c = 0$ or in homogeneous terms

$$\mathbf{l}\tilde{\mathbf{x}} = 0,$$

where $\mathbf{l} = [a, b, c]$. If points are transformed so that

$$\tilde{\mathbf{x}}' = \mathbf{T}\tilde{\mathbf{x}},$$

what is the equation of the transformed line?

15.3 Using your solution from Problem 15.2, develop a linear algorithm for estimating a homography based on a number of matched lines between the two images (i.e., the analogue of the DLT algorithm for matched lines).

15.4 A conic (see Problem 14.6) is defined by

$$\tilde{\mathbf{x}}^T\mathbf{C}\tilde{\mathbf{x}} = 0,$$

where $\mathbf{C}$ is a 3×3 matrix. If the points in the image undergo the transformation

$$\tilde{\mathbf{x}}' = \mathbf{T}\tilde{\mathbf{x}},$$

then what is the equation of the transformed conic?

15.5 All of the 2D transformations in this chapter (Euclidean, similarity, affine, projective) have 3D equivalents. For each class write out the 4×4 matrix that describes the 3D transformation in homogeneous coordinates. How many independent parameters does each model have?

15.6 Devise an algorithm to estimate a 3D affine transformation based on two sets of matching 3D points. What is the minimum number of points required to get a unique estimate of the parameters of this model?

15.7 A 1D affine transformation acts on 1D points x as $x' = ax + b$. Show that the ratio of two distances is *invariant* to a 1D affine transformation so that

$$I = \frac{x_1 - x_2}{x_2 - x_3} = \frac{x'_1 - x'_2}{x'_2 - x'_3}.$$

15.8 A 1D projective transformation acts on 1D points x as $x' = (ax + b)/(cx + d)$. Show that the *cross-ratio* of distances is *invariant* to a 1D projective transformation so that

$$I = \frac{(x_3 - x_1)(x_4 - x_2)}{(x_3 - x_2)(x_4 - x_1)} = \frac{(x'_3 - x'_1)(x'_4 - x'_2)}{(x'_3 - x'_2)(x'_4 - x'_1)}.$$

It was proposed at one point to exploit this type of invariance to recognize planar objects under different transformations (Rothwell et al. 1995). However, this is rather impractical as it assumes that we can identify a number of the points on the object in a first place.

15.9 Show that Equation 15.36 follows from Equation 15.35.

15.10 A camera with intrinsic matrix λ and extrinsic parameters $\mathbf{\Omega} = \mathbf{I}, \boldsymbol{\tau} = \mathbf{0}$ takes an image and then rotates to a new position $\mathbf{\Omega} = \mathbf{\Omega}_1, \boldsymbol{\tau} = \mathbf{0}$ and takes a second image. Show that the homography relating these two images is given by

$$\mathbf{\Phi} = \mathbf{\Lambda}\mathbf{\Omega}_1\mathbf{\Lambda}^{-1}.$$

15.11 Consider two images of the same scene taken from a camera that rotates, but does not translate between taking the images. What is the minimum number of point matches required to recover a 3D rotation between two images taken using a camera where the intrinsic matrix is known?

15.12 Consider the problem of computing a homography from point matches that include outliers. If 50 percent of the initial matches are correct, how many iterations of the RANSAC algorithm would we expect to have to run in order to have a 95 percent chance of computing the correct homography?

15.13 A different approach to fitting transformations in the presence of outliers is to model the uncertainty as a mixture of two Gaussians. The first Gaussian models the image noise, and the second Gaussian, which has a very large variance, accounts for the outliers. For example, for the affine transformation we would have

$$Pr(\mathbf{x}|\mathbf{w}) = \lambda\text{Norm}_\mathbf{x}\left[\mathbf{aff}[\mathbf{w}, \mathbf{\Phi}, \boldsymbol{\tau}], \sigma^2\mathbf{I}\right] + (1 - \lambda)\text{Norm}_\mathbf{x}\left[\mathbf{aff}[\mathbf{w}, \mathbf{\Phi}, \boldsymbol{\tau}], \sigma_0^2\mathbf{I}\right] +$$

where λ is the probability of being an inlier, σ^2 is the image noise, and σ_0^2 is the large variance that accounts for the outliers. Sketch an approach to learning the parameters $\sigma^2, \boldsymbol{\Phi}, \boldsymbol{\tau}$, and λ of this model. You may assume that σ_0^2 is fixed. Identify a possible weakness of this model.

15.14 In the description of how to compute the panorama (Section 15.7.2), it is suggested that we take each pixel in the central image and transform it into the other images and then copy the color. What is wrong with the alternate strategy of taking each pixel from the other images and transforming them into the central image?

Chapter 16

Multiple cameras

This chapter extends the discussion of the pinhole camera model. In Chapter 14 we showed how to find the 3D position of a point based on its projections into multiple cameras. However, this approach was contingent on knowing the intrinsic and extrinsic parameters of these cameras, and this information is often unknown. In this chapter we discuss methods for reconstruction in the absence of such information. Before reading this chapter, readers should ensure that they are familiar with the mathematical formulation of the pinhole camera (Section 14.1).

To motivate these methods, consider a single camera moving around a static object. The goal is to build a 3D model from the images taken by the camera. To do this, we will also need to simultaneously establish the properties of the camera and its position in each frame. This problem is widely known as *structure from motion*, although this is something of a misnomer as both "structure" and "motion" are recovered simultaneously.

The structure from motion problem can be stated formally as follows. We are given J images of a rigid object that is characterized by I distinct 3D points $\{\mathbf{w}_i\}_{i=1}^{I}$. The images are taken with the same camera at a series of unknown positions. Given the projections $\{\mathbf{x}_{ij}\}_{i=1,j=1}^{I,J}$ of the I points in the J images, establish the 3D positions $\{\mathbf{w}_i\}_{i=1}^{I}$ of the points in the world, the fixed intrinsic parameters $\mathbf{\Lambda}$, and the extrinsic parameters $\{\mathbf{\Omega}_j, \boldsymbol{\tau}_j\}_{j=1}^{J}$ for each image:

$$\{\hat{\mathbf{w}}_i\}_{i=1}^{I}, \{\hat{\mathbf{\Omega}}_j, \hat{\boldsymbol{\tau}}_j\}_{j=1}^{J}, \hat{\mathbf{\Lambda}} \qquad (16.1)$$

$$= \underset{\mathbf{w},\mathbf{\Omega},\boldsymbol{\tau},\mathbf{\Lambda}}{\operatorname{argmax}} \left[\sum_{i=1}^{I} \sum_{j=1}^{J} \log[Pr(\mathbf{x}_{ij}|\mathbf{w}_i, \mathbf{\Lambda}, \mathbf{\Omega}_j, \boldsymbol{\tau}_j)] \right]$$

$$= \underset{\mathbf{w},\mathbf{\Omega},\boldsymbol{\tau},\mathbf{\Lambda}}{\operatorname{argmax}} \left[\sum_{i=1}^{I} \sum_{j=1}^{J} \log \left[\text{Norm}_{\mathbf{x}_{ij}} \left[\mathbf{pinhole}[\mathbf{w}_i, \mathbf{\Lambda}, \mathbf{\Omega}_j, \boldsymbol{\tau}_j], \sigma^2 \mathbf{I}] \right] \right].$$

Since this objective function is a based on the normal distribution we can reformulate it as a least squares problem of the form

$$\{\hat{\mathbf{w}}_i\}_{i=1}^{I}, \{\hat{\mathbf{\Omega}}_j, \hat{\boldsymbol{\tau}}_j\}_{j=1}^{J}, \hat{\mathbf{\Lambda}} = \qquad (16.2)$$

$$\underset{\mathbf{w},\mathbf{\Omega},\boldsymbol{\tau},\mathbf{\Lambda}}{\operatorname{argmin}} \left[\sum_{i=1}^{I} \sum_{j=1}^{J} (\mathbf{x}_{ij} - \mathbf{pinhole}[\mathbf{w}_i, \mathbf{\Lambda}, \mathbf{\Omega}_j, \boldsymbol{\tau}_j])^T (\mathbf{x}_{ij} - \mathbf{pinhole}[\mathbf{w}_i, \mathbf{\Lambda}, \mathbf{\Omega}_j, \boldsymbol{\tau}_j]) \right],$$

in which the goal is to minimize the total squared distance between the observed image points and those predicted by the model. This is known as the *squared reprojection error*. Unfortunately, there is no simple closed form solution for this problem, and we must ultimately rely on nonlinear optimization. However, to ensure that the optimization converges, we need good initial estimates of the unknown parameters.

To simplify our discussion, we will concentrate first on the case where we have $J = 2$ views, and the intrinsic matrix Λ is known. We already saw how to estimate 3D points given known camera positions in Section 14.6, so the unresolved problem is to get good initial estimates of the extrinsic parameters. Surprisingly, it is possible to do this based on just examining the positions of corresponding points without having to reconstruct their 3D world positions. To understand why, we must first learn more about the geometry of two views.

16.1 Two-view geometry

In this section, we show that there is a geometric relationship between corresponding points in two images of the same scene. This relationship depends only on the intrinsic parameters of the two cameras and their relative translation and rotation.

16.1.1 The epipolar constraint

Consider a single camera viewing a 3D point $\mathbf{w}$ in the world. We know that $\mathbf{w}$ must lie somewhere on the ray that passes through the optical center and position $\mathbf{x}_1$ on the image plane (Figure 16.1). However, from one camera alone, we cannot know how far along this ray the point is.

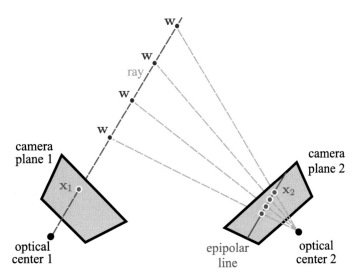

Figure 16.1 Epipolar line. Consider point $\mathbf{x}_1$ in the first image. The 3D point $\mathbf{w}$ that projected to $\mathbf{x}_1$ must lie somewhere along the ray that passes from the optical center of camera 1 through the position $\mathbf{x}_1$ in the image plane (dashed green line). However, we don't know where along that ray it lies (4 possibilities shown). It follows that $\mathbf{x}_2$, the projected position in camera 2, must lie somewhere on the projection of this ray. The projection of this ray is a line in image 2 and is referred to as an epipolar line.

Now consider a second camera viewing the same 3D world point. We know from the first camera that this point must lie along a particular ray in 3D space. It follows that the projected position x_2 of this point in the second image must lie somewhere along the projection of this ray in the second image. The ray in 3D projects to a 2D line which is known as an *epipolar line*.

This geometric relationship tells us something important: for any point in the first image, the corresponding point in the second image is constrained to lie on a line. This is known as the *epipolar constraint*. The particular line that it is constrained to lie on depends on the intrinsic parameters of the cameras and the extrinsic parameters (i.e., the relative translation and rotation of the two cameras).

The epipolar constraint has two important practical implications.

1. Given the intrinsic and extrinsic parameters, we can find point correspondences relatively easily: for a given point in the first image, we only need to perform a 1D search along the epipolar line in the second image for the corresponding position.
2. The constraint on corresponding points is a function of the intrinsic and extrinsic parameters; given the intrinsic parameters, we can use the observed pattern of point correspondences to determine the extrinsic parameters and hence establish the geometric relationship between the two cameras.

16.1.2 Epipoles

Now consider a number of points in the first image. Each is associated with a ray in 3D space. Each ray projects to form an epipolar line in the second image. Since all the rays converge at the optical center of the first camera, the epipolar lines must converge at a single point in the second image plane; this is the image in the second camera of the optical center of the first camera and is known as the *epipole* (Figure 16.2).

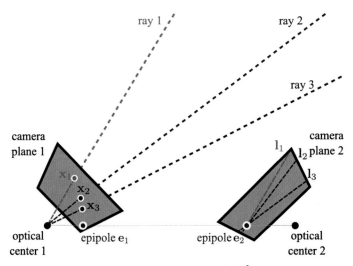

Figure 16.2 Epipoles. Consider several observed points $\{x_i\}_{i=1}^I$ in image 1. For each point, the corresponding 3D world position w_i lies on a different ray. Each ray projects to an epipolar line l_i in image 2. Since the rays converge in 3D space at the optical center of camera 1, the epipolar lines must also converge. The point where they converge is known as the epipole e_2. It is the projection of the optical center of camera 1 into camera 2. Similarly, the epipole e_1 is the projection of the optical center of camera 2 into camera 1.

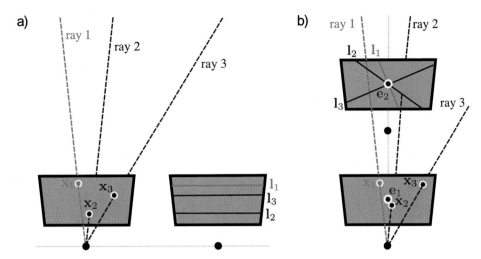

Figure 16.3 Epipolar lines and epipoles. a) When the camera movement is a pure translation perpendicular to the optical axis (parallel to the image plane), the epipolar lines are parallel and the epipole is at infinity. b) When the camera movement is a pure translation along the optical axis, the epipoles are in the center of the image and the epipolar lines form a radial pattern.

Similarly, points in image 2 induce epipolar lines in image 1, and these epipolar lines converge at the epipole in image 1. This is the image in camera 1 of the optical center of camera 2.

The epipoles are not necessarily within the observed images: the epipolar lines may converge to a point outside the visible area. Two common cases are illustrated in Figure 16.3. When the cameras are oriented in the same direction (i.e., no relative rotation) and the displacement is perpendicular to their optical axes (Figure 16.3a), then the epipolar lines are parallel and the epipoles (where they converge) are hence at infinity. When the cameras are oriented in the same direction and the displacement is parallel to their optical axes (Figure 16.3b), then the epipoles are in the middle of the images, and the epipolar lines form a radial pattern. These examples illustrate that the pattern of epipolar lines provides information about the relative position and orientation of the cameras.

16.2   The essential matrix

Now we will capture these geometric intuitions in the form of a mathematical model. For simplicity, we will assume that the world coordinate system is centered on the first camera so that the extrinsic parameters (rotation and translation) of the first camera are $\{\mathbf{I}, \mathbf{0}\}$. The second camera may be in any general position $\{\mathbf{\Omega}, \boldsymbol{\tau}\}$. We will further assume that the cameras are normalized so that $\mathbf{\Lambda}_1 = \mathbf{\Lambda}_2 = \mathbf{I}$. In homogeneous coordinates, a 3D point $\mathbf{w}$ is projected into the two cameras as

$$\lambda_1 \tilde{\mathbf{x}}_1 = [\mathbf{I}, \mathbf{0}]\tilde{\mathbf{w}} \qquad (16.3)$$
$$\lambda_2 \tilde{\mathbf{x}}_2 = [\mathbf{\Omega}, \boldsymbol{\tau}]\tilde{\mathbf{w}}.$$

where $\tilde{\mathbf{x}}_1$ is the observed position in the first camera, $\tilde{\mathbf{x}}_2$ is the observed position in the second camera, and both are expressed in homogeneous coordinates.

Expanding the first of these relations, we get

$$\lambda_1 \begin{bmatrix} x_1 \\ y_1 \\ 1 \end{bmatrix} = \begin{bmatrix} 1 & 0 & 0 & 0 \\ 0 & 1 & 0 & 0 \\ 0 & 0 & 1 & 0 \end{bmatrix} \begin{bmatrix} u \\ v \\ w \\ 1 \end{bmatrix} = \begin{bmatrix} u \\ v \\ w \end{bmatrix}. \tag{16.4}$$

This simplifies to

$$\lambda_1 \tilde{\mathbf{x}}_1 = \mathbf{w}. \tag{16.5}$$

By a similar process, the projection in the second camera can be written as

$$\lambda_2 \tilde{\mathbf{x}}_2 = \boldsymbol{\Omega}\mathbf{w} + \boldsymbol{\tau}. \tag{16.6}$$

Finally, substituting Equation 16.5 into Equation 16.6 yields

$$\lambda_2 \tilde{\mathbf{x}}_2 = \lambda_1 \boldsymbol{\Omega} \tilde{\mathbf{x}}_1 + \boldsymbol{\tau}. \tag{16.7}$$

This relationship represents a constraint between the possible positions of corresponding points $\mathbf{x}_1$ and $\mathbf{x}_2$ in the two images. The constraint is parameterized by the rotation and translation $\{\boldsymbol{\Omega}, \boldsymbol{\tau}\}$ of the second camera relative to the first.

We will now manipulate the relationship in Equation 16.7 into a form that can be more easily related to the epipolar lines and the epipoles. We first take the cross product of both sides with the translation vector $\boldsymbol{\tau}$. This removes the last term as the cross product of any vector with itself is zero. Now we have

$$\lambda_2 \boldsymbol{\tau} \times \tilde{\mathbf{x}}_2 = \lambda_1 \boldsymbol{\tau} \times \boldsymbol{\Omega} \tilde{\mathbf{x}}_1. \tag{16.8}$$

Then we take the inner product of both sides with $\tilde{\mathbf{x}}_2$. The left-hand side disappears since $\boldsymbol{\tau} \times \tilde{\mathbf{x}}_2$ must be perpendicular to $\tilde{\mathbf{x}}_2$, and so we have

$$\tilde{\mathbf{x}}_2^T \boldsymbol{\tau} \times \boldsymbol{\Omega} \tilde{\mathbf{x}}_1 = 0, \tag{16.9}$$

where we have also divided by the scaling factors λ_1 and λ_2. Finally, we note that the cross product operation $\boldsymbol{\tau} \times$ can be expressed as multiplication by the rank 2 skew-symmetric 3×3 matrix $\boldsymbol{\tau}_\times$:

$$\boldsymbol{\tau}_\times = \begin{bmatrix} 0 & -\tau_z & \tau_y \\ \tau_z & 0 & -\tau_x \\ -\tau_y & \tau_x & 0 \end{bmatrix}. \tag{16.10}$$

Hence Equation 16.9 has the form

$$\tilde{\mathbf{x}}_2^T \mathbf{E} \tilde{\mathbf{x}}_1 = 0, \tag{16.11}$$

where $\mathbf{E} = \boldsymbol{\tau}_\times \boldsymbol{\Omega}$ is known as the *essential matrix*. Equation 16.11 is an elegant formulation of the mathematical constraint between the positions of corresponding points $\mathbf{x}_1$ and $\mathbf{x}_2$ in two normalized cameras.

16.2.1   Properties of the essential matrix

The 3×3 essential matrix captures the geometric relationship between the two cameras and has rank 2 so that $\det[\mathbf{E}] = 0$. The first two singular values of the essential matrix are always identical, and the third is zero. It depends only on the rotation and translation between the cameras, each of which has three parameters, and so one might think it would have 6 degrees of freedom. However, it operates on homogeneous variables $\tilde{\mathbf{x}}_1$ and $\tilde{\mathbf{x}}_2$ and is hence ambiguous up to scale: multiplying all of the entries of the essential matrix by any constant does not change its properties. For this reason, it is usually considered as having 5 degrees of freedom.

Since there are fewer degrees of freedom than there are unknowns, the nine entries of the matrix must obey a set of algebraic constraints. These can be expressed compactly as

$$2\mathbf{E}\mathbf{E}^T\mathbf{E} - \text{trace}[\mathbf{E}\mathbf{E}^T]\mathbf{E} = \mathbf{0}. \tag{16.12}$$

These constraints are sometimes exploited in the computation of the essential matrix, although in this volume we use a simpler method (Section 16.4).

The epipolar lines are easily retrieved from the essential matrix. The condition for a point being on a line is $ax + by + c = 0$ or

$$\begin{bmatrix} a & b & c \end{bmatrix} \begin{bmatrix} x \\ y \\ 1 \end{bmatrix} = 0. \tag{16.13}$$

In homogeneous co-ordinates, this can be written as $\mathbf{l}\tilde{\mathbf{x}} = 0$ where $\mathbf{l} = [a, b, c]$ is a 1×3 vector representing the line.

Now consider the essential matrix relation

$$\tilde{\mathbf{x}}_2^T \mathbf{E} \tilde{\mathbf{x}}_1 = 0. \tag{16.14}$$

Since $\tilde{\mathbf{x}}_2^T \mathbf{E}$ is a 1×3 vector, this relationship has the form $\mathbf{l}_1 \tilde{\mathbf{x}}_1 = 0$. The line $\mathbf{l}_1 = \tilde{\mathbf{x}}_2^T \mathbf{E}$ is the epipolar line in image 1 due to the point $\mathbf{x}_2$ in image 2. By a similar argument, we can find the epipolar line $\mathbf{l}_2$ in the second camera due to the point $\mathbf{x}_1$ in the first camera. The final relations are

$$\begin{aligned} \mathbf{l}_1 &= \tilde{\mathbf{x}}_2^T \mathbf{E} \\ \mathbf{l}_2 &= \tilde{\mathbf{x}}_1^T \mathbf{E}^T. \end{aligned} \tag{16.15}$$

The epipoles can also be extracted from the essential matrix. Every epipolar line in image 1 passes through the epipole $\tilde{\mathbf{e}}_1$, so at the epipole $\tilde{\mathbf{e}}_1$ we have $\tilde{\mathbf{x}}_2^T \mathbf{E} \tilde{\mathbf{e}}_1 = 0$ for all $\tilde{\mathbf{x}}_2$. This implies that $\tilde{\mathbf{e}}_1$ must lie in the right null-space of $\mathbf{E}$ (see Appendix C.2.7). By a similar argument, the epipole $\tilde{\mathbf{e}}_2$ in the second image must lie in the left null space of $\mathbf{E}$. Hence, we have the relations

$$\begin{aligned} \tilde{\mathbf{e}}_1 &= \mathbf{null}[\mathbf{E}] \\ \tilde{\mathbf{e}}_2 &= \mathbf{null}[\mathbf{E}^T]. \end{aligned} \tag{16.16}$$

In practice, the epipoles can be retrieved by computing the singular value decomposition $\mathbf{E} = \mathbf{U}\mathbf{L}\mathbf{V}^T$ of the essential matrix and setting $\tilde{\mathbf{e}}_1$ to the last column of $\mathbf{V}$ and $\tilde{\mathbf{e}}_2$ to the last row of $\mathbf{U}$.

16.2.2 Decomposition of essential matrix

We saw previously that the essential matrix is defined as

⊙ 16.1

$$\mathbf{E} = \boldsymbol{\tau}_\times \boldsymbol{\Omega}, \tag{16.17}$$

where $\boldsymbol{\Omega}$ and $\boldsymbol{\tau}$ are the rotation matrix and translation vector that map points in the coordinate system of camera 2 to the coordinate system of camera 1, and $\boldsymbol{\tau}_\times$ is a 3×3 matrix derived from the translation vector.

We will defer the question of how to compute the essential matrix from a set of corresponding points until Section 16.3. For now, we will concentrate on how to decompose a given essential matrix $\mathbf{E}$ to recover this rotation $\boldsymbol{\Omega}$ and translation $\boldsymbol{\tau}$. This is known as the *relative orientation* problem.

In due course, we shall see that whereas we can compute the rotation exactly, it is only possible to compute the translation up to an unknown scaling factor. This remaining uncertainty reflects the geometric ambiguity of the system; from the images alone, we cannot tell if these cameras are far apart and looking at a large distant object or close together and looking at a small nearby object.

To decompose $\mathbf{E}$, we define the matrix

$$\mathbf{W} = \begin{bmatrix} 0 & -1 & 0 \\ 1 & 0 & 0 \\ 0 & 0 & 1 \end{bmatrix} \tag{16.18}$$

and then take the singular value decomposition $\mathbf{E} = \mathbf{ULV}^T$. We now choose

$$\boldsymbol{\tau}_\times = \mathbf{ULWU}^T$$
$$\boldsymbol{\Omega} = \mathbf{UW}^{-1}\mathbf{V}^T. \tag{16.19}$$

It is convention to set the magnitude of the translation vector $\boldsymbol{\tau}$ that is recovered from the matrix $\boldsymbol{\tau}_\times$ to unity.

The preceding decomposition is not obvious, but it is easily checked that multplying the derived expressions for $\boldsymbol{\tau}_\times$ and $\boldsymbol{\Omega}$ yields $\mathbf{E} = \mathbf{ULV}^T$. This method assumes that we started with a valid essential matrix where the first two singular values are identical and the third is zero. If this is not the case (due to noise), then we can substitute $\mathbf{L}' = \mathbf{diag}[1,1,0]$ for $\mathbf{L}$ in the solution for $\boldsymbol{\tau}_\times$. For a detailed proof of this decomposition, consult Hartley and Zisserman (2004).

This solution is only one of four possible combinations of $\boldsymbol{\Omega}$ and $\boldsymbol{\tau}$ that are compatible with $\mathbf{E}$ (Figure 16.4). This fourfold ambiguity is due to the fact that the pinhole model cannot distinguish between objects that are behind the camera (and are not imaged in real cameras) and those that are in front of the camera.

Part of the uncertainty is captured mathematically by our lack of knowledge of the sign of the essential matrix (recall it is ambiguous up to scale) and hence the sign of the recovered translation. Hence, we can generate a second solution by multiplying the translation vector by -1. The other component of the uncertainty results from an ambiguity in the decomposition of the essential matrix; we can equivalently replace $\mathbf{W}$ for $\mathbf{W}^{-1}$ in the decomposition procedure, and this leads to two more solutions.

Fortunately, we can resolve this ambiguity using a corresponding pair of points from the two images. For each putative solution, we reconstruct the 3D position associated with this pair (Section 14.6). For one of the four possible combinations of $\boldsymbol{\Omega}, \boldsymbol{\tau}$, the point

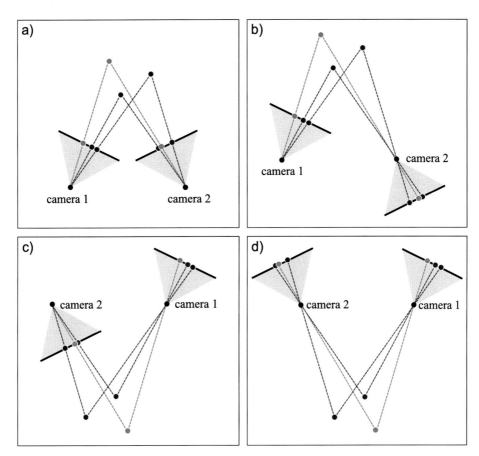

Figure 16.4 Fourfold ambiguity of reconstruction from two pinhole cameras. The mathematical model for the pinhole camera does not distinguish between points that are in front of and points that are behind the camera. This leads to a fourfold ambiguity when we extract the rotation Ω and translation τ relating the cameras from the essential matrix. a) Correct solution. Points are in front of both cameras. b) Incorrect solution. The images are identical, but with this interpretation the points are behind camera 2. c) Incorrect solution with points behind camera 1. d) Incorrect solution with points behind both cameras.

will be in front of both cameras, and this is the correct solution. In each of the other three cases, the point will be reconstructed behind one or both of the cameras (Figure 16.4). For a robust estimate, we would repeat this procedure with a number of corresponding points and base our decision on the total number of votes for each of the four interpretations.

16.3   The fundamental matrix

The derivation of the essential matrix in Section 16.2 used normalized cameras (where $\Lambda_1 = \Lambda_2 = I$). The fundamental matrix plays the role of the essential matrix for cameras with arbitrary intrinsic matrices Λ_1 and Λ_2. The general projection equations for the two cameras are

$$\lambda_1 \tilde{\mathbf{x}}_1 = \mathbf{\Lambda}_1 [\mathbf{I}, \mathbf{0}] \tilde{\mathbf{w}} \tag{16.20}$$
$$\lambda_2 \tilde{\mathbf{x}}_2 = \mathbf{\Lambda}_2 [\mathbf{\Omega}, \boldsymbol{\tau}] \tilde{\mathbf{w}},$$

and we can use similar manipulations to those presented in Section 16.2 to derive the constraint

$$\tilde{\mathbf{x}}_2^T \mathbf{\Lambda}_2^{-T} \mathbf{E} \mathbf{\Lambda}_1^{-1} \tilde{\mathbf{x}}_1 = 0, \tag{16.21}$$

or

$$\tilde{\mathbf{x}}_2^T \mathbf{F} \tilde{\mathbf{x}}_1 = 0, \tag{16.22}$$

where the 3×3 matrix $\mathbf{F} = \mathbf{\Lambda}_2^{-T} \mathbf{E} \mathbf{\Lambda}_1^{-1} = \mathbf{\Lambda}_2^{-T} \boldsymbol{\tau}_\times \mathbf{\Omega} \mathbf{\Lambda}_1^{-1}$ is termed the *fundamental matrix*. Like the essential matrix, it also has rank two, but unlike the essential matrix it has 7 degrees of freedom.

If we know the fundamental matrix $\mathbf{F}$ and the intrinsic matrices $\mathbf{\Lambda}_1$ and $\mathbf{\Lambda}_2$, it is possible to recover the essential matrix $\mathbf{E}$ using the relation

$$\mathbf{E} = \mathbf{\Lambda}_2^T \mathbf{F} \mathbf{\Lambda}_1, \tag{16.23}$$

and this can further be decomposed to find the rotation and translation between the cameras using the method of Section 16.2.2. It follows that for calibrated cameras, if we can estimate the fundamental matrix, then we can find the rotation and translation between the cameras. Hence, we now turn our attention on how to compute the fundamental matrix.

16.3.1 Estimation of the fundamental matrix

The fundamental matrix relation (Equation 16.22) is a constraint on the possible positions of corresponding points in the first and second images. This constraint is parameterized by the nine entries of $\mathbf{F}$. It follows that if we analyze a set of corresponding points, we can observe *how* they are constrained, and from this we can deduce the entries of the fundamental matrix $\mathbf{F}$.

A suitable cost function for the fundamental matrix can be found by considering the epipolar lines. Consider a pair of matching points $\{\mathbf{x}_{i1}, \mathbf{x}_{i2}\}$ in images 1 and 2, respectively. Each point induces an epipolar line in the other image: the point $\mathbf{x}_{i1}$ induces line $\mathbf{l}_{i2}$ in image 2 and the point $\mathbf{x}_{i2}$ induces the line $\mathbf{l}_{i1}$ in image 1. When the fundamental matrix is correct, each point should lie exactly on the epipolar line induced by the corresponding point in the other image (Figure 16.5). We hence minimize the squared distance between every point and the epipolar line predicted by its match in the other image so that

$$\hat{\mathbf{F}} = \underset{\mathbf{F}}{\operatorname{argmin}} \left[\sum_{i=1}^{I} \left((\operatorname{dist}[\mathbf{x}_{i1}, \mathbf{l}_{i1}])^2 + (\operatorname{dist}[\mathbf{x}_{i2}, \mathbf{l}_{i2}])^2 \right) \right], \tag{16.24}$$

where the distance between a 2D point $\mathbf{x} = [x, y]^T$ and a line $\mathbf{l} = [a, b, c]$ is

$$\operatorname{dist}[\mathbf{x}, \mathbf{l}] = \frac{ax + by + c}{\sqrt{a^2 + b^2}}. \tag{16.25}$$

Figure 16.5 Cost function for estimating fundamental matrix. The point $\mathbf{x}_{i1}$ in image 1 induces the epipolar line $\mathbf{l}_{i2}$ in image 2. When the fundamental matrix is correct, the matching point $\mathbf{x}_{i2}$ will be on this line. Similarly the point $\mathbf{x}_{i2}$ in image 2 induces the epipolar line $\mathbf{l}_{i1}$ in image 1. When the fundamental matrix is correct, the point $\mathbf{x}_{i1}$ will be on this line. The cost function is the sum of the squares of the distances between these epipolar lines and points (yellow arrows). This is termed *symmetric epipolar distance*.

Here too, it is not possible to find the minimum of Equation 16.24 in closed form, and we must rely on nonlinear optimization methods. It is possible to get a good starting point for this optimization using the *eight-point algorithm*.

16.3.2   The eight-point algorithm

The eight-point algorithm converts the corresponding 2D points to homogeneous coordinates and then solves for the fundamental matrix in closed form. It does not directly optimize the cost function in Equation 16.24, but instead minimizes an algebraic error. However, the solution to this problem is usually very close to the value that optimizes the desired cost function.

In homogeneous coordinates, the relationship between the ith point $\mathbf{x}_{i1} = [x_{i1}, y_{i1}]^T$ in image 1 and the ith point $\mathbf{x}_{i2} = [x_{i2}, y_{i2}]^T$ in image 2 is

$$
\begin{bmatrix} x_{i2} & y_{i2} & 1 \end{bmatrix}
\begin{bmatrix} f_{11} & f_{12} & f_{13} \\ f_{21} & f_{22} & f_{23} \\ f_{31} & f_{32} & f_{33} \end{bmatrix}
\begin{bmatrix} x_{i1} \\ y_{i1} \\ 1 \end{bmatrix} = 0,
\tag{16.26}
$$

where f_{pq} represents one of the entries in the fundamental matrix. When we write this constraint out in full, we get

$$
x_{i2}x_{i1}f_{11} + x_{i2}y_{i1}f_{12} + x_{i2}f_{13} + y_{i2}x_{i1}f_{21} + y_{i2}y_{i1}f_{22} + y_{i2}f_{23}
$$
$$
+ x_{i1}f_{31} + y_{i1}f_{32} + f_{33} = 0.
\tag{16.27}
$$

This can be expressed as an inner product

$$
[x_{i2}x_{i1}, x_{i2}y_{i1}, x_{i2}, y_{i2}x_{i1}, y_{i2}y_{i1}, y_{i2}, x_{i1}, y_{i1}, 1]\mathbf{f} = 0,
\tag{16.28}
$$

where $\mathbf{f} = [f_{11}, f_{12}, f_{13}, f_{21}, f_{22}, f_{23}, f_{31}, f_{32}, f_{33}]^T$ is a vectorized version of the fundamental matrix, $\mathbf{F}$.

This provides one linear constraint on the elements of $\mathbf{F}$. Consequently, given I matching points, we can stack these constraints to form the system

$$\mathbf{Af} = \begin{bmatrix} x_{12}x_{11} & x_{12}y_{11} & x_{12} & y_{12}x_{11} & y_{12}y_{11} & y_{12} & x_{11} & y_{11} & 1 \\ x_{22}x_{21} & x_{22}y_{21} & x_{22} & y_{22}x_{21} & y_{22}y_{21} & y_{22} & x_{21} & y_{21} & 1 \\ \vdots & \vdots & \vdots & \vdots & \vdots & \vdots & \vdots & \vdots & \vdots \\ x_{I2}x_{I1} & x_{I2}y_{I1} & x_{I2} & y_{I2}x_{I1} & y_{I2}y_{I1} & y_{I2} & x_{I1} & y_{I1} & 1 \end{bmatrix} \mathbf{f} = \mathbf{0}.$$
(16.29)

Since the elements of $\mathbf{f}$ are ambiguous up to scale, we solve this system with the constraint that $|\mathbf{f}| = 1$. This also avoids the trivial solution $\mathbf{f} = \mathbf{0}$. This is a minimum direction problem (see Appendix C.7.2). The solution can be found by taking the singular value decomposition, $\mathbf{A} = \mathbf{ULV}^T$ and setting $\mathbf{f}$ to be the last column of $\mathbf{V}$. The matrix $\mathbf{F}$ is then formed by reshaping $\mathbf{f}$ to form a 3×3 matrix.

There are 8 degrees of freedom in the fundamental matrix (it is ambiguous with respect to scale) and so we require a minimum of $I = 8$ pairs of points. For this reason, this algorithm is called the *eight-point algorithm*.

In practice, there are several further concerns in implementing this algorithm:

- Since the data are noisy, the singularity constraint of the resulting fundamental matrix will not be obeyed in general (i.e., the estimated matrix will be full rank, not rank two). We reintroduce this constraint by taking the singular decomposition of $\mathbf{F}$, setting the last singular value to zero, and multiplying the terms back out. This provides the closest singular matrix under a Frobenius norm.

- Equation 16.29 is badly scaled since some terms are on the order of pixels squared (~ 10000) and some are of the order ~ 1. To improve the quality of the solution, it is wise to prenormalize the data (see Hartley 1997). We transform the points in image 1 as $\tilde{\mathbf{x}}'_{i1} = \mathbf{T}_1 \tilde{\mathbf{x}}_{i1}$ and the points in image 2 as $\tilde{\mathbf{x}}'_{i2} = \mathbf{T}_2 \tilde{\mathbf{x}}_{i2}$. The transformations $\mathbf{T}_1$ and $\mathbf{T}_2$ are chosen to map the mean of the points in their respective image to zero, and to ensure that the variance in the x- and y-dimensions is one. We then compute the matrix $\mathbf{F}'$ from the transformed data using the eight-point algorithm, and recover the original fundamental matrix as $\mathbf{F} = \mathbf{T}_2^T \mathbf{F}' \mathbf{T}_1$.

- The algorithm will only work if the three-dimensional positions $\mathbf{w}_i$ corresponding to the eight pairs of points $\mathbf{x}_{i1}, \mathbf{x}_{i2}$ are in general position. For example, if they all fall on a plane then the equations become degenerate, and we cannot get a unique solution; here the relation between the points in the two images is given by a homography (see Chapter 15). Similarly, in the case where there is no translation (i.e., $\boldsymbol{\tau} = \mathbf{0}$), the relation between the two images is a homography, and there is no unique solution for the fundamental matrix.

- In the subsequent nonlinear optimization, we must also ensure that the rank of $\mathbf{F}$ is two. In order to do this, it is usual to reparameterize the fundamental matrix to ensure that this will be the case.

16.4 Two-view reconstruction pipeline

We now put all of these ideas together and present a rudimentary pipeline for the reconstruction of a static 3D scene based on two images taken from unknown positions, but with cameras where we know the intrinsic parameters. We apply the following steps (Figures 16.6 and 16.7).

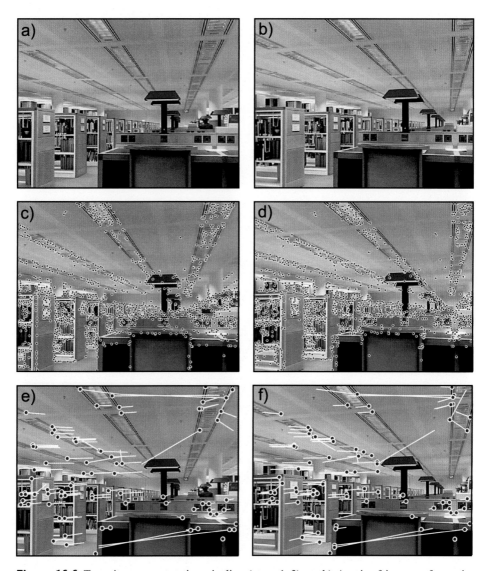

Figure 16.6 Two-view reconstruction pipeline (steps 1–3). a–b) A pair of images of a static scene, captured from two slightly different positions. c–d) SIFT features are computed in each image. A region descriptor is calculated for each feature point that provides a low dimensional characterization of the region around the point. Points in the left and right images are matched using a greedy procedure; the pair of points for which the region descriptors are most similar in a least squares sense are chosen first. Then the pair of remaining points for which the descriptors are most similar are chosen, and so on. This continues until the minimum squared distance between the descriptors exceeds a threshold. e–f) Results of greedy matching procedure: the lines represent the offset to the matching point. Most matches are correct, but there are clearly also some outliers.

Figure 16.7 Two-view reconstruction pipeline (steps 4–8). A fundamental matrix is fitted using a robust estimation procedure such as RANSAC. a–b) Eight matches with maximum agreement from the rest of the data. For each feature, the epipolar line is plotted in the other image. In each case, the matching point lies on or very near the epipolar line. The resulting fundamental matrix can be decomposed to get estimates for the relative rotation and translation between the cameras. c–d) Result of greedily matching original feature points taking into account the epipolar geometry. Matches where the symmetric epipolar distance exceeds a threshold are rejected. e–f) Computed w coordinate (depth) relative to first camera for each feature. Red features are closer, and blue features are further away. Almost all of the distances agree with our perceived understanding of the scene.

1. **Compute image features**. We find salient points in each image using an interest point detector such as the SIFT detector (Section 13.2.3).

2. **Compute feature descriptors**. We characterize the region around each feature in each image with a low-dimensional vector. One possibility would be to use the SIFT descriptor (Section 13.3.2).

3. **Find initial matches**. We greedily match features between the two images. For example, we might base this on the squared distance between their region descriptors and stop this procedure when the squared distance exceeds a predefined threshold to minimize false matches. We might also reject points where the ratio between the quality of the best and second best match in the other image is too close to one (suggesting that alternative matches are plausible).

4. **Compute fundamental matrix.** We compute the fundamental matrix using the eight-point algorithm. Since some matches are likely to be incorrect, we use a robust estimation procedure such as RANSAC (Section 15.6).

5. **Refine matches.** We again greedily match features, but this time we exploit our knowledge of the epipolar geometry: if a putative match is not close to the induced epipolar line, it is rejected. We recompute the fundamental matrix based on all of the remaining point matches.

6. **Estimate essential matrix.** We estimate the essential matrix from the fundamental matrix using Equation 16.23.

7. **Decompose essential matrix.** We extract estimates of the rotation and translation between the cameras (i.e., the extrinsic parameters) by decomposing the essential matrix (Section 16.2.2). This provides four possible solutions.

8. **Estimate 3D points.** For each solution, we reconstruct the 3D position of the points using the linear solution from Section 14.6. We retain the extrinsic parameters where most of the reconstructed points are in front of both cameras.

After this procedure, we have a set of I points $\{\mathbf{x}_{i1}\}_{i=1}^{I}$ in the first image, a set of I corresponding points $\{\mathbf{x}_{i2}\}_{i=1}^{I}$ in the second image, and a good initial estimate of the 3D world positions $\{\mathbf{w}_i\}_{i=1}^{I}$ that were responsible for them. We also have initial estimates of the extrinsic parameters $\{\mathbf{\Omega}, \boldsymbol{\tau}\}$. We now optimize the true cost function

$$
\hat{\mathbf{w}}_{1\ldots I}, \hat{\mathbf{\Omega}}, \hat{\boldsymbol{\tau}} = \underset{\mathbf{w}, \mathbf{\Omega}, \boldsymbol{\tau}}{\operatorname{argmax}} \left[\sum_{i=1}^{I} \sum_{j=1}^{2} \log[Pr(\mathbf{x}_{ij} | \mathbf{w}_i, \mathbf{\Lambda}_j, \mathbf{\Omega}, \boldsymbol{\tau})] \right] \tag{16.30}
$$

$$
= \underset{\mathbf{w}, \mathbf{\Omega}, \boldsymbol{\tau}}{\operatorname{argmax}} \left[\sum_{i=1}^{I} \log \left[\mathrm{Norm}_{\mathbf{x}_{i1}} [\mathbf{pinhole}[\mathbf{w}_i, \mathbf{\Lambda}_1, \mathbf{I}, 0], \sigma^2 \mathbf{I}] \right] \right.
$$

$$
\left. + \sum_{i=1}^{I} \log \left[\mathrm{Norm}_{\mathbf{x}_{i2}} [\mathbf{pinhole}[\mathbf{w}_i, \mathbf{\Lambda}_2, \mathbf{\Omega}, \boldsymbol{\tau}], \sigma^2 \mathbf{I}] \right] \right]
$$

to refine these estimates. In doing so, we must ensure to enforce the constraints that $|\boldsymbol{\tau}| = 1$ and $\mathbf{\Omega}$ is a valid rotation matrix (see Appendix B).

16.4.1   Minimal solutions

The pipeline described previously is rather naïve; in practice the fundamental and essential matrices can be estimated considerably more efficiently.

For example, the fundamental matrix contains seven degrees of freedom, and so it is actually possible to solve for it using only seven pairs of points. Unsurprisingly, this is known as the *seven point algorithm*. It is is more complex as it relies on the seven linear constraints and the nonlinear constraint $\det[\mathbf{F}] = 0$. However, a robust solution can be computed much more efficiently using RANSAC if only seven points are required.

Even if we use this seven-point algorithm, it is still inefficient. When we know the intrinsic parameters of the cameras, it is possible to compute the essential matrix (and hence the relative orientation of the cameras) using a minimal five-point solution. This is based on five linear constraints from observed corresponding points and the nonlinear constraints relating the nine parameters of the essential matrix (Equation 16.12). This method has the advantages of being much quicker to estimate in the context of a RANSAC algorithm and being robust to non-general configurations of the scene points.

16.5 Rectification

The preceding procedure provides a set of sparse matches between the two images. These may suffice for some tasks such as navigation, but if we wish to build an accurate model of the scene, we need to estimate the depth at every point in the image. This is known as *dense stereo reconstruction*.

Dense stereo reconstruction algorithms (see Sections 11.8.2 and 12.8.3) generally assume that the corresponding point lies on the same horizontal scanline in the other image. The goal of *rectification* is to preprocess the image pair so that this is true. In other words, we will transform the images so that each epipolar line is horizontal and so that the epipolar lines associated with a point fall on the same scanline to that point in the other image. We will describe two different approaches to this problem.

16.5.1 Planar rectification

We note that the epipolar lines are naturally horizontal and aligned when the camera motion is purely horizontal and both image planes are perpendicular to the w-axis (Figure 16.3a). The key idea of planar rectification is to manipulate the two images to recreate these viewing conditions. We apply homographies $\boldsymbol{\Phi}_1$ and $\boldsymbol{\Phi}_2$ to the two images so that they cut their respective ray bundles in the desired way (Figure 16.8).

In fact there is an entire family of homographies that accomplish this goal. One possible way to select a suitable pair is to first work with image 2. We apply a series of transformations $\boldsymbol{\Phi}_2 = \mathbf{T}_3\mathbf{T}_2\mathbf{T}_1$, which collectively move the epipole $\mathbf{e}_2$ to a position at infinity $[1,0,0]^T$.

We first center the coordinate system on the principal point,

$$\mathbf{T}_1 = \begin{bmatrix} 1 & 0 & -\delta_x \\ 0 & 1 & -\delta_y \\ 0 & 0 & 1 \end{bmatrix}. \tag{16.31}$$

Then we rotate the image about this center until the epipole lies on the x-axis,

$$\mathbf{T}_2 = \begin{bmatrix} \cos[-\theta] & -\sin[-\theta] & 0 \\ \sin[-\theta] & \cos[-\theta] & 0 \\ 0 & 0 & 1 \end{bmatrix}, \tag{16.32}$$

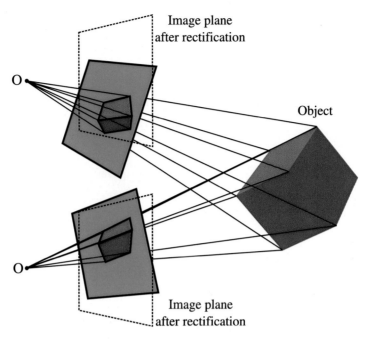

Figure 16.8 Planar rectification. Green quadrilaterals represent image planes of two cameras viewing a 3D object (cube). The goal of planar rectification is to transform each of these planes so that the final configuration replicates Figure 16.3a. After this transformation (dotted lines), the image planes are coplanar, and the translation between the cameras is parallel to this plane. Now the epipolar lines are horizontal and aligned. Since the transformed planes are just different cuts through the respective ray bundles, each transformation can be accomplished using a homography.

where $\theta = \mathrm{atan2}[e_y, e_x]$ is the angle of the translated epipole $\mathbf{e} = [e_x, e_y]$. Finally, we translate the epipole to infinity, using the transformation

$$\mathbf{T}_3 = \begin{bmatrix} 1 & 0 & 0 \\ 0 & 1 & 0 \\ -1/e_x & 0 & 1 \end{bmatrix}, \tag{16.33}$$

where e_x is the x-coordinate of the epipole after the previous two transformations.

After these transformations, the epipole in the second image is at infinity in the horizontal direction. The epipolar lines in this image must converge at the epipole, and are consequently parallel and horizontal as desired.

Now we consider the first image. We cannot simply apply the same procedure as this will not guarantee that the epipolar lines in the first image will be aligned with those in the second. It transpires, however, that there is a family of possible transformations that do make the epipolar lines of this image horizontal and aligned with those in the second image. This family can (not obviously) be parameterized as

$$\mathbf{\Phi}_1[\boldsymbol{\alpha}] = (\mathbf{I} + \mathbf{e}_2 \boldsymbol{\alpha}^T) \mathbf{\Phi}_2 \mathbf{M}, \tag{16.34}$$

where $\mathbf{e}_2 = [1, 0, 0]^T$ is the transformed epipole in the second image, and $\boldsymbol{\alpha} = [\alpha_1, \alpha_2, \alpha_3]^T$ is a 3D vector that selects the particular transformation from the family. The matrix $\mathbf{M}$ comes from the decomposition of the fundamental matrix into $\mathbf{F} = \mathbf{SM}$, where $\mathbf{S}$ is skew symmetric (see below). A proof of the relation in Equation 16.34 can be found in Hartley and Zisserman (2004).

A sensible criterion is to choose α so that it minimizes the disparity,

$$\hat{\alpha} = \underset{\alpha}{\mathrm{argmax}} \left[\sum_{i=1}^{I} (\mathbf{hom}[\mathbf{x}_{i1}, \mathbf{\Phi}_1[\alpha]] - \mathbf{hom}[\mathbf{x}_{i2}, \mathbf{\Phi}_2])^T (\mathbf{hom}[\mathbf{x}_{i1}, \mathbf{\Phi}_1[\alpha]] - \mathbf{hom}[\mathbf{x}_{i2}, \mathbf{\Phi}_2]) \right].$$

(16.35)

This criterion simplifies to solving the least squares problem $|\mathbf{A}\alpha - \mathbf{b}|^2$ where

$$\mathbf{A} = \begin{bmatrix} x'_{11} & y'_{11} & 1 \\ x'_{21} & y'_{21} & 1 \\ \vdots & \vdots & \vdots \\ x'_{I1} & y'_{I1} & 1 \end{bmatrix} \text{ and } \mathbf{b} = \begin{bmatrix} x'_{12} \\ x'_{22} \\ \vdots \\ x'_{I2} \end{bmatrix},$$

(16.36)

where the vectors $\mathbf{x}'_{ij} = [x'_{ij}, y'_{ij}]^T$ are defined by

$$\mathbf{x}'_{i1} = \mathbf{hom}[\mathbf{x}_{i1}, \mathbf{\Phi}_2\mathbf{M}]$$
$$\mathbf{x}'_{i2} = \mathbf{hom}[\mathbf{x}_{i2}, \mathbf{\Phi}_2].$$

(16.37)

This least squares problem can be solved using the standard approach (Appendix C.7.1). Figure 16.9 shows example rectified images. After these transformations, the corresponding points are guaranteed to be on the same horizontal scanline, and dense stereo reconstruction can proceed.

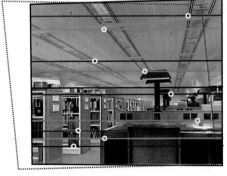

Figure 16.9 Planar rectification. The images from Figures 16.6 and 16.7 have been rectified by applying homographies. After rectification, each point induces an epipolar line in the other image that is horizontal and on the same scanline (compare to Figure 16.7a). This means that the match is guaranteed to be on the same scanline. In this figure, the red dotted line is the superimposed outline of the other image.

Decomposition of the fundamental matrix

The preceding algorithm requires the matrix $\mathbf{M}$ from the decomposition of the fundamental matrix as $\mathbf{F} = \mathbf{SM}$, where $\mathbf{S}$ is skew symmetric. A suitable way to do this is to compute the singular value decomposition of the fundamental matrix $\mathbf{F} = \mathbf{ULV}^T$. We then define the matrices

$$\mathbf{L}' = \begin{bmatrix} l_{11} & 0 & 0 \\ 0 & l_{22} & 0 \\ 0 & 0 & \frac{l_{11}+l_{22}}{2} \end{bmatrix} \text{ and } \mathbf{W} = \begin{bmatrix} 0 & -1 & 0 \\ 1 & 0 & 0 \\ 0 & 0 & 1 \end{bmatrix}, \tag{16.38}$$

where l_{ii} denotes the ith element from the diagonal of $\mathbf{L}$. Finally, we choose

$$\mathbf{M} = \mathbf{UWL}'\mathbf{V}^T. \tag{16.39}$$

16.5.2 Polar rectification

The planar rectification method described in Section 16.5.1 is suitable when the epipole is sufficiently far outside the image. Since the basis of this method is to map the epipoles to infinity, it cannot work when the epipole is inside the image and distorts the image a great deal if it is close to the image. Under these circumstances, a *polar rectification* is preferred.

Polar rectification applies a nonlinear warp to each image so that corresponding points are mapped to the same scanline. Each new image is formed by resampling the original images so that the first new axis is the distance from the epipole and the second new axis is the angle from the epipole (Figure 16.10). This approach can distort the image significantly but works for all camera configurations.

This method is conceptually simple but should be implemented with caution; when the epipole lies within the camera image, it is important to ensure that the correct half of the epipolar line is aligned with the appropriate part of the other image. The reader is encouraged to consult the original description (Pollefeys et al. 1999b) before implementing this algorithm.

16.5.3 After rectification

After rectification, the horizontal offset between every point in the first image and its corresponding point in the second image can be computed using a dense stereo algorithm (see Sections 11.8.2 and 12.8.3). Typical results are shown in Figure 16.11. Each point and its match are then warped back to their original positions (i.e., their image positions are "un-rectified"). For each pair of 2D points, the depth can then be computed using the algorithm of Section 14.6.

Finally, we may wish to view the model from a novel direction. For the two-view case, a simple way to do this is to form a 3D triangular mesh and to texture this mesh using the information from one or the other image. If we have computed dense matches using a stereo-matching algorithm, then the mesh can be computed from the perspective of one camera with two triangles per pixel and cut where there are sharp depth discontinuities. If we have only a sparse correspondence between the two images, then it is usual to triangulate the projections of the 3D points in one image using a technique such as Delaunay triangulation to form the mesh. The textured mesh can now be viewed from a novel direction using the standard computer graphics pipeline.

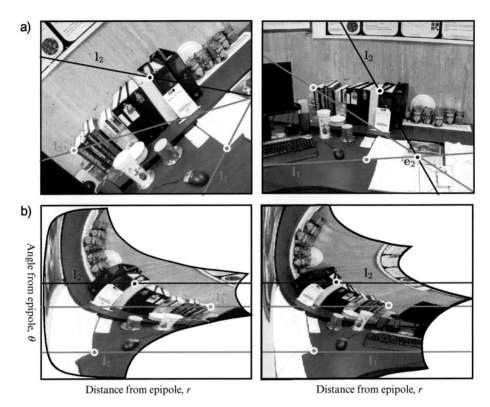

Figure 16.10 Polar rectification. When the epipole is inside one of the images, the planar rectification method is no longer suitable. An alternative in this situation is to perform a nonlinear warp of each image, in which the two new dimensions correspond to the distance and angle from the epipole, respectively. This is known as *polar rectification*.

16.6 Multiview reconstruction

So far, we have considered reconstruction based on two views of a scene. Of course, it is common to have more than two views. For example, we might want to build 3D models using a video sequence taken by a single moving camera, or equivalently from a video sequence from a static camera of a rigidly moving object (Figure 16.12). This problem is often referred to as *structure from motion* or *multiview reconstruction*.

The problem is conceptually very similar to the two camera case. Once again, the solution ultimately relies on a nonlinear optimization in which we manipulate the camera position and the three-dimensional points to minimize the squared reprojection error (Equation 16.2), and hence maximize the likelihood of the model. However, the multiview case does bring several new aspects to the problem.

First, if we have a number of frames all taken with the same camera, there are now sufficient constraints to estimate the intrinsic parameters as well. We initialize the camera matrix with sensible values and add this to the final optimization. This process is known as *auto-calibration*. Second, matching points in video footage is easier because the changes between adjacent frames tend to be small, and so the features can be explicitly tracked in two dimensions. However, it is usual for some points to be occluded in

Figure 16.11 Disparity. After rectification, the horizontal offset at each point can be computed using a dense stereo algorithm. Here we used the method of Sizintsev et al. (2010). Color indicates the horizontal shift (disparity) between images. Black regions indicate places where the matching was ambiguous or where the corresponding part of the scene was occluded. Given these horizontal correspondences, we undo the rectification to get a dense set of matching points with 2D offsets. The 3D position can now be computed using the method from Section 14.6.

any given frame, so we must keep track of which points are present at which time (Figure 16.12f).

Third, there are now additional constraints on feature matching, which make it easier to eliminate outliers in the matching set of points. Consider a point that is matched between three frames. The point in the third frame will be constrained to lie on an epipolar line due to the first frame and another epipolar line due to the second frame: its position has to be at the intersection of the two lines and so is determined exactly. Unfortunately, this method will not work when the two predicted epipolar lines are the same as there is not a unique intersection. Consequently, the position in the third view is computed in a different way in practice. Just as we derived the fundamental matrix relation (Equation 16.22) constraining the positions of matching points between two views, it is possible to derive a closed-form relation that constrains the positions across three images. The three-view analogue of the fundamental matrix is called the *tri-focal tensor*. It can be used to predict the position of the point in a third image given its position in the first and second images even when the epipolar lines are parallel. There is also a relation between four images, which is captured by the quadri-focal tensor, but there are no further relations between points in $J > 5$ images.

Finally, there are new ways to get initial estimates of the unknown quantities. It may not be practical to get the initial estimates of camera position by computing the transformation between adjacent frames and chaining these through the sequence. The translation between adjacent frames may be too small to reliably estimate the motion, and errors accrue as we move through the sequence. Moreover, it is difficult to maintain a consistent estimate of the (ambiguous) scale throughout. To this end, methods have been developed that simultaneously provide an initial estimate of all the camera positions and

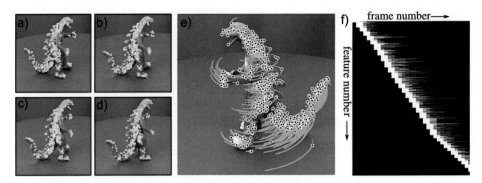

Figure 16.12 Multiframe structure from motion. The goal is to construct a 3D model from a continuous video stream of a moving camera viewing a static object, or a static camera viewing a moving rigid object. a–d) Features are computed in each frame and tracked through the sequence. e) Features in current frame and their history. f) In each new frame a number of new features is identified, and these are tracked until they are occluded or the correspondence is lost. Here, the white pixels indicate that a feature was present in a frame, and black pixels indicate that it was absent.

3D points, some of which are based on factorization of a matrix containing all the (x, y) positions of every point tracked throughout the sequence.

16.6.1 Bundle adjustment

After finding the initial estimates of the 3D positions (structure) and the camera positions (motion), we must again resort to a large nonlinear optimization problem to fine-tune these parameters. With I tracked points over J frames, the problem is formulated as

$$
\hat{\boldsymbol{\theta}} = \underset{\boldsymbol{\theta}}{\operatorname{argmax}} \left[\sum_{i=1}^{I} \sum_{j=1}^{J} \log[Pr(\mathbf{x}_{ij}|\mathbf{w}_i, \boldsymbol{\Lambda}, \boldsymbol{\Omega}_j, \boldsymbol{\tau}_j)] \right] \tag{16.40}
$$

$$
= \underset{\boldsymbol{\theta}}{\operatorname{argmax}} \left[\sum_{i=1}^{I} \sum_{j=1}^{J} \log \left[\operatorname{Norm}_{\mathbf{x}_{ij}} [\mathbf{pinhole}[\mathbf{w}_i, \boldsymbol{\Lambda}, \boldsymbol{\Omega}_j, \boldsymbol{\tau}_j], \sigma^2 \mathbf{I}] \right] \right],
$$

where $\boldsymbol{\theta}$ contains the unknown world points $\{\mathbf{w}_i\}_{i=1}^{I}$, the intrinsic matrix $\boldsymbol{\Lambda}$, and the extrinsic parameters $\{\boldsymbol{\Omega}_j, \boldsymbol{\tau}_j\}_{j=1}^{J}$. This optimization problem is known as *Euclidean bundle adjustment*. As for the two-view case, it is necessary to constrain the overall scale of the solution in some way.

One way to solve this optimization problem is to use an alternating approach. We first improve the log likelihood with respect to each of the extrinsic sets of parameters $\{\boldsymbol{\Omega}_j, \boldsymbol{\tau}_j\}$ (and possibly the intrinsic matrix $\boldsymbol{\Lambda}$ if unknown) and then update each 3D position $\mathbf{w}_i$. This is known as *resection-intersection*. It seems attractive as it only involves optimizing over a small subset of parameters at any one time. However, this type of *coordinate ascent* is inefficient: it cannot take advantage of the large gains that come from varying all of the parameters at once.

To make progress, we note that the cost function is based on the normal distribution and so can be rewritten in the least squares form

$$\hat{\boldsymbol{\theta}} = \underset{\boldsymbol{\theta}}{\operatorname{argmin}} \left[\mathbf{z}^T \mathbf{z} \right], \tag{16.41}$$

where the vector $\mathbf{z}$ contains the squared differences between the observed feature positions $\mathbf{x}_{ij}$ and the positions $\textbf{pinhole}[\mathbf{w}_i, \boldsymbol{\Lambda}, \boldsymbol{\Omega}_j, \boldsymbol{\tau}_j]$ predicted by the model with the current parameters:

$$\mathbf{z} = \begin{bmatrix} \mathbf{x}_{11} - \textbf{pinhole}[\mathbf{w}_1, \boldsymbol{\Lambda}, \boldsymbol{\Omega}_1, \boldsymbol{\tau}_1] \\ \mathbf{x}_{12} - \textbf{pinhole}[\mathbf{w}_1, \boldsymbol{\Lambda}, \boldsymbol{\Omega}_2, \boldsymbol{\tau}_2] \\ \vdots \\ \mathbf{x}_{IJ} - \textbf{pinhole}[\mathbf{w}_I, \boldsymbol{\Lambda}, \boldsymbol{\Omega}_J, \boldsymbol{\tau}_J] \end{bmatrix}. \tag{16.42}$$

The Gauss-Newton method (Appendix B.2.3) is specialized to this type of problem and updates the current estimate $\boldsymbol{\theta}^{[t]}$ of the parameters using

$$\boldsymbol{\theta}^{[t]} = \boldsymbol{\theta}^{[t-1]} + \lambda (\mathbf{J}^T \mathbf{J})^{-1} \frac{\partial f}{\partial \boldsymbol{\theta}}, \tag{16.43}$$

where $\mathbf{J}$ is the Jacobian matrix. The entry in the mth row and n^{th} column of $\mathbf{J}$ consists of the derivative of the mth element of $\mathbf{z}$ with respect to the nth element of the parameter vector $\boldsymbol{\theta}$:

$$J_{mn} = \frac{\partial z_m}{\partial \theta_n}. \tag{16.44}$$

In a real structure from motion problem, there might be thousands of scene points, each with three unknowns, and also thousands of camera positions, each with six unknowns. At each stage of the optimization, we must invert $\mathbf{J}^T \mathbf{J}$, which is a square matrix whose dimension is the same as the number of unknowns. When the number of unknowns is large, inverting this matrix becomes expensive.

However, it is possible to build a practical system by exploiting the sparse structure of $\mathbf{J}^T \mathbf{J}$. This sparsity results from the fact that every squared error term does not depend on every unknown. There is one contributing error term per observed 2D point, and this depends only on the associated 3D point, the intrinsic parameters, and the camera position in that frame.

To exploit this structure, we order the elements of the Jacobian matrix as $\mathbf{J} = [\mathbf{J}_{\mathbf{w}}, \mathbf{J}_{\boldsymbol{\Omega}}]$, where $\mathbf{J}_{\mathbf{w}}$ contains the terms that relate to the unknown world points $\{\mathbf{w}_i\}_{i=1}^I$ in turn, and $\mathbf{J}_{\boldsymbol{\Omega}}$ contains the terms that relate to the unknown camera positions $\{\boldsymbol{\Omega}_j, \boldsymbol{\tau}_j\}_{j=1}^J$. For pedagogical reasons, we will assume that the intrinsic matrix $\boldsymbol{\Lambda}$ is known here and hence has no entries in the Jacobian. We see that the matrix to be inverted becomes

$$\mathbf{J}^T \mathbf{J} = \begin{bmatrix} \mathbf{J}_{\mathbf{w}}^T \mathbf{J}_{\mathbf{w}} & \mathbf{J}_{\mathbf{w}}^T \mathbf{J}_{\boldsymbol{\Omega}} \\ \mathbf{J}_{\boldsymbol{\Omega}}^T \mathbf{J}_{\mathbf{w}} & \mathbf{J}_{\boldsymbol{\Omega}}^T \mathbf{J}_{\boldsymbol{\Omega}} \end{bmatrix}. \tag{16.45}$$

We now note that the matrices in the top-left and bottom-right of this matrix are block-diagonal (different world points do not interact with one another, and neither do the parameters from different cameras). Hence, these two submatrices can be inverted very efficiently. The Schur complement relation (Appendix C.8.2), allows us to exploit this fact to reduce the complexity of the larger matrix inversion.

The preceding description is only a sketch of a real bundle adjustment algorithm; in a real system, additional sparseness in $\mathbf{J}^T\mathbf{J}$ would be exploited, a more sophisticated optimization method such as Levenberg-Marquardt would be employed, and a robust cost function would be used to reduce the effect of outliers.

16.7   Applications

We first describe a typical pipeline for recovering a 3D mesh model from a sequence of video frames. We then discuss a system that can extract 3D information about a scene from images gathered by a search engine on the Internet, and use this information to help navigate through the set of photos. Finally, we discuss a multicamera system for capturing 3D objects that uses a volumetric representation and exploits a Markov random field prior to get a smooth reconstruction.

16.7.1   3D reconstruction pipeline

Pollefeys and Van Gool (2002) present a complete pipeline for constructing 3D models from a sequence of images taken from an uncalibrated hand-held camera (Figure 16.13). In the first stage, they compute a set of interest points (corners) in each image. When the image data consist of individual still photos, these points are matched between images. When the image data consist of continuous video, they are tracked between frames. In either case, a sparse set of potential correspondences is obtained. The multiview relations are estimated using a robust procedure, and these are then used to eliminate outliers from the correspondence set.

To estimate the motion of the cameras, two images are chosen, and a projective reconstruction is computed (i.e., a reconstruction that is ambiguous up to a 3D projective transformation because the intrinsic parameters are not known). For each of the other images in turn, the pose for the camera is determined relative to this reconstruction, and the reconstruction is refined. In this way, it is possible to incorporate views that have no common features with the original two frames.

A subsequent bundle adjustment procedure minimizes the reprojection errors to get more accurate estimates of the camera positions and the points in the 3D world. At this stage, the reconstruction is still ambiguous up to a projective ambiguity and only now are initial estimates of the intrinsic parameters computed using a specialized procedure (see Pollefeys et al. 1999a). Finally, a full bundle adjustment method is applied; it simultaneously refines the estimates of the intrinsic parameters, camera positions, and 3D structure of the scene.

Successive pairs of images are rectified, and a dense set of disparities are computed using a multiresolution dynamic programming technique. Given these dense correspondences, it is possible to compute an estimate of the 3D scene from the point of view of both cameras. A final estimate of the 3D structure relative to a reference frame is computed by fusing all of these independent estimates using a Kalman filter (see Chapter 19).

For relatively simple scenes, a 3D mesh is computed by placing the vertices of the triangles in 3D space according to the values found in the depth map of the reference frame. The associated texture map can be retrieved from one or more of the original images. For more complex scenes, a single reference frame may not suffice and so several meshes are computed from different reference frames and fused together. Figures 16.13g–h show

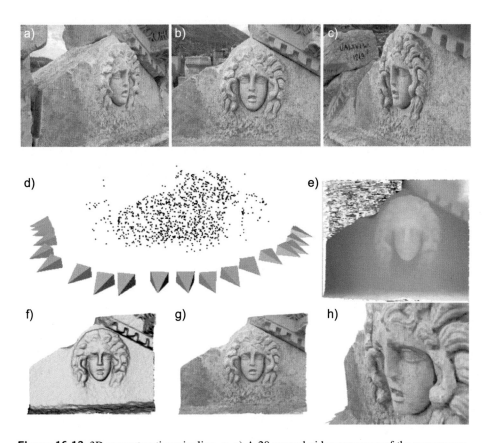

Figure 16.13 3D reconstruction pipeline. a–c) A 20-second video sequence of the camera panning around the Medusa carving was captured. Every 20th frame was used for the reconstruction, three of which are shown here. d) Sparse reconstruction (points) and estimated camera positions (pyramids) after bundle adjustment procedure. e) Depth map after dense stereo matching. f) Shaded 3D mesh model. g–h) Two views of textured 3D mesh model. Adapted from Pollefeys and Van Gool (2002). ©2002 Wiley.

examples of the resulting textured 3D model of a Medusa head at the ancient site of Sagalassos in Turkey. More details concerning this pipeline can be found in Pollefeys et al. (2004).

16.7.2 Photo-tourism

Snavely et al. (2006) present a system for browsing a collection of images of an object that were gathered from the Internet. A sparse 3D model of the object is created by locating SIFT features in each image and finding a set of correspondences between pairs of images by computing the fundamental matrix using the eight point algorithm with RANSAC.

A bundle adjustment procedure is then applied to estimate the camera positions and a sparse 3D model of the scene (Figure 16.14a). This optimization procedure starts with only a single pair of images and gradually includes images based on their overlap with

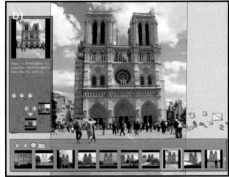

Figure 16.14 Photo-tourism. a) A sparse 3D model of an object is computed from a set of photographs retrieved from the Internet and the relative positions of the cameras (pyramids) are estimated. b) This 3D model is used as the basis of an interface that provides novel ways to explore the photo-collection by moving from image to image in 3D space. Adapted from Snavely et al. (2006). ©2006 ACM.

the current reconstruction, "rebundling" at each stage. The intrinsic matrix of each camera is also estimated in this step, but this is simplified by assuming that the center of projection is coincident with the image center, that the skew is zero, and that the pixels are square, leaving a single focal length parameter. This is initialized in the optimization using information from the EXIF tags of the image when they are present. The bundle adjustment procedure was lengthy; for the model of NotreDame, it took two weeks to compute a model from 2635 photos of which 597 images were ultimately included. However, more recent approaches to reconstruction from Internet photos such as that of Frahm et al. (2010) are considerably faster.

This sparse 3D model of the scene is exploited to create a set of tools for navigating around the set of photographs. For example, it is possible to

- Select a particular view based on a 3D rendering (as in Figure 16.14a),
- Find images of the object that are similar to the current view,
- Retrieve images of the object taken from the left or the right of the current position (effectively pan around the object),
- Find images that are from a similar viewpoint but closer or further from the object (zoom into/away from the object),
- Annotate objects and have these annotations transferred to other images.

This system was extended by Snavely et al. (2008) to allow more natural interaction with the space of images. For example, in this system it is possible to pan smoothly around objects by warping the original photos, so that they appear to define a smooth path through space.

16.7.3 Volumetric graph cuts

The reconstruction pipeline described in Section 16.7.1 has the potential disadvantage that it requires the merging of multiple meshes of the object computed from different viewpoints. Vogiatzis et al. (2007) presented a system that uses a volumetric representation of depth to avoid this problem. In other words, the 3D space that we wish to

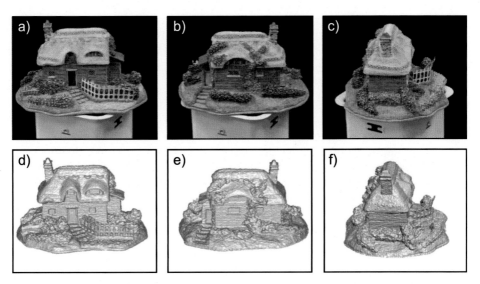

Figure 16.15 Volumetric graph cuts. a–c) Three of the original photos used to build the 3D model. d–f) Renderings of the resulting model from similar viewpoints. Adapted from Vogiatzis et al. (2007). ©2007 IEEE.

reconstruct is divided into a 3D grid, and each constituent element (voxel) is simply labeled as being inside or outside the object. Hence, reconstruction can be viewed as a binary segmentation of the 3D space.

The relative positions of the cameras are computed using a standard bundle adjustment approach. However, the reconstruction problem is now formulated in terms of an energy function consisting of two terms and optimized using graph cuts. First, there is an occupation cost for labeling each voxel as either foreground or background. Second, there is a discontinuity cost for lying at the boundary between the two partitions. We will now examine each of these terms in more detail.

The cost of labeling a voxel as being within the object is set to a very high value if this voxel does not project into the silhouette of the object in each image (i.e., it is not within the visual hull). Conversely, it is assumed that concavities in the object do not extend beyond a fixed distance from this visual hull, so a very high cost is paid if voxels close to the center of the visual hull are labeled as being outside the object. For the remaining voxels, a data-independent cost is set that favors the voxel being part of the object and produces a ballooning tendency that counters the shrinking bias of the graph cut solution, which pays a cost at transitions between the object and the space around it.

The discontinuity cost for lying on the boundary of the object depends on the *photo-consistency* of the voxel; a voxel is deemed photo-consistent if it projects to positions with similar RGB values in all of the cameras from which it is visible. Of course, to evaluate this, we must estimate the set of cameras in which this point is visible. One approach to this is to approximate the shape of the object using the visual hull. However, Vogiatzis et al. (2007) propose a more sophisticated method in which each camera votes for the photo-consistency of the voxel based on its pattern of correlation with the other images.

The final optimization problem now takes the form of a sum of unary occupation costs and pairwise terms that encourage the final voxel label field to be smooth. These pairwise terms are modified by the discontinuity cost (an example of using geodesic distance in graph cuts) so that the transition from foreground to background is more likely in regions where the photo-consistency is high. Figure 16.15 shows an example of a volumetric 3D model computed in this way.

Discussion

This chapter has not introduced any truly new models; rather we have explored the ramifications of using multiple projective pinhole camera models simultaneously. It is now possible to use these ideas to reconstruct 3D models from camera sequences of rigid objects with well-behaved optical properties. However, 3D reconstruction in more general cases remains an open research problem.

Notes

Multiview geometry: For more information about general issues in multiview geometry consult the books by Faugeras et al. (2001), Hartley and Zisserman (2004), and Ma et al. (2004) and the online tutorial by Pollefeys (2002). A summary of multiview relations was presented by Moons (1998).

Essential and fundamental matrices: The essential matrix was described by Longuet-Higgins (1981) and its properties were explored by Huang and Faugeras (1989), Horn (1990), and Maybank (1998) among others. The fundamental matrix was discussed in Faugeras (1992), Faugeras et al. (1992), and Hartley (1992), (1994). The eight-point algorithm for computing the essential matrix is due to Longuet-Higgins (1981). Hartley (1997) described a method for rescaling in the eight-point algorithm that improved its accuracy. Details of the seven-point algorithm for computing the fundamental matrix can be found in Hartley and Zisserman (2004). Nistér (2004) and Stewénius et al. (2006) describe methods for the relative orientation problem that work directly with five-point correspondences between the cameras.

Rectification: The planar rectification algorithm described in the text is adapted from the description in Hartley and Zisserman (2004). Other variations on planar rectification can be found in Fusiello et al. (2000), Loop and Zhang (1999), and Ma et al. (2004). The polar rectification procedure is due to Pollefeys et al. (1999b).

Features and feature tracking: The algorithms in this chapter rely on the computation of distinctive points in the image. Typically, these are found using the Harris corner detector (Harris and Stephens 1988) or the SIFT detector (Lowe 2004). A more detailed discussion of how these points are computed can be found in Section 13.2. Methods for tracking points in smooth video sequences (as opposed to matching them across views with a wide baseline) are discussed in Lucas and Kanade (1981), Tomasi and Kanade (1991), and Shi and Tomasi (1994).

Reconstruction pipelines: Several authors have described pipelines for computing 3D structure based on a set of images of a rigid object including Fitzgibbon and Zisserman (1998), Pollefeys et al. (2004), Brown and Lowe (2005), and Agarwal et al. (2009). Newcombe and Davison (2010) present a recent system that runs at interactive speeds. A summary of this area can be found in Moons et al. (2009).

Factorization: Tomasi and Kanade (1992) developed an exact ML solution for the projection matrices and 3D points in a set of images based on factorization. This solution assumes that the projection process is affine (a simplification of the full pinhole model) and that every point is visible in every image. Sturm and Triggs (1996) developed a similar method that could be used for the full projective camera. Buchanan and Fitzgibbon (2005) discuss approaches to this problem when the complete set of data is not available.

Bundle adjustment: Bundle adjustment is a complex topic, which is reviewed in Triggs et al. (1999). More recently Engels et al. (2006) discuss a real-time bundle adjustment approach that works with temporal subwindows from a video sequence. Recent approaches to bundle adjustment have adopted a conjugate gradient optimization strategy (Byröd and Åström 2010; Agarwal et al. 2010). A public implementation of bundle adjustment has been made available by Lourakis and Argyros (2009). A system which is cutting edge at the time of writing is described in Jeong et al. (2010), and recent methods that use multicore processing have also been developed (Wu et al. 2011).

Multiview reconstruction: The stereo algorithms in Chapters 11 and 12 compute an estimate of depth at each pixel of one or both of the input images. An alternative strategy is to use an image-independent representation of shape. Examples of such representations include voxel occupancy grids (Vogiatzis et al. 2007; Kutulakos and Seitz 2000), level sets (Faugeras and Keriven 1998; Pons et al. 2007), and polygonal meshes (Fua and Leclerc 1995, Hernández and Schmitt 2004). Many multiview reconstruction techniques also enforce the constraints imposed by the silhouettes (see Section 14.7.2) on the final solution (e.g., Sinha and Pollefeys 2005; Sinha et al. 2007; Kolev and Cremers 2008). A review of multiview reconstruction techniques can be found in Seitz et al. (2006).

Problems

16.1 Sketch the pattern of epipolar lines on the images in Figure 16.17a.

16.2 Show that the cross product relation can be written in terms of a matrix multiplication so that

$$\mathbf{a} \times \mathbf{b} = \begin{bmatrix} 0 & -a_3 & a_2 \\ a_3 & 0 & -a_1 \\ -a_2 & a_1 & 0 \end{bmatrix} \begin{bmatrix} b_1 \\ b_2 \\ b_3 \end{bmatrix}.$$

16.3 Consider figure 16.16. Write the direction of the three 3D vectors $\mathbf{O}_1\mathbf{O}_2$, $\mathbf{O}_1\mathbf{w}$, and $\mathbf{O}_2\mathbf{w}$ in terms of the observed image positions $\mathbf{x}_1$,$\mathbf{x}_2$ and the rotation $\mathbf{\Omega}$ and translation $\mathbf{\tau}$ between the cameras. The scale of the vectors is unimportant.

The three vectors that you have found must be coplanar. The criterion for three 3D vectors $\mathbf{a}, \mathbf{b}, \mathbf{c}$ being coplanar can be written as $\mathbf{a}.(\mathbf{b} \times \mathbf{c}) = 0$. Use this criterion to derive the essential matrix.

16.4 A clueless computer vision professor writes:

"The essential matrix is a 3×3 matrix that relates image coordinates between two images of the same scene. It contains 8 independent degrees of freedom (it is ambiguous up to scale). It has rank 2. If we know the intrinsic matrices of the two cameras, we can use the essential matrix to recover the rotation and translation between the cameras exactly."

Edit this statement to make it factually correct.

16.5 The essential matrix relates points in two cameras so that

$$\mathbf{x}_2^T \mathbf{E} \mathbf{x}_1 = 0$$

is given by

$$\mathbf{E} = \begin{bmatrix} 0 & 0 & 10 \\ 0 & 0 & 0 \\ -10 & 0 & 0 \end{bmatrix}.$$

What is the epipolar line in image 2 corresponding to the point $x_1 = [1, -1, 1]$? What is the epipolar line in image 2 corresponding to the points $x_1 = [-5, -2, 1]$? Determine the position of the epipole in image 2. What can you say about the motion of the cameras?

16.6 Show that we can retrieve the essential matrix by multiplying together the expressions from the decomposition (Equations 16.19) as $\mathbf{E} = \mathbf{\tau}_\times \mathbf{\Omega}$.

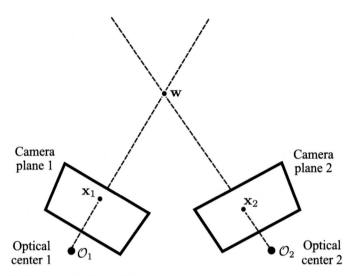

Figure 16.16 Figure for Problem 16.3.

16.7 Derive the fundamental matrix relation:

$$\tilde{\mathbf{x}}_2^T \boldsymbol{\Lambda}_2^{-T} \mathbf{E} \boldsymbol{\Lambda}_1^{-1} \tilde{\mathbf{x}}_1 = 0.$$

16.8 I intend to compute the fundamental matrix using the eight-point algorithm. Unfortunately, my data set is polluted by 30 percent outliers. How many iterations of the RANSAC algorithm will I need to run to have a 99 percent probability of success (i.e., computing the fundamental matrix from eight inliers at least once)? How many iterations will I need if I use an algorithm based on seven points?

16.9 We are given the fundamental matrix $\mathbf{F}_{13}$ relating images 1 and 3 and the fundamental matrix $\mathbf{F}_{23}$ relating images 2 and 3. I am now given corresponding points $\mathbf{x}_1$ and $\mathbf{x}_2$ in images 1 and 2, respectively. Derive a formula for the position of the corresponding point in image 3.

16.10 Tomasi-Kanade factorization. In the orthographic camera (figure 14.19), the projection process can be described as

$$\begin{bmatrix} x \\ y \end{bmatrix} = \begin{bmatrix} \phi_x & \gamma & \delta_x \\ 0 & \phi_y & \delta_y \end{bmatrix} \begin{bmatrix} \omega_{11} & \omega_{12} & \omega_{13} & \tau_x \\ \omega_{21} & \omega_{22} & \omega_{23} & \tau_y \\ 0 & 0 & 0 & 1 \end{bmatrix} \begin{bmatrix} u \\ v \\ w \\ 1 \end{bmatrix}$$

$$= \begin{bmatrix} \pi_{11} & \pi_{12} & \pi_{13} \\ \pi_{21} & \pi_{22} & \pi_{23} \end{bmatrix} \begin{bmatrix} u \\ v \\ w \end{bmatrix} + \begin{bmatrix} \tau_x' \\ \tau_y' \end{bmatrix},$$

or in matrix form

$$\mathbf{x} = \boldsymbol{\Pi}\mathbf{w} + \boldsymbol{\tau}'.$$

Now consider a data matrix $\mathbf{X}$ containing the positions $\{\mathbf{x}_{ij}\}_{i,j=1}^{I,J}$ of J points as seen in I images so that

$$\mathbf{X} = \begin{bmatrix} \mathbf{x}_{11} & \mathbf{x}_{12} & \cdots & \mathbf{x}_{iJ} \\ \mathbf{x}_{21} & \mathbf{x}_{22} & \cdots & \mathbf{x}_{2J} \\ \vdots & \vdots & \ddots & \vdots \\ \mathbf{x}_{I1} & \mathbf{x}_{I2} & \cdots & \mathbf{x}_{IJ}, \end{bmatrix}$$

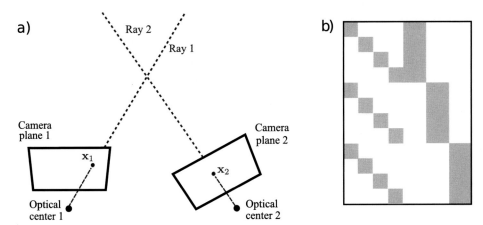

Figure 16.17 a) Figure for Problem 16.1. c) Figure for Problem 16.11. Gray regions represent nonzero entries in this portrait Jacobian matrix.

and where $\mathbf{x}_{ij} = [x_{ij}, y_{ij}]^T$.

    (i) Show that the matrix $\mathbf{X}$ can be written in the form

$$\mathbf{X} = \mathbf{PW} + \mathbf{T}$$

    where $\mathbf{P}$ contains all of the I 3×2 projection matrices $\{\mathbf{\Pi}_i\}_{i=1}^I$, $\mathbf{W}$ contains all of the J 3D world positions $\{\mathbf{w}_j\}_{j=1}^J$ and $\mathbf{T}$ contains the translation vectors $\{\boldsymbol{\tau}'_i\}_{i=1}^I$.

    (ii) Devise an algorithm to recover the matrices $\mathbf{P}, \mathbf{W}$ and $\mathbf{T}$ from the measurements $\mathbf{X}$. Is your solution unique?

16.11 Consider a Jacobian that has a structure of nonzero entries as shown in Figure 16.17b. Draw an equivalent image that shows the structure of the nonzero entries in the matrix $\mathbf{J}^T\mathbf{J}$. Describe how you would use the Schur complement relation to invert this matrix efficiently.

Part VI
Models for vision

In the final part of this book, we discuss four families of models. There is very little new theoretical material; these models are straight applications of the learning and inference techniques introduced in the first nine chapters. Nonetheless, this material addresses some of the most important machine vision applications: shape modeling, face recognition, tracking, and object recognition.

In Chapter 17 we discuss models that characterize the shape of objects. This is a useful goal in itself as knowledge of shape can help localize or segment an object. Furthermore, shape models can be used in combination with models for the RGB values to provide a more accurate generative account of the observed data.

In Chapter 18 we investigate models that distinguish between the identities of objects and the style in which they are observed; a prototypical example of this type of application would be face recognition. Here the goal is to build a generative model of the data that can separate critical information about identity from the irrelevant image changes due to pose, expression and lighting.

In Chapter 19 we discuss a family of models for tracking visual objects through time sequences. These are essentially graphical models based on chains such as those discussed in Chapter 11. However, there are two main differences. First, we focus here on the case where the unknown variable is continuous rather than discrete. Second, we do not usually have the benefit of observing the full sequence; we must make a decision at each time based on information from only the past.

Finally, in Chapter 20 we consider models for object and scene recognition. An important recent discovery is that good object recognition performance can be achieved using a discrete representation where the image is characterized as an unstructured histogram of *visual words*. Hence, this chapter considers models where the observed data are discrete.

It is notable that all of these families of models are generative; it has proven difficult to integrate complex knowledge about the structure of visual problems into discriminative models.

Chapter 17

Models for shape

This chapter concerns models for 2D and 3D shape. The motivation for shape models is twofold. First, we may wish to identify exactly which pixels in the scene belong to a given object. One approach to this *segmentation* problem, is to model the outer contour of the object (i.e., the shape) explicitly. Second, the shape may provide information about the identity or other characteristics of the object: it can be used as an intermediate representation for inferring higher-level properties.

Unfortunately, modeling the shape of an object is challenging; we must account for deformations of the object, the possible absence of some parts of the object and even changes in the object topology. Furthermore, the object may be partially occluded, making it difficult to relate the shape model to the observed data.

One possible approach to establishing 2D object shape is to use a *bottom-up approach*; here, a set of boundary fragments are identified using an edge detector (Section 13.2.1) and the goal is to connect these fragments to form a coherent object contour. Unfortunately, achieving this goal has proved surprisingly elusive. In practice, the edge detector finds extraneous edge fragments that are not part of the object contour and misses others that are part of the true contour. Hence it is difficult to connect the edge fragments in a way that correctly reconstructs the contour of an object.

The methods in this chapter adopt the *top-down approach*. Here, we impose prior information about the object that constrains the possible contour shapes and hence reduces the search space. We will investigate a range of different types of prior information; in some models this will be very weak (e.g., the object boundary is smooth) and in others it will be very strong (e.g., the object boundary is a 2D projection of a particular 3D shape).

To motivate these models, consider the problem of fitting a 2D geometric model of the spine to medical imaging data (Figure 17.1). Our goal is to characterize this complex shape with only a few parameters, which could subsequently be used as a basis for diagnosing medical problems. This is challenging because the local edge information in the image is weak. However, in our favor we have very strong prior knowledge about the possible shapes of the spine.

17.1   Shape and its representation

Before we can introduce concrete models for identifying shape in images, we should
define exactly what we mean by the word "shape." A commonly used definition comes
from Kendall (1984) who states that shape "is all the geometrical information that
remains when location, scale and rotational effects are filtered out from an object." In
other words, the shape consists of whatever geometric information is invariant to a similarity transformation. Depending on the situation, we may generalize this definition to
other transformation types such as Euclidean or affine.

We will also need a way to represent the shape. One approach is to directly define
an algebraic expression that describes the contour. For example, a *conic* defines points
$\mathbf{x} = [x, y]^T$ as lying on the contour if they obey

$$\begin{bmatrix} x & y & 1 \end{bmatrix} \begin{bmatrix} \alpha & \beta & \gamma \\ \beta & \delta & \epsilon \\ \gamma & \epsilon & \zeta \end{bmatrix} \begin{bmatrix} x \\ y \\ 1 \end{bmatrix} = 0. \tag{17.1}$$

This family of shapes includes circles, ellipses, parabolas, and hyperbolas, where the
choice of shape depends on the parameters $\boldsymbol{\theta} = \{\alpha, \beta, \gamma, \delta, \epsilon, \zeta\}$.

Algebraic models are attractive in that they provide a closed form expression for the
contour, but their applicability is extremely limited; it is difficult to define a mathematical
expression that describes a family of complex shapes such as the spine in Figure 17.1.
It *is* possible to model complex objects as superimposed collections of geometric primitives like conics, but the resulting models are unwieldy and lose many of the desirable
properties of the closed form representation.

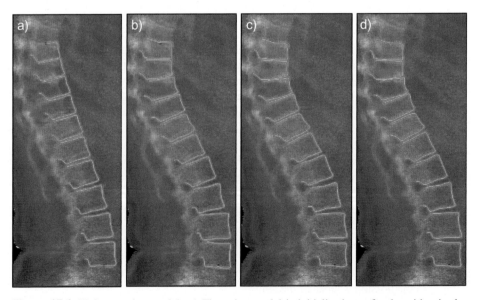

Figure 17.1 Fitting a spine model. a) The spine model is initialized at a fixed position in the
image. b–d) The model then adapts to the image until it describes the data as well as possible. Models that "crawl" across the image in this way are known as *active shape models*. Figure
provided by Tim Cootes and Martin Roberts.

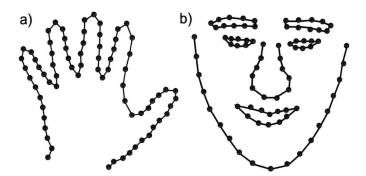

Figure 17.2 Landmark points. Object shape can be represented with sets of landmark points. a) Here the landmark points (red dots) define a single open contour that describes the shape of a hand. b) In this example the landmark points are connected into sets of open and closed contours that describe the regions of the face.

Most of the models in this chapter adopt a different approach; they define the shape using a set of *landmark points* (Figure 17.2). One way to think of landmark points is as a set of discrete samples from one or more underlying continuous contours. The connectivity of the landmark points varies according to the model: they may be ordered and hence represent a single continuous contour, ordered with wrapping, so they represent a closed contour or may have a more complex organization so that they can represent a collection of closed and open contours.

The contour can be reconstituted from the landmark points by interpolating between them according to the connectivity. For example, in Figure 17.2, the contours have been formed by connecting adjacent landmark points with straight lines. In more sophisticated schemes, the landmark points may indirectly determine the position of a smooth curve by acting as the control points of a spline model.

17.2 Snakes

As a base model, we will consider *parametric contour models*, which are sometimes also referred to as *active contour models* or *snakes*. These provide only very weak a priori geometric information; they assume that we know the topology of the contour (i.e., open or closed) and that it is smooth but nothing else. Hence they are suitable for situations where little is known about the contents of the image. We will consider a closed contour defined by a set of N 2D landmark points $\mathbf{W} = [\mathbf{w}_1, \mathbf{w}_2, \ldots, \mathbf{w}_N]$, which are unknown.

Our goal is to find the configuration of landmark points that best explains the shape of an object in the image. We construct a generative model for the landmark positions, which is determined by a likelihood term (which indicates the agreement of this configuration with the image data) and a prior term (which encompasses our prior knowledge about the frequency with which different configurations occur).

The likelihood $Pr(\mathbf{x}|\mathbf{W})$ of the RGB image data $\mathbf{x}$ given the landmark points $\mathbf{W}$ should be high when the landmark points $\mathbf{w}$ lie on or close to edges in the image, and low when they lie in flat regions. One possibility for the likelihood is hence

$$Pr(\mathbf{x}|\mathbf{W}) \propto \prod_{n=1}^{N} \exp\left[\text{sobel}\left[\mathbf{x}, \mathbf{w}_n\right]\right], \tag{17.2}$$

where the function sobel$[\mathbf{x}, \mathbf{w}]$ returns the magnitude of the Sobel edge operator (i.e., the square root of the sum of the squared responses to the horizontal and vertical Sobel filters – see Section 13.1.3) at 2D position $\mathbf{w}$ in the image.

This likelihood will be high when the landmark points are on a contour and low otherwise, as required. However, it has a rather serious disadvantage in practice; in completely flat parts of the image, the Sobel edge operator returns a value of zero. Consequently, if the landmark points lie in flat parts of the image, there is no information about which way to move them to improve the fit (Figures 17.3a–b).

A better approach is to find a set of discrete edges using the Canny edge detector (Section 13.2.1) and then compute a *distance transform*; each pixel is allotted a value according to its squared distance from the nearest edge pixel. The likelihood now becomes

$$Pr(\mathbf{x}|\mathbf{W}) \propto \prod_{n=1}^{N} \exp\left[-(\text{dist}\,[\mathbf{x}, \mathbf{w}_n])^2\right], \qquad (17.3)$$

where the function dist$[\mathbf{x}, \mathbf{w}]$ returns the value of the distance transform at position $\mathbf{w}$ in the image. Now the likelihood is large when the landmark points all fall close to edges in the image (where the distance transform is low) and smoothly decreases as the distance between the landmark points and the edges increases (Figures 17.3c–d). In addition to being pragmatic, this approach also has an attractive interpretation; the "squared distance" objective function is equivalent to assuming that the measured position of the edge is a noisy estimate of the true edge position and that the noise is additive and normally distributed.

If we were to find the landmark points $\mathbf{W}$ based on this criterion alone, then each point would be separately attracted to a strong edge in the image, and the result would probably not form a coherent shape; they might even all be attracted to the same position. To avoid this problem and complete the model, we define a prior that favors smooth contours with low curvature. There are various ways to do this, but one possibility is to choose a prior with two terms

$$Pr(\mathbf{W}) \propto \prod_{n=1}^{N} \exp\left[\alpha \, \text{space}[\mathbf{w}, n] + \beta \, \text{curve}[\mathbf{w}, n]\right], \qquad (17.4)$$

where the scalars α and β control the relative contribution of these terms.

The first term encourages the spacing of the points around the contour to be even; the function space$[\mathbf{w}, n]$ returns a high value if spacing between the nth contour point $\mathbf{w}_n$ and its neighbors is close to the average spacing between neighboring points along the contour:

$$\text{space}[\mathbf{w}, n] = \qquad (17.5)$$

$$-\left(\frac{\sum_{n=1}^{N} \sqrt{(\mathbf{w}_n - \mathbf{w}_{n-1})^T (\mathbf{w}_n - \mathbf{w}_{n-1})}}{N} - \sqrt{(\mathbf{w}_n - \mathbf{w}_{n-1})^T (\mathbf{w}_n - \mathbf{w}_{n-1})}\right)^2,$$

where we assume that the contour is closed so that $\mathbf{w}_0 = \mathbf{w}_N$.

The second term in the prior, curve$, [\mathbf{w}, n]$ returns larger values when the curvature is small and so encourages the contour to be smooth. It is defined as

$$\text{curve}[\mathbf{w}, n] = -(\mathbf{w}_{n-1} - 2\mathbf{w}_n + \mathbf{w}_{n+1})^T (\mathbf{w}_{n-1} - 2\mathbf{w}_n + \mathbf{w}_{n+1}), \qquad (17.6)$$

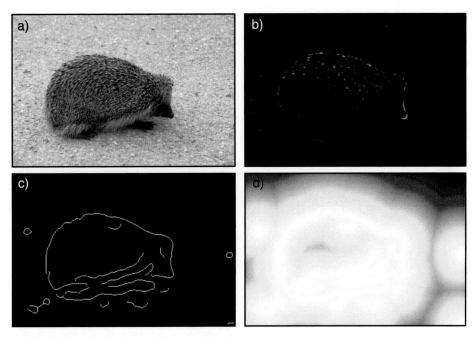

Figure 17.3 Likelihood for landmark points. a) Original image. b) Output of Sobel edge opera-tor – one possible scheme is to assign the landmark points a high likelihood if the Sobel response is strong at their position. This encourages the landmark points to lie on boundaries, in the image but the response is flat in regions away from the boundaries and this makes it difficult to apply gradient methods to fit the model c) Results of applying Canny edge detector. d) Negative distance from nearest Canny edge. This function is also high at boundaries in the image but varies smoothly in regions away from the boundaries.

where again we assume that the contour is closed so $\mathbf{w}_0 = \mathbf{w}_N$ and $\mathbf{w}_{N+1} = \mathbf{w}_1$.

There are only two parameters in this model (the weighting terms, α and β). These can be learned from training examples, but for simplicity, we will assume that they were set by hand so there is no need for an explicit learning procedure.

17.2.1 Inference

In inference, we observe a new image $\mathbf{x}$ and try to fit the points $\{\mathbf{w}_i\}$ on the contour so that they describe the image as well as possible. To this end, we use a maximum a posteriori criterion

$$\hat{\mathbf{W}} = \underset{\mathbf{W}}{\operatorname{argmax}}\left[Pr(\mathbf{W}|\mathbf{x})\right] = \underset{\mathbf{W}}{\operatorname{argmax}}\left[Pr(\mathbf{x}|\mathbf{W})Pr(\mathbf{W})\right]$$
$$= \underset{\mathbf{W}}{\operatorname{argmax}}\left[\log[Pr(\mathbf{x}|\mathbf{W})] + \log[Pr(\mathbf{W})]\right]. \quad (17.7)$$

The optimum of this objective function cannot be found in closed form, and we must apply a general nonlinear optimization procedure such as the Newton method (Appendix B). The number of unknowns is twice the number of the landmark points as each point has an x and y coordinate.

An example of this fitting procedure is illustrated in Figure 17.4. As the minimization proceeds, the contour crawls around the image, seeking the set of landmark points with

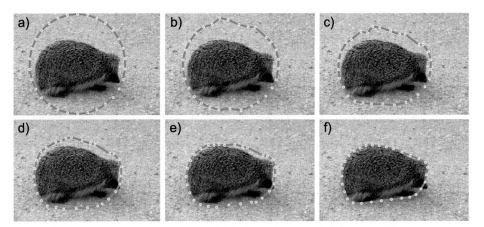

Figure 17.4 Snakes. The snake is defined by a series of connected landmark points. a–f) As the optimization proceeds and the posterior probability of these points increases, the snake contour crawls across the image. The objective function is chosen so that the landmark points are attracted to edges in the image, but also try to remain equidistant from one another and form a shape with low curvature.

highest posterior probability. For this reason, this type of contour model is sometimes known as a *snake* or *active contour model*.

The final contour in Figure 17.4 fits snugly around the outer boundary of the hedgehog. However, it has not correctly delineated the nose region; this is an area of high curvature and the scale of the nose is smaller than the distance between adjacent landmark points. The model can be improved by using a likelihood that depends on the image at positions along the contour between the landmark points. In this way, we can develop a model that has few unknowns but that depends on the image in a dense way.

A second problem with this model is that the optimization procedure can get stuck in local optima. One possibility is to restart the optimization from a number of different initial conditions, and choose the final solution with the highest probability. Alternatively, it is possible to modify the prior to make inference more tractable. For example, the spacing term can be redefined as

$$\text{space}[\mathbf{w}, n] = -\left(\mu_s - \sqrt{(\mathbf{w}_n - \mathbf{w}_{n-1})^T(\mathbf{w}_n - \mathbf{w}_{n-1})}\right)^2, \qquad (17.8)$$

which encourages the spacing of the points to be close to a predefined value μ_s and hence encourages solutions at a certain scale. This small change makes inference in the model much easier: the prior is now a 1D Markov random field, with cliques that consist of each element and its two neighbors (due to the term in the curve[$\bullet, \bullet$]). The problem can now be discretized and solved efficiently using dynamic programming methods (see Section 11.8.4).

17.2.2 Problems with the snake model

The simple snake model described previously has a number of limitations; it embodies only weak information about the smoothness of the object boundary and as such:

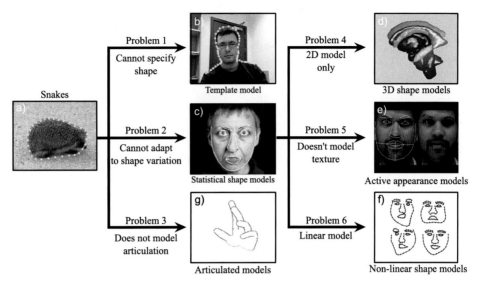

Figure 17.5 Shape models. a) The snake model only assumes that the contour is smooth. b) The template model assumes a priori knowledge of the object shape. c) Active shape models are a compromise in which some information about the object class is known, but the model can adapt to the particular image. d–f) We consider three extensions to the active shape models describe 3D shape, simultaneously model intensity variation, and describe more complex shape variation, respectively. g) Finally, we investigate models in which a priori information about the structure of an articulated object is provided.

- It is not useful where we know the object shape but not its position within the image.
- It is not useful where we know the class of the object (e.g., a face) but not the particular instance (e.g., whose face).
- The snake model is 2D and does not understand that some contours are created by projecting a 3D surface through the camera model.
- It cannot model articulated objects such as the human body.

We remedy these various problems in the subsequent parts of this chapter (Figure 17.5). In Section 17.3, we investigate a model in which we know exactly the shape we are looking for, and the only problem is to find its position in the image. In Sections 17.4–17.8, we investigate models that describe the statistical variation in a class of objects and can find unseen examples of the same class. Finally, in Section 17.9 we discuss articulated models.

17.3 Shape templates

We will now consider *shape template* models. These impose the strongest possible form of geometric information; it is assumed that we know the shape exactly. So, whereas the snake model started with a circular configuration and adapted this to fit the image, the template model starts with the correct shape of the object and merely tries to identify its position, scale, and orientation in the image. More generally, the problem is to determine the parameters $\mathbf{\Psi}$ of the transformation that maps this shape onto the current image.

We will now develop a generative model that determines the likelihood of the observed image data as a function of these transformation parameters. The underlying representation of the shape is again a set $\mathbf{W} = \{\mathbf{w}_n\}_{n=1}^N$ of 2D landmark points, which are now assumed known. However, to explain the observed data, the points must be mapped into the image by a 2D transformation $\mathbf{trans}[\mathbf{w}, \mathbf{\Psi}]$, where $\mathbf{\Psi}$ contains the parameters of the transformation model. For example, with a similarity transformation, $\mathbf{\Psi}$ would consist of the rotation angle, scaling factor, and 2D translation vector.

As with the snake model, we choose the likelihood of image data $\mathbf{x}$ to be dependent on the negative distance from the closest edge in the image

$$Pr(\mathbf{x}|\mathbf{W}, \mathbf{\Psi}) \propto \prod_{n=1}^N \exp\left[-\left(\text{dist}\left[\mathbf{x}, \mathbf{trans}\left[\mathbf{w}_n, \mathbf{\Psi}\right]\right]\right)^2\right], \qquad (17.9)$$

where the function $\text{dist}[\mathbf{x}, \mathbf{w}]$ returns the distance transform of the image $\mathbf{x}$ at position $\mathbf{w}$. Again the likelihood is larger when the landmark points all fall in regions where the distance transform is low (i.e., close to edges in the image).

17.3.1 Inference

The only unknown variables in the template model are the transformation parameters $\mathbf{\Psi}$. For simplicity, we will assume that we have no prior knowledge of these parameters and adopt the maximum likelihood approach in which we maximize the log-likelihood L:

$$\hat{\mathbf{\Psi}} = \underset{\mathbf{\Psi}}{\text{argmax}}[L] = \underset{\mathbf{\Psi}}{\text{argmax}}\left[\log\left[Pr(\mathbf{x}|\mathbf{W}, \mathbf{\Psi})\right]\right]$$

$$= \underset{\mathbf{\Psi}}{\text{argmax}}\left[\sum_{n=1}^N -\left(\text{dist}\left[\mathbf{x}, \mathbf{trans}[\mathbf{w}_n, \mathbf{\Psi}]\right]\right)^2\right]. \qquad (17.10)$$

There is no closed form solution to this problem, so we must rely on nonlinear optimization. To this end, we must take the derivative of the objective function with respect to the unknowns, and for this we employ the chain rule:

$$\frac{\partial L}{\partial \mathbf{\Psi}} = -\sum_{n=1}^N \sum_{j=1}^2 \frac{\partial(\text{dist}[\mathbf{x}, \mathbf{w}_n'])^2}{\partial w_{jn}'} \frac{\partial w_{jn}'}{\partial \mathbf{\Psi}}, \qquad (17.11)$$

where $\mathbf{w}_n' = \mathbf{trans}[\mathbf{w}_n, \mathbf{\Psi}]$ is the transformed point, and w_{jn}' is the jth entry in this 2D vector.

The first term on the right-hand side of Equation 17.11 is easy to compute. The derivative of the distance image can be approximated in each direction by evaluating horizontal or vertical derivative filters (Section 13.1.3) at the current position $\mathbf{w}_n'$. In general this will not exactly fall on the center of a pixel and so the derivative values should be interpolated from nearby pixels. The second term depends on the transformation in question.

Figure 17.6 illustrates the fitting procedure for a template model based on an affine transform. As the optimization proceeds, the contour crawls over the image as it tries to

Figure 17.6 Shape templates. Here the shape of the object is known and only the affine transformation relating the shape to the image is unknown. a) Original image. b) Results of applying Canny edge detector. c) Distance transformed image. The intensity represents the distance to the nearest edge. d) Fitting a shape template. The template is initialized with a randomly chosen affine transformation (blue curve). After optimization (green curve) the landmark points, which define the curve, have moved toward positions with lower values in the distance image. In this case, the fitting procedure has converged to a local optimum, and the correct silhouette has not been identified. e) When we start the optimization from nearer the true optimum, it converges to the global maximum. f) Final fit of template.

find a more optimal position. Unfortunately, there is no guarantee that the optimization will converge to the true position. As for the snake model, one way to deal with this problem is to restart the optimization from many different places and choose the solution with the overall maximum log likelihood. Alternatively, we could initialize the template position more intelligently; in this example the initial position might be based on the output of a face detector. It is also possible to restrict the possible solutions by imposing prior knowledge about the possible transformation parameters and using a maximum a posteriori formulation.

17.3.2 Inference with iterative closest point algorithm

In Chapter 15 we saw that the transformation mapping one set of points to another can be computed in closed form for several common families of transformations. However, the template model cannot be fit in closed form because we do not know which edge points in the image correspond to each landmark point in the model.

This suggests a different approach to inference for this model. The *iterative closest point (ICP)* algorithm alternately matches points in the image to the landmark points and computes the best transformation. More precisely:

- Each landmark point $\mathbf{w}_n$ is transformed into the image as $\mathbf{w}'_n = \mathbf{trans}[\mathbf{w}_n, \boldsymbol{\Psi}]$ using the current parameters $\boldsymbol{\Psi}$.
- Each transformed point $\mathbf{w}'_n$ is associated with the *closest* image point $\mathbf{y}_n$ that lies on an edge.

Figure 17.7 Iterative closest point algorithm. We associate each landmark point (positions where the red normals join the blue contour) with a single edge point in the image. In this example, we search along the normal direction to the contour (red lines). There are usually several points identified by an edge detector along each normal (circles). In each case we choose the closest – a process known as data association. We compute the transformation that best maps the landmark points to these closest edge positions. This moves the contour and potentially changes the closest points in the next iteration.

- The transformation parameters $\boldsymbol{\Psi}$ that best map the landmark points $\{\mathbf{w}_n\}_{n=1}^N$ to the image points $\{\mathbf{y}_n\}_{n=1}^N$ are computed in closed form.

This procedure is repeated until convergence. As the optimization proceeds, the choice of closest points changes – a process known as *data association* – and so the computed transformation parameters also evolve.

A variation of this approach considers matching the landmark points to edges in a direction that is perpendicular to the contour (Figure 17.7). This means that the search for the nearest edge point is now only in 1D, and this can also make the fitting more robust in some circumstances. This is most practical for smooth contour models where the normals can be computed in closed form.

17.4 Statistical shape models

The template model is useful when we know exactly what the object is. Conversely, the snake model is useful when we have very little prior information about the object. In this section we describe a model that lies in between these two extremes. *Statistical shape models*, *active shape models*, or *point distribution models* describe the variation within a class of objects, and so can adapt to an individual shape from that class even if they have not seen this specific example before.

As with the template and snake models, the shape is described in terms of the positions of the N landmark points $\{\mathbf{w}_n\}_{n=1}^N$, and the likelihood of these points depends on their proximity to edges in the image. For example, we might choose the likelihood of the ith training image data $\mathbf{x}_i$ to be

$$Pr(\mathbf{x}_i|\mathbf{w}_i) \propto \prod_{n=1}^N \exp\left[-(\text{dist}\,[\mathbf{x}_i, \mathbf{trans}[\mathbf{w}_{in}, \boldsymbol{\Psi}_i]])^2\right], \qquad (17.12)$$

where $\mathbf{w}_{in}$ is the nth landmark point in the ith training image and dist$[\bullet, \bullet]$ is a function that computes the distance to the nearest Canny edge in the image.

However, we now define a more sophisticated prior model over the landmark positions, which are characterized as a compound vector $\mathbf{w}_i = [\mathbf{w}_{i1}^T, \mathbf{w}_{i2}^T \ldots, \mathbf{w}_{iN}^T]^T$ containing all of the x- and y-positions of the landmark points in the ith image. In particular, we model the density $Pr(\mathbf{w}_i)$ as a normal distribution so that

$$Pr(\mathbf{w}_i) = \text{Norm}_{\mathbf{w}_i}[\boldsymbol{\mu}, \boldsymbol{\Sigma}], \tag{17.13}$$

where the mean $\boldsymbol{\mu}$ captures the average shape and the covariance $\boldsymbol{\Sigma}$ captures how different instances vary around this mean.

17.4.1 Learning

In learning, our goal is to estimate the parameters $\boldsymbol{\theta} = \{\boldsymbol{\mu}, \boldsymbol{\Sigma}\}$ based on training data. Each training example consists of a set of landmark points that have been hand-annotated on one of the training images.

Unfortunately, the training examples are not usually geometrically aligned when we receive them. In other words, we receive the transformed data examples $\mathbf{w}_i' = [\mathbf{w}_{i1}'^T, \mathbf{w}_{i2}'^T, \ldots, \mathbf{w}_{iN}'^T]^T$, where

$$\mathbf{w}_{in}' = \mathbf{trans}[\mathbf{w}_{in}, \boldsymbol{\Psi}_i]. \tag{17.14}$$

Before we can learn the parameters $\boldsymbol{\mu}$ and $\boldsymbol{\Sigma}$ of the normal, we must align the examples using the inverse of this transformation

$$\mathbf{w}_{in} = \mathbf{trans}[\mathbf{w}_{in}', \boldsymbol{\Psi}_i^-], \tag{17.15}$$

where $\{\boldsymbol{\Psi}_i^-\}_{i=1}^I$ are the parameters of the inverse transformations.

Alignment of training examples

⚙ 17.1 The method for aligning the training examples is known as *generalized Procrustes analysis* (Figure 17.8) and exploits the "chicken and egg" structure of the underlying problem; if we knew the mean shape $\boldsymbol{\mu}$, then it would be easy to estimate the parameters $\{\boldsymbol{\Psi}_i^-\}_{i=1}^I$ of the transformations that best map the observed points to this mean. Similarly, if we knew these transformations, we could easily compute the mean shape by transforming the observed points and taking the mean of the resulting shapes. Generalized Procrustes analysis takes an alternating approach to this problem in which we repeatedly

1. Update the transformations using the criterion

$$\hat{\boldsymbol{\Psi}}_i^- = \underset{\boldsymbol{\Psi}_i^-}{\text{argmin}} \left[\sum_{n=1}^N \left| \mathbf{trans}[\mathbf{w}_{in}', \boldsymbol{\Psi}_i^-] - \boldsymbol{\mu}_n \right|^2 \right], \tag{17.16}$$

   where $\boldsymbol{\mu} = [\boldsymbol{\mu}_1^T, \boldsymbol{\mu}_2^T, \ldots, \boldsymbol{\mu}_N^T]^T$. This can be achieved in closed form for common transformation families such as the Euclidean, similarity, or affine transformations (see Section 15.2).
2. Update the mean template

$$\hat{\boldsymbol{\mu}} = \underset{\boldsymbol{\mu}}{\text{argmin}} \left[\sum_{n=1}^N \left| \mathbf{trans}[\mathbf{w}_{in}', \boldsymbol{\Psi}_i^-] - \boldsymbol{\mu}_n \right|^2 \right]. \tag{17.17}$$

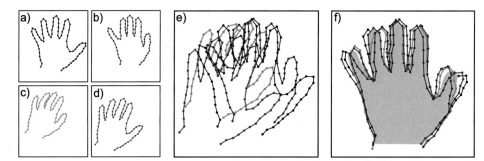

Figure 17.8 Generalized Procrustes analysis. a–d) Four training shapes. e) Superimposing the training shapes shows that they are not aligned well. f) The goal of generalized Procrustes analysis is simultaneously to align all of the training shapes with respect to a chosen transformation family. Here, the images are aligned with respect to a similarity transformation (gray region illustrates mean shape). After this procedure, the remaining variation is described by a statistical shape model.

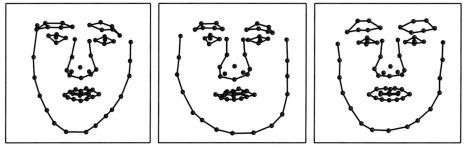

Figure 17.9 Statistical model of face shape. Three samples drawn from normally distributed model of landmark vectors $\mathbf{w}$. Each generated 136-dimensional vector was reshaped to create a 68×2 matrix containing 68 (x,y) points, which are plotted in the figure. The samples look like plausible examples of face shapes.

In practice, to optimize this criterion we inversely transform each set of points using Equation 17.15 and take the average of the resulting shape vectors. It is important to normalize the mean vector $\boldsymbol{\mu}$ after this stage to define the absolute scale uniquely.

Typically, we would initialize the mean vector $\boldsymbol{\mu}$ to be one of the training examples and iterate between these steps until there was no further improvement.

After convergence, we can fit the statistical model

$$Pr(\mathbf{w}_i) = \text{Norm}_{\mathbf{w}_i}[\boldsymbol{\mu}, \boldsymbol{\Sigma}]. \tag{17.18}$$

We already know the mean $\boldsymbol{\mu}$. We can compute the covariance $\boldsymbol{\Sigma}$ using the maximum likelihood approach from the aligned shapes $\{\mathbf{w}_i\}_{i=1}^{I}$. Figure 17.9 visualizes a shape model for the human face that was learned using this technique.

17.4.2   Inference

In inference, we fit the model to a new image. The simplest way to do this is to take a brute force optimization approach in which we estimate the unknown landmark points $\mathbf{w} = \{\mathbf{w}_n\}_{n=1}^N$ and the parameters $\boldsymbol{\Psi}$ of the transformation model so that

$$\hat{\mathbf{w}} = \underset{\mathbf{w}}{\operatorname{argmax}} \left[\max_{\boldsymbol{\Psi}} \left[\sum_{n=1}^N -(\operatorname{dist}[\mathbf{x}_i, \mathbf{trans}[\mathbf{w}_n, \boldsymbol{\Psi}]])^2 + \log[\operatorname{Norm}_{\mathbf{w}}[\boldsymbol{\mu}, \boldsymbol{\Sigma}]] \right] \right]. \quad (17.19)$$

One way to optimize this objective function is to alternate between estimating the transformation parameters and the landmark points. For fixed landmark points $\{\mathbf{w}_n\}_{n=1}^N$, we are effectively fitting a shape template model, and we can use the methods of Sections 17.3.1 and 17.3.2 to find the transformation parameters $\boldsymbol{\Psi}$. For fixed transformation parameters, it is possible to estimate the landmark points by nonlinear optimization of the objective function.

As with the template model, the statistical shape model "crawls" across the image as the optimization discovers improved ways to make the model agree with the image. However, unlike the template model, it can adapt its shape to match the idiosyncrasies of the particular object in this image as in Figure 17.1.

Unfortunately this statistical shape model has some practical disadvantages due to the number of variables involved. In the fitting procedure, we must optimize over the landmark points, themselves. If there are N landmark points, then there are $2N$ variables over which to optimize. For the face model in Figure 15.9, there would be 136 variables, and the resulting optimization is quite costly. Moreover, we will require a large number of training examples to accurately estimate the covariance $\boldsymbol{\Sigma}$ of these variables.

Furthermore, it is not clear that all these parameters are needed; the classes of object that are suited to this normally distributed model (hands, faces, spines, etc.) are quite constrained in their shape variation and so many of the parameters of this full model are merely describing noise in the training shape annotation. In the next section we describe a related model which uses fewer unknown variables (and can be fit more efficiently) and fewer parameters (and so can be learned from less data).

17.5   Subspace shape models

The subspace shape model exploits the structure inherent in the covariance of the landmark points. In particular, it assumes that the shape vectors $\{\mathbf{w}_i\}_{i=1}^I$ all lie very close to a K-dimensional linear subspace (see Figure 7.19) and describes the shape vectors as resulting from the process:

$$\mathbf{w}_i = \boldsymbol{\mu} + \boldsymbol{\Phi}\mathbf{h}_i + \boldsymbol{\epsilon}_i, \quad (17.20)$$

where $\boldsymbol{\mu}$ is the mean shape, $\boldsymbol{\Phi} = [\boldsymbol{\phi}_1, \boldsymbol{\phi}_2, \ldots, \boldsymbol{\phi}_K]$ is a portrait matrix containing K basis functions $\{\boldsymbol{\phi}_k\}_{k=1}^K$ that define the subspace in its columns, and $\boldsymbol{\epsilon}_i$ is an additive normal noise term with spherical covariance $\sigma^2\mathbf{I}$. The term $\mathbf{h}_i$ is a $K \times 1$ hidden variable where each element is responsible for weighting one of the basis functions. This can be seen more clearly by rewriting Equation 17.20 as

$$\mathbf{w}_i = \boldsymbol{\mu} + \sum_{k=1}^K \boldsymbol{\phi}_k h_{ik} + \boldsymbol{\epsilon}_i, \quad (17.21)$$

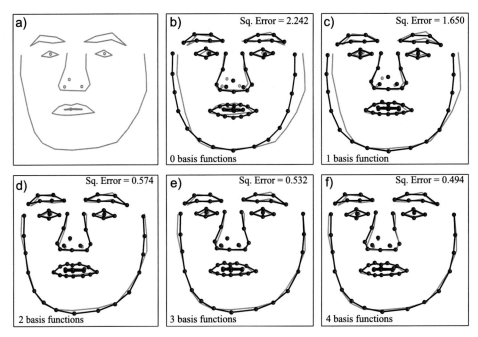

Figure 17.10 Approximation of face by weighting basis functions. a) Original face. b) Approximating original (gray) by mean face $\boldsymbol{\mu}$. c) Approximating original by mean face plus optimal weighting h_{i1} of basis function $\boldsymbol{\phi}_1$. d–f) Adding further weighted basis functions. As more terms are added, the approximation becomes closer to the original. With only four basis functions, the model can explain 78 percent of the variation of the original face around the mean.

where h_{ik} is the kth element of the vector $\mathbf{h}_i$.

The principle of the subspace model is to approximate the shape vector by the deterministic part of this process so that

$$\mathbf{w}_i \approx \boldsymbol{\mu} + \sum_{k=1}^{K} \boldsymbol{\phi}_k h_{ik}, \tag{17.22}$$

and so now we can represent the $2N \times 1$ vector $\mathbf{w}_i$ using only the $K \times 1$ vector $\mathbf{h}_i$.

For constrained data sets such as the spine, hand, and face models, it is remarkable how good this approximation can be, even when K is set to quite a small number. For example, in Figure 17.10 the face is very well approximated by taking a weighted sum of only $K = 4$ basis functions. We will exploit this phenomenon when we fit the shape model; we now optimize over the weights of the basis functions rather than the landmark points themselves, and this results in considerable computational savings.

Of course, the approximation in Figure 17.10 only works because (i) we have selected a set of basis functions $\boldsymbol{\Phi}$ that are suitable for representing faces and (ii) we have chosen the weights $\mathbf{h}_i$ appropriately to describe this face. We will now take a closer look at the model and how to find these quantities.

17.5.1 Probabilistic principal component analysis

The particular subspace model that we will apply here is known as *probabilistic principal component analysis* or PPCA for short. To define the model, we reexpress Equation 17.20 in probabilistic terms:

$$Pr(\mathbf{w}_i|\mathbf{h}_i, \boldsymbol{\mu}, \boldsymbol{\Phi}, \sigma^2) = \text{Norm}_{\mathbf{w}_i}[\boldsymbol{\mu} + \boldsymbol{\Phi}\mathbf{h}_i, \sigma^2\mathbf{I}], \tag{17.23}$$

where $\boldsymbol{\mu}$ is a $2N \times 1$ mean vector, $\boldsymbol{\Phi}$ is a $2N \times K$ matrix containing K basis functions in its columns, and σ^2 controls the degree of additive noise. In the context of this model, the basis functions are known as *principal components*. The $K \times 1$ hidden variable $\mathbf{h}_i$ weights the basis functions and determines the final positions on the subspace, before the additive noise component is added.

To complete the model, we also define a prior over the hidden variable $\mathbf{h}_i$, and we choose a spherical normal distribution for this:

$$Pr(\mathbf{h}_i) = \text{Norm}_{\mathbf{h}_i}[\mathbf{0}, \mathbf{I}]. \tag{17.24}$$

By marginalizing the joint distribution $Pr(\mathbf{w}_i, \mathbf{h}_i)$ with respect to the hidden variable $\mathbf{h}_i$, we can retrieve the prior density $Pr(\mathbf{w}_i)$, and this is given by

$$
\begin{aligned}
Pr(\mathbf{w}_i) &= \int Pr(\mathbf{w}_i|\mathbf{h}_i)Pr(\mathbf{h}_i)d\mathbf{h}_i \\
&= \int \text{Norm}_{\mathbf{w}_i}[\boldsymbol{\mu} + \boldsymbol{\Phi}\mathbf{h}_i, \sigma^2\mathbf{I}]\text{Norm}_{\mathbf{h}_i}[\mathbf{0}, \mathbf{I}]d\mathbf{h}_i \\
&= \text{Norm}_{\mathbf{w}_i}[\boldsymbol{\mu}, \boldsymbol{\Phi}\boldsymbol{\Phi}^T + \sigma^2\mathbf{I}].
\end{aligned}
\tag{17.25}
$$

This algebraic result is not obvious; however, it has a simple interpretation. The prior over the landmark points $\mathbf{w}_i$ is once more normally distributed, but now the covariance is divided into two parts: the term $\boldsymbol{\Phi}\boldsymbol{\Phi}^T$, which explains the variation in the subspace (due to shape changes), and the term $\sigma^2\mathbf{I}$, which explains any remaining variation in the data (mainly noise in the training points).

17.5.2 Learning

The PPCA model is very closely related to factor analysis (Section 7.6). The only difference is that the noise term $\sigma^2\mathbf{I}$ is spherical in the PPCA model, but has the diagonal form in factor analysis. Surprisingly, this difference has important implications; it is possible to learn the PPCA model in closed form whereas the factor analysis model needs an iterative strategy such as the EM algorithm.

In learning we are given a set of aligned training data $\{\mathbf{w}_i\}_{i=1}^I$ where $\mathbf{w}_i = [\mathbf{w}_{i1}^T, \mathbf{w}_{i2}^T \ldots, \mathbf{w}_{iN}^T]^T$ is a vector containing all of the x and y positions of the landmark points in the ith example. We wish to estimate the parameters $\boldsymbol{\mu}, \boldsymbol{\Phi}$, and σ^2 of the PPCA model.

To this end, we first set the mean parameter $\boldsymbol{\mu}$ to be the mean of the training examples $\mathbf{w}_i$:

$$\boldsymbol{\mu} = \frac{\sum_{i=1}^I \mathbf{w}_i}{I}. \tag{17.26}$$

We then form a matrix $\mathbf{W} = [\mathbf{w}_1 - \boldsymbol{\mu}, \mathbf{w}_2 - \boldsymbol{\mu}, \ldots, \mathbf{w}_I - \boldsymbol{\mu}]$ containing the zero-centered data and compute the singular value decomposition of $\mathbf{W}\mathbf{W}^T$

$$\mathbf{W}\mathbf{W}^T = \mathbf{U}\mathbf{L}^2\mathbf{U}^T, \tag{17.27}$$

where $\mathbf{U}$ is an orthogonal matrix and $\mathbf{L}^2$ is diagonal. For a model that explains D dimensional data with K principal components, we compute the parameters using

$$\hat{\sigma}^2 = \frac{1}{D-K} \sum_{j=K+1}^{D} L_{jj}^2$$

$$\hat{\boldsymbol{\Phi}} = \mathbf{U}_K (\mathbf{L}_K^2 - \hat{\sigma}^2 \mathbf{I})^{1/2}, \tag{17.28}$$

where $\mathbf{U}_K$ denotes a truncation of $\mathbf{U}$ where we have retained only the first K columns, $\mathbf{L}_K^2$ represents a truncation of $\mathbf{L}^2$ to retain only the first K columns and K rows, and L_{jj} is the jth element from the diagonal of $\mathbf{L}$.

If the dimensionality D of the data is very high, then the eigenvalue decomposition of the $D \times D$ matrix $\mathbf{W}\mathbf{W}^T$ will be computationally expensive. If the number of training examples I is less than the dimensionality D, then a more efficient approach is to compute the singular value decomposition of the $I \times I$ scatter matrix $\mathbf{W}^T\mathbf{W}$

$$\mathbf{W}^T\mathbf{W} = \mathbf{V}\mathbf{L}^2\mathbf{V}^T \tag{17.29}$$

and then rearrange the SVD relation $\mathbf{W} = \mathbf{U}\mathbf{L}\mathbf{V}^T$ to compute $\mathbf{U}$.

There are two things to notice about the estimated basis functions $\boldsymbol{\Phi}$:

1. The basis functions (principal components) in the columns of $\boldsymbol{\Phi}$ are all orthogonal to one another. This can be easily seen because the solution for $\boldsymbol{\Phi}$ (Equation 17.28) is the product of the truncated orthogonal matrix $\mathbf{U}_K$ and the diagonal matrix $(\mathbf{L}_K^2 - \hat{\sigma}^2\mathbf{I})^{1/2}$.
2. The basis functions are ordered: the first column of $\boldsymbol{\Phi}$ represents the direction in the space of $\mathbf{w}$ that contained the most variance, and each subsequent direction explains less variation. This is a consequence of the SVD algorithm, which orders the elements of $\mathbf{L}^2$ so that they decrease.

We could visualize the PPCA model by drawing samples from the marginal density (Equation 17.25). However, the properties of the basis functions permit a more systematic way to examine the model. In Figure 17.11 we visualize the PPCA model by manipulating the hidden variable $\mathbf{h}_i$ and then illustrating the vector $\boldsymbol{\mu} + \boldsymbol{\Phi}\mathbf{h}_i$. We can choose $\mathbf{h}_i$ to elucidate each basis function $\{\phi_k\}_{k=1}^K$ in turn. For example, by setting $\mathbf{h}_i = \pm[1, 0, 0, 0, ..., 0]$ we investigate the first basis function.

Figure 17.11 shows that the principal components ϕ_k sometimes have surprisingly clear interpretations. For example, the first principal component clearly encodes the opening and closing of the fingers. A second example that visualizes the spine model from Figure 17.1 is illustrated in Figure 17.12.

17.5.3 Inference

In inference, we fit the shape to a new image by manipulating the weights $\mathbf{h}$ of the basis functions $\boldsymbol{\Phi}$. A suitable objective function is

$$\hat{\mathbf{h}} = \underset{\mathbf{h}}{\operatorname{argmax}} \left[\underset{\boldsymbol{\Psi}}{\max} \left[\sum_{n=1}^{N} \left(-\frac{(\text{dist}\,[\mathbf{x}_i, \mathbf{trans}[\boldsymbol{\mu}_n + \boldsymbol{\Phi}_n\mathbf{h}, \boldsymbol{\Psi}]])^2}{\sigma^2} \right) + \log[\text{Norm}_{\mathbf{h}}\,[\mathbf{0}, \mathbf{I}]] \right] \right], \tag{17.30}$$

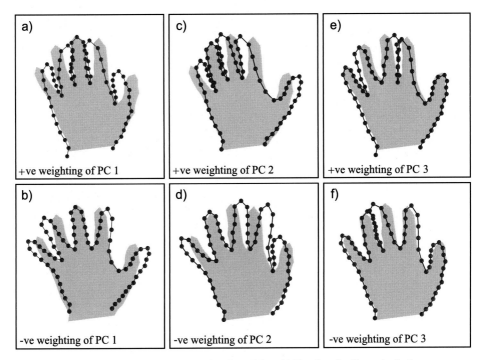

Figure 17.11 Principal components for hand model. a–b) Varying the first principal component. In panel (a) we have added a multiple λ of the first principal component ϕ_1 to the mean vector μ. In panel (b) we have subtracted the same multiple of the first principal component from the mean. In each case the shaded area indicates the mean vector. The first principal component has a clear interpretation: it controls the opening and closing of the fingers. Panels (c–d) and (e–f) show similar manipulations of the second and third principal components, respectively.

where μ_n contains the two elements of μ that pertain to the nth point and Φ_n contains the two rows of Φ that pertain to the nth point. There are a number of ways to optimize this model, including a straightforward nonlinear optimization over the unknowns $\mathbf{h}$ and Ψ. We will briefly describe an iterative closest point approach. This consists of iteratively repeating these steps:

- The current landmark points are computed as $\mathbf{w} = \mu + \Phi\mathbf{h}$.
- Each landmark point is transformed into the image as $\mathbf{w}'_n = \mathbf{trans}[\mathbf{w}_n, \Psi]$.
- Each transformed point $\mathbf{w}'_n$ is associated with the *closest* edge point $\mathbf{y}_n$ in the image.
- The transformation parameters Ψ that best map the original landmark points $\{\mathbf{w}_n\}_{n=1}^N$ to the edge points $\{\mathbf{y}_n\}_{n=1}^N$ are computed.
- Each point is transformed again using the updated parameters Ψ.
- The *closest* edge points $\{\mathbf{y}_n\}_{n=1}^N$ are found once more.
- The hidden variables $\mathbf{h}$ are updated (see below).

We repeat these steps until convergence. After optimization, the landmark points can be recovered as $\mathbf{w} = \mu + \Phi\mathbf{h}$.

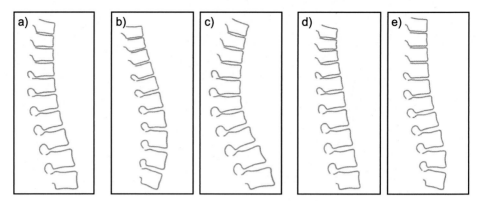

Figure 17.12 Learned spine model. a) Mean spine shape. b–c) Manipulating first principal component. d–e) Manipulating second principal component. Figure provided by Tim Cootes.

In the last step of the iterative algorithm we must update the hidden variables. This can be achieved using the objective function:

$$\hat{\mathbf{h}} = \underset{\mathbf{h}}{\mathrm{argmax}} \left[\sum_{n=1}^{N} \log[Pr(\mathbf{y}_n|\mathbf{h}), \boldsymbol{\Psi}] + \log[Pr(\mathbf{h})] \right] \tag{17.31}$$

$$= \underset{\mathbf{h}}{\mathrm{argmax}} \left[\sum_{n=1}^{N} -(\mathbf{y}_n - \mathrm{trans}[\boldsymbol{\mu}_n + \boldsymbol{\Phi}_n \mathbf{h}, \boldsymbol{\Psi}])^2 / \sigma^2 - \log[\mathbf{h}^T \mathbf{h}] \right],$$

where $\boldsymbol{\mu}_n$ contains the two elements of $\boldsymbol{\mu}$ associated with the nth landmark point and $\boldsymbol{\Phi}_n$ contains the two rows of $\boldsymbol{\Phi}$ associated with the nth landmark point. If the transformation is linear so that $\mathrm{trans}[\mathbf{w}_n, \boldsymbol{\Psi}]$ can be written in the form $\mathbf{A}\mathbf{w}_n + \mathbf{b}$, then this update can be computed in closed form and is given by

$$\hat{\mathbf{h}} = \left(\sigma^2 \mathbf{I} + \sum_{n=1}^{N} \boldsymbol{\Phi}_n^T \mathbf{A}^T \mathbf{A} \boldsymbol{\Phi}_n \right)^{-1} \sum_{n=1}^{N} \mathbf{A} \boldsymbol{\Phi}_n (\mathbf{y}_n - \mathbf{A}\boldsymbol{\mu} - \mathbf{b}). \tag{17.32}$$

Examples of performing inference in subspace shape models are illustrated in Figures 17.1 and 17.13. As the optimization proceeds, the shape model moves across the surface of the image and adapts itself to the shape of the object. For this reason, these models are often referred to as *active shape models*.

We note that there are many variations of this model and many strategies that help fitting the model robustly. One particularly weak aspect of the model is that it assumes that each landmark point maps to a generic edge in the image; it does not even distinguish between the polarity or orientation of this edge, let alone take advantage of other nearby image information that might help identify the correct position. A more sensible approach is to build a generative model that describes the likelihood of the local image data when the nth feature $\mathbf{w}_n$ is present. A second important concept is *coarse-to-fine* fitting, in which a coarse model is fitted to a low-resolution image. The result is then used as a starting point for a more detailed model at a higher resolution. In this way, it is possible to increase the probability of converging to the true fit without getting stuck in a local minimum.

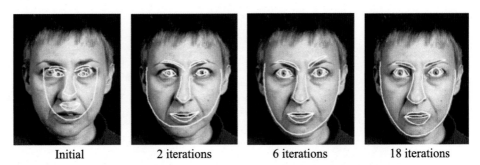

| Initial | 2 iterations | 6 iterations | 18 iterations |

Figure 17.13 Several iterations of fitting a subspace shape model to a face image. After convergence, both the global transformation of the model and the details of the shape are correct. When a statistical shape model is fit to an image in this way, it is referred to as an *active shape model*. Figure provided by Tim Cootes.

17.6   Three-dimensional shape models

The subspace shape model can be easily extended to three dimensions. For 3D data, the model works in almost exactly the same way as it did in 2D. However, the landmark points $\mathbf{w}$ become 3×1 vectors determining the position within 3D space, and the global transformation that maps these into the image must also be generalized to 3D. For example, a 3D affine transformation encompasses 3D translations, rotations, shearing, and scaling in 3D and is determined by 12 parameters.

Finally, the likelihood must also be adapted for 3D. A trivial way to do this would be to create the 3D analogue of an edge operator by taking the root mean square of three derivative filters in the coordinate directions. We then construct an expression so that the likelihood is high in regions where the 3D edge operator returns a high value. An example of a 3D shape model is shown in Figure 17.14.

17.7   Statistical models for shape and appearance

In Chapter 7 we discussed the use of subspace models to describe the pixel intensities of a class of images such as faces. However, it was concluded that these were very poor models of this high-dimensional data. In this section, we consider models that describe both the intensity of the pixels and the shape of the object simultaneously. Moreover, they describe correlations between these aspects of the image: the shape tells us something about the intensity values and vice versa (Figure 17.15). When we fit these models to new images, they deform and adapt to the shape and intensity of the image, and so they are known as *active appearance models*.

As before, we characterize the shape with a vector of N landmark points $\mathbf{w} = [\mathbf{w}_1^T, \mathbf{w}_2^T, \dots, \mathbf{w}_N^T]$. However, we now also describe a model of the pixel intensity values $\mathbf{x}$ where this vector contains the concatenated RGB data from the image. The full model can best be described as a sequence of conditional probability statements:

$$Pr(\mathbf{h}_i) = \text{Norm}_{\mathbf{h}_i}[\mathbf{0}, \mathbf{I}]$$
$$Pr(\mathbf{w}_i | \mathbf{h}_i) = \text{Norm}_{\mathbf{w}_i}[\boldsymbol{\mu}_w + \boldsymbol{\Phi}_w \mathbf{h}_i, \sigma_w^2 \mathbf{I}]$$
$$Pr(\mathbf{x}_i | \mathbf{w}_i, \mathbf{h}_i) = \text{Norm}_{\mathbf{x}_i}[\mathbf{warp}[\boldsymbol{\mu}_x + \boldsymbol{\Phi}_x \mathbf{h}_i, \mathbf{w}_i, \boldsymbol{\Psi}_i], \sigma_x^2 \mathbf{I}]. \qquad (17.33)$$

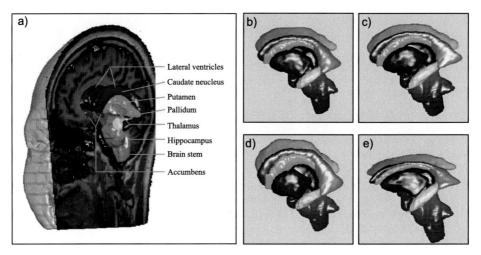

Figure 17.14 Three-dimensional statistical shape model. a) The model describes regions of the human brain. It is again defined by a set of landmark points. These are visualized by triangulating them to form a surface. b–c) Changing the weighting of the first principal component. d–e) Changing weighting of second component. Adapted from Babalola et al. (2008).

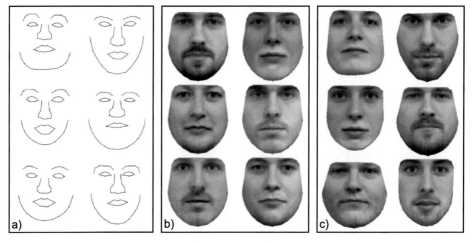

Figure 17.15 Modeling both shape and texture. We learn a model in which we a) parameterize shape using a subspace model (results of manipulating weights of shape basis functions shown) and b) parameterize intensity values for fixed shape using a different subspace model (results of manipulating weights of texture basis functions shown). c) The subspace models are connected in that the weightings of the basis functions (principal components) in each model are always the same. In this way, correlations between shape and texture are described (results of manipulating weights of basis functions for both shape and texture together shown). Adapted from Stegmann (2002).

This is quite a complex model, so we will break it down into its constituent parts. At the core of the model is a hidden variable $\mathbf{h}_i$. This can be thought of as a low-dimensional explanation that underpins both the shape and the pixel intensity values. In the first equation, we define a prior over this hidden variable.

In the second equation, the shape data $\mathbf{w}$ is created by weighting a set of basis functions $\mathbf{\Phi}_w$ by the hidden variable and adding a mean vector $\boldsymbol{\mu}_w$. The result is corrupted with spherically distributed normal noise with covariance $\sigma^2 \mathbf{I}$. This is exactly the same as for the statistical shape model.

The third equation describes how the observed pixel values $\mathbf{x}_i$ in the ith image depend on the shape $\mathbf{w}_i$, the global transformation parameters $\mathbf{\Psi}_i$ and the hidden variable $\mathbf{h}_i$. There are three stages in this process:

1. The intensity values are generated for the mean shape $\boldsymbol{\mu}_w$; pixel values are described as a weighted sum $\boldsymbol{\mu}_x + \mathbf{\Phi}_x \mathbf{h}_i$ of a second set of basis functions $\mathbf{\Phi}_x$ which is added to a mean intensity $\boldsymbol{\mu}_x$.
2. These generated intensity values are then warped to the final desired shape; the operation $\mathbf{warp}[\boldsymbol{\mu}_x + \mathbf{\Phi}_x \mathbf{h}_i, \mathbf{w}_i, \mathbf{\Psi}_i]$ warps the resulting intensity image $\boldsymbol{\mu}_x + \mathbf{\Phi}_x \mathbf{h}_i$ to the desired shape based on the landmark points $\mathbf{w}_i$ and the global transformation parameters $\mathbf{\Psi}_i$.
3. Finally, the observed data $\mathbf{x}_i$ is corrupted by normally distributed noise with spherical covariance $\sigma_x^2 \mathbf{I}$.

Notice that both the intensity values and the shape depend on the same underlying hidden variable $\mathbf{h}_i$. This means that the model can describe correlations in the shape and appearance; for example, the texture might change to include teeth when the mouth region expands. Figure 17.15 shows examples of manipulating the shape and texture components of a face model and illustrates the correlation between the two. Notice that the resulting images are much sharper than the factor analysis model for faces (Figure 7.22); by explicitly accounting for the shape component, we get a superior model of the texture.

Warping images

A simple approach to warping the images is to triangulate the landmark points and then use a piecewise affine warp; each triangle is warped from the canonical position to the desired final position using a separate affine transformation (Figure 17.16). The coordinates of the canonical triangle vertices are held in $\boldsymbol{\mu}$. The coordinates of the triangle vertices after the warp are held in $\mathbf{trans}[\boldsymbol{\mu}_w + \mathbf{\Phi}_w \mathbf{h}_i, \mathbf{\Psi}_i]$.

17.7.1 Learning

In learning we are given a set of I images in which we know the transformed landmark points $\{\mathbf{w}_i\}_{i=1}^I$ and the associated warped and transformed pixel data $\{\mathbf{x}_i\}_{i=1}^I$, and we aim to learn the parameters $\{\boldsymbol{\mu}_w, \mathbf{\Phi}_w, \sigma_w^2, \boldsymbol{\mu}_x, \mathbf{\Phi}_x, \sigma_x^2\}$. The model is too complex to learn directly; we take the approach of simplifying it by eliminating (i) the effect of the

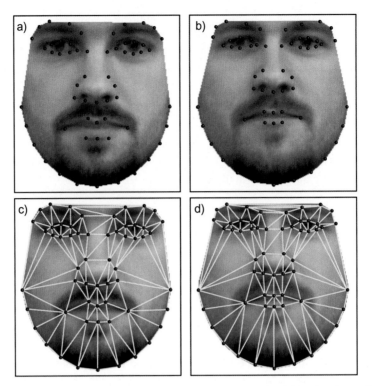

Figure 17.16 Piecewise affine warping. a) The texture is synthesized for a fixed canonical shape. b) This shape is then warped to create the final image. c) One technique for warping the image is to use a piecewise affine transformation. We first triangulate the landmark points. d) Then each triangle undergoes a separate affine transformation such that the three points that define it move to their final positions. Adapted from Stegmann (2002).

transformation on the landmark points and (ii) both the warp and the transformation on the image data. Then we estimate the parameters in this simplified model.

To eliminate the effect of the transformations $\{\boldsymbol{\Psi}_i\}_{i=1}^{I}$ on the landmark points, we perform generalized Procrustes analysis. To eliminate the effect of the transformation and warps and the observed images, we now warp each training image to the average shape $\boldsymbol{\mu}_w = \sum_{i=1}^{I} \mathbf{w}_i / I$ using piecewise affine transformations.

The result of these operations is to generate training data consisting of aligned sets of landmark points $\{\mathbf{w}_i\}_{i=1}^{I}$ representing the shape (similar to Figure 17.15a) and a set of face images $\{\mathbf{x}_i\}_{i=1}^{I}$ that all have the same shape (similar to Figure 17.15b). These data are explained using the simpler model:

$$
\begin{aligned}
Pr(\mathbf{h}_i) &= \mathrm{Norm}_{\mathbf{h}_i}[\mathbf{0}, \mathbf{I}] \\
Pr(\mathbf{w}_i|\mathbf{h}_i) &= \mathrm{Norm}_{\mathbf{w}_i}[\boldsymbol{\mu}_w + \boldsymbol{\Phi}_w \mathbf{h}_i, \sigma_w^2 \mathbf{I}] \\
Pr(\mathbf{x}_i|\mathbf{h}_i) &= \mathrm{Norm}_{\mathbf{x}_i}[\boldsymbol{\mu}_x + \boldsymbol{\Phi}_x \mathbf{h}_i, \sigma_x^2 \mathbf{I}].
\end{aligned}
\qquad (17.34)
$$

To learn the parameters, we write the last two equations in the generative form

$$
\begin{bmatrix} \mathbf{w}_i \\ \mathbf{x}_i \end{bmatrix} = \begin{bmatrix} \boldsymbol{\mu}_w \\ \boldsymbol{\mu}_x \end{bmatrix} + \begin{bmatrix} \boldsymbol{\Phi}_w \\ \boldsymbol{\Phi}_x \end{bmatrix} \mathbf{h}_i + \begin{bmatrix} \boldsymbol{\epsilon}_{wi} \\ \boldsymbol{\epsilon}_{xi} \end{bmatrix},
\tag{17.35}
$$

where $\boldsymbol{\epsilon}_{wi}$ is a normally distributed noise term with spherical covariance $\sigma_w^2 \mathbf{I}$ and $\boldsymbol{\epsilon}_{xi}$ is a normally distributed noise term with spherical covariance $\sigma_x^2 \mathbf{I}$.

We now observe that the system is very similar to the standard form of a PPCA model or factor analyzer $\mathbf{x}' = \boldsymbol{\mu}' + \boldsymbol{\Phi}' \mathbf{h} + \boldsymbol{\epsilon}'$. Unlike PPCA, the noise term is structured and contains two values (σ_w^2 and σ_x^2). However, each dimension of the data does not have a separate variance as for factor analysis.

Unfortunately, there is no closed form solution as there was for the PPCA model. This model can be learned with a modified version of the EM algorithm for factor analysis (see Section 7.6.2), where the update step for the variance terms σ^2 and σ_x^2 differs from the usual equation.

17.7.2   Inference

In inference we fit the model to new data by finding the values of the hidden variable $\mathbf{h}$, which are responsible for both the shape and appearance of the image. This low-dimensional representation of the object could then be used as an input to a second algorithm that analyzes its characteristics. For example, in a face model it might be used as the basis for discriminating gender.

Inference in this model can be simplified by assuming that the landmark points lie exactly on the subspace so that we have the deterministic relation $\mathbf{w}_i = \boldsymbol{\mu} + \boldsymbol{\Phi}\mathbf{h}$. This means that the likelihood of the observed data given the hidden variable $\mathbf{h}$ can be expressed as

$$
Pr(\mathbf{x}|\mathbf{h}) = \text{Norm}_{\mathbf{x}}[\mathbf{warp}[\boldsymbol{\mu}_x + \boldsymbol{\Phi}_x\mathbf{h}, \boldsymbol{\mu}_w + \boldsymbol{\Phi}_w\mathbf{h}, \boldsymbol{\Psi}], \sigma_x^2 \mathbf{I}].
\tag{17.36}
$$

We adopt a maximum likelihood procedure and note that this criterion is based on the normal distribution so the result is a least squares cost function:

$$
\hat{\mathbf{h}}, \hat{\boldsymbol{\Psi}} = \underset{\mathbf{h}, \boldsymbol{\Psi}}{\operatorname{argmax}} \left[\log \left[Pr(\mathbf{x}|\mathbf{h}) \right] \right]
\tag{17.37}
$$

$$
= \underset{\mathbf{h}, \boldsymbol{\Psi}}{\operatorname{argmin}} \left[\left(\mathbf{x} - \mathbf{warp}[\boldsymbol{\mu}_x + \boldsymbol{\Phi}_x\mathbf{h}, \boldsymbol{\mu}_w + \boldsymbol{\Phi}_w\mathbf{h}, \boldsymbol{\Psi}] \right)^T \right.
$$
$$
\left. \left(\mathbf{x} - \mathbf{warp}[\boldsymbol{\mu}_x + \boldsymbol{\Phi}_x\mathbf{h}, \boldsymbol{\mu}_w + \boldsymbol{\Phi}_w\mathbf{h}, \boldsymbol{\Psi}] \right) \right].
$$

Denoting the unknown quantities by $\boldsymbol{\theta} = \{\mathbf{h}, \boldsymbol{\Psi}\}$, we observe that this cost function takes the general form of $f[\boldsymbol{\theta}] = \mathbf{z}[\boldsymbol{\theta}]^T \mathbf{z}[\boldsymbol{\theta}]$ and can hence be optimized using the Gauss-Newton method (Appendix B.2.3). We initialize the unknown quantities to some sensible values and then iteratively update these values using the relation

$$
\boldsymbol{\theta}^{[t]} = \boldsymbol{\theta}^{[t-1]} + \lambda (\mathbf{J}^T \mathbf{J})^{-1} \frac{\partial f}{\partial \boldsymbol{\theta}},
\tag{17.38}
$$

where $\mathbf{J}$ is the Jacobian matrix. The entry in the mth row and n^{th} column of $\mathbf{J}$ consists of the derivative of the mth element of $\mathbf{z}$ with respect to the nth element of the parameter vector $\boldsymbol{\theta}$:

$$
J_{mn} = \frac{\partial z_m}{\partial \theta_n}.
\tag{17.39}
$$

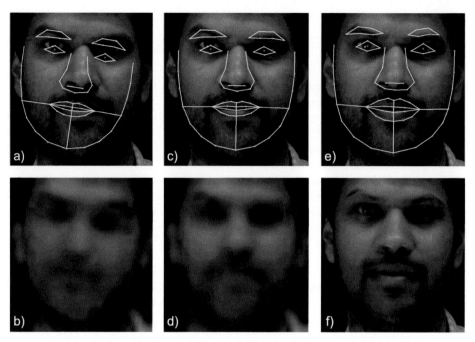

Figure 17.17 Fitting a statistical model of shape and appearance. a) Shape model at start of fitting process superimposed on the observed image. b) Shape and appearance model (synthesized image **x**) at start of fitting process. c–d) After several iterations. e–f) At the end of the fitting procedure. The synthesized face (f) looks very similar to the observed image in (a),(c), and (e). Such models are known as *active appearance models* as they can be seen to adapt to the image. Figure provided by Tim Cootes.

Figure 17.17 shows an example of a statistical shape and appearance model being fit to face data. The spine model in Figure 17.1 was also a model of this kind although only the shape component was shown. As usual, the success of this fitting procedure relies on having a good starting point for the optimization process and a course-to-fine strategy can help the optimization converge.

17.8   Non-Gaussian statistical shape models

The statistical shape model discussed in Section 17.4 is effective for objects where the shape variation is relatively constrained and is well described by the normally distributed prior. However, in some situations a normal distribution will not suffice, and we must turn to more complex models. One possibility is to use a mixture of PPCAs, and this is straightforward to implement. However, we will use this opportunity to introduce an alternative model for describing non-Gaussian densities.

The *Gaussian process latent variable model* or *GPLVM* is a density model that can model complex non-normal distributions. The GPLVM extends the PPCA model so that the hidden variables $\mathbf{h}_i$ are transformed through a fixed nonlinearity before being weighted by the basis functions $\boldsymbol{\Phi}$.

17.8.1 PPCA as regression

To help understand the GPLVM, we will reconsider subspace models in terms of regression. Consider the PPCA model, which can be expressed as

$$
\begin{aligned}
Pr(\mathbf{w}|\boldsymbol{\mu},\boldsymbol{\Phi},\sigma^2) &= \int Pr(\mathbf{w},\mathbf{h}|\boldsymbol{\mu},\boldsymbol{\Phi},\sigma^2)d\mathbf{h} \\
&= \int Pr(\mathbf{w}|\mathbf{h},\boldsymbol{\mu},\boldsymbol{\Phi},\sigma^2)Pr(\mathbf{h})d\mathbf{h} \\
&= \int \mathrm{Norm}_{\mathbf{w}}[\boldsymbol{\mu}+\boldsymbol{\Phi}\mathbf{h},\sigma^2\mathbf{I}]\mathrm{Norm}_{\mathbf{h}}[\mathbf{0},\mathbf{I}]d\mathbf{h}. \quad (17.40)
\end{aligned}
$$

The first term in the last line of this expression has a close relationship to linear regression (Section 8.1); it is a model for predicting $\mathbf{w}$ given the variable $\mathbf{h}$. Indeed if we consider just the dth element w_d of $\mathbf{w}$ then this term has the form

$$
Pr(w_d|\mathbf{h},\boldsymbol{\mu},\boldsymbol{\Phi},\sigma^2) = \mathrm{Norm}_{\mathbf{w}_d}[\mu_d+\boldsymbol{\phi}_{d\bullet}^T\mathbf{h},\sigma^2], \quad (17.41)
$$

where μ_d is the dth dimension of $\boldsymbol{\mu}$ and $\boldsymbol{\phi}_{d\bullet}^T$ is the dth row of $\boldsymbol{\Phi}$; this is exactly the linear regression model for w_d against $\mathbf{h}$.

This insight provides a new way of looking at the model. Figure 17.18 shows a 2D data set $\{w_i\}_{i=1}^I$, which is explained by a set of 1D hidden variables $\{h_i\}_{i=1}^I$. Each dimension of the 2D data $\mathbf{w}$ is created by a different regression model, but in each case we are regressing against the common set of hidden variables $\{h_i\}_{i=1}^I$. So, the first dimension w_1 of $\mathbf{w}$ is described as $\mu_1+\boldsymbol{\phi}_{1\bullet}^T h$ and the second dimension w_2 is modeled as $\mu_2+\boldsymbol{\phi}_{2\bullet}^T h$. The common underlying hidden variable induces the correlation we see in the distribution $Pr(\mathbf{w})$.

Now let us consider how the overall density is formed. For a fixed value of h, we get a prediction for w_1 and a prediction for w_2 each of which has additive normal

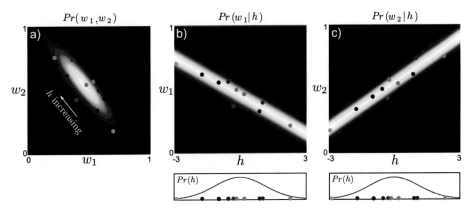

Figure 17.18 PPCA model as regression. a) We consider a 2D data set that is explained by a PPCA model with a single hidden variable. The data are explained by a 2D normal distribution with mean $\boldsymbol{\mu}$ and covariance $\boldsymbol{\phi}\boldsymbol{\phi}^T+\sigma^2\mathbf{I}$. b) One way to think of this PPCA model is that the 2D data are explained by two underlying regression models. The first data dimension $\mathbf{w}_1$ is formed from a regression against h and c) the second data dimension $\mathbf{w}_2$ is formed from a different regression against the same values h.

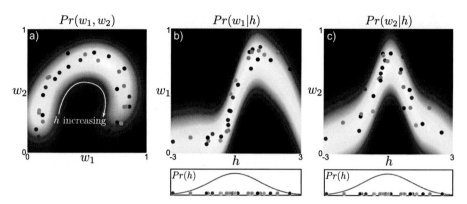

Figure 17.19 Gaussian process latent variable model as regression. a) We consider a 2D data set that is explained by a GPLVM with a single variable. b) One way to consider this model is that the 2D data are explained by two underlying regression models. The first data dimension w_1 is formed from a Gaussian process regression against the hidden variable h. c) The second data dimension w_2 is formed from a different Gaussian process regression model against the same values h.

noise with the same variance (Figures 17.18b–c). The result is a 2D spherical normal distribution in $\mathbf{w}$. To create the density, we integrate over all possible values of h, weighted by a the normal prior; the final density is hence an infinite weighted sum of the 2D spherical normal distributions predicted by each value of h, and this happens to have the form of the normal distribution with nonspherical covariance $\phi\phi^2 + \sigma^2\mathbf{I}$, which is seen in Figure 17.18a.

17.8.2 Gaussian process latent variable model

This interpretation of PPCA provides an obvious approach to describing more complex densities; we simply replace the linear regression model with a more sophisticated nonlinear regression model. As the name suggests, the Gaussian process latent variable model makes use of the Gaussian process regression model (see Section 8.5).

Figure 17.19 illustrates the GPLVM. Each dimension of the density in Figure 17.19a once again results from a regression against a common underlying variable h. However, in this model, the two regression curves are nonlinear (Figures 17.19b–c) and this accounts for the complexity of the original density.

There are two major practical changes in the GPLVM:

1. In Gaussian process regression, we marginalize over the regression parameters $\boldsymbol{\mu}$ and $\boldsymbol{\Phi}$ so we do not have to estimate these in the learning procedure.
2. Conversely, it is no longer possible to marginalize over the hidden variables $\mathbf{h}$ in closed form; we must estimate the hidden variables during the training procedure. The inability to marginalize over the hidden variables also creates some difficulties in evaluating the final density.

We will now consider learning and inference in this model in turn.

Learning

In the original Gaussian process regression model (Section 8.5), we aimed to predict the univariate world states $\mathbf{w} = [w_1, w_2, \ldots, w_I]^T$ from multivariate data $\mathbf{X} =$

$[\mathbf{x}_1, \mathbf{x}_2, \ldots, \mathbf{x}_I]$. The parameter vector ϕ was marginalized out of the model, and the noise parameter σ^2 was found by maximizing the marginal likelihood:

$$\hat{\sigma^2} = \underset{\sigma^2}{\operatorname{argmax}} \left[Pr(\mathbf{w}|\mathbf{X}, \sigma^2) \right] \tag{17.42}$$

$$= \underset{\sigma^2}{\operatorname{argmax}} \left[\int Pr(\mathbf{w}|\mathbf{X}, \mathbf{\Phi}, \sigma^2) Pr(\mathbf{\Phi}) d\mathbf{\Phi} \right]$$

$$= \underset{\sigma^2}{\operatorname{argmax}} \left[\operatorname{Norm}_{\mathbf{w}}[\mathbf{0}, \sigma_p^2 \mathbf{K}[\mathbf{X}, \mathbf{X}] + \sigma^2 \mathbf{I}] \right],$$

where σ_p^2 controls the prior variance of the parameter vector ϕ and $\mathbf{K}[\bullet, \bullet]$ is the chosen kernel function.

In the GPLVM we have a similar situation. We aim to predict multivariate world values $\mathbf{W} = [\mathbf{w}_1, \mathbf{w}_2, \ldots, \mathbf{w}_I]^T$ from multivariate hidden variables $\mathbf{H} = [\mathbf{h}_1, \mathbf{h}_2, \ldots, \mathbf{h}_I]$. Once more, we marginalize the basis functions $\mathbf{\Phi}$ out of the model and maximize over the noise parameters σ^2. However, this time, we do not know the values of the hidden variables $\mathbf{H}$ that we are regressing against; these must be simultaneously estimated, giving the objective function:

$$\hat{\mathbf{H}}, \hat{\sigma^2} = \underset{\mathbf{H}, \sigma^2}{\operatorname{argmax}} \left[Pr(\mathbf{W}, \mathbf{H}, \sigma^2) \right] \tag{17.43}$$

$$= \underset{\mathbf{H}, \sigma^2}{\operatorname{argmax}} \left[\int Pr(\mathbf{W}|\mathbf{H}, \mathbf{\Phi}, \sigma^2) Pr(\mathbf{\Phi}) Pr(\mathbf{H}) d\mathbf{\Phi} \right]$$

$$= \underset{\mathbf{H}, \sigma^2}{\operatorname{argmax}} \left[\prod_{d=1}^{D} \operatorname{Norm}_{\mathbf{w}_{d\bullet}}[\mathbf{0}, \sigma_p^2 \mathbf{K}[\mathbf{H}, \mathbf{H}] + \sigma^2 \mathbf{I}] \prod_{i=1}^{I} \operatorname{Norm}_{\mathbf{h}_i}[\mathbf{0}, \mathbf{I}] \right],$$

where there is one term in the first product for each of the D dimensions of the world and one term in the second product for each of the training examples.

Unfortunately, there is no closed form solution to this optimization problem; to learn the model we must use one of the general-purpose nonlinear optimization techniques discussed in Appendix B. Sometimes, the kernel $\mathbf{K}[\bullet, \bullet]$ also contains parameters, and these should be simultaneously optimized.

Inference

For a new value of the hidden variable $\mathbf{h}^*$ the distribution over the dth dimension of the world w_d^* is given by the analogue of Equation 8.24:

$$Pr(w_d^*|\mathbf{h}^*, \mathbf{H}, \mathbf{W}) = \tag{17.44}$$

$$\operatorname{Norm}_{w_d^*} \left[\frac{\sigma_p^2}{\sigma^2} \mathbf{K}[\mathbf{h}^*, \mathbf{H}] \mathbf{w}_{d\bullet} - \frac{\sigma_p^2}{\sigma^2} \mathbf{K}[\mathbf{h}^*, \mathbf{H}] \left(\mathbf{K}[\mathbf{H}, \mathbf{H}] + \frac{\sigma_p^2}{\sigma^2} \mathbf{I} \right)^{-1} \mathbf{K}[\mathbf{H}, \mathbf{H}] \mathbf{w}_{d\bullet}, \right.$$

$$\left. \sigma_p^2 \mathbf{K}[\mathbf{h}^*, \mathbf{h}^*] - \sigma_p^2 \mathbf{K}[\mathbf{h}^*, \mathbf{H}] \left(\mathbf{K}[\mathbf{H}, \mathbf{H}] + \frac{\sigma_p^2}{\sigma^2} \mathbf{I} \right)^{-1} \mathbf{K}[\mathbf{H}, \mathbf{h}^*] + \sigma^2 \right].$$

To sample from the model, we select the hidden variable $\mathbf{h}^*$ from the prior and then predict a probability distribution over the landmarks $\mathbf{w}^*$ using this equation.

To assess the probability of the a new sample $\mathbf{w}^*$, we should use the relation

$$Pr(\mathbf{w}) = \prod_{d=1}^{D} \int Pr(w_d^*|\mathbf{h}^*, \mathbf{H}, \mathbf{W}) Pr(\mathbf{h}^*) d\mathbf{h}^*. \tag{17.45}$$

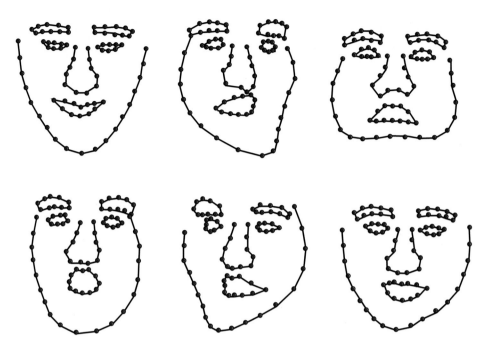

Figure 17.20 Samples from a non-Gaussian face model based on a GPLVM. The samples represent more significant distortions to the shape than could be realistically described by the original statistical shape model. Adapted from Huang et al. (2011). ©2011 IEEE.

Unfortunately, this integral cannot be computed in closed form. One possibility is to maximize over $\mathbf{h}^*$ rather than marginalize over it. Another possibility is to approximate the density $Pr(\mathbf{h}^*)$ by a set of delta functions at the positions of the training data $\{\mathbf{h}_i\}_{i=1}^{I}$ and we can then replace the integral with a sum over the individual predictions from these examples.

Application to shape models

Figure 17.20 illustrates several examples of sampling from a shape model for a face that is based on the GPLVM. This more sophisticated model can cope with modeling larger variations in the shape than the original PPCA, which was based on a single normal distribution.

17.9   Articulated models

Statistical shape models work well when the shape variation is relatively small. However, there are other situations where we have much stronger a priori knowledge about the object. For example, in a body model, we know that there are two arms and two legs and that these are connected in a certain way to the main body. An *articulated model* parameterizes the model in terms of the joint angles and the overall transformation relating one root component to the camera.

The core idea of an articulated model is that the transformations of the parts are cumulative; the position of the foot depends on the position of the lower leg, which depends on the position of the upper leg and so on. This is known as a *kinematic chain*.

To compute the global transformation of the foot relative to the camera, we chain the transformations relating each of the body parts in the appropriate order.

There are many approaches to constructing articulated models. They may be two dimensional (e.g., the pictorial structures discussed in Chapter 11) or exist in three dimensions. We will consider a 3D hand model that is constructed from *truncated quadrics*. The quadric is the 3D generalization of the conic (see Section 17.1) and can represent cylinders, spheres, ellipsoids, a pair of planes, and other shapes in 3D. Points in 3D which lie on the surface of the quadric satisfy the relation

$$\begin{bmatrix} x & y & z & 1 \end{bmatrix} \begin{bmatrix} \psi_1 & \psi_2 & \psi_3 & \psi_4 \\ \psi_2 & \psi_5 & \psi_6 & \psi_7 \\ \psi_3 & \psi_6 & \psi_8 & \psi_9 \\ \psi_4 & \psi_7 & \psi_9 & \psi_{10} \end{bmatrix} \begin{bmatrix} x \\ y \\ z \\ 1 \end{bmatrix} = 0. \tag{17.46}$$

Figure 17.21 illustrates a hand model that was constructed from a set of 39 *quadrics*. Some of these quadrics are truncated; to make a tube shape of finite length, a cylinder or ellipsoid is clipped by a pair of planes in 3D so that only parts of the quadric that are between the planes are retained. The pair of planes is represented by a second quadric, so each part of the model is actually represented by two quadrics. This model has 27 degrees of freedom, 6 for the global hand position, 4 for the pose of each finger, and 5 for the pose of the thumb.

The quadric is a sensible choice because its projection through a pinhole camera takes the form of a conic and can be computed in closed form. Typically, an ellipsoid (represented by a quadric) would project down to an ellipse in the image (represented by a conic), and we can find a closed form expression for the parameters of this conic in terms of the quadric parameters.

Given the camera position relative to the model, it is possible to project the collection of quadrics that form the 3D model into the camera image. Self occlusion can be handled neatly by testing the depth along each ray and not rendering the resulting conic if the associated quadric lies behind another part of the model. This leads to a straightforward method for fitting the model to an image of the object (i.e., finding the joint angles and overall pose relative to the camera). We simulate a set of contours for the model (as in Figure 17.21d) and then evaluate an expression for the likelihood that increases when these match the observed edges in the image. To fit the model, we simply optimize this cost function.

Unfortunately, this algorithm is prone to converging to local minima; it is hard to find a good starting point for the optimization. Moreover, the visual data may be genuinely ambiguous in a particular image, and there may be more than one configuration of the object that is compatible with the observed image. The situation becomes more manageable if we view the object from more than one camera (as in Figures 17.21e–f and h–i) as much of the ambiguity is resolved. Fitting the model is also easier when we are tracking the model through a series of frames; we can initialize the model fitting at each time based on the known position of the hand at the previous time. This kind of temporal model is investigated in Chapter 19.

17.10 Applications

We will now look at two applications that extend the ideas of this chapter into 3D. First, we will consider a face model that is essentially a 3D version of the active appearance

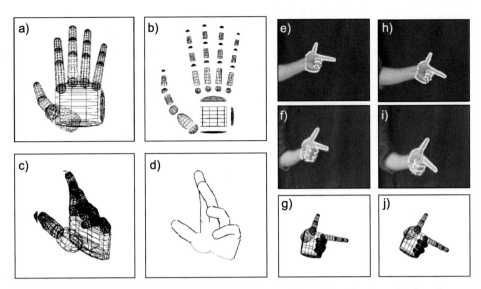

Figure 17.21 Articulated model for a human hand. a) A three-dimensional model for a human hand is constructed from 39 truncated quadrics. b) Exploded view. c) The model has 27 degrees of freedom that control the joint angles. d) It is easy to project this model into an image and find the outer and occluding contours, which can then be aligned with contours in an image. e–f) Two views of a hand taken simultaneously from different cameras g) Estimated state of hand model. h–j) Two more views and another estimate of the position. Adapted from Stenger et al. (2001a). ©2001 IEEE.

model. Second, we will discuss a model for the human body that combines the ideas of the articulated model and the subspace representation of shape.

17.10.1 Three dimensional morphable models

Blanz and Vetter (1999) developed a statistical model of the 3D shape and appearance of faces. Their model was based on 200 laser scans. Each face was represented by approximately 70,000 3D vertices and an RGB texture map. The captured faces were preprocessed so that the global 3D transformation between them was removed, and the vertices were registered using a method based on optical flow.

A statistical shape model was built where the 3D vertices now take on the role of the landmark points. As with most of the statistical shape models in this chapter, this model was based on a linear combination of basis functions (principal components). Similarly, the texture maps were described as a linear combination of a set of basis images (principal components). Figure 17.22 illustrates the mean face and the effect of varying the shape and texture components independently.

The model, as described so far, is thus a 3D version of the model for shape and appearance that we described in Section 17.7. However, in addition, Blanz and Vetter (1999) model the rendering process using the *Phong shading model* which includes both ambient and directional lighting effects.

To fit this model to a photograph of a face, the square error between the observed pixel intensities and those predicted from the model is minimized. The goal then is to

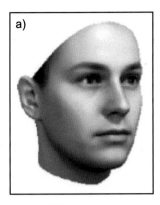 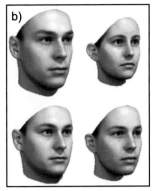 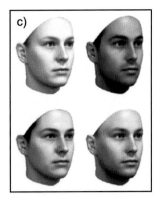

Figure 17.22 3D morphable model of a face. The model was trained from laser scans of 200 individuals and is represented as a set of 70,000 vertex positions and an associated texture map. a) Mean face. b) As for the 2D subspace shape model, the final shape is described as a linear combination of basis shapes (principal components). In this model, however, these basis shapes are three dimensional. The figure shows the effect of changing the weighting of these basis functions while keeping the texture constant. c) The texture is also modeled as a linear combination of basis shapes. The figure shows the effect of changing the texture while keeping the shape constant. Adapted from Blanz and Vetter (2003). ©2003 IEEE.

manipulate the parameters of the model so that the rendered image matches the observed image as closely as possible. These parameters include:

- The weightings of the basis functions that determine the shape,
- The weightings of the basis functions that determine the texture,
- The relative position of the camera and the object,
- The RGB intensities of the ambient and directed light, and
- The offsets and gains for each image RGB channel.

Other parameters such as the camera distance, light direction, and surface shininess were fixed by hand. In practice, the fitting was accomplished using a nonlinear optimization technique. Figure 17.23 illustrates the process of fitting the model to a real image. After convergence, the shape and texture closely replicate the original image. At the end of this process, we have full knowledge of the shape and texture of the face. This can now be viewed from different angles, relit and even have realistic shadows superimposed.

Blanz and Vetter (Blanz and Vetter 2003; Blanz et al. 2005) applied this model to face recognition. In the simplest case, they described the fitted face using a vector containing the weighting functions for both the shape and texture. Two faces can be compared by examining the distance between the vector associated with each. This method has the advantage that the faces can be originally presented in very different lighting conditions and with very different poses as neither of these factors is reflected in the final representation. However, the method is limited in practice by the model-fitting procedure, which does not always converge for real images that may suffer from complex lighting conditions and partial occlusion.

Matthews et al. (2007) presented a simplified version of the same model; this was still 3D but had a sparser mesh and did not include a reflectance model. However, they describe an algorithm for fitting this face model to video sequences that can run at more than 60 frames per second. This permits real-time tracking of the pose and expression of

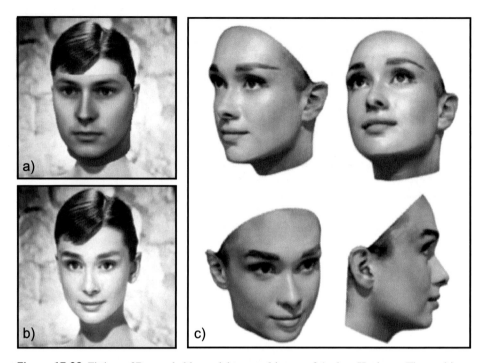

Figure 17.23 Fitting a 3D morphable model to a real image of Audrey Hepburn. The goal is to find the parameters of the 3D model that best describe the 2D face. Once we have done this, we can manipulate the image. For example we could relight the face or view it from different angles. a) Simulated image from model with initial parameters. b) Simulated image from model after fitting procedure. This closely replicates the original image in terms of both texture and shape. c) Images from fitted model generated under several different viewing conditions. Adapted from Blanz and Vetter (1999). ©1999 ACM.

faces (Figure 17.24). This technique has been used to capture facial expressions for CGI characters in movies and video games.

17.10.2 Three-dimensional body model

Anguelov et al. (2005) presented a 3D body model that combines an articulated structure with a subspace model. The articulated model describes the skeleton of the body, and the subspace model describes the variation of the shape of the individual around this skeleton (Figure 17.25).

At its core, this model is represented by a set of triangles that define the surface of the body. The model is best explained in terms of generation in which each triangle undergoes a series of transformations. First, the position is deformed in a way that depends on the configuration of the nearest joints in the body. The deformation is determined using a regression model and creates subtle effects such as the deformation of muscles. Second, the position of the triangle is deformed according to a PCA model which determines the individuals characteristics (body shape, etc.). Finally, the triangle is warped in 3D space depending on the position of the skeleton.

Two applications of this model are shown in Figure 17.26. First, the model can be used to fill in missing parts of partial scans of human beings. Many scanners cannot

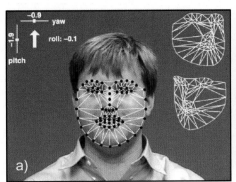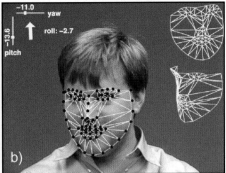

Figure 17.24 Real-time facial tracking using a 3D active appearance model. a–b) Two examples from tracking sequence. The pose of the face is indicated in the top left-hand corner. The superimposed mesh shown to the right of the face illustrates two different views of the shape component of the model. Adapted from Matthews et al. (2007). ©2007 Springer.

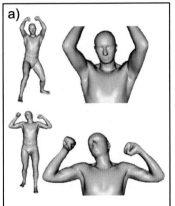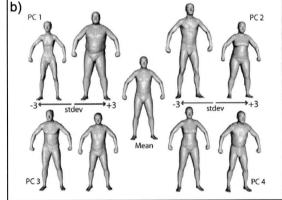

Figure 17.25 3D body model. a) The final position of the skin surface is regressed against the nearest joint angles; this produces subtle effects such as the bulging of muscles. b) The final position of the skin surface also depends on a PCA model which describes between-individual variation in body shape. Adapted from Anguelov et al. (2005). ©2005 ACM.

capture a full 3D model at once; they may only capture the front of the object and so several scans must be combined to get a full model. This is problematic for moving objects such as human beings. Even for models that can capture 360° of shape, there are often missing or noisy parts of the data. Figure 17.26a shows an example of fitting the model to a partial scan; the position of the skeleton and the weighting of the PCA components are adapted until the synthesized shape agrees with the partial scan. The remaining part of the synthesized shape plausibly fills in the missing elements.

Figures 17.26b–d illustrate the use of the model for motion capture based animation. An actor in a motion capture studio has his body position tracked, and this body position can be used to determine the position of the skeleton of the 3D model. The regression model then adjusts the vertices of the skin model appropriately to model muscle deformation while the PCA model allows the identity of the resulting model to vary.

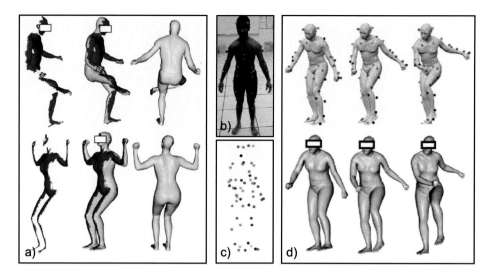

Figure 17.26 Applications of 3D body model. a) Interpolation of partial scans. In each case, the purple region represents the original scan and the green region is the interpolated part after fitting a 3D body model (viewed from two angles). b) Motion capture animation. An actor is tracked in a conventional motion capture studio. c) This results in the known position of a number of markers on the body. d) These markers are used to position the skeletal aspect of the model. The PCA part of the model can control the shape of the final body (two examples shown). Adapted from Anguelov et al. (2005). ©2005 ACM.

This type of system can be used to generate character animations for video games and movies.

Discussion

In this chapter, we have presented a number of models for describing the shape of visual objects. These ideas relate closely to the subsequent chapters in this book. These shape models are often tracked in video sequences and the machinery for this tracking is developed in Chapter 19. Several of the shape models have a subspace (principal component) representation at their core. In Chapter 18 we investigate models that exploit this type of representation for identity recognition.

Notes

Snakes and active contour models: Snakes were first introduced by Kass et al. (1987). Various modifications have been made to encourage them to converge to a sensible answer including the addition of a ballooning term (Cohen 1991) and a new type of external force field called gradient vector flow (Xu and Prince 1998). The original description treated the contour as a continuous object, but subsequent work also considered it as discrete and used greedy algorithms or dynamic programming methods for optimization (Amini et al. 1990; Williams and Shah 1992). Subsequent work has investigated the use of prior information about object shape and led to active contour models (Cootes et al. 1995). This is still an open research area (e.g., Bergtholdt et al. 2005; Freifeld et al. 2010).

The contour models discussed in this chapter are known as parametric because the shape is explicitly represented. A summary of early work on parametric active contours can be found in Blake and Isard (1998). A parallel strand of research investigates implicit or nonparametric contours in which the contour is implicitly defined by the level sets of a function defined on the image domain (Malladi et al. 1994; Caselles et al. 1997). There has also been considerable interest in applying prior knowledge to these models (Leventon et al. 2000; Rousson and Paragios 2002).

Bottom-up models: This chapter has concerned top-down approaches to contour detection in which a generative model for the object is specified that explains the observed edges in the image. However, there has also been a recent surge of research progress into bottom-up approaches, in which edge fragments are combined to form coherent shapes. For example, Opelt et al. (2006) introduced the "Boundary fragment model" in which pairs of edge fragments vote for the position of the centroid of the object and the object is detected by finding the position with the most support. Shotton et al. (2008a) present a similar model that incorporates scale invariance and searches through local regions of the image to identify objects that form only a small part of a larger scene. Pairwise constraints between features were introduced by Leordeanu et al. (2007). Other work has investigated reconstructing pieces of the contour as combinations of local geometric primitives such as line segments and ellipses (Chia et al. 2010).

Subspace models: The statistical models in this chapter are based on subspace models such as probabilistic PCA (Tipping 2001) although in their original presentation they used regular (non-probabilistic) PCA (see Section 13.4.2). The models could equally have been built using factor analysis (Rubin and Thayer 1982). This has the disadvantage that it cannot be learned in closed form but can cope with modeling the joint distribution of quantities that are expressed in different units (e.g., shape and texture in active appearance models). Nonlinear generalizations of PCA (Schölkopf et al. 1998) and factor analysis (Lawrence 2005) have extended these statistical models to the non-Gaussian case.

Active shape and appearance models: More details about active shape models can be found in Cootes et al. (1995). More details about active appearance models can be found in Cootes et al. (2001) and Stegmann (2002). Jones and Soatto (2005) presented an interesting extension to active appearance models in which the objects was modeled as a number of superimposed layers. Recent interest in active appearance models has focussed on improving the efficiency of fitting algorithms (Matthews and Baker 2004; Matthews et al. 2007; Amberg et al. 2009). They have been applied to many tasks including face recognition, face pose estimation and expression recognition (Lanitis et al. 1997), and lip reading (Matthews et al. 2002). Several authors have investigated nonlinear approaches including systems based on mixture models (Cootes and Taylor 1997), kernel PCA (Romdhani et al. 1999), and the GPLVM (Huang et al. 2011).

3D Morphable models: Morphable models for faces were first introduced by Blanz and Vetter (1999) and were subsequently applied to editing images and video (Blanz et al. 2003), for face recognition (Blanz and Vetter 2003; Blanz et al. 2005), and for tracking 3D faces (Matthews et al. 2007). A related model has been developed for vehicles (Leotta and Mundy 2011).

Body Tracking: Generative models for tracking human bodies have been developed based on a number of representations including cylinders (Hogg 1983), ellipsoids (Bregler and Malik 1998), stick men (Mori et al. 2004), and meshes (Shakhnarovich et al. 2003). As well as 3D models, attempts have also been made to fit purely 2D models (e.g., Felzenszwalb and Huttenlocher 2005, and see Rehg et al. 2003). Some research has focused on multicamera setups which help disambiguate the observed data (e.g., Gavrila and Davis 1996). Models for tracking the body in time sequences have attracted a lot of attention (e.g., Deutscher et al. 2000; Sidenbladh et al. 2000 and see Chapter 19). Recent work has attempted to leverage knowledge of the physics of the body movement to improve the results (Brubaker et al. 2010). There are also a number of approaches to body tracking based on regression (see Chapter 8). Reviews of human motion tracking can be found in Forsyth et al. (2006), Moeslund et al. (2006), Poppe (2007), and Sigal et al. (2010).

Body models for graphics: The work of Anguelov et al. (2005), who combined the skeletal and statistical shape models, was preceeded by Allen et al. (2003) and Seo and Magnenat-Thalmann

(2003), who also applied PCA to skeletal models for the human body, although they do not include a component that models deformations due to muscle movement.

Hand models: Many authors have developed models for tracking hands including Rehg and Kanade (1994), (1995), Heap and Hogg (1996), Stenger et al. (2001a), Wu et al. (2001), and Lu et al. (2003). De La Gorce *et al.* (2008) present a very sophisticated model that describes texture, shading, and self-occlusions of the hand.

Problems

17.1 A conic is defined as the set of points where

$$
\begin{bmatrix} x & y & 1 \end{bmatrix}
\begin{bmatrix} \alpha & \beta & \gamma \\ \beta & \delta & \epsilon \\ \gamma & \epsilon & \zeta \end{bmatrix}
\begin{bmatrix} x \\ y \\ 1 \end{bmatrix} = 0,
$$

or

$$
\tilde{\mathbf{x}}^T \mathbf{C} \tilde{\mathbf{x}} = 0.
$$

Use MATLAB to draw the 2D function $\tilde{\mathbf{x}}^T \mathbf{C} \tilde{\mathbf{x}}$ and identify the set of positions where this function is zero for the following matrices:

$$
\mathbf{C}_1 = \begin{bmatrix} 3 & 0 & 0 \\ 0 & 2 & 0 \\ 0 & 0 & -1 \end{bmatrix} \qquad
\mathbf{C}_2 = \begin{bmatrix} 0 & 0 & 1 \\ 0 & 0 & 0 \\ 1 & 0 & -2 \end{bmatrix} \qquad
\mathbf{C}_3 = \begin{bmatrix} -1 & 0 & 0 \\ 0 & 0 & 1 \\ 0 & 1 & 0 \end{bmatrix}.
$$

17.2 Devise an efficient algorithm to compute the distance transform. The algorithm should take a binary image and return at each pixel the city block distance to the nearest nonzero element of the original image. The city block distance d between pixels (x_1, y_1) and pixel (x_2, y_2) is defined as

$$
d = |x_1 - x_2| + |y_1 - y_2|.
$$

17.3 Consider a prior that is based in the curvature term:

$$
\text{curve}[\mathbf{w}, n] = -(\mathbf{w}_{n-1} - 2\mathbf{w}_n + \mathbf{w}_{n+1})^T (\mathbf{w}_{n-1} - 2\mathbf{w}_n + \mathbf{w}_{n+1}).
$$

If landmark point $\mathbf{w}_1 = [100, 100]$, and landmark point $\mathbf{w}_3$ is at position $\mathbf{w}_3 = [200, 300]$, what position $\mathbf{w}_2$ will minimize the function $\text{curve}[\mathbf{w}, 2]$?

17.4 If the snake as described in Section 17.2 is initialized in an empty image, how would you expect it to evolve during the fitting procedure?

17.5 The spacing element of the snake prior (Equation 17.5) encourages all of the control points of the snake to be the equidistant. An alternative approach is to give the snake a tendency to shrink (so that it collapses around objects). Write out an alternative expression for the spacing term that accomplishes this goal.

17.6 Devise a method to find the "best" weight vector $\mathbf{h}$ given a new vector $\mathbf{w}$ and the parameters $\{\boldsymbol{\mu}, \boldsymbol{\Phi}, \sigma^2\}$ of the PPCA model (see Figure 17.10).

17.7 Show that if the singular value decomposition of a matrix $\mathbf{W}$ can be written as $\mathbf{W} = \mathbf{U}\mathbf{L}\mathbf{V}^T$, then it follows that

$$
\mathbf{W}\mathbf{W}^T = \mathbf{U}\mathbf{L}^2\mathbf{U}^T
$$
$$
\mathbf{W}^T\mathbf{W} = \mathbf{V}\mathbf{L}^2\mathbf{V}^T.
$$

17.8 Devise a method to learn the PPCA model using the EM algorithm, giving details of both the E- and M-steps. Are you guaranteed to get the same answer as the method based on the SVD?

17.9 Show that the maximum a posteriori solution for the hidden weight variable $\mathbf{h}$ is as given in Equation 17.32.

17.10 You are given a set of 100 male faces and 100 female faces. By hand you mark 50 landmark points on each image. Describe how to use this data to develop a generative approach to gender classification based on shape alone. Describe both the training process and how you would infer the gender for a new face that does not contain landmark points.

17.11 Imagine that we have learned a point distribution for the shape of the human face. Now we see a new face where everything below the nose is occluded by a scarf. How could you exploit the model to estimate both the positions of the landmark points in the top half of the face and the landmark points in the (missing) bottom half of the face?

17.12 An alternative approach to building a nonlinear model of shape is to use a mixture model. Describe an approach to training a statistical shape model based on the mixture of probabilistic principal component analyzers. How would you fit this model to a new image?

17.13 One way to warp one image to another is to implement a piecewise affine warp. Assume that we have a number of points in image 1 and their corresponding points in image 2. We first triangulate each set of points in the same way. We now represent the position $\mathbf{x}_1$ in image 1 as a weighted sum of the three vertices of the triangle $\mathbf{a}_1, \mathbf{b}_1, \mathbf{c}_1$ that it lies in so that

$$\mathbf{x}_1 = \alpha \mathbf{a}_1 + \beta \mathbf{b}_1 + \gamma \mathbf{c}_1,$$

where the weights are constrained to be positive with $\alpha + \beta + \gamma = 1$. These weights are known as *barycentric coordinates*.

To find the position in the second image, we then compute the position relative to the three vertices $\mathbf{a}_2, \mathbf{b}_2, \mathbf{c}_2$ of the warped triangle so that

$$\mathbf{x}_2 = \alpha \mathbf{a}_2 + \beta \mathbf{b}_2 + \gamma \mathbf{c}_2.$$

How can we compute the weights α, β, γ? Devise a method to warp the whole image in this manner.

17.14 Consider an ellipsoid in 3D space that is represented by the quadric

$$\tilde{\mathbf{w}}^T \begin{bmatrix} \mathbf{A} & \mathbf{b} \\ \mathbf{b}^T & c \end{bmatrix} \tilde{\mathbf{w}} = 0,$$

where $\mathbf{A}$ is a 3×3 matrix, $\mathbf{b}$ is a 3×1 vector, and c is a scalar.

For a normalized camera we can write the world point $\tilde{\mathbf{w}}$ in terms of the image point $\tilde{\mathbf{x}}$ as $\tilde{\mathbf{w}} = [\tilde{\mathbf{x}}^T, s]^T$ where s is a scaling factor that determines the distance along the ray $\tilde{\mathbf{x}}$.

(i) Combine these conditions to produce a criterion that must be true for an image point $\tilde{\mathbf{x}}$ to lie within the projection of the conic.

(ii) The edge of the image of the conic is the locus of points for which there is a single solution for the distance s. Outside the conic there is no real solution for s and inside it there are two possible solutions corresponding to the front and back face of the quadric. Use this intuition to derive an expression for the conic in terms of $\mathbf{A}, \mathbf{b}$ and c. If the camera has intrinsic matrix $\mathbf{\Lambda}$, what would the new expression for the conic be?

Chapter 18

Models for style and identity

In this chapter we discuss a family of models that explain observed data in terms of several underlying causes. These causes can be divided into three types: the identity of the object, the style in which it is observed, and the remaining variation.

To motivate these models, consider *face recognition*. For a facial image, the identity of the face (i.e., whose face it is) obviously influences the observed data. However, the style in which the face is viewed is also important. The pose, expression, and illumination are all style elements that might be modeled. Unfortunately, many other things also contribute to the final observed data: the person may have applied cosmetics, put on glasses, grown a beard, or dyed his or her hair. These myriad contributory elements are usually too difficult to model and are hence explained with a generic noise term.

In face recognition tasks, our goal is to infer whether the identities of face images are the same or different. For example, in *face verification*, we aim to infer a binary variable $w \in \{0,1\}$, where $w=0$ indicates that the identities differ and $w=1$ indicates that they are the same. This task is extremely challenging when there are large changes in pose, illumination, or expression; the change in the image due to style may dwarf the change due to identity (Figure 18.1).

The models in this chapter are generative, so the focus is on building separate density models over the observed image data cases where the faces do and don't have the same identity. They are all *subspace models* and describe data as a linear combination of basis vectors. We have previously encountered several models of this type, including factor analysis (Section 7.6) and PPCA (Section 17.5.1). The models in this chapter are most closely related to factor analysis, so we will start by reviewing this.

Factor analysis

Recall that the factor analysis model explained the ith data example $\mathbf{x}_i$ as

$$\mathbf{x}_i = \boldsymbol{\mu} + \boldsymbol{\Phi}\mathbf{h}_i + \boldsymbol{\epsilon}_i, \tag{18.1}$$

where $\boldsymbol{\mu}$ is the overall mean of the data. The matrix $\boldsymbol{\Phi} = [\boldsymbol{\phi}_1, \boldsymbol{\phi}_2, \ldots, \boldsymbol{\phi}_K]$ contains K factors in its columns. Each factor can be thought of as a basis vector in a high-dimensional space, and so together they define a subspace. The K elements of the hidden variable $\mathbf{h}_i$ weight the K factors to explain the observed deviations of the data from the

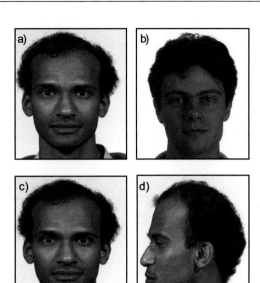

Figure 18.1 Face recognition. In face recognition the goal is to draw inferences about the identities of face images. This is difficult because the style in which the picture was taken can have a more drastic effect on the observed data than the identities themselves. For example, the images in (a–b) are more similar to one another by most measures than the images in (c–d) because the style (pose) has changed in the latter case. Nonetheless, the identities in (a–b) are different but the identities in (c–d) are the same. We must build models that tease apart the contributions of identity and style to make accurate inferences about whether the identities match.

mean. Remaining differences that cannot be explained in this way are ascribed to additive noise ϵ_i which is normally distributed with diagonal covariance Σ.

In probabilistic terms, we write

$$Pr(\mathbf{x}_i|\mathbf{h}_i) = \text{Norm}_{\mathbf{x}_i}[\boldsymbol{\mu} + \boldsymbol{\Phi}\mathbf{h}_i, \boldsymbol{\Sigma}]$$
$$Pr(\mathbf{h}_i) = \text{Norm}_{\mathbf{h}_i}[\mathbf{0}, \mathbf{I}], \tag{18.2}$$

where we have also defined a suitable prior over the hidden variable $\mathbf{h}_i$. Ancestral sampling from this model is illustrated in Figure 18.2.

We can compute the likelihood of observing a new data example by marginalizing over the hidden variable to get a final probability model

$$Pr(\mathbf{x}_i) = \int Pr(\mathbf{x}_i, \mathbf{h}_i) \, d\mathbf{h}_i = \int Pr(\mathbf{x}_i|\mathbf{h}_i) Pr(\mathbf{h}_i) \, d\mathbf{h}_i$$
$$= \text{Norm}_{\mathbf{x}_i}[\boldsymbol{\mu}, \boldsymbol{\Phi}\boldsymbol{\Phi}^T + \boldsymbol{\Sigma}]. \tag{18.3}$$

To learn this model from training data $\{\mathbf{x}_i\}_{i=1}^I$, we use the expectation maximization algorithm. In the E-step, we compute the posterior distribution $Pr(\mathbf{h}_i|\mathbf{x}_i)$ over each hidden variable $\mathbf{h}_i$,

$$Pr(\mathbf{h}_i|\mathbf{x}_i) = \text{Norm}_{\mathbf{h}_i}[(\boldsymbol{\Phi}^T\boldsymbol{\Sigma}^{-1}\boldsymbol{\Phi} + \mathbf{I})^{-1}\boldsymbol{\Phi}^T\boldsymbol{\Sigma}^{-1}(\mathbf{x}_i - \boldsymbol{\mu}), (\boldsymbol{\Phi}^T\boldsymbol{\Sigma}^{-1}\boldsymbol{\Phi} + \mathbf{I})^{-1}]. \tag{18.4}$$

In the M-step we update the parameters as

$$\hat{\boldsymbol{\mu}} = \frac{\sum_{i=1}^I \mathbf{x}_i}{I}$$

$$\hat{\boldsymbol{\Phi}} = \left(\sum_{i=1}^I (\mathbf{x}_i - \hat{\boldsymbol{\mu}})\text{E}[\mathbf{h}_i]^T\right)\left(\sum_{i=1}^I \text{E}[\mathbf{h}_i\mathbf{h}_i^T]\right)^{-1}$$

$$\hat{\boldsymbol{\Sigma}} = \frac{1}{I}\sum_{i=1}^I \text{diag}\left[(\mathbf{x}_i - \hat{\boldsymbol{\mu}})(\mathbf{x}_i - \hat{\boldsymbol{\mu}})^T - \hat{\boldsymbol{\Phi}}\text{E}[\mathbf{h}_i](\mathbf{x}_i - \hat{\boldsymbol{\mu}})^T\right], \tag{18.5}$$

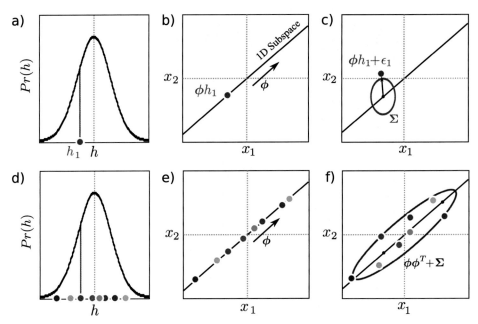

Figure 18.2 Ancestral sampling from factor analyzer. In both this figure and other subsequent figures in this chapter, we assume that the mean μ is zero. a) To generate from a factor analyzer defined over 2D data we first choose the hidden variable $\mathbf{h}_i$ from the normally distributed prior. Here h_i is a 1D variable and a small negative value is drawn. b) For each case we weight the factors Φ by the hidden variable. This generates a point on the subspace (here a 1D subspace indicated by black line). c) Then we add the noise term ϵ_i, which is normally distributed with covariance Σ. Finally, we would add a mean term μ (not shown). d–f) This process is repeated many times. f) The final distribution of the data is a normal distribution that is oriented along the subspace. Deviations from this subspace are due to the noise term. The final covariance is $\Phi\Phi^T + \Sigma$.

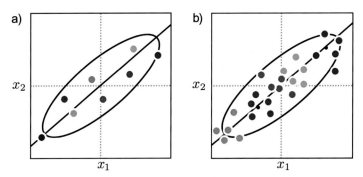

Figure 18.3 Subspace model vs. subspace identity model. a) The subspace model generates data that are roughly aligned along a subspace (here a 1D subspace defined by the black line) as illustrated in Figure 18.2. b) In the identity subspace model, the overall data distribution is the same, but there is additional structure: points that belong to the same identity (same color) are generated in the same region of space.

where the expectations $E[\mathbf{h}_i]$ and $E[\mathbf{h}_i\mathbf{h}_i^T]$ over the hidden variable are extracted from the posterior distribution computed in the E-step. More details about factor analysis can be found in Section 7.6.

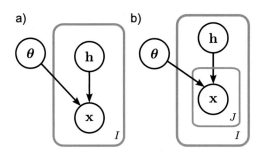

Figure 18.4 Graphical models for subspace model and subspace identity model. a) In the subspace model (factor analysis), there is one data example $\mathbf{x}_i$ per hidden variable $\mathbf{h}_i$ and some other parameters $\theta = \{\boldsymbol{\mu}, \boldsymbol{\Phi}, \boldsymbol{\Sigma}\}$ that describe the subspace. b) In the subspace identity model, there are J data examples $\mathbf{x}_{ij}$ per hidden variable $\mathbf{h}_i$, and all of these J examples have the same identity.

18.1   Subspace identity model

The factor analysis model provides a good description of the intensity data in frontal face images: they really do lie close to a linear subspace (see Figure 7.22). However, this description of the data does not account for identity. For images that have the same style (e.g., pose, lighting), we expect faces that have the same identity to lie in a similar part of the space (Figure 18.3), but there is no mechanism to accomplish this in the original model.

We now extend the factor analysis model to take account of data examples which are known to have the same identity and show how to exploit this to make inferences about the identity of new data examples. We adopt the notation $\mathbf{x}_{ij}$ to denote the jth of J observed data examples from the ith of I identities (individuals). In real-world data sets, it is unlikely that we will have exactly J examples for every individual, and the models we present do not require this, but this assumption simplifies the notation.

The generative explanation for the observed data $\mathbf{x}_{ij}$ is now

$$\mathbf{x}_{ij} = \boldsymbol{\mu} + \boldsymbol{\Phi}\mathbf{h}_i + \boldsymbol{\epsilon}_{ij}, \tag{18.6}$$

where all of the terms have the same interpretations as before. The key difference is that now all of the J data examples from the same individual are formed by taking the *same* linear combination $\mathbf{h}_i$ of the basis functions $\boldsymbol{\phi}_1 \ldots \boldsymbol{\phi}_K$. However, a different noise term is added for each data example, and this explains the differences between the J face images of a given individual. We can write this in probabilistic form as

$$Pr(\mathbf{h}_i) = \text{Norm}_{\mathbf{h}_i}[\mathbf{0}, \mathbf{I}] \tag{18.7}$$
$$Pr(\mathbf{x}_{ij}|\mathbf{h}_i) = \text{Norm}_{\mathbf{x}_{ij}}[\boldsymbol{\mu} + \boldsymbol{\Phi}\mathbf{h}_i, \boldsymbol{\Sigma}],$$

where as before we have defined a prior over the hidden variables. The graphical models for both factor analysis and the subspace identity model are illustrated in Figure 18.4. Figure 18.5 illustrates ancestral sampling from the subspace identity model; as desired this produces data points that lie close together when the identity is the same.

One way to think of this is that we have decomposed the variance in the model into two parts. The *between-individual* variation explains the differences between data due to different identities and the *within-individual* variation explains the differences between data examples due to all other factors. The data density for a single datapoint remains

$$Pr(\mathbf{x}_{ij}) = \text{Norm}_{\mathbf{x}_{ij}}[\boldsymbol{\mu}, \boldsymbol{\Phi}\boldsymbol{\Phi}^T + \boldsymbol{\Sigma}]. \tag{18.8}$$

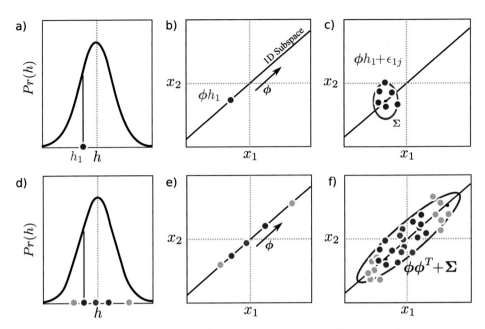

Figure 18.5 Ancestral sampling from identity subspace model. a) To generate from this model we first choose the hidden variable $\mathbf{h}_i$ from the normally distributed prior. Here h_i is a 1D variable and a small negative number is drawn. b) We weight the factors $\boldsymbol{\Phi}$ by the hidden variable. This generates a point on the subspace. c) Then we add different noise terms $\{\boldsymbol{\epsilon}_{ij}\}_{j=1}^{J}$ to create each of the J examples $\{\mathbf{x}_{ij}\}_{j=1}^{J}$. In each case, the noise is normally distributed with covariance $\boldsymbol{\Sigma}$. Finally, we would add a mean term $\boldsymbol{\mu}$ (not shown). d–f) This process is repeated several times. f) The final distribution of the data is a normal distribution with covariance $\boldsymbol{\Phi}\boldsymbol{\Phi}^T + \boldsymbol{\Sigma}$. However, it is structured so that points with the same hidden variable (identity) are close to one another.

However, the two components of the variance now have clear interpretations. The term $\boldsymbol{\Phi}\boldsymbol{\Phi}^T$ corresponds to the between-individual variation, and the term $\boldsymbol{\Sigma}$ is the within-individual variation.

18.1.1 Learning

Before we consider how to use this model to draw inferences about identity in face recognition tasks, we will briefly discuss how to learn the parameters $\boldsymbol{\theta} = \{\boldsymbol{\mu}, \boldsymbol{\Phi}, \boldsymbol{\Sigma}\}$. As for the factor analysis model, we exploit the EM algorithm to iteratively increase a bound on the log likelihood. In the E-step we compute the posterior probability distribution over each of the hidden variables $\mathbf{h}_i$ given all of the data $\mathbf{x}_{i\bullet} = \{\mathbf{x}_{ij}\}_{j=1}^{J}$ associated with that particular identity,

$$Pr(\mathbf{h}_i|\mathbf{x}_{i\bullet}) = \frac{\prod_{j=1}^{J} Pr(\mathbf{x}_{ij}|\mathbf{h}_i)Pr(\mathbf{h}_i)}{\int \prod_{j=1}^{J} Pr(\mathbf{x}_{ij}|\mathbf{h}_i)Pr(\mathbf{h}_i)\,d\mathbf{h}_i} \qquad (18.9)$$

$$= \mathrm{Norm}_{\mathbf{h}_i}\left[(J\boldsymbol{\Phi}^T\boldsymbol{\Sigma}^{-1}\boldsymbol{\Phi}+\mathbf{I})^{-1}\boldsymbol{\Phi}^T\boldsymbol{\Sigma}^{-1}\sum_{j=1}^{J}(\mathbf{x}_{ij}-\boldsymbol{\mu}), (J\boldsymbol{\Phi}^T\boldsymbol{\Sigma}^{-1}\boldsymbol{\Phi}+\mathbf{I})^{-1}\right].$$

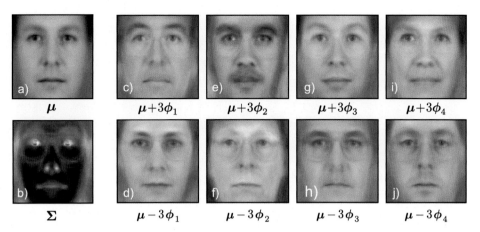

Figure 18.6 Subspace identity model parameters. These parameters were learned from $J = 3$ images of $I = 195$ individuals from the XM2VTS data set. a) Estimated mean μ. b) Estimated covariance, Σ. c–j) Four of 32 subspace directions explored by adding and subtracting multiples of each dimension to the mean.

From this we extract the moments that will be needed in the M-step,

$$\mathrm{E}[\mathbf{h}_i] = (J\mathbf{\Phi}^T\mathbf{\Sigma}^{-1}\mathbf{\Phi} + \mathbf{I})^{-1}\mathbf{\Phi}^T\mathbf{\Sigma}^{-1}\sum_{j=1}^{J}(\mathbf{x}_{ij} - \mu)$$

$$\mathrm{E}[\mathbf{h}_i\mathbf{h}_i^T] = (J\mathbf{\Phi}^T\mathbf{\Sigma}^{-1}\mathbf{\Phi} + \mathbf{I})^{-1} + \mathrm{E}[\mathbf{h}_i]\mathrm{E}[\mathbf{h}_i]^T. \tag{18.10}$$

In the M-step we update the parameters using the relations

$$\hat{\mu} = \frac{\sum_{i=1}^{I}\sum_{j=1}^{J}\mathbf{x}_{ij}}{IJ} \tag{18.11}$$

$$\hat{\mathbf{\Phi}} = \left(\sum_{i=1}^{I}\sum_{j=1}^{J}(\mathbf{x}_{ij} - \hat{\mu})\mathrm{E}[\mathbf{h}_i]^T\right)\left(\sum_{i=1}^{I}J\mathrm{E}[\mathbf{h}_i\mathbf{h}_i^T]\right)^{-1}$$

$$\mathbf{\Sigma} = \frac{1}{IJ}\sum_{i=1}^{I}\sum_{j=1}^{J}\mathrm{diag}\left[(\mathbf{x}_{ij} - \hat{\mu})(\mathbf{x}_{ij} - \hat{\mu})^T - \hat{\mathbf{\Phi}}\mathrm{E}[\mathbf{h}_i](\mathbf{x}_{ij} - \hat{\mu})^T\right],$$

which were generated by taking the derivative of the EM bound with respect to the relevant quantities, equating the results to zero, and rearranging. We alternate the E- and M-steps until the loglikelihood of the data no longer increases.

Figure 18.6 shows parameters learned from 70×70 pixel face images from the XM2VTS database. A model with a $K = 32$ dimensional hidden space was learned with 195 identities and 3 images per person. The subspace directions capture major changes that correlate with identity. For example, ethnicity and gender are clearly represented. The noise describes whatever remains. It is most prominent around high-contrast features such as the eyes.

In Figure 18.7 we decompose pairs of matching images into their identity and noise components. To accomplish this, we compute the MAP hidden variable $\hat{\mathbf{h}}_i$. The posterior over $\mathbf{h}$ is normal (Equation 18.9) and so the MAP estimate is simply the mean of this

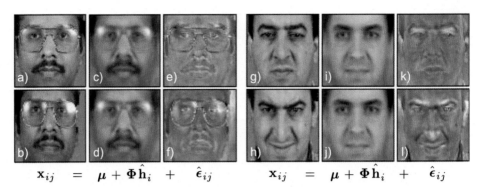

$$\mathbf{x}_{ij} \quad = \quad \boldsymbol{\mu} + \boldsymbol{\Phi}\hat{\mathbf{h}}_i \quad + \quad \hat{\boldsymbol{\epsilon}}_{ij} \qquad\qquad \mathbf{x}_{ij} \quad = \quad \boldsymbol{\mu} + \boldsymbol{\Phi}\hat{\mathbf{h}}_i \quad + \quad \hat{\boldsymbol{\epsilon}}_{ij}$$

Figure 18.7 Fitting subspace identity model to new data. a–b) Original images $\mathbf{x}_{i1}$ and $\mathbf{x}_{i2}$. These faces can be decomposed into the sum of c–d) an identity component and e–f) a within-individual noise component. To decompose the image in this way, we computed the MAP estimate $\hat{\mathbf{h}}_i$ of the hidden variable and set the identity component to be $\boldsymbol{\mu} + \boldsymbol{\Phi}\hat{\mathbf{h}}_i$. The noise comprises whatever cannot be explained by the identity. g–l) A second example.

normal. We can then visualize the identity component $\boldsymbol{\mu} + \boldsymbol{\Phi}\hat{\mathbf{h}}_i$, which is the same for each image of the same individual and looks like a prototypical view of that person. We can also visualize the within-individual noise $\hat{\boldsymbol{\epsilon}}_{ij} = \mathbf{x}_{ij} - \boldsymbol{\mu} - \boldsymbol{\Phi}\hat{\mathbf{h}}_i$, which explains how each image of the same person differs.

18.1.2 Inference

We will now discuss how to exploit the model to make inferences about new faces that were not part of the training data set. In face verification problems, we observe two data examples $\mathbf{x}_1$ and $\mathbf{x}_2$ and wish to infer the state of the world $w \in \{0,1\}$, where $w = 0$ denotes the case where the data examples have different identities and $w = 1$ denotes the case where the data examples have the same identity.

This is a generative model, and so we calculate the posterior $Pr(w|\mathbf{x}_1,\mathbf{x}_2)$ over the world state using Bayes' rule

$$Pr(w = 1|\mathbf{x}_1,\mathbf{x}_2) = \frac{Pr(\mathbf{x}_1,\mathbf{x}_2|w = 1)Pr(w = 1)}{\sum_{n=0}^{1} Pr(\mathbf{x}_1,\mathbf{x}_2|w = n)Pr(w = n)}. \tag{18.12}$$

To compute this we need the prior probabilities $Pr(w = 0)$ and $Pr(w = 1)$ of the data examples having different identities or the same identity. In the absence of any other information, we might set these both to 0.5. We also need expressions for the likelihoods $Pr(\mathbf{x}_1,\mathbf{x}_2|w = 0)$ and $Pr(\mathbf{x}_1,\mathbf{x}_2|w = 1)$.

We will first consider the likelihood $Pr(\mathbf{x}_1,\mathbf{x}_2|w = 0)$ when the two datapoints have different identities. Here, each image is explained by a different hidden variable and so the generative equation looks like

$$\begin{bmatrix} \mathbf{x}_1 \\ \mathbf{x}_2 \end{bmatrix} = \begin{bmatrix} \boldsymbol{\mu} \\ \boldsymbol{\mu} \end{bmatrix} + \begin{bmatrix} \boldsymbol{\Phi} & \mathbf{0} \\ \mathbf{0} & \boldsymbol{\Phi} \end{bmatrix} \begin{bmatrix} \mathbf{h}_1 \\ \mathbf{h}_2 \end{bmatrix} + \begin{bmatrix} \boldsymbol{\epsilon}_1 \\ \boldsymbol{\epsilon}_2 \end{bmatrix}, \tag{18.13}$$

We note that this has the form of a factor analyzer:

$$\mathbf{x}' = \boldsymbol{\mu}' + \boldsymbol{\Phi}'\mathbf{h}' + \boldsymbol{\epsilon}'. \tag{18.14}$$

We can reexpress this in probabilistic terms as

$$Pr(\mathbf{x}'|\mathbf{h}') = \text{Norm}_{\mathbf{x}'}[\boldsymbol{\mu}' + \boldsymbol{\Phi}'\mathbf{h}', \boldsymbol{\Sigma}']$$
$$Pr(\mathbf{h}') = \text{Norm}_{\mathbf{h}'}[\mathbf{0}, \mathbf{I}], \tag{18.15}$$

where $\boldsymbol{\Sigma}'$ is defined as

$$\boldsymbol{\Sigma}' = \begin{bmatrix} \boldsymbol{\Sigma} & \mathbf{0} \\ \mathbf{0} & \boldsymbol{\Sigma} \end{bmatrix}. \tag{18.16}$$

We can now compute the likelihood $Pr(\mathbf{x}_1, \mathbf{x}_2 | w = 0)$ by writing the joint likelihood of the compound variables $\mathbf{x}'$ and $\mathbf{h}'$ and marginalizing over $\mathbf{h}'$, so that

$$Pr(\mathbf{x}_1, \mathbf{x}_2 | w = 0) = \int Pr(\mathbf{x}'|\mathbf{h}')Pr(\mathbf{h}') \, d\mathbf{h}'$$
$$= \text{Norm}_{\mathbf{x}'}[\boldsymbol{\mu}', \boldsymbol{\Phi}'\boldsymbol{\Phi}'^T + \boldsymbol{\Sigma}'], \tag{18.17}$$

where we have used the standard factor analysis result for the integration.

For the case where the faces match ($w = 1$), we know that both data examples must have been created from the same hidden variable. To compute the likelihood $Pr(\mathbf{x}_1, \mathbf{x}_2 | w = 1)$, we write the compound generative equation

$$\begin{bmatrix} \mathbf{x}_1 \\ \mathbf{x}_2 \end{bmatrix} = \begin{bmatrix} \boldsymbol{\mu} \\ \boldsymbol{\mu} \end{bmatrix} + \begin{bmatrix} \boldsymbol{\Phi} \\ \boldsymbol{\Phi} \end{bmatrix} \mathbf{h}_{12} + \begin{bmatrix} \boldsymbol{\epsilon}_1 \\ \boldsymbol{\epsilon}_2 \end{bmatrix}, \tag{18.18}$$

which we notice also has the form of a standard factor analyzer (Equation 18.14), and so we can compute the likelihood using the same method.

One way to think about this process is that we are comparing the likelihood for two different models of the data (Figure 18.8a). However, it should be noted that the model that categorizes the faces as different ($w = 0$) has two variables ($\mathbf{h}_1$ and $\mathbf{h}_2$), whereas the model that categorizes the faces as the same ($w = 1$) has only one ($\mathbf{h}_{12}$). One might expect then that the model with more variables would always provide a superior explanation of the data. In fact this does not happen here, because we marginalized these variables out of the likelihoods, and so the final expressions do not include these hidden variables. This is an example of *Bayesian model selection*: it is valid to compare models with different numbers of parameters as long as they are marginalized out of the final solution.

18.1.3   Inference in other recognition tasks

Face verification is only one of several possible face recognition problems. Others include:

- *Closed set identification:* Find which one of N gallery faces matches a given probe face.
- *Open set identification:* Choose one of N gallery faces that matches a probe, or identify that there is no match in the gallery.
- *Clustering:* Given N faces, find how many different people are present and which face belongs to each person.

All of these models can be thought of in terms of model comparison (Figure 18.8). For example, consider a clustering task in which we have three faces $\mathbf{x}_1, \mathbf{x}_2, \mathbf{x}_3$ and wish to

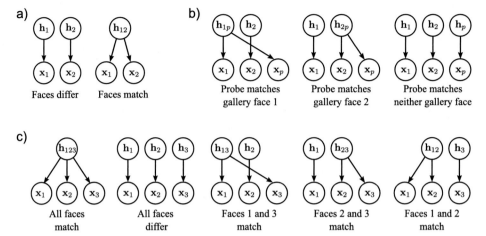

Figure 18.8 Inference as model comparison. a) Verification task. Given two faces x_1 and x_2, we must decide whether (i) they belong to different people and hence have separate hidden variables h_1, h_2 or (ii) they belong to the same person and hence share a single hidden variable h_{12}. These two hypotheses are illustrated as the two graphical models. b) Open set identification task. We are given a library $\{x_i\}_{i=1}^I$ of faces that belong to different people and a probe face x_p. In this case (where $I = 2$), we must decide whether the probe matches (i) gallery face 1, (ii) gallery face 2, or (iii) none of the gallery faces. In closed set identification, we simply omit the latter model. c) Clustering task. Given three faces x_1, x_2, and x_3, we must decide whether (i) they are all from the same person, (ii) all from different people, or (iii–v) two of the three match.

know if (i) there are three different identities, or (ii) all of the images belong to the same person, or (iii) two images belong to the same person and the third belongs to someone different (distinguishing between the three different ways that this can happen). The world can take five states $w \in \{1, 2, 3, 4, 5\}$ corresponding to these five situations, and each is explained by a different compound generative equation. For example, if the first two images are the same person, but the third is different we would write

$$\begin{bmatrix} x_1 \\ x_2 \\ x_3 \end{bmatrix} = \begin{bmatrix} \mu \\ \mu \\ \mu \end{bmatrix} + \begin{bmatrix} \Phi & 0 \\ \Phi & 0 \\ 0 & \Phi \end{bmatrix} \begin{bmatrix} h_{12} \\ h_3 \end{bmatrix} + \begin{bmatrix} \epsilon_1 \\ \epsilon_2 \\ \epsilon_3 \end{bmatrix}, \tag{18.19}$$

which again has the form of a factor analyzer, and so we can compute the likelihood using the method described earlier. We compare the likelihood for this model to the likelihoods for the other models using Bayes' rule with suitable priors.

18.1.4 Limitations of identity subspace model

The subspace identity model has three main limitations (Figure 18.9).

1. The model of within-individual covariance (diagonal) is inadequate.
2. It is a linear model and cannot model non-Gaussian densities.
3. It cannot model large changes in style (e.g., frontal vs. profile faces).

We tackle these problems by introducing probabilistic linear discriminant analysis (Section 18.2), nonlinear identity models (Section 18.3), and multilinear models (Sections 18.4–18.5), respectively.

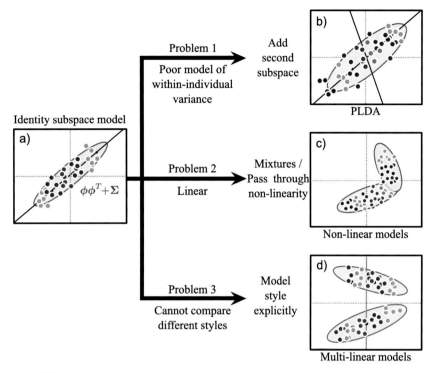

Figure 18.9 Identity models. a) There are three limitations to the subspace identity model. b) First, it has an impoverished model of the within-individual noise. To remedy this we develop probabilistic linear discriminant analysis. c) Second, it is linear and can only describe the distribution of faces as a normal distribution. Hence, we develop nonlinear models based on mixtures and kernels. d) Third, it does not work well when there are large style changes. To cope with this, we introduce multilinear models.

18.2   Probabilistic linear discriminant analysis

The subspace identity model explains the data as the sum of a component due to the identity and an additive noise term. However, the noise term is rather simple: it describes the within-individual variation as a normal distribution with diagonal covariance. The estimated noise components that we visualized in Figure 18.7 contain considerable structure, which suggests that modeling the within-individual variation at each pixel as independent is insufficient.

Probabilistic linear discriminant analysis (PLDA) uses a more sophisticated model for the within-individual variation. This model adds a new term to the generative equation that describes the within-individual variation as also lying on a subspace determined by a second factor matrix $\boldsymbol{\Psi}$. The jth image $\mathbf{x}_{ij}$ of the ith individual is now described as

$$\mathbf{x}_{ij} = \boldsymbol{\mu} + \boldsymbol{\Phi}\mathbf{h}_i + \boldsymbol{\Psi}\mathbf{s}_{ij} + \boldsymbol{\epsilon}, \tag{18.20}$$

where $\mathbf{s}_{ij}$ is a hidden variable that represents the *style* of this face: it describes systematic contributions to the image from uncontrolled viewing parameters. Notice that it differs for each instance j, and so it tells us nothing about identity.

The columns of $\boldsymbol{\Phi}$ describe the space of between-individual variation, and $\mathbf{h}_i$ determines a point in this space. The columns of $\boldsymbol{\Psi}$ describe the space of within-individual

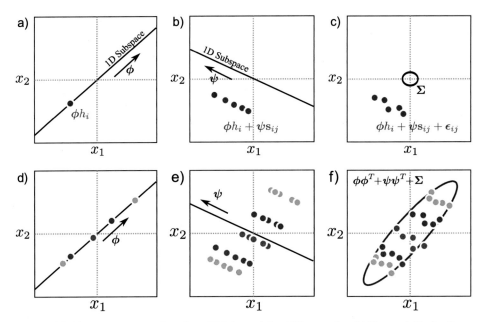

Figure 18.10 Ancestral sampling from PLDA model. a) We sample a hidden variable $\mathbf{h}_i$ from the identity prior and use this to weight the between-individual factors $\mathbf{\Phi}$. b) We sample J hidden variables $\{\mathbf{s}_{ij}\}_{j=1}^{J}$ from the style prior and use these to weight the within-individual factors $\mathbf{\Psi}$. c) Finally, we add normal noise with diagonal covariance, $\mathbf{\Sigma}$. d–f) This process is repeated for several individuals. Notice that the clusters associated with each identity in (f) are now oriented (compare to Figure 18.5f); we have constructed a more sophisticated model of within-individual variation.

variation, and $\mathbf{s}_{ij}$ determines a point in this space. A given face is now modeled as the sum of a term $\boldsymbol{\mu} + \mathbf{\Phi}\mathbf{h}_i$ that derives from the identity of the individual, a term $\mathbf{\Psi}\mathbf{s}_{ij}$ that models the style of this particular image, and a noise term $\boldsymbol{\epsilon}_{ij}$ that explains any remaining variation (Figure 18.10).

Once again, we can write the model in probabilistic terms:

$$Pr(\mathbf{h}_i) = \text{Norm}_{\mathbf{h}_i}[\mathbf{0}, \mathbf{I}]$$
$$Pr(\mathbf{s}_{ij}) = \text{Norm}_{\mathbf{s}_{ij}}[\mathbf{0}, \mathbf{I}]$$
$$Pr(\mathbf{x}_{ij}|\mathbf{h}_i, \mathbf{s}_{ij}) = \text{Norm}_{\mathbf{x}_{ij}}[\boldsymbol{\mu} + \mathbf{\Phi}\mathbf{h}_i + \mathbf{\Psi}\mathbf{s}_{ij}, \mathbf{\Sigma}], \qquad (18.21)$$

where now we have defined priors over both hidden variables.

18.2.1 Learning

In the E-step, we collect together all the J observations $\{\mathbf{x}_{ij}\}_{j=1}^{J}$ associated with the same identity to form the compound system

$$
\begin{bmatrix} \mathbf{x}_{i1} \\ \mathbf{x}_{i2} \\ \vdots \\ \mathbf{x}_{iJ} \end{bmatrix}
=
\begin{bmatrix} \boldsymbol{\mu} \\ \boldsymbol{\mu} \\ \vdots \\ \boldsymbol{\mu} \end{bmatrix}
+
\begin{bmatrix} \mathbf{\Phi} & \mathbf{\Psi} & \mathbf{0} & \dots & \mathbf{0} \\ \mathbf{\Phi} & \mathbf{0} & \mathbf{\Psi} & \dots & \mathbf{0} \\ \vdots & \vdots & \vdots & \ddots & \vdots \\ \mathbf{\Phi} & \mathbf{0} & \mathbf{0} & \dots & \mathbf{\Psi} \end{bmatrix}
\begin{bmatrix} \mathbf{h}_i \\ \mathbf{s}_{i1} \\ \mathbf{s}_{i2} \\ \vdots \\ \mathbf{s}_{iJ} \end{bmatrix}
+
\begin{bmatrix} \boldsymbol{\epsilon}_{i1} \\ \boldsymbol{\epsilon}_{i2} \\ \vdots \\ \boldsymbol{\epsilon}_{iJ} \end{bmatrix}, \qquad (18.22)
$$

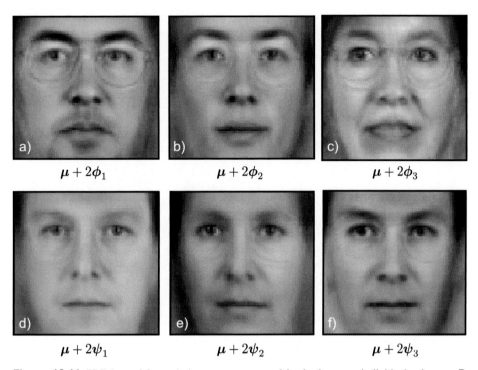

Figure 18.11 PLDA model. a–c) As we move around in the between-individual subspace $\boldsymbol{\Phi}$ the images look like different people. d–f) As we move around in the within-individual subspace $\boldsymbol{\Psi}$ the images look like the same person viewed in slightly different poses and under different illuminations. The PLDA model has successfully separated out contributions that correlate with identity form those that don't. Adapted from Li et al. (2012). ©2012 IEEE.

which takes the form of the original subspace identity model $\mathbf{x}'_i = \boldsymbol{\mu}' + \boldsymbol{\Phi}'\mathbf{h}'_i + \boldsymbol{\epsilon}'$. We can hence compute the joint posterior probability distribution over all of the hidden variables in $\mathbf{h}'$ using Equation 18.9.

In the M-step we write a compound generative equation for each image,

$$\mathbf{x}_{ij} = \boldsymbol{\mu} + \begin{bmatrix} \boldsymbol{\Phi} & \boldsymbol{\Psi} \end{bmatrix} \begin{bmatrix} \mathbf{h}_i \\ \mathbf{s}_{ij} \end{bmatrix} + \boldsymbol{\epsilon}_{ij}. \tag{18.23}$$

On noting that this has the form $\mathbf{x}_{ij} = \boldsymbol{\mu} + \boldsymbol{\Phi}''\mathbf{h}''_{ij} + \boldsymbol{\epsilon}_{ij}$ of the standard factor analysis model, we can solve for the unknown parameters using Equations 18.5. The computations require the expectations $E[\mathbf{h}''_{ij}]$ and $E[\mathbf{h}''_{ij}\mathbf{h}''^{T}_{ij}]$, and these can be extracted from the posterior computed in the E-step.

Figure 18.11 shows parameters learned from $J = 3$ examples each of $I = 195$ people from the XM2VTS database with 16 between-individual basis functions in $\boldsymbol{\Phi}$ and 16 within-individual basis functions in $\boldsymbol{\Psi}$. The figure demonstrates that the model has distinguished these two components.

18.2.2 Inference

As for the subspace identity model, we perform inference by comparing the likelihoods of models using Bayes's rule. For example, in the verification task we compare models that explain the two data examples $\mathbf{x}_1$ and $\mathbf{x}_2$ as having either their own identities $\mathbf{h}_1$ and $\mathbf{h}_2$ or sharing a single identity $\mathbf{h}_{12}$. When the identities are different ($w=0$), the data are generated as

$$
\begin{bmatrix} \mathbf{x}_1 \\ \mathbf{x}_2 \end{bmatrix} = \begin{bmatrix} \boldsymbol{\mu} \\ \boldsymbol{\mu} \end{bmatrix} + \begin{bmatrix} \boldsymbol{\Phi} & \mathbf{0} & \boldsymbol{\Psi} & \mathbf{0} \\ \mathbf{0} & \boldsymbol{\Phi} & \mathbf{0} & \boldsymbol{\Psi} \end{bmatrix} \begin{bmatrix} \mathbf{h}_1 \\ \mathbf{h}_2 \\ \mathbf{s}_1 \\ \mathbf{s}_2 \end{bmatrix} + \begin{bmatrix} \boldsymbol{\epsilon}_1 \\ \boldsymbol{\epsilon}_2 \end{bmatrix} . \tag{18.24}
$$

When the identities are the same ($w=1$), the data are generated as

$$
\begin{bmatrix} \mathbf{x}_1 \\ \mathbf{x}_2 \end{bmatrix} = \begin{bmatrix} \boldsymbol{\mu} \\ \boldsymbol{\mu} \end{bmatrix} + \begin{bmatrix} \boldsymbol{\Phi} & \boldsymbol{\Psi} & \mathbf{0} \\ \boldsymbol{\Phi} & \mathbf{0} & \boldsymbol{\Psi} \end{bmatrix} \begin{bmatrix} \mathbf{h}_{12} \\ \mathbf{s}_1 \\ \mathbf{s}_2 \end{bmatrix} + \begin{bmatrix} \boldsymbol{\epsilon}_1 \\ \boldsymbol{\epsilon}_2 \end{bmatrix} . \tag{18.25}
$$

Both of these formulae have the same form $\mathbf{x}' = \boldsymbol{\mu}' + \boldsymbol{\Phi}'\mathbf{h}' + \boldsymbol{\epsilon}'$ as the original factor analysis model, and so the likelihood of the data $\mathbf{x}'$ after marginalizing out the hidden variables $\mathbf{h}'$ is given by

$$
Pr(\mathbf{x}') = \mathrm{Norm}_{\mathbf{x}'}[\boldsymbol{\mu}', \boldsymbol{\Phi}'\boldsymbol{\Phi}'^T + \boldsymbol{\Sigma}'], \tag{18.26}
$$

where the particular choice of $\boldsymbol{\Phi}'$ comes from Equations 18.24 or 18.25, respectively. Other inference tasks concerning identity such as closed set recognition and clustering can be formulated in a similar way; we associate one value of the discrete world variable $w = \{1, \ldots, K\}$ with each possible configuration of identities, construct a generative model for each, and compare the likelihoods via Bayes' rule.

Figure 18.12 compares closed set identification performance for several models as a function of the subspace size (for the PLDA models, the size of $\boldsymbol{\Psi}$ and $\boldsymbol{\Phi}$ were always the same). The results are not state of the art: the images were not properly preprocessed, and anyway, this data set is considered relatively unchallenging. Nonetheless, the pattern of results nicely demonstrates an important point The %-correct classification improves

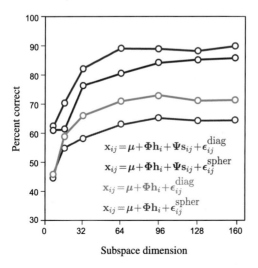

Figure 18.12 Face recognition results. The models were trained using three 70×70 RGB images each from 195 people from the XM2VTS database and tested using two images each from 100 different people. A gallery was formed from one image of each of the test individuals. For each of the remaining 100 test images the system had to identify the match in the gallery. Plots show %-correct performance as a function of subspace dimensionality (number of columns in $\boldsymbol{\Phi}$ and $\boldsymbol{\Psi}$). Results show that as the noise model becomes more complex (adding within-individual subspace, using diagonal rather than spherical additive noise) the results improve systematically.

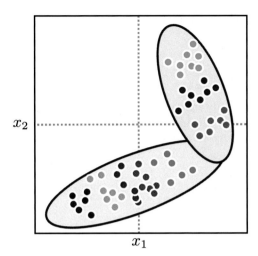

Figure 18.13 Mixture models. One way to create more complex models is to use a mixture of subspace identity models, or a mixture of PLDAs. A discrete variable is associated with each datapoint that indicates to which mixture component it belongs. If two faces belong to the same person, this must be the same; every image of the same person is associated with one mixture component. The within-individual model may also vary between components. Consequently, the within-individual variation may differ depending on the identity of the face.

as we increases the model's ability to describe within-individual noise: building more complex models is worth the time and effort!

18.3   Nonlinear identity models

The models discussed so far describe the between-individual and within-individual variance by means of linear models and produce final densities that are normally distributed. However, there is no particular reason to believe that the distribution of faces is normal. We now briefly discuss two methods to generalize the preceding models to the nonlinear case.

The first approach is to note that since the identity subspace model and PLDA are both valid probabilistic models, we can easily describe a more complex distribution in terms of mixtures of these elements. For example, a mixture of PLDAs model (Figure 18.13) can be written as

$$Pr(c_i) = \text{Cat}_{c_i}[\boldsymbol{\lambda}]$$
$$Pr(\mathbf{h}_i) = \text{Norm}_{\mathbf{h}_i}[\mathbf{0}, \mathbf{I}]$$
$$Pr(\mathbf{s}_{ij}) = \text{Norm}_{\mathbf{s}_{ij}}[\mathbf{0}, \mathbf{I}]$$
$$Pr(\mathbf{x}_{ij}|c_i, \mathbf{h}_i, \mathbf{s}_{ij}) = \text{Norm}_{\mathbf{x}_{ij}}[\boldsymbol{\mu}_{c_i} + \boldsymbol{\Phi}_{c_i}\mathbf{h}_i + \boldsymbol{\Psi}_{c_i}\mathbf{s}_{ij}, \boldsymbol{\Sigma}_{c_i}], \qquad (18.27)$$

where $c_i \in [1 \dots C]$ is a hidden variable that determines to which of the c clusters the data belong. Each cluster has different parameters, so the full model is nonlinear. To learn this model, we embed the existing learning algorithm inside a second EM loop that associates each identity with a cluster. In inference, we assume that faces must belong to the same cluster if they match.

A second approach is based on the Gaussian process latent variable model (see Section 17.8). The idea is to induce a complex density by passing the hidden variable through a nonlinear function $\mathbf{f}[\bullet]$ before using the result to weight the basis functions. For example, the generalization of the subspace identity model to the nonlinear case can be written as

$$Pr(\mathbf{h}_i) = \text{Norm}_{\mathbf{h}_i}[\mathbf{0}, \mathbf{I}]$$
$$Pr(\mathbf{x}_{ij}|\mathbf{h}_i, \boldsymbol{\mu}, \boldsymbol{\Phi}, \boldsymbol{\Sigma}) = \text{Norm}_{\mathbf{x}_{ij}}[\boldsymbol{\mu} + \boldsymbol{\Phi}\mathbf{f}[\mathbf{h}_i], \boldsymbol{\Sigma}]. \tag{18.28}$$

Although this model is conceptually simple, it is harder to work with in practice: it is no longer possible to marginalize over the hidden variables. However, the model is still linear with respect to the factor matrix $\boldsymbol{\Phi}$, and it is possible to marginalize over this and the mean $\boldsymbol{\mu}$, giving a likelihood term of the form

$$Pr(\mathbf{x}_{ij}|\mathbf{h}_i, \boldsymbol{\Sigma}) = \int\int \text{Norm}_{\mathbf{x}_{ij}}[\boldsymbol{\mu} + \boldsymbol{\Phi}\mathbf{f}[\mathbf{h}_i], \boldsymbol{\Sigma}] d\boldsymbol{\mu} d\boldsymbol{\Phi}. \tag{18.29}$$

This model can be expressed in terms of inner products of the transformed hidden variables $\mathbf{f}[\mathbf{h}]$ and so is amenable to kernelization. Unfortunately, because we cannot marginalize over $\mathbf{h}_i$, it is no longer possible exactly to compare model likelihoods directly in the inference stage. However, in practice there are ways to approximate this process.

18.4 Asymmetric bilinear models

The models that we have discussed so far are sufficient if the within-individual variation is small. However, there are other situations where the style of the data may change considerably. For example, consider the problem of face recognition when some of the faces are frontal and others profile. Unfortunately, any given frontal face has more in common visually with other non-matching frontal faces than it does with a matching profile face.

Motivated by this problem, we now develop the *asymmetric bilinear model* for modeling identity and style: as before, we treat the identity $\mathbf{h}_i$ as continuous, but now we treat the style $s \in \{1 \ldots S\}$ as discrete taking one of S possible values. For example, in the cross-pose face recognition example, $s = 0$ might indicate a frontal face, and $s = 1$ might indicate a profile face. The model is hence asymmetric as it treats identity and style differently. The expression of the identity depends on the style category so that the same identity may produce completely different data in different styles.

We adopt the notation $\mathbf{x}_{ijs}$ to denote the jth of J examples of the ith of I identities in the sth of S styles. The data are generated as

$$\mathbf{x}_{ijs} = \boldsymbol{\mu}_s + \boldsymbol{\Phi}_s\mathbf{h}_i + \boldsymbol{\epsilon}_{ijs}, \tag{18.30}$$

where $\boldsymbol{\mu}_s$ is a mean vector associated with the sth style, $\boldsymbol{\Phi}_s$ contains basis functions associated with the sth style, and $\boldsymbol{\epsilon}_{ijs}$ is additive normal noise with a covariance $\boldsymbol{\Sigma}_s$ that also depends on the style. When the noise covariances are spherical, this model is a probabilistic form of *canonical correlation analysis*. When the noise is diagonal, it is known as *tied factor analysis*. We will use the generic term *asymmetric bilinear model* to cover both situations.

Equation 18.30 is easy to parse; for a given individual, the identity $\mathbf{h}_i$ is constant. The data are explained as a weighted linear sum of basis functions, where the weights

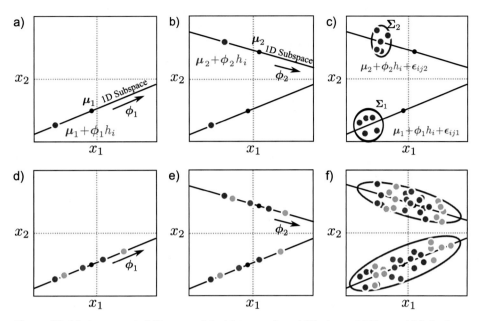

Figure 18.14 Asymmetric bilinear model with two styles. a) We draw a hidden variable $\mathbf{h}_i$ from the prior and use this to weight basis functions $\boldsymbol{\Phi}_1$ (one basis function ϕ_1 shown). The result is added to the mean $\boldsymbol{\mu}_1$. b) We use the same value of $\mathbf{h}_i$ to weight a second set of basis functions $\boldsymbol{\Phi}_2$ and add the result to $\boldsymbol{\mu}_2$. c) We add normally distributed noise with a diagonal covariance $\boldsymbol{\Sigma}_s$ that depends on the style. d–f) When we repeat this procedure, it produces one normal distribution per style. The data within each style are structured so that nearby points have the same identity (color) and identities that are close in one cluster are also close in the other cluster.

determine the identity. However, the basis functions (and other aspects of the model) are now contingent on the style.

We can write the model in probabilistic terms as

$$Pr(s) = \text{Cat}_s[\boldsymbol{\lambda}]$$
$$Pr(\mathbf{h}_i) = \text{Norm}_{\mathbf{h}_i}[\mathbf{0}, \mathbf{I}]$$
$$Pr(\mathbf{x}_{ijs}|\mathbf{h}_i, s) = \text{Norm}_{\mathbf{x}_{ijs}}[\boldsymbol{\mu}_s + \boldsymbol{\Phi}_s \mathbf{h}_i, \boldsymbol{\Sigma}_s], \tag{18.31}$$

where $\boldsymbol{\lambda}$ contains parameters that determine the probability of observing data in each style. Figure 18.14 demonstrates ancestral sampling from this model. If we marginalize over the identity parameter $\mathbf{h}$ and the style parameter s, the overall data distribution (without regard to the structure of the style clusters) is a mixture of factor analyzers,

$$Pr(\mathbf{x}) = \sum_{s=1}^{S} \lambda_s \text{Norm}_{\mathbf{x}}[\boldsymbol{\mu}_s, \boldsymbol{\Phi}_s \boldsymbol{\Phi}_s^T + \boldsymbol{\Sigma}_s]. \tag{18.32}$$

18.4.1 Learning

For simplicity, we will assume that the styles of each training example are known and so it is also trivial to estimate the categorical parameters $\boldsymbol{\lambda}$. As for the previous models in this chapter, we employ the EM algorithm.

In the E-step, we compute a posterior distribution over the hidden variable $\mathbf{h}_i$ that represents the identity, using all of the training data for that individual regardless of the style. Employing Bayes' rule, we have

$$Pr(\mathbf{h}_i|\mathbf{x}_{i\bullet\bullet}) = \frac{\prod_{j=1}^{J}\prod_{s=1}^{S}Pr(\mathbf{x}_{ijs}|\mathbf{h}_i)Pr(\mathbf{h}_i)}{\int\prod_{j=1}^{J}\prod_{s=1}^{S}Pr(\mathbf{x}_{ijs}|\mathbf{h}_i)Pr(\mathbf{h}_i)\,d\mathbf{h}_i}, \tag{18.33}$$

where $\mathbf{x}_{i\bullet\bullet} = \{\mathbf{x}_{ijs}\}_{j,s=1}^{J,S}$ denotes all the data associated with the ith individual.

One way to compute this is to write a compound generative equation for $\mathbf{x}_{i\bullet\bullet}$. For example, with $J = 2$ images at each of $S = 2$ styles we would have

$$\begin{bmatrix} \mathbf{x}_{i11} \\ \mathbf{x}_{i12} \\ \mathbf{x}_{i21} \\ \mathbf{x}_{i22} \end{bmatrix} = \begin{bmatrix} \boldsymbol{\mu}_1 \\ \boldsymbol{\mu}_2 \\ \boldsymbol{\mu}_1 \\ \boldsymbol{\mu}_2 \end{bmatrix} + \begin{bmatrix} \boldsymbol{\Phi}_1 \\ \boldsymbol{\Phi}_2 \\ \boldsymbol{\Phi}_1 \\ \boldsymbol{\Phi}_2 \end{bmatrix}\mathbf{h}_i + \begin{bmatrix} \boldsymbol{\epsilon}_{11} \\ \boldsymbol{\epsilon}_{12} \\ \boldsymbol{\epsilon}_{21} \\ \boldsymbol{\epsilon}_{22} \end{bmatrix}, \tag{18.34}$$

which has the same form as the identity subspace model, $\mathbf{x}'_{ij} = \boldsymbol{\mu}' + \boldsymbol{\Phi}'\mathbf{h}_i + \boldsymbol{\epsilon}'_{ij}$. We can hence compute the posterior distribution using Equation 18.9 and extract the expected values needed for the M-step using Equation 18.10.

In the M-step we update the parameters $\boldsymbol{\theta}_s = \{\boldsymbol{\mu}_s, \boldsymbol{\Phi}_s, \boldsymbol{\Sigma}_s\}$ for each style separately using all of the relevant data. This gives the updates

$$\hat{\boldsymbol{\mu}}_s = \frac{\sum_{i=1}^{I}\sum_{j=1}^{J}\mathbf{x}_{ijs}}{IJ}$$

$$\hat{\boldsymbol{\Phi}}_s = \left(\sum_{i=1}^{I}\sum_{j=1}^{J}(\mathbf{x}_{ijs} - \hat{\boldsymbol{\mu}}_s)\mathrm{E}[\mathbf{h}_i]^T\right)\left(J\sum_{i=1}^{I}\mathrm{E}[\mathbf{h}_i\mathbf{h}_i^T]\right)^{-1}$$

$$\hat{\boldsymbol{\Sigma}}_s = \frac{1}{IJ}\sum_{i=1}^{I}\sum_{j=1}^{J}\mathrm{diag}\left[(\mathbf{x}_{ijs} - \hat{\boldsymbol{\mu}}_s)^T(\mathbf{x}_{ijs} - \hat{\boldsymbol{\mu}}_s) - \hat{\boldsymbol{\Phi}}_s\mathrm{E}[\mathbf{h}_i]\mathbf{x}_{ijs}^T\right]. \tag{18.35}$$

As usual, we iterate these two steps until the system converges and the log likelihood ceases to improve. Figure 18.15 shows examples of the learned parameters for a data set that includes faces at two poses.

18.4.2 Inference

There are a number of possible forms of inference in this model. These include:

1. Given $\mathbf{x}$, infer the style $s \in \{1,\ldots,S\}$.
2. Given $\mathbf{x}$, infer the parameterized identity $\mathbf{h}$.
3. Given $\mathbf{x}_1$ and $\mathbf{x}_2$, infer whether they have the same identity or not.
4. Given $\mathbf{x}_1$ in style s_1, translate the style to s_2 to create $\hat{\mathbf{x}}_2$.

We will consider each in turn.

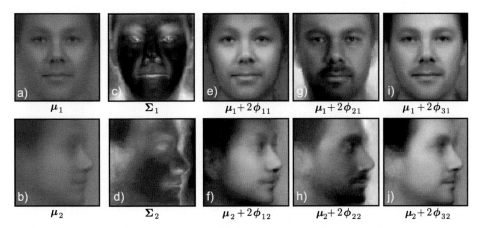

Figure 18.15 Learned parameters of asymmetric bilinear model with two styles (frontal and profile faces). This model was learned from one 70×70 image of each style in 200 individuals from the FERET data set. a–b) Mean vector for each style. c–d) Diagonal covariance for each style. e–f) Varying first basis function in each style (notation ϕ_{ks} denotes k^{th} basis function of sth style). g–h) Varying second basis function in each style. i–l) Varying third basis function in each style. Manipulating the two sets of basis functions in the same way produces images that look like the same person, viewed in each of the styles. Adapted from Prince et al. (2008). ©2008 IEEE.

Inferring style

The likelihood of the data given style s but regardless of identity $\mathbf{h}$ is

$$
\begin{aligned}
Pr(\mathbf{x}|s) &= \int Pr(\mathbf{x}|\mathbf{h}, s) Pr(\mathbf{h}) \, d\mathbf{h} \\
&= \int \text{Norm}_{\mathbf{x}}[\boldsymbol{\mu}_s + \boldsymbol{\Phi}_s \mathbf{h}, \boldsymbol{\Sigma}_s] Pr(\mathbf{h}) \, d\mathbf{h} \\
&= \text{Norm}_{\mathbf{x}}[\boldsymbol{\mu}_s, \boldsymbol{\Phi}_s \boldsymbol{\Phi}_s^T + \boldsymbol{\Sigma}_s].
\end{aligned}
\tag{18.36}
$$

The posterior $Pr(s|\mathbf{x})$ over style s can be computed by combining this likelihood with the prior $Pr(s)$ using Bayes' rule. The prior for style s is given by

$$
Pr(s) = \text{Cat}_s[\boldsymbol{\lambda}].
\tag{18.37}
$$

Inferring identity

The likelihood of the data for a fixed identity $\mathbf{h}$ but regardless of style s is

$$
\begin{aligned}
Pr(\mathbf{x}|\mathbf{h}) &= \sum_{s=1}^{S} Pr(\mathbf{x}|\mathbf{h}, s) Pr(s) \\
&= \sum_{s=1}^{S} \text{Norm}_x[\boldsymbol{\mu}_s + \boldsymbol{\Phi}_s \mathbf{h}, \boldsymbol{\Sigma}_s] \lambda_s.
\end{aligned}
\tag{18.38}
$$

The posterior over identity can now be combined with the prior $Pr(\mathbf{h})$ using Bayes' rule and is given by

$$Pr(\mathbf{h}|\mathbf{x}) = \sum_{s=1}^{S} \lambda_s \text{Norm}_{\mathbf{h}_i}[(\boldsymbol{\Phi}_s^T \boldsymbol{\Sigma}_s^{-1} \boldsymbol{\Phi}_s + \mathbf{I})^{-1} \boldsymbol{\Phi}_s^T \boldsymbol{\Sigma}_s^{-1} (\mathbf{x}_i - \boldsymbol{\mu}_s), (\boldsymbol{\Phi}_s^T \boldsymbol{\Sigma}_s^{-1} \boldsymbol{\Phi}_s + \mathbf{I})].$$

(18.39)

Note that this posterior distribution is a mixture of Gaussians, with one component for each possible style.

Identity matching

Given two examples $\mathbf{x}_1, \mathbf{x}_2$, compute the posterior probability that they have the same identity, even though they may be viewed in different styles. We will initially assume the styles are known and are s_1 and s_2, respectively. We first build the compound model

$$\begin{bmatrix} \mathbf{x}_1 \\ \mathbf{x}_2 \end{bmatrix} = \begin{bmatrix} \boldsymbol{\mu}_{s_1} \\ \boldsymbol{\mu}_{s_2} \end{bmatrix} + \begin{bmatrix} \boldsymbol{\Phi}_{s_1} & \mathbf{0} \\ \mathbf{0} & \boldsymbol{\Phi}_{s_2} \end{bmatrix} \begin{bmatrix} \mathbf{h}_1 \\ \mathbf{h}_2 \end{bmatrix} + \begin{bmatrix} \boldsymbol{\epsilon}_1 \\ \boldsymbol{\epsilon}_2 \end{bmatrix},$$

(18.40)

which represents the case where the identities differ $(w = 0)$. We compute the likelihood by noting that this has the form $\mathbf{x}' = \boldsymbol{\mu}' + \boldsymbol{\Phi}'\mathbf{h}' + \boldsymbol{\epsilon}'$ of the original factor analyzer, and so we can write

$$Pr(\mathbf{x}'|w = 0) = \text{Norm}_{\mathbf{x}'}[\boldsymbol{\mu}', \boldsymbol{\Phi}'\boldsymbol{\Phi}'^T + \boldsymbol{\Sigma}'],$$

(18.41)

where $\boldsymbol{\Sigma}'$ is a diagonal matrix containing the (diagonal) covariances of the elements of $\boldsymbol{\epsilon}'$ (as in Equation 18.16).

Similarly, we can build a system for when the identities match $(w = 1)$

$$\begin{bmatrix} \mathbf{x}_1 \\ \mathbf{x}_2 \end{bmatrix} = \begin{bmatrix} \boldsymbol{\mu}_{s_1} \\ \boldsymbol{\mu}_{s_2} \end{bmatrix} + \begin{bmatrix} \boldsymbol{\Phi}_{s_1} \\ \boldsymbol{\Phi}_{s_2} \end{bmatrix} \mathbf{h}_{12} + \begin{bmatrix} \boldsymbol{\epsilon}_1 \\ \boldsymbol{\epsilon}_2 \end{bmatrix}$$

(18.42)

and compute its likelihood $Pr(\mathbf{x}'|w = 1)$ in the same way. The posterior probability $Pr(w = 1|\mathbf{x}')$ can then be computed using Bayes' rule.

If we do not know the styles, then each likelihood term will become a mixture of Gaussians where each component has the form of Equation 18.41. There will be one component for every one of the S^2 combinations of the two styles. The mixing weights will be given by the probability of observing that combination so that $Pr(s_1 = m, s_2 = n) = \lambda_m \lambda_n$.

Style translation

Finally, let us consider style translation. Given observed data $\mathbf{x}$ in style s_1 translate to the style s_2 while maintaining the same identity. A simple way to get a point estimate of the translated styles is to first estimate the identity variable $\mathbf{h}$ based on the observed image $\mathbf{x}_{s1}$. To do this, we compute the posterior distribution over the hidden variable

$$Pr(\mathbf{h}|\mathbf{x}, s_1) = \text{Norm}_{\mathbf{h}_i}[(\boldsymbol{\Phi}_{s_1}^T \boldsymbol{\Sigma}_{s_1}^{-1} \boldsymbol{\Phi}_{s_1} + \mathbf{I})^{-1} \boldsymbol{\Phi}_{s_1}^T \boldsymbol{\Sigma}_{s_1}^{-1} (\mathbf{x}_i - \boldsymbol{\mu}_{s_1}), (\boldsymbol{\Phi}_{s_1}^T \boldsymbol{\Sigma}_{s_1}^{-1} \boldsymbol{\Phi}_{s_1} + \mathbf{I})],$$

(18.43)

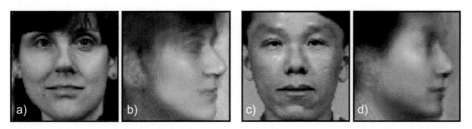

Figure 18.16 Style translation based on asymmetric bilinear model from Figure 18.15. a) Original face in style 1 (frontal). b) Translated to style 2 (profile). c–d) A second example. Adapted from Prince et al. (2008). ©2008 IEEE.

and then set $\mathbf{h}$ to the MAP estimate

$$\hat{\mathbf{h}}_{MAP} = \underset{\mathbf{h}}{\operatorname{argmax}} \left[Pr(\mathbf{h}|\mathbf{x}, s_1) \right]$$
$$= (\mathbf{\Phi}_{s_1}^T \mathbf{\Sigma}_{s_1}^{-1} \mathbf{\Phi}_{s_1})^{-1} \mathbf{\Phi}_{s_1}^T \mathbf{\Sigma}_{s_1}^{-1} (\mathbf{x}_i - \boldsymbol{\mu}_{s_1}), \tag{18.44}$$

which is just the mean of this distribution.

We then generate the image in the second style as

$$\mathbf{x}_{s_2} = \boldsymbol{\mu}_{s_2} + \mathbf{\Phi}_{s_2} \hat{\mathbf{h}}_{MAP}, \tag{18.45}$$

which is the original generative equation with the noise term omitted.

18.5 Symmetric bilinear and multilinear models

As the name suggests, symmetric bilinear models treat both style and identity equivalently. Both are continuous variables, and the model is linear in each. To write these models in a compact way, it is necessary to introduce tensor product notation. In this notation (see Appendix C.3), the generative equation for the subspace identity model (Equation 18.6) is written as

$$\mathbf{x}_{ij} = \boldsymbol{\mu} + \mathbf{\Phi} \times_2 \mathbf{h}_i + \boldsymbol{\epsilon}_{ij}, \tag{18.46}$$

where the notation $\mathbf{\Phi} \times_2 \mathbf{h}_i$ means take the dot product of the second dimension of $\mathbf{\Phi}$ with $\mathbf{h}_i$. Since $\mathbf{\Phi}$ was originally a 2D matrix, this returns a vector.

In the symmetric bilinear model, the generative equation for the jth example of the ith identity in the kth style is given by

$$\mathbf{x}_{ijk} = \boldsymbol{\mu} + \mathbf{\Phi} \times_2 \mathbf{h}_i \times_3 \mathbf{s}_k + \boldsymbol{\epsilon}_{ijk}, \tag{18.47}$$

where $\mathbf{h}_i$ is a 1D vector representing the identity, $\mathbf{s}_k$ is a 1D vector representing the style, and $\mathbf{\Phi}$ is now a 3D tensor. In the expression $\mathbf{\Phi} \times_2 \mathbf{h}_i \times_3 \mathbf{s}_k$ we take the dot product with two of these three dimensions, leaving a column vector as desired.

In probabilistic form, we write

$$Pr(\mathbf{h}_i) = \operatorname{Norm}_{\mathbf{h}_i}[\mathbf{0}, \mathbf{I}]$$
$$Pr(\mathbf{s}_k) = \operatorname{Norm}_{\mathbf{s}_k}[\mathbf{0}, \mathbf{I}]$$
$$Pr(\mathbf{x}_{ijk}|\mathbf{h}_i, \mathbf{s}_k) = \operatorname{Norm}_{\mathbf{x}_{ijk}}[\boldsymbol{\mu} + \mathbf{\Phi} \times_2 \mathbf{h}_i \times_3 \mathbf{s}_k, \mathbf{\Sigma}]. \tag{18.48}$$

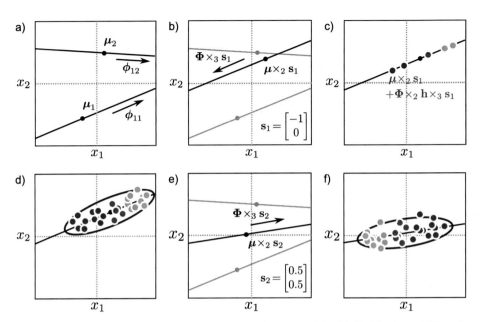

Figure 18.17 Ancestral sampling from symmetric bilinear model, with 1D identity and 2D style. a) In this model each style dimension consists of a subspace identity model with a 1D subspace. b) For a given style vector s_1, we weight these models to create a new subspace identity model. c) We then generate from this by weighting the factor by the hidden variable h and d) adding noise to generate different instances of this identity in this style. e) A different weighting induced by the style vector s_2 creates a different subspace model. f) Generation from the resulting subspace identity model.

For a fixed style vector s_k this model is exactly a subspace identity model with hidden variable h_i The choice of style determines the factors by weighting a set of basis functions to create them. It is also possible to make the mean vector depend on the style by using the model

$$\mathbf{x}_{ijk} = \boldsymbol{\mu} \times_2 \mathbf{s}_k + \boldsymbol{\Phi} \times_2 \mathbf{h}_i \times_3 \mathbf{s}_k + \boldsymbol{\epsilon}_{ijk}, \qquad (18.49)$$

where $\boldsymbol{\mu}$ is now a matrix with basis functions in the columns that are weighted by the style s. Ancestral sampling from this model is illustrated in Figure 18.17.

It is instructive to compare the asymmetric and symmetric bilinear models. In the asymmetric bilinear model, there were a discrete number of styles each of which generated data that individually looked like a subspace identity model, but the model induced a relationship between the position of an identity in one style cluster and in another. In the symmetric bilinear model, there is a continuous family of styles that produces a continuous family of subspace identity models. Again the model induces a relationship between the position of an identity in each.

Up to this point, we have described the model as a subspace identity model for fixed style. The model is symmetric, and so it is possible to reverse the roles of the variables. For a fixed identity, the model looks like a subspace model where the basis functions are weighted by the variable s_k. In other words, the model is linear in both sets of hidden variables when the other is fixed. It is *not*, however, simultaneously linear in both h and s together. These variables have a nonlinear interaction, and overall the model is nonlinear.

18.5.1 Learning

Unfortunately, is not possible to compute the likelihood of the bilinear model in closed form; we cannot simultaneously marginalize over both sets of hidden variables and compute

$$Pr(\mathbf{x}_{ijk}|\boldsymbol{\theta}) = \int\int Pr(\mathbf{x}_{ijk},\mathbf{h}_i,\mathbf{s}_k|\boldsymbol{\theta})\,d\mathbf{h}_i ds_k, \qquad (18.50)$$

where $\boldsymbol{\theta} = \{\boldsymbol{\mu},\boldsymbol{\Phi},\boldsymbol{\Sigma}\}$ represents all of the unknown parameters. The usual approach for learning models with hidden variables is to use the EM algorithm, but this is no longer suitable because we cannot compute the joint posterior distribution over the hidden variables $Pr(\mathbf{h}_i,\mathbf{s}_k|\{\mathbf{x}_{ijk}\}_{j=1}^J)$ in closed form either.

For the special case of spherical additive noise $\boldsymbol{\Sigma} = \sigma^2\mathbf{I}$, and complete data (where we see J examples of each of the I individuals in each of K styles), it is possible to solve for the parameters in closed form using a method similar to that used for PPCA (Section 17.5.1). This technique relies on the *N-mode singular value decomposition*, which is the generalization of the SVD to higher dimensions.

For models with diagonal noise, we can approximate by maximizing over one of the hidden variables rather than marginalizing over them. For example, if we maximize over the style parameters so that

$$\boldsymbol{\theta} = \underset{\boldsymbol{\theta}}{\operatorname{argmax}}\left[\sum_{k=1}^K\underset{\mathbf{s}_k}{\max}\left[\sum_{i=1}^I\sum_{j=1}^J\log\left[\int Pr(\mathbf{x}_{ijk},\mathbf{h}_i,\mathbf{s}_k|\boldsymbol{\theta})\,d\mathbf{h}_i\right]\right]\right], \qquad (18.51)$$

then the remaining model is linear in the hidden variables $\mathbf{h}_i$. It would hence be possible to apply an alternating approach in which we first fix the styles and learn the parameters with the EM algorithm and then fix the parameters and update the style parameters using optimization.

18.5.2 Inference

Various forms of inference are possible, including all of those discussed for the asymmetric bilinear model. We can, for example, make decisions about whether identities match by comparing different compound models. It is not possible to marginalize over both the identity and style variables in these models, and so we maximize over the style variable in a similar manner to the learning procedure. Similarly, we can translate from one style to another by estimating the identity variable $\mathbf{h}$ (and the current style variable $\mathbf{s}$ if unknown) from the observed data. We then use the generative equation with a different style vector $\mathbf{s}$ to simulate a new example in a different style.

The symmetric bilinear model has a continuous parameterization of style, and so it is also possible to perform a new translation task: given an example whose identity we have not previously seen *and* whose style we have not previously seen, we can translate either its style or identity as required. We first compute the current identity and style which can be done using a nonlinear optimization approach,

$$\hat{\mathbf{h}},\hat{\mathbf{s}} = \underset{\mathbf{h},\mathbf{s}}{\operatorname{argmax}}\left[Pr(\mathbf{x}|\boldsymbol{\theta},\mathbf{h},\mathbf{s})Pr(\mathbf{h})Pr(\mathbf{s})\right]. \qquad (18.52)$$

Then we simulate new examples using the generative equation, modifying the style $\mathbf{s}$ or identity $\mathbf{h}$ as required. An example of this is shown in Figure 18.18.

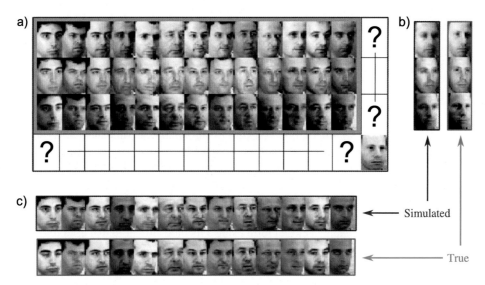

Figure 18.18 Translation of styles using symmetric bilinear model. a) We learn the model from a set of images, where the styles (rows) and identities (columns) are known. Then we are given a new image which has a previously unseen identity and style. b) The symmetric bilinear model can estimate the identity parameters and simulate the image in new styles, or c) estimate the style parameters and simulate new identities. In both cases, the simulated results are close to the ground truth. Adapted from Tenenbaum and Freeman (2000). ©2000 MIT Press.

18.5.3 Multilinear models

The symmetric bilinear model can be extended to create *multilinear* or *multifactor* models. For example, we might describe our data as depending on three hidden variables, $\mathbf{h}, \mathbf{s}$ and $\mathbf{t}$, so the generative equation becomes

$$\mathbf{x}_{ijkl} = \boldsymbol{\mu} + \boldsymbol{\Phi} \times_2 \mathbf{h}_i \times_3 \mathbf{s}_k \times_4 \mathbf{t}_l + \boldsymbol{\epsilon}_{ijkl}, \qquad (18.53)$$

and now the tensor $\boldsymbol{\Phi}$ becomes four-dimensional. As in the symmetric bilinear model, it is not possible to marginalize over all of the hidden variables in closed form, and this constrains the possible methods for learning and inference.

18.6   Applications

We have illustrated many of the models in this chapter with examples from face recognition. In this section, we will describe face recognition in more detail and talk about some of the practicalities of building a recognition system. Subsequently, we will discuss an application in which a visual texture is compactly represented as a multilinear model. Finally, we will describe a nonlinear version of the multilinear model that can be used to synthesize animation data.

18.6.1 Face recognition

To provide a more concrete idea of how well these algorithms work in practice, we will discuss a recent application in detail. Li et al. (2012) present a recognition system based on probabilistic linear discriminant analysis.

Eight keypoints on each face were identified, and the images were registered using a piecewise affine warp. The final image size was 400×400. Feature vectors were extracted from the area of the image around each keypoint. The feature vectors consisted of image gradients at 8 orientations and three scales at points in a 6×6 grid centered on the keypoint. A separate recognition model was built for each keypoint and these were treated as independent in the final recognition decision.

The system was trained using only the first 195 individuals from the XM2VTS database and signal and noise subspaces of size 64. In testing, the algorithm was presented with 80 images taken from the remaining 100 individuals in the database and was required to cluster them into groups according to identity. There may be 80 images of the same person or 80 images of different people or any permutation between these extremes.

In principle it is possible to calculate the likelihood for each possible clustering of the data. Unfortunately, in practice there are far too many possible configurations. Hence, Li et al. (2012) adopted a greedy agglomerative strategy. They started with the hypothesis that there are 80 different individuals. They considered merging all pairs of individuals and chose the combination that increased the likelihood the most. They repeated this process until the likelihood could not be improved. Example clustering results are illustrated in Figure 18.19 and are typical of state-of-the-art recognition algorithms; they cope relatively easily with frontal faces under controlled lighting conditions.

However, for more natural images the same algorithms struggle even with more sophisticated preprocessing. For example, Li et al. (2012) applied the PLDA model to face verification in the "Labeled Faces in the Wild" dataset (Huang et al. 2007b), which

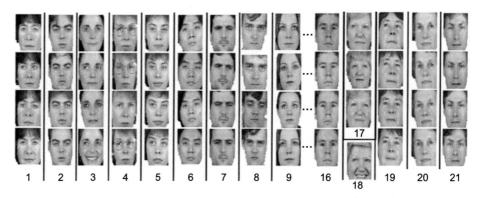

Figure 18.19 Face clustering results from Li et al. (2012). The algorithm was presented with a set of 80 faces consisting of with 4 pictures each of 20 people and clustered these almost perfectly; it correctly found 19 of these 20 groups of images but erroneously divided the data from one individual into two separate clusters. The algorithm works well for these frontal faces despite changes in expression (e.g., cluster 3), changes in hairstyle (e.g., cluster 9) and the addition or removal of glasses (e.g., cluster 4). Adapted from Li et al. (2012). ©2012 IEEE.

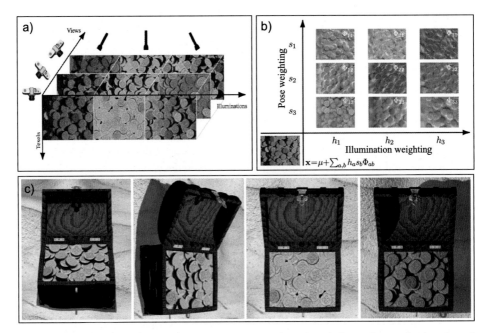

Figure 18.20 Tensor textures. a) The training set consists of renderings of a set of coins viewed from several different directions and with several different lighting directions. b) A new texture (bottom-left corner) is computed as a weighted sum of the learned basis functions stored in the 3D tensor Φ. c) Several frames of a video sequence in which the texture is synthesized appropriately from the model. Adapted from Vasilescu and Terzopoulos (2004). ©2003 ACM.

contains images of famous people collected from the Internet, and obtained an equal-error rate of approximately 10 percent. This is typical of the state of the art at the time of writing and is much worse than for faces captured under controlled conditions.

18.6.2 Modeling texture

The interaction of light with a surface can be described by the bi-directional reflectance distribution function; essentially, this describes the outgoing light at each angle from the surface given incoming light at a particular angle to the surface. The bi-directional texture function (BTF) generalizes this model to also depend on the 2D position on the surface of the object. If we know the BTF, then we know how a textured surface will appear from every angle and under every lighting combination.

This function could be approximated by taking several thousand images of the surface viewed from different angles and under different lighting conditions. However, the resulting data are clearly highly redundant. Vasilescu and Terzopoulos (2004) described the BTF using a multilinear model known as "TensorTextures." It contained style factors that represent the lighting and viewing directions (Figure 18.20a–b). Although both of these quantities are naturally 2D, they represented them as vectors of size 21 and 37, respectively, where each training example was transformed to one coordinate axis.

Figure 18.20c shows images generated from the TensorTextures model; the hidden variables associated in each style were chosen by linearly interpolating between the hidden variables of nearby training examples, and the image was synthesized without the addition of noise. It can be seen that the TensorTextures model has learned a compact representation of the appearance variation under changes in viewpoint and illumination, including complex effects due to self-occlusion, inter-reflection, and self-shadowing.

18.6.3 Animation synthesis

Wang et al. (2007) developed a multifactor model that depended nonlinearly on the identity and style components. Their approach was based on the Gaussian process latent variable model; the style and identity factors were transformed through nonlinear functions before weighting the tensor $\boldsymbol{\Phi}$. In this type of model, the likelihood might be given by

$$Pr(\mathbf{x}_{ijk}|\boldsymbol{\Sigma},\mathbf{h}_i,\mathbf{s}_k) = \int\int \text{Norm}_{\mathbf{x}_{ijk}}[\boldsymbol{\mu}+\boldsymbol{\Phi}\times_2\mathbf{f}[\mathbf{h}_i]\times_3\mathbf{g}[\mathbf{s}_k],\boldsymbol{\Sigma}]\,d\boldsymbol{\Phi}d\boldsymbol{\mu}, \quad (18.54)$$

where $\mathbf{f}[\bullet]$ and $\mathbf{g}[\bullet]$ are nonlinear functions that transform the identity and style parameters, respectively. In practice, the tensor $\boldsymbol{\Phi}$ can be marginalized out of the final likelihood computation in closed form along with the overall mean $\boldsymbol{\mu}$. This model can be expressed in terms of inner products of the identity and style parameters and can hence be kernelized. It is known as the *multifactor Gaussian process latent variable model* or the *multifactor GPLVM*.

Wang et al. (2007) used this model to describe human locomotion. A single pose was described as an 89-dimensional vector, which consisted of 43 joint angles, the corresponding 43 angular velocities and the global translational velocity. They built a model consisting of three factors; the identity of the individual, the gait of locomotion (walk, stride, or run), and the current state in the motion sequence. Each was represented as a 3D vector. They learned the model from human capture data using an RBF kernel.

Figure 18.21 shows the results of style translation in this model. The system can predict realistic body poses in styles that have not been observed in the training data.

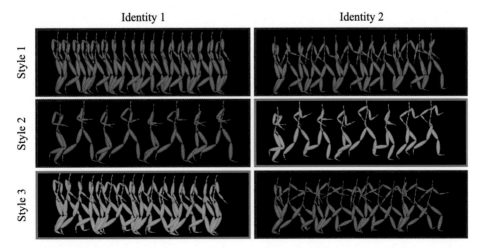

Figure 18.21 Multifactor GPLVM applied to animation synthesis. A three-factor model was learned with factors for identity, style, and position in the gait sequence. The figures shows training data (red boxes) and synthesized data from the learned model (green boxes). In each case, it manages to simulate the style and identity well. Adapted from Wang et al. (2007).

Since the system is generative, it can also be used to synthesize novel motion sequences for a given individual in which the gait varies over time.

Discussion

In this chapter, we have examined a number of models that describe image data as a function of style and content variables. During training, these variables are forced to take the same value for examples where we know the style or content are the same. We have demonstrated a number of different forms of inference including identity recognition and style translation.

Notes

Face recognition: For a readable introduction to face recognition consult Chellappa et al. (2010). For more details, consult the review paper by Zhao et al. (2003) or the edited book by Li and Jain (2005).

Subspace methods for face recognition: Turk and Pentland (2001) developed the *eigenfaces* method in which the pixel data were reduced in dimension by linearly projecting it onto a subspace corresponding to the principal components of the training data. The decision about whether two faces matched or not was based on the distance between these low-dimensional representations. This approach quickly supplanted earlier techniques that had been based on measuring the relative distance between facial features (Brunelli and Poggio 1993).

The subsequent history of face recognition has been dominated by other *subspace methods*. Researchers have variously investigated the choice of basis functions (e.g., Bartlett et al. 1998; Belhumeur et al. 1997; He et al. 2005; Cai et al. 2007), analogous nonlinear techniques (Yang 2002), and the choice of distance metric (Perlibakas 2004). The relationship between different subspace models is discussed in (Wang and Tang 2004b). A review of subspace methods (without particular reference to face recognition) can be found in De La Torre (2011).

Linear discriminant analysis A notable subcategory of these subspace methods consists of approaches based on linear discriminant analysis (LDA). The Fisherfaces algorithm (Belhumeur et al. 1997) projected face data to a space where the ratio of between-individual variation to within-individual variation was maximized. Fisherfaces is limited to directions in which at least some within-individual variance has been observed (the small-sample problem). The null-space LDA approach (Chen et al. 2000) exploited the signal in the remaining subspace. The Dual-Space LDA approach (Wang and Tang 2004a) combined these two sources of information.

Probabilistic approaches: The identity models in this chapter are probabilistic reinterpretations of earlier non-probabilistic techniques. For example, the subspace identity model is very similar to the eigenfaces algorithm (Turk and Pentland 2001), and probabilistic LDA is very similar to the Fisherfaces algorithm (Belhumeur et al. 1997). For more details about these probabilistic versions, consult Li et al. (2012) and Ioffe (2006), who presented a slightly different probabilistic LDA algorithm. There have also been many other probabilistic approaches to face recognition (Liu and Wechsler 1998; Moghaddam et al. 2000; Wang and Tang 2003; Zhou and Chellappa 2004).

Alignment and pose changes: An important part of most face recognition pipelines is to accurately identify facial features so that either (i) the face image can be aligned to a fixed template or (ii) the separate parts of the face can be treated independently (Wiskott et al. 1997; Moghaddam and Pentland 1997). Common methods to identify facial features include the use of active shape models (Edwards et al. 1998) or pictorial structures (Everingham et al. 2006; Li et al. 2010).

For larger pose changes, it may not be possible to warp the face accurately to a common template, and explicit methods are required to compare the faces. These include fitting 3D morphable models to the images and then simulating a frontal image from a non-frontal one (Blanz et al. 2005), predicting the face at one pose from another using statistical methods (Gross et al. 2002; Lucey and Chen 2006) or using the tied factor analysis model discussed in this chapter (Prince et al. 2008). A review of face recognition across large pose changes can be found in Zhang and Gao (2009).

Current work in face recognition: It is now considered that face recognition for frontal faces in constant lighting and with no pose or expression changes is almost solved. Earlier databases that have these characteristics (e.g., Messer et al. 1999; Phillips et al. 2000) have now been supplanted by test databases containing more variation (Huang et al. 2007b).

Several recent trends have emerged in face recognition. These include a resurgence of interest in discriminative models (e.g., Wolf et al. 2009; Taigman et al. 2009; Kumar et al. 2009), the application of learning of metrics to discriminate identity (e.g., Nowak and Jurie 2007; Ferencz et al. 2008; Guillaumin et al. 2009; Nguyen and Bai 2010), the use of sparse representations (e.g., Wright et al. 2009), and a strong interest in preprocessing techniques. In particular, many current methods are based on Gabor features (e.g., Wang and Tang 2003), local binary patterns (Ojala et al. 2002; Ahonen et al. 2004), three-patch local binary patterns (Wolf et al. 2009), or SIFT features (Lowe 2004). Some of the most successful methods combine or select several different preprocessing techniques (Li et al. 2012; Taigman et al. 2009; Pinto and Cox 2011).

Bilinear and multilinear models: Bilinear models were introduced to computer vision by Tenenbaum and Freeman (2000), and multilinear models were explored by Vasilescu and Terzopoulos (2002). Kernelized multilinear models were discussed by Li et al. (2005) and Wang et al. (2007). An alternative approach to nonlinear multifactor models was presnented in Elgammal and Lee (2004). The most common use of bilinear and multilinear models in computer vision has been for face recognition in situations where the capture conditions vary (Grimes et al. 2003; Lee et al. 2005; Cuzzolin 2006; Prince et al. 2008).

Problems

18.1 Prove that the posterior distribution over the hidden variable in the subspace identity model is as given in Equation 18.9.

18.2 Show that the M-step updates for the subspace identity model are as given in Equation 18.11.

18.3 Develop a closed form solution for learning the parameters $\{\boldsymbol{\mu}, \boldsymbol{\Phi}, \sigma^2\}$ of a subspace identity model where the noise is spherical:

$$Pr(\mathbf{x}_{ij}) = \text{Norm}_{\mathbf{x}_{ij}}[\boldsymbol{\mu}, \boldsymbol{\Phi}\boldsymbol{\Phi}^T + \sigma^2\mathbf{I}].$$

Hint: Assume you have exactly $J = 2$ examples of each of the I training images and base your solution on probabilistic PCA.

18.4 In a face clustering problem, how many possible models of the data are there with 2, 3, 4, 10, and 100 faces?

18.5 An alternative approach to face verification using the identity subspace model is to compute the probability of the observed data $\mathbf{x}_1$ and $\mathbf{x}_2$ under the models:

$$Pr(\mathbf{x}_1, \mathbf{x}_2 | w = 0) = Pr(\mathbf{x}_1)Pr(\mathbf{x}_2)$$
$$Pr(\mathbf{x}_1, \mathbf{x}_2 | w = 1) = Pr(\mathbf{x}_1)Pr(\mathbf{x}_2 | \mathbf{x}_1).$$

Write down expressions for the marginal probability terms $Pr(\mathbf{x}_1)$, $Pr(\mathbf{x}_2)$ and the conditional probability $Pr(\mathbf{x}_2 | \mathbf{x}_1)$. How could you use these expressions to compute the posterior $Pr(w | \mathbf{x}_1, \mathbf{x}_2)$ over the world state?

18.6 Propose a version of the subspace identity model that is robust to outliers in the training data.

18.7 Moghaddam et al. (2000) took a different probabilistic approach to face verification. They took the difference $\mathbf{x}_\Delta = \mathbf{x}_2 - \mathbf{x}_1$ and modeled the likelihoods of this vector $Pr(\mathbf{x}_\Delta|w=0)$ and $Pr(\mathbf{x}_\Delta|w=1)$ when the two faces match or don't. Propose expressions for these likelihoods and discuss learning and inference in this model. Identify one possible disadvantage of this model.

18.8 Develop a model that combines the advantages of PLDA and the asymmetric bilinear model; it should be able to model the within-individual covariance with a subspace but also be able to compare data between disparate styles. Discuss learning and inference in your model.

18.9 In the asymmetric bilinear model, how would you infer whether the style of two examples is the same or not, regardless of whether the images matched?

Chapter 19

Temporal models

This chapter concerns temporal models and tracking. The goal is to infer a sequence of world states $\{\mathbf{w}_t\}_{t=1}^T$ from a noisy sequence of measurements $\{\mathbf{x}_t\}_{t=1}^T$. The world states are not independent; each is modeled as being contingent on the previous one. We exploit this statistical dependency to help estimate the state $\mathbf{w}_t$ even when the associated observation $\mathbf{x}_t$ is partially or completely uninformative.

Since the states form a chain, the resulting models are similar to those in Chapter 11. However, there are two major differences. First, in this chapter, we consider models where the world state is continuous rather than discrete. Second, the models here are designed for real-time applications; a judgment is made based on only the past and present measurements and without knowledge of those in the future.

A prototypical use of these temporal models is for *contour tracking*. Consider a parameterized model of an object contour (Figure 19.1). The goal is to track this contour through a sequence of images so that it remains firmly attached to the object. A good model should be able to cope with nonrigid deformations of the object, background clutter, blurring, and occasional occlusion.

19.1 Temporal estimation framework

Each model in this chapter consists of two components.

- The *measurement model* describes the relationship between the measurements $\mathbf{x}_t$ and the state $\mathbf{w}_t$ at time t. We treat this as generative, and model the likelihood $Pr(\mathbf{x}_t|\mathbf{w}_t)$. We assume that the data at time t depend only on the state at time t and not those at any other time. In mathematical terms, we assume that $\mathbf{x}_t$ is conditionally independent of $\mathbf{w}_{1...t-1}$ given $\mathbf{w}_t$.

- The *temporal model* describes the relationship between states. Typically, we make the *Markov assumption*: we assume that each state depends only upon its predecessor. More formally, we assume that $\mathbf{w}_t$ is conditionally independent of the states $\mathbf{w}_{1...t-2}$ given its immediate predecessor $\mathbf{w}_{t-1}$, and just model the relationship $Pr(\mathbf{w}_t|\mathbf{w}_{t-1})$.

Together, these assumptions lead to the graphical model shown in Figure 19.2.

Figure 19.1 Contour tracking. The goal is to track the contour (solid blue line) through the sequence of images so that it remains firmly attached to the object (see Chapter 17 for more information about contour models). The estimation of the contour parameters is based on a temporal model relating nearby frames, and local measurements from the image (e.g., between the dashed blue lines). Adapted from Blake and Isard (1998). ©1998 Springer.

19.1.1 Inference

In inference, the general problem is to compute the marginal posterior distribution $Pr(\mathbf{w}_t|\mathbf{x}_{1...t})$ over the world state $\mathbf{w}_t$ at time t, given all of the measurements $\mathbf{x}_{1...t}$ up until this time. At time $t=1$, we have only observed a single measurement $\mathbf{x}_1$, so our prediction is based entirely on this datum. To compute the posterior distribution $Pr(\mathbf{w}_1|\mathbf{x}_1)$, Bayes' rule is applied:

$$Pr(\mathbf{w}_1|\mathbf{x}_1) = \frac{Pr(\mathbf{x}_1|\mathbf{w}_1)Pr(\mathbf{w}_1)}{\int Pr(\mathbf{x}_1|\mathbf{w}_1)Pr(\mathbf{w}_1)\,d\mathbf{w}_1}, \tag{19.1}$$

where the distribution $Pr(\mathbf{w}_1)$ contains our prior knowledge about the initial state.

At time $t=2$ we observe a second measurement $\mathbf{x}_2$. We now aim to compute the posterior distribution of the state at time $t=2$ based on both $\mathbf{x}_1$ and $\mathbf{x}_2$. Again, we apply Bayes' rule,

$$Pr(\mathbf{w}_2|\mathbf{x}_1,\mathbf{x}_2) = \frac{Pr(\mathbf{x}_2|\mathbf{w}_2)Pr(\mathbf{w}_2|\mathbf{x}_1)}{\int Pr(\mathbf{x}_2|\mathbf{w}_2)Pr(\mathbf{w}_2|\mathbf{x}_1)\,d\mathbf{w}_2}. \tag{19.2}$$

Notice that the likelihood term $Pr(\mathbf{x}_2|\mathbf{w}_2)$ is only dependent on the current measurement $\mathbf{x}_2$ (according to the assumption stated earlier). The prior $Pr(\mathbf{w}_2|\mathbf{x}_1)$ is now based on what we have learned from the previous measurement; the possible values of the state at this time depend on our knowledge of what happened at the previous time and how these are affected by the temporal model.

Generalizing this procedure to time t, we have

$$Pr(\mathbf{w}_t|\mathbf{x}_{1...t}) = \frac{Pr(\mathbf{x}_t|\mathbf{w}_t)Pr(\mathbf{w}_t|\mathbf{x}_{1...t-1})}{\int Pr(\mathbf{x}_t|\mathbf{w}_t)Pr(\mathbf{w}_t|\mathbf{x}_{1...t-1})\,d\mathbf{w}_t}. \tag{19.3}$$

To evaluate this, we must compute $Pr(\mathbf{w}_t|\mathbf{x}_{1...t-1})$, which represents our prior knowledge about $\mathbf{w}_t$ before we look at the associated measurement $\mathbf{x}_t$. This prior depends on our knowledge $Pr(\mathbf{w}_{t-1}|\mathbf{x}_{1...t-1})$ of the state at the previous time and the temporal model $Pr(\mathbf{w}_t|\mathbf{w}_{t-1})$, and is computed recursively as

$$Pr(\mathbf{w}_t|\mathbf{x}_{1...t-1}) = \int Pr(\mathbf{w}_t|\mathbf{w}_{t-1})Pr(\mathbf{w}_{t-1}|\mathbf{x}_{1...t-1})\,d\mathbf{w}_{t-1}, \tag{19.4}$$

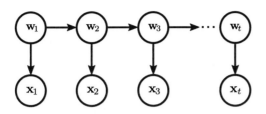

Figure 19.2 Graphical model for Kalman filter and other temporal models in this chapter. This implies the following conditional independence relation: the state $\mathbf{w}_t$ is conditionally independent of the states $\mathbf{w}_{1\ldots t-2}$ and the measurements $\mathbf{x}_{1\ldots t-1}$ given the previous state $\mathbf{w}_{t-1}$.

which is known as the *Chapman–Kolmogorov* relation. The first term in the integral represents the prediction for the state at time t given a known state $\mathbf{w}_{t-1}$ at time $t-1$. The second term represents the uncertainty about what the state actually was at time $t-1$. The Chapman–Kolmogorov equation amalgamates these two pieces of information to predict what will happen at time t.

Hence, inference consists of two alternating steps. In the *prediction step*, we compute the prior $Pr(\mathbf{w}_t|\mathbf{x}_{1\ldots t-1})$ using the Chapman–Kolmogorov relation (Equation 19.4). In the *measurement incorporation* step, we combine this prior with the new information from the measurement $\mathbf{x}_t$ using Bayes's rule (Equation 19.3).

19.1.2   Learning

The goal of learning is to estimate the parameters $\boldsymbol{\theta}$ that determine the relationship $Pr(\mathbf{w}_t|\mathbf{w}_{t-1})$ between adjacent states and the relationship $Pr(\mathbf{x}_t|\mathbf{w}_t)$ between the state and the data, based on several observed time sequences.

If we know the states for these sequences, then this can be achieved using the maximum likelihood method. If the states are unknown, then they can be treated as *hidden variables*, and the model can be learned using the EM algorithm (Section 7.8). In the E-step, we compute the posterior distribution over the states for each time sequence. This is a process similar to the inference method described earlier, except that it also uses data from later in the sequence (Section 19.2.6). In the M-step, we update the EM bound with respect to $\boldsymbol{\theta}$.

The rest of this chapter focusses on inference in this type of temporal model. We will first consider the *Kalman filter*. Here the uncertainty over the world state is described by a normal distribution,[1] the relationship between the measurements and the world is linear with additive normal noise, and the relationship between the state at adjacent times is also linear with additive normal noise.

19.2   Kalman filter

To define the Kalman filter, we must specify the temporal and measurement models. The temporal model relates the states at times $t-1$ and t and is given by

$$\mathbf{w}_t = \boldsymbol{\mu}_p + \boldsymbol{\Psi}\mathbf{w}_{t-1} + \boldsymbol{\epsilon}_p, \tag{19.5}$$

---

[1]In the original formulation of the Kalman filter, it was only assumed that the noise was white; however, if the distribution is normal, we can compute the exact marginal posterior distributions, so we will favor this assumption.

where $\boldsymbol{\mu}_p$ is a $D_\mathbf{w} \times 1$ vector, which represents the mean change in the state, and $\boldsymbol{\Psi}$ is a $D_\mathbf{w} \times D_\mathbf{w}$ matrix, which relates the mean of the state at time t to the state at time $t-1$. This is known as the *transition* matrix. The term $\boldsymbol{\epsilon}_p$ is a realization of the transition noise, which is normally distributed with covariance $\boldsymbol{\Sigma}_p$ and determines how closely related the states are at times t and $t-1$. Alternately, we can write this in probabilistic form:

$$Pr(\mathbf{w}_t|\mathbf{w}_{t-1}) = \text{Norm}_{\mathbf{w}_t}[\boldsymbol{\mu}_p + \boldsymbol{\Psi}\mathbf{w}_{t-1}, \boldsymbol{\Sigma}_p]. \tag{19.6}$$

The measurement model relates the data $\mathbf{x}_t$ at time t to the state $\mathbf{w}_t$,

$$\mathbf{x}_t = \boldsymbol{\mu}_m + \boldsymbol{\Phi}\mathbf{w}_t + \boldsymbol{\epsilon}_m, \tag{19.7}$$

where $\boldsymbol{\mu}_m$ is a $D_\mathbf{x} \times 1$ mean vector and $\boldsymbol{\Phi}$ is a $D_\mathbf{x} \times D_\mathbf{w}$ matrix relating the $D_\mathbf{x} \times 1$ measurement vector to the $D_\mathbf{w} \times 1$ state. The term $\boldsymbol{\epsilon}_m$ is a realization of the measurement noise that is normally distributed with covariance $\boldsymbol{\Sigma}_m$. In probabilistic notation, we have

$$Pr(\mathbf{x}_t|\mathbf{w}_t) = \text{Norm}_{\mathbf{x}_t}[\boldsymbol{\mu}_m + \boldsymbol{\Phi}\mathbf{w}_t, \boldsymbol{\Sigma}_m]. \tag{19.8}$$

Notice that the measurement equation is identical to the relation between the data and the hidden variable in the factor analysis model (Section 7.6); here the state $\mathbf{w}$ replaces the hidden variable $\mathbf{h}$. In the context of the Kalman filter, the dimension $D_\mathbf{w}$ of the state $\mathbf{w}$ is often larger than the dimension $D_\mathbf{x}$ of the measurements $\mathbf{x}$, so $\boldsymbol{\Phi}$ is a *landscape* matrix, and the measurement noise $\boldsymbol{\Sigma}_m$ is not necessarily diagonal.

The form of both the temporal and measurement equations is the same: each is a normal probability distribution where the mean is a linear function of another variable and the variance is constant. This form has been carefully chosen because it ensures that if the marginal posterior $Pr(\mathbf{w}_{t-1}|\mathbf{x}_{1...t-1})$ at time $t-1$ was normal, then so is the marginal posterior $Pr(\mathbf{w}_t|\mathbf{x}_{1...t})$ at time t. Hence, the inference procedure consists of a recursive updating of the means and variances of these normal distributions. We now elaborate on this procedure.

19.2.1 Inference

In inference, the goal is to compute the posterior probability $Pr(\mathbf{w}_t|\mathbf{x}_{1...t})$ over the state $\mathbf{w}_t$ given all of the measurements $\mathbf{x}_{1...t}$ so far. As before, we apply the prediction and measurement-incorporation steps to recursively estimate $Pr(\mathbf{w}_t|\mathbf{x}_{1...t})$ from $Pr(\mathbf{w}_{t-1}|\mathbf{x}_{1...t-1})$. The latter distribution is assumed to be normal with mean $\boldsymbol{\mu}_{t-1}$ and variance $\boldsymbol{\Sigma}_{t-1}$.

In the prediction step, we compute the prior at time t using the Chapman–Kolmogorov equation

$$\begin{aligned}
Pr(\mathbf{w}_t|\mathbf{x}_{1...t-1}) &= \int Pr(\mathbf{w}_t|\mathbf{w}_{t-1})Pr(\mathbf{w}_{t-1}|\mathbf{x}_{1...t-1})\,d\mathbf{w}_{t-1} \\
&= \int \text{Norm}_{\mathbf{w}_t}[\boldsymbol{\mu}_p + \boldsymbol{\Psi}\mathbf{w}_{t-1}, \boldsymbol{\Sigma}_p]\text{Norm}_{\mathbf{w}_{t-1}}[\boldsymbol{\mu}_{t-1}, \boldsymbol{\Sigma}_{t-1}]\,d\mathbf{w}_{t-1} \\
&= \text{Norm}_{\mathbf{w}_t}[\boldsymbol{\mu}_p + \boldsymbol{\Psi}\boldsymbol{\mu}_{t-1}, \boldsymbol{\Sigma}_p + \boldsymbol{\Psi}\boldsymbol{\Sigma}_{t-1}\boldsymbol{\Psi}^T] \\
&= \text{Norm}_{\mathbf{w}_t}[\boldsymbol{\mu}_+, \boldsymbol{\Sigma}_+], \tag{19.9}
\end{aligned}$$

where we have denoted the predicted mean and variance of the state by $\boldsymbol{\mu}_+$ and $\boldsymbol{\Sigma}_+$. The integral between lines 2 and 3 was solved by using Equations 5.17 and 5.14 to rewrite the integrand as proportional to a normal distribution in $\mathbf{w}_{t-1}$. Since the integral of any pdf is one, the result is the constant of proportionality, which is itself a normal distribution in $\mathbf{w}_t$.

In the measurement incorporation step, we apply Bayes' rule,

$$
\begin{aligned}
Pr(\mathbf{w}_t|\mathbf{x}_{1\ldots t}) &= \frac{Pr(\mathbf{x}_t|\mathbf{w}_t)Pr(\mathbf{w}_t|\mathbf{x}_{1\ldots t-1})}{Pr(\mathbf{x}_{1\ldots t})} \\
&= \frac{\text{Norm}_{\mathbf{x}_t}[\boldsymbol{\mu}_m + \boldsymbol{\Phi}\mathbf{w}_t, \boldsymbol{\Sigma}_m]\text{Norm}_{\mathbf{w}_t}[\boldsymbol{\mu}_+, \boldsymbol{\Sigma}_+]}{Pr(\mathbf{x}_{1\ldots t})} \\
&= \text{Norm}_{\mathbf{w}_t}\left[\left(\boldsymbol{\Phi}^T\boldsymbol{\Sigma}_m^{-1}\boldsymbol{\Phi} + \boldsymbol{\Sigma}_+^{-1}\right)^{-1}\left(\boldsymbol{\Phi}^T\boldsymbol{\Sigma}_m^{-1}(\mathbf{x}_t - \boldsymbol{\mu}_m) + \boldsymbol{\Sigma}_+^{-1}\boldsymbol{\mu}_+\right),\right. \\
&\qquad\qquad \left.\left(\boldsymbol{\Phi}^T\boldsymbol{\Sigma}_m^{-1}\boldsymbol{\Phi} + \boldsymbol{\Sigma}_+^{-1}\right)^{-1}\right] \\
&= \text{Norm}_{\mathbf{w}_t}[\boldsymbol{\mu}_t, \boldsymbol{\Sigma}_t],
\end{aligned} \tag{19.10}
$$

where we have used Equation 5.17 on the likelihood term and then combined the likelihood and prior using Equation 5.14. The right-hand side is now proportional to a normal distribution in $\mathbf{w}_t$, and the constant of proportionality must be one to ensure that the posterior on the left-hand side is a valid distribution.

Notice that the posterior $Pr(\mathbf{w}_t|\mathbf{x}_{1\ldots t})$ is normal with mean $\boldsymbol{\mu}_t$ and covariance $\boldsymbol{\Sigma}_t$. We are in the same situation as at the start, so the procedure can be repeated for the next time step.

It can be shown that the mean of the posterior is a weighted sum of the values predicted by the measurements and the prior knowledge, and the covariance is smaller than either. However, this is not particularly obvious from the equations. In the following section we rewrite the equation for the posterior in a form that makes these properties more obvious.

19.2.2   Rewriting measurement incorporation step

The measurement incorporation step is rarely presented in the above form in practice. One reason for this is that the equations for $\boldsymbol{\mu}_t$ and $\boldsymbol{\Sigma}_t$ contain an inversion that is of size $D_{\mathbf{w}} \times D_{\mathbf{w}}$. If the world state is much higher dimensional than the observed data, then it would be more efficient to reformulate this as an inverse of size $D_{\mathbf{x}} \times D_{\mathbf{x}}$. To this end, we define the *Kalman gain* as

$$
\mathbf{K} = \boldsymbol{\Sigma}_+ \boldsymbol{\Phi}^T(\boldsymbol{\Sigma}_m + \boldsymbol{\Phi}\boldsymbol{\Sigma}_+\boldsymbol{\Phi}^T)^{-1}. \tag{19.11}
$$

We will use this to modify the expressions for $\boldsymbol{\mu}_t$ and $\boldsymbol{\Sigma}_t$ from Equation 19.10. Starting with $\boldsymbol{\mu}_t$, we apply the matrix inversion lemma (Appendix C.8.4):

$$
\begin{aligned}
(\boldsymbol{\Phi}^T\boldsymbol{\Sigma}_m^{-1}\boldsymbol{\Phi} + \boldsymbol{\Sigma}_+^{-1})^{-1}&(\boldsymbol{\Phi}^T\boldsymbol{\Sigma}_m^{-1}(\mathbf{x}_t - \boldsymbol{\mu}_m) + \boldsymbol{\Sigma}_+^{-1}\boldsymbol{\mu}_+) \\
&= \mathbf{K}(\mathbf{x}_t - \boldsymbol{\mu}_m) + (\boldsymbol{\Phi}^T\boldsymbol{\Sigma}_m^{-1}\boldsymbol{\Phi} + \boldsymbol{\Sigma}_+^{-1})^{-1}\boldsymbol{\Sigma}_+^{-1}\boldsymbol{\mu}_+ \\
&= \mathbf{K}(\mathbf{x}_t - \boldsymbol{\mu}_m) + (\boldsymbol{\Sigma}_+ - \boldsymbol{\Sigma}_+\boldsymbol{\Phi}^T(\boldsymbol{\Phi}\boldsymbol{\Sigma}_+\boldsymbol{\Phi}^T + \boldsymbol{\Sigma}_m)^{-1}\boldsymbol{\Phi}\boldsymbol{\Sigma}_+)\boldsymbol{\Sigma}_+^{-1}\boldsymbol{\mu}_+ \\
&= \mathbf{K}(\mathbf{x}_t - \boldsymbol{\mu}_m) + \boldsymbol{\mu}_+ - \boldsymbol{\Sigma}_+\boldsymbol{\Phi}^T(\boldsymbol{\Phi}\boldsymbol{\Sigma}_+\boldsymbol{\Phi}^T + \boldsymbol{\Sigma}_m)^{-1}\boldsymbol{\Phi}\boldsymbol{\mu}_+ \\
&= \mathbf{K}(\mathbf{x}_t - \boldsymbol{\mu}_m) + \boldsymbol{\mu}_+ - \mathbf{K}\boldsymbol{\Phi}\boldsymbol{\mu}_+ \\
&= \boldsymbol{\mu}_+ + \mathbf{K}\left(\mathbf{x}_t - \boldsymbol{\mu}_m - \boldsymbol{\Phi}\boldsymbol{\mu}_+\right).
\end{aligned} \tag{19.12}
$$

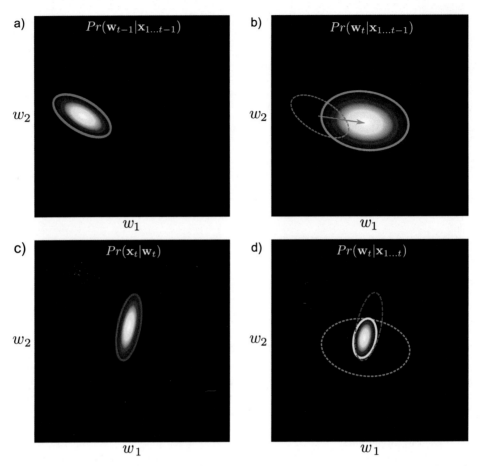

Figure 19.3 Recursive inference in the Kalman filter. a) The posterior probability $Pr(\mathbf{w}_{t-1}|$ $\mathbf{x}_{1...t-1})$ of the state $\mathbf{w}_{t-1}$ given all of the measurements $\mathbf{x}_{1...t-1}$ up to that time takes the form of a normal distribution (green ellipse). b) In the prediction step, we apply the Chapman–Kolmogorov relation to estimate the prior $Pr(\mathbf{w}_t|\mathbf{x}_{1...t-1})$, which is also a normal distribution (cyan ellipse). c) The measurement likelihood $Pr(\mathbf{x}_t|\mathbf{w}_t)$ is proportional to a normal distribution (magenta ellipse). d) To compute the posterior probability $Pr(\mathbf{w}_t|\mathbf{x}_{1...t})$, we apply Bayes' rule by taking the product of the prior from panel (b) and the likelihood from panel (c) and normalizing. This yields a new normal distribution (yellow ellipse) and the procedure can begin anew.

The expression in brackets in the final line is known as the *innovation* and is the difference between the actual measurements $\mathbf{x}_t$ and the predicted measurements $\boldsymbol{\mu}_m +$ $\boldsymbol{\Phi}\boldsymbol{\mu}_+$ based on the prior estimate of the state. It is easy to see why $\mathbf{K}$ is termed the Kalman gain: it determines the amount that the measurements contribute to the new estimate in each direction in state space. If the Kalman gain is small in a given direction, then this implies that the measurements are unreliable relative to the prior and should not influence the mean of the state too much. If the Kalman gain is large in a given direction, then this suggests that the measurements are more reliable than the prior and should be weighted more highly.

We now return to the covariance term of Equation 19.10. Using the matrix inversion lemma, we get

$$(\mathbf{\Phi}^T\mathbf{\Sigma}_m\mathbf{\Phi} + \mathbf{\Sigma}_+^{-1})^{-1} = \mathbf{\Sigma}_+ - \mathbf{\Sigma}_+\mathbf{\Phi}^T(\mathbf{\Phi}\mathbf{\Sigma}_+\mathbf{\Phi}^T + \mathbf{\Sigma}_m)^{-1}\mathbf{\Phi}\mathbf{\Sigma}_+$$
$$= \mathbf{\Sigma}_+ - \mathbf{K}\mathbf{\Phi}\mathbf{\Sigma}_+$$
$$= (\mathbf{I} - \mathbf{K}\mathbf{\Phi})\mathbf{\Sigma}_+, \tag{19.13}$$

which also has a clear interpretation: the posterior covariance is equal to the prior covariance less a term that depends on the Kalman gain: we are always more certain about the state after incorporating information due to the measurement, and the Kalman gain modifies how much more certain we are. When the measurements are more reliable, the Kalman gain is high, and the covariance decreases more.

After these manipulations, we can rewrite Equation 19.10 as

$$Pr(\mathbf{w}_t|\mathbf{x}_{1...t}) = \text{Norm}_{\mathbf{w}_t}\left[\boldsymbol{\mu}_+ + \mathbf{K}(\mathbf{x}_t - \boldsymbol{\mu}_m - \mathbf{\Phi}\boldsymbol{\mu}_+), (\mathbf{I} - \mathbf{K}\mathbf{\Phi})\mathbf{\Sigma}_+\right]. \tag{19.14}$$

19.2.3 Inference summary

Developing the inference equations was rather long-winded, so here we summarize the inference process in the Kalman filter (see also Figure 19.3). We aim to compute the marginal posterior probability $Pr(\mathbf{w}_t|\mathbf{x}_{1...t})$ based on a normally distributed estimate of the marginal posterior probability $Pr(\mathbf{w}_{t-1}|\mathbf{x}_{1...t-1})$ at the previous time and a new measurement $\mathbf{x}_t$. If the posterior probability at time $t-1$ has mean $\boldsymbol{\mu}_{t-1}$ and variance $\mathbf{\Sigma}_{t-1}$, then the Kalman filter updates take the form

$$\begin{array}{rll}
\text{State Prediction:} & \boldsymbol{\mu}_+ = \boldsymbol{\mu}_p + \mathbf{\Psi}\boldsymbol{\mu}_{t-1} & \tag{19.15} \\
\text{Covariance Prediction:} & \mathbf{\Sigma}_+ = \mathbf{\Sigma}_p + \mathbf{\Psi}\mathbf{\Sigma}_{t-1}\mathbf{\Psi}^T & \\
\text{State Update:} & \boldsymbol{\mu}_t = \boldsymbol{\mu}_+ + \mathbf{K}(\mathbf{x}_t - \boldsymbol{\mu}_m - \mathbf{\Phi}\boldsymbol{\mu}_+) & \\
\text{Covariance Update:} & \mathbf{\Sigma}_t = (\mathbf{I} - \mathbf{K}\mathbf{\Phi})\mathbf{\Sigma}_+, &
\end{array}$$

where

$$\mathbf{K} = \mathbf{\Sigma}_+\mathbf{\Phi}^T(\mathbf{\Sigma}_m + \mathbf{\Phi}\mathbf{\Sigma}_+\mathbf{\Phi}^T)^{-1}. \tag{19.16}$$

In the absence of prior information at time $t=1$, it is usual to initialize the prior mean $\boldsymbol{\mu}_0$ to any reasonable value and the covariance $\mathbf{\Sigma}_0$ to a large multiple of the identity matrix representing our lack of knowledge.

19.2.4 Example 1

The Kalman filter update equations are not very intuitive. To help understand the properties of this model, we present two toy examples. In the first case, we consider an object that is approximately circling a central point in two dimensions. The state consists of the two-dimensional position of the object. The actual set of states can be seen in Figure 19.4a.

Let us assume that we do not have a good temporal model that describes this motion. Instead, we will assume the simplest possible model. The Brownian motion model assumes that the state at time $t+1$ is similar to the state at time t:

$$Pr(\mathbf{w}_t|\mathbf{w}_{t-1}) = \text{Norm}_{\mathbf{w}_t}[\mathbf{w}_{t-1}, \sigma_p^2\mathbf{I}]. \tag{19.17}$$

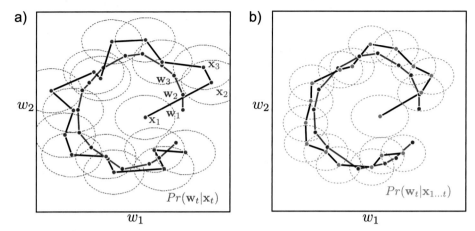

Figure 19.4 Kalman filter example 1. The true state (red dots) evolves in a 2D circle. The measurements (magenta dots) consist of direct noisy observations of the state. a) Posterior probability $Pr(\mathbf{w}_t|\mathbf{x}_t)$ of state using measurements alone (uniform prior assumed). The mean of each distribution is centered on the associated datapoint, and the covariance depends on the measurement noise. b) Posterior probabilities based on Kalman filter. Here the temporal equation describes the state as a random perturbation of the previous state. Although this is not a good model (the circular movement is not accounted for), the posterior covariances (blue ellipses) are smaller than without the Kalman filter (magenta ellipses in (a)) and the posterior means (blue dots) are closer to the true states (red dots) than the estimates due to the measurements alone (magenta dots in (a)).

This is a special case of the more general formulation in Equation 19.6. Notice that this model has no insight into the fact that the object is rotating.

For ease of visualization, we will assume that the observations are just noisy realizations of the true 2D state so that

$$Pr(\mathbf{x}_t|\mathbf{w}_t) = \text{Norm}_{\mathbf{x}_t}[\mathbf{w}_t, \mathbf{\Sigma}_m], \qquad (19.18)$$

where $\mathbf{\Sigma}_m$ is diagonal. This is a special case of the general formulation in 19.8.

In inference, the goal is to estimate the posterior probability over the state at each time step given the observed sequence so far. Figure 19.4b shows the sequence of posterior probabilities $Pr(\mathbf{w}_t|\mathbf{x}_{1...t})$ over the state after running the Kalman recursions. It is now easy to understand why this is referred to as the Kalman *filter*: the MAP states (the peaks of the marginal posteriors) are smoothed relative to estimates from the measurements alone. Notice that the Kalman filter estimate has a lower covariance than the estimate due to the measurements alone (Figure 19.4a). In this example, the inclusion of the temporal model makes the estimates both more accurate and more certain, even though the particular choice of temporal model is wrong.

19.2.5 Example 2

Figure 19.5 shows a second example where the setup is the same except that the observation equation differs at alternate time steps. At even time steps, we observe a noisy estimate of just the first dimension of the state $\mathbf{w}$. At odd time steps, we observe only a

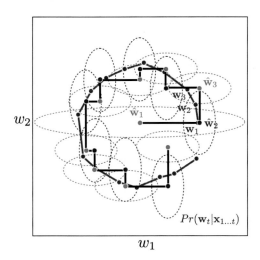

Figure 19.5 Kalman filter example 2. As for example 1, the true state (red points) proceeds in an approximate circle. We don't have access to this temporal model and just assume that the new state is a perturbation of the previous state. At even time steps, the measurement is a noisy realization of the first dimension (horizontal coordinate) of the state. At odd time steps, it is a noisy realization of the second dimension (vertical coordinate). The Kalman filter produces plausible estimates (blue and cyan points and ellipses) even though a single measurement is being used to determine a 2D state at any time step.

noisy estimate of the second dimension. The measurement equations are

$$Pr(x_t|\mathbf{w}_t) = \text{Norm}_{x_t}\left[\begin{bmatrix} 1 & 0 \end{bmatrix}\mathbf{w}_t, \sigma_m^2\right], \qquad \text{for } t = 1, 3, 5 \dots$$
$$Pr(x_t|\mathbf{w}_t) = \text{Norm}_{x_t}\left[\begin{bmatrix} 0 & 1 \end{bmatrix}\mathbf{w}_t, \sigma_m^2\right], \qquad \text{for } t = 2, 4, 6 \dots. \quad (19.19)$$

This is an example of a *nonstationary model*: the model changes over time.

We use the same set of ground truth 2D states as for example 1 and simulate the associated measurements using Equation 19.19. The posterior probability over the state was computed using the Kalman filter recursions with the relevant measurement matrix $\boldsymbol{\Phi}$ at each time step.

The results (Figure 19.5) show that the Kalman filter maintains a good estimate of the 2D state despite having only a 1D measurement at each time step. At odd time steps, the variance in the first dimension decreases (due to the information from the measurement), but the variance in the second dimension increases (due to the uncertainty in the temporal model). At even time steps, the opposite occurs.

This model may seem esoteric, but it is common in many imaging modalities for different aspects of the measurements to arrive at different times. One option is to wait until a full set of measurements is present before estimating the state, but this means that many of them are out of date. Incorporation of each measurement when it arrives using a Kalman filter is a superior approach.

19.2.6 Smoothing

The preceding inference procedure is designed for real-time applications where the estimation of the state is based only on measurements from the past and present. However, there may be occasions where we wish to infer the state using measurements that lie in the future. In the parlance of Kalman filters, this is known as *smoothing*.

We consider two cases. The *fixed lag smoother* is still intended for on-line estimation, but it delays the decision about the state by a fixed number of time steps. The *fixed interval smoother* assumes that we have observed all of the measurements in the entire sequence before we make a judgment about the world state.

Fixed lag smoother

The fixed lag smoother relies on a simple trick. To estimate the state delayed by τ time steps, we *augment* the state vector to contain the delayed estimates of the previous τ times. The time update equation now takes the form

$$
\begin{bmatrix} \mathbf{w}_t \\ \mathbf{w}_t^{[1]} \\ \mathbf{w}_t^{[2]} \\ \vdots \\ \mathbf{w}_t^{[\tau]} \end{bmatrix} = \begin{bmatrix} \boldsymbol{\Psi} & \mathbf{0} & \dots & \mathbf{0} & \mathbf{0} \\ \mathbf{I} & \mathbf{0} & \dots & \mathbf{0} & \mathbf{0} \\ \mathbf{0} & \mathbf{I} & \dots & \mathbf{0} & \mathbf{0} \\ \vdots & \vdots & \ddots & \vdots & \vdots \\ \mathbf{0} & \mathbf{0} & \dots & \mathbf{I} & \mathbf{0} \end{bmatrix} \begin{bmatrix} \mathbf{w}_{t-1} \\ \mathbf{w}_{t-1}^{[1]} \\ \mathbf{w}_{t-1}^{[2]} \\ \vdots \\ \mathbf{w}_{t-1}^{[\tau]} \end{bmatrix} + \begin{bmatrix} \boldsymbol{\epsilon}_p \\ \mathbf{0} \\ \mathbf{0} \\ \vdots \\ \mathbf{0}, \end{bmatrix}, \tag{19.20}
$$

where the notation $\mathbf{w}_t^{[m]}$ refers to the state at time $t - m$ based on measurements up to time t, and $\mathbf{w}_t^{[\tau]}$ is the quantity we wish to estimate. This state evolution equation clearly fits the general form of the Kalman filter (Equation 19.5). It can be parsed as follows: in the first equation of this system, the temporal model is applied to the current estimate of the state. In the remaining equations, the delayed states are created by simply copying the previous state.

The associated measurement equation is

$$
\mathbf{x}_t = \begin{bmatrix} \boldsymbol{\Phi} & \mathbf{0} & \mathbf{0} & \dots & \mathbf{0} \end{bmatrix} \begin{bmatrix} \mathbf{w}_t \\ \mathbf{w}_t^{[1]} \\ \mathbf{w}_t^{[2]} \\ \vdots \\ \mathbf{w}_t^{[\tau]}, \end{bmatrix} + \boldsymbol{\epsilon}_m, \tag{19.21}
$$

which fits the form of the Kalman filter measurement model (Equation 19.7). The current measurements are based on the current state, and the time-delayed versions play no part. Applying the Kalman recursions with these equations computes not just the current estimate of the state but also the time-delayed estimates.

Fixed interval smoother

The fixed interval smoother consists of a backward set of recursions that estimate the marginal posterior distributions $Pr(\mathbf{w}_t|\mathbf{x}_{1\ldots T})$ of the state at each time step, taking into account all of the measurements $\mathbf{x}_{1\ldots T}$. In these recursions, the marginal posterior distribution $Pr(\mathbf{w}_t|\mathbf{x}_{1\ldots T})$ of the state at time t is updated. Based on this result, the marginal posterior $Pr(\mathbf{w}_{t-1}|\mathbf{x}_{1\ldots T})$ at time $t - 1$ is updated and so on. We denote the mean and variance of the marginal posterior $Pr(\mathbf{w}_t|\mathbf{x}_{1\ldots T})$ at time t by $\boldsymbol{\mu}_{t|T}$ and $\boldsymbol{\Sigma}_{t|T}$, respectively, and use

$$
\begin{aligned}
\boldsymbol{\mu}_{t|T} &= \boldsymbol{\mu}_t + \mathbf{C}_t(\boldsymbol{\mu}_{t+1|T} - \boldsymbol{\mu}_{+|t}) \\
\boldsymbol{\Sigma}_{t|T} &= \boldsymbol{\Sigma}_t + \mathbf{C}_t(\boldsymbol{\Sigma}_{t+1|T} - \boldsymbol{\Sigma}_{+|t})\mathbf{C}_t^T,
\end{aligned} \tag{19.22}
$$

where $\boldsymbol{\mu}_t$ and $\boldsymbol{\Sigma}_t$ are the estimates of the mean and covariance from the forward pass. The notation $\boldsymbol{\mu}_{+|t}$ and $\boldsymbol{\Sigma}_{+|t}$ denotes the mean and variance of the posterior distribution $Pr(\mathbf{w}_t|\mathbf{x}_{1\ldots t-1})$ of the state at time t based on the measurements up to time $t - 1$ (i.e., what we denoted as $\boldsymbol{\mu}_+$ and $\boldsymbol{\Sigma}_+$ during the forward Kalman filter recursions) and

$$
\mathbf{C}_t = \boldsymbol{\Sigma}_{t|t}\boldsymbol{\Psi}^T\boldsymbol{\Sigma}_{+|t}^{-1}. \tag{19.23}
$$

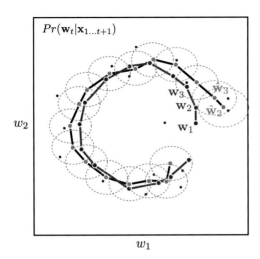

$Pr(\mathbf{w}_t|\mathbf{x}_{1...t+1})$

w_2

w_1

Figure 19.6 Fixed lag Kalman smoothing. The estimated state (light blue dots) and the associated covariance (light blue ellipses) were estimated using a lag of 1 time step: each estimate is based on all of the data in the past, the present observation and the observation one step into the future. The resulting estimated states have a smaller variance than for the standard Kalman filter (Compare to Figure 19.4b) and are closer to the true state (red dots). In effect, the estimate averages out the noise in the measurements (dark blue dots). The cost of this improvement is that there is a delay of one time step.

It can be shown that the backward recursions correspond to the backward pass of sum-product belief propagation in the Kalman filter graphical model.

19.2.7   Temporal and measurement models

The choice of temporal model in the Kalman filter is restricted to be linear and is dictated by the matrix $\mathbf{\Psi}$. Despite this limitation, it is possible to build a surprisingly versatile family of models within this framework. In this section we review a few of the best-known examples.

1. *Brownian motion:* The simplest model is Brownian motion Figure 19.7a in which the state is operated upon by the identity matrix so that

$$\mathbf{w}_t = \mathbf{w}_{t-1} + \boldsymbol{\epsilon}_p. \tag{19.24}$$

2. *Geometric transformations:* The family of linear filters includes geometric transformations such as rotations, stretches, and shears. For example, choosing $\mathbf{\Psi}$ so that $\mathbf{\Psi}^T\mathbf{\Psi} = \mathbf{I}$ and $|\mathbf{\Psi}| = 1$ creates a rotation around the origin Figure 19.7b: this is the true temporal model in Figures 19.4–19.6.

3. *Velocities and accelerations:* The Brownian motion model can be extended by adding a constant velocity $\mathbf{v}$ to the motion model (Figure 19.7c) so that.

$$\mathbf{w}_t = \mathbf{v} + \mathbf{w}_{t-1} + \boldsymbol{\epsilon}_p. \tag{19.25}$$

To incorporate a changing velocity, we can enhance the state vector to include the velocity term so that

$$\begin{bmatrix} \mathbf{w}_t \\ \dot{\mathbf{w}}_t \end{bmatrix} = \begin{bmatrix} \mathbf{I} & \mathbf{I} \\ \mathbf{0} & \mathbf{I} \end{bmatrix} \begin{bmatrix} \mathbf{w}_{t-1} \\ \dot{\mathbf{w}}_{t-1} \end{bmatrix} + \boldsymbol{\epsilon}_p. \tag{19.26}$$

This has the natural interpretation that the velocity term $\dot{\mathbf{w}}$ contributes an offset to the state at each time. However, the velocity is itself uncertain and is related

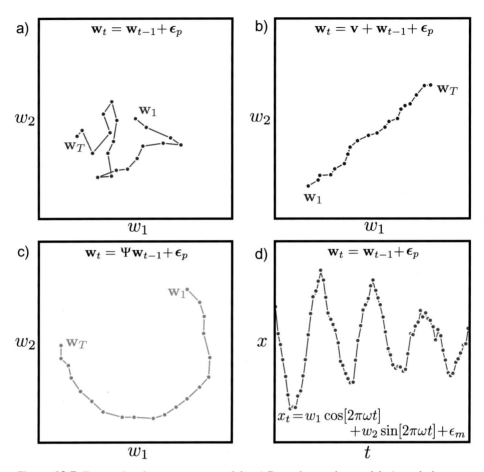

Figure 19.7 Temporal and measurement models. a) Brownian motion model. At each time step the state is randomly perturbed from the previous position, so a drunken walk through state space occurs. b) Constant velocity model. At each time step, a constant velocity is applied in addition to the noise. c) Transformation model. At each time step, the state is rotated about the origin and noise is added. d) Oscillatory measurements. These quasi-sinusoidal measurements are created from a two-dimensional state that itself undergoes Brownian motion. The two elements of the state control the sinusoidal and co-sinusoidal parts of the measurements.

by a Brownian motion model to the velocity at the previous time step. For the measurement equation, we have

$$\mathbf{x}_t = \begin{bmatrix} \mathbf{I} & \mathbf{0} \end{bmatrix} \begin{bmatrix} \mathbf{w}_t \\ \dot{\mathbf{w}}_t \end{bmatrix} + \boldsymbol{\epsilon}_m. \tag{19.27}$$

In other words, the measurements at time t do not directly depend on the velocity term, only the state itself. This idea can be easily extended to include an acceleration term as well.

4. *Oscillatory data:* Some data are naturally oscillatory. To describe oscillatory 1D data, we could use a state containing a 2×1 state vector $\mathbf{w}$ using Brownian motion as the temporal model. We then implement the nonstationary measurement

equation

$$x_t = \begin{bmatrix} \cos[2\pi\omega t] & \sin[2\pi\omega t] \end{bmatrix} \mathbf{w}_t + \epsilon_m. \qquad (19.28)$$

For a fixed state $\mathbf{w}$, this model produces noisy sinusoidal data. As the state varies due to the Brownian motion of the temporal model, the phase and amplitude of the quasi-sinusoidal output will change (19.7d).

19.2.8 Problems with the Kalman filter

Although the Kalman filter is a flexible tool, it has a number of shortcomings (Figure 19.8). Most notably,

- It requires the temporal and measurement equations to be linear, and
- It assumes that the marginal posterior is unimodal and can be well captured by a mean and covariance; hence, it can only ever have one hypothesis about the position of the object.

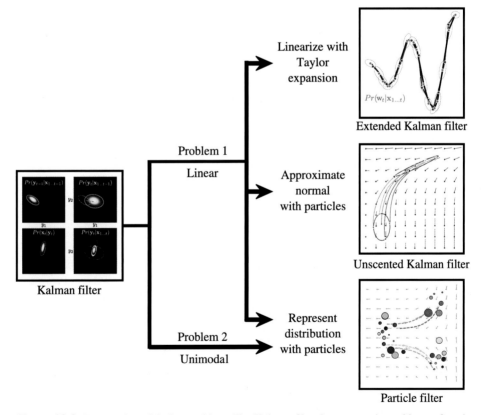

Figure 19.8 Temporal models for tracking. The Kalman filter has two main problems: first, it requires the temporal and measurement models to be linear. This problem is directly addressed by the extended and unscented Kalman filters. Second, it represents the uncertainty with a normal distribution that is uni-modal and so cannot maintain multiple hypotheses about the state. This problem is tackled by particle filters.

In the following sections, we discuss models that address these problems. The *extended Kalman filter* and the *unscented Kalman filter* both allow nonlinear state update and measurement equations. *Particle filtering* abandons the use of the normal distribution and describes the state as a complex multimodal distribution.

19.3 Extended Kalman filter

The extended Kalman filter (EKF) is designed to cope with more general temporal models, where the relationship between the states at time t is an arbitrary nonlinear function $\mathbf{f}[\bullet,\bullet]$ of the state at the previous time step and a stochastic contribution ϵ_p

$$\mathbf{w}_t = \mathbf{f}[\mathbf{w}_{t-1}, \epsilon_p], \tag{19.29}$$

where the covariance of the noise term ϵ_p is Σ_p as before. Similarly, it can cope with a nonlinear relationship $\mathbf{g}[\bullet,\bullet]$ between the state and the measurements

$$\mathbf{x}_t = \mathbf{g}[\mathbf{w}_t, \epsilon_m], \tag{19.30}$$

where the covariance of ϵ_m is Σ_m.

The extended Kalman filter works by taking linear approximations to the nonlinear functions at the peak μ_t of the current estimate using the Taylor expansion. If the function is not too nonlinear, then this approximation will adequately represent the function in the region of the current estimate and we can proceed as usual. We define the Jacobian matrices,

$$\Psi = \left.\frac{\partial \mathbf{f}[\mathbf{w}_{t-1}, \epsilon_p]}{\partial \mathbf{w}_{t-1}}\right|_{\mu_{t-1},0}$$

$$\Upsilon_p = \left.\frac{\partial \mathbf{f}[\mathbf{w}_{t-1}, \epsilon_p]}{\partial \epsilon_p}\right|_{\mu_{t-1},0}$$

$$\Phi = \left.\frac{\partial \mathbf{g}[\mathbf{w}_t, \epsilon_m]}{\partial \mathbf{w}_t}\right|_{\mu_+,0}$$

$$\Upsilon_m = \left.\frac{\partial \mathbf{g}[\mathbf{w}_t, \epsilon_m]}{\partial \epsilon_m}\right|_{\mu_+,0}, \tag{19.31}$$

where the notation $|_{\mu_+,0}$ denotes that the derivative is computed at position $\mathbf{w} = \mu_+$ and $\epsilon = 0$. Note that we have overloaded the meaning of Φ and Ψ here. Previously they represented the linear transformations between states at adjacent times, and between the state and the measurements, respectively. Now they represent the local linear approximation of the nonlinear functions relating these quantities.

The update equations for the extended Kalman filter are

$$\begin{aligned}
\text{State Prediction:} \quad & \mu_+ = \mathbf{f}[\mu_{t-1}, \mathbf{0}] \\
\text{Covariance Prediction:} \quad & \Sigma_+ = \Psi \Sigma_{t-1} \Psi^T + \Upsilon_p \Sigma_p \Upsilon_p^T \\
\text{State Update:} \quad & \mu_t = \mu_+ + \mathbf{K}(\mathbf{x}_t - \mathbf{g}[\mu_+, \mathbf{0}]) \\
\text{Covariance Update:} \quad & \Sigma_t = (\mathbf{I} - \mathbf{K}\Phi)\Sigma_+,
\end{aligned} \tag{19.32}$$

where

$$\mathbf{K} = \Sigma_+ \Phi^T (\Upsilon_m \Sigma_m \Upsilon_m^T + \Phi \Sigma_+ \Phi^T)^{-1}. \tag{19.33}$$

In the context of fixed interval smoothing, the results can be improved by performing several passes back and forth through the data, relinearizing around the previous estimates of the state in each sweep. This is called the *iterated extended Kalman filter*.

⚙ 19.4   In conclusion, the extended Kalman filter is conceptually simple, but only copes with relatively benign nonlinearities. It is a heuristic solution to the nonlinear tracking problem and may diverge from the true solution.

19.3.1 Example

Figure 19.9 shows a worked example of the extended Kalman filter. In this case, the time update model is nonlinear, but the observation model is still linear:

$$\mathbf{w}_t = \mathbf{f}[\mathbf{w}_{t-1}, \boldsymbol{\epsilon}_p]$$
$$\mathbf{x}_t = \mathbf{w} + \boldsymbol{\epsilon}_m, \tag{19.34}$$

where $\boldsymbol{\epsilon}_p$ is a normal noise term with covariance $\boldsymbol{\Sigma}_p$, $\boldsymbol{\epsilon}_m$ is a normal noise term with covariance $\boldsymbol{\Sigma}_m$, and the nonlinear function $\mathbf{f}[\bullet, \bullet]$ is given by

$$\mathbf{f}[\mathbf{w}, \boldsymbol{\epsilon}_p] = \begin{bmatrix} w_1 \\ w_1 \sin[w_1] + \boldsymbol{\epsilon}_p \end{bmatrix}. \tag{19.35}$$

The Jacobian matrices for this model are easily computed. The matrices $\boldsymbol{\Upsilon}_p$, $\boldsymbol{\Phi}$, and $\boldsymbol{\Upsilon}_m$ are all equal to the identity. The Jacobian matrix $\boldsymbol{\Psi}$ is

$$\boldsymbol{\Psi} = \begin{bmatrix} 1 & 0 \\ \sin[w_1] + w_1 \cos[w_1] & 0 \end{bmatrix}. \tag{19.36}$$

The results of using this system for tracking are illustrated in Figure 19.9. The extended Kalman filter successfully tracks this nonlinear model giving results that are both closer to the true state and more confident than estimates based on the individual measurements alone. The EKF works well here because the nonlinear function is smooth and departs from linearity slowly relative to the time steps: consequently, the linear approximation is reasonable.

19.4   Unscented Kalman filter

The extended Kalman filter is only reliable if the linear approximations to the functions $\mathbf{f}[\bullet, \bullet]$ or $\mathbf{g}[\bullet, \bullet]$ describe them well in the region of the current position. Figure 19.10 shows a situation where the local properties of the temporal function are not representative and so the EKF estimate of the covariance is inaccurate.

⚙ 19.5   The unscented Kalman filter (UKF) is a derivative-free approach that partially circumvents this problem. It is suited to nonlinear models with additive normally distributed noise so that the temporal and measurement equations are

$$\mathbf{w}_t = \mathbf{f}[\mathbf{w}_{t-1}] + \boldsymbol{\epsilon}_p$$
$$\mathbf{x}_t = \mathbf{g}[\mathbf{w}_t] + \boldsymbol{\epsilon}_m. \tag{19.37}$$

To understand how the UKF works, consider a nonlinear temporal model. Given the mean and covariance of the normally distributed posterior distribution

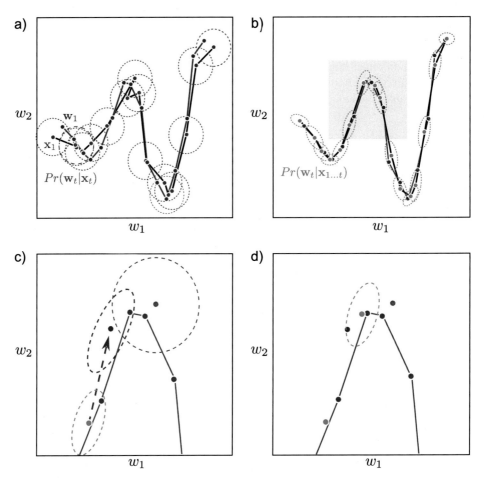

Figure 19.9 The extended Kalman filter. a) The temporal model that transforms the state (red dots) here is nonlinear. Each observed data point (magenta dots) is a noisy copy of the state at that time. Based on the data alone, the posterior probability over the state is given by the magenta ellipses. b) Estimated marginal posterior distributions using the extended Kalman filter: the estimates are more certain and more accurate than using the measurements alone. c) Close-up of shaded region from (b). The EKF makes a normal prediction (dark blue ellipse) based on the previous state (light blue ellipse) and the linearized motion model. The measurement makes a different prediction (magenta ellipse). d) The EKF combines these two predictions to get an improved estimate (light blue ellipse).

$Pr(\mathbf{w}_{t-1}|\mathbf{x}_{1...t-1})$ over the state at time $t-1$, we wish to predict a normally distributed prior $Pr(\mathbf{w}_t|\mathbf{x}_{1...t-1})$ over the state at time t. We proceed by

- Approximating the normally distributed posterior $Pr(\mathbf{w}_{t-1}|\mathbf{x}_{1...t-1})$ with a set of point masses that are deterministically chosen so that they have the same mean $\boldsymbol{\mu}_{t-1}$ and covariance $\boldsymbol{\Sigma}_{t-1}$ as the original distribution,
- Passing each of the point masses through the nonlinear function, and then
- Setting the predicted distribution $Pr(\mathbf{w}_t|\mathbf{x}_{1...t-1})$ at time t to be a normal distribution with the mean and covariance of the transformed point masses.

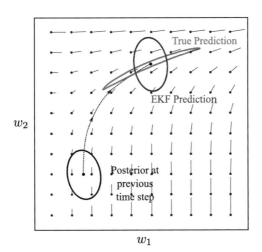

Figure 19.10 Problems with the EKF. A 2D temporal function $\mathbf{f}[\bullet,\bullet]$ operates on the state (red lines indicate gradient direction). In the prediction step, the previous estimate (blue ellipse) should be passed through this function (to create distorted green ellipse) and noise added (not shown). The EKF approximates this by passing the mean through the function and updating the covariance based on a linear approximation of the function at the previous state estimate. Here, the function changes quite nonlinearly, and so this approximation is bad, and the predicted covariance (magenta ellipse) is inaccurate.

This process is illustrated in Figure 19.11.

As for the extended Kalman filter, the predicted state $Pr(\mathbf{w}_t|\mathbf{x}_{1...t-1})$ in the UKF is a normal distribution. However, this normal distribution is a provably better approximation to the true distribution than that provided by the EKF. A similar approach is applied to cope with a nonlinearity in the measurement equations. We will now consider each of these steps in more detail.

19.4.1 State evolution

As for the standard Kalman filter, the goal of the state evolution step is to form a prediction $Pr(\mathbf{w}_t|\mathbf{x}_{1...t-1})$ about the state at time t by applying the temporal model to the posterior distribution $Pr(\mathbf{w}_{t-1}|\mathbf{x}_{1...t-1})$ at the previous time step. This posterior distribution is normal with mean $\boldsymbol{\mu}_{t-1}$ and covariance $\boldsymbol{\Sigma}_{t-1}$, and the prediction will also be normal with mean $\boldsymbol{\mu}_+$ and covariance $\boldsymbol{\Sigma}_+$.

We proceed as follows. We approximate the marginal posterior at the previous time step by a weighted sum of $2D_\mathbf{w}+1$ delta functions, where $D_\mathbf{w}$ is the dimensionality of the state, so that

$$Pr(\mathbf{w}_{t-1}|\mathbf{x}_{1...t-1}) = \text{Norm}_{\mathbf{w}_{t-1}}[\boldsymbol{\mu}_{t-1}, \boldsymbol{\Sigma}_{t-1}]$$

$$\approx \sum_{j=0}^{2D_\mathbf{w}} a_j \delta[\mathbf{w}_{t-1} - \hat{\mathbf{w}}^{[j]}], \qquad (19.38)$$

where the weights $\{a_j\}_{j=0}^{2D_\mathbf{w}}$ are positive and sum to one. In this context, the delta functions are referred to as *sigma points*. The positions $\{\hat{\mathbf{w}}^{[j]}\}_{j=0}^{2D_\mathbf{w}}$ of the sigma points are carefully chosen so that

$$\boldsymbol{\mu}_{t-1} = \sum_{j=0}^{2D_\mathbf{w}} a_j \hat{\mathbf{w}}^{[j]}$$

$$\boldsymbol{\Sigma}_{t-1} = \sum_{j=0}^{2D_\mathbf{w}} a_j (\hat{\mathbf{w}}^{[j]} - \boldsymbol{\mu}_{t-1})(\hat{\mathbf{w}}^{[j]} - \boldsymbol{\mu}_{t-1})^T. \qquad (19.39)$$

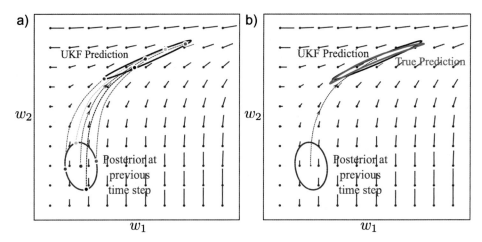

Figure 19.11 Temporal update for unscented Kalman filter. a) In the temporal update step, the posterior distribution from the previous time step (which is a normal) is approximated by a weighted set of point masses that collectively have the same mean and covariance as this normal. Each of these is passed through the temporal model (dashed lines). A normal prediction is formed by estimating the mean and the covariance of the transformed point masses. In a real system, the variance would subsequently be inflated to account for additive uncertainty in the position. b) The resulting prediction is quite close to the true prediction and for this case is much better than that of the extended Kalman filter (see Figure 19.10).

One possible scheme is to choose sigma points

$$\hat{\mathbf{w}}^{[0]} = \boldsymbol{\mu}_{t-1}$$

$$\hat{\mathbf{w}}^{[j]} = \boldsymbol{\mu}_{t-1} + \sqrt{\frac{D_{\mathbf{w}}}{1-a_0}} \boldsymbol{\Sigma}_{t-1}^{1/2} \mathbf{e}_j \qquad \text{for all } j \in \{1 \dots D_{\mathbf{w}}\}$$

$$\hat{\mathbf{w}}^{[D_{\mathbf{w}}+j]} = \boldsymbol{\mu}_{t-1} - \sqrt{\frac{D_{\mathbf{w}}}{1-a_0}} \boldsymbol{\Sigma}_{t-1}^{1/2} \mathbf{e}_j \qquad \text{for all } j \in \{1 \dots D_{\mathbf{w}}\}, \qquad (19.40)$$

where $\mathbf{e}_j$ is the unit vector in the jth direction. The associated weights are chosen so that $a_0 \in [0,1]$ and

$$a_j = \frac{1-a_0}{2D_{\mathbf{w}}}, \qquad (19.41)$$

for all a_j. The choice of weight a_0 of the first sigma point determines how far the remaining sigma points are from the mean.

We pass the sigma points through the nonlinearity, to create a new set of samples $\hat{\mathbf{w}}_+^{[j]} = \mathbf{f}[\hat{\mathbf{w}}^{[j]}]$ that collectively form a prediction for the state. We then compute the mean and the variance of the predicted distribution $Pr(\mathbf{w}_t|\mathbf{x}_{1\dots t-1})$ from the mean and variance of the transformed points so that

$$\boldsymbol{\mu}_+ = \sum_{j=0}^{2D_{\mathbf{w}}} a_j \hat{\mathbf{w}}_+^{[j]}$$

$$\boldsymbol{\Sigma}_+ = \sum_{j=0}^{2D_{\mathbf{w}}} a_j (\hat{\mathbf{w}}_+^{[j]} - \boldsymbol{\mu}_+)(\hat{\mathbf{w}}_+^{[j]} - \boldsymbol{\mu}_+)^T + \boldsymbol{\Sigma}_p, \qquad (19.42)$$

where we have added an extra term $\boldsymbol{\Sigma}_p$ to the predicted covariance to account for the additive noise in the temporal model.

19.4.2 Measurement incorporation

The measurement incorporation process in the UKF uses a similar idea: we approximate the predicted distribution $Pr(\mathbf{w}_t|\mathbf{x}_{1...t-1})$ as a set of delta functions or sigma points

$$Pr(\mathbf{w}_t|\mathbf{x}_{1...t-1}) = \text{Norm}_{\mathbf{w}_{t-1}}[\boldsymbol{\mu}_+, \boldsymbol{\Sigma}_+]$$

$$\approx \sum_{j=0}^{2D_{\mathbf{w}}} a_j \delta[\mathbf{w}_t - \hat{\mathbf{w}}^{[j]}], \tag{19.43}$$

where we choose the centers of the sigma points and the weights so that

$$\boldsymbol{\mu}_+ = \sum_{j=0}^{2D_{\mathbf{w}}} a_j \hat{\mathbf{w}}^{[j]}$$

$$\boldsymbol{\Sigma}_+ = \sum_{j=0}^{2D_{\mathbf{w}}} a_j (\hat{\mathbf{w}}^{[j]} - \boldsymbol{\mu}_+)(\hat{\mathbf{w}}^{[j]} - \boldsymbol{\mu}_+)^T. \tag{19.44}$$

For example, we could use the scheme outlined in Equations 19.40 and 19.41.

Then the sigma points are passed through the measurement model $\hat{\mathbf{x}}^{[j]} = \mathbf{g}[\hat{\mathbf{w}}^{[j]}]$ to create a new set of points $\{\hat{\mathbf{x}}^{[j]}\}_{j=0}^{2D_{\mathbf{w}}}$ in the measurement space. We compute the mean and covariance of these predicted measurements using the relations

$$\boldsymbol{\mu}_x = \sum_{j=0}^{2D_{\mathbf{w}}} a_j \hat{\mathbf{x}}^{[j]}$$

$$\boldsymbol{\Sigma}_x = \sum_{j=0}^{2D_{\mathbf{w}}} a_j (\hat{\mathbf{x}}^{[j]} - \boldsymbol{\mu}_x)(\hat{\mathbf{x}}^{[j]} - \boldsymbol{\mu}_x)^T + \boldsymbol{\Sigma}_m. \tag{19.45}$$

The measurement incorporation equations are now

$$\boldsymbol{\mu}_t = \boldsymbol{\mu}_+ + \mathbf{K}\,(\mathbf{x}_t - \boldsymbol{\mu}_x)$$

$$\boldsymbol{\Sigma}_t = \boldsymbol{\Sigma}_+ - \mathbf{K}\boldsymbol{\Sigma}_x\mathbf{K}^T, \tag{19.46}$$

where the Kalman gain $\mathbf{K}$ is now redefined as

$$\mathbf{K} = \left(\sum_{j=0}^{2D_{\mathbf{w}}} a_j (\hat{\mathbf{w}}^{[j]} - \boldsymbol{\mu}_+)^T (\hat{\mathbf{x}}^{[j]} - \boldsymbol{\mu}_x)^T \right) \boldsymbol{\Sigma}_x^{-1}. \tag{19.47}$$

As for the prediction step, it can be shown that the UKF approximation is better than that of the EKF.

19.5   Particle filtering

The extended and unscented Kalman filters can partially cope with nonlinear temporal and measurement models. However, they both represent the uncertainty over the state as a normal distribution. They are hence ill-equipped to deal with situations where the true probability distribution over the state is multimodal. Figure 19.12 illustrates a temporal model that maps nearby states into two distinct regions. In this situation, neither the EKF nor the UKF suffice: the EKF models only one of the resulting clusters and the UKF

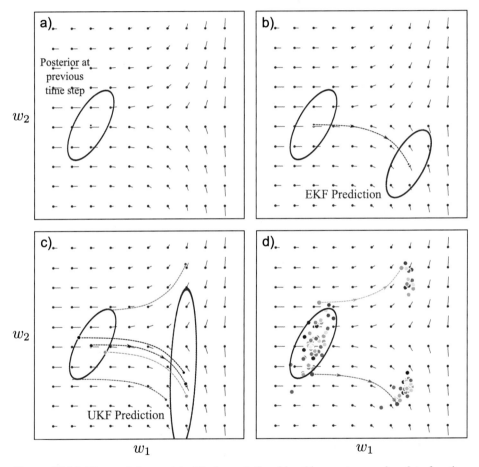

Figure 19.12 The need for particle filtering. a) Consider this new temporal update function (change of state with time indicated by red pointers), which bifurcates around the horizontal midline. b) With the EKF, the predicted distribution after the time update is toward the bottom, as the initial mean was below the bifurcation. The linear approximation is not good here and so the covariance estimate is inaccurate. c) In the UKF, one of the sigma points that approximates the prior is above the midline and so it is moved upward (green dashed line), whereas the others are below the midline and are moved downward (other dashed lines). The estimated covariance is very large. d) We can get an idea of the true predicted distribution by sampling the posterior at the previous time step and passing the samples through the nonlinear temporal model. It is clear that the resulting distribution is bimodal and can never be well approximated with a normal distribution. The particle filter represents the distribution in terms of particles throughout the tracking process and so it can describe multimodal distributions like this.

tries to model both with a single normal model, assigning a large probability to the empty region between the clusters.

Particle filtering resolves this problem by representing the probability density as a set of particles in the state space. Each particle can be thought of as representing a hypothesis about the possible state. When the state is tightly constrained by the data, all of these particles will lie close to one another. In more ambiguous cases, they will be widely distributed or clustered into groups of competing hypotheses.

The particles can be evolved through time or projected down to simulate measurements regardless of how nonlinear the functions are. The latter exercise leads us to another nice property of the particle filter: since the state is multimodal, so are the predicted measurements. In turn, the measurement density may also be multimodal. In vision systems, this means that the system copes much better with clutter in the scene (Figure 19.14). As long as some of the predicted measurements agree with the measurement density, the tracker should remain stable.

One of the simplest particle filter methods is the *conditional density propagation* or *condensation* algorithm. The probability distribution $Pr(\mathbf{w}_{t-1}|\mathbf{x}_{1...t-1})$ is represented by a weighted sum of J weighted particles:

$$Pr(\mathbf{w}_{t-1}|\mathbf{x}_{1...t-1}) = \sum_{j=1}^{J} a_j \delta[\mathbf{w}_{t-1} - \hat{\mathbf{w}}_{t-1}^{[j]}], \qquad (19.48)$$

where the weights are positive and sum to one. Each particle represents a hypothesis about the state and the weight of the particle indicates our confidence in that hypothesis. Our goal is to compute the probability distribution $Pr(\mathbf{w}_t|\mathbf{x}_{1...t})$ at the next time step, which will be represented in a similar fashion. As usual this process is divided into a time evolution and a measurement incorporation step, which we now consider in turn.

19.5.1   Time evolution

In the time evolution step, we create J predictions $\hat{\mathbf{w}}_+^{[j]}$ for the time-evolved state. Each is represented by an *unweighted particle*. We create each prediction by re-sampling so that we

- choose an index $n \in \{1 \ldots J\}$ of the original weighted particles where the probability is according to the weights. In other words, we draw a sample from $\text{Cat}_n[\mathbf{a}]$ and
- draw the sample $\hat{\mathbf{w}}_+^{[j]}$ from the temporal update distribution $Pr(\mathbf{w}_t|\mathbf{w}_{t-1} = \hat{\mathbf{w}}_{t-1}^{[n]})$ (Equation 19.37).

In this process, the final unweighted particles $\hat{\mathbf{w}}_+^{[j]}$ are created from the original weighted particles $\hat{\mathbf{w}}_{t-1}^{[j]}$ according to the weights $\mathbf{a} = [a_1, a_2, \ldots, a_J]$. Hence, the highest weighted original particles may contribute repeatedly to the final set, and the lowest weighted ones may not contribute at all.

19.5.2   Measurement incorporation

In the measurement incorporation step we weight the new set of particles according to how well they agree with the observed data. To this end, we

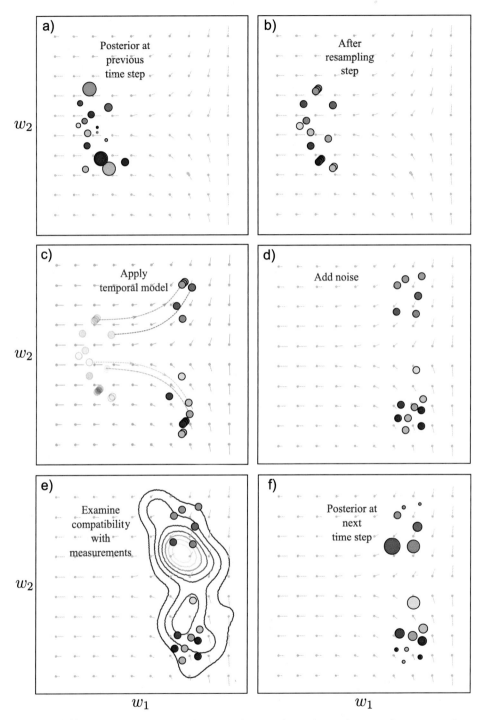

Figure 19.13 The condensation algorithm. a) The posterior at the previous step is represented as a set of weighted particles. b) The particles are re-sampled according to their weights to produce a new set of unweighted particles. c) These particles are passed through the nonlinear temporal function. d) Noise is added according to the temporal model. e) The particles are passed through the measurement model and compared to the measurement density. f) The particles are reweighted according to their compatibility with the measurements, and the process can begin again.

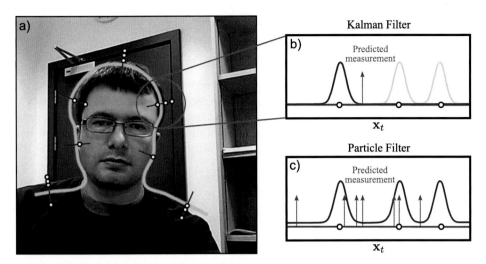

Figure 19.14 Data association. a) Consider the problem of tracking this contour. The contour from the previous frame is shown in cyan, and the problem is to incorporate the measurements in this frame. These measurements take the form of edges along one-dimensional slices perpendicular to the contour. In most cases, there are multiple possible edges that might be due to the contour. b) In the Kalman filter, the measurement density is constrained to be normal: we are forced to choose between the different possible hypotheses. A sensible way to do this is to select the one that is closest to the predicted measurement. This is known as data association. c) In the particle filter, there are multiple predicted measurements and it is not necessary that the measurement density is normal. We can effectively take into account all of the possible measurements.

- Pass the particles through the measurement model $\hat{\mathbf{x}}_+^{[j]} = \mathbf{g}[\hat{\mathbf{w}}_+^{[j]}]$.
- Weight the particles according to their agreement with the observation density. For example, with a Gaussian measurement model, we could use

$$a_j \propto Pr(\mathbf{x}_t|\hat{\mathbf{w}}_+^{[j]}) = \text{Norm}_{\mathbf{x}_t}[\hat{\mathbf{x}}_+^{[j]}, \Sigma_m]. \qquad (19.49)$$

- Normalize the resulting weights $\{a_j\}_{j=1}^J$ to sum to one.
- Finally, set the new states $\hat{\mathbf{w}}_t^{[j]}$ to the predicted states $\hat{\mathbf{w}}_+^{[j]}$ and the new weights to a_j.

Figure 19.13 demonstrates the action of the particle filter. The filter copes elegantly with the multimodal probability distribution. It is also suitable for situations where it is not obvious which aspect of the data is the true measurement. This is known as the *data association* problem (Figure 19.14).

The main disadvantage of particle filters is their cost: in high dimensions, a very large number of particles may be required to get an accurate representation of the true distribution over the state.

19.5.3 Extensions

There are many variations and extensions to the particle filter. In many schemes, the particles are not resampled on each iteration, but only occasionally so the main scheme operates with weighted particles. The resampling process can also be improved by applying *importance sampling*. Here, the new samples are generated in concert with the measurement process, so that particles that agree with the measurements are more likely to be produced. This helps prevent the situation where none of the unweighted samples after the prediction stage agree with the measurements.

The process of *Rao-Blackwellization* partitions the state into two subsets of variables. The first subset is tracked using a particle filter, but the other subset is conditioned on the first subset and evaluated analytically using a process more like the Kalman filter. Careful choice of these subsets can result in a tracking algorithm that is both efficient and accurate.

19.6   Applications

Tracking algorithms can be used in combination with any model that is being reesti-mated over a time sequence. For example, they are often used in combination with 3D body models to track the pose of a person in video footage. In this section, we will describe three example applications. First we will consider tracking the 3D position of a pedestrian in a scene. Second, we will describe *simultaneous localization and mapping (SLAM)* in which both a 3D representation of a scene and the pose of the camera viewing it are estimated through a time sequence. Finally, we will consider contour tracking for an object with complex motion against a cluttered background.

19.6.1   Pedestrian Tracking

Rosales and Sclaroff (1999) described a system to track pedestrians in 2D from a fixed static camera using the extended Kalman filter. For each frame, the measurements $\mathbf{x}$ consisted of a 2D bounding box $\mathbf{x} = \{x_1, y_1, x_2, y_2\}$ around the pedestrian. This was found by segmenting the pedestrian from the background using a background subtraction model, and finding a connected region of foreground pixels.

The state of the world $\mathbf{w}$ was considered to be the 3D position of a bounding box of constant depth $\{u_1, v_1, u_2, v_2, w\}$ and the velocities associated with these five quantities. The state update equation assumed first-order Newtonian dynamics in 3D space. The relationship between the state and measurements was

$$\begin{bmatrix} x_1 \\ y_1 \\ x_2 \\ y_2 \end{bmatrix} = \begin{bmatrix} u_1 \\ v_1 \\ u_2 \\ v_2 \end{bmatrix} \frac{1}{1+w} + \boldsymbol{\epsilon}, \tag{19.50}$$

which mimics the nonlinear action of the pinhole camera.

Results from the tracking procedure are illustrated in Figure 19.15. The system successfully tracks pedestrians and was extended to cope with occlusions (which are predicted by the EKF based on the estimated trajectory of the objects). In the full sys-tem, the estimated bounding boxes are used to warp the images of the pedestrians to a fixed size, and the resulting registered images were used as input to an action recognition algorithm

Figure 19.15 Pedestrian tracking results. a–f) Six frames from a sequence in which a 3D bounding plane of constant depth was used to track each person. Adapted from Rosales and Sclaroff (1999). ©1999 IEEE.

19.6.2 Monocular SLAM

The goal of *simultaneous localization and mapping* or *SLAM* is to build a map of an unknown environment based on measurements from a moving sensor (usually attached to a robot) and to establish where the sensor is in the world at any given time. Hence, the system must simultaneously estimate the structure of the world and its own position and orientation within that model. SLAM was originally based on range sensors but in the last decade it has become possible to build systems based on a monocular camera that work in real time. In essence it is a real-time version of the sparse 3D reconstruction algorithms discussed in Chapter 16.

Davison et al. (2007) presented one such system which was based on the extended Kalman filter. Here the world state **w** contains

- The camera position (u, v, w),
- The orientation of the camera as represented by a 4D quaternion **q**,
- The velocity and angular velocity, and
- A set of 3D points $\{\mathbf{p}_k\}$ where $\mathbf{p}_k = [p_{uk}, p_{vk}, p_{wk}]$. This set generally expands during the sequence as more parts of the world are seen.

The state update equation modifies the position and orientation according to their respective velocities, and allows these velocities themselves to change. The observation equation maps each 3D point through a pinhole camera model to create a predicted 2D image position (i.e., similar to Equation 19.50). The actual measurements consist of interest points in the image, which are uniquely identified and associated with the predicted measurements by considering their surrounding region. The system is very efficient as it is only necessary to search the image in regions close to the 2D point predicted by the measurement equation from the current state.

The full system is more complex, and includes special procedures for initializing new feature points, modeling the local region of each point as a plane, selecting which

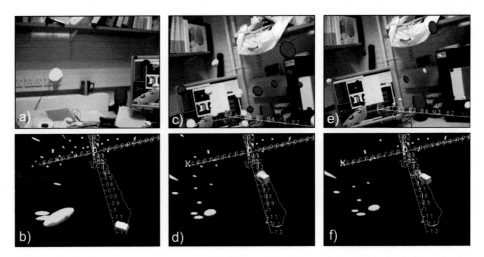

Figure 19.16 Monocular SLAM model of Davison et al. (2007). a) Current view of world with visual features and their 3D covariance ellipse superimposed. Yellow points are features in the model that were actually measured. Blue points are features in the model that were not detected in this frame. Red points are new features that can potentially be incorporated into the model. b) Model of world at the time this frame was captured, showing the position of the camera and the position and uncertainty of visual features. c–f) Two more pairs of images and associated models from later in the same time sequence. Notice that the uncertainty in the feature positions gradually decreases over time. Adapted from Davison et al. (2007). ©2007 IEEE.

features to measure in this frame, and managing the resulting map by deleting extraneous features to reduce the complexity. A series of frames from the system is illustrated in Figure 19.16.

19.6.3 Tracking a contour through clutter

In Section 17.3 we discussed fitting a template shape model to an image. It was noted that this was a challenging problem as the template frequently fell into local minima when the object was observed in clutter. In principle, this problem should be easier in a temporal sequence; if we know the template position in the current frame, then we can hypothesize quite accurately where it is in the next frame. Nonetheless, tracking methods based on the Kalman filter still fail to maintain a lock on the object; sooner or later, part of the contour becomes erroneously associated with the background and the tracking fails.

Blake and Isard (1998) describe a system based on the condensation algorithm that can cope with tracking a contour undergoing rapid motions against a cluttered background. The state of the system consists of the parameters of an affine transformation that maps the template into the scene and the measurements are similar to those illustrated in Figure 19.14. The state is represented as 100 weighted particles, each of which represents a different hypothesis about the current position of the template. This system was used to track the head of a child dancing in front of a cluttered background (Figure 19.17).

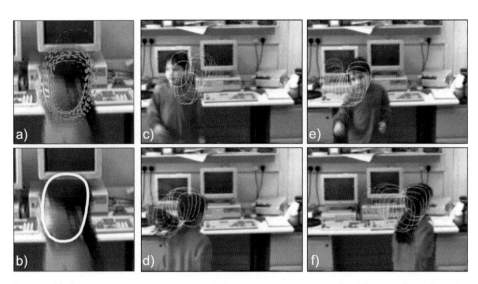

Figure 19.17 Tracking a contour through clutter. a) The representation of uncertainty about the contour consists of a set of weighted particles, each of which represents a hypothesis about the current position. In this frame, the different contours represent different hypotheses, and their weight indicates our relative belief that the system takes this state. b) The overall estimate of the current position can be illustrated by taking a weighted mean of the hypotheses. c–f) Four frames of sequence tracked by condensation algorithm showing the current estimate and the estimates from previous frames. Adapted from Blake and Isard (1998). ©1998 Springer.

Discussion

In this chapter we have discussed a family of models that allow us to estimate a set of continuous parameters throughout a time sequence by exploiting the temporal coherence of the estimates. In principle these methods can be applied to any model in this book that estimates a set of parameters from a single frame. These models have a close relationship with the chain-based models discussed in Chapter 11. The latter models used discrete parameters and generally estimated the state from the whole sequence rather than just the observed data up until the current time.

Notes

Applications of tracking: Tracking models are used for a variety of tasks in vision including tracking pedestrians (Rosales and Sclaroff 1999; Beymer and Konolige 1999), contours (Terzopolous and Szeliski 1992; Blake et al. 1993; 1995; Blake and Isard 1996; 1998), points (Broida and Chellappa 1986), 3D hand models (Stenger et al. 2001b), and 3D body models (Wang et al. 2008). They have also been used for activity recognition (Vaswani et al. 2003), estimating depth (Matthies et al. 1989), SLAM (Davison et al. 2007), and object recognition (Zhou et al. 2004). Reviews of tracking methods and applications can be found in Blake (2006) and Yilmaz et al. (2006). Approaches to tracking the human body are reviewed in Poppe (2007).

Tracking models: The Kalman filter was originally developed by Kalman (1960) and Kalman and Bucy (1961). The unscented Kalman filter was developed by Julier and Uhlmann (1997). The condensation algorithm is due to Blake and Isard (1996). For more information about the Kalman filter and its variants, consult Maybeck (1990), Gelb (1974), and Jazwinski (1970). Roweis and

Ghahramani (1999) provide a unifying review of linear models, which provides information about how the Kalman filter relates to other methods. Arulampalam et al. (2002) provide a detailed review of the use of particle filters. A summary of tracking models and different approaches to inference within them can be found in Minka (2002).

There are a large number of variants on the standard Kalman filter. Many of these involve switching between different state space models or propagating mixtures (Shumway and Stoffer 1991; Ghahramani and Hinton 1996b; Murphy 1998; Chen and Liu 2000; Isard and Blake 1998). A notable recent extension has been to develop a nonlinear tracking algorithm based on the GPLVM (Wang et al. 2008).

One topic that has not been discussed in this chapter is how to learn the parameters of the tracking models. In practice, it is not uncommon to set these parameters by hand. However, information about learning in these temporal models can be found in Shumway and Stoffer (1982), Ghahramani and Hinton (1996a), Roweis and Ghahramani (2001), and Oh et al. (2005).

Simultaneous localization and mapping: Simultaneous localization and mapping has its roots in the robotics community who were concerned with the representation of spatial uncertainty by vehicles exploring an environment (Durrant-Whyte 1988; Smith and Cheeseman 1987), although the term SLAM was coined much later by Durrant-Whyte et al. (1996). Smith et al. (1990) had the important insight that the errors in mapped positions were correlated due to uncertainty in the camera position. The roots of vision-based SLAM are to be found in the pioneering work of Harris and Pike (1987), Ayache (1991), and Beardsley et al. (1995).

SLAM systems are usually based on either the extended Kalman filter (Guivant and Nebot 2001; Leonard and Feder 2000; Davison et al. 2007) or a Rao-Blackwellized particle filter (Montemerlo et al. 2002; Montemerlo et al. 2003; Sim et al. 2005). However, it currently the subject of some debate as to whether a tracking method of this type is necessary at all, or whether repeated bundle adjustments on tactically chosen subsets of 3D points will suffice (Strasdat et al. 2010).

Recent examples of efficient visual SLAM systems can be found in Nistér et al. (2004), Davison et al. (2007), Klein and Murray (2007), Mei et al. (2009), and Newcombe et al. (2011), and most of these include a bundle adjustment procedure into the algorithm. Current research issues in SLAM include how to efficiently match features in the image with features in the current model (Handa et al. 2010) and how to close loops (i.e., recognize that the robot has returned to a familiar place) in a map (Newman and Ho 2005). A review of SLAM techniques can be found in Durrant-Whyte and Bailey (2006) and Bailey and Durrant-Whyte (2006).

Problems

19.1 Prove the Chapman–Kolmogorov relation:

$$Pr(\mathbf{w}_t|\mathbf{x}_{1\ldots t-1}) = \int Pr(\mathbf{w}_t|\mathbf{w}_{t-1})Pr(\mathbf{w}_{t-1}|\mathbf{x}_{1\ldots t-1})\, d\mathbf{w}_{t-1}$$

$$= \int \text{Norm}_{\mathbf{w}_t}[\boldsymbol{\mu}_p + \boldsymbol{\Psi}\mathbf{w}_{t-1}, \boldsymbol{\Sigma}_p]\text{Norm}_{\mathbf{w}_{t-1}}[\boldsymbol{\mu}_{t-1}, \boldsymbol{\Sigma}_{t-1}]\, d\mathbf{w}_{t-1}$$

$$= \text{Norm}_{\mathbf{w}_t}[\boldsymbol{\mu}_p + \boldsymbol{\Psi}\boldsymbol{\mu}_{t-1}, \boldsymbol{\Sigma}_p + \boldsymbol{\Psi}\boldsymbol{\Sigma}_{t-1}\boldsymbol{\Psi}^T].$$

19.2 Derive the measurement incorporation step for the Kalman filter. In other words, show that

$$
\begin{aligned}
Pr(\mathbf{w}_t|\mathbf{x}_{1\ldots t}) &= \frac{Pr(\mathbf{x}_t|\mathbf{w}_t)Pr(\mathbf{w}_t|\mathbf{w}_{1\ldots t-1},\mathbf{x}_{1\ldots t})}{Pr(\mathbf{x}_{1\ldots t})} \\
&= \frac{\mathrm{Norm}_{\mathbf{x}_t}[\boldsymbol{\mu}_m + \boldsymbol{\Phi}\mathbf{w}_t, \boldsymbol{\Sigma}_m]\mathrm{Norm}_{\mathbf{w}_t}[\boldsymbol{\mu}_+, \boldsymbol{\Sigma}_+]}{Pr(\mathbf{x}_{1\ldots t})} \\
&= \mathrm{Norm}_{\mathbf{w}_t}\left[\left(\boldsymbol{\Phi}^T\boldsymbol{\Sigma}_m^{-1}\boldsymbol{\Phi} + \boldsymbol{\Sigma}_+^{-1}\right)^{-1}\left(\boldsymbol{\Phi}^T\boldsymbol{\Sigma}_m^{-1}(\mathbf{x}_t - \boldsymbol{\mu}_m) + \boldsymbol{\Sigma}_+^{-1}\boldsymbol{\mu}_+\right),\right. \\
&\qquad\qquad\left. \left(\boldsymbol{\Phi}^T\boldsymbol{\Sigma}_m^{-1}\boldsymbol{\Phi} + \boldsymbol{\Sigma}_+^{-1}\right)^{-1}\right].
\end{aligned}
$$

19.3 Consider a variation of the Kalman filter where the prior based on the previous time step is a mixture of K Gaussians

$$
Pr(\mathbf{w}_t|\mathbf{x}_{1\ldots t-1}) = \sum_{k=1}^K \lambda_k \mathrm{Norm}_{\mathbf{w}_t}[\boldsymbol{\mu}_{+k}, \boldsymbol{\Sigma}_{+k}].
$$

What will happen in the subsequent measurement incorporation step? What will happen in the next time update step?

19.4 Consider a model where there are two possible temporal update equations represented by state transition matrices $\boldsymbol{\Psi}_1$ and $\boldsymbol{\Psi}_2$ and the system periodically switches from one regime to the other. Write a set of equations that describe this model and discuss a strategy for max-marginals inference.

19.5 In a Kalman filter model, discuss how you would compute the joint posterior distribution $Pr(\mathbf{w}_{1\ldots T}|\mathbf{x}_{1\ldots T})$ over all of the unknown world states. What form will this posterior distribution take? In the Kalman filter we choose to compute the marginal posteriors instead. Why is this?

19.6 Apply the sum-product algorithm (Section 11.4.3) to the Kalman filter model and show that the result is equivalent to applying the Kalman filter recursions.

19.7 Prove the Kalman smoother recursions:

$$
\begin{aligned}
\boldsymbol{\mu}_{t|T} &= \boldsymbol{\mu}_t + \mathbf{C}_t(\boldsymbol{\mu}_{t+1|T} - \boldsymbol{\mu}_{+|t}) \\
\boldsymbol{\Sigma}_{t|T} &= \boldsymbol{\Sigma}_t + \mathbf{C}_t(\boldsymbol{\Sigma}_{t+1|T} - \boldsymbol{\Sigma}_{+|t})\mathbf{C}_t^T,
\end{aligned}
$$

where

$$
\mathbf{C}_t = \boldsymbol{\Sigma}_{t|t}\boldsymbol{\Psi}^T\boldsymbol{\Sigma}_{+|t}^{-1}.
$$

Hint: It may help to examine the proof of the forward-backward algorithm for HMMs (Section 11.4.2).

19.8 Discuss how you would learn the parameters of the Kalman filter model given training sequences consisting of (i) both the known world state and the observed data and (ii) just the observed data alone.

19.9 In the unscented Kalman filter we represented a Gaussian with mean $\boldsymbol{\mu}$ and covariance $\boldsymbol{\Sigma}$ with a set of delta functions

$$
\begin{aligned}
\hat{\mathbf{w}}^{[0]} &= \boldsymbol{\mu}_{t-1} \\
\hat{\mathbf{w}}^{[j]} &= \boldsymbol{\mu}_{t-1} + \sqrt{\frac{D_{\mathbf{w}}}{1 - a_0}}\boldsymbol{\Sigma}_{t-1}^{1/2}\mathbf{e}_j &&\text{for all } j \in \{1\ldots D_{\mathbf{w}}\} \\
\hat{\mathbf{w}}^{[D_{\mathbf{w}}+j]} &= \boldsymbol{\mu}_{t-1} - \sqrt{\frac{D_{\mathbf{w}}}{1 - a_0}}\boldsymbol{\Sigma}_{t-1}^{1/2}\mathbf{e}_j &&\text{for all } j \in \{1\ldots D_{\mathbf{w}}\},
\end{aligned}
$$

with associated weights

$$a_j = \frac{1 - a_0}{2D_\mathbf{w}}.$$

Show that the mean and covariance of these points are indeed $\boldsymbol{\mu}_{t-1}$ and $\boldsymbol{\Sigma}_{t-1}$ so that

$$\boldsymbol{\mu}_{t-1} = \sum_{j=0}^{2D_\mathbf{w}} a_j \hat{\mathbf{w}}^{[j]}$$

$$\boldsymbol{\Sigma}_{t-1} = \sum_{j=0}^{2D_\mathbf{w}} a_j (\hat{\mathbf{w}}^{[j]} - \boldsymbol{\mu}_{t-1})(\hat{\mathbf{w}}^{[j]} - \boldsymbol{\mu}_{t-1})^T.$$

19.10 The extended Kalman filter requires the Jacobian matrix describing how small changes in the data create small changes in the measurements. Compute the Jacobian matrix for the measurement model for the pedestrian-tracking application (Equation 19.50).

Chapter 20

Models for visual words

In most of the models in this book, the observed data are treated as continuous. Hence, for generative models the data likelihood is usually based on the normal distribution. In this chapter, we explore generative models that treat the observed data as discrete. The data likelihoods are now based on the categorical distribution; they describe the probability of observing the different possible values of the discrete variable.

As a motivating example for the models in this chapter, consider the problem of *scene classification* (Figure 20.1). We are given example training images of different scene categories (e.g., office, coastline, forest, mountain) and we are asked to learn a model that can classify new examples. Studying the scenes in Figure 20.1 demonstrates how challenging a problem this is. Different images of the same scene may have very little in common with one another, yet we must somehow learn to identify them as the same. In this chapter, we will also discuss object recognition, which has many of the same characteristics; the appearance of an object such as a tree, bicycle, or chair can vary dramatically from one image to another, and we must somehow capture this variation.

The key to modeling these complex scenes is to encode the image as a collection of *visual words*, and use the frequencies with which these words occur as the substrate for further calculations. We start this chapter by describing this transformation.

20.1 Images as collections of visual words

To encode an image in terms of visual words, we need first to establish a *dictionary*. This is computed from a large set of training images that are unlabeled, but known to contain examples of all of the scenes or objects that will ultimately be classified. To compute the dictionary, we take the following steps:

1. For every one of the I training images, select a set of J_i spatial locations. One possibility is to identify interest points (Section 13.2) in the image. Alternately, the image can be sampled in a regular grid.
2. Compute a descriptor at each spatial location in each image that characterizes the surrounding region with a low dimensional vector. For example, we might compute the SIFT descriptor (Section 13.3.2).
3. Cluster all of these descriptor vectors into K groups using a method such as the K-means algorithm (Section 13.4.4).
4. The means of the K clusters are used as the K prototype vectors in the dictionary.

Figure 20.1 Scene recognition. The goal of scene recognition is to assign a discrete category to an image according to the type or content. In this case, the data includes images of a) street scenes, b) the sea, and c) forests. Scene recognition is a useful precursor to object recognition; if we know that the scene is a street, then the probability of a car being present is high, but the probability of a boat being present is small. Unfortunately, scene recognition is quite a challenging task in itself. Different examples from the same scene class may have very little in common visually.

Typically, several hundred thousand descriptors would be used to compute the dictionary, which might consist of several hundred prototype words.

Having computed the dictionary, we are now in a position to take a new image and convert it into a set of visual words. To compute the visual words, we take the following steps:

1. Select a set of J spatial locations in the image using the same method as for the dictionary.
2. Compute the descriptor at each of the J spatial locations.
3. Compare each descriptor to the set of K prototype descriptors in the dictionary and find the closest prototype (visual word).
4. Assign to this location a discrete index that corresponds to the index of the closest word in the dictionary.

After computing the visual words, the data $\mathbf{x}$ from a single image consist of a set $\mathbf{x} = \{f_j, x_j, y_j\}_{j=1}^{J}$ of J word indices $f_j \in \{1 \dots K\}$ and their 2D image positions (x_j, y_j). This is a highly compressed representation that nonetheless contains the critical information about the image appearance and layout. In the remaining part of the chapter, we will develop a series of generative models that attempt to explain the pattern of this data when different objects or scenes are present.

20.2 Bag of words

One of the simplest possible representations for an image in terms of visual words is the
⚙ 20.1 *bag of words*. Here we entirely discard the spatial information held in the word positions

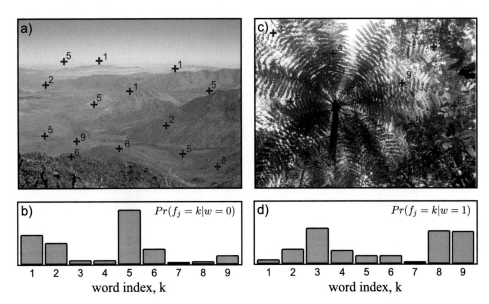

Figure 20.2 Scene recognition using bags of words. a) A set of interest points is found in this desert scene and a descriptor is calculated at each. These descriptors are compared to a dictionary containing K prototypes and the index of the nearest prototype is chosen (red numbers). Here $K = 9$, but in real applications it might be several hundred. b) The scene-type "desert" implies a certain distribution over the observed visual words. c) A second image containing a jungle scene, and the associated visual words. d) The scene type "jungle" implies a different distribution over the visual words. A new image can be classified as belonging to one scene type or another by assessing the likelihood that the observed visual words were drawn from the "desert" or "jungle" distribution.

(x_j, y_j) and just retain the word indices f_j, so that the observed data are $\mathbf{x} = \{f_j\}_{j=1}^{J}$. The image is simply represented by the frequency with which each word appears. It is assumed that different types of object or scene will tend to contain different words and that this can be exploited to perform scene or object recognition (Figure 20.2).

More formally, the goal is to infer a discrete variable $w \in \{1, 2, \ldots, N\}$ indicating which of N classes is present in this image. We take a generative approach and model each of the N classes separately. Since the data $\{f_j\}_{j=1}^{J}$ are discrete, we describe its probability with a categorical distribution and make the parameters $\boldsymbol{\lambda}$ of this distribution a function of the discrete world state:

$$Pr(\mathbf{x}|w=n) = \prod_{j=1}^{J} \text{Cat}_{f_j}[\boldsymbol{\lambda}_n]$$

$$= \prod_{k=1}^{K} \lambda_{kn}^{T_k}, \tag{20.1}$$

where T_k is the total number of times that the kth word was observed, so that

$$T_k = \sum_{j=1}^{J} \delta[f_j - k]. \tag{20.2}$$

We will now consider the learning and inference algorithms for this model.

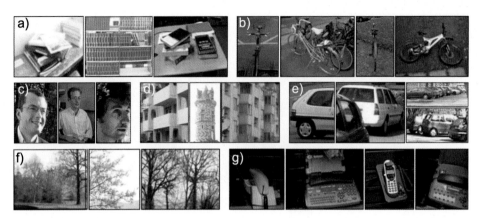

Figure 20.3 Object recognition using bags of words. Csurka et al. (2004) built a generative bag of visual words model to distinguish between examples of a) books, b) bicycles, c) people, d) buildings, e) cars, f) trees, and g) phones. Despite the wide variety of visual appearance within each class, they achieved 72 percent correct classification. By applying a discriminative approach to the same problem, they managed to improve performance further.

20.2.1 Learning

In learning, our goal is to estimate the parameters $\{\boldsymbol{\lambda}_n\}_{n=1}^N$ based on labeled pairs $\{\mathbf{x}_i, w_i\}$ of the observed data $\mathbf{x}_i = \{f_{ij}\}_{j=1}^{J_i}$ and the world state w_i. We note that the nth parameter vector $\boldsymbol{\lambda}_n$ is used only when the world state $w_i = n$. Hence, we can learn each parameter vector separately; we learn the parameter $\boldsymbol{\lambda}_n$ from the subset $\mathcal{S}_n$ of training images where $w_i = n$.

Making use of the results in Section 4.5, we see that if we apply a Dirichlet prior with uniform parameter $\boldsymbol{\alpha} = [\alpha, \alpha, \ldots, \alpha]$, then the MAP estimate of the categorical parameters is given by

$$\hat{\lambda}_{nk} = \frac{\sum_{i \in \mathcal{S}_n} T_{ik} + \alpha - 1}{\sum_{k=1}^K (\sum_{i \in \mathcal{S}_n} T_{ik} + \alpha - 1)}, \tag{20.3}$$

where λ_{nk} is the kth entry in the categorical distribution for the nth class and T_{ik} is the total number of times that word k was observed in the ith training image.

20.2.2 Inference

To infer the world state, we apply Bayes' rule:

$$Pr(w=n|\mathbf{x}) = \frac{Pr(\mathbf{x}|w=n)Pr(w=n)}{\sum_{n=1}^N Pr(\mathbf{x}|w=n)Pr(w=n)}, \tag{20.4}$$

where we allocate suitable prior probabilities $Pr(w=n)$ according to the relative frequencies with which each world type is present.

Discussion

Despite discarding all spatial information, the bag of words model works remarkably well for object recognition. For example, Csurka et al. (2004) achieved 72 percent correct performance at classifying images of the seven classes found in Figure 20.3. It should

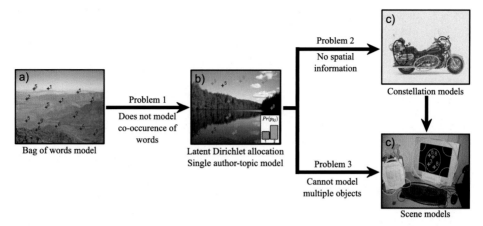

Figure 20.4 Problems with bag of words model. a) The bag of words model is quite effective for object and scene recognition, but it can be improved upon by b) modeling the cooccurence of visual words (creating the latent Dirichlet allocation model). c) This model can be extended to describe the relative positions of different parts of the object (creating a constellation model) and d) extended again to describe the relative position of objects in the scene (creating a scene model).

be noted that it is possible to improve performance further by treating the vector $\mathbf{z} = [T_1, T_2, \ldots, T_K]/\sum_k T_k$ of normalized word frequencies as continuous and subjecting it to a kernelized discriminative classifier (see Chapter 9). Regardless, we will continue to investigate the (more theoretically interesting) generative approach.

20.2.3 Problems with the bag of words model

There are a number of drawbacks to the generative bag of words model:

- It assumes that the words are generated independently, within a given object class although this is not necessarily true. The presence of a particular visual word tells us about the likelihood of observing other words.
- It ignores spatial information; consequently, when applied to object recognition, it cannot tell us where the object is in the image.
- It is unsuited to describing multiple objects in a single image.

We devote the remaining part of this chapter to building a series of generative models that improve on these weaknesses (Figure 20.4).

20.3   Latent Dirichlet allocation

We will now develop an intermediate model known as *latent Dirichlet allocation*. This model has limited utility for visual applications in its most basic form, but it underpins more interesting models that are discussed subsequently.

There are two important differences between the bag of words and latent Dirichlet allocation models. First, the bag of words model describes the relative frequency of visual words in a single image, whereas latent Dirichlet allocation describes the occurrence of visual words across a number of images. Second, the bag of words model assumes that each word in the image is generated completely independently; having observed word f_{i1}, we are none the wiser about word f_{i2}. However, in the latent Dirichlet allocation model, a hidden variable associated with each image induces a more complex distribution over the word frequencies.

Latent Dirichlet allocation can be best understood by analogy to text documents. Each document is considered as a certain mixture of *topics*. For example, this book might contain the topics "machine learning", "vision," and "computer science" in proportions of $0.3, 0.5$, and 0.2, respectively. Each topic defines a probability distribution over words; the words "image" and "pixel" might be more probable under the topic of vision, and the words "algorithm" and "complexity" might be more probable under the topic of computer science.

To generate a word, we first choose a topic according to the topic probabilities for the current document. Then we choose a word according to a distribution that depends on the chosen topic. Notice how this model induces correlations between the probability of observing different words. For example, if we see the word "image", then this implies that the topic "vision" has a significant probability and hence observing the word "pixel" becomes more likely.

Now let us convert these ideas back to the vision domain. The document becomes an image, and the words become visual words. The topic does not have an absolutely clear interpretation, but we will refer to it as a *part*. It is a cluster of visual words that tend to co-occur in images. They may or may not be spatially close to one another in the image, and they may or may not correspond to an actual "part" of an object (Figure 20.5).

Formally, the model represents the words in an image as a mixture of categorical distributions. The mixing weights depend on the image, but the parameters of the categorical distributions are shared across all of the images:

$$Pr(p_{ij}) = \text{Cat}_{p_{ij}}[\boldsymbol{\pi}_i]$$
$$Pr(f_{ij}|p_{ij}) = \text{Cat}_{f_{ij}}[\boldsymbol{\lambda}_{p_{ij}}], \qquad (20.5)$$

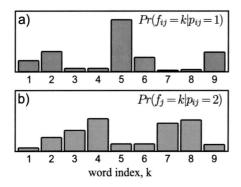

Figure 20.5 Latent Dirichlet allocation. This model treats each word as belonging to one of M different parts (here $M = 2$). a) The distribution over the words given that the part is 1 is described by a categorical distribution. b) The distribution over the words given that the part is 2 is described by a different categorical distribution. c) In each image, the tendency for the observed words to belong to each part is different. In this case, part 1 is more likely than part 2 and so most of the words belong to part 1 (are red as opposed to green).

where i indexes the image and j indexes the word. The first equation says that the part label $p_{ij} \in \{1, 2, \ldots, M\}$ associated with the jth word in the ith image is drawn from a categorical distribution with parameters $\boldsymbol{\pi}_i$ that are unique to this image. The second equation says that the actual choice of visual word f_{ij} is a categorical distribution where the parameters $\boldsymbol{\lambda}_{p_{ij}}$ depend on the part. For short, we will refer to $\{\boldsymbol{\pi}_i\}_{i=1}^I$ and $\{\boldsymbol{\lambda}_m\}_{m=1}^M$ as the part probabilities and the word probabilities, respectively.

The final density over the words comes from marginalizing over the part labels, which are hidden variables, so that

$$Pr(f_{ij}) = \sum_{m=1}^{M} Pr(f_{ij}|p_{ij} = m)Pr(p_{ij} = m). \tag{20.6}$$

To complete the model, we define priors on the parameters $\{\boldsymbol{\pi}_i\}_{i=1}^I$, $\{\boldsymbol{\lambda}_m\}_{m=1}^M$, where I is the number of images and M is the total number of parts. In each case, we choose the conjugate Dirichlet prior with a uniform parameter vector so that

$$Pr(\boldsymbol{\pi}_i) = \text{Dir}_{\boldsymbol{\pi}_i}[\boldsymbol{\alpha}]$$
$$Pr(\boldsymbol{\lambda}_m) = \text{Dir}_{\boldsymbol{\lambda}_m}[\boldsymbol{\beta}], \tag{20.7}$$

where $\boldsymbol{\alpha} = [\alpha, \alpha, \ldots, \alpha]$ and $\boldsymbol{\beta} = [\beta, \beta, \ldots, \beta]$. The associated graphical model is shown in Figure 20.6.

Notice that latent Dirichlet allocation is a density model for the data in a set of images. It does not involve a "world" term that we wish to infer. In the subsequent models, we will reintroduce the world term and use the model for inference in visual problems. However, for now we will concentrate on how to learn the relatively simple latent Dirichlet allocation model.

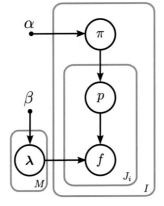

Probability of selecting each of M parts in i^{th} image

Part label for j^{th} word in i^{th} image

Probability of observing each of K possible words under part label m

Word label for j^{th} feature in i^{th} image

Figure 20.6 Graphical model for latent Dirichlet allocation. The likelihood of the jth word f_{ij} in the ith image taking each of the K different values depends on which of M parts it belongs to, and this is determined by the associated part label p_{ij}. The tendency of the part label to take different values is different for each image and is determined by the parameters $\boldsymbol{\pi}_i$. The hyperparameters α and β determine the Dirichlet priors over the part probabilities and word probabilities, respectively.

20.3.1 Learning

In learning, the goal is to estimate the part probabilities $\{\pi_i\}_{i=1}^{I}$ for each of the I training images and the word probabilities for each of the M parts $\{\lambda_m\}_{m=1}^{M}$ based on a set of training data $\{f_{ij}\}_{i=1,j=1}^{I,J_i}$, where J_i denotes the number of words found in the ith image.

If we knew the values of the hidden part labels $\{p_{ij}\}_{i=1,j=1}^{I,J_i}$, then it would be easy to learn the unknown parameters. Adopting the approach of Section 4.4, the exact expressions would be

$$\hat{\pi}_{im} = \frac{\sum_j \delta[p_{ij} - m] + \alpha}{\sum_{j,m} \delta[p_{ij} - m] + M\alpha}$$

$$\hat{\lambda}_{mk} = \frac{\sum_{i,j} \delta[p_{ij} - m]\delta[f_{ij} - k] + \beta}{\sum_{i,j,k} \delta[p_{ij} - m]\delta[f_{ij} - k] + K\beta}. \tag{20.8}$$

Unfortunately, we do not know these part labels and so we cannot use this direct technique. One possible approach would be to adopt the EM algorithm in which we alternately compute the posterior distribution over the part labels and update the parameters. Unfortunately, this is also problematic; all of the part labels $\{p_{ij}\}_{j=1}^{J_i}$ in the ith image share a parent π_i in the graphical model. This means we cannot treat them as independent. In theory, we could compute their joint posterior distribution, but there may be several hundred words per image, each of which takes several hundred values and so this is not practical.

Hence, our strategy will be to:

- Write an expression for the posterior distribution over the part labels,
- Develop an MCMC method to draw samples from this distribution, and then
- use the samples to estimate the parameters.

These three steps are expanded upon in the next three sections.

Posterior distribution over part labels

The posterior distribution over the part labels $\mathbf{p} = \{p_{ij}\}_{i=1,j=1}^{I,J_i}$ results from applying Bayes' rule:

$$Pr(\mathbf{p}|\mathbf{f}) = \frac{Pr(\mathbf{f}|\mathbf{p})Pr(\mathbf{p})}{\sum_{\mathbf{f}} Pr(\mathbf{f}|\mathbf{p})Pr(\mathbf{p})}, \tag{20.9}$$

where $\mathbf{f} = \{f_{ij}\}_{i=1,j=1}^{I,J_i}$ denotes the observed words.

The two terms in the numerator depend on the word probabilities $\{\lambda_m\}_{m=1}^{M}$ and the part probabilities $\{\pi_i\}_{i=1}^{I}$, respectively. However, since each of these quantities has a conjugate prior, we can marginalize over them and remove them from the computation entirely. Hence, the likelihood $Pr(\mathbf{f}|\mathbf{p})$ can be written as

$$Pr(\mathbf{f}|\mathbf{p}) = \int \prod_{i=1}^{I} \prod_{j=1}^{J_i} Pr(f_{ij}|p_{ij}, \lambda_{1...M})Pr(\lambda_{1...M}) \, d\lambda_{1...M} \tag{20.10}$$

$$= \left(\frac{\Gamma[K\beta]}{\Gamma[\beta]^K}\right)^M \prod_{m=1}^{M} \frac{\prod_{k=1}^{K} \Gamma\left[\sum_{i,j} \delta[f_{ij} - k]\delta[p_{ij} - m] + \beta\right]}{\Gamma\left[\sum_{i,j,k} \delta[f_{ij} - k]\delta[p_{ij} - m] + K\beta\right]},$$

and the prior can be written as

$$Pr(\mathbf{p}) = \prod_{i=1}^{I} \int \prod_{j=1}^{J_i} Pr(p_{ij}|\boldsymbol{\pi}_i) Pr(\boldsymbol{\pi}_i) \, d\boldsymbol{\pi}_i \qquad (20.11)$$

$$= \left(\frac{\Gamma[M\alpha]}{\Gamma[\alpha]^M} \right)^I \prod_{i=1}^{I} \frac{\prod_{m=1}^{M} \Gamma\left[\sum_j \delta[p_{ij} - m] + \alpha\right]}{\Gamma\left[\sum_{j,m} \delta[p_{ij} - m] + M\alpha\right]},$$

where we exploited conjugate relations to help solve the integral (see Problem 3.10).

Unfortunately, we cannot compute the denominator of Equation 20.9 as this involves summing over every possible assignment of the word labels $\mathbf{f}$. Consequently, we can only compute the posterior probability for part labels $\mathbf{p}$ up to an unknown scaling factor. We encountered a similar situation before in the MRF labeling problem (Chapter 12). In that case there was a polynomial time algorithm to find the MAP estimate, but here that is not possible; the cost function for this problem cannot be expressed as a sum of unary and pairwise terms.

Drawing samples from posterior distribution

To make progress, we will use a Monte Carlo Markov chain method to generate a set of samples $\{\mathbf{p}^{[1]}\mathbf{p}^{[2]}, \ldots, \mathbf{p}^{[T]}\}$ from the posterior distribution. More specifically, we will use a Gibbs sampling approach (see Section 10.7.2) in which we update each part label p_{ij} in turn. To do this, we compute the posterior probability of the current part label assuming that all of the others are fixed and then draw a sample from this distribution. We repeat this for every part label to generate a new sample of $\mathbf{p}$. This posterior probability of a single part label assuming that the others are fixed has M elements that are computed as

$$Pr(p_{ij} = m | \mathbf{p}_{\backslash ij}, \mathbf{f}) = \frac{Pr(p_{ij} = m, \mathbf{p}_{\backslash ij}, \mathbf{f})}{\sum_{m=1}^{M} Pr(p_{ij} = m, \mathbf{p}_{\backslash ij}, \mathbf{f})}, \qquad (20.12)$$

where the notation $\mathbf{p}_{\backslash ij}$ denotes all of the elements of $\mathbf{p}$ except p_{ij}. To estimate this, we must compute joint probabilities $Pr(\mathbf{f}, \mathbf{p}) = Pr(\mathbf{f}|\mathbf{p}) Pr(\mathbf{p})$ using Equations 20.10 and 20.11. In practice, the resulting expression simplifies considerably to

$$Pr(p_{ij} = m | \mathbf{p}_{\backslash ij}, \mathbf{f}) \propto \left(\frac{\sum_{a,b \backslash i,j} \delta[f_{ab} - f_{ij}] \delta[p_{ab} - m] + \beta}{\sum_k \sum_{a,b \backslash i,j} \delta[f_{ab} - k] \delta[p_{ab} - m] + K\beta} \right) \qquad (20.13)$$

$$\times \left(\frac{\sum_{b \backslash j} \delta[p_{ib} - m] + \alpha}{\sum_m \sum_{b \backslash j} \delta[p_{ib} - m] + M\alpha} \right),$$

where the notation $\sum_{a,b \backslash i,j}$ means sum over all values of $\{a,b\}$ except i,j. Although it looks rather complex, this expression has a simple interpretation. The first term is the probability of observing the word f_{ij} given that part $p_{ij} = m$. The second term is the proportion of the time that part m is present in the current document.

To sample from the posterior distribution, we initialize the part labels $\{p_{ij}\}_{i=1,j=1}^{I,J_i}$ and alternately update each part label in turn. After a reasonable burn in period (several thousand iterations over all of the variables), the resulting samples can be assumed to be drawn from the posterior. We then take a subset of samples from this chain, where each is separated by a reasonable distance to ensure that their correlation is low.

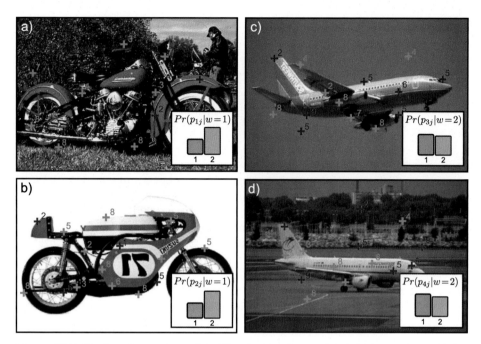

Figure 20.7 Single author–topic model. The single author–topic model is a variant of latent Dirichlet allocation that includes a variable $w_i \in \{1 \ldots N\}$ that represents which of N possible objects is in the image. It is assumed that the part probabilities $\{\pi_n\}_{n=1}^N$ are contingent on the particular choice of object. a) Image 1 contains a motorbike and this induces the part probabilities shown in the bottom right hand corner. The parts are drawn from this probability distribution (color of crosses) and the words (numbers) are drawn based on the parts chosen. b) A second image of a motorbike induces the same part probabilities. c–d) These two images contain a different object and hence have different part probabilities (bottom right).

Using samples to estimate parameters

Finally, we estimate the unknown parameters using the expressions

$$\hat{\pi}_{im} = \frac{\sum_{t,j} \delta[p_{ij}^{[t]} - m] + \alpha}{\sum_{t,j,m} \delta[p_{ij}^{[t]} - m] + M\alpha}$$

$$\hat{\lambda}_{mk} = \frac{\sum_{t,i,j} \delta[p_{ij}^{[t]} - m]\delta[f_{ij} - k] + \beta}{\sum_{t,i,j,k} \delta[p_{ij}^{[t]} - m]\delta[f_{ij} - k] + K\beta}, \tag{20.14}$$

which are very similar to the original expressions (Equation 20.8) for estimating the parameters given known part labels.

20.3.2 Unsupervised object discovery

The preceding model can been used to help analyze the structure of a set of images. Consider fitting this model to an unlabeled data set containing several images each of a number of different object categories. After fitting, each of the I images is modeled as a mixture of parts, and we have an estimate of the mixture weights λ_i for each. We now

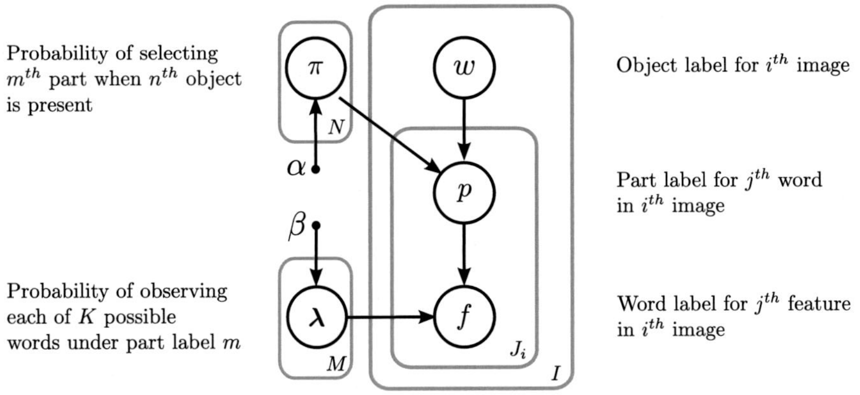

Figure 20.8 Graphical model for the single author–topic model. The likelihood of the jth word in the ith image f_{ij} being categorized as one word or another depends on which of M parts it belongs to, and this is determined by the associated part label p_{ij}. The tendency of the part label to take different values is different for each object $w_i \in \{1 \ldots N\}$ is determined by the parameters π_n, where it is assumed there is a single object in each image.

cluster the images according to the dominant part in this mixtures. For small data sets, it has been shown that this method can separate out different object classes with a high degree of accuracy; this model allows the discovery of object classes in unlabeled data sets.

20.4   Single author–topic model

Latent Dirichlet allocation is simply a density model for images containing sets of discrete words. We will now describe an extension to this model that assumes there is a single object in each image, and the identity of this object is characterized by a label $w_i \in \{1 \ldots N\}$. In the *single author–topic model* (Figure 20.7), we make the assumption that each image of the same object contains the same part probabilities:

$$Pr(p_{ij}|w_i = n) = \text{Cat}_{p_{ij}}[\boldsymbol{\pi}_n]$$
$$Pr(f_{ij}|p_{ij}) = \text{Cat}_{f_{ij}}[\boldsymbol{\lambda}_{p_{ij}}]. \tag{20.15}$$

To complete the model, we add Dirichlet priors to the unknown parameters $\{\boldsymbol{\pi}_n\}_{n=1}^N$ and $\{\boldsymbol{\lambda}_m\}_{m=1}^M$:

$$Pr(\boldsymbol{\pi}_n) = \text{Dir}_{\boldsymbol{\pi}_n}[\boldsymbol{\alpha}]$$
$$Pr(\boldsymbol{\lambda}_m) = \text{Dir}_{\boldsymbol{\lambda}_m}[\boldsymbol{\beta}], \tag{20.16}$$

where $\boldsymbol{\alpha} = [\alpha, \alpha, \ldots, \alpha]$ and $\boldsymbol{\beta} = [\beta, \beta, \ldots, \beta]$. For simplicity we will assume that the prior over the object label w is uniform and not discuss this further. The associated graphical model is illustrated in Figure 20.8.

Like the bag of words and latent Dirichlet allocation models, this model was originally used for describing text documents; it assumes that each document was written by one author (each image contains one object), and this determines the relative frequency of topics (of parts). It is a special case of the more general *author–topic* model, which allows multiple authors for each document.

20.4.1 Learning

Learning proceeds in much the same way as in latent Dirichlet allocation. We are given a set of I images, each of which has a known object label $w_i \in \{1 \ldots N\}$ and a set of visual words $\{f_{ij}\}_{j=1}^{J_i}$, where $f_{ij} \in \{1 \ldots M\}$. It would be easy to estimate the part probabilities for each object $\{\boldsymbol{\pi}_n\}_{n=1}^{N}$ and the word probabilities for each part $\{\boldsymbol{\lambda}_m\}_{m=1}^{M}$ if we knew the hidden part labels p_{ij} associated with each word. As before we take the approach of drawing samples from the posterior distribution over the part labels and using these to estimate the unknown parameters. This posterior is computed via Bayes' rule:

$$Pr(\mathbf{p}|\mathbf{f}, \mathbf{w}) = \frac{Pr(\mathbf{f}|\mathbf{p})Pr(\mathbf{p}|\mathbf{w})}{\sum_{\mathbf{f}} Pr(\mathbf{f}|\mathbf{p})Pr(\mathbf{p}|\mathbf{w})}, \tag{20.17}$$

where $\mathbf{w} = \{w_i\}_{i=1}^{I}$ contains all of the object labels.

The likelihood term $Pr(\mathbf{f}|\mathbf{p})$ is the same as for latent Dirichlet allocation and is given by Equation 20.10. The prior term becomes

$$Pr(\mathbf{p}|\mathbf{w}) = \int \prod_{i=1}^{I} \prod_{j=1}^{J_i} Pr(p_{ij}|w_i, \boldsymbol{\pi}_{1\ldots N}) Pr(\boldsymbol{\pi}_{1\ldots N}) \, d\boldsymbol{\pi}_{1\ldots N} \tag{20.18}$$

$$= \left(\frac{\Gamma[M\alpha]}{\Gamma[\alpha]^M} \right)^N \prod_{n=1}^{N} \frac{\prod_{m=1}^{M} \Gamma\left[\sum_{i,j} \delta[p_{ij} - m]\delta[w_i - n] + \alpha \right]}{\Gamma\left[\sum_{i,j,m} \delta[p_{ij} - m]\delta[w_i - n] + M\alpha \right]}.$$

As before, we cannot compute the denominator of Bayes' rule as it involves an intractable summation over all possible words. Hence, we use a Gibbs sampling method in which we repeatedly draw samples $\mathbf{p}^{[1]} \ldots \mathbf{p}^{[T]}$ from each marginal posterior in turn using the relation:

$$Pr(p_{ij} = m|\mathbf{p}_{\backslash ij}, \mathbf{f}, w_i = n) \propto \left(\frac{\sum_{a,b\backslash i,j} \delta[f_{ab} - f_{ij}]\delta[p_{ab} - m] + \beta}{\sum_k \sum_{a,b\backslash i,j} \delta[f_{ab} - k]\delta[p_{ab} - m] + K\beta} \right) \tag{20.19}$$

$$\times \left(\frac{\sum_{a,b\backslash i,j} \delta[p_{ab} - m]\delta[w_i - n] + \alpha}{\sum_m \sum_{a,b\backslash i,j} \delta[p_{ab} - m]\delta[w_i - n] + M\alpha} \right),$$

where the notation $\sum_{a,b\backslash i,j}$ denotes a sum over all valid values of a, b except for the combination i, j. This expression has a simple interpretation. The first term is the probability of observing the word f_{ij} given that part $p_{ij} = m$. The second term is the proportion of the time that part m is present for the nth object.

Finally, we estimate the unknown parameters using the relations:

$$\hat{\pi}_{nm} = \frac{\sum_{t,i,j} \delta[p_{ij}^{[t]} - m]\delta[w_i - n] + \alpha}{\sum_{t,i,j,m} \delta[p_{ij}^{[t]} - m]\delta[w_i - n] + M\alpha}$$

$$\hat{\lambda}_{mk} = \frac{\sum_{t,i,j} \delta[p_{ij}^{[t]} - m]\delta[f_{ij} - k] + \beta}{\sum_{t,i,j,k} \delta[p_{ij}^{[t]} - m]\delta[f_{ij} - k] + K\beta}. \tag{20.20}$$

20.4.2   Inference

In inference, we compute the likelihood of new image data $\mathbf{f} = \{f_j\}_{j=1}^J$ under each possible object $w \in \{1 \dots N\}$ using

$$Pr(\mathbf{f}|w = n) = \prod_{j=1}^J \sum_{p_j=1}^M Pr(p_j|w = n)Pr(f_j|p_j)$$

$$= \prod_{j=1}^J \sum_{p_j=1}^M \text{Cat}_{p_j}[\boldsymbol{\pi}_n]\text{Cat}_{f_j}[\boldsymbol{\lambda}_{p_j}]. \tag{20.21}$$

We now define suitable priors $Pr(w)$ over the possible objects and use Bayes' rule to compute the posterior distribution,

$$Pr(w = n|\mathbf{f}) = \frac{Pr(\mathbf{f}|w = n)Pr(w = n)}{\sum_{n=1}^N Pr(\mathbf{f}|w = n)Pr(w = n)}. \tag{20.22}$$

20.5   Constellation models

The single author–topic model described in Section 20.4 is still a very weak description of an object as it contains no spatial information. Constellation models are a general class of model that describe objects in terms of a set of parts and their spatial relations. For example, the pictorial structures model described in Section 11.8.3 can be considered a constellation model. Here, we will develop a different type of constellation model that extends the latent Dirichlet allocation model (Figure 20.9).

We assume that a part retains the same meaning as before; it is a cluster of co-occurring words. However, each part now induces a spatial distribution over its associated words, which we will model with a 2D normal distribution so that

$$Pr(p_{ij}|w_i = n) = \text{Cat}_{p_{ij}}[\boldsymbol{\pi}_n]$$
$$Pr(f_{ij}|p_{ij} = m) = \text{Cat}_{f_{ij}}[\boldsymbol{\lambda}_m]$$
$$Pr(\mathbf{x}_{ij}|p_{ij} = m) = \text{Norm}_{\mathbf{x}_{ij}}[\boldsymbol{\mu}_m, \boldsymbol{\Sigma}_m], \tag{20.23}$$

where $\mathbf{x}_{ij} = [x_{ij}, y_{ij}]^T$ is the two-dimensional position of the jth word in the ith image. As before, we also define Dirichlet priors over the unknown categorical parameters so that

$$Pr(\boldsymbol{\pi}_n) = \text{Dir}_{\boldsymbol{\pi}_n}[\boldsymbol{\alpha}]$$
$$Pr(\boldsymbol{\lambda}_m) = \text{Dir}_{\boldsymbol{\lambda}_m}[\boldsymbol{\beta}], \tag{20.24}$$

Figure 20.9 Constellation model. In the constellation model the object or scene is again described as consisting of set of different parts (colors). A number of words are associated with each part, and the word probabilities depend on the part label. However, unlike in the previous models, each part now has a particular range of locations associated with it, which are described as a normal distribution. In this sense it conforms more closely to the normal use of the English word "part."

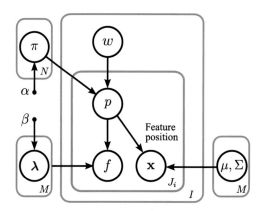

Figure 20.10 Constellation model. In addition to all of the other variables in the single author–topic model (compare to Figure 20.8), the position $\mathbf{x}_{ij}$ of the jth word in the ith image is also modeled. This position is contingent on which of the M parts that the current word is assigned to (determined by the variable p_{ij}). When the word is assigned to the mth part, the position $\mathbf{x}_{ij}$ is modeled as being drawn from a normal distribution with mean and variance $\boldsymbol{\mu}_m, \boldsymbol{\Sigma}_m$.

where $\boldsymbol{\alpha} = [\alpha, \alpha, \ldots, \alpha]$ and $\boldsymbol{\beta} = [\beta, \beta, \ldots, \beta]$. The associated graphical model is shown in Figure 20.10.

This model extends latent Dirichlet allocation to allow it to represent the relative positions of parts of an object or scene. For example, it might learn that words associated with trees usually occur in the center of the image and that those associated with the sky usually occur near the top of the image.

20.5.1 Learning

As for latent Dirichlet allocation, the model would be easy to learn if we knew the part assignments $\mathbf{p} = \{p_{ij}\}_{i=1,j=1}^{I,J_i}$. By the same logic as before, we hence draw samples from posterior distribution $Pr(\mathbf{p}|\mathbf{f}, \mathbf{X}, \mathbf{w})$ over the part assignments given the observed word labels $\mathbf{f} = \{f_{ij}\}_{j=1}^{I,J_i}$, their associated positions $\mathbf{X} = \{\mathbf{x}_{ij}\}_{i=1,j=1}^{I,J_i}$, and the known object labels $\mathbf{w} = \{w_i\}_{i=1}^{I}$. The expression for the posterior is computed via Bayes' rule

$$Pr(\mathbf{p}|\mathbf{f}, \mathbf{X}, \mathbf{w}) = \frac{Pr(\mathbf{f}, \mathbf{X}|\mathbf{p})Pr(\mathbf{p}|\mathbf{w})}{\sum_p Pr(\mathbf{f}, \mathbf{X}|\mathbf{p})Pr(\mathbf{p}|\mathbf{w})}, \qquad (20.25)$$

and once again, the terms in the numerator can be computed, but the denominator contains an intractable sum of exponentially many terms. This means that the posterior cannot be computed in closed form, but we can still evaluate the posterior probability for any particular assignment $\mathbf{p}$ up to an unknown scale factor. This is sufficient to draw samples from the distribution using Gibbs sampling.

The prior probability $Pr(\mathbf{p}|\mathbf{w})$ of the part assignments is the same as before and is given in Equation 20.18. However, the likelihood term $Pr(\mathbf{f}, \mathbf{X}|\mathbf{p})$ now has an additional component due to the requirement for the word position $\mathbf{x}_{ij}$ to agree with the normal distribution induced by the part:

$$Pr(\mathbf{f}, \mathbf{X}|\mathbf{p}) \tag{20.26}$$

$$= \int \prod_{i=1}^{I} \prod_{j=1}^{J_i} Pr(f_{ij}|p_{ij}, \boldsymbol{\lambda}_{1\ldots M}) Pr(\boldsymbol{\lambda}_{1\ldots M}) Pr(\mathbf{x}_{ij}|p_{ij}, \boldsymbol{\mu}_{1\ldots M}, \boldsymbol{\Sigma}_{1\ldots M}) \, d\boldsymbol{\lambda}_{1\ldots M}$$

$$= \left(\frac{\Gamma[K\beta]}{\Gamma[\beta]^K}\right)^M \prod_{m=1}^{M} \frac{\prod_{k=1}^{K} \Gamma\left[\sum_{i,j} \delta[p_{ij} - m]\delta[f_{ij} - k] + \beta\right]}{\Gamma\left[\sum_{i,j,k} \delta[p_{ij} - m]\delta[f_{ij} - k] + K\beta\right]} \mathrm{Norm}_{\mathbf{x}_{ij}}[\boldsymbol{\mu}_{p_{ij}}, \boldsymbol{\Sigma}_{p_{ij}}].$$

In Gibbs sampling, we choose one data example $\{f_{ij}, \mathbf{x}_{ij}\}$ and draw from the posterior distribution assuming that all of the other parts are fixed. An approximate[1] expression to compute this posterior is given by

$$Pr(p_{ij} = m|\mathbf{p}_{\backslash ij}, \mathbf{f}, \mathbf{x}_{ij}, w_i = n) \propto \tag{20.27}$$

$$\left(\frac{\sum_{a,b\backslash i,j} \delta[f_{ab} - f_{ij}]\delta[p_{ab} - m] + \beta}{\sum_k \sum_{a,b\backslash i,j} \delta[f_{ab} - k]\delta[p_{ab} - m] + K\beta}\right) \mathrm{Norm}_{\mathbf{x}_{ij}}[\tilde{\boldsymbol{\mu}}_m, \tilde{\boldsymbol{\Sigma}}_m]$$

$$\times \left(\frac{\sum_{a,b\backslash i,j} \delta[p_{ab} - m]\delta[w_i - n] + \alpha}{\sum_m \sum_{a,b\backslash i,j} \delta[p_{ab} - m]\delta[w_i - n] + M\alpha}\right),$$

where the notation $\sum_{a,b\backslash i,j}$ denotes summation over all values of $\{a, b\}$ except i, j. The terms $\tilde{\boldsymbol{\mu}}_m$ and $\tilde{\boldsymbol{\Sigma}}_m$ are the mean and covariance of all of the word positions associated with the mth part *ignoring* the contribution of the current position $\mathbf{x}_{ij}$.

At the end of the procedure, the probabilities are computed using the relations in Equation 20.20 and the part locations as

$$\hat{\boldsymbol{\mu}}_m = \frac{\sum_{i,j,t} \mathbf{x}_{ij} \delta[p_{ij}^{[t]} - m]}{\sum_{i,j,t} \delta[p_{ij}^{[t]} - m]}$$

$$\hat{\boldsymbol{\Sigma}}_m = \frac{\sum_{i,j,t} (\mathbf{x}_{ij} - \boldsymbol{\mu}_m)^T (\mathbf{x}_{ij} - \boldsymbol{\mu}_m) \delta[p_{ij}^{[t]} - m]}{\sum_{i,j,t} \delta[p_{ij}^{[t]} - m]}. \tag{20.28}$$

Example learning results can be seen in Figure 20.11. Each part is a spatially localized cluster of words, and these often correspond to real-world objects such as "legs" or "wheels." The parts are shared between the objects and so there is no need for a different set of parameters to learn the appearance of wheels for bicycles and wheels for motorbikes.

---

[1] More properly, we should define a prior over the mean and variance of the parts and marginalize over these parameters as well. This also avoids problems when no features are assigned to a certain part and hence the mean and covariance cannot be computed.

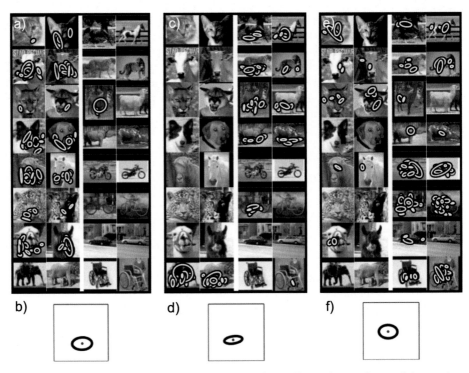

Figure 20.11 Sharing words in the constellation model. a) Sixteen images from training set (two from each class). Yellow ellipses depict words identified in the image associated with one part of the image (i.e., they are equivalent of the crosses in Figure 20.9). It is notable that the words associated with this part mainly belong to the lower part of the faces of the animal images. b) The mean μ and variance Σ of this object part. c,d) A second part seems to correspond to the legs of animals in profile. e,f) A third part contains many words associated with the wheels of objects. Adapted from Sudderth et al. (2008). ©2008 IEEE.

20.5.2 Inference

In inference, we compute the likelihood of new image data $\{f_j, \mathbf{x}_j\}_{j=1}^{J}$ under each possible object $w \in \{1 \ldots N\}$ using

$$Pr(\mathbf{f}, \mathbf{X}|w = n) = \prod_{j=1}^{J} \sum_{m=1}^{M} Pr(p_j = m|w = n) Pr(f_j|p_j = m) Pr(\mathbf{x}_j|p_j = m)$$

$$= \prod_{j=1}^{J} \sum_{p_j=1}^{M} \mathrm{Cat}_{p_j}[\boldsymbol{\pi}_n] \mathrm{Cat}_{f_j}[\boldsymbol{\lambda}_{p_j}] \mathrm{Norm}_{\mathbf{x}_{ij}}[\boldsymbol{\mu}_{p_j}, \boldsymbol{\Sigma}_{p_j}]. \tag{20.29}$$

We now define suitable priors $Pr(w)$ over the possible objects and use Bayes' rule to compute the posterior distribution

$$Pr(w = n|\mathbf{f}, \mathbf{X}) = \frac{Pr(\mathbf{f}, \mathbf{X}|w = n) Pr(w = n)}{\sum_{n=1}^{N} Pr(\mathbf{f}, \mathbf{X}|w = n) Pr(w = n)}. \tag{20.30}$$

20.6 Scene models

One limitation of the constellation model is that it assumes that the image contains a single object. However, real images generally contain a number of spatially offset objects. Just as the object determined the probability of the different parts, so the scene determines the relative likelihood of observing different objects (Figure 20.12). For example, an office scene might include desks, computers, and chairs, but it is very unlikely to include tigers or icebergs.

To this end we introduce a new set of variables that represent the choice of scene $\{s_i\}_{i=1}^{I} \in \{1 \ldots C\}$

$$Pr(w_{ij}|s_i = c) = \text{Cat}_{w_{ij}}[\boldsymbol{\phi}_c]$$
$$Pr(p_{ij}|w_{ij} = n) = \text{Cat}_{p_{ij}}[\boldsymbol{\pi}_{w_n}]$$
$$Pr(f_{ij}|p_{ij} = m) = \text{Cat}_{f_{ij}}[\boldsymbol{\lambda}_m]$$
$$Pr(\mathbf{x}_{ij}|p_{ij} = m, w_{ij} = n) = \text{Norm}_{\mathbf{x}_{ij}}[\boldsymbol{\mu}_n^{(w)} + \boldsymbol{\mu}_m^{(p)}, \boldsymbol{\Sigma}_n^{(w)} + \boldsymbol{\Sigma}_m^{(p)}]. \quad (20.31)$$

Each word has an object label $\{w_{ij}\}_{i=1,j=1}^{I,J_I}$, which denotes which of the L objects it corresponds to. The scene label $\{s_i\}$ determines the relative propensity for each object to be present, and these probabilities are held in the categorical parameters $\{\boldsymbol{\phi}_c\}_{c=1}^{C}$. Each object type also has a position that is normally distributed with mean and covariance $\boldsymbol{\mu}_m^{(w)}$ and $\boldsymbol{\Sigma}_m^{(w)}$. As before, each object defines a probability distribution over the M shared parts where the part assignment is held in the label p_{ij}. Each part has a position that is measured relative to the object position and has mean and covariance $\boldsymbol{\mu}_m^{(p)}$, and $\boldsymbol{\Sigma}_m^{(p)}$, respectively.

We leave the details of the learning and inference algorithms as an exercise for the reader; the principles are the same as for the constellation model; we generate a series of samples from the posterior over the hidden variables w_{ij} and p_{ij} using Gibbs sampling and update the mean and covariances based on the samples.

Figure 20.13 shows several examples of scenes that have been interpreted using a scene model very similar to that described. In each case, the scene is parsed into a number of objects that are likely to co-occur and are in a sensible relative spatial configuration.

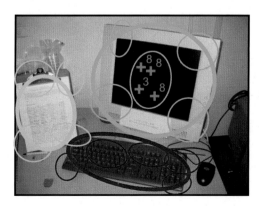

Figure 20.12 Scene model. Each image consists of a single scene. A scene induces a probability distribution over the presence of different objects (different colors) such as the monitor, piece of paper, and keyboard in this scene and their relative positions (thick ellipses). Each object is itself composed of spatially separate parts (thin ellipses). Each part has a number of words associated with it (crosses, shown only for one part for clarity).

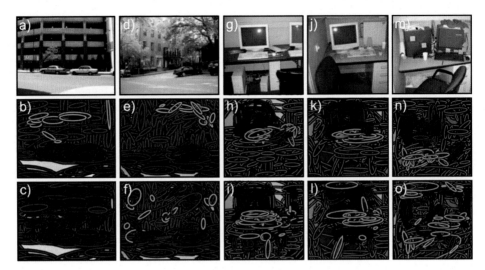

Figure 20.13 Scene recognition. a) Example street image. b) Results of scene parsing model. Each ellipse represents one word (i.e., the equivalent of the crosses in Figure 20.12). The ellipse color denotes the object label to which that word is assigned (part labels not shown). c) Results of the bag of words model, which makes elementary mistakes such as putting car labels at the top of the image as it has no spatial information. d) Another street scene. e) Interpretation with scene model and f) bag of words model. g–o) Three more office scenes parsed by the scene model and bag of words models. Adapted from Sudderth et al. (2008). ©2008 Springer.

20.7 Applications

In this chapter we have described a series of generative models for visual words of increasing complexity. Although these models are interesting, it should be emphasized that many applications use only the basic bag of words approach combined with a discriminative classifier. We now describe two representative examples of such systems.

20.7.1 Video Google

Sivic and Zisserman (2003) presented a system based on the bag of words, which can retrieve frames from a movie very efficiently based on a visual query; the user draws a bounding box around the object of interest and the system returns other images that contain the same object (Figure 20.14).

The system starts by identifying feature positions in each frame of the video. Unlike conventional bag of words models, these feature positions are tracked through several frames of video and rejected if this cannot be done. The averaged SIFT descriptor over each track is used to represent the image contents in the neighborhood of the feature. These descriptors are then clustered using K-means to create of the order of 6,000–10,000 possible visual words. Each feature is then assigned to one of these words based on the distance to the nearest cluster. Finally, each image or region is characterized by a vector containing the frequencies with which each visual word is found.

When the system receives a query, it compares the vector for the identified region to those for each potential region in the remaining video stream and retrieves those that are closest.

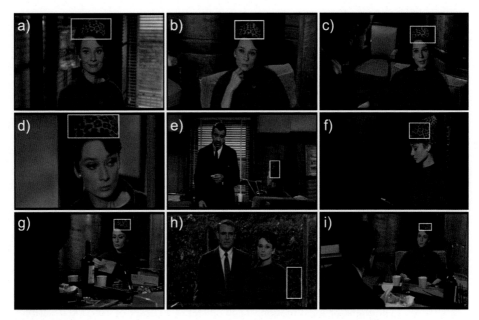

Figure 20.14 Video Google. a) The user identifies part of one frame of a video by drawing a bounding box around part of the scene. b–i) The system returns a ranked list of frames that contain the same object and identifies where it is in the image (white bounding boxes). The system correctly identifies the leopard-skin patterned hat in a variety of contexts despite changes in scale and position. In (h) it mistakes the texture of the vegetation in the background for an instance of the hat.

The implementation includes several features that make this process more reliable. First, it discards the top 5 percent and bottom 10 percent of words according to their frequency. This eliminates very common words that do not distinguish between frames and words that are very rare and are hence inefficient to search on. Second, it weights the distance measure using the *term-frequency inverse document frequency* scheme: the weight increases if the word is relatively rare in the database (the word is discriminative) and if it is used relatively frequently in this region (it is particularly representative of the region). Finally, the matches are considered more reliable if the spatial arrangement of visual words is similar. The final retrieved results are re-ranked based on their spatial consistency with the query.

The final system reliably returns plausible regions for a feature length movie in less than 0.1 seconds using an inverted file structure to facilitate efficient retrieval.

20.7.2 Action recognition

Laptev et al. (2008) applied a bag of words approach to action recognition in video sequences. They used a space-time extension of the Harris corner detector to find interest points in the video frames and extracted descriptors at multiple scales around each point. They eliminated detections at boundaries between shots.

To characterize the local motion and appearance, they computed histogram-based descriptors of the space time volumes surrounding these feature points. These were either based on the histogram of oriented gradients (HOG) descriptor (Section 13.3.3) or based

Figure 20.15 Example images from the KTH database (Schüldt et al. 2004). Images in (a–f) each show three examples of the six categories of walking, jogging, running, boxing, waving, and clapping, respectively. Using the bag of words approach of Laptev et al. (2008), these actions can be classified with over 90 percent accuracy.

on histograms of local motion. They clustered a subset of 100,000 descriptors from the training data using the K-means algorithm to create 4000 clusters and each feature in the test and training data was represented by the index of the nearest cluster center.

They binned these quantized feature indices over a number of different space-time windows. The final decision about the action was based on a *one-against-all* binary classifier in which each action was separately considered and rated as being present or absent. The kernelized binary classifier combined information from the two different feature types and the different space time windows.

Laptev et al. (2008) first considered discriminating between six actions from the KTH database (Schüldt et al. 2004). This is a relatively simple dataset in which the camera is static and the action occurs against a relatively empty background (Figure 20.15). They discriminated between these classes with an average of 91.8 percent accuracy, with the major confusion being between jogging and running.

They also considered a more complex database containing eight different actions from movie sequences (Figure 20.16). It was notable that the performance here relied more on the HOG descriptors than the motion information, suggesting that the local context was providing considerable information (e.g., the action "get out of car" is more likely when a car is present). For this database, the performance was much worse, but it was significantly better than chance; action recognition "in the wild" is an open problem in computer vision research.

Discussion

The models in this chapter treat each image as a set of discrete features. The bag of features model, latent Dirichlet allocation, and single author–topic models do not explicitly describe the position of objects in the scene. Although they are effective for recognizing objects, they cannot locate them in the image. The constellation model improves this by allowing the parts of object to have spatial relations, and the scene model describes a scene as a collection of displaced parts.

Answer phone Get out car Shake hands Hug Kiss Sit down Sit up Stand up

Figure 20.16 Action recognition in movie database of Laptev et al. (2008). a) Example true positives (correct detections), b) true negatives (action correctly identified as being absent), c) false positives (action classified as occurring but didn't) d) false negatives (action classified as not occurring but did). This type of real-world action classification task is still considered very challenging.

Notes

Bag of words models: Sivic and Zisserman (2003) introduced the term "visual words" and first made the connection with text retrieval. Csurka et al. (2004) applied the bag of words methodology to object recognition. A number of other studies then exploited developments in the document search community. For example, Sivic et al. (2005) exploited probabilistic latent semantic analysis (Hofmann 1999) and latent Dirichlet allocation (Blei et al. 2003) for unsupervised learning of object classes. Sivic et al. (2008) extended this work to learn hierarchies of object classes. Li and Perona (2005) constructed a model very similar to the original author–topic model (Rosen-Zvi et al. 2004) for learning scene categories. Sudderth et al. (2005) and Sudderth et al. (2008) extended the author–topic model to contain information about the spatial layout of objects. The constellation and scene models presented in this chapter are somewhat simplified versions of this work. They also extended these models to cope with varying numbers of objects and or parts.

Applications of bag of words: Applications of the bag of words model include object recognition (Csurka et al. 2004), searching through video (Sivic and Zisserman 2003), scene recognition (Li and Perona 2005), and action recognition (Schüldt et al. 2004), and similar approaches have been applied to texture classfiication (Varma and Zisserman 2004) and labeling facial attributes (Aghajanian et al. 2009). Recent progress in object recognition can be reviewed by examining a recent summary of the PASCAL visual object classes challenge (Everingham et al. 2010). In the 2007 competition, bag of words approaches with no spatial information at all were still common. Several authors (Nistér and Stewénius 2006; Philbin et al. 2007; Jegou et al. 2008) have now presented large-scale demonstrations of object instance recognition based on bag of words, and this idea has been used in commercial applications such as "Google Goggles."

Bag of words variants: Although we have discussed mainly generative models for visual words in this chapter, discriminative approaches generally yield somewhat better performance. Grauman and Darrell (2005) introduced the pyramid match kernel, which maps unordered data in a high-dimensional feature space into multiresolution histograms and computes a weighted histogram intersection in this space. This effectively performs the clustering and feature comparison steps simultaneously. This idea was extended to the spatial domain of the image itself by Lazebnik et al. (2006).

Improving the pipeline: Yang et al. (2007) and Zhang et al. (2007) provide quantitative comparisons showing how the various parts of the pipeline (e.g., the matching kernel, interest point detector, clustering method) affect object recognition results.

The focus of recent research has moved on to addressing various weaknesses of the pipeline such as the arbitrariness of the initial vector quantization step and the problem of regular patterns (Chum et al. 2007; Philbin et al. 2007, 2010; Jégou et al. 2009; Mikulik et al. 2010; Makadia 2010). The current trend is to increase the problem to realistic sizes and to this end new databases for object recognition (Deng et al. 2010) and scene recognition have been released (Xiao et al. 2010).

Action recognition: There has been a progression in recent years from testing action recognition algorithms in specially captured databases where the subject can easily be separated from the background (Schüldt et al. 2004), to movie footage (Laptev et al. 2008), and finally to completely unconstrained footage that may not be professionally shot and may have considerable camera shake. As this progression has taken place, the dominant approach has gradually become to base the system on visual words that capture the context of the scene as well as the action itself (Laptev et al. 2008). A comparison between approaches based on visual words and those that used explicit parts for action recognition in a still frame is presented by Delaitre et al. (2010). Recent work in this area has addressed unsupervised learning of action categories (Niebles et al. 2008).

Problems

20.1 The bag of words method in this chapter uses a generative approach to model the frequencies of the visual words. Develop a discriminative approach that models the probability of the object class as a function of the word frequencies.

20.2 Prove the relations in Equation 20.8, which show how to learn the latent Dirichlet allocation model in the case where we do know the part labels $\{p_{ij}\}_{i=1,j=1}^{I,J_i}$.

20.3 Show that the likelihood and prior terms are given by Equations 20.10 and 20.11, respectively.

20.4 Li and Perona (2005) developed an alternative model to the single author–topic model in which the hyperparameter α was different for each value of the object label $\mathbf{w}$. Modify the graphical model for latent Dirichlet allocation to include this change.

20.5 Write out generative equations for the author–topic model in which multiple authors are allowed for each document. Draw the associated graphical model.

20.6 In real objects, we might expect visual words f that are adjacent to one another to take the same part label. How would you modify the author–topic model to encourage nearby part labels to be the same. How would the Gibbs sampling procedure for drawing samples from the posterior probability over parts be affected?

20.7 Draw a graphical model for the scene model described in Section 20.6.

20.8 All of the models in this chapter have dealt with classification; we wish to infer a discrete variable representing the state of the world based on discrete observed features $\{f_j\}$. Develop a generative model that can be used to infer a continuous variable based on discrete observed features (i.e., a regression model that uses visual words).

Part VII

Appendices

Appendix A

Notation

This is a brief guide to the notational conventions used in this text.

Scalars, vectors, and matrices

We denote scalars by either small or capital letters a, A, α. We denote column vectors by bold small letters $\mathbf{a}, \phi$. When we need a row vector we usually present this as the transpose of a column vector $\mathbf{a}^T, \phi^T$.

We represent matrices by bold capital letters $\mathbf{B}, \mathbf{\Phi}$. The ith row and j^{th} column of matrix $\mathbf{A}$ is written as a_{ij}. The jth column of matrix $\mathbf{A}$ is written as $\mathbf{a}_j$. When we need to refer to the ith row of a matrix, we write this as $\mathbf{a}_{i\bullet}$ where the bullet $\bullet$ indicates that we are considering all possible values of the column index.

We concatenate two $D \times 1$ column vectors horizontally as $\mathbf{a} = [\mathbf{b}, \mathbf{c}]$ to form the $D \times 2$ matrix $\mathbf{A}$. We concatenate two $D \times 1$ column vectors vertically as $\mathbf{a} = [\mathbf{b}^T, \mathbf{c}^T]^T$ to form the $2D \times 1$ vector $\mathbf{a}$. Although this notation is cumbersome, it allows us to represent vertical concatenations within a single line of text.

Variables and parameters

We denote variables with Roman letters $\mathbf{a}, \mathbf{b}$. The most common examples are the observed data which is always denoted by $\mathbf{x}$ and the state of the world which is always denoted by $\mathbf{w}$. However, other hidden or latent variables are also represented by Roman letters. We denote parameters of the model by Greek letters $\mu, \mathbf{\Phi}, \sigma^2$. These are distinguished from variables in that there is usually a single set of parameters that explains the relation between many sets of variables.

Functions

We write functions as a name, followed by square brackets that contain the arguments of the function. For example, $\log[x]$ returns the logarithm of the scalar variable x. Sometimes we will write a function with bullets $\bullet$ as arguments (e.g., $\text{atan2}[\bullet, \bullet]$) to focus the interest on the function itself rather than the arguments.

When the function returns one or more vector or matrix arguments, it is written in bold. For example, the function $\mathbf{aff}[\mathbf{x}, \mathbf{\Phi}, \boldsymbol{\tau}]$ applies an affine transformation to the 2D point $\mathbf{x}$ with parameters $\mathbf{\Phi}, \boldsymbol{\tau}$ and returns a new 2D vector output. When a function returns multiple outputs, we write this in Matlab notation so $[\mathbf{U}, \mathbf{L}, \mathbf{V}] = \mathbf{svd}[\mathbf{X}]$ returns the three parts $\mathbf{U}, \mathbf{L}, \mathbf{V}$ of the singular value decomposition of $\mathbf{X}$.

Some functions are used repeatedly throughout the text. These include:

- $\min_x f[x]$, which returns the minimum possible value of the function $f[x]$ as we vary x over its entire valid range,
- $\operatorname{argmin}_x f[x]$, which returns the value of the argument x that minimizes $f[x]$,
- $\max_x$ and argmax_x, which fulfill the same roles as $\min_x$ and argmin_x but where we are maximizing the function,
- $\mathbf{diag}[\mathbf{A}]$, which returns a column vector containing the elements on the diagonal of matrix $\mathbf{A}$,
- $\delta[x]$ for continuous x, which is a Dirac delta function and has the key property $\int f[x]\delta[x - x_0]dx = f[x_0]$,
- $\delta[x]$ for discrete x, which returns 1 when the argument x is 0 and returns 0 otherwise, and
- heaviside$[x]$, which represents the Heaviside step function. It returns 0 when the argument $x < 0$ and returns 1 otherwise.

Probability distributions

We write the probability of a random variable x as $Pr(x)$. We write the joint probability of two variables a, b as $Pr(a, b)$ and the conditional probability of a given b as $Pr(a|b)$. Sometimes, we wish to specify the exact value b^* that a is conditioned upon and here we write $Pr(a|b = b^*)$. Occasionally, we denote that variables a and b are independent by writing $a \perp\!\!\!\perp b$. Similarly we indicate that a and b are conditionally independent given c by writing $a \perp\!\!\!\perp b|c$.

Probability distributions are written in the style $Pr(\mathbf{x}|\boldsymbol{\mu}, \boldsymbol{\Sigma}) = \operatorname{Norm}_{\mathbf{x}}[\boldsymbol{\mu}, \boldsymbol{\Sigma}]$. This returns the value of the multivariate normal distribution for data $\mathbf{x}$ when the distribution has mean $\boldsymbol{\mu}$ and covariance $\boldsymbol{\Sigma}$. In this way, we always distinguish the argument of the distribution (here $\mathbf{x}$) from the parameters (here $\boldsymbol{\mu}, \boldsymbol{\Sigma}$).

Sets

We denote sets with calligraphic letters $\mathcal{S}$. The notation $\mathcal{S} \subset \mathcal{T}$ indicates that $\mathcal{S}$ is a subset of $\mathcal{T}$. The notation $x \in \mathcal{S}$ indicates that x is a member of the set $\mathcal{S}$. The notation $\mathcal{A} = \mathcal{B} \cup \mathcal{C}$ indicates that set $\mathcal{A}$ is the union of sets $\mathcal{B}$ and $\mathcal{C}$. The notation $\mathcal{A} = \mathcal{B} \setminus \mathcal{C}$ indicates that set $\mathcal{A}$ consists of all of the elements of $\mathcal{B}$ except those that are in $\mathcal{C}$.

Often we write out a set explicitly in terms of the elements and for this we use curly brackets so that $\mathcal{A} = \{x, y, z\}$ indicates that the set $\mathcal{A}$ contains x, y, and z and nothing else. When a set is empty, we write $\mathcal{A} = \{\}$. We use the notation $\{x_i\}_{i=1}^I$ as shorthand to represent the set $\{x_1, x_2, \ldots, x_I\}$, and we may write the same set in the compact form $x_{1\ldots I}$ if it is part of an equation.

Appendix B

Optimization

Throughout this book, we have used iterative nonlinear optimization methods to find the maximum likelihood or MAP parameter estimates. We now provide more details about these methods. It is impossible to do full justice to this topic in the space available; many entire books have been written about nonlinear optimization. Our goal is merely to provide a brief introduction to the main ideas.

B.1 Problem statement

Continuous nonlinear optimization techniques aim to find the set of parameters $\hat{\theta}$ that minimize a function $f[\bullet]$. In other words, they try to compute

$$\hat{\theta} = \underset{\theta}{\operatorname{argmin}} \left[f[\theta] \right], \tag{B.1}$$

where $f[\bullet]$ is termed a *cost function* or *objective function*.

Although optimization techniques are usually described in terms of minimizing a function, most optimization problems in this book involve *maximizing* an objective function based on log probability. To turn a maximization problem into a minimization, we multiply the objective function by minus one. In other words, instead of maximizing the log probability, we minimize the negative log probability.

B.1.1 Convexity

The optimization techniques that we consider here are iterative: they start with an estimate $\theta^{[0]}$ and improve it by finding successive new estimates $\theta^{[1]}, \theta^{[2]}, \ldots, \theta^{[\infty]}$ each of which is better than the last until no more improvement can be made. The techniques are purely local in the sense that the decision about where to move next is based on only the properties of the function at the current position. Consequently, these techniques cannot guarantee the correct solution: they may find an estimate $\theta^{[\infty]}$ from which no local change improves the cost. However, this does not mean there is not a better solution in some distant part of the function that has not yet been explored (Figure B.1). In optimization parlance, they can only find *local minima*. One way to mitigate this problem is to start the optimization from a number of different places and choose the final solution with the lowest cost.

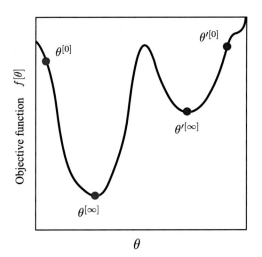

Figure B.1 Local minima. Optimization methods aim to find the minimum of the objective function $f[\theta]$ with respect to parameters θ. Roughly, they work by starting with an initial estimate $\theta^{[0]}$ and moving iteratively downhill until no more progress can be made (final position represented by $\theta^{[\infty]}$). Unfortunately, it is possible to terminate in a local minimum. For example, if we start at $\theta'^{[0]}$ and move downhill, we wind up in position $\theta'^{[\infty]}$.

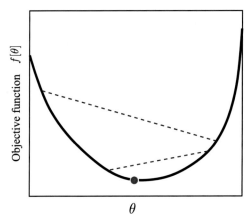

Figure B.2 Convex functions. If the function is convex, then the global minimum can be found. A function is convex if no chord (line between two points on the function) intersects the function. The figure shows two example chords (blue dashed lines). The convexity of a function can be established algebraically by considering the matrix of second derivatives. If this is positive definite for all values of $\boldsymbol{\theta}$, then the function is convex.

In the special case where the function is *convex*, there will only be a single minimum, and we are guaranteed to find it with sufficient iterations (Figure B.2). For a 1D function, it is possible to establish the convexity by looking at the second derivative of the function; if this is positive everywhere (i.e., the slope is continuously increasing), then the function is convex and the global minimum can be found. The equivalent test in higher dimensions is to examine the *Hessian matrix* (the matrix of second derivatives of the cost function with respect to the parameters). If this is positive definite everywhere (see Appendix C.2.6), then the function is convex and the global minimum will be found. Some of the cost functions in this book are convex, but this is unusual; most optimization problems found in vision do not have this convenient property.

B.1.2 Overview of approach

In general the parameters $\boldsymbol{\theta}$ over which we search are multidimensional. For example, when $\boldsymbol{\theta}$ has two dimensions, we can think of the function as a two-dimensional surface (Figure B.3). With this in mind, the principles behind the methods we will discuss are simple. We alternately

- Choose a search direction **s** based on the local properties of the function, and
- Search to find the minimum along the chosen direction. In other words, we seek the distance λ to move such that

$$\hat{\lambda} = \underset{\lambda}{\operatorname{argmin}} \left[f[\boldsymbol{\theta}^{[t]} + \lambda \mathbf{s}] \right], \tag{B.2}$$

and then set $\boldsymbol{\theta}^{[t+1]} = \boldsymbol{\theta}^{[t]} + \hat{\lambda}\mathbf{s}$. This is termed a *line search*.

We now consider each of these stages in turn.

B.2   Choosing a search direction

We will describe two general methods for choosing a search direction (*steepest descent* and *Newton's method*) and one method which is specialized for least squares problems (the *Gauss-Newton method*). Both methods rely on computing derivatives of the function with respect to the parameters at the current position. To this end, we are relying on the function being smooth so that the derivatives are well behaved.

For most models, it is easy to find a closed form expression for the derivatives. If this is not the case, then an alternative is to approximate them using finite differences. For example, the first derivative of $f[\bullet]$ with respect to the jth element of $\boldsymbol{\theta}$ can be approximated by

$$\frac{\partial f}{\partial \theta_j} \approx \frac{f[\boldsymbol{\theta} + a\mathbf{e}_j] - f[\boldsymbol{\theta}]}{a}, \tag{B.3}$$

where a is a small number and $\mathbf{e}_j$ is the unit vector in the jth direction. In principle as a tends to zero, this estimate becomes more accurate. However, in practice the calculation is limited by the floating point precision of the computer, so a must be chosen with care.

B.2.1   Steepest descent

An intuitive way to choose the search direction is to measure the gradient and select the direction which moves us downhill fastest. We could move in this direction until the function no longer decreases, then recompute the steepest direction and move again. In this way, we gradually move toward a local minimum of the function (Figure B.3a). The algorithm terminates when the gradient is zero and the second derivative is positive, indicating that we are at the minimum point, and any further local changes would not result in further improvement. This approach is termed *steepest descent*. More precisely, we choose

$$\boldsymbol{\theta}^{[t+1]} = \boldsymbol{\theta}^{[t]} - \lambda \left. \frac{\partial f}{\partial \boldsymbol{\theta}} \right|_{\boldsymbol{\theta}^{[t]}}, \tag{B.4}$$

where the derivative $\partial f / \partial \boldsymbol{\theta}$ is the *gradient vector* that points uphill and λ is the distance moved downhill in the opposite direction $-\partial f / \partial \boldsymbol{\theta}$. The line search procedure (Section B.3) selects the value of λ.

Steepest descent sounds like a good idea but can be very inefficient in certain situations (Figure B.3b). For example, in a descending valley, it can oscillate ineffectually from one side to the other rather than proceeding straight down the center: the method approaches the bottom of the valley from one side, but overshoots because the valley itself is descending, so the minimum along the search direction is not exactly in

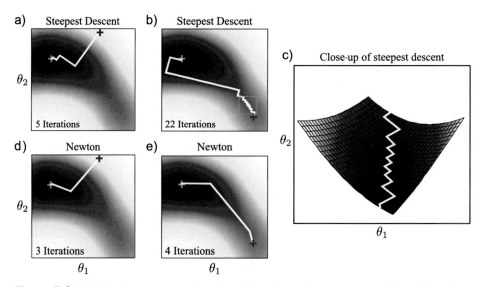

Figure B.3 Optimization on a two-dimensional function (color represents height of function). We wish to find the parameters that minimize the function (green cross). Given an initial starting point θ^0 (blue cross), we choose a direction and then perform a local search to find the optimal point in that direction. a) One way to chose the direction is steepest descent: at each iteration, we head in the direction where the function changes the fastest. b) When we initialize from a different position, the steepest descent method takes many iterations to converge due to oscillatory behavior. c) Close-up of oscillatory region (see main text). d) Setting the direction using Newton's method results in faster convergence. e) Newton's method does not undergo oscillatory behavior when we initialize from the second position.

the valley center (Figure B.3c). When we remeasure the gradient and perform a second line search, we overshoot in the other direction. This is not an unusual situation: it is guaranteed that the gradient at the new point will be perpendicular to the previous one, so the only way to avoid this oscillation is to hit the valley at exactly right angles.

B.2.2   Newton's method

Newton's method is an improved approach that also exploits the second derivatives at the current point: it considers both the gradient of the function and how that gradient is changing.

To motivate the use of second derivatives, consider a one-dimensional function (Figure B.4). If the magnitude of the second derivative is low, then the gradient is changing slowly. Consequently, it will probably take a while before it completely flattens out and becomes a minimum, and so it is safe to move a long distance. Conversely, if the magnitude of the second derivative is high, then things are changing rapidly, and we should move only a small distance.

Now consider the same argument in two dimensions. Imagine we are at a point where the gradient is identical in both dimensions. For steepest descent, we would move equally in both dimensions. However, if the magnitude of the second derivative in the

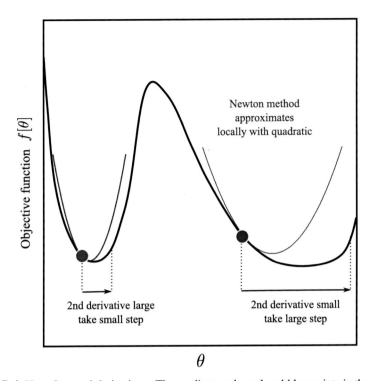

Figure B.4 Use of second derivatives. The gradient at the red and blue points is the same, but the magnitude of the second derivative is larger at the red point than the blue point: the gradient is changing faster at the red point than the blue point. The distance we move should be moderated by the second derivative: if the gradient is changing fast, then the minimum may be nearby and we should move a small distance. If it is changing slowly, then it is safe to move further. Newton's method takes into account the second derivative: it uses a Taylor expansion to create a quadratic approximation to the function and then moves toward the minimum.

first direction is much greater than that in the second, we would nonetheless wish to move further in the second direction.

To see how to exploit the second derivatives algebraically, consider a truncated Taylor expansion around the current estimate $\boldsymbol{\theta}^{[t]}$:

$$f[\boldsymbol{\theta}] \approx f[\boldsymbol{\theta}^{[t]}] + (\boldsymbol{\theta} - \boldsymbol{\theta}^{[t]})^T \left. \frac{\partial f}{\partial \boldsymbol{\theta}} \right|_{\boldsymbol{\theta}^{[t]}} + \frac{1}{2}(\boldsymbol{\theta} - \boldsymbol{\theta}^{[t]})^T \left. \frac{\partial^2 f}{\partial \boldsymbol{\theta}^2} \right|_{\boldsymbol{\theta}^{[t]}} (\boldsymbol{\theta} - \boldsymbol{\theta}^{[t]}), \qquad \text{(B.5)}$$

where $\boldsymbol{\theta}$ is a $D \times 1$ variable, the first derivative vector is of size $D \times 1$, and the Hessian matrix of second derivatives is $D \times D$. To find the local extrema, we now take derivatives with respect to $\boldsymbol{\theta}$ and set the result to zero

$$\frac{\partial f}{\partial \boldsymbol{\theta}} \approx \left. \frac{\partial f}{\partial \boldsymbol{\theta}} \right|_{\boldsymbol{\theta}^{[t]}} + \left. \frac{\partial^2 f}{\partial \boldsymbol{\theta}^2} \right|_{\boldsymbol{\theta}^{[t]}} (\boldsymbol{\theta} - \boldsymbol{\theta}^{[t]}) = 0. \qquad \text{(B.6)}$$

By rearranging this equation, we get an expression for the minimum $\hat{\boldsymbol{\theta}}$,

$$\hat{\boldsymbol{\theta}} = \boldsymbol{\theta}^{[t]} - \left(\frac{\partial^2 f}{\partial \boldsymbol{\theta}^2} \right)^{-1} \frac{\partial f}{\partial \boldsymbol{\theta}}, \qquad \text{(B.7)}$$

where the derivatives are still taken at $\boldsymbol{\theta}^{[t]}$, but we have stopped writing this for clarity. In practice we would implement Newton's method as a series of iterations

$$\boldsymbol{\theta}^{[t+1]} = \boldsymbol{\theta}^{[t]} - \lambda \left(\frac{\partial^2 f}{\partial \boldsymbol{\theta}^2}\right)^{-1} \frac{\partial f}{\partial \boldsymbol{\theta}}, \tag{B.8}$$

where the λ is the step size. This can be set to one, or we can find the optimal value using line search.

One interpretation of Newton's method is that we have locally approximated the function as a quadratic. On each iteration, we move toward its extremum (or move exactly to it if we fix $\lambda = 1$). Note that we are assuming that we are close enough to the correct solution that the nearby extremum *is* a minimum and not a saddle point or maximum. In particular, if the Hessian is not positive definite, then a direction that is not downhill may be chosen. In this sense Newton's method is not as robust as steepest descent.

Subject to this limitation, Newton's method converges in fewer iterations than steepest descent (Figure B.3d–e). However, it requires more computation per iteration as we have to invert the $D \times D$ Hessian matrix at each step. Choosing this method usually implies that we can write the Hessian in closed form; approximating the Hessian from finite derivatives requires many function evaluations and so is potentially very costly.

B.2.3 Gauss-Newton method

Cost functions in computer vision often take the special form of a least squares problem

$$f[\boldsymbol{\theta}] = \sum_{i=1}^{I} (\mathbf{x}_i - \mathbf{g}[\mathbf{w}_i, \boldsymbol{\theta}])^T (\mathbf{x}_i - \mathbf{g}[\mathbf{w}_i, \boldsymbol{\theta}]), \tag{B.9}$$

where $\mathbf{g}[\bullet, \bullet]$ is a function that transfers the variables $\{\mathbf{w}_i\}$ into the space of the variables $\{\mathbf{x}_i\}$, and is parameterized by $\boldsymbol{\theta}$. In other words, we seek the values of $\boldsymbol{\theta}$ that most closely map $\{\mathbf{w}_i\}$ to $\{\mathbf{x}_i\}$ in a least squares sense. This cost function is a special case of the more general form $f[\boldsymbol{\theta}] = \mathbf{z}^T \mathbf{z}$, where

$$\mathbf{z} = \begin{bmatrix} \mathbf{x}_1 - \mathbf{g}[\mathbf{w}_1, \boldsymbol{\theta}] \\ \mathbf{x}_2 - \mathbf{g}[\mathbf{w}_2, \boldsymbol{\theta}]| \\ \vdots \\ \mathbf{x}_I - \mathbf{g}[\mathbf{w}_I, \boldsymbol{\theta}] \end{bmatrix}. \tag{B.10}$$

The *Gauss-Newton method* is an optimization technique that is used to solve least squares problems of the form

$$\hat{\boldsymbol{\theta}} = \operatorname{argmin}[f[\boldsymbol{\theta}]] \qquad \text{where } f[\boldsymbol{\theta}] = \mathbf{z}[\boldsymbol{\theta}]^T \mathbf{z}[\boldsymbol{\theta}]. \tag{B.11}$$

To minimize this objective function, we approximate the term $\mathbf{z}[\boldsymbol{\theta}]$ with a Taylor series expansion around the current estimate $\boldsymbol{\theta}^{[t]}$ of the parameters:

$$\mathbf{z}[\boldsymbol{\theta}] \approx \mathbf{z}[\boldsymbol{\theta}^{[t]}] + \mathbf{J}(\boldsymbol{\theta} - \boldsymbol{\theta}^{[t]}), \tag{B.12}$$

where $\mathbf{J}$ is the Jacobian matrix. The entry j_{mn} at the mth row and the nth column of $\mathbf{J}$ contains the derivative of the mth element of $\mathbf{z}$ with respect to the nth parameter so that

$$j_{mn} = \frac{\partial z_m}{\partial \theta_n}. \tag{B.13}$$

Now we substitute the approximation for $\mathbf{z}[\boldsymbol{\theta}]$ into the original cost function $f[\boldsymbol{\theta}] = \mathbf{z}^T\mathbf{z}$ to yield

$$f[\boldsymbol{\theta}] \approx (\mathbf{z}[\boldsymbol{\theta}^{[t]}] + \mathbf{J}(\boldsymbol{\theta} - \boldsymbol{\theta}^{[t]}))^T(\mathbf{z}[\boldsymbol{\theta}^{[t]}] + \mathbf{J}(\boldsymbol{\theta} - \boldsymbol{\theta}^{[t]})) \tag{B.14}$$
$$= \mathbf{z}[\boldsymbol{\theta}^{[t]}]^T\mathbf{z}[\boldsymbol{\theta}^{[t]}] + 2(\boldsymbol{\theta} - \boldsymbol{\theta}^{[t]})^T\mathbf{J}^T\mathbf{z}[\boldsymbol{\theta}^{[t]}] + (\boldsymbol{\theta} - \boldsymbol{\theta}^{[t]})^T\mathbf{J}^T\mathbf{J}(\boldsymbol{\theta} - \boldsymbol{\theta}^{[t]}).$$

Finally, we take derivatives of this expression with respect to the parameters $\boldsymbol{\theta}$ and equate to zero to get the relation

$$\frac{\partial f}{\partial \boldsymbol{\theta}} \approx 2\mathbf{J}^T\mathbf{z}[\boldsymbol{\theta}^{[t]}] + 2\mathbf{J}^T\mathbf{J}(\boldsymbol{\theta} - \boldsymbol{\theta}^{[t]}) = 0. \tag{B.15}$$

Rearranging, we get the update rule:

$$\boldsymbol{\theta} = \boldsymbol{\theta}^{[t]} - (\mathbf{J}^T\mathbf{J})^{-1}\mathbf{J}^T\mathbf{z}[\boldsymbol{\theta}^{[t]}]. \tag{B.16}$$

We can rewrite this by noting that

$$\left.\frac{\partial f}{\partial \boldsymbol{\theta}}\right|_{\boldsymbol{\theta}^{[t]}} = \left.\frac{\partial \mathbf{z}^T\mathbf{z}}{\partial \boldsymbol{\theta}}\right|_{\boldsymbol{\theta}^{[t]}} = 2\mathbf{J}^T\mathbf{z}[\boldsymbol{\theta}^{[t]}] \tag{B.17}$$

to give the final Gauss-Newton update

$$\boldsymbol{\theta}^{[t+1]} = \boldsymbol{\theta}^{[t]} - \lambda(\mathbf{J}^T\mathbf{J})^{-1}\frac{\partial f}{\partial \boldsymbol{\theta}}, \tag{B.18}$$

where the derivative is taken at $\boldsymbol{\theta}^{[t]}$ and λ is the step size.

Comparing with the Newton update (Equation B.8), we see that we can consider this update as approximating the Hessian matrix as $\mathbf{H} \approx \mathbf{J}^T\mathbf{J}$. It provides better results than gradient descent without ever computing second derivatives. Moreover, the term $\mathbf{J}^T\mathbf{J}$ is normally positive definite resulting in increased stability.

B.2.4   Other methods

There are numerous other methods for choosing the optimization direction. Many of these involve approximating the Hessian in some way with the goal of either ensuring that a downhill direction is always chosen or reducing the computational burden. For example, if computation of the Hessian is prohibitive, a practical approach is to approximate it with its own diagonal. This usually provides a better direction than steepest descent.

Quasi-Newton methods such as the *Broyden Fletcher Goldfarb Shanno (BFGS) method* approximate the Hessian with information gathered by analyzing successive gradient vectors. The *Levenberg-Marquardt* algorithm interpolates between the Gauss-Newton algorithm and steepest descent with the aim of producing a method that requires few iterations and is also robust. *Damped Newton* and *trust-region methods* also attempt to improve the robustness of Newton's method. The nonlinear *conjugate gradient algorithm* is another valuable method when only first derivatives are available.

B.3   Line search

Having chosen a sensible direction using steepest descent, Newton's method or some other approach, we must now decide how far to move: we need an efficient method to

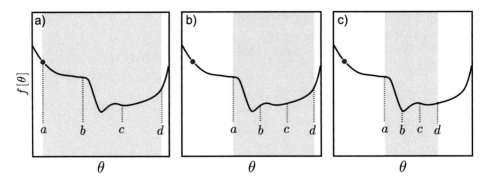

Figure B.5 Line search over region $[a, d]$ using bracketing approach. Gray region indicates current search region. a) We define two points b, c that are interior to the search region and evaluate the function at these points. Here $f[b] > f[c]$ so we eliminate the range $[a, b]$. b) We evaluate two points $[b, c]$ interior to the new range and compare their values. This time we find that $f[b] < f[c]$ so we eliminate the range $[c, d]$. c) We repeat this process until the minimum is closely bracketed.

find the minimum of the function in the chosen direction. Line search methods start by determining the range over which to search for the minimum. This is usually guided by the magnitude of the second derivative along the line that provides information about the likely search range (see Figure B.4).

There are many heuristics to find the minimum, but we will discuss only the direct search method (Figure B.5). Consider searching over the region $[a, d]$. We compute the function at two internal points b and c where $a < b < c < d$. If $f[b] < f[c]$, we eliminate the range $[c, d]$ and search over the new region $[a, c]$ at the next iteration. Conversely, if $f[b] > f[c]$, we eliminate the range $[a, b]$ and search over a new region $[b, d]$.

This method is applied iteratively until the minimum is closely bracketed. It is typically not worth exactly locating the minimum; the line search direction is rarely optimal and so the minimum of the line search is usually far from the overall minimum of the function. Once the remaining interval is sufficiently small, an estimate of the minimum position can be computed by making a parabolic fit to the three points that remain after eliminating one region or the other and selecting the position of the minimum of this parabola.

B.4   Reparameterization

Often in vision problems, we must find the best parameters θ subject to one or more constraints. Typical examples include optimizing variances σ^2 that must be positive, covariance matrices that must be positive definite, and matrices that represent geometric rotations which must be orthogonal. The general topic of constrained optimization is beyond the scope of this volume, but we briefly describe a trick that can be used to convert constrained optimization problems into unconstrained ones that can be solved using the techniques already described.

The idea of reparameterization is to represent the parameters θ in terms of a new set of parameters ϕ, which do not have any constraints on them, so that

$$\theta = \mathrm{g}[\phi], \qquad\qquad (\text{B}.19)$$

where $\mathrm{g}[\bullet]$ is a carefully chosen function.

Then we optimize with respect to the new unconstrained parameters ϕ. The objective function becomes $f[\mathbf{g}[\phi]]$ and the derivatives are computed using the chain rule so that the first derivative would be

$$\frac{\partial f}{\partial \phi} = \sum_{k=1}^{K} \frac{\partial f}{\partial \theta_k} \frac{\partial \theta_k}{\partial \phi}. \tag{B.20}$$

where θ_k is the kth element of $\boldsymbol{\theta}$. This strategy is easier to understand with some concrete examples.

Parameters that must be positive

When we optimize a variance parameter $\theta = \sigma^2$ we must ensure that the final answer is positive. To this end, we use the relation

$$\theta = \exp[\phi], \tag{B.21}$$

and now optimize with respect to the new scalar parameter ϕ. Alternatively, we can use the square relation:

$$\theta = \phi^2, \tag{B.22}$$

and again optimize with respect to the parameters ϕ.

Parameters that must lie between 0 and 1

To ensure that a scalar parameter θ lies between zero and one, we use the logistic sigmoid function:

$$\theta = \frac{1}{1 + \exp[-\phi]}, \tag{B.23}$$

and optimize with respect to the new scalar parameter ϕ.

Parameters that must be positive and sum to one

To ensure that the elements of a $K \times 1$ multivariable parameter $\boldsymbol{\theta}$ sum to one and are all positive we use the softmax function:

$$\theta_k = \frac{\exp[\phi_k]}{\sum_{j=1}^{K} \exp[\phi_j]}, \tag{B.24}$$

and optimize with respect to the new $K \times 1$ variable ϕ.

3D rotation matrices

A 3×3 rotation matrix contains three independent quantities spread throughout its nine entries. A number of nonlinear constraints exist between the entries: the norm of each column and row must be one, each column is perpendicular to the other columns, each row is perpendicular to the other rows, and the determinant is one.

One way to enforce these constraints is to reparameterize the rotation matrix as a *quaternion* and optimize with respect to this new representation. A quaternion $\mathbf{q}$ is a 4D quantity $\mathbf{q} = [q_0, q_1, q_2, q_3]$. Mathematically speaking, they are a four-dimensional extension of complex numbers, but the relevance for vision is that they can be used to represent 3D rotations. We use the relation:

$$
\Theta = \frac{1}{q_0^2 + q_1^2 + q_2^2 + q_3^2} \begin{bmatrix} q_0^2 + q_1^2 - q_2^2 - q_3^2 & 2q_1q_2 - 2q_0q_3 & 2q_1q_3 + 2q_0q_2 \\ 2q_1q_2 + 2q_0q_3 & q_0^2 - q_1^2 + q_2^2 - q_3^2 & 2q_2q_3 - 2q_0q_1 \\ 2q_1q_3 - 2q_0q_2 & 2q_2q_3 + 2q_0q_1 & q_0^2 - q_1^2 - q_2^2 + q_3^2 \end{bmatrix}.
$$
(B.25)

Although the quaternion contains four numbers, only the ratios of those numbers are important (giving 3 degrees of freedom): each element of equation B.25 consists of squared terms, which are normalized by the squared amplitude constant, and so and constant that multiplies the elements of $\mathbf{q}$ is canceled out when we convert back to a rotation matrix.

Now we optimize with respect to the quaternion $\mathbf{q}$. The derivatives with respect to the kth element of $\mathbf{q}$ can be computed as

$$
\frac{\partial f}{\partial q_k} = \sum_{i=1}^{3} \sum_{j=1}^{3} \frac{\partial f}{\partial \Theta_{ij}} \frac{\partial \Theta_{ij}}{\partial q_k}.
$$
(B.26)

The quaternion optimization is stable as long as we do not approach the singularity at $\mathbf{q} = \mathbf{0}$. One way to achieve this is to periodically renormalize the quaternion to length 1 during the optimization procedure.

Positive definite matrices

When we optimize over a $K \times K$ covariance matrix $\Theta = \Sigma$, we must ensure that the result is positive definite. A simple way to do this is to use the relation:

$$
\Theta = \Phi\Phi^T,
$$
(B.27)

where Φ is an arbitrary $K \times K$ matrix.

Appendix C

Linear algebra

C.1 Vectors

A vector is a geometric entity in D dimensional space that has both a direction and a magnitude. It is represented by a $D \times 1$ array of numbers. In this book, we write vectors as bold, small, Roman or Greek letters (e.g., $\mathbf{a}, \phi$). The transpose $\mathbf{a}^T$ of vector $\mathbf{a}$ is a $1 \times D$ array of numbers where the order of the numbers is retained.

C.1.1 Dot product

The *dot product* or *scalar product* between two vectors $\mathbf{a}$ and $\mathbf{b}$ is defined as

$$c = \mathbf{a}^T \mathbf{b} = \sum_{d=1}^{D} a_d b_d, \tag{C.1}$$

where $\mathbf{a}^T$ is the transpose of $\mathbf{a}$ (i.e., $\mathbf{a}$ converted to a row vector) and the returned value c is a scalar. Two vectors are said to be *orthogonal* if the dot product between them is zero.

C.1.2 Norm of a vector

The *magnitude* or *norm* of a vector is the square root of the sum of the square of the D elements so that

$$\text{norm}[\mathbf{a}] = |\mathbf{a}| = \left(\sum_{d=1}^{D} a_d^2 \right)^{1/2} = (\mathbf{a}^T \mathbf{a})^{1/2}. \tag{C.2}$$

C.1.3 Cross product

The *cross product* or *vector product* is specialized to three dimensions. The operation $\mathbf{c} = \mathbf{a} \times \mathbf{b}$ is equivalent to the matrix multiplication (Section C.2.1):

$$\begin{bmatrix} c_1 \\ c_2 \\ c_3 \end{bmatrix} = \begin{bmatrix} 0 & -a_3 & a_2 \\ a_3 & 0 & -a_1 \\ -a_2 & a_1 & 0 \end{bmatrix} \begin{bmatrix} b_1 \\ b_2 \\ b_3 \end{bmatrix}, \tag{C.3}$$

or for short

$$\mathbf{c} = \mathbf{A}_\times \mathbf{b}, \tag{C.4}$$

where $\mathbf{A}_\times$ is the 3×3 matrix from Equation C.3 that implements the cross product.

It is easily shown that the result $\mathbf{c}$ of the cross product is orthogonal to both $\mathbf{a}$ and $\mathbf{b}$. In other words,

$$\mathbf{a}^T(\mathbf{a}\times\mathbf{b}) = \mathbf{b}^T(\mathbf{a}\times\mathbf{b}) = 0. \tag{C.5}$$

C.2 Matrices

Matrices are used extensively throughout the book and are written as bold, capital, Roman or Greek letters (e.g., $\mathbf{A},\mathbf{\Phi}$). We categorize matrices as *landscape* (more columns than rows), *square* (the same number of columns and rows), or *portrait* (more rows than columns). They are always indexed by row first and then column, so a_{ij} denotes the element of matrix $\mathbf{A}$ at the ith row and the jth column.

A *diagonal* matrix is a square matrix with zeros everywhere except on the diagonal (i.e., elements a_{ii}) where the elements may take any value. An important special case of a diagonal matrix is the *identity* matrix $\mathbf{I}$. This has zeros everywhere except for the diagonal, where all the elements are ones.

C.2.1 Matrix multiplication

To take the matrix product $\mathbf{C} = \mathbf{AB}$, we compute the elements of $\mathbf{C}$ as

$$c_{ij} = \sum_{k=1}^{K} a_{ik}b_{kj}. \tag{C.6}$$

This can only be done when the number of columns in $\mathbf{A}$ equals the number of rows in $\mathbf{B}$. Matrix multiplication is associative so that $\mathbf{A}(\mathbf{BC}) = (\mathbf{AB})\mathbf{C} = \mathbf{ABC}$. However, it is not commutative so that in general $\mathbf{AB} \neq \mathbf{BA}$.

C.2.2 Transpose

The transpose of a matrix $\mathbf{A}$ is written as $\mathbf{A}^T$ and is formed by reflecting it around the principal diagonal, so that the kth column becomes the kth row and vice versa. If we take the transpose of a matrix product $\mathbf{AB}$, then we take the transpose of the original matrices but reverse the order so that

$$(\mathbf{AB})^T = \mathbf{B}^T\mathbf{A}^T. \tag{C.7}$$

C.2.3 Inverse

A square matrix $\mathbf{A}$ may or may not have an inverse $\mathbf{A}^{-1}$ such that $\mathbf{A}^{-1}\mathbf{A} = \mathbf{A}\mathbf{A}^{-1} = \mathbf{I}$. If a matrix does not have an inverse, it is called *singular*.

Diagonal matrices are particularly easy to invert: the inverse is also a diagonal matrix, with each diagonal value d_{ii} replaced by $1/d_{ii}$. Hence, any diagonal matrix that has nonzero values on the diagonal is invertible. It follows that the inverse of the identity matrix is the identity matrix itself.

If we take the inverse of a matrix product $\mathbf{AB}$, then we can equivalently take the inverse of each matrix individually, and reverse the order of multiplication

$$(\mathbf{AB})^{-1} = \mathbf{B}^{-1}\mathbf{A}^{-1}. \tag{C.8}$$

C.2.4   Determinant and trace

Every square matrix $\mathbf{A}$ has a scalar associated with it called the determinant and denoted by $|\mathbf{A}|$ or $\det[\mathbf{A}]$. It is (loosely) related to the scaling applied by the matrix. Matrices where the magnitude of the determinant is small tend to make vectors smaller upon multiplication. Matrices where the magnitude of the determinants is large tend to make them larger. If a matrix is singular, the determinant will be zero and there will be at least one direction in space that is mapped to the origin when the matrix is applied. For a diagonal matrix, the determinant is the product of the diagonal values. It follows that the determinant of the identity matrix is 1. Determinants of matrix expressions can be computed using the following rules:

$$|\mathbf{A}^T| = |\mathbf{A}| \tag{C.9}$$

$$|\mathbf{AB}| = |\mathbf{A}||\mathbf{B}| \tag{C.10}$$

$$|\mathbf{A}^{-1}| = 1/|\mathbf{A}|. \tag{C.11}$$

The trace of a matrix is a second number associated with a square matrix $\mathbf{A}$. It is the sum of the diagonal values (the matrix itself need not be diagonal). The traces of compound terms are bound by the following rules:

$$\mathrm{tr}[\mathbf{A^T}] = \mathrm{tr}[\mathbf{A}] \tag{C.12}$$

$$\mathrm{tr}[\mathbf{AB}] = \mathrm{tr}[\mathbf{BA}] \tag{C.13}$$

$$\mathrm{tr}[\mathbf{A} + \mathbf{B}] = \mathrm{tr}[\mathbf{A}] + \mathrm{tr}[\mathbf{B}] \tag{C.14}$$

$$\mathrm{tr}[\mathbf{ABC}] = \mathrm{tr}[\mathbf{BCA}] = \mathrm{tr}[\mathbf{CAB}], \tag{C.15}$$

where in the last relation, the trace is invariant for cyclic permutations only, so that in general $\mathrm{tr}[\mathbf{ABC}] \neq \mathrm{tr}[\mathbf{BAC}]$.

C.2.5   Orthogonal and rotation matrices

An important class of square matrix is the orthogonal matrix. Orthogonal matrices have the following special properties:

1. Each column has norm one, and each row has norm one.
2. Each column is orthogonal to every other column, and each row is orthogonal to every other row.

The inverse of an orthogonal matrix $\boldsymbol{\Omega}$ is its own transpose, so $\boldsymbol{\Omega}^T\boldsymbol{\Omega} = \boldsymbol{\Omega}^{-1}\boldsymbol{\Omega} = \mathbf{I}$; orthogonal matrices are easy to invert! When this class of matrix premultiplies a vector, the effect is to rotate it around the origin and possibly reflect it.

Rotation matrices are a subclass of orthogonal matrices that have the additional property that the determinant is one. As the name suggests when this class of matrix premultiplies a vector, the effect is to rotate it around the origin with no reflection.

C.2.6   Positive definite matrices

A $D \times D$ real symmetric matrix $\mathbf{A}$ is *positive definite* if $\mathbf{x}^T\mathbf{A}\mathbf{x} > 0$ for all nonzero vectors $\mathbf{x}$. Every positive definite matrix is invertible and its inverse is also positive definite. The determinant and trace of a symmetric positive definite matrix are always positive. The covariance matrix $\boldsymbol{\Sigma}$ of a normal distribution is always positive definite.

C.2.7 Null space of a matrix

The right null space of a matrix $\mathbf{A}$ consists of the set of vectors $\mathbf{x}$ for which

$$\mathbf{A}\mathbf{x} = \mathbf{0}. \tag{C.16}$$

Similarly, the left null space of a matrix $\mathbf{A}$ consists of the set of vectors $\mathbf{x}$ for which

$$\mathbf{x}^T \mathbf{A} = \mathbf{0}^T. \tag{C.17}$$

A square matrix only has a nontrivial null space (i.e., not just $\mathbf{x} = \mathbf{0}$) if the matrix is singular (non-invertible) and hence the determinant is zero.

C.3 Tensors

We will occasionally have need for $D > 2$ dimensional quantities that we shall refer to as D-dimensional tensors. For our purposes a matrix can be thought of as the special case of a two-dimensional tensor, and a vector as the special case of a 1D tensor.

The idea of taking matrix products generalizes to higher dimensions and is denoted using the special notion $\times_n$ where n is the dimension over which we take the product. For example, the lth element f_l of the tensor product $\mathbf{f} = \mathbf{A} \times_2 \mathbf{b} \times_3 \mathbf{c}$ is given by

$$f_l = \sum_m \sum_n A_{lmn} b_m c_n, \tag{C.18}$$

where l, m and n index the 3D tensor $\mathbf{A}$, and $\mathbf{b}$ and $\mathbf{c}$ are vectors.

C.4 Linear transformations

When we premultiply a vector by a matrix this is called a linear transformation. Figure C.1 shows the results of applying several different 2D linear transformations (randomly chosen 2×2 matrices) to the 2D vectors that represent the points of the unit square. We can deduce several things from this figure. First, the point (0,0) at the origin in always mapped back onto itself. Second, collinear points remain collinear. Third, parallel lines are always mapped to parallel lines. Viewed as a geometric transformation, premultiplication by a matrix can account for shearing, scaling, reflection and rotation around the origin.

A different perspective on linear transformations comes from applying different transformations to points on the unit circle (Figure C.2). In each case, the circle is transformed to an ellipse. The ellipse can be characterized by its major axis (most elongated axis) and its minor axis (most compact axis), which are perpendicular to one another. This tells us something interesting: in general, there is a special direction in space (position on the original circle) that gets stretched the most (or compressed the least) by the transformation. Likewise there is a second direction that gets stretched the least or compressed the most.

C.5 Singular value decomposition

The singular value decomposition (SVD) is a factorization of a $M \times N$ matrix $\mathbf{A}$ such that

$$\mathbf{A} = \mathbf{U}\mathbf{L}\mathbf{V}^T, \tag{C.19}$$

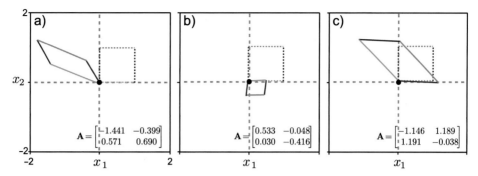

Figure C.1 Effect of applying three linear transformations to a unit square. Dashed square is before transformation. Solid square is after. The origin is always mapped to the origin. Colinear points remain colinear. Parallel lines remain parallel. The linear transformation encompasses shears, reflections, rotations, and scalings.

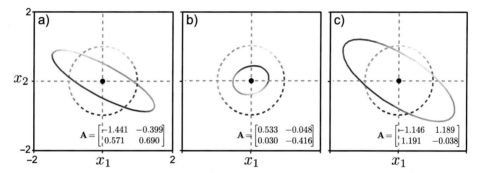

Figure C.2 Effect of applying three linear transformations to a circle. Dashed circle is before transformation. Solid ellipse is after. After the transformation, the circle is mapped to an ellipse. This demonstrates that there is one special direction that is expanded the most (becomes the major axis of the ellipse), and one special direction that is expanded the least (becomes the minor axis of the ellipse).

where $\mathbf{U}$ is a $M \times M$ orthogonal matrix, $\mathbf{L}$ is a $M \times N$ diagonal matrix, and $\mathbf{V}$ is a $N \times N$ orthogonal matrix. It is always possible to compute this factorization, although a description of how to do so is beyond the scope of this book.

The best way to get the flavor of the SVD is to consider some examples. First let us consider a square matrix:

$$\mathbf{A}_1 = \begin{bmatrix} 0.183 & 0.307 & 0.261 \\ -1.029 & 0.135 & -0.941 \\ 0.949 & 0.515 & -0.162 \end{bmatrix} = \mathbf{ULV}^T \tag{C.20}$$

$$= \begin{bmatrix} -0.204 & -0.061 & -0.977 \\ 0.832 & -0.535 & -0.140 \\ -0.514 & -0.842 & 0.160 \end{bmatrix} \begin{bmatrix} 1.590 & 0 & 0 \\ 0 & 0.856 & 0 \\ 0 & 0 & 0.303 \end{bmatrix} \begin{bmatrix} -0.870 & -0.302 & 0.389 \\ -0.135 & -0.613 & -0.778 \\ -0.474 & 0.729 & -0.492 \end{bmatrix}.$$

Notice that by convention the nonnegative values on the principal diagonal of $\mathbf{L}$ decrease monotonically as we move from top-left to bottom-right. These are known as the *singular values*.

Now consider the singular value decomposition of a portrait matrix:

$$\mathbf{A}_2 = \begin{bmatrix} 0.537 & 0.862 \\ 1.839 & 0.318 \\ -2.258 & -1.307 \end{bmatrix} = \mathbf{ULV}^T \tag{C.21}$$

$$= \begin{bmatrix} -0.263 & 0.698 & 0.665 \\ -0.545 & -0.676 & 0.493 \\ 0.795 & -0.233 & 0.559 \end{bmatrix} \begin{bmatrix} 3.273 & 0 \\ 0 & 0.76 \\ 0 & 0 \end{bmatrix} \begin{bmatrix} -0.898 & -0.440 \\ -0.440 & 0.898 \end{bmatrix}.$$

For this rectangular matrix, the orthogonal matrices $\mathbf{U}$ and $\mathbf{V}$ are different sizes and the diagonal matrix $\mathbf{L}$ is the same size as the original matrix. The singular values are still found on the diagonal, but the number is determined by the smallest dimension. In other words, if the original matrix was $M \times N$ then there will be $\min[M, N]$ singular values.

To further understand the SVD, let us consider a third example:

$$\mathbf{A}_3 = \begin{bmatrix} -0.147 & 0.357 \\ -0.668 & 0.811 \end{bmatrix} = \begin{bmatrix} 0.189 & 0.981 \\ 0.981 & -0.189 \end{bmatrix} \begin{bmatrix} 1.068 & 0 \\ 0 & 0.335 \end{bmatrix} \begin{bmatrix} -0.587 & 0.8091 \\ 0.809 & 0.587 \end{bmatrix}. \tag{C.22}$$

Figure C.3 illustrates the cumulative effect of the transformations in the decomposition $\mathbf{A}_3 = \mathbf{ULV}^T$. The matrix $\mathbf{V}^T$ rotates and reflects the original points. The matrix $\mathbf{L}$ scales the result differently along each dimension. In this case, it is stretched along the first dimension and shrunk along the second. Finally, the matrix $\mathbf{U}$ rotates the result.

Figure C.4 provides a second perspective on this process. Each pair of panels depicts what happens when we modify a different part of the SVD but keep the remaining parts the same. When we change $\mathbf{V}$, the shape of the final ellipse is the same, but the mapping from original directions to points on the ellipse changes (observe the color change along the major axis). When we modify the first element of $\mathbf{L}$, the length of the major axis changes. When we change the other nonzero element of $\mathbf{L}$, the length of the minor axis changes. When we change the matrix $\mathbf{U}$, the orientation of the ellipse changes.

C.5.1 Analyzing the singular values

We can learn a lot about a matrix by looking at the singular values. We saw in Section C.4, that as we decrease the smallest singular value the minor axis of the ellipse becomes progressively smaller. When it actually becomes zero, both sides of the unit circle collapse into one another (as do points from circles of all radii). Now there is a many-to-one mapping from the original points to the transformed ones and the matrix is no longer invertible. In general, a matrix is only invertible if all of the singular values are nonzero.

The number of nonzero singular values is called the rank of the matrix. The ratio of the smallest to the largest singular values is known as the condition number: it is roughly a measure of how 'invertible' the matrix is. As it becomes close to zero, our ability to invert the matrix decreases.

The singular values scale the different axes of the ellipse by different amounts (Figure C.3c). Hence, the area of a unit circle is changed by a factor that is equal to the product of the singular values. In fact, this scaling factor is the determinant (Section C.2.4). When the matrix is singular, at least one of the singular values is zero and hence the determinant is also zero. The right null space consists of all of the vectors that can be reached by taking a weighted sum of those columns of $\mathbf{V}$ whose corresponding singular values are zero. Similarly, the left null space consists of all the vectors that can be

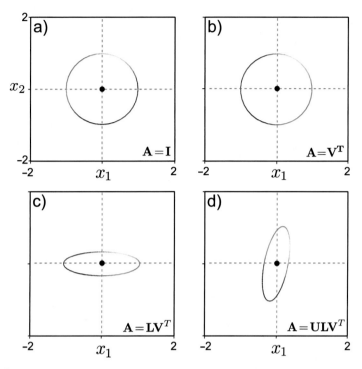

Figure C.3 Cumulative effect of SVD components for matrix $\mathbf{A}_3$. a) Original object. b) Applying matrix $\mathbf{V}^T$ rotates and reflects the object around the origin. c) Subsequently applying $\mathbf{L}$ causes stretching/compression along the coordinate axes. d) Finally, applying matrix $\mathbf{U}$ rotates and reflects this distorted structure.

reached by taking a weighted sum of those columns of $\mathbf{U}$ whose corresponding singular values are zero.

Orthogonal matrices only rotate and reflect points, and rotation matrices just rotate them. In either case, there is no change in area to the unit circle: all the singular values are one for these matrices and the determinant is also one.

C.5.2   Inverse of a matrix

We can also see what happens when we invert a square matrix in terms of the singular value decomposition. Using the rule $(\mathbf{AB})^{-1} = \mathbf{B}^{-1}\mathbf{A}^{-1}$, we have

$$\mathbf{A}^{-1} = (\mathbf{ULV}^T)^{-1} = (\mathbf{V}^T)^{-1}\mathbf{L}^{-1}\mathbf{U}^{-1} = \mathbf{VL}^{-1}\mathbf{U}^T, \tag{C.23}$$

where we have used the fact that $\mathbf{U}$ and $\mathbf{V}$ are orthogonal matrices so $\mathbf{U}^{-1} = \mathbf{U}^T$ and $\mathbf{V}^{-1} = \mathbf{V}^T$. The matrix $\mathbf{L}$ is diagonal so $\mathbf{L}^{-1}$ will also be diagonal with new nonzero entries that are the reciprocal of the original values. This also shows that the matrix is not invertible when any of the singular values are zero: we cannot take the reciprocal of 0.

Expressed in this way, the inverse has the opposite geometric effect to that of the original matrix: if we consider the effect on the transformed ellipse in Figure C.3d, it first rotates by $\mathbf{U}^T$ so its major and minor axis are aligned with the coordinate axes (Figure C.3c). Then it scales these axes (using the elements of $\mathbf{L}^{-1}$), so that the ellipse

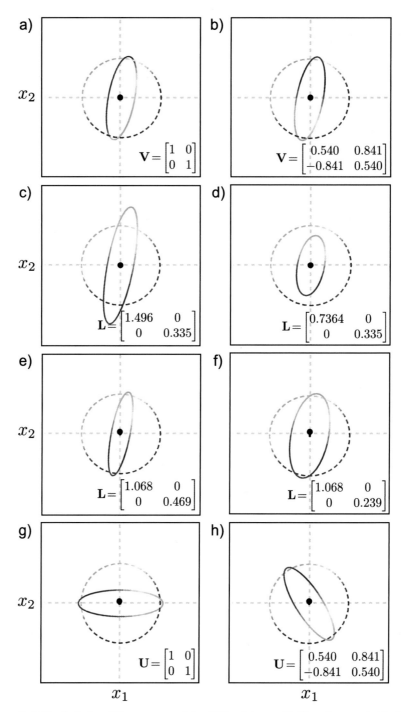

Figure C.4 Manipulating different parts of the SVD of $\mathbf{A}_3$. a–b) Changing matrix $\mathbf{V}$ does not affect the final ellipse, but changes which directions (colors) are mapped to the minor and major axes. c–d) Changing the first diagonal element of $\mathbf{L}$ changes the length of the major axis of the ellipse. e–f) Changing the second diagonal element of $\mathbf{L}$ changes the length of the minor axis. g–h) Changing $\mathbf{U}$ affects the final orientation of the ellipse.

becomes a circle (Figure C.3b). Finally, it rotates the result by $\mathbf{V}$ to get back to the original position (Figure C.3a).

C.6 Matrix calculus

We are often called upon to take derivatives of compound matrix expressions. The derivative of a function f[$\mathbf{a}$] that takes a vector as its argument and returns a scalar is a vector $\mathbf{b}$ with elements

$$b_i = \frac{\partial f}{\partial a_i} \tag{C.24}$$

The derivative of a function f[$\mathbf{A}$] that returns a scalar, with respect to an $M \times N$ matrix $\mathbf{A}$ will be a $M \times N$ matrix $\mathbf{B}$ with elements

$$b_{ij} = \frac{\partial f}{\partial a_{ij}}. \tag{C.25}$$

The derivative of a function $\mathbf{f}[\mathbf{a}]$ that returns a vector with respect to vector $\mathbf{a}$ is a matrix $\mathbf{B}$ with elements

$$b_{ij} = \frac{\partial f_i}{\partial a_j}. \tag{C.26}$$

where f_i is the ith element of the vector returned by the function $\mathbf{f}[\mathbf{a}]$.

We now provide several commonly used results for reference.

1. Derivative of linear function:

$$\frac{\partial \mathbf{x}^T \mathbf{a}}{\partial \mathbf{x}} = \mathbf{a} \tag{C.27}$$

$$\frac{\partial \mathbf{a}^T \mathbf{x}}{\partial \mathbf{x}} = \mathbf{a} \tag{C.28}$$

$$\frac{\partial \mathbf{a}^T \mathbf{X} \mathbf{b}}{\partial \mathbf{X}} = \mathbf{a}\mathbf{b}^T \tag{C.29}$$

$$\frac{\partial \mathbf{a}^T \mathbf{X}^T \mathbf{b}}{\partial \mathbf{X}} = \mathbf{b}\mathbf{a}^T. \tag{C.30}$$

2. Derivative of quadratic function:

$$\frac{\partial \mathbf{b}^T \mathbf{X}^T \mathbf{X} \mathbf{c}}{\partial \mathbf{X}} = \mathbf{X}(\mathbf{b}\mathbf{c}^T + \mathbf{c}\mathbf{b}^T) \tag{C.31}$$

$$\frac{\partial (\mathbf{B}\mathbf{x} + \mathbf{b})^T \mathbf{C}(\mathbf{D}\mathbf{x} + \mathbf{d})}{\partial \mathbf{x}} = \mathbf{B}^T \mathbf{C}(\mathbf{D}\mathbf{x} + \mathbf{d}) + \mathbf{D}^T \mathbf{C}^T (\mathbf{B}\mathbf{x} + \mathbf{b}) \tag{C.32}$$

$$\frac{\partial \mathbf{x}^T \mathbf{B} \mathbf{x}}{\partial \mathbf{x}} = (\mathbf{B} + \mathbf{B}^T)\mathbf{x} \tag{C.33}$$

$$\frac{\partial \mathbf{b}^T \mathbf{X}^T \mathbf{D} \mathbf{X} \mathbf{c}}{\partial \mathbf{X}} = \mathbf{D}^T \mathbf{X}\mathbf{b}\mathbf{c}^T + \mathbf{D}\mathbf{X}\mathbf{c}\mathbf{b}^T \tag{C.34}$$

$$\frac{\partial (\mathbf{X}\mathbf{b} + \mathbf{c})^T \mathbf{D}(\mathbf{X}\mathbf{b} + \mathbf{c})}{\partial \mathbf{X}} = (\mathbf{D} + \mathbf{D}^T)(\mathbf{X}\mathbf{b} + \mathbf{c})\mathbf{b}^T. \tag{C.35}$$

3. Derivative of determinant:

$$\frac{\partial \det[\mathbf{Y}]}{\partial x} = \det[\mathbf{Y}]\text{tr}\left[\mathbf{Y}^{-1}\frac{\partial \mathbf{Y}}{\partial x}\right], \tag{C.36}$$

which leads to the relation

$$\frac{\partial \det[\mathbf{Y}]}{\partial \mathbf{Y}} = \det[\mathbf{Y}]\mathbf{Y}^{-T}. \tag{C.37}$$

4. Derivative of log determinant:

$$\frac{\partial \log[\det[\mathbf{Y}]]}{\partial \mathbf{Y}} = \mathbf{Y}^{-T}. \tag{C.38}$$

5. Derivative of inverse:

$$\frac{\partial \mathbf{Y}^{-1}}{\partial x} = -\mathbf{Y}^{-1}\frac{\partial \mathbf{Y}}{\partial x}\mathbf{Y}^{-1}. \tag{C.39}$$

6. Derivative of trace:

$$\frac{\partial \operatorname{tr}[\mathbf{F}[\mathbf{X}]]}{\partial \mathbf{X}} = \left(\frac{\partial \mathbf{F}[\mathbf{X}]}{\partial \mathbf{X}}\right)^T. \tag{C.40}$$

More information about matrix calculus can be found in Petersen et al. (2006).

C.7 Common problems

In this section, we discuss several standard linear algebra problems that are found repeatedly in computer vision.

C.7.1 Least squares problems

Many inference and learning tasks in computer vision result in least squares problems. The most frequent context is when we use maximum likelihood methods with the normal distribution. The least squares problem may be formulated in a number of ways. We may be asked to find the vector $\mathbf{x}$ that solves the system

$$\mathbf{A}\mathbf{x} = \mathbf{b} \tag{C.41}$$

in a least squares sense. Alternatively, we may be given i of smaller sets of equations of the form

$$\mathbf{A}_i\mathbf{x} = \mathbf{b}_i, \tag{C.42}$$

and again asked to solve for $\mathbf{x}$. In this latter case, we form the compound matrix $\mathbf{A} = [\mathbf{A}_1^T, \mathbf{A}_2^T \dots \mathbf{A}_I^T]^T$ and compound vector $\mathbf{b} = [\mathbf{b}_1^T, \mathbf{b}_2^T \dots \mathbf{b}_I^T]^T$, and the problem is the same as in Equation C.41.

We may equivalently see the same problem in an explicit least squares form,

$$\hat{\mathbf{x}} = \underset{\mathbf{x}}{\operatorname{argmin}} \left[(\mathbf{A}\mathbf{x} - \mathbf{b})^T (\mathbf{A}\mathbf{x} - \mathbf{b})\right]. \tag{C.43}$$

Finally, we may be presented the problem as a sum of smaller terms

$$\hat{\mathbf{x}} = \underset{\mathbf{x}}{\operatorname{argmin}} \left[\sum_{i=1}^{I} (\mathbf{A}_i\mathbf{x} - \mathbf{b}_i)^T (\mathbf{A}_i\mathbf{x} - \mathbf{b}_i)\right], \tag{C.44}$$

in which case we form compound matrices $\mathbf{A}$ and $\mathbf{b}$, which changes the problem back to that in Equation C.43.

To make progress, we multiply out the terms in Equation C.43

$$\hat{\mathbf{x}} = \underset{\mathbf{x}}{\text{argmin}} \left[(\mathbf{A}\mathbf{x} - \mathbf{b})^T (\mathbf{A}\mathbf{x} - \mathbf{b}) \right].$$
$$= \underset{\mathbf{x}}{\text{argmin}} \left[\mathbf{x}^T \mathbf{A}^T \mathbf{A}\mathbf{x} - \mathbf{b}^T \mathbf{A}\mathbf{x} - \mathbf{x}^T \mathbf{A}^T \mathbf{b} + \mathbf{b}^T \mathbf{b} \right]$$
$$= \underset{\mathbf{x}}{\text{argmin}} \left[\mathbf{x}^T \mathbf{A}^T \mathbf{A}\mathbf{x} - 2\mathbf{x}^T \mathbf{A}^T \mathbf{b} + \mathbf{b}^T \mathbf{b} \right], \quad (C.45)$$

where we have combined two terms in the last line by noting that they are both the same: they are transposes of one another, but they are also scalars, so they equal their own transpose. Now we take the derivative with respect to $\mathbf{x}$ and equate the result to zero to give

$$2\mathbf{A}^T \mathbf{A}\mathbf{x} - 2\mathbf{A}^T \mathbf{b} = 0, \quad (C.46)$$

which we can rearrange to give the standard least squares result

$$\mathbf{x} = (\mathbf{A}^T \mathbf{A})^{-1} \mathbf{A}^T \mathbf{b}. \quad (C.47)$$

This result can only be computed if there are at least as many rows in $\mathbf{A}$ as there are unknown values in $\mathbf{x}$ (i.e., if the matrix $\mathbf{A}$ is square or portrait). Otherwise, the matrix $\mathbf{A}^T \mathbf{A}$ will be singular. For implementations in Matlab, it is better to make use of the backslash operator '\' rather than explicitly implement Equation C.47.

C.7.2 Principal direction/minimum direction

We define the principal and minimal directions as

$$\hat{\mathbf{b}} = \underset{\mathbf{b}}{\text{argmax}} \left[||\mathbf{A}\mathbf{b}|| \right] \qquad \text{subject to } |\mathbf{b}| = 1$$
$$\hat{\mathbf{b}} = \underset{\mathbf{b}}{\text{argmin}} \left[||\mathbf{A}\mathbf{b}|| \right] \qquad \text{subject to } |\mathbf{b}| = 1, \quad (C.48)$$

respectively. This problem has exactly the geometric form of Figure C.2. The constraint that $|\mathbf{b}| = 1$ means that $\mathbf{b}$ has to lie on the circle (or sphere or hypersphere in higher dimensions). In the principal direction problem, we are hence seeking the direction that is mapped to the major axis of the resulting ellipse/ellipsoid. In the minimum direction problem, we seek the direction that is mapped to the minor axis of the ellipsoid.

We saw in Figure C.4 that it is the matrix $\mathbf{V}$ from the singular value decomposition of $\mathbf{A}$ that controls which direction is mapped to the different axes of the ellipsoid. To solve the principal direction problem, we hence compute the SVD, $\mathbf{A} = \mathbf{U}\mathbf{L}\mathbf{V}^T$ and set $\mathbf{b}$ to be the first column of $\mathbf{V}$. To solve the minimum direction problem, we set $\mathbf{b}$ to be the last column of $\mathbf{V}$.

C.7.3 Orthogonal Procrustes problem

The orthogonal Procrustes problem is to find the closest linear mapping $\boldsymbol{\Omega}$ between one set of vectors $\mathbf{A}$ and another $\mathbf{B}$ such that $\boldsymbol{\Omega}$ is an orthogonal matrix. In layman's terms, we seek the best Euclidean rotation (possibly including mirroring) that maps points $\mathbf{A}$ to points $\mathbf{B}$.

$$\hat{\boldsymbol{\Omega}} = \underset{\boldsymbol{\Omega}}{\text{argmin}} \left[|\boldsymbol{\Omega}\mathbf{A} - \mathbf{B}|_F \right], \quad (C.49)$$

where $|\bullet|_F$ denotes the Frobenius norm of a matrix – the sum of the square of all of the elements. To make progress, we recall that the trace of a matrix is the sum of its diagonal entries and so $|\mathbf{X}|_F = \mathrm{tr}[\mathbf{X}^T\mathbf{X}]$, which gives the new criterion

$$
\begin{aligned}
\hat{\boldsymbol{\Omega}} &= \underset{\boldsymbol{\Omega}}{\operatorname{argmin}} \left[\mathrm{tr}[\mathbf{A}^T\mathbf{A}] + \mathrm{tr}[\mathbf{B}^T\mathbf{B}] - 2\mathrm{tr}[\mathbf{A}^T\boldsymbol{\Omega}^T\mathbf{B}] \right] \\
&= \underset{\boldsymbol{\Omega}}{\operatorname{argmax}} \left[\mathrm{tr}[\mathbf{A}^T\boldsymbol{\Omega}^T\mathbf{B}] \right] \\
&= \underset{\boldsymbol{\Omega}}{\operatorname{argmax}} \left[\mathrm{tr}[\boldsymbol{\Omega}^T\mathbf{B}\mathbf{A}^T] \right],
\end{aligned}
\tag{C.50}
$$

where we have used relation C.15 between the last two lines. We now compute the SVD $\mathbf{B}\mathbf{A}^T = \mathbf{U}\mathbf{L}\mathbf{V}^T$ to get the criterion

$$
\begin{aligned}
\hat{\boldsymbol{\Omega}} &= \underset{\boldsymbol{\Omega}}{\operatorname{argmax}} \left[\mathrm{tr}[\boldsymbol{\Omega}^T\mathbf{U}\mathbf{L}\mathbf{V}^T] \right] \\
&= \underset{\boldsymbol{\Omega}}{\operatorname{argmax}} \left[\mathrm{tr}[\mathbf{V}^T\boldsymbol{\Omega}^T\mathbf{U}\mathbf{L}] \right]
\end{aligned}
\tag{C.51}
$$

and notice that

$$
\mathrm{tr}[\mathbf{V}^T\boldsymbol{\Omega}^T\mathbf{U}\mathbf{L}] = \mathrm{tr}[\mathbf{Z}\mathbf{L}] = \sum_{i=1}^{I} z_{ii}l_{ii},
\tag{C.52}
$$

where we defined $\mathbf{Z} = \mathbf{V}^T\boldsymbol{\Omega}^T\mathbf{U}$ and used the fact that the $\mathbf{L}$ is a diagonal matrix, so each entry scales the diagonal of $\mathbf{Z}$ on multiplication.

We note that the matrix $\mathbf{Z}$ is orthogonal (it is the product of three orthogonal matrices). Hence, every value on the diagonal of the orthogonal matrix $\mathbf{Z}$ must be less than or equal to one (the norms of each column are exactly one), and so we maximize the criterion in Equation C.52 by choosing $\mathbf{Z} = \mathbf{I}$ when the diagonal values are equal to one. To achieve this, we set $\boldsymbol{\Omega}^T = \mathbf{V}\mathbf{U}^T$ so that the overall solution is

$$
\hat{\boldsymbol{\Omega}} = \mathbf{U}\mathbf{V}^T.
\tag{C.53}
$$

A special case of this problem is to find the closest orthogonal matrix $\boldsymbol{\Omega}$ to a given square matrix $\mathbf{B}$ in a least squares sense. In other words, we seek to optimize

$$
\hat{\boldsymbol{\Omega}} = \underset{\boldsymbol{\Omega}}{\operatorname{argmin}} \left[|\boldsymbol{\Omega} - \mathbf{B}|_F \right].
\tag{C.54}
$$

This is clearly equivalent to optimizing the criterion in Equation C.49 but with $\mathbf{A} = \mathbf{I}$. It follows that the solution can be found by computing the singular value decomposition $\mathbf{B} = \mathbf{U}\mathbf{L}\mathbf{V}^T$ and setting $\boldsymbol{\Omega} = \mathbf{U}\mathbf{V}^T$.

C.8 Tricks for inverting large matrices

Inversion of a $D \times D$ matrix has a complexity of $\mathcal{O}(D^3)$. In practice, this means it is difficult to invert matrices whose dimension is larger than a few thousand. Fortunately, matrices are often highly structured, and we can exploit that structure using a number of tricks to speed up the process.

C.8.1   Diagonal and block-diagonal matrices

Diagonal matrices can be inverted by forming a new diagonal matrix, where the values on the diagonal are reciprocal of the original values. Block diagonal matrices are matrices of the form

$$\mathbf{A} = \begin{bmatrix} \mathbf{A}_1 & \mathbf{0} & \cdots & \mathbf{0} \\ \mathbf{0} & \mathbf{A}_2 & \cdots & \mathbf{0} \\ \vdots & \vdots & \ddots & \vdots \\ \mathbf{0} & \mathbf{0} & \cdots & \mathbf{A}_N \end{bmatrix}. \tag{C.55}$$

The inverse of a block-diagonal matrix can be computed by taking the inverse of each block separately so that

$$\mathbf{A}^{-1} = \begin{bmatrix} \mathbf{A}_1^{-1} & \mathbf{0} & \cdots & \mathbf{0} \\ \mathbf{0} & \mathbf{A}_2^{-1} & \cdots & \mathbf{0} \\ \vdots & \vdots & \ddots & \vdots \\ \mathbf{0} & \mathbf{0} & \cdots & \mathbf{A}_N^{-1} \end{bmatrix}. \tag{C.56}$$

C.8.2   Inversion relation #1: Schur complement identity

The inverse of a matrix with sub-blocks $\mathbf{A}$, $\mathbf{B}$, $\mathbf{C}$, and $\mathbf{D}$ in the top-left, top-right, bottom-left, and bottom-right positions, respectively, can easily be shown to be

$$\begin{bmatrix} \mathbf{A} & \mathbf{B} \\ \mathbf{C} & \mathbf{D} \end{bmatrix}^{-1} = \begin{bmatrix} (\mathbf{A} - \mathbf{B}\mathbf{D}^{-1}\mathbf{C})^{-1} & -(\mathbf{A} - \mathbf{B}\mathbf{D}^{-1}\mathbf{C})^{-1}\mathbf{B}\mathbf{D}^{-1} \\ -\mathbf{D}^{-1}\mathbf{C}(\mathbf{A} - \mathbf{B}\mathbf{D}^{-1}\mathbf{C})^{-1} & \mathbf{D}^{-1} + \mathbf{D}^{-1}\mathbf{C}(\mathbf{A} - \mathbf{B}\mathbf{D}^{-1}\mathbf{C})^{-1}\mathbf{B}\mathbf{D}^{-1} \end{bmatrix} \tag{C.57}$$

by multiplying the original matrix with the right-hand side and showing that the result is the identity matrix.

     This result is extremely useful when the matrix $\mathbf{D}$ is diagonal or block-diagonal (Figure C.5). In this circumstance, $\mathbf{D}^{-1}$ is fast to compute, and the remaining inverse quantity $(\mathbf{A} - \mathbf{B}\mathbf{D}^{-1}\mathbf{C})^{-1}$ is much smaller and easier to invert than the original matrix. The quantity $\mathbf{A} - \mathbf{B}\mathbf{D}^{-1}\mathbf{C}$ is known as the Schur complement.

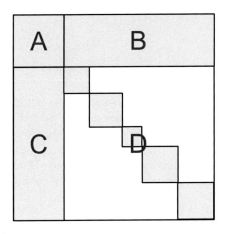

Figure C.5 Inversion relation #1. Gray regions indicate parts of matrix with nonzero values, white regions represent zeros. This relation is suited to the case where the matrix can be divided into four submatrices $\mathbf{A}, \mathbf{B}, \mathbf{C}, \mathbf{D}$, and the bottom right block is easy to invert (e.g., diagonal, block diagonal or structured in another way that means that inversion is efficient). After applying this relation, the remaining inverse is the size of submatrix $\mathbf{A}$.

C.8.3   Inversion relation #2

Consider the $d \times d$ matrix $\mathbf{A}$, the $k \times k$ matrix $\mathbf{C}$, and the $k \times d$ matrix $\mathbf{B}$ where $\mathbf{A}$ and $\mathbf{C}$ are symmetric, positive definite matrices. The following equality holds:

$$(\mathbf{A}^{-1} + \mathbf{B}^T\mathbf{C}^{-1}\mathbf{B})^{-1}\mathbf{B}^T\mathbf{C}^{-1} = \mathbf{A}\mathbf{B}^T(\mathbf{B}\mathbf{A}\mathbf{B}^T + \mathbf{C})^{-1}. \tag{C.58}$$

Proof:

$$\mathbf{B}^T\mathbf{C}^{-1}\mathbf{B}\mathbf{A}\mathbf{B}^T + \mathbf{B}^T = \mathbf{B}^T + \mathbf{B}^T\mathbf{C}^{-1}\mathbf{B}\mathbf{A}\mathbf{B}^T$$

$$\mathbf{B}^T\mathbf{C}^{-1}(\mathbf{B}\mathbf{A}\mathbf{B}^T + \mathbf{C}) = (\mathbf{A}^{-1} + \mathbf{B}^T\mathbf{C}^{-1}\mathbf{B})\mathbf{A}\mathbf{B}^T. \tag{C.59}$$

Taking the inverse of both sides we get

$$(\mathbf{A}^{-1} + \mathbf{B}^T\mathbf{C}^{-1}\mathbf{B})^{-1}\mathbf{B}^T\mathbf{C}^{-1} = \mathbf{A}\mathbf{B}^T(\mathbf{B}\mathbf{A}\mathbf{B}^T + \mathbf{C})^{-1}, \tag{C.60}$$

as required.

This relation is very useful when $\mathbf{B}$ is a landscape matrix with many more columns C than rows R. On the left-hand side, the term we must invert is of size $C \times C$, which might be very costly. However, on the right-hand side, the inversion is only of size $R \times R$, which might be considerably more cost efficient.

C.8.4   Inversion relation #3: Sherman–Morrison–Woodbury

Consider the $d \times d$ matrix $\mathbf{A}$, the $k \times k$ matrix $\mathbf{C}$, and the $k \times d$ matrix $\mathbf{B}$ where $\mathbf{A}$ and $\mathbf{C}$ are symmetric, positive definite matrices. The following equality holds:

$$(\mathbf{A}^{-1} + \mathbf{B}^T\mathbf{C}^{-1}\mathbf{B})^{-1} = \mathbf{A} - \mathbf{A}\mathbf{B}^T(\mathbf{B}\mathbf{A}\mathbf{B}^T + \mathbf{C})^{-1}\mathbf{B}\mathbf{A}. \tag{C.61}$$

This is sometimes known as the *matrix inversion lemma*.

Proof:

$$
\begin{aligned}
(\mathbf{A}^{-1} + \mathbf{B}^T\mathbf{C}^{-1}\mathbf{B})^{-1} &= (\mathbf{A}^{-1} + \mathbf{B}^T\mathbf{C}^{-1}\mathbf{B})^{-1}(\mathbf{I} + \mathbf{B}^T\mathbf{C}^{-1}\mathbf{B}\mathbf{A} - \mathbf{B}^T\mathbf{C}^{-1}\mathbf{B}\mathbf{A}) \\
&= (\mathbf{A}^{-1} + \mathbf{B}^T\mathbf{C}^{-1}\mathbf{B})^{-1}\big((\mathbf{A}^{-1} + \mathbf{B}^T\mathbf{C}^{-1}\mathbf{B})\mathbf{A} - \mathbf{B}^T\mathbf{C}^{-1}\mathbf{B}\mathbf{A}\big) \\
&= \mathbf{A} - (\mathbf{A}^{-1} + \mathbf{B}^T\mathbf{C}^{-1}\mathbf{B})^{-1}\mathbf{B}^T\mathbf{C}^{-1}\mathbf{B}\mathbf{A}.
\end{aligned} \tag{C.62}
$$

Now, applying inversion relation #2 to the term in brackets:

$$
\begin{aligned}
(\mathbf{A}^{-1} + \mathbf{B}^T\mathbf{C}^{-1}\mathbf{B})^{-1} &= \mathbf{A} - (\mathbf{A}^{-1} + \mathbf{B}^T\mathbf{C}^{-1}\mathbf{B})^{-1}\mathbf{B}^T\mathbf{C}^{-1}\mathbf{B}\mathbf{A} \\
&= \mathbf{A} - \mathbf{A}\mathbf{B}^T(\mathbf{B}\mathbf{A}\mathbf{B}^T + \mathbf{C})^{-1}\mathbf{B}\mathbf{A},
\end{aligned} \tag{C.63}
$$

as required.

C.8.5   Matrix determinant lemma

The matrices that we need to invert are often the covariances in the normal distribution. When this is the case, we sometimes also need to compute the determinant of the same matrix. Fortunately, there is a direct analogy of the matrix inversion lemma for determinants.

Consider the $d \times d$ matrix $\mathbf{A}$, the $k \times k$ matrix $\mathbf{C}$ and the $k \times d$ matrix $\mathbf{B}$ where $\mathbf{A}$ and $\mathbf{C}$ are symmetric, positive definite covariance matrices. The following equality holds:

$$|\mathbf{A}^{-1} + \mathbf{B}^T\mathbf{C}^{-1}\mathbf{B}| = |\mathbf{I} + \mathbf{B}\mathbf{A}\mathbf{B}^T||\mathbf{C}|^{-1}|\mathbf{A}|^{-1}. \tag{C.64}$$

Bibliography

Aeschliman, C., Park, J., & Kak, A. C. (2010) A novel parameter estimation algorithm for the multivariate t-distribution and its application to computer vision. In *European Conference on Computer Vision*, pp. 594–607. 100, 105

Agarwal, A., & Triggs, B. (2006) Recovering 3D human pose from monocular images. *IEEE Transactions on Pattern Analysis & Machine Intelligence* **28** (1): 44–48. 109, 129, 131

Agarwal, S., Snavely, N., Seitz, S. M., & Szeliski, R. (2010) Bundle adjustment in the large. In *European Conference on Computer Vision*, pp. 29–42. 381

Agarwal, S., Snavely, N., Simon, I., Seitz, S. M., & Szeliski, R. (2009) Building Rome in a day. In *IEEE International Conference on Computer Vision*, pp. 72–79. 380

Agarwala, A., Dontcheva, M., Agrawala, M., Drucker, S. M., Colburn, A., Curless, B., Salesin, D., & Cohen, M. F. (2004) Interactive digital photomontage. *ACM Transactions on Graphics* **23** (3): 294–302. 261

Aghajanian, J., Warrell, J., Prince, S. J. D., Li, P., Rohn, J. L., & Baum, B. (2009) Patch-based within-object classification. In *IEEE International Conference on Computer Vision*, pp. 1125–1132. 503

Ahonen, T., Hadid, A., & Pietikäinen, M. (2004) Face recognition with local binary patterns. In *European Conference on Computer Vision*, pp. 469–481. 451

Alahari, K., Kohli, P., & Torr, P. H. S. (2008) Reduce, reuse & recycle: Efficiently solving multi-label MRFs. In *IEEE Computer Vision & Pattern Recognition*. 262

Allen, B., Curless, B., & Popovic, Z. (2003) The space of human body shapes: reconstruction and parameterization from range scans. *ACM Transactions on Graphics* **22** (3): 587–594. 421

Aloimonos, J. Y. (1990) Perspective approximations. *Image and Vision Computing* **8** (3): 177–192. 319

Amberg, B., Blake, A., & Vetter, T. (2009) On compositional image alignment, with an application to active appearance models. In *IEEE Computer Vision & Pattern Recognition*, pp. 1714–1721. 421

Amini, A., Weymouth, T., & Jain, R. (1990) Using dynamic programming for solving variational problems in vision. *IEEE Transactions on Pattern Analysis & Machine Intelligence* **12** (9): 855–867. 223, 420

Amit, Y., & Geman, D. (1997) Shape quantization and recognition with randomized trees. *Neural Computation* **9** (7): 1545–1588. 167

Amit, Y., & Kong, A. (1996) Graphical templates for model registration. *IEEE Transactions on Pattern Analysis & Machine Intelligence* **18** (3): 225–236. 222

Andriluka, M., Roth, S., & Schiele, B. (2009) Pictorial structures revisited: People detection and articulated pose estimation. In *IEEE Computer Vision & Pattern Recognition*. 222

Anguelov, D., Srinivasan, P., Koller, D., Thrun, S., Rodgers, J., & Davis, J. (2005) SCAPE: Shape completion and animation of people. *ACM Transactions on Graphics* **24** (3): 408–416. 418, 419, 420, 421

Arulampalam, M., Maskell, S., Gordon, N., & Clapp, T. (2002) A tutorial on particle filters for online nonlinear/non-Gaussian Bayesian tracking. *IEEE Transactions on Signal Processing* **50** (2): 174–188. 480

Avidan, S., & Shamir, A. (2007) Seam carving for content-aware image resizing. *ACM Transactions on Graphics* **26** (3): 10. 222

Ayache, N. (1991) *Artificial Vision for Mobile Robots: Stereo Vision and Multisensory Perception*. MIT Press. 480

Babalola, K., Cootes, T., Twining, C., Petrovic, V., & Taylor, C. (2008) 3D brain segmentation using active appearance models and local regressors. In *Medical Image Computing and Computer-Assisted Intervention 2008*, ed. by D. Metaxas, L. Axel, G. Fichtinger, & G. Székely, volume 5241 of *Lecture Notes in Computer Science*, pp. 401–408. Springer. 406

Bailey, T., & Durrant-Whyte, H. (2006) Simultaneous localization and mapping (SLAM): Part II. *Robotics & Automation Magazine, IEEE* **13** (3): 108–117. 480

Baker, H. H., & Binford, T. O. (1981) Depth from edge and intensity-based stereo. In *International Joint Conference on Artificial Intelligence*, pp. 631–636. 222

Ballan, L., & Cortelazzo, G. M. (2008) Marker-less motion capture of skinned models in a four camera set-up using optical flow and silhouettes. In *3D Data Processing, Visualization and Transmission*. 319

Baluja, S., & Rowley, H. A. (2003) Boosting sex identification performance. *International Journal of Computer Vision* **71** (1): 111–119. 167

Barber, D. (2012) *Bayesian Reasoning and Machine Learning*. Cambridge University Press. 181, 192, 223

Bartlett, M. S., Lades, H. M., & Sejnowski, T. J. (1998) Independent component representations for face recognition. In *Proceedings of the SPIE Symposium on Electronic Imaging: Science and Technology: Conference on Human Vision and Electronic Imaging III*, pp. 528–539. 450

Basri, R., Costa, L., Geiger, D., & Jacobs, D. (1998) Determining the similarity of deformable shapes. *Vision Research* **38** (15–16): 2365–2385. 222

Batlle, J., Mouaddib, E., & Salvi, J. (1998) Recent progress in coded structured light as a technique to solve the correspondence problem: A survey. *Pattern Recognition* **31** (7): 963–982. 319

Baumgart, B. G. (1974) *Geometric modeling for computer vision*. Stanford University PhD dissertation. 319

Bay, H., Ess, A., Tuytelaars, T., & Gool, L. J. V. (2008) Speeded-up robust features (SURF). *Computer Vision and Image Understanding* **110** (3): 346–359. 293

Beardsley, P. A., Reid, I. D., Zisserman, A., & Murray, D. W. (1995) Active visual navigation using non-metric structure. In *IEEE International Conference on Computer Vision*, pp. 58–65. 480

Bekios-Calfa, J., Buenaposada, J. M., & Baumela, L. (2011) Revisiting linear discriminant techniques in gender recognition. *IEEE Transactions on Pattern Analysis & Machine Intelligence* **33** (4): 858–864. 167

Belhumeur, P. N., Hespanha, J. P., & Kriegman, D. J. (1997) Eigenfaces vs. Fisherfaces: Recognition using class specific linear projection. *IEEE Transactions on Pattern Analysis & Machine Intelligence* **19** (7): 711–720. 450

Belkin, M., & Niyogi, P. (2001) Laplacian eigenmaps and spectral techniques for embedding and clustering. In *Advances in Neural Information Processing Systems*, pp. 585–591. 293

Belongie, S., Carson, C., Greenspan, H., & Malik, J. (1998) Color- and texture-based image segmentation using EM and its application to content based image retrieval. In *IEEE International Conference on Computer Vision*, pp. 675–682. 106

Belongie, S., Malik, J., & Puzicha, J. (2002) Shape matching and object recognition using shape contexts. *IEEE Transactions on Pattern Analysis & Machine Intelligence* **24** (4): 509–522. 293

Bengio, Y., & Delalleau, O. (2009) Justifying and generalizing contrastive divergence. *Neural Computation* **21** (6): 1601–1621. 192

Bergtholdt, M., Cremers, D., & Schörr, C. (2005) Variational segmentation with shape priors. In *Handbook of Mathematical Models in Computer Vision*, ed. by Y. C. N. Paragios & O. Faugeras, 131–144. 420

Beymer, D., & Konolige, K. (1999) Real-time tracking of multiple people using continuous detection. In *IEEE Frame Rate Workshop*. 479

Birchfield, S., & Tomasi, C. (1998) Depth discontinuities by pixel-to-pixel stereo. In *IEEE International Conference on Computer Vision*, pp. 1073–1080. 222

Bishop, C. M. (2006) *Pattern Recognition and Machine Learning*. Springer, 2nd edition. 5, 16, 25, 51, 67, 166, 192, 223

Blake, A. (2006) Visual tracking: a short research roadmap. In *Handbook of Mathematical Models in Computer Vision*, ed. by N. Paragios & Y. C. and. O. Faugeras, pp. 293–307. Springer. 479

Blake, A., Curwen, R. W., & Zisserman, A. (1993) A framework for spatiotemporal control in the tracking of visual contours. *International Journal of Computer Vision* **11** (2): 127–145. 262

Blake, A., & Isard, M. (1996) The CONDENSATION algorithm – conditional density propagation and applications to visual tracking. In *Advances in Neural Information Processing Systems*, pp. 361–367. 479

Blake, A., & Isard, M. (1998) *Active Contours*. Springer. 420, 454, 478, 479

Blake, A., Isard, M., & Reynard, D. (1995) Learning to track the visual motion of contours. *Artificial Intelligence* **78** (1–2): 179–212. 262

Blake, A., Kohli, P., & Rother, C., eds. (2011) *Advances in Markov Random Fields for Vision and Image Processing*. MIT Press. 262

Blanz, V., Basso, C., Poggio, T., & Vetter, T. (2003) Reanimating faces in images and video. *Computer Graphics Forum* **22** (3): 641–650. 421

Blanz, V., Grother, P., Phillips, P. J., & Vetter, T. (2005) Face recognition based on frontal views generated from non-frontal images. In *IEEE Computer Vision & Pattern Recognition*, pp. 454–461. 417, 421, 451

Blanz, V., & Vetter, T. (1999) A morphable model for the synthesis of 3D faces. In *SIGGRAPH*, pp. 187–194. 416, 418, 421

Blanz, V., & Vetter, T. (2003) Face recognition based on fitting a 3D morphable model. *IEEE Transactions on Pattern Analysis & Machine Intelligence* **25** (9): 1063–1074. 417, 421

Blei, D. M., Ng, A. Y., & Jordan, M. I. (2003) Latent Dirichlet allocation. *Journal of Machine Learning Research* **3**: 993–1022. 503

Bleyer, M., & Chambon, S. (2010) Does color really help in dense stereo matching? In *International Symposiumon 3D Data Processing, Visualization and Transmission*. 263

Bor Wang, S., Quattoni, A., Morency, L. P., Demirdjian, D., & Darrell, T. (2006) Hidden conditional random fields for gesture recognition. In *IEEE Computer Vision & Pattern Recognition*, pp. 1521–1527. 223

Bosch, A., Zisserman, A., & Munoz, X. (2007) Image classification using random forests and ferns. In *IEEE International Conference on Computer Vision*. 167

Bouwmans, T., Baf, F. E., & Vachon, B. (2010) Statistical background modeling for foreground detection: A survey. In *Handbook of Pattern Recognition and Computer Vision*, ed. by C. H. Chen, L. F. Pau, & P. S. P. Wang, pp. 181–199. World Scientific Publishing. 67

Boykov, Y., & Funka Lea, G. (2006) Graph cuts and efficient N-D image segmentation. *International Journal of Computer Vision* **70** (2): 109–131. 263

Boykov, Y., & Jolly, M.-P. (2001) Interactive graph cuts for optimal boundary and region segmentation of objects in N-D images. In *IEEE International Conference on Computer Vision*, pp. 105–112. 263

Boykov, Y., & Kolmogorov, V. (2004) An experimental comparison of min-cut/max-flow algorithms for energy minimization in vision. *IEEE Transactions on Pattern Analysis & Machine Intelligence* **26** (9): 1124–1137. 262

Boykov, Y., & Veksler, O. (2006) Graph cuts in vision and graphics: Theories and applications. In *Handbook of Mathematical Models in Computer Vision*, ed. by Y. C. N. Paragios & O. Faugeras, pp. 79–96. Springer. 262

Boykov, Y., Veksler, O., & Zabih, R. (1999) Fast approximate energy minimization via graph cuts. In *IEEE International Conference on Computer Vision*, pp. 377–384. 254

Boykov, Y., Veksler, O., & Zabih, R. (2001) Fast approximate energy minimization via graph cuts. *IEEE Transactions on Pattern Analysis & Machine Intelligence* **23** (11): 1222–1239. 261

Brand, J., & Mason, J. (2000) A comparative assessment of three approaches to pixel-level skin-detection. In *International Conference on Pattern Recognition*, pp. 1056–1059. 67

Brand, M. (2002) Charting a manifold. In *Advances in Neural Information Processing Systems*, pp. 961–968. 293

Bregler, C., & Malik, J. (1998) Tracking people with twists and exponential maps. In *IEEE Computer Vision & Pattern Recognition*, pp. 8–15. 421

Breiman, L. (2001) Random forests. *Machine Learning* **45**: 5–32. 167

Brishnapuram, B., Figueiredo, M., Carin, L., & Hartemink, A. (2005) Sparse multinomial logistic regression: Fast algorithms and generalization bounds. *IEEE Transactions on Pattern Analysis & Machine Intelligence* **27** (6): 957–968. 167

Broida, T. J., & Chellappa, R. (1986) Estimation of object motion parameters from noisy images. *IEEE Transactions on Pattern Analysis & Machine Intelligence* **8** (1): 90–99. 479

Brown, M., Hua, G., & Winder, S. A. J. (2011) Discriminative learning of local image descriptors. *IEEE Transactions on Pattern Analysis & Machine Intelligence* **33** (1): 43–57. 293

Brown, M., & Lowe, D. G. (2005) Unsupervised 3D object recognition and reconstruction in unordered datasets. In *3D Digital Imaging and Modeling*, pp. 56–63. 380

Brown, M., & Lowe, D. G. (2007) Automatic panoramic image stitching using invariant features. *International Journal of Computer Vision* **74** (1): 59–73. 351

Brown, M. Z., Burschka, D., & Hager, G. D. (2003) Advances in computational stereo. *IEEE Transactions on Pattern Analysis & Machine Intelligence* **25** (8): 993–1008. 264

Brubaker, M. A., Fleet, D. J., & Hertzmann, A. (2010) Physics-based person tracking using the anthropomorphic walker. *International Journal of Computer Vision* **87** (1–2): 140–155. 421

Brunelli, R., & Poggio, T. (1993) Face recognition: Features versus templates. *IEEE Transactions on Pattern Analysis & Machine Intelligence* **15** (10): 1042–1052. 450

Buchanan, A. M., & Fitzgibbon, A. W. (2005) Damped Newton algorithms for matrix factorization with missing data. In *IEEE Computer Vision & Pattern Recognition*, pp. 316–322. 380

Burgess, C. J. C. (2010) Dimension reduction: a guided tour. *Foundations and Trends in Machine Learning* **2** (4): 275–365. 293

Byröd, M., & Åström, K. (2010) Conjugate gradient bundle adjustment. In *European Conference on Computer Vision*, pp. 114–127. 381

Cai, D., He, X., Hu, Y., Han, J., & Huang, T. S. (2007) Learning a spatially smooth subspace for face recognition. In *IEEE Computer Vision & Pattern Recognition*. 450

Canny, J. (1986) A computational approach to edge detection. *IEEE Transactions on Pattern Analysis & Machine Intelligence* **8** (6): 679–698. 292

Carreira-Perpiñán., M. Á., & Hinton, G. E. (2005) On contrastive divergence learning. In *Artificial Intelligence and Statistics*, volume 2005, p. 17. Citeseer. 192

Caselles, V., Kimmel, R., & Sapiro, G. (1997) Geodesic active contours. *International Journal of Computer Vision* **22** (1): 61–79. 421

Chellappa, R., Sinha, P., & Phillips, P. J. (2010) Face recognition by computers and humans. *IEEE Computer* **43** (2): 46–55. 450

Chen, L.-F., Liao, H.-Y. M., Ko, M.-T., Lin, J.-C., & Yu, G.-J. (2000) A new LDA-based face recognition system which can solve the small sample size problem. *Pattern Recognition* **33** (10): 1713–1726. 450

Chen, R., & Liu, J. S. (2000) Mixture Kalman filters. *Journal of the Royal Statistical Society B.* **62** (3): 493–508. 480

Chen, S. E. (1995) QuickTime VR: An image-based approach to virtual environment navigation. In *SIGGRAPH*, pp. 29–38. 351

Cheung, G. K. M., Baker, S., & Kanade, T. (2004) Shape-from-silhouette across time. Part I: Theory and algorithms. *International Journal of Computer Vision* **62** (3): 221–247. 319

Chia, A. Y. S., Rahardja, S., Rajan, D., & Leung, M. K. H. (2010) Object recognition by discriminative combinations of line segments and ellipses. In *IEEE Computer Vision & Pattern Recognition*, pp. 2225–2232. 421

Chittajallu, D. R., Shah, S. K., & Kakadiaris, I. A. (2010) A shape-driven MRF model for the segmentation of organs in medical images. In *IEEE Computer Vision & Pattern Recognition*, pp. 3233–3240. 263

Cho, Y., Lee, J., & Neumann, U. (1998) A multi-ring color fiducial system and an intensity-invariant detection method for scalable fiducial-tracking augmented reality. In *International Workshop on Augmented Reality*, pp. 147–165. 350

Choi, S., Kim, T., & Yu, W. (2009) Performance evaluation of RANSAC family. In *British Machine Vision Conference*. BMVA Press, pp. 110–119. 350

Chum, O., Philbin, J., Sivic, J., Isard, M., & Zisserman, A. (2007) Total recall: Automatic query expansion with a generative feature model for object retrieval. In *IEEE International Conference on Computer Vision*, pp. 1–8. 504

Chum, O., Werner, T., & Matas, J. (2005) Two-view geometry estimation unaffected by a dominant plane. In *IEEE Computer Vision & Pattern Recognition*, pp. 772–779. 350

Claus, D., & Fitzgibbon, A. W. (2005) A rational function lens distortion model for general cameras. In *IEEE Computer Vision & Pattern Recognition*, pp. 213–219. 319

Cohen, L. (1991) On active contour models and balloons. *CGVIP: Image Understanding* **53** (2): 211–218. 420

Cootes, T. F., Edwards, G. J., & Taylor, C. J. (2001) Active appearance models. *IEEE Transactions on Pattern Analysis & Machine Intelligence* **23** (6): 681–685. 421

Cootes, T. F., & Taylor, C. J. (1997) A mixture model for representing shape variation. In *British Machine Vision Conference*. BMVG Press, pp. 110–119. 421

Cootes, T. F., Taylor, C. J., Cooper, D. H., & Graham, J. (1995) Active shape models – their training and application. *Computer Vision & Image Understanding* **61** (1): 38–59. 420, 421

Cormen, T. H., Leiserson, C. E., Rivest, R. L., & Stein, C. (2001) *Introduction to Algorithms*. MIT Press, 2nd edition. 219, 262

Coughlan, J., Yuille, A., English, C., & Snow, D. (2000) Efficient deformable template detection and localization without user interaction. *Computer Vision & Image Understanding* **78** (3): 303–319. 222

Cristianini, M., & Shawe-Taylor, J. (2000) *An Introduction to Support Vector Machines*. Cambridge University Press. 167

Csurka, G., Dance, C., Fan, L., Williamowski, J., & Bray, C. (2004) Visual categorization with bags of keypoints. In *ECCV International Workshop on Statistical Learning in Computer Vision*. 166, 486, 503

Cuzzolin, F. (2006) Using bilinear models for view-invariant action and identity recognition. In *IEEE Computer Vision & Pattern Recognition*, pp. 1701–1708. 451

Dalal, N., & Triggs, B. (2005) Histograms of oriented gradients for human detection. In *IEEE Computer Vision & Pattern Recognition*, pp. 886–893. 293

Davison, A. J., Reid, I. D., Molton, N., & Stasse, O. (2007) MonoSLAM: Real-time single camera SLAM. *IEEE Transactions on Pattern Analysis & Machine Intelligence* **29** (6): 1052–1067. 477, 478, 479, 480

de Aguiar, E., Stoll, C., Theobalt, C., Ahmed, N., Seidel, H.-P., & Thrun, S. (2008) Performance capture from sparse multi-view video. *ACM Transactions on Graphics* **27** (3): 98:1–98:10. 319

De La Gorce, M., Paragios, N., & Fleet, D. J. (2008) Model-based hand tracking with texture, shading and self-occlusions. In *IEEE Computer Vision & Pattern Recognition*.

De La Torre, F. (2011) A least-squares framework for component analysis. *IEEE Transactions on Pattern Analysis & Machine Intelligence*. 293, 450

De Ridder, D., & Franc, V. (2003) Robust subspace mixture models using t-distributions. In *British Machine Vision Conference*, pp. 319–328. 106

Delaitre, V., Laptev, I., & Sivic, J. (2010) Recognizing human actions in still images: A study of bag-of-features and part-based representations. In *British Machine Vision Conference*. 504

Delong, A., & Boykov, Y. (2009) Globally optimal segmentation of multi-region objects. In *IEEE International Conference on Computer Vision*, pp. 285–292. 263

Dempster, A. P., Laird, M. N., & Rubin, D. B. (1977) Maximum likelihood from incomplete data via the EM algorithm. *Journal of the Royal Statistical Society, Series B* **39** (1): 1–38. 105

Deng, J., Berg, A., Li, K., & Fei-Fei, L. (2010) What does classifying more than 10,000 image categories tell us? *European Conference on Computer Vision*, pp. 71–84. 504

Deng, Y., & Lin, X. (2006) A fast line segment based stereo algorithm using tree dynamic programming. In *European Conference on Computer Vision*, pp. 201–212. 222

Deutscher, J., Blake, A., & Reid, I. D. (2000) Articulated body motion capture by annealed particle filtering. In *IEEE Computer Vision & Pattern Recognition*, pp. 2126–2133. 421

Devernay, F., & Faugeras, O. D. (2001) Straight lines have to be straight. *Mach. Vis. Appl.* **13** (1): 14–24. 319

Dollár, P., Tu, Z., & Belongie, S. (2006) Supervised learning of edges and object boundaries. In *IEEE Computer Vision & Pattern Recognition*, pp. 1964–1971. 166, 292

Domke, J., Karapurkar, A., & Aloimonos, Y. (2008) Who killed the directed model? In *IEEE Computer Vision & Pattern Recognition*. 263

Duda, R. O., Hart, P. E., & Stork, D. G. (2001) *Pattern Classification*. John Wiley and Sons, 2nd edition. 67

Durrant-Whyte, H., & Bailey, T. (2006) Simultaneous localization and mapping (SLAM): Part I. *Robotics & Automation Magazine, IEEE* **13** (2): 99–110. 480

Durrant-Whyte, H., Rye, D., & Nebot, E. (1996) Localisation of automatic guided vehicles. In *International Symposium on Robotics Research*, pp. 613–625. 480

Durrant-Whyte, H. F. (1988) Uncertain geometry in robotics. *IEEE Transactions on Robot Automation* **4** (1): 23–31. 480

Edwards, G. J., Taylor, C. J., & Cootes, T. F. (1998) Interpreting face images using active appearance models. In *IEEE International Conference on Automatic Face & Gesture Recognition*, pp. 300–305. 450

Efros, A. A., & Freeman, W. T. (2001) Image quilting for texture synthesis and transfer. In *SIGGRAPH*, pp. 341–346. 258, 263

Efros, A. A., & Leung, T. K. (1999) Texture synthesis by non-parametric sampling. In *IEEE International Conference on Computer Vision*, pp. 1033–1038. 263

Eichner, M., & Ferrari, V. (2009) Better appearance models for pictorial structures. In *British Machine Vision Conference*. 222

Elder, J. H. (1999) Are edges incomplete? *International Journal of Computer Vision* **34** (2–3): 97–122. 279, 292

Elgammal, A. (2011) Figure-ground segmentation – Pixel-based. In *Guide to Visual Analysis of Humans: Looking at People*, ed. by T. Moeslund, A. Hilton, Krüger, & L. Sigal. Springer. 67

Elgammal, A., Harwood, D., & Davis, L. (2000) Non-parametric model for background subtraction. In *European Conference on Computer Vision*, pp. 751–767. 68

Elgammal, A. M., & Lee, C.-S. (2004) Separating style and content on a nonlinear manifold. In *IEEE Computer Vision & Pattern Recognition*, pp. 478–485. 451

Engels, C., Stewénius, H., & Nistér, D. (2006) Bundle adjustment rules. *Photogrammetric Computer Vision* . 381

Everingham, M., Sivic, J., & Zisserman, A. (2006) Hello! My name is Buffy – Automatic naming of characters in TV video. In *British Machine Vision Conference*, pp. 889–908. 222, 450

Everingham, M., Van Gool, L., Williams, C., Winn, J., & Zisserman, A. (2010) The PASCAL visual object classes (VOC) challenge. *International Journal of Computer Vision* **88** (2): 303–338. 503

Faugeras, O. (1993) *Three-Dimensional Computer Vision: A Geometric Viewpoint*. MIT Press. 319

Faugeras, O., Luong, Q., & Papadopoulo, T. (2001) *The Geometry of Multiple Images*. MIT PRESS. 319, 380

Faugeras, O. D. (1992) What can be seen in three dimensions with an uncalibrated stereo rig. In *European Conference on Computer Vision*, pp. 563–578. 380

Faugeras, O. D., & Keriven, R. (1998) Variational principles, surface evolution, PDEs, level set methods, and the stereo problem. *IEEE Transactions on Image Processing* **7** (3): 336–344. 381

Faugeras, O. D., Luong, Q.-T., & Maybank, S. J. (1992) Camera self-calibration: Theory and experiments. In *European Conference on Computer Vision*, pp. 321–334. 380

Felzenszwalb, P., & Zabih, R. (2011) Dynamic programming and graph algorithms in computer vision. *IEEE Transactions on Pattern Analysis & Machine Intelligence* **33** (4): 721–740. 221, 222, 262

Felzenszwalb, P. F., Girshick, R. B., McAllester, D. A., & Ramanan, D. (2010) Object detection with discriminatively trained part-based models. *IEEE Transactions on Pattern Analysis & Machine Intelligence* **32** (9): 1627–1645. 222, 223

Felzenszwalb, P. F., & Huttenlocher, D. P. (2005) Pictorial structures for object recognition. *International Journal of Computer Vision* **61** (1): 55–79. 219, 220, 221, 222, 421

Felzenszwalb, P. F., & Veksler, O. (2010) Tiered scene labeling with dynamic programming. In *IEEE Computer Vision & Pattern Recognition*. 222, 263

Ferencz, A., Learned-Miller, E. G., & Malik, J. (2008) Learning to locate informative features for visual identification. *International Journal of Computer Vision* **77** (1–3): 3–24. 451

Fischler, M., & Bolles, R. (1981) Random sample consensus: a paradigm for model fitting with application to image analysis and automated cartography. *Communications of the ACM* **24** (6): 381–395. 350

Fischler, M. A., & Erschlager, R. A. (1973) The representation and matching of pictorial structures. *IEEE Transactions on Computers* **22** (1): 67–92. 222

Fitzgibbon, A. W., & Zisserman, A. (1998) Automatic camera recovery for closed or open image sequences. In *European Conference on Computer Vision*, pp. 311–326. 380

Ford, L., & Fulkerson, D. (1962) *Flows in Networks*. Princeton University Press. 262

Forssén, P.-E., & Lowe, D. G. (2007) Shape descriptors for maximally stable extremal regions. In *IEEE International Conference on Computer Vision*, pp. 1–8. 293

Förstner, W. (1986) A feature-based correspondence algorithm for image matching. *International Archives of Photogrammetry and Remote Sensing* **26** (3): 150–166. 292

Forsyth, D. A., Arikan, O., Ikemoto, L., O'Brien, J., & Ramanan, D. (2006) Computational studies of human motion: Part 1, Tracking and motion synthesis. *Foundations and Trends in Computer Graphics and Computer Vision* **1** (2/2): 77–254. 421

Frahm, J.-M., Georgel, P. F., Gallup, D., Johnson, T., Raguram, R., Wu, C., Jen, Y.-H., Dunn, E., Clipp, B., & Lazebnik, S. (2010) Building Rome on a cloudless day. In *European Conference on Computer Vision*, pp. 368–381. 378

Frahm, J.-M., & Pollefeys, M. (2006) RANSAC for (quasi-)degenerate data (QDEGSAC). In *IEEE Computer Vision & Pattern Recognition*, pp. 453–460. 350

Franco, J.-S., & Boyer, E. (2005) Fusion of multi-view silhouette cues using a space occupancy grid. In *IEEE International Conference on Computer Vision*, pp. 1747–1753. 319

Freeman, W. T., Pasztor, E. C., & Carmichael, O. T. (2000) Learning low-level vision. *International Journal of Computer Vision* **40**: 25–47. 223, 257, 261

Freifeld, O., Weiss, A., Zuffi, S., & Black, M. J. (2010) Contour people: A parameterized model of 2D articulated human shape. In *IEEE Computer Vision & Pattern Recognition*, pp. 639–646. 420

Freiman, M., Kronman, A., Esses, S. J., Joskowicz, L., & Sosna, J. (2010) Non-parametric iterative model constraint graph min-cut for automatic kidney segmentation. In *Medical Image Computing and Computer-Assisted Intervention*, pp. 73–80. 263

Freund, Y., & Schapire, R. (1996) Experiments with a new boosting algorithm. In *International Conference on Machine Learning*, pp. 148–156. 167

Freund, Y., & Schapire, R. E. (1995) A decision-theoretic generalization of on-line learning and an application to boosting. In *Computational Learning Theory: Eurocolt '95*, pp. 23–37. 167

Frey, B., Kschischang, F., Loeliger, H., & Wiberg, N. (1997) Factor graphs and algorithms. In *Allerton Conference on Communication, Control and Computing*. 223

Frey, B. J., & Jojic, N. (1999a) Estimating mixture models of images and inferring spatial transformations using the EM algorithm. In *IEEE Computer Vision & Pattern Recognition*, pp. 416–422. 106

Frey, B. J., & Jojic, N. (1999b) Transformed component analysis: Joint estimation of spatial transformations and image components. In *IEEE Computer Vision & Pattern Recognition*, pp. 1190–1196. 106

Friedman, J., Hastie, T., & Tibshirani, R. (2000) Additive logistic regression: A statistical view of boosting. *Annals of Statistics* **28** (2): 337–407. 167

Friedman, J. H. (1999) Greedy function approximation: A gradient boosting machine. Technical report, Department of Statistics, Stanford University. 167

Friedman, N., & Russell, S. J. (1997) Image segmentation in video sequences: A probabilistic approach. In *Uncertainty in Artificial Intelligence*, pp. 175–181. 68

Fua, P., & Leclerc, Y. G. (1995) Object-centered surface reconstruction: Combining multi-image stereo and shading. *International Journal of Computer Vision* **16** (1): 35–56. 381

Fusiello, A., Trucco, E., & Verri, A. (2000) A compact algorithm for rectification of stereo pairs. *Machine Vision and Applications* **12** (1): 16–22. 380

Gao, X.-S., Hou, X., Tang, J., & Cheng, H.-F. (2003) Complete solution classification for the perspective-three-point problem. *IEEE Transactions on Pattern Analysis & Machine Intelligence* **25** (8): 930–943. 319

Gavrila, D., & Davis, L. S. (1996) 3-D model-based tracking of humans in action: A multi-view approach. In *IEEE Computer Vision & Pattern Recognition*, pp. 73–80. 421

Geiger, B., Ladendorf, B., & Yuille, A. (1992) Occlusions and binocular stereo. In *European Conference on Computer Vision*, pp. 425–433. 222

Geiger, D., Gupta, A., Costa, L. A., & Vlontzos, J. (1995) Dynamic-programming for detecting, tracking and matching deformable contours. *IEEE Transactions on Pattern Analysis & Machine Intelligence* **17** (3): 294–302. 223

Gelb, A. (1974) *Applied Optimal Estimation*. MIT Press. 479

Gelman, A., Carlin, J. B., Stern, H. S., & Rubin, D. B. (2004) *Bayesian Data Analysis*. Chapman and Hall / CRC. 25, 41

Geman, S., & Geman, D. (1984) Stochastic relaxation, Gibbs distributions, and the Bayesian restoration of images. *IEEE Transactions on Pattern Analysis & Machine Intelligence* **6** (6): 721–741. 260

Geyer, C., & Daniilidis, K. (2001) Catadioptric projective geometry. *International Journal of Computer Vision* **45** (3): 223–243. 319

Ghahramani, Z. (2001) An introduction to hidden Markov models and Bayesian networks. In *Hidden Markov Models: Applications in Computer Vision*, ed. by B. H. Juang, pp. 9–42. World Scientific Publishing. 223

Ghahramani, Z., & Hinton, G. (1996a) Parameter estimation for linear dynamical systems. Technical Report CRG–TR–96–2, Department of Computer Science, University of Toronto. 480

Ghahramani, Z., & Hinton, G. (1996b) Switching state-space models. Technical Report CRG–TR–96–3, Department of Computer Science, University of Toronto. 480

Ghahramani, Z., & Hinton, G. E. (1996c) The EM algorithm for mixtures of factor analyzers. Technical Report CRG–TR–96–1, University of Toronto. 105

Goldberg, A., & Tarjan, R. (1988) A new approach to the maximum flow problem. *Journal of the Association for Computing Machinery* **35** (4): 921–940. 262

Golomb, B. A., Lawrence, D. T., & Sejnowski, T. (1990) SEXNET: a neural network identifies sex from human faces. In *Advances in Neural Information Processing Systems*, pp. 572–579. 167

Gong, M., & Yang, Y. H. (2005) Near real-time reliable stereo matching using programmable graphics hardware. In *IEEE Computer Vision & Pattern Recognition*, pp. 924–931. 222

Gonzalez, R. C., & Woods, R. E. (2002) *Digital Image Processing*. Prentice Hall, 2nd edition. 292

Gower, J. C., & Dijksterhuis, G. B. (2004) *Procrustes Problems*. Oxford University Press. 350

Grady, L. (2006) Random walks for image segmentation. *IEEE Transactions on Pattern Analysis & Machine Intelligence* **28** (11): 1768–1783. 263

Grauman, K., & Darrell, T. (2005) The pyramid match kernel: Discriminative classification with sets of image features. In *IEEE International Conference on Computer Vision*, pp. 1458–1465. 503

Grauman, K., Shakhnarovich, G., & Darrell, T. (2003) A Bayesian approach to image-based visual hull reconstruction. In *IEEE Computer Vision & Pattern Recognition*, pp. 187–194. 319

Greig, D. M., Porteous, B. T., & Seheult, A. H. (1989) Exact maximum a posteriori estimation for binary images. *Journal of the Royal Statistical Society. Series B* **51** (2): 271–279. 261

Grimes, D. B., Shon, A. P., & Rao, R. P. N. (2003) Probabilistic bilinear models for appearance-based vision. In *IEEE International Conference on Computer Vision*, pp. 1478–1485. 451

Gross, R., Matthews, I., & Baker, S. (2002) Eigen light-fields and face recognition across pose. In *Automated Face and Gestured Recongnition*, pp. 3–9. 451

Guesebroek, J. M., Bughouts, G. J., & Smeulders, A. W. M. (2005) The Amsterdam library of object images. *International Journal of Computer Vision* **61** (1): 103–112. 100, 101

Guillaumin, M., Verbeek, J. J., & Schmid, C. (2009) Is that you? Metric learning approaches for face identification. In *IEEE International Conference on Computer Vision*, pp. 498–505. 451

Guivant, J. E., & Nebot, E. M. (2001) Optimization of the simultaneous localization and map-building algorithm for real-time implementation. *IEEE Transactions on Robotics* **17** (3): 242–257. 480

Handa, A., Chli, M., Strasdat, H., & Davison, A. J. (2010) Scalable active matching. In *IEEE Computer Vision & Pattern Recognition*, pp. 1546–1553. 480

Harris, C. (1992) Tracking with rigid objects. In *Active Vision*, ed. by A. Blake & A. L. Yuille, pp. 59–73. 350

Harris, C., & Stephens, M. J. (1988) A combined corner and edge detector. In *Alvey Vision Conference*, pp. 147–152. 292, 380

Harris, C. G., & Pike, J. M. (1987) 3D positional integration from image sequences. In *Alvey Vision Conference*, pp. 233–236. 480

Hartley, R. I. (1992) Estimation of relative camera positions for uncalibrated cameras. In *European Conference on Computer Vision*, pp. 579–587. 380 380

Hartley, R. I. (1994) Projective reconstruction from line correspondence. In *IEEE Computer Vision & Pattern Recognition*, pp. 579–587.

Hartley, R. I. (1997) In defense of the eight-point algorithm. *IEEE Transactions on Pattern Analysis & Machine Intelligence* **19** (6): 580–593. 364, 380

Hartley, R. I., & Gupta, R. (1994) Linear pushbroom cameras. In *European Conference on Computer Vision*, pp. 555–566. 319

Hartley, R. I., & Zisserman, A. (2004) *Multiple View Geometry in Computer Vision.* Cambridge University Press, 2nd edition. 5, 306, 319, 338, 350, 360, 370, 380

He, X., Yan, S., Hu, Y., Niyogi, P., & Zhang, H. (2005) Face recognition using Laplacianfaces. *IEEE Transactions on Pattern Analysis & Machine Intelligence* **27** (3): 328–340. 450

He, X., Zemel, R. S., & Carreira-Perpiñán, M. Á. (2004) Multiscale conditional random fields for image labeling. In *IEEE Computer Vision & Pattern Recognition*, pp. 695–702. 166, 167

He, X., Zemel, R. S., & Ray, D. (2006) Learning and incorporating top-down cues in image segmentation. In *European Conference on Computer Vision*, pp. 338–351. 167

Heap, T., & Hogg, D. (1996) Towards 3D hand tracking using a deformable model. In *IEEE International Conference on Automatic Face & Gesture Recognition*, pp. 140–145. 422

Heeger, D., & Bergen, J. (1995) Pyramid-based texture analysis/synthesis. In *Computer Graphics and Interactive Techniques*, pp. 229–238. ACM. 263

Heess, N., Williams, C. K. I., & Hinton, G. E. (2009) Learning generative texture models with extended fields of experts. In *British Machine Vision Conference*. 263

Hernández, C., & Schmitt, F. (2004) Silhouette and stereo fusion for 3D object modeling. *Computer Vision & Image Understanding* **96** (3): 367–392. 381

Hinton, G. E. (2002) Training products of experts by minimizing contrastive divergence. *Neural Computation* **14** (8): 1771–1800. 192

Hirschmüller, H. (2005) Accurate and efficient stereo processing by semi-global matching and mutual information. In *IEEE Computer Vision & Pattern Recognition*, pp. 807–814. 264

Hirschmüller, H., & Scharstein, D. (2009) Evaluation of stereo matching costs on images with radiometric differences. *IEEE Transactions on Pattern Analysis & Machine Intelligence* **31** (9): 1582–1599. 263

Hofmann, T. (1999) Probabilistic latent semantic analysis. In *Uncertainty in Artificial Intelligence*, pp. 289–296. 503

Hogg, D. (1983) Model-based vision: a program to see a walking person. *Image and Vision Computing* **1** (1): 5–20. 421

Hoiem, D., Efros, A., & Hebert, M. (2005) Automatic photo pop-up. *ACM Transcations on Graphics (SIGGRAPH)* **24** (3): 577–584. 164

Hoiem, D., Efros, A. A., & Hebert, M. (2007) Recovering surface layout from an image. *International Journal of Computer Vision* **75** (1): 151–172. 163, 165, 166

Horn, B. K. P. (1990) Relative orientation. *International Journal of Computer Vision* **4** (1): 59–78. 380

Horn, E., & Kiryati, N. (1999) Toward optimal structured light patterns. *Image and Vision Computing* **17** (2): 87–97. 319

Horprasert, T., Harwood, D., & Davis, L. S. (2000) A robust background subtraction and shadow detection. In *Asian Conference on Computer Vision*, pp. 983–988. 68

Hsu, R. L., Abdel-Mottaleb, M., & Jain, A. K. (2002) Face detection in color images. *IEEE Transactions on Pattern Analysis & Machine Intelligence* **24** (5): 696–707. 67

Huang, C., Ai, H., Li, Y., & Lao, S. (2007a) High-performance rotation invariant multi-view face detection. *IEEE Transactions on Pattern Analysis & Machine Intelligence* **29** (4): 671–686. 167

Huang, G. B., Ramesh, M., Berg, T., & Learned-Miller, E. (2007b) Labeled faces in the wild: A database for studying face recognition in unconstrained environments. Technical Report Technical Report 07–49, University of Massachusetts, Amherst. 447, 451

Huang, T. S., & Faugeras, O. D. (1989) Some properties of the E matrix in two-view motion estimation. *IEEE Transactions on Pattern Analysis & Machine Intelligence* **11** (12): 1310–1312. 380

Huang, Y., Liu, Q., & Metaxas, D. N. (2011) A component-based framework for generalized face alignment. *IEEE Transactions on Systems, Man, and Cybernetics, Part B* **41** (1): 287–298. 414, 421

Huber, P. J. (2009) *Robust Statistics*. John Wiley and Sons, 2nd edition. 350

Humayun, A., Oisin, M. A., & Brostow, G. J., (2011) *Learning to Find Occlusion Regions*, In *IEEE Computer Vision and Pattern Recognition*.

Ioffe, S. (2006) Probabilistic linear discriminant analysis. In *European Conference on Computer Vision*, pp. 531–542. 450

Isack, H., & Boykov, Y. (2012) Energy-based geometric multi-model fitting. *International Journal of Computer Vision* **97** (2), pp. 123–147. 261, 347, 350

Isard, M., & Blake, A. (1998) A mixed-state CONDENSATION tracker with automatic model-switching. In *IEEE International Conference on Computer Vision*, pp. 107–112. 480

Ishikawa, H. (2003) Exact optimization for Markov random fields with convex priors. *IEEE Transactions on Pattern Analysis & Machine Intelligence* **25** (10): 1333–1336. 261

Ishikawa, H. (2009) Higher order clique reduction in binary graph cut. In *IEEE Computer Vision & Pattern Recognition*. 263

Jazwinski, A. H. (1970) *Stochastic Processes and Filtering Theory*. Academic Press. 479

Jegou, H., Douze, M., & Schmid, C. (2008) Recent advances in large scale image search. In *Emerging Trends in Visual Computing*, pp. 305–326. 503

Jégou, H., Douze, M., & Schmid, C. (2009) Packing bag-of-features. In *IEEE International Conference on Computer Vision*, pp. 2357–2364. 504

Jeong, Y., Nistér, D., Steedly, D., Szeliski, R., & Kweon, I.-S. (2010) Pushing the envelope of modern methods for bundle adjustment. In *IEEE Computer Vision & Pattern Recognition*, pp. 1474–1481. 381

Jiang, H., & Martin, D. R. (2008) Global pose estimation using non-tree models. In *IEEE Computer Vision & Pattern Recognition*. 222

Jojic, N., & Frey, B. J. (2001) Learning flexible sprites in video layers. In *IEEE Computer Vision & Pattern Recognition*, pp. 199–206. 106

Jojic, N., Frey, B. J., & Kannan, A. (2003) Epitomic analysis of appearance and shape. In *IEEE International Conference on Computer Vision*, pp. 34–41. 106

Jones, E., & Soatto, S. (2005) Layered active appearance models. In *IEEE International Conference on Computer Vision*, pp. 1097–1102. 421

Jones, M. J., & Rehg, J. M. (2002) Statistical color models with application to skin detection. *International Journal of Computer Vision* **46** (1): 81–96. 67, 105

Jordan, M. I. (2004) Graphical models. *Statistical science* **19** (1): 140–155. 192

Jordan, M. I., & Jacobs, R. A. (1994) Hierarchical mixtures of experts and the EM algorithm. *Neural Computation* **6** (2): 181–214. 168

Juan, O., & Boykov, Y. (2006) Active graph cuts. In *IEEE Computer Vision & Pattern Recognition*, pp. 1023–1029. 262

Julier, S., & Uhlmann, J. (1997) A new extension of the Kalman filter to nonlinear systems. In *International Symposium on Aerospace/Defense Sensing, Simulation and Controls*, volume 3, p. 26. 479

Kadir, T., & Brady, M. (2001) Saliency, scale and image description. *International Journal of Computer Vision* **45** (2): 83–105. 292

Kakumanu, P., Makrogiannis, S., & Bourbakis, N. G. (2007) A survey of skin-colour modeling and detection methods. *Pattern Recognition* **40** (3): 1106–1122. 67

Kalman, R. E. (1960) A new approach to linear filtering and prediction problems. *Journal of Basic Engineering* **82** (1): 35–45. 479

Kalman, R. E., & Bucy, R. S. (1961) New results in linear filtering and prediction theory. *Transactions of the American Society for Mechanical Engineering D* **83** (1): 95–108. 479

Kanade, T., Rander, P., & Narayanan, P. J. (1997) Virtualized reality: Constructing virtual worlds from real scenes. *IEEE MultiMedia* **4** (1): 34–47. 319

Kass, M., Witkin, A., & Terzopolous, D. (1987) Snakes: Active contour models. *International Journal of Computer Vision* **1** (4): 321–331. 223, 420

Kato, H., & Billinghurst, M. (1999) Marker tracking and HMD calibration for a video-based augmented reality conferencing system. In *International Workshop on Augmented Reality*, pp. 85–94. 350

Kato, H., Billinghurst, M., Poupyrev, I., Imamoto, K., & Tachibana, K. (2000) Virtual object manipulation on a table-top AR environment. In *International Symposium on Augmented Reality*, pp. 111–119. 350

Kendall, D. G. (1984) Shape manifolds, Procrustean metrics, and complex projective spaces. *Bulletin of the London Mathematical Society* **16** (2): 81–121. 388

Khan, Z., & Dellaert, F. (2004) Robust generative subspace modelling: The subspace t-distribution. Technical Report GIT–GVU–04–11, Georgia Institute of Technology. 105

Kim, J. C., Lee, K. M., Choi, B., & Lee, S. U. (2005) A dense stereo matching using two pass dynamic programming with generalized control points. In *IEEE Computer Vision & Pattern Recognition*, pp. 1075–1082. 222

Klein, G., & Murray, D. (2007) Parallel tracking and mapping for small AR workspaces. In *Proc. Sixth IEEE and ACM International Symposium on Mixed and Augmented Reality (ISMAR'07)*. 480

Kohli, P., Kumar, M. P., & Torr, P. H. S. (2009a) P3 & beyond: Move making algorithms for solving higher order functions. *IEEE Transactions on Pattern Analysis & Machine Intelligence* **31** (9): 1645–1656. 263

Kohli, P., Ladicky, L., & Torr, P. H. S. (2009b) Robust higher order potentials for enforcing label consistency. *International Journal of Computer Vision* **82** (3): 302–324. 263

Kohli, P., & Torr, P. H. S. (2005) Efficiently solving dynamic Markov random fields using graph cuts. In *IEEE International Conference on Computer Vision*, pp. 922–929. 262

Kolev, K., & Cremers, D. (2008) Integration of multiview stereo and silhouettes via convex functionals on convex domains. In *European Conference on Computer Vision*, pp. 752–765. 381

Koller, D., & Friedman, N. (2009) *Probabilistic Graphical Models*. MIT Press. 181, 192, 223

Koller, D., Klinker, G., Rose, E., Breen, D., Whitaker, R., & Tuceryan, M. (1997) Real-time vision-based camera tracking for augmented reality applications. In *ACM Symposium on Virtual Reality Software and Technology*, pp. 87–94. 350

Kolmogorov, V. (2006) Convergent tree-reweighted message passing for energy minimization. *IEEE Transactions on Pattern Analysis & Machine Intelligence* **28** (10): 1568–1583. 263

Kolmogorov, V., Criminisi, A., Blake, A., Cross, G., & Rother, C. (2006) Probabilistic fusion of stereo with color and contrast for bi-layer segmentation. *IEEE Transactions on Pattern Analysis & Machine Intelligence* **28** (9): 1480–1492. 261

Kolmogorov, V., & Rother, C. (2007) Minimizing non-submodular graph functions with graph-cuts – A review. *IEEE Transactions on Pattern Analysis & Machine Intelligence* **29** (7): 1274–1279. 262, 263

Kolmogorov, V., & Zabih, R. (2001) Computing visual correspondence with occlusions via graph cuts. In *IEEE International Conference on Computer Vision*, pp. 508–515. 255, 261, 263

Kolmogorov, V., & Zabih, R. (2002) Multi-camera scene reconstruction via graph cuts. In *European Conference on Computer Vision*, pp. 82–96. 261

Kolmogorov, V., & Zabih, R. (2004) What energy functions can be minimized via graph cuts? *IEEE Transactions on Pattern Analysis & Machine Intelligence* **26** (2): 147–159. 262

Komodakis, N., Tziritas, G., & Paragios, N. (2008) Performance vs computational efficiency for optimizing single and dynamic MRFs: Setting the state of the art with primal-dual strategies. *Computer Vision & Image Understanding* **112** (1): 14–29. 262

Kotz, S., & Nadarajah, S. (2004) *Multivariate t Distributions and Their Applications*. Cambridge University Press. 105

Kschischang, F. R., Frey, B., & Loeliger, H. A. (2001) Factor graphs and the sum-product algorithm. *IEEE Transactions on Information Theory* **47** (2): 498–519. 223

Kumar, M. P., Torr, P., & Zisserman, A. (2004) Extending pictorial structures for object recognition. In *British Machine Vision Conference*, pp. 789–798. 222

Kumar, M. P., Torr, P. H. S., & Zisserman, A. (2005) OBJ CUT. In *IEEE Computer Vision & Pattern Recognition*, pp. 18–25. 263

Kumar, M. P., Veksler, O., & Torr, P. H. S. (2011) Improved moves for truncated convex models. *Journal of Machine Learning Research* **12**: 31–67. 262

Kumar, N., Belhumeur, P., & Nayar, S. K. (2008) Face tracer: A search engine for large collections of images with faces. In *European Conference on Computer Vision*. 166, 167

Kumar, N., Berg, A. C., Belhumeur, P. N., & Nayar, S. K. (2009) Attribute and simile classifiers for face verification. In *IEEE International Conference on Computer Vision*, pp. 365–372. 451

Kumar, S., & Hebert, M. (2003) Discriminative random fields: A discriminative framework for contextual interaction in classification. In *IEEE International Conference on Computer Vision*, pp. 1150–1159. 261

Kutulakos, K. N., & Seitz, S. M. (2000) A theory of shape by space carving. *International Journal of Computer Vision* **38** (3): 199–218. 381

Kwatra, V., Schödl, A., Essa, I., Turk, G., & Bobick, A. (2003) Graphcut textures: Image and video synthesis using graph cuts. *ACM Transactions on Graphics (SIGGRAPH 2003)* **22** (3): 277–286. 261, 263

Lanitis, A., Taylor, C. J., & Cootes, T. F. (1997) Automatic interpretation and coding of face images using flexible models. *IEEE Transactions on Pattern Analysis & Machine Intelligence* **19** (7): 743–756. 421

Laptev, I., Marszałek, M., Schmid, C., & Rozenfeld, B. (2008) Learning realistic human actions from movies. In *IEEE Computer Vision & Pattern Recognition.* 501, 502, 503, 504

Laurentini, A. (1994) The visual hull concept for silhouette-based image understanding. *IEEE Transactions on Pattern Analysis & Machine Intelligence* **16** (2): 150–162. 319

Lawrence, N. D. (2004) Probabilistic non-linear principal component analysis with Gaussian process latent variable models. Technical Report CS–04–08, University of Sheffield. 105, 293

Lawrence, N. D. (2005) Probabilistic non-linear principal component analysis with Gaussian process latent variable models. *Journal of Machine Learning Research* **6**: 1783–1816. 421

Lazebnik, S., Schmid, C., & Ponce, J. (2006) Beyond bags of features: Spatial pyramid matching for recognizing natural scene categories. In *IEEE Computer Vision & Pattern Recognition*, pp. 2169–2178. 503

Lee, J., Moghaddam, B., Pfister, H., & Machiraju, R. (2005) A bilinear illumination model for robust face recognition. In *IEEE International Conference on Computer Vision*, pp. 1177–1184. 451

Lempitsky, V., Blake, A., & Rother, C. (2008) Image segmentation by branch-and-mincut. In *European Conference on Computer Vision*, pp. 15–29. 263

Lempitsky, V., Rother, C., Roth, S., & Blake, A. (2010) Fusion moves for Markov random field optimization. *IEEE Transactions on Pattern Analysis & Machine Intelligence* **32** (8): 1392–1405. 262

Leonard, J. J., & Feder, H. J. S. (2000) A computational efficient method for large-scale concurrent mapping and localisation. In *International Symposium on Robotics Research*, pp. 169–176. 480

Leordeanu, M., Hebert, M., & Sukthankar, R. (2007) Beyond local appearance: Category recognition from pairwise interactions of simple features. In *IEEE Computer Vision & Pattern Recognition.* 421

Leotta, M. J., & Mundy, J. L. (2011) Vehicle surveillance with a generic, adaptive, 3D vehicle model. *IEEE Transactions on Pattern Analysis & Machine Intelligence* **33** (7): 1457–1469. 421

Lepetit, V., & Fua, P. (2005) Monocular model-based 3D tracking of rigid objects: A survey. *Foundations and Trends in Computer Graphics and Vision* **1** (1): 1–89. 351

Lepetit, V., & Fua, P. (2006) Keypoint recognition using randomized trees. *IEEE Transactions on Pattern Analysis & Machine Intelligence* **28** (9): 1465–1479. 350

Lepetit, V., Lagger, P., & Fua, P. (2005) Randomized trees for real-time keypoint recognition. In *IEEE Computer Vision & Pattern Recognition*, pp. 775–781. 166, 167, 348

Lepetit, V., Moreno-Noguer, F., & Fua, P. (2009) EPnP: An accurate $O(n)$ solution to the PnP problem. *International Journal of Computer Vision* **81** (2): 155–166. 319

Leventon, M. E., Grimson, W. E. L., & Faugeras, O. D. (2000) Statistical shape influence in geodesic active contours. In *IEEE Computer Vision & Pattern Recognition*, pp. 1316–1323. 421

Levin, A., Lischinski, D., & Weiss, Y. (2004) Colorization using optimization. *ACM Transactions on Graphics* **23** (3): 689–694. 261

Lhuillier, M., & Quan, L. (2002) Match propagation for image-based modeling and rendering. *IEEE Transactions on Pattern Analysis & Machine Intelligence* **24** (8): 1140–1146. 264

Li, F.-F., & Perona, P. (2005) A Bayesian hierarchical model for learning natural scene categories. In *IEEE Computer Vision & Pattern Recognition*, pp. 524–531. 503, 504

Li, J., & Allinson, N. M. (2008) A comprehensive review of current local features for computer vision. *Neurocomputing* **71** (10–12): 1771–1787. 292

Li, P., Fu, Y., Mohammed, U., Elder, J., & Prince, S. J. D. (2012) Probabilistic models for inference about identity. *IEEE Transactions on Pattern Analysis & Machine Intelligence* **34**(1): 144–157. 435, 447, 450, 451

Li, P., Warrell, J., Aghajanian, J., & Prince, S. (2010) Context-based additive logistic model for facial keypoint localization. In *British Machine Vision Conference*, pp. 1–11. 450

Li, S. Z. (2010) *Markov Random Field Modeling in Image Analysis*. Springer, 3rd edition. 261

Li, S. Z., & Jain, A. K. eds. (2005) *Handbook of Face Recognition*. Springer. 450

Li, S. Z., & Zhang, Z. (2004) Floatboost learning and statistical face detection. *IEEE Transactions on Pattern Analysis & Machine Intelligence* **26** (9): 1112–1123. 167

Li, S. Z., Zhang, Z. Q., Shum, H. Y., & Zhang, H. J. (2003) Floatboost learning for classification. In *Advances in Neural Information Processing Systems*, pp. 993–1000. 167

Li, S. Z., Zhuang, Z., Blake, A., Zhang, H., & Shum, H. (2002) Statistical learning of multi-view face detection. In *European Conference on Computer Vision*, pp. 67–82. 167

Li, Y., Du, Y., & Lin, X. (2005) Kernel-based multifactor analysis for image synthesis and recognition. In *IEEE International Conference on Computer Vision*, pp. 114–119. 451

Li, Y., Sun, J., Tang, C.-K., & Shum, H.-Y. (2004) Lazy snapping. *ACM Transactions on Graphics* **23** (3): 303–308. 263

Lienhart, R., Kuranov, A., & Pisarevsky, V. (2003) Empirical analysis of detection cascades of boosted classifiers for rapid object detection. In *Deutsche Arbeitsgemeinschaft für Mustererkennung*, pp. 297–304. 167

Liu, C., & Rubin, D. B. (1995) ML estimation of the t distribution using EM and its extensions ECM and ECME. *Statistica Sinica* **5** (1): 19–39. 105

Liu, C., & Shum, H. Y. (2003) Kullback-Leibler boosting. In *IEEE Computer Vision & Pattern Recognition*, pp. 407–411. 167

Liu, C., & Wechsler, H. (1998) Probabilistic reasoning models for face recognition. In *IEEE Computer Vision & Pattern Recognition*, pp. 827–832. 450

Liu, J., Sun, J., & Shum, H.-Y. (2009) Paint selection. *ACM Transactions on Graphics* **28** (3): 69:1–68:7. 263

Longuet-Higgins, H. C. (1981) A computer algorithm for reconstructing a scene from two projections. *Nature* **293**: 133–135. 380

Loop, C. T., & Zhang, Z. (1999) Computing rectifying homographies for stereo vision. In *IEEE Computer Vision & Pattern Recognition*, pp. 1125–1131. 380

Lourakis, M. I. A., & Argyros, A. A. (2009) SBA: A software package for generic sparse bundle adjustment. *ACM Transactions on Mathematical Software* **36**(1): 2:2:30. 381

Lowe, D. G. (2004) Distinctive image features from scale-invariant keypoints. *International Journal of Computer Vision* **60** (2): 91–110. 292, 293, 380, 451

Loxam, J., & Drummond, T. (2008) Student-t mixture filter for robust, real-time visual tracking. In *European Conference on Computer Vision*, pp. 372–385. 105

Lu, S., Metaxas, D. N., Samaras, D., & Oliensis, J. (2003) Using multiple cues for hand tracking and model refinement. In *IEEE Computer Vision & Pattern Recognition*, pp. 443–450. 422

Lucas, B. D., & Kanade, T. (1981) An iterative image registration technique with an application to stereo vision. In *International Joint Conference on Artificial Intelligence*, pp. 647–679. 380

Lucey, S., & Chen, T. (2006) Learning patch dependencies for improved pose mismatched face verification. In *IEEE Computer Vision & Pattern Recognition*, pp. 909–915. 451

Ma, Y., Derksen, H., Hong, W., & Wright, J. (2007) Segmentation of multivariate mixed data via lossy data coding and compression. *IEEE Transactions on Pattern Analysis & Machine Intelligence* **29** (9): 1546–1562. 106

Ma, Y., Soatto, S., & Kosecká, J. (2004) *An Invitation to 3-D Vision*. Springer. 319, 380

Mac Aodha, O., Brostow, G. J. and Pollefeys, M. (2010) Segmenting video into classes of algorithm suitability, In *IEEE Computer Vision and Pattern Recognition*. 167

Mackay, D. J. (2003) *Information Theory, Learning and Inference Algorithms*. Cambridge University Press. 41

Makadia, A. (2010) Feature tracking for wide-baseline image retrieval. In *European Conference on Computer Vision*, pp. 310–323. 504

Mäkinen, E., & Raisamo, R. (2008a) Evaluation of gender classification methods with automatically detected and aligned faces. *IEEE Transactions on Pattern Analysis & Machine Intelligence* **30** (3): 541–547. 167

Mäkinen, E., & Raisamo, R. (2008b) An experimental comparison of gender classification methods. *Pattern Recognition Methods* **29** (10): 1544–1556. 167

Malcolm, J. G., Rathi, Y., & Tannenbaum, A. (2007) Graph cut segmentation with nonlinear shape priors. In *IEEE International Conference on Image Processing*, pp. 365–368. 263

Malladi, R., Sethian, J. A., & Vemuri, B. C. (1994) Evolutionary fronts for topology-independent shape modeling and recoveery. In *European Conference on Computer Vision*, pp. 3–13. 421

Matas, J., Chum, O., Urban, M., & Pajdla, T. (2002) Robust wide baseline stereo from maximally stable extremal regions. In *British Machine Vision Conference*, pp. 348–393. 292

Matthews, I., & Baker, S. (2004) Active appearance models revisited. *International Journal of Computer Vision* **60** (2): 135–164. 421

Matthews, I., Cootes, T. F., Bangham, J. A., Cox, S., & Harvey, R. (2002) Extraction of visual features for lipreading. *IEEE Transactions on Pattern Analysis & Machine Intelligence* **24** (2): 198–213. 421

Matthews, I., Xiao, J., & Baker, S. (2007) 2D vs. 3D deformable face models: Representational power, construction, and real-time fitting. *International Journal of Computer Vision* **75** (1): 93–113. 417, 419, 421

Matthies, L., Kanade, T., & Szeliski, R. (1989) Kalman filter-based algorithms for estimating depth from image sequences. *International Journal of Computer Vision* **3** (3): 209–238. 479

Matusik, W., Buehler, C., Raskar, R., Gortler, S. J., & McMillan, L. (2000) Image-based visual hulls. In *SIGGRAPH*, pp. 369–374. 319

Maybank, S. J. (1998) *Theory of Reconstruction from Image Motion*. Springer-Verlag. 380

Maybeck, P. S. (1990) The Kalman filter: An introduction to concepts. In *Autonomous Robot Vehicles*, ed. by I. J. Cox & G. T. Wilfong, pp. 194–204. Springer-Verlag. 479

McLachlan, G. J., & Krishnan, T. (2008) *The EM Algorithm and Extensions*. Wiley, 2nd edition. 105

Mei, C., Sibley, G., Cummins, M., Newman, P., & Reid, I. (2009) A constant time efficient stereo SLAM system. In *British Machine Vision Conference*. 480

Meir, R., & Mätsch, G. (2003) An introduction to boosting and leveraging. In *Advanced Lectures on Machine Learning*, ed. by S. Mendelson & A. Smola, pp. 119–184. Springer. 167

Messer, K., Matas, J., Kittler, J., Luettin, J., & Maitre, G. (1999) XM2VTS: The extended M2VTS database. In *Conference on Audio and Video-based Biometric Personal Verification*, pp. 72–77. 451

Mikolajczyk, K., & Schmid, C. (2002) An affine invariant interest point detector. In *European Conference on Computer Vision*, pp. 128–142. 292

Mikolajczyk, K., & Schmid, C. (2004) Scale & affine invariant interest point detectors. *International Journal of Computer Vision* **60** (1): 63–86. 292

Mikolajczyk, K., & Schmid, C. (2005) A performance evaluation of local descriptors. *IEEE Transactions on Pattern Analysis & Machine Intelligence* **27** (10): 1615–1630. 293

Mikolajczyk, K., Tuytelaars, T., Schmid, C., Zisserman, A., Matas, J., Schaffalitzky, F., Kadir, T., & Gool, L. J. V. (2005) A comparison of affine region detectors. *International Journal of Computer Vision* **65** (1–2): 43–72. 292

Mikulík, A., Perdoch, M., Chum, O., & Matas, J. (2010) Learning a fine vocabulary. In *European Conference on Computer Vision*, pp. 1–14. 504

Minka, T. (2002) Bayesian inference in dynamic models: an overview. Technical report, Carnegie Mellon University. 480

Moeslund, T. B., Hilton, A., & Krüger, V. (2006) A survey of advances in vision-based human motion capture and analysis. *Computer Vision & Image Understanding* **104** (2–3): 90–126. 421

Moghaddam, B., Jebara, T., & Pentland, A. (2000) Bayesian face recognition. *Pattern Recognition* **33** (11): 1771–1782. 450, 452

Moghaddam, B., & Pentland, A. (1997) Probabilistic visual learning for object representation. *IEEE Transactions on Pattern Analysis & Machine Intelligence* **19** (7): 696–710. 106, 450

Moghaddam, B., & Yang, M. H. (2002) Learning gender with support faces. *IEEE Transactions on Pattern Analysis & Machine Intelligence* **24** (5): 707–711. 167

Mohammed, U., Prince, S. J. D., & Kautz, J. (2009) Visio-lization: Generating novel facial images. *ACM Transactions on Graphics (SIGGRAPH)* **28**(3). 259, 261

Moni, M. A., & Ali, A. B. M. S. (2009) HMM based hand gesture recognition: A review on techniques and approaches. In *International Conference on Computer Science and Information Technology*, pp. 433–437. 223

Montemerlo, M., Thrun, S., Koller, D., & Wegbreit, B. (2002) FastSLAM: A factored solution to the simultaneous localization and mapping problem. In *Proceedings of AAAI National Conference on Artifical Intelligence*, pp. 593–598. 480

Montemerlo, M., Thrun, S., Koller, D., & Wegbreit, B. (2003) FastSLAM 2.0: An improved particle filtering algorithm for simultaneous localization and mapping that provably converges. In *International Joint Conference on Artifical Intelligence*, pp. 1151–1156. 480

Moons, T. (1998) A guided tour through multiview relations. In *SMILE*, ed. by R. Koch & L. J. V. Gool, volume 1506 of *Lecture Notes in Computer Science*, pp. 304–346. Springer. 380

Moons, T., Van Gool, L. J., & Vergauwen, M. (2009) 3D reconstruction from multiple images: Part 1 – Principles. *Foundations and Trends in Computer Graphics and Vision* **4** (4): 287–404. 380

Moore, A. P., Prince, S. J. D., & Warrell, J. (2010) "Lattice Cut" – constructing superpixels using layer constraints. In *IEEE Computer Vision & Pattern Recognition*, pp. 2117–2124. 261, 263

Moore, A. P., Prince, S. J. D., Warrell, J., Mohammed, U., & Jones, G. (2008) Superpixel lattices. In *IEEE Computer Vision & Pattern Recognition*. 222

Moosmann, F., Nowak, E., & Jurie, F. (2008) Randomized clustering forests for image classification. *IEEE Transactions on Pattern Analysis & Machine Intelligence* **30** (9): 1632–1646. 167

Moosmann, F., Triggs, B., & Jurie, F. (2006) Fast discriminative visual codebooks using randomized clustering forests. In *Advances in Neural Information Processing Systems*, pp. 985–992. 167

Moravec, H. (1983) The Stanford cart and the CMU rover. *Proceedings of the IEEE* **71** (7): 872–884. 292

Mori, G., Ren, X., Efros, A. A., & Malik, J. (2004) Recovering human body configurations: Combining segmentation and recognition. In *IEEE Computer Vision & Pattern Recognition*, pp. 326–333. 421

Mundy, J., & Zisserman, A. (1992) *Geometric Invariance in Computer Vision*. MIT Press. 319

Murase, H., & Nayar, S. K. (1995) Visual learning and recognition of 3-d objects from appearance. *International Journal of Computer Vision* **14** (1): 5–24. 106

Murino, V., Castellani, U., Etrari, E., & Fusiello, A. (2002) Registration of very time-distant aerial images. In *IEEE International Conference on Image Processing*, pp. 989–992. 350

Murphy, K., Weiss, Y., & Jordan, M. (1999) Loopy belief propagation for approximate inference: An empirical study. In *Uncertainty in Artificial Intelligence*, pp. 467–475. 223

Murphy, K. P. (1998) Switching Kalman Filters. Technical report. Department of Computer Science, University of California, Berkeley. 480

Mǐcušík, B., & Pajdla, T. (2003) Estimation of omnidirectional camera model from epipolar geometry. In *IEEE Computer Vision & Pattern Recognition*, pp. 485–490. 319

Nadarajah, S., & Kotz, S. (2008) Estimation methods for the multivariate t distribution. *Acta Applicandae Mathematicae: An International Survey Journal on Applying Mathematics and Mathematical Applications* **102** (1): 99–118. 105

Navaratnam, R., Fitzgibbon, A. W., & Cippola, R. (2007) The joint manifold model for semi-supervised multi-valued regression. In *IEEE International Conference on Computer Vision*, pp. 1–8. 131

Neal, R., & Hinton, G. (1999) A view of the EM algorithm that justifies incremental, sparse and other variants. In *Learning in Graphical Models*, ed. by M. I. Jordan. MIT PRess. 105

Newcombe, R. A., & Davison, A. J. (2010) Live dense reconstruction with a single moving camera. In *IEEE Computer Vision & Pattern Recognition*, pp. 1498–1505. 380

Newcombe, R. A., Lovegrove, S., & Davison, A. J. (2011) DTAM: Dense tracking and mapping in real-time. In *IEEE International Conference on Computer Vision*. 480

Newman, P., & Ho, K. L. (2005) SLAM – Loop closing with visually salient features. In *IEEE International Conference on Robotics and Automation*. 480

Nguyen, H. V., & Bai, L. (2010) Cosine similarity metric learning for face verification. In *Asian Conference on Computer Vision*, pp. 709–720. 451

Niebles, J. C., Wang, H., & 0002, Li, F.-.F. (2008) Unsupervised learning of human action categories using spatial-temporal words. *International Journal of Computer Vision* **79** (3): 299–318. 504

Nistér, D. (2004) An efficient solution to the five-point relative pose problem. *IEEE Transactions on Pattern Analysis & Machine Intelligence* **26** (6): 756–777. 380

Nistér, D., Naroditsky, O., & Bergen, J. R. (2004) Visual odometry. In *IEEE Computer Vision & Pattern Recognition*, pp. 652–659. 480

Nistér, D., & Stewénius, H. (2006) Scalable recognition with a vocabulary tree. In *IEEE Computer Vision & Pattern Recognition*, pp. 2161–2168. 503

Nixon, M., & Aguado, A. S. (2008) *Feature Extraction and Image Processing*. Academic Press, 2nd edition. 5, 292

Nowak, E., & Jurie, F. (2007) Learning visual similarity measures for comparing never seen objects. In *IEEE Computer Vision & Pattern Recognition*. 451

O'Gorman, L., Sammon, M. J., & Seul, M. (2008) *Practical Algorithms for Image Analysis*. Cambridge University Press, 2nd edition. 292

Oh, S. M., Rehg, J. M., Balch, T. R., & Dellaert, F. (2005) Learning and inference in parametric switching linear dynamical systems. In *IEEE International Conference on Computer Vision*, pp. 1161–1168. 480

Ohta, Y., & Kanade, T. (1985) Stereo by intra- and inter-scanline search using dynamic programming. *IEEE Transactions on Pattern Analysis & Machine Intelligence* **7** (2): 139–154. 217, 222

Ojala, T., Pietikäinen, M., & Mäenpää, T. (2002) Multiresolution gray-scale and rotation invariant texture classification with local binary patterns. *IEEE Transactions on Pattern Analysis & Machine Intelligence* **24** (7): 971–987. 293, 451

Oliver, N., Rosario, B., & Pentland, A. (2000) A Bayesian computer vision system for modeling human interactions. *IEEE Transactions on Pattern Analysis & Machine Intelligence* **22** (8): 831–843. 68, 223

Opelt, A., Pinz, A., & Zisserman, A. (2006) A boundary-fragment-model for object detection. In *European Conference on Computer Vision*, pp. 575–588. 421

Osuna, E., Freund, R., & Girosi, F. (1997) Training support vector machines: An application to face detection. In *IEEE Computer Vision & Pattern Recognition*, pp. 746–751. 167

Özuysal, M., Calonder, M., Lepetit, V., & Fua, P. (2010) Fast keypoint recognition using random ferns. *IEEE Transactions on Pattern Analysis & Machine Intelligence* **32** (3): 448–461. 350

Papoulis, A. (1991) *Probability, Random Variables and Stochastic Processes*. McGraw Hill, 3rd edition. 16

Pearl, J. (1988) *Probabilistic Reasoning in Intelligent Systems*. Morgan Kaufmann. 223

Peel, D., & McLachlan, G. (2000) Robust mixture modelling using the t distribution. *Statistics and Computing* **10** (4): 339–348. 105

Perlibakas, V. (2004) Distance measures for PCA-based face recognition. *Pattern Recognition Letters* **25** (6): 711–724. 450

Petersen, K. B., Pedersen, M. S., Larsen, J., Strimmer, K., Christiansen, L., Hansen, K., He, L., Thibaut, L., Baro, M., Hattinger, S., Sima, V., & The, W. (2006) The matrix cookbook. Technical University of Denmark. 528

Pham, M., & Cham, T. (2007a) Fast training and selection of Haar features using statistics in boosting-based face detection. In *IEEE International Conference on Computer Vision*. 167

Pham, M., & Cham, T. (2007b) Online learning asymmetric boosted classifiers for object detection. In *IEEE Computer Vision & Pattern Recognition*. 167

Philbin, J., Chum, O., Isard, M., Sivic, J., & Zisserman, A. (2007) Object retrieval with large vocabularies and fast spatial matching. In *IEEE Computer Vision & Pattern Recognition*. 503

Philbin, J., Isard, M., Sivic, J., & Zisserman, A. (2010) Descriptor learning for efficient retrieval. In *European Conference on Computer Vision*, pp. 677–691. 293

Phillips, P. J., Moon, H., Rizvi, S. A., & Rauss, P. J. (2000) The FERET evaluation methodology for face-recognition algorithms. *IEEE Transactions on Pattern Analysis & Machine Intelligence* **22** (10): 1090–1104. 451

Phung, S., Bouzerdoum, A., & Chai, D. (2005) Skin segmentation using color pixel classification: Analysis and comparison. *IEEE Transactions on Pattern Analysis & Machine Intelligence* **27** (1): 147–154. 67

Piccardi, M. (2004) Background subtraction techniques: a review. In *IEEE Int. Conf. Systems, Man and Cybernetics*, pp. 3099–3105. 67

Pinto, N., & Cox, D. (2011) Beyond simple features: A large-scale feature search approach to unconstrained face recognition. In *IEEE International Conference on Automatic Face & Gesture Recognition*. 451

Pollefeys, M. (2002) Visual 3D modeling from images. *On-line tutorial: http://www.cs. unc.edu/marc/tutorial* . 380

Pollefeys, M., Koch, R., & Van Gool, L. J. (1999a) Self-calibration and metric reconstruction inspite of varying and unknown intrinsic camera parameters. *International Journal of Computer Vision* **32** (1): 7–25. 376

Pollefeys, M., Koch, R., & Van Gool, L. J. (1999b) A simple and efficient rectification method for general motion. In *IEEE International Conference on Computer Vision*, pp. 496–501. 371, 380

Pollefeys, M., & Van Gool, L. J. (2002) Visual modelling: From images to images. *Journal of Visualization and Computer Animation* **13** (4): 199–209. 376, 377

Pollefeys, M., Van Gool, L. J., Vergauwen, M., Verbiest, F., Cornelis, K., Tops, J., & Koch, R. (2004) Visual modeling with a hand-held camera. *International Journal of Computer Vision* **59** (3): 207–232. 377, 380

Pons, J.-P., Keriven, R., & Faugeras, O. D. (2007) Multi-view stereo reconstruction and scene flow estimation with a global image-based matching score. *International Journal of Computer Vision* **72** (2): 179–193. 381

Poppe, R. (2007) Vision-based human motion analysis: An overview. *Computer Vision and Image Understanding* **108** (1–2): 4–18. 421, 479

Portilla, J., & Simoncelli, E. (2000) A parametric texture model based on joint statistics of complex wavelet coefficients. *International Journal of Computer Vision* **40** (1): 49–70. 263

Pratt, W. H. (2007) *Digital Image Processing*. Wiley Interscience, 3rd edition. 292

Prince, S., Cheok, A. D., Farbiz, F., Williamson, T., Johnson, N., Billinghurst, M., & Kato, H. (2002) 3D live: Real time captured content for mixed reality. In *International Symposium on Mixed and Augmented Reality*, pp. 317–324. 317, 318, 319

Prince, S. J. D., & Aghajanian, J. (2009) Gender classification in uncontrolled settings using additive logistic models. In *IEEE International Conference on Image Processing*, pp. 2557–2560. 160, 167

Prince, S. J. D., Elder, J. H., Warrell, J., & Felisberti, F. M. (2008) Tied factor analysis for face recognition across large pose differences. *IEEE Transactions on Pattern Analysis & Machine Intelligence* **30** (6): 970–984. 441, 443, 451

Prinzie, A., & Van den Poel, D. (2008) Random forests for multiclass classification: Random multinomial logit. *Expert Systems with Applications* **35** (3): 1721–1732. 167

Pritch, Y., Kav-Venaki, E., & Peleg, S. (2009) Shift-map image editing. In *IEEE International Conference on Computer Vision*, pp. 151–158. 255, 256, 261

Quan, L., & Lan, Z.-D. (1999) Linear n-point camera pose determination. *IEEE Transactions on Pattern Analysis & Machine Intelligence* **21** (8): 774–780. 319

Rabiner, L. (1989) A tutorial on hidden Markov models and selected applications in speech recognition. *Proceedings of the IEEE* **77** (2): 257–286. 223

Rae, R., & Ritter, H. (1998) Recognition of human head orientation based on artificial neural networks. *IEEE Transactions on Neural Networks* **9** (2): 257–265. 131

Raguram, R., Frahm, J.-M., & Pollefeys, M. (2008) A comparative analysis of RANSAC techniques leading to adaptive real-time random sample consensus. In *European Conference on Computer Vision*, pp. 500–513. 350

Ramanan, D., Forsyth, D. A., & Zisserman, A. (2008) Tracking people by learning their appearance. *IEEE Transactions on Pattern Analysis & Machine Intelligence* **29** (1): 65–81. 222

Ranganathan, A. (2009) Semantic scene segmentation using random multinomial logit. In *British Machine Vision Conference*. 167

Ranganathan, A., & Yang, M. (2008) Online sparse matrix Gaussian process regression and vision applications. In *European Conference on Computer Vision*, pp. 468–482. 131

Raphael, C. (2001) Course-to-fine dynamic programming. *IEEE Transactions on Pattern Analysis & Machine Intelligence* **23** (12): 1379–1390. 222

Rasmussen, C. E., & Williams, C. K. I. (2006) *Gaussian Processes for Machine Learning.* MIT Press. 131, 167

Rehg, J., & Kanade, T. (1994) Visual tracking of high DOF articulated structures: an application to human hand tracking. In *European Conference on Computer Vision*, pp. 35–46. 422

Rehg, J. M., & Kanade, T. (1995) Model-based tracking of self-occluding articulated objects. In *IEEE International Conference on Computer Vision*, pp. 612–617. 422

Rehg, J. M., Morris, D. D., & Kanade, T. (2003) Ambiguities in visual tracking of articulated objects using two- and three-dimensional models. *International Journal of Robotics Research* **22**(6): 393–418. 421

Rekimoto, J. (1998) MATRIX: A realtime object identification and registration method for augmented reality. In *Asia Pacific Computer Human Interaction*, pp. 63–69. 350

Ren, X., Berg, A. C., & Malik, J. (2005) Recovering human body configurations using pairwise constraints between parts. In *IEEE International Conference on Computer Vision*, pp. 824–831. 222

Rigoll, G., Kosmala, A., & Eickeler, S. (1998) High performance real-time gesture recognition using hidden Markov models. In *International Workshop on Gesture and Sign language in Human-Computer Interaction*. 223

Rogez, G., Rihan, J., Ramalingam, S., Orrite, C., & Torr, P. (2006) Randomized trees for human pose detection. In *Advances in Neural Information Processing Systems*, pp. 985–992. 167

Romdhani, S., Cong, S., & Psarrou, A. (1999) A multi-view non-linear active shape model using kernel PCA. In *British Machine Vision Conference*. 421

Rosales, R., & Sclaroff, S. (1999) 3D trajectory recovery for tracking multiple objects and trajectory guided recognition of actions. In *IEEE Computer Vision & Pattern Recognition*, pp. 2117–2123. 476, 477, 479

Rosen-Zvi, M., Griffiths, T. L., Steyvers, M., & Smyth, P. (2004) The author–topic model for authors and documents. In *Uncertainty in Artificial Intelligence*, pp. 487–494. 503

Rosenblatt, F. (1958) The Perceptron: A probabilistic model for information storage and organization in the brain. *Psychological Review* **65** (6): 386–408. 167

Rosten, E., & Drummond, T. (2006) Machine learning for high-speed corner detection. In *European Conference on Computer Vision*, volume 1, pp. 430–443. 292

Roth, S., & Black, M. J. (2009) Fields of experts. *International Journal of Computer Vision* **82** (2): 205–229. 105, 263

Rother, C., Bordeaux, L., Hamadi, Y., & Blake, A. (2006) Autocollage. *ACM Transactions on Graphics* **25** (3): 847–852.

Rother, C., Kohli, P., Feng, W., & Jia, J. (2009) Minimizing sparse higher order energy functions of discrete variables. In *IEEE Computer Vision & Pattern Recognition*, pp. 1382–1389.

Rother, C., Kolmogorov, V., & Blake, A. (2004) Grabcut – Interactive foreground extraction using iterated graph cuts. *ACM Transactions on Graphics (SIGGRAPH 2004)* **23** (3): 309–314. 261, 263

Rother, C., Kolmogorov, V., Lempitsky, V. S., & Szummer, M. (2007) Optimizing binary MRFs via extended roof duality. In *IEEE Computer Vision & Pattern Recognition*. 262

Rother, C., Kumar, S., Kolmogorov, V., & Blake, A. (2005) Digital tapestry. In *IEEE Computer Vision & Pattern Recognition*, pp. 589–586. 253

Rothwell, C. A., Zisserman, A., Forsyth, D. A., & Mundy, J. L. (1995) Planar object recognition using projective shape representation. *International Journal of Computer Vision* **16** (1): 57–99. 352

Rousseeuw, P. J. (1984) Least median of squares regression. *Journal of the American Statistical Association* **79** (388): 871–880. 350

Rousson, M., & Paragios, N. (2002) Shape priors for level set representations. In *European Conference on Computer Vision*, pp. 78–92. 421

Roweis, S., & Saul, L. (2000) Nonlinear dimensionality reduction by locally linear embedding. *Science* **290** (5500): 2323–2326. 293

Roweis, S. T., & Ghahramani, Z. (1999) A unifying review of linear Gaussian models. *Neural Computation* **11** (2): 305–345. 480

Roweis, S. T., & Ghahramani, Z. (2001) Learning nonlinear dynamical systems using the expectation-maximization algorithm. In *Kalman Filtering and Neural Networks*, ed. by S. Haykin, pp. 175–220. Wiley. 480

Rubin, D., & Thayer, D. (1982) EM algorithms for ML factor analysis. *Psychometrica* **47** (1): 69–76. 105, 421

Rumelhart, D. E., Hinton, G. E., & Williams, R. (1986) Learning internal representations by error propagation. In *Parallel Distributed Processing: Explorations in the Microstructure of Cognition. Volume 1: Foundations*, ed. by D. Rumelhart, J. McLelland, & The PDP Research Group, pp. 318–362. MIT Press. 167

Salmen, J., Schlipsing, M., Edelbrunner, J., Hegemann, S., & Lüke, S. (2009) Real-time stereo vision: Making more out of dynamic programming. In *Proceedings of the 13th International Conference on Computer Analysis of Images and Patterns*, CAIP '09, pp. 1096–1103. Springer-Verlag. 222

Salvi, J., Pags, J., & Batlle, J. (2004) Pattern codification strategies in structured light systems. *Pattern Recognition* **37** (4): 827 – 849. 319

Schaffalitzky, F., & Zisserman, A. (2002) Multi-view matching for unordered image sets, or "how do i organize my holiday snaps?". In *European Conference on Computer Vision*, pp. 414–431.

Schapire, R., & Singer, Y. (1998) Improved boosting algorithms using confidence-rated predictions. In *Conference on Computational Learning Theory*, pp. 80–91. 167

Scharstein, D., & Szeliski, R. (2002) A taxonomy and evaluation of dense two-frame stereo correspondence algorithms. *International Journal of Computer Vision* **47** (1): 7–42. 264

Scharstein, D., & Szeliski, R. (2003) High-accuracy depth maps using structured light. In *IEEE Computer Vision & Pattern Recognition*, pp. 194–202. 314, 315, 316, 319

Schlesinger, D., & Flach, B. (2006) Transforming an arbitrary minsum problem into a binary one. Technical Report TUD–FI06–01, Dresden University of Technology. 261

Schmugge, S. J., Jayaram, S., Shin, M., & Tsap, L. (2007) Objective evaluation of approaches to skin detection using roc analysis. *Computer Vision & Image Understanding* **108** (1–2): 41–51. 67

Schneiderman, H., & Kanade, T. (2000) A statistical method for 3D object detection applied to faces and cards. In *IEEE International Conference on Computer Vision*, pp. 746–751. 167

Schölkopf, B., Smola, A. J., & Müller, K.-R. (1997) Kernel principal component analysis. In *International Conference on Artificial Neural Networks*, pp. 583–588. 293

Schölkopf, B., Smola, A. J., & Müller, K.-R. (1998) Nonlinear component analysis as a kernel eigenvalue problem. *Neural Computation* **10** (5): 1299–1319. 421

Schüldt, C., Laptev, I., & Caputo, B. (2004) Recognizing human actions: A local SVM approach. In *International Conference on Pattern Recognition*, pp. 32–36. 502, 503, 504

Seitz, S. M., Curless, B., Diebel, J., Scharstein, D., & Szeliski, R. (2006) A comparison and evaluation of multi-view stereo reconstruction algorithms. In *IEEE Computer Vision & Pattern Recognition*, pp. 519–528. 381

Seo, H., & Magnenat-Thalmann, N. (2003) An automatic modeling of human bodies from sizing parameters. In *ACM Symposium on Interactive 3D Graphics*, pp. 19–26. 422

Sfikas, G., Nikou, C., & Galatsanos, N. (2007) Robust image segmentation with mixtures of Student's t-distributions. In *IEEE International Conference on Image Processing*, pp. 273–276. 102, 106

Sha'ashua, A., & Ullman, S. (1988) Structural saliency: The detection of globally salient structures using a locally connected network. In *IEEE International Conference on Computer Vision*, pp. 321–327. 222

Shakhnarovich, G., Viola, P. A., & Darrell, T. (2003) Fast pose estimation with parameter-sensitive hashing. In *IEEE International Conference on Computer Vision*, pp. 750–759. 421

Shan, C. (2012) Learning local binary patterns for gender classification on real-world face images. *Pattern Recognition Letters*, **33** (4), pp. 431–437. 167

Shepherd, B. (1983) An appraisal of a decision tree approach to image classification. In *International Joint Conferences on Artificial Intelligence*, pp. 473–475. 167

Shi, J., & Tomasi, C. (1994) Good features to track. In *IEEE Computer Vision & Pattern Recognition*, pp. 311–326. 380

Shotton, J., Blake, A., & Cipolla, R. (2008a) Multiscale categorical object recognition using contour fragments. *IEEE Transactions on Pattern Analysis & Machine Intelligence* **30** (7): 1270–1281. 421

Shotton, J., Fitzgibbon, A. W., Cook, M., Sharp, T., Finoccio, M., Moore, R., Kipman, A., & Blake, A. (2011) Real-time human pose recognition in parts from single depth images. In *IEEE Computer Vision & Pattern Recognition*. 164, 166, 167

Shotton, J., Johnson, M., & Cipolla, R. (2008b) Semantic texton forests for image categorization and segmentation. In *IEEE Computer Vision & Pattern Recognition*. 167

Shotton, J., Winn, J., Rother, C., & Criminisi, A. (2009) Textonboost for image understanding: Multi-class object recognition and segmentation by jointly modeling texture, layout and context. *International Journal of Computer Vision* **81** (1): 2–23. 163, 164, 167, 261, 278

Shum, H.-Y., & Szeliski, R. (2000) Construction of panoramic image mosaics with global and local alignment. *International Journal of Computer Vision* **36** (2): 101–130. 351

Shumway, R. H., & Stoffer, D. S. (1991) Dynamic linear models with switching. *Journal of the American Statistical Association* **86** (415): 763–769. 480

Shumway, R. H., & Stoffer, D. S. (1982) An approach to time series smoothing and forecasting using the EM algorithm. *J. Time Series Analysis* **3** (4): 253–264. 480

Sidenbladh, H., Black, M. J., & Fleet, D. J. (2000) Stochastic tracking of 3D human figures using 2D image motion. In *European Conference on Computer Vision*, pp. 702–718. 421

Sigal, L., Balan, A. O., & Black, M. J. (2010) HumanEva: Synchronized video and motion capture dataset and baseline algorithm for evaluation of articulated human motion. *International Journal of Computer Vision* **87** (1–2): 4–27. 421

Sigal, L., & Black, M. J. (2006) Measure locally, reason globally: Occlusion-sensitive articulated pose estimation. In *IEEE Computer Vision & Pattern Recognition*, pp. 2041–2048. 222

Sim, R., Elinas, P., Griffin, M., & Little, J. (2005) Vision-based SLAM using the Rao-Blackwellised particle filter. In *IJCAI Workshop on Reasoning with Uncertainty in Robotics*, pp. 9–16. 480

Simon, G., & Berger, M.-O. (2002) Pose estimation for planar structures. *IEEE Computer Graphics and Applications* **22** (6): 46–53. 350

Simon, G., Fitzgibbon, A. W., & Zisserman, A. (2000) Markerless tracking using planar structures in the scene. In *International Symposium on Mixed and Augmented Reality*, pp. 120–128. 350

Sinha, S. N., Mordohai, P., & Pollefeys, M. (2007) Multi-view stereo via graph cuts on the dual of an adaptive tetrahedral mesh. In *IEEE International Conference on Computer Vision*, pp. 1–8. 381

Sinha, S. N., & Pollefeys, M. (2005) Multi-view reconstruction using photo-consistency and exact silhouette constraints: A maximum-flow formulation. In *IEEE International Conference on Computer Vision*, pp. 349–356. 381

Sivic, J., Russell, B. C., Efros, A. A., Zisserman, A., & Freeman, W. T. (2005) Discovering objects and their localization in images. In *IEEE International Conference on Computer Vision*, pp. 370–377. 503

Sivic, J., Russell, B. C., Zisserman, A., Freeman, W. T., & Efros, A. A. (2008) Unsupervised discovery of visual object class hierarchies. In *IEEE Computer Vision & Pattern Recognition*. 503

Sivic, J., & Zisserman, A. (2003) Video google: A text retrieval approach to object matching in videos. In *IEEE International Conference on Computer Vision*, pp. 1470–1477. 500, 503

Sizintsev, M., Kuthirummal, S., Sawhney, H., Chaudhry, A., Samarasekera, S., & Kumar, R. (2010) GPU accelerated realtime stereo for augmented reality. In *International Symposium 3D Data Processing, Visualization and Transmission*. 373

Sizintsev, M., & Wildes, R. P. (2010) Coarse-to-fine stereo vision with accurate 3d boundaries. *Image and Vision Computing* **28** (3): 352–366. 264

Skrypnyk, I., & Lowe, D. G. (2004) Scene modelling, recognition and tracking with invariant image features. In *International Symposium on Mixed and Augmented Reality*, pp. 110–119. 350

Smith, R., & Cheeseman, P. (1987) On the representation of spatial uncertainty. *International Journal of Robotics Research* **5** (4): 56–68. 480

Smith, R., Self, M., & Cheeseman, P. (1990) Estimating uncertain spatial relationships in robotics. In *Autonomous Robot Vehicles*, ed. by I. J. Cox & G. T. Wilton, pp. 167–193. Springer. 480

Smith, S. M., & Brady, J. M. (1997) Susan - A new approach to low level image processing. *International Journal of Computer Vision* **23** (1): 45–78. 292

Snavely, N., Garg, R., Seitz, S. M., & Szeliski, R. (2008) Finding paths through the world's photos. *ACM Transactions on Graphics (Proceedings of SIGGRAPH 2008)* **27** (3): 11–21. 378

Snavely, N., Seitz, S. M., & Szeliski, R. (2006) Photo tourism: Exploring photo collections in 3D. In *SIGGRAPH Conference Proceedings*, pp. 835–846. ACM Press. 377, 378

Starck, J., Maki, A., Nobuhura, S., Hilton, A., & Mastuyama, T. (2009) The multiple-camera 3-D production studio. *IEEE Transactions on Circuits and Systems for Video Technology* **19** (6): 856–869. 319

Starner, T., Weaver, J., & Pentland, A. (1998) A wearable computer based American sign language recognizer. In *Assistive Technology and Artificial Intelligence*, Lecture Notes in Computer Science, volume 1458, pp. 84–96. 216, 217, 223

State, A., Hirota, G., Chen, D. T., Garrett, W. F., & Livingston, M. A. (1996) Superior augmented reality registration by integrating landmark tracking and magnetic tracking. In *ACM SIGGRAPH*, pp. 429–438. 350

Stauffer, C., & Grimson, E. (1999) Adaptive background classification using time-based co-occurences. In *IEEE Computer Vision & Pattern Recognition*, pp. 246–252. 68, 105

Stegmann, M. B. (2002) Analysis and segmentation of face images using point annotations and linear subspace techniques. Technical report, Informatics and Mathematical Modelling, Technical University of Denmark, DTU, Richard Petersens Plads, Building 321, DK–2800 Kgs. Lyngby. 406, 408, 421

Stenger, B., Mendonça, P. R. S., & Cipolla, R. (2001a) Model-based 3D tracking of an articulated hand. In *IEEE Computer Vision & Pattern Recognition*, pp. 310–315. 416, 422

Stenger, B., Mendonça, P. R. S., & Cipolla, R. (2001b) Model-based hand tracking using an unscented Kalman filter. In *British Machine Vision Conference*. 479

Stewénius, H., Engels, C., & Nistér, D. (2006) Recent developments on direct relative orientation. *ISPRS Journal of Photogrammetry and Remote Sensing* **60**: 284–294. 380

Strasdat, H., Montiel, J. M. M., & Davison, A. J. (2010) Real-time monocular SLAM: Why filter? In *IEEE International Conference on Robotics and Automation*, pp. 2657–2664. 480

Sturm, P. F. (2000) Algorithms for plane-based pose estimation. In *IEEE Computer Vision & Pattern Recognition*, pp. 1706–1711. 350

Sturm, P. F., & Maybank, S. J. (1999) On plane-based camera calibration: A general algorithm, singularities, applications. In *IEEE Computer Vision & Pattern Recognition*, pp. 1432–1437. 351

Sturm, P. F., Ramalingam, S., Tardif, J.-P., Gasparini, S., & Barreto, J. (2011) Camera models and fundamental concepts used in geometric computer vision. *Foundations and Trends in Computer Graphics and Vision* **6** (1-2): 1–183. 319

Sturm, P. F., & Triggs, B. (1996) A factorization based algorithm for multi-image projective structure and motion. In *European Conference on Computer Vision*, pp. 709–720. 380

Sudderth, E. B., Torralba, A., Freeman, W. T., & Willsky, A. S. (2005) Learning Hierarchical Models of Scenes, Objects, and Parts, In *IEEE International Conference on Computer Vision*, pp. 1331–1338.

Sudderth, E. B., Torralba, A., Freeman, W. T., & Willsky, A. S. (2008) Describing visual scenes using transformed objects and parts. *International Journal of Computer Vision* **77** (1–3): 291–330. 498, 500

Sugimoto, A. (2000) A linear algorithm for computing the homography for conics in correspondence. *Journal of Mathematical Imaging and Vision* **13** (2): 115–130. 350

Sun, J., Zhang, W., Tang, X., & Shum, H. Y. (2006) Background cut. In *European Conference on Computer Vision*, pp. 628–641. 68

Sun, J., Zheng, N., & Shum, H. Y. (2003) Stereo matching using belief propagation. *IEEE Transactions on Pattern Analysis & Machine Intelligence* **25** (7): 787–800. 223, 263

Sutherland, I. E. (1963) Sketchpad: a man-machine graphical communications system. Technical Report 296, MIT Lincoln Laboratories. 350

Sutton, C., & McCallum, A. (2011) An introduction to conditional random fields. *Foundations and Trends in Machine Learning.* 261

Szeliski, R. (1996) Video mosaics for virtual environments. *IEEE Computer Graphics and Applications* **16** (2): 22–30. 351

Szeliski, R. (2006) Image alignment and stitching: A tutorial. *Foundations and Trends in Computer Graphics and Vision* **2** (1). 351

Szeliski, R. (2010) *Computer vision: algorithms and applications.* Springer. 2, 5, 264, 351

Szeliski, R., & Shum, H.-Y. (1997) Creating full view panoramic image mosaics and environment maps. In *ACM SIGGRAPH*, pp. 251–258. 351

Szeliski, R., Zabih, R., Scharstein, D., Veksler, O., Kolmogorov, V., Agarwala, A., Tappen, M., & Rother, C. (2008) A comparative study of energy minimization methods for Markov random fields. *IEEE Transactions on Pattern Analysis & Machine Intelligence* **30** (6): 1068–1080. 263

Taigman, Y., Wolf, L., & Hassner, T. (2009) Multiple one-shots for utilizing class label information. In *British Machine Vision Conference.* 451

Tappen, M. F., & Freeman, W. T. (2003) Comparison of graph cuts with belief propagation for stereo, using identical MRF parameters. In *IEEE International Conference on Computer Vision*, pp. 900–907. 263

Tarlow, D., Givoni, I., Zemel, R., & Frey, B. (2011) Graph cuts is a max-product algorithms. In *Uncertainty in Artificial Intelligence.* 262

Tenenbaum, J., Silva, V., & Langford, J. (2000) A global geometric framework for nonlinear dimensionality reduction. *Science* **290** (5500): 2319–2315. 293

Tenenbaum, J. B., & Freeman, W. T. (2000) Separating style and content with bilinear models. *Neural Computation* **12** (6): 1247–1283. 446, 451

Terzopolous, D., & Szeliski, R. (1992) Tracking with Kalman snakes. In *Active Vision*, ed. by A. Blake & A. Y. Yuile, pp. 3–29. MIT Press.

Thayananthan, A., Navatnam, R., Stenger, B., Torr, P., & Cipolla, R. (2006) Multivariate relevance vector machines for tracking. In *European Conference on Computer Vision*, pp. 124–138. 131

Theobalt, C., Ahmed, N., Lensch, H. P. A., Magnor, M. A., & Seidel, H.-P. (2007) Seeing people in different light-joint shape, motion, and reflectance capture. *IEEE Transactions on Visualization and Computer Graphics* **13** (4): 663–674. 319

Tipping, M., & Bishop, C. M. (1999) Probabilistic principal component analysis. *Journal of the Royal Statistical Society: Series B* **61** (3): 611–622. 105

Tipping, M. E. (2001) Sparse Bayesian learning and the relevance vector machine. *Journal Machine Learning Research* **1**: 211–244. 131, 167, 421

Tomasi, C., & Kanade, T. (1991) Detection and tracking of point features. Technical Report CMU–SC–91–132, Carnegie Mellon. 380

Tomasi, C., & Kanade, T. (1992) Shape and motion from image streams under orthography: A factorization method. *International Journal of Computer Vision* **9** (2): 137–154. 380

Tombari, F., Mattoccia, S., di Stefano, L., & Addimanda, E. (2008) Classification and evaluation of cost aggregation methods for stereo correspondence. In *IEEE Computer Vision & Pattern Recognition*. 263

Torr, P. (1998) Geometric motion segmentation and model selection. *Philosophical Transactions of the Royal Society A* **356** (1740): 1321–1340. 350

Torr, P. H. S., & Criminisi, A. (2004) Dense stereo using pivoted dynamic programming. *Image and vision computing* **22** (10): 795–806. 222

Torr, P. H. S., & Zisserman, A. (2000) MLESAC: A new robust estimator with application to estimating image geometry. *Computer Vision & Image Understanding* **78**(1): 138–156. 350

Torralba, A., Murphy, K., & Freeman, W. T. (2007) Sharing visual features for multiclass and multi-view object detection. *IEEE Transactions on Pattern Analysis & Machine Intelligence* **29** (5): 854–869. 163, 167

Treibitz, T., Schechner, Y. Y., & Singh, H. (2008) Flat refractive geometry. In *IEEE Computer Vision & Pattern Recognition*. 319

Triggs, B., McLauchlan, P. F., Hartley, R. I., & Fitzgibbon, A. W. (1999) Bundle adjustment – A modern synthesis. In *Workshop on Vision Algorithms*, pp. 298–372. 381

Tsai, R. (1987) A versatile cameras calibration technique for high accuracy 3D machine vision metrology using off-the-shelf TV cameras and lenses. *Journal of Robotics and Automation* **3** (4): 323–344. 319

Turk, M., & Pentland, A. P. (2001) Face recognition using eigenfaces. In *IEEE Computer Vision & Pattern Recognition*, pp. 586–591. 450

Tuytelaars, T., & Mikolajczyk, K. (2007) Local invariant feature detectors: A survey. *Foundations and Trends in Computer Graphics and Vision* **3** (3): 177–280. 292

Urtasun, R., Fleet, D. J., & Fua, P. (2006) 3D people tracking with Gaussian process dynamical models. In *IEEE Computer Vision & Pattern Recognition*, pp. 238–245. 131

Vapnik, V. (1995) *The Nature of Statistical Learning Theory*. Springer Verlag. 167

Varma, M., & Zisserman, A. (2004) Unifying statistical texture classification frameworks. *Image and Vision Computing* **22** (14): 1175–1183. 503

Vasilescu, M. A. O., & Terzopoulos, D. (2002) Multilinear analysis of image ensembles: Tensorfaces. In *European Conference on Computer Vision*, pp. 447–460. 451

Vasilescu, M. A. O., & Terzopoulos, D. (2004) Tensortextures: Multilinear image-based rendering. *ACM Transactions on Graphics* **23** (3): 336–342. 448

Vaswani, N., Chowdhury, A. K. R., & Chellappa, R. (2003) Activity recognition using the dynamics of the configuration of interacting objects. In *IEEE Computer Vision & Pattern Recognition*, pp. 633–642. 479

Veksler, O. (2005) Stereo correspondence by dynamic programming on a tree. In *IEEE Computer Vision & Pattern Recognition*, pp. 384–390. 219, 222

Veksler, O. (2008) Star shape prior for graph-cut image segmentation. In *European Conference on Computer Vision*, pp. 454–467. 263

Veksler, O., Boykov, Y., & Mehrani, P. (2010) Superpixels and supervoxels in an energy optimization framework. In *European Conference on Computer Vision*, pp. 211–224. 261

Vezhnevets, V., Sazonov, V., & Andreeva, A. (2003) A survey on pixel-based skin color detection techniques. In *Graphicon*, pp. 85–92. 67

Vicente, S., Kolmogorov, V., & Rother, C. (2008) Graph cut based image segmentation with connectivity priors. In *IEEE Computer Vision & Pattern Recognition*, pp. 1–8. 263

Vincent, E., & Laganiere, R. (2001) Detecting planar homographies in an image pair. In *IEEE International Symposium on Image and Signal Processing Analysis*, pp. 182–187. 350

Viola, P., & Jones, M. (2002) Fast and robust classification using asymmetric adaboost and a detector cascade. In *Advances in Neural Information Processing Systems*, pp. 1311–1318. 167

Viola, P. A., & Jones, M. J. (2004) Robust real-time face detection. *International Journal of Computer Vision* **57** (2): 137–154. 161, 162, 166, 167

Viola, P. A., Jones, M. J., & Snow, D. (2005) Detecting pedestrians using patterns of motion and appearance. *International Journal of Computer Vision* **63** (2): 153–161. 162

Vlasic, D., Baran, I., Matusik, W., & Popovic, J. (2008) Articulated mesh animation from multi-view silhouettes. *ACM Transactions on Graphics* **27** (3). 319

Vogiatzis, G., Esteban, C. H., Torr, P. H. S., & Cipolla, R. (2007) Multiview stereo via volumetric graph-cuts and occlusion robust photo-consistency. *IEEE Transactions on Pattern Analysis & Machine Intelligence* **29** (12): 2241–2246. 261, 378, 379, 381

Vuylsteke, P., & Oosterlinck, A. (1990) Range image acquisition with a single binary-encoded light pattern. *IEEE Transactions on Pattern Analysis & Machine Intelligence* **12** (2): 148–164. 319

Wagner, D., Reitmayr, G., Mulloni, A., Drummond, T., & Schmalstieg, D. (2008) Pose tracking from natural features on mobile phones. In *International Symposium on Mixed and Augmented Reality*, pp. 125–134. 351

Wainright, M., Jaakkola, T., & Willsky, A. (2005) MAP estimation via agreement on trees: Message passing and linear programming. *IEEE Transactions on Information Theory* **5** (11): 3697–3717. 263

Wang, J. M., Fleet, D. J., & Hertzmann, A. (2007) Multifactor Gaussian process models for style-content separation. In *International Conference on Machine Learning*, pp. 975–982. 449, 451

Wang, J. M., Fleet, D. J., & Hertzmann, A. (2008) Gaussian process dynamical models for human motion. *IEEE Transactions on Pattern Analysis & Machine Intelligence* **30** (2): 283–298. 479, 480

Wang, X., & Tang, X. (2003) Bayesian face recognition using Gabor features. In *Proceedings of the 2003 ACM SIGMM Workshop on Biometrics Methods and Applications*, pp. 70–73. ACM. 450, 451

Wang, X., & Tang, X. (2004a) Dual-space linear discriminant analysis for face recognition. In *IEEE Computer Vision & Pattern Recognition*, pp. 564–569. 450

Wang, X., & Tang, X. (2004b) A unified framework for subspace face recognition. *IEEE Transactions on Pattern Analysis & Machine Intelligence* **26** (9): 1222–1228. 450

Wei, L.-Y., & Levoy, M. (2000) Fast texture synthesis using tree-structured vector quantization. In *ACM SIGGRAPH*, pp. 479–488. 263

Weiss, Y., & Freeman, W. (2001) On the optimality of solutions of the max-product belief propagation algorithm in arbitrary graphs. *IEEE Transactions on Information Theory* **47** (2): 723–735. 223, 263

Weiss, Y., Yanover, C., & Meltzer, T. (2011) Linear programming and variants of belief propagation. In *Advances in Markov Random Fields*, ed. by A. Blake, P. Kohli, & C. Rother. MIT Press. 263

Wilbur, R. B., & Kak, A. C. (2006) Purdue RVL-SLLL American sign language database. Technical Report TR–06–12, Purdue University, School of Electrical and Computer Engineering. 196

Williams, C., & Barber, D. (1998) Bayesian classification with Gaussian priors. *IEEE Transactions on Pattern Analysis & Machine Intelligence* **20** (2): 1342–1351. 166

Williams, D., & Shah, M. (1992) A fast algorithm for active contours and curvature estimation. *CVGIP: Image Understanding* **55** (1): 14–26. 420

Williams, O. M. C., Blake, A., & Cipolla, R. (2005) Sparse Bayesian learning for efficient tracking. *IEEE Transactions on Pattern Analysis & Machine Intelligence* **27** (8): 1292–1304. 130, 131

Williams, O. M. C., Blake, A., & Cipolla, R. (2006) Sparse and semi-supervised visual mapping with the S3P. In *IEEE Computer Vision & Pattern Recognition*, pp. 230–237. 131

Wiskott, L., Fellous, J.-M., Krüger, N., & von der Malsburg, C. (1997) Face recognition by elastic bunch graph matching. In *IEEE International Conference on Image Processing*, pp. 129–132. 450

Wolf, L., Hassner, T., & Taigman, Y. (2009) The one-shot similarity kernel. In *IEEE International Conference on Computer Vision*, pp. 897–902. 451

Woodford, O., Torr, P. H. S., Reid, I., & Fitzgibbon, A. W. (2009) Global stereo reconstruction under second-order smoothness priors. *IEEE Transactions on Pattern Analysis & Machine Intelligence* **31** (12): 2115–2128. 261

Wren, C. R., Aazarbayejani, A., Darrell, T., & Pentland, A. P. (1997) Pfinder: Real-time tracking of the human body. *IEEE Transactions on Pattern Analysis & Machine Intelligence* **19** (7): 780–785. 68

Wright, J., Yang, A. Y., Ganesh, A., Sastry, S. S., & Ma, Y. (2009) Robust face recognition via sparse representation. *IEEE Transactions on Pattern Analysis & Machine Intelligence* **31** (2): 210–227. 451

Wu, B., Ai, H., Huang, C., & Lao, S. (2007) Fast rotation invariant multi-view face detection based on real adaboost. In *IEEE Workshop on Automated Face and Gesture Recognition*, pp. 79–84. 167

Wu, C., Agarwal, S., Curless, B., & Seitz, S. (2011) Multicore bundle adjustment. In *IEEE Computer Vision & Pattern Recognition*, pp. 3057–3064. 381

Wu, Y., Lin, J. Y., & Huang, T. S. (2001) Capturing natural hand articulation. In *IEEE International Conference on Computer Vision*, pp. 426–432. 422

Xiao, J., Hays, J., Ehinger, K. A., Oliva, A., & Torralba, A. (2010) Sun database: Large-scale scene recognition from abbey to zoo. In *IEEE Computer Vision & Pattern Recognition*, pp. 3485–3492. 504

Xu, C., & Prince, J. L. (1998) Snakes, shapes, and gradient vector flow. *IEEE Transactions on Image Processing* **7** (3): 359–369. 420

Yang, J., Jiang, Y.-G., Hauptmann, A. G., & Ngo, C.-W. (2007) Evaluating bag-of-visual-words representations in scene classification. In *Multimedia Information Retrieval*, pp. 197–206. 504

Yang, M.-H. (2002) Kernel eigenfaces vs. kernel fisherfaces: Face recognition using kernel methods. In *IEEE International Conference on Automatic Face & Gesture Recognition*, pp. 215–220. 450

Yilmaz, A., Javed, O., & Shah, M. (2006) Object tracking: A survey. *Acm Computing Surveys (CSUR)* **38** (4): 1–45. 479

Yin, P., Criminisi, A., Winn, J., & Essa, I. (2007) Tree based classifiers for bilayer video segmentation. In *IEEE Computer Vision & Pattern Recognition*. 167

Yoon, K.-J., & Kweon, I.-S. (2006) Adaptive support-weight approach for correspondence search. *IEEE Transactions on Pattern Analysis & Machine Intelligence* **28** (4): 650–656. 263

Zhang, C., & Zhang, Z. (2010) A survey of recent advances in face detection. Technical Report MSR–TR–2010–66, Microsoft Research, Redmond. 167

Zhang, J., Marszalek, M., Lazebnik, S., & Schmid, C. (2007) Local features and kernels for classification of texture and object categories: A comprehensive study. *International Journal of Computer Vision* **73** (2): 213–238. 504

Zhang, X., & Gao, Y. (2009) Face recognition across pose: A review. *Pattern Recognition* **42** (11): 2876–2896. 451

Zhang, Z. (2000) A flexible new technique for camera calibration. *IEEE Transactions on Pattern Analysis & Machine Intelligence* **22** (11): 1330–1334. 351

Zhao, J., & Jiang, Q. (2006) Probabilistic PCA for t distributions. *Neurocomputing* **69** (16–18): 2217–2226. 105

Zhao, W.-Y., Chellappa, R., Phillips, P. J., & Rosenfeld, A. (2003) Face recognition: A literature survey. *ACM Comput. Surv.* **35** (4): 399–458. 450

Zhou, S., Chellappa, R., & Moghaddam, B. (2004) Visual tracking and recognition using appearance-adaptive models in particle filters. *IEEE Transactions on Image Processing,* **13** (11): 1491–1506. 479

Zhou, S. K., & Chellappa, R. (2004) Probabilistic identity characterization for face recognition. In *IEEE Computer Vision & Pattern Recognition*, pp. 805–812. 450

Zhu, X., Yang, J., & Waibel, A.   (2000)   Segmenting hands of arbitrary colour. In *IEEE International Conference on Automatic Face & Gesture Recognition*, pp. 446–453. 67

Zitnick, C. L., & Kanade, T. (2000) A cooperative algorithm for stereo matching and occlusion detection. *IEEE Transactions on Pattern Analysis & Machine Intelligence* **22** (7): 675–684. 264

Index

Printed in the United States
by Baker & Taylor Publisher Services